Motion Graphic Design

Applied History and Aesthetics

Third Edition

Jon Krasner

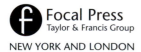

Focal Press
Taylor & Francis Group

NEW YORK AND LONDON

Third edition first published 2013 by Focal Press
70 Blanchard Road, Suite 402, Burlington, MA 01803

Simultaneously published in the UK by Focal Press
2 Park Square, Milton Park, Abingdon, Oxon OX14 4RN

Focal Press is an imprint of the Taylor & Francis Group, an informa business.

Notices
Knowledge and best practice in this field are constantly changing. As new research and experience broaden our understanding, changes in research methods, professional practices, or medical treatment may become necessary.

Practitioners and researchers must always rely on their own experience and knowledge in evaluating and using any information, methods, compounds, or experiments described herein. In using such information or methods they should be mindful of their own safety and the safety of others, including parties for whom they have a professional responsibility.

Product or corporate names may be trademarks or registered trademarks, and are used only for identification and explanation without intent to infringe.

Library of Congress Cataloging in Publication Data
Krasner, Jon S.

Motion graphic design : applied history and aesthetics / Jon Krasner. -- Third edition.

pages cm

Includes index.

1. Animation (Cinematography) 2. Television graphics. I. Title.

TR897.5.K73 2013

006.6'96--dc23

2012041137

ISBN: 978-0-240-82113-9 (pbk)
ISBN: 978-0-240-82470-3 (ebk)

Typeset in Utopia
by Jon Krasner

Printed and bound in India by Replika Press Pvt. Ltd.

To my mother, **Lee Krasner**, who taught me perseverance and the art of giving.

To my father, **Robert Krasner**, who has also been a source of encouragement, inspiration, and admiration.

To my children, **Harris**, **Simon**, and **Julina Krasner**. You continue to amaze me every day, and I look forward to our journey together in a life of adventure.

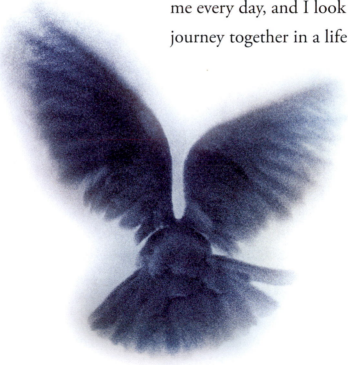

Table of Contents

4 Motion Graphics in Interactive Media

5 Motion Graphics in Public Spaces

6 Motion Literacy

Preface

Enclosed DVD

This book's companion DVD features student work from schools including Massachusetts College of Art, and Design, Ringling College of Art + Design, New York University, Kent State University, California Institute of The Arts, and Fitchburg State University. Additionally, it contains many examples of today's, cutting-edge motion graphics from the following studios and designers across the globe:

twenty2product

Blur

Digital Kitchen

Fuel TV

METAphrenie

Addikt

Freestyle Collective

Studio Dialog

Viewpoint Creative

Capacity, Inc.

Kemistry

ZONA Design

Local Projects

Trollbäck + Company

The Ebeling Group

Heavenspot

Belief

Velvet

ONESIZE

Dvein

Minivegas

Flightphase

Eallin

Stardust Studios

Studio Blanc

KRAFTHAUS

Buck

Shilo

L.inc Design

Flying Machine

Giant Octopus

Elastic

Humunculus

The Ebeling Group

ritxi

Daniel Jenett

David Carson

Susan Detrie

Adam Swaab

Kook Ewo

Varun Chawla

Reality Check Studios

Renascent

Kohler & Griffiths

G'Raffe

Acknowledgments

Mom and Dad, I am grateful for the ongoing support and encouragement you have always given me. I could not ask for more loving and supportive parents.

Meagan, Harris, Simon, Julina, thank you for your support and patience with me throughout my past editions.

Thank you **Bob Harris**, my friend and colleague at Fitchburg State University, for introducing me to many experimental film/animation pioneers who inspired generations of motion designers.

I want to give special thanks to **Professor Ed Cheetham, faculty, and students in the Motion Design department at Ringling College of Art + Design**. Your work is truly inspirational, and I look forward to many more future collaborations!

Thanks to **Jakob Trollbäck** for writing the foreword and contributing your outstanding work to my book.

Students and colleagues at Fitchburg State University; you continue to be a joy to work with. Every day you teach me more about the art of teaching and learning.

I would like to express my gratitude to my editors at Focal Press, **Peter Linsley**, **Emma Elder** and **Dennis McGonagle**. It has been a pleasure working with you.

Finally, thanks to the designers, students, and studios across the world who generously contributed to my book. You will continue to serve as a source of inspiration to my readers.

Introduction

Time—the fourth dimension—has been recognized as a vital force in visual communication. Its powerful impact as a vehicle for communication and artistic expression has enhanced the landscape of thinking among motion graphic designers.

Since the late 1970s, graphic design has evolved from a static publishing discipline to a practice that incorporates a broad range of communications technologies in the film, television, and interactive media industries. The extraordinary evolution of motion graphics has captured the imagination of designers and viewers in the twenty-first century. Motion is now a key component of our complex, contemporary visual landscape with its integrative technologies and immersive environments.

Motion graphics presents a set of unique, creative challenges that combine the language of traditional graphic design with the dynamic visual language of cinema into a hybridized system of communication. The objectives of this text are to provide a foundation for understanding the essence of motion graphic design, to examine principles that are unique to choreographing images and motion, and to explore how to tell stories with meaning, expression, and clarity. Further, this book strives to address how fine artists and designers have shaped the landscape of visual communication.

Having said that, this book should not be mistaken for a software-specific guide, it should be viewed as a historical and critical overview of how motion graphics has evolved as a commercial practice in the motion picture, broadcast, and interactive media industries.

Throughout each chapter, case studies and engaging examples of works of high artistic merit from students and professionals across the globe offer insight into how designers formulate ideas, solve problems, and search for artistic expression. Assignments are intended to challenge and motivate you to develop a greater understanding of motion literacy, kinetic images and typography, and the pictorial and sequential aspects of motion graphic compositions.

The human imagination has no limits. The artistic impulse to experiment and innovate burns inside all of us. This text is written with the hope of inspiring you artistically. I encourage you to examine this comprehensive text and push ahead into the boundless possibilities of motion graphics as an independent and commercial enterprise.

—Jon Krasner

Foreword

Life is linear. Regardless of how much we at times yearn to go back and relive jewel-like events or fast forward past bleak ones or towards milestones, time stubbornly moves on in the same old direction, at the same old pace. Fortunately, our perception of time is far less rigid. How we feel about time does not, of course, always work to our advantage. A great experience usually melts into the past way too fast, while adversity feels endless. To make our existence more gentle, however, our imagination can whisk us forward or backward. This unique human ability to warp the timeline allows us to reflect on the past, process the present, and picture the future. And when you capture and retell a small moment from along the way, suddenly you are delivering a story.

Stories are at the core of humanity. They are our most fundamental and richest means of exploring, shaping, and sharing our reality. Without our narratives, life would make no sense. But the greatest blessing is a good story's ability to rupture monotony and infuse new emotions and new ideas into our lives. Stories not only result from the power of our imagination but fuel it too, conjuring up a wonderful, free world of relative space and time from which we derive our sense of both purpose and possibility.

Tools for creating time-based design are increasingly easy to access and use. We've therefore seen a giant surge in the number of designers beginning to explore animation and filmmaking. If you're a designer who has spent a lot of time creating static expressions, the addition of motion can be both liberating and confusing.

A self-taught graphic designer from Sweden, Jakob Trollbäck creates seminal and award-winning designs, and is an acknowledged industry leader in branding and motion graphic design.

Trollbäck + Company, currently in its eighth year, produces film titles, television commercials, environmental design, music videos, and short films. Clients include top TV networks (CBS, AMC, HBO, TCM, TNT, and Sundance Channel); film companies (HBO Films, Fox Searchlight, and Miramax); and advertising clients (Nike, Volvo, and Fidelity).

On the one hand, it's rewarding to see how images can unfold over time and working with this new axis can make a designer feel very powerful. On the other, it's easy to get carried away by all the cool possibilities at your fingertips. No matter what, however, the crux of all visual communication, either motion or static, is still actually having something to say. We tend to be instantly hooked by design in motion. Humans are hardwired from our days as hunters and gatherers to be captivated by anything that moves. If a TV is on in a bar, we have to strain to avoid looking at it, no matter how interesting the conversation or how pointless the animation on the screen.

While it's our duty to respect this innate drive to watch, we must also honor the ancient art of storytelling. In these pages, you will find a rich understanding of the history, theory and practice of motion graphics. But after you are done reading, it's all up to you. Make your motion narratives seductive, shocking, useful, beautiful. Whatever you do, be passionate. And if you really want to do something that matters, tell us your best stories.

Jakob Trollbäck
President/Creative Director
Trollbäck + Company, NY
http://www.trollback.com

Trollbäck + Company has received numerous creative industry awards, including the Primetime Emmy Awards, the AICP Show, the Art Directors Club, Arts Design Annual, British D&AD, Broadcast Designers Association, Type Directors Club, and the One Show. Recently, Trollbäck + Company was included in the 2006–2007 Cooper-Hewitt National Design Triennial.

1

a brief history of motion graphics

early practices and pioneers

"*It seems inevitable to me that some day, in an elegant new hi-tech museum, someone will holler out in recognition and affection: 'Hey look, a whole room of Fischingers!'—or Len Lyes—or any of the great artist-animators of our century. They are the undiscovered treasures of our time.*"
—Cecile Starr

The moving image in cinema occupies a unique niche in the history of twentieth-century art. Experimental film pioneers of the 1920s exerted a tremendous influence on succeeding generations of animators and graphic designers. In the motion picture industry, the development of animated film titles in the 1950s established a new form of graphic design called motion graphics.

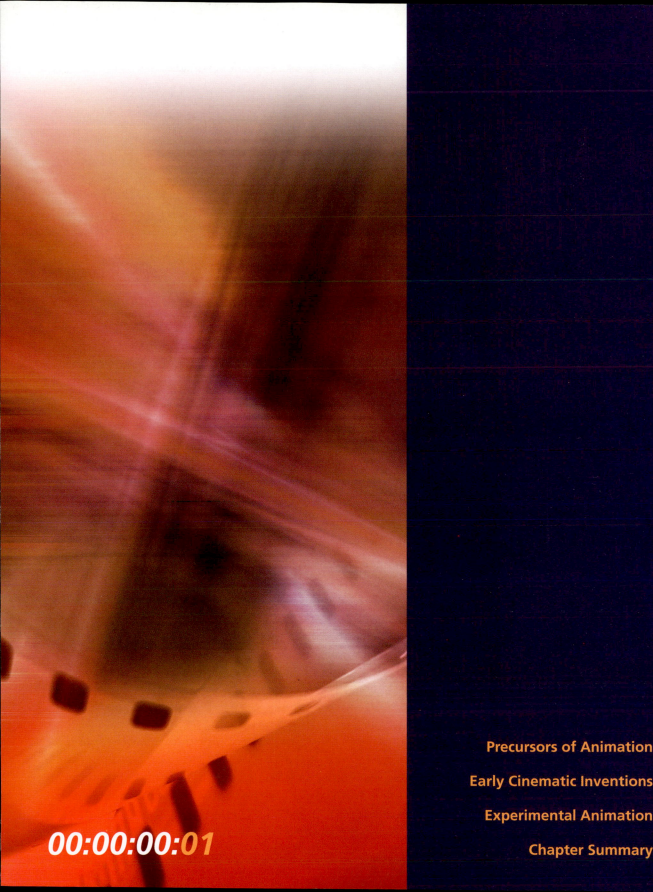

00:00:00:01

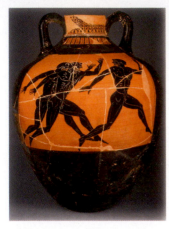

1.1
Panathenaic amphora, c.500 BC. Photo by H. Lewandowski, Louvre, Paris, France. Réunion des Musées Nationaux. © Art Resource, NY.

Several individuals have been credited with the discovery of persistence of vision. They include Greek mathematician Euclid, Greek astronomer Claudius Ptolemy, Roman poet Titus Lucretius Carus, British physicist Isaac Newton, Belgian physicist Joseph Plateau, and Swiss physician Peter Roget.

Precursors of Animation

Since the beginning of our existence, we have endeavored to achieve a sense of motion in art. Our quest for telling stories through the use of moving images can be traced back to cave paintings found in Lascaux, France and Altamira, Spain, that depict animals with multiple legs to suggest movement. Attempts to imply motion were also evident in early Egyptian wall decoration and Greek vessel painting.

persistence of vision

Animation cannot be achieved without understanding a fundamental principle of the human eye: *persistence of vision*. This phenomenon involves our eye's ability to retain an image for a fraction of a second after it disappears. Our brain is tricked into perceiving a rapid succession of different still images as a continuous picture.

early optical inventions

Although the concept of persistence of vision had been firmly established by the nineteenth century, the illusion of motion was not achieved until optical devices emerged. They appeared throughout Europe to provide animated entertainment. Illusionistic theatre boxes, for example, became a popular parlor game in France. They contained a variety of effects that allowed elements to be moved across the stage or lit from behind to create the illusion of depth. Another early form of popular entertainment was the magic lantern, a device that scientists began experimenting with in the 1600s (**1.2**). Magic lantern slide shows involved the projection of hand-painted or photographic glass slides. Using fire (and later gas light), magic lanterns often contained built-in mechanical levers, gears, belts, and pulleys that allowed the slides (sometimes measuring over a foot long) to be moved within the projector. Slides containing images that showed progressive motion could be projected in rapid sequence to create animation.

One of the first successful devices for creating the illusion of motion was the thaumatrope, made popular in Europe during the 1820s by London physicist Dr. John A. Paris. (Its actual invention has often been credited to the astronomer Sir John Herschel.) This simple apparatus was a small paper disc that was attached to two pieces of string and held on opposite sides (**1.3**). Each side of the disc showed an image, and the two images appeared to become merged together when the

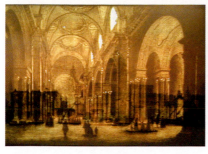
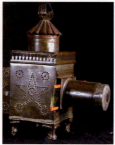
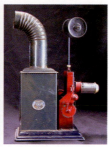

1.2
Magic lantern slide and projectors.
Photos by Dick Waghorne.
Courtesy of the Wileman
Collection of Optical Toys.

disc was spun rapidly. This was accomplished by twirling the disc to wind the string and gently stretching the strings in opposite directions. As a result, the disc would rotate in one direction and then in the other. The faster the rotation, the more believable the illusion.

In 1832, a Belgian physicist named Joseph Plateau introduced the phenakistoscope to Europe. (During the same year, Simon von Stampfer of Vienna, Austria invented a similar device called the stroboscope.) This mechanism consisted of two circular discs mounted on the same axis of a spindle. The outer disc contained vertical slots around the circumference, and the inner disc contained drawings that depicted successive stages of movement. Both discs spun together in the same direction, and when held up to a mirror and peered at through the slots, the progression of images on the second disc appeared to move. Plateau derived his inspiration from Michael Faraday, who invented a device called Michael Faraday's Wheel, and Peter Mark Roget, the compiler of Roget's Thesaurus. The phenakistoscope was in wide circulation in Europe and America during the nineteenth century until William George Horner invented the zoetrope, which did not require a viewing mirror. Referred to as the "wheel of life," the zoetrope was a short cylinder with an open top that rotated on a central axis. Long slots were cut at equal distances into the outer sides of the drum, and a sequence of drawings on strips of paper were placed around the inside, directly below the slots. When the cylinder was spun, viewers gazed through the slots at the images on the opposite wall of the cylinder, which appeared to spring to life in an endless loop (**1.4**).

The popularity of the zoetrope declined when Parisian engineer Emile Reynaud invented the praxinoscope. A precursor of the film projector, it offered a clearer image, overcoming picture distortion by placing images around the inner walls of an exterior cylinder. Each image was reflected by a set of mirrors attached to the outer walls of an interior

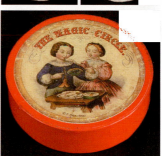

1.3
Thaumatrope discs and case.
Photo by Dick Waghorne.
Courtesy of the Wileman
Collection of Optical Toys.

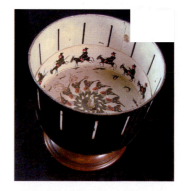

1.4
Zoetrope, top view. Photo by Dick
Waghorne. Courtesy of the
Wileman Collection of Optical Toys.

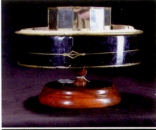

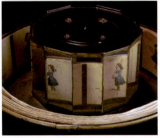

1.5
Praxinoscope views. Photos by
Dick Waghorne. Courtesy of
the Wileman Collection of
Optical Toys.

cylinder (**1.5**). When the outer cylinder was rotated, the illusion of movement was seen on any one of the mirrored surfaces. Two years later, Reynaud developed the praxinoscope theatre, a large wooden box containing the praxinoscope. The viewer peered through a small hole in the box's lid at a theatrical background scene that created a narrative context for the moving imagery.

Early Cinematic Inventions

During the late 1860s, former California governor Leland Stanford became interested in the research of Etienne Marey, a French physiologist who suggested that the movements of horses were different from what most people believed. Determined to investigate Marey's claim, Stanford hired Eadward Muybridge, who had earned a reputation for his photographs of the American West, to record the moving gait of his racehorse with a sequence of still cameras (**1.6**). Muybridge continued to conduct motion experiments, some of which were published in an 1878 article in *Scientific American*. This article suggested that its readers cut the pictures out and place them in a zoetrope to recreate the illusion of motion. This fueled Muybridge to invent the zoopraxiscope, an instrument that allowed him to project up to 200 single images on a screen. This forerunner of the motion picture was received with great enthusiasm in America and England. In 1884, Muybridge was commissioned by the University of Pennsylvania to further his study of animal and human locomotion and produced an enormous compilation of over 100,000 detailed studies of animals and humans engaging in various physical activities. These volumes were a great aid to visual artists, helping them understand movement.

In 1889, Hannibal W. Goodwin, an American clergyman, developed a transparent, celluloid film base that George Eastman began to manufacture. For the first time in history, long sequences of images could be contained on a single reel. (Zoetrope and praxinoscope strips were limited to approximately 15 images per strip.) In Britain, Louis and Auguste Lumière developed the kinora, a home movie device that consisted of a 14 centimeter wheel that held a series of pictures. When the wheel was rotated by a handle, the rapid succession of pictures in front of a lens gave the illusion of motion (**1.7**). By 1894, coin-operated

Muybridge's books, Animals in Motion (1899) and The Human Figure in Motion (1901), are available from Dover Publishers. Many of his plates are exhibited at the Kingston upon Thames Museum as well as in the collection of the Royal Photographic Society.

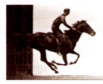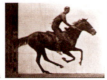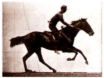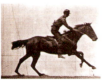

1.6
Motion study, by Eadweard Muybridge. Courtesy of the National Museum of American History.

kinetoscope parlors could be seen in New York City, London, and Paris. This eventually led to the brothers' invention of the cinématographe, the first mass-produced camera-printer-projector of modern cinema (**1.8**). For the first time in history, cinematographic films were projected onto a large screen for a paying public.

In addition to filming movies, new developments led to the concept of creating drawings that were specifically designed to move on the big screen. Prior to Warner Brothers, MGM, and Disney, the origins of classical animation can be traced back to newspapers and magazines that displayed political caricatures and comic strips. One of the most famous cartoon personalities before Mickey Mouse was Felix the Cat. Created by Australian cartoonist Pat Sullivan and animated by Otto Mesmer, Felix was the first animated character to have an identifiable screen personality. In 1914, American newspaper cartoonist Winsor McCay introduced a new animated character to the big screen—Gertie the Dinosaur. Developing a likeable personality from a living creature had a galvanizing impact upon audiences. As the film was projected on screen, McCay would stand nearby and interact with his character.

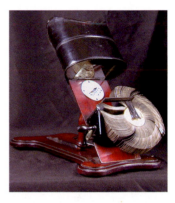

1.7
A kinora. Photo by Dick Waghorne. Courtesy of the Wileman Collection of Optical Toys.

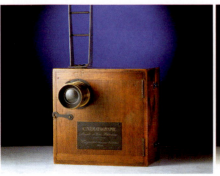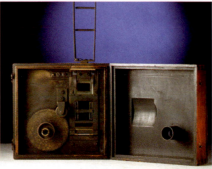

1.8
The cinématographe, the first mass-produced camera-printer-projector in modern cinema. Photos courtesy of the National Museum of American History.

Kinora Ltd. was a British factory that sold and rented kinora reels for personal home viewing. It allowed people to have "motion portraits" taken in a photographic studio to be viewed on their home kinora. The company supplied an amateur camera that allowed people to create their own movies. In 1914, the factory burned down, and the company decided not to rebuild itself, since public interest in the kinora had faded.

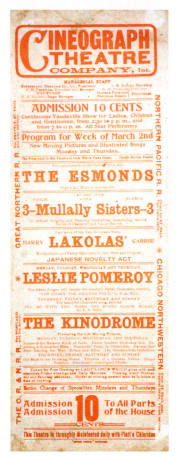

1.9
Ad for "Cineograph Theatre" showing a daily program of motion picture shows (1899–1900). Courtesy of the National Museum of American History.

The cell animation process, developed in 1910 by Earl Hurd at John Bray studios, was a major technical breakthrough in figurative animation that involved the use of translucent sheets of celluloid for overlaying images. Early artists who utilized Bray's process included Max Fleischer (Betty Boop), Paul Terry (Terrytoons), and Walter Lantz (Woody Woodpecker). Stop-motion animation, which can be traced back to the invention of stop-action photography, was used by French filmmaker Georges Méliès, a Paris magician. In Méliès' classic film, A Trip to the Moon (1902), stop-action photography allowed Méliès to apply his techniques, which were derived from magic and the theatre, to film. Additional effects, such as the use of superimposed images, double exposures, dissolves, and fades, allowed a series of magical transformations to take place.

Four years later, J. Stuart Blackton, an Englishman who had immigrated to the United States, discovered that by exposing one frame of film at a time, a subject could be manipulated between exposures to produce the illusion of motion. In 1906, his company, Vitagraph, released an animated short titled "Humorous Phases of Funny Faces," one of the earliest surviving American animated films. Blackton's hand is seen creating a line drawing of a male and female character with chalk on a blackboard. The animation of each face's changing expression was accomplished through single-frame exposures of each slight variation. When the artist's hand exits the frame, the faces roll their eyes and smoke issues from a cigar in the man's mouth. At the end of the film, Blackton's hand reappears to erase the figures. This new stop-motion technique shocked audiences as the drawings magically came to life.

1.10
Postage stamp with portrait of Georges Méliès. Courtesy of Anthology Film Archives.

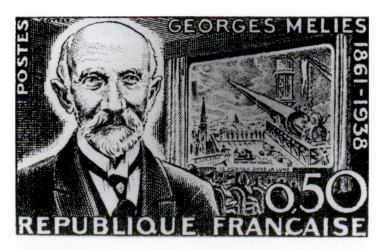

Emile Cohl and Max Fleischer expanded the resources of animation by mixing live footage with hand-drawn elements. Considered to be the father of French animation, Emile Cohl, a newspaper cartoonist, is known for his classic film, "Fantasmagorie" (1908). Cohl's subsequent short animations were a product of the Absurdist school of art that derived inspiration from drug-induced fantasies and hallucinations. These works combined hand-drawn animated content and live action.

Around 1917, Max Fleischer, an admirer of McCay's realistic style, patented the technique of "rotoscoping." This process involved drawing frames by tracing over previously filmed live-action footage, allowing animators to produce smooth, lifelike movements. Fleischer's next invention, the Rotograph, enabled animated characters to be placed into live, realistic settings. A live-action background would be filmed and projected one frame at a time onto a piece of glass. A cel containing an animated character would be placed on the front side of the glass, and the composite scene would be filmed. Fleischer went on to develop the personalities of famous characters such as Koko the Clown, Betty Boop, Popeye, and Superman.

Experimental Animation

At the turn of the twentieth century, postwar industrial advances and the changing social, economic, and cultural conditions of capitalism throughout Europe fueled artists to reject classical representation. Revolutionary Cubist painters began expressing space in geometric terms. Italian Futurists became interested in depicting motion on the canvas as a means of liberating the masses from the cruel treatment they were receiving from the government. Dadaist and Surrealist artists sought to overthrow traditional constraints by exploring the spontaneous and the irrational. These forms of Modernism abandoned the laws of beauty in an attempt to demolish current standards of art. This manifested in music, poetry, sculpture, painting, graphic design, and experimental filmmaking.

pioneers of "pure cinema"

During the 1920s, huge movie palaces, fan magazines, and studio publicity departments projected wholesome images of stars. (Few people knew the names of the directors!) Hollywood's mass-produced

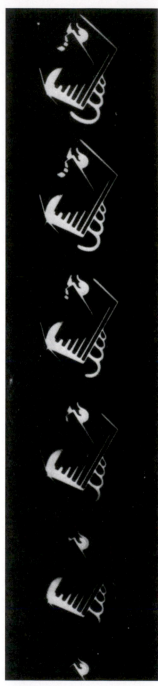

1.11
Filmstrip from the work of Viking
Eggeling. From *Experimental
Animation*, courtesy of Cecile Starr.

romances and genre films reaffirmed values such as the family and patriotism. In Germany, France, and Denmark, filmmakers began to embrace a more personal attitude toward film through the medium of animation. Their basic motivation was not commercial gain; rather, it came from a personal drive to create art. "Pure cinema," as the first abstract animated films were called, won the respect of the art community which viewed film as an expressive medium.

During the early 1900s, Swedish musician and painter Viking Eggeling described his theory of painting by way of music, in terms of "instruments" and "orchestration." His desire was to establish what he referred to as a "universal language" of abstract symbols, and he strived to accomplish this by emphasizing musical structure and avoiding representation. The nihilistic tendencies of the Dadaist movement gave Eggeling the freedom to break from conventional schools of thought, and he collaborated with German filmmaker Hans Richter on a series of "scroll drawings" that utilized straight lines and curves of varying orientations and thicknesses. These structures were arranged in a linear progression across a long scroll of paper, forcing viewers to see them in a temporal context. Driven by the need to integrate time into his work, he turned his attention to film and produced *Symphonie diagonale* in 1924. Taking almost four years to complete, this frame-by-frame animation showed a strong correlation between music and painting in the movements of the figures, which were created from paper cutouts and tin foil (**1.11**). Eggeling died in Berlin approximately two weeks after his film was released.

A major contributor to the Cubist movement, Fernand Léger has been described as "a painter who linked industry to art." Born in northwestern France, he desired to express his love for city life, common people, and everyday objects in painting. By 1911, he had become identified with his tubular and curvilinear structures, which contrasted with the more angular shapes produced by other cubists such as Picasso and Braque. During the 1920s, Léger began to pursue film and produced his classic, *Ballet Mécanique* (1924). Created without a script, this masterpiece demonstrated a desire to combine the energy of the machine with the elegance of classical ballet. Fragments of reflective metal machinery, disembodied figures, and camera reflections were orchestrated into a seductive, rhythmic mechanical dance. Conceptually, this film has been interpreted as a personal statement in a world of accelerating technological advancement and sexual liberation. From an artistic perspective, it represented a daring jump into the territory of kinetic abstraction.

German Dadaist Hans Richter had collaborated with Viking Eggeling to produce their many scroll drawings which depict sequential transformations of geometric forms which he described as "the music of the orchestrated form." Richter saw film animation as the next logical step for expressing the kinetic interplay between positive and negative forms. Richter's silent films of the late 1920s demonstrated a more surreal approach that combined animation with live-action footage. At the time, these shocking films challenged artistic conventions by exploring fantasy through the use of special effects, many of which are used in contemporary filmmaking. In *Ghosts Before Breakfast* (1927), people and objects engage in unusual behavior set in bizarre and often disturbing settings. Flying hats continually reappear, in conjunction with live images of men's beards magically appearing and disappearing, teacups filling up by themselves, men disappearing behind street signs, and objects moving in reverse. In a scene containing a bull's eye, a man's head becomes detached from his body and floats inside the target. In another scene of a blossoming tree branch, fast-motion photography was used. Richter also played back the film in reverse and used negatives to defy the laws of the natural world.

After World War I, German painter Walter Ruttmann became impatient with the static quality of his artwork and saw the potential of film as a medium for abstraction, motion, and the passage of time. In 1920, he founded his own film company in Munich and pioneered a series of playful animated films entitled *Opus,* which explored the interaction of geometric forms (**1.13**). (*Opus I* [1919–1921] was one of the earliest abstract films produced and one of the few that was filmed in black and white and hand-tinted.) The technical process that Ruttmann employed remains uncertain, although it is known that he painted directly onto glass and used clay forms molded on sticks that, when turned, changed their appearance. Ruttmann's later documentary, *Berlin: Symphony of a City*, gives a cross-section impression of life in Berlin in the late 1920s. The dynamism of urbanization in motion is portrayed in bustling trains, horses, masses of people, spinning wheels, and machines, offering an intimate model of Berlin.

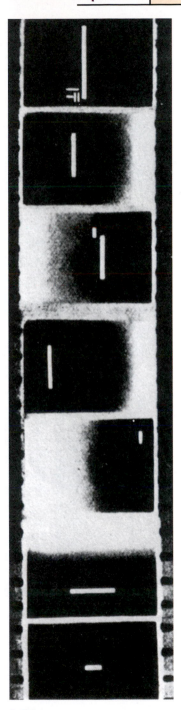

1.12
Filmstrip from *Rhythm 23* (1923) by Hans Richter. From *Experimental Animation*, courtesy of Cecile Starr.

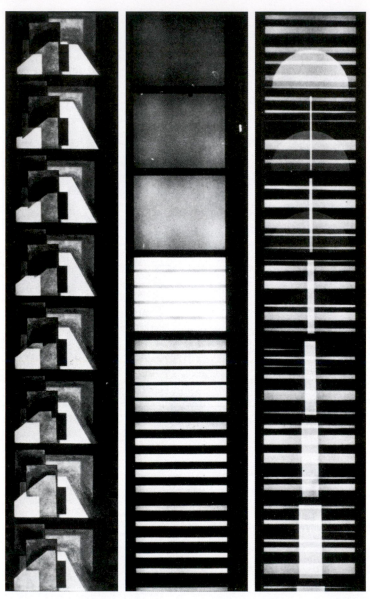

1.13
Frames from *Opus III* (c.1923) and *Opus IV* (c.1924), by Walter Ruttmann. From *Experimental Animation*, courtesy of Cecile Starr.

Born in Brooklyn, New York, Man Ray (born Emanuel Radnitsky), became an enigmatic leader of the Dadaist, Surrealist and American avant-garde movements of the 1920s and 1930s. After establishing Dadaism in New York City with Marcel Duchamp and Francis Picabia, he moved to Paris and became a portrait photographer for the wealthy avant-garde. By the early 1920s, he had developed a reputation for his use of natural light and informal poses during a time when Pictorialism was the predominant style of photography in Europe. Commercial success gave him the freedom to experiment, and his discovery of the "Rayograph" (later called the photogram) made a significant contribution to the field of photography. Throughout the 1920s, Man Ray produced Surrealist films that were created without a camera, such as *Anemic Cinema* (1925–1926) and *L'Etoile de Mer* (1928). He often described them as "inventions of light forms and movements."

In the 1930s, Russian-born filmmaker Alexander Alexeieff and American Claire Parker invented the pinboard (later named the pinscreen), one of the most eccentric traditional animation techniques. This contraption consisted of thousands of closely-spaced pins that were pushed and pulled into a perforated screen, using rollers to achieve varying heights. When subject to lighting, cast shadows from the pins produced a wide range of tones, creating dramatic textural effects that resembled a mezzotint, wood carving, or etching. The extraordinary results of this process are evident in classic pieces such as *Night on Bald Mountain* and *The Nose*, a film based on a story about a Russian major whose nose is discovered by a barber in a loaf of bread.

According to Parker, "Instead of brushes we use different sized rollers; for instance, bed casters, ball-bearings, etc., to push the pins toward either surface, thus obtaining the shades or lines of gray, black, or white, which we need to compose the picture."

Revolutionary New Zealand animator Len Lye, who referred to himself as "an artist for the twenty-first century," pioneered the direct-on-film technique of cameraless animation by painting and scratching onto 35 millemeter celluloid. His abstract, metaphorical images are a product of his association with Surrealism, Futurism, Constructivism, and Abstract Expressionism, and his affinity for jazz, Oceanic art, and calligraphy. His use of percussive music, saturated color, and organic forms had a major impact on a genre that later became known as music video. Living in Samoa between 1922 and 1923, Lye became inspired by Aboriginal motifs and produced his first animated silent film, *Tusalava* (1929), which expressed "the beginnings of organic life" (**1.14**). Taking almost two years to complete, each frame was hand painted and photographed. In another 16 millimeter abstract film, *Free Radicals* (1958), Lye scratched the imagery onto a few thousand feet of black film leader using tools such as sewing needles and Indian arrowheads.

Inspired by master filmmakers Eisenstein and Pudovkin, Norman McLaren began animating directly onto film, scratching into its emulsion to make the stock transparent. (He was unaware that Len Lye was conducting similar experiments.) In 1941, he joined the newly formed National Film Board of Canada (NFB) and founded its animation department. Films such as *Fiddle-de-Dee* (1947) and *Begone Dull Care* (1949) were made by painting on both sides of 35 millimeter celluloid. Incredibly rich textures and patterns were achieved through brushing, spraying, scratching, and pressing cloths into the paint before it dried. For over four decades, McLaren produced films for the NFB that inspired animators throughout the world. In 1989, the head office building of the NFB was renamed the Norman McLaren Building.

Berlin animator Lotte Reiniger is known for her silhouette cut-out animation style during the sound-on film era of the 1930s. Her full-length feature film *The Adventures of Prince Achmed* was among the first animated motion pictures to be produced, taking approximately three years to complete. The main characters were marionettes that were composed of black cardboard figures cut out with scissors and photographed frame by frame.

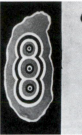

1.14
Frame from *Tusalava* (1929), by Len Lye. From *Experimental Animation*, courtesy of Cecile Starr.

Len Lye was always fascinated with the idea of composition with motion. As a teenager, he used an old box as a frame and devised a pulley mechanism with a phonograph handle attached to a string. An object would be attached to the other end of the string, and when the handle was turned, the pulley wheels would make the object revolve inside the frame.

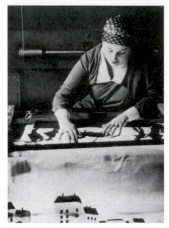

1.15
Lotte Reiniger in the 1920s.
From *Experimental Animation*,
courtesy of Cecile Starr.

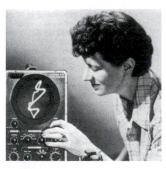

1.16
Mary Ellen Bute, c.1954. From
Experimental Animation, courtesy
of Cecile Starr.

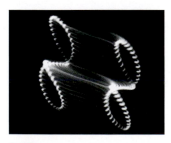

1.17
Frame from *Abstronic* (1954)
by Mary Ellen Bute. From
Experimental Animation,
courtesy of Cecile Starr.

Born in Texas, Mary Ellen Bute developed an interest in filmmaking as a means of exploring kinetic art. In collaboration with Joseph Schillinger, a musician and composer who had developed a theory about reducing musical structures to mathematical formulas, she began animating a film that would prove that music could be expressed visually. (Because of the intricacy of the imagery, this ambitious film was never completed.) Bute incorporated many types of found objects in her work including combs, colanders, Ping-Pong balls, and eggbeaters, and photographed them frame by frame at various speeds. She distorted them to conceal their origin by filming their reflections against a wall. Bute's first film from the 1930s, *Rhythm in Light,* involved shooting paper and cardboard models through mirrors and glass ashtrays to achieve multiple reflections. She also explored oscilloscope patterns as a means of controlling light to produce rhythm (**1.17**). Between 1934 and 1959, her abstract films played in regular movie theaters around the country.

Born in Germany, Oskar Fischinger was exiled to Los Angeles when Hitler came to power and the Nazis censured abstract art. An innovator of experimental film, he believed that visual music was the future of art. During the early 1920s, he developed a series of film studies created from charcoal drawings of pure geometric shapes and lines. Constructed from approximately 5,000 drawings, they demonstrated a desire to marry sound and image. Fischinger also experimented with images produced from a wax-slicing machine and explored color film techniques, cardboard cutouts, liquids, and structural wire supports. In 1938, he was hired by Disney Studios to animate portions of *Fantasia.* His presence in Hollywood helped shape the work of generations of West Coast artists, filmmakers, graphic designers, and musicians.

Born in Portland, Oregon, Harry Smith began recording Native American songs and rituals as a teenager and emerged as a complex artistic figure in sound recording, filmmaking, painting, and ethnographic collecting. Intrigued by the occult, he often spoke of his art in alchemical and cosmological terms. His process involved hand-painting onto 35 millimeter film stock in combination with stop-motion and collage. Echoing his life and personality, his compositions are complex and mysterious and have been interpreted as explorations of unconscious mental processes. Like an alchemist, he worked diligently on his films secretly for almost 30 years. At times, Smith spoke of synesthesia and the search for correspondences among color, sound, and movement.

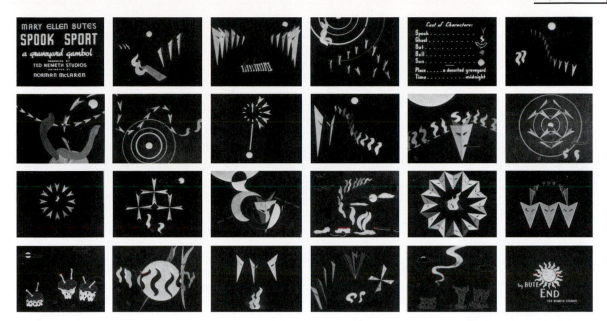

1.18
Frames from *Spook Sport* (1939), by Mary Ellen Bute and Norman McLaren. From *Experimental Animation*, courtesy of Cecile Starr.

His painstaking direct-on-film process involved a wide range of non-conventional tools and techniques, ranging from adhesive gum dots to Vaseline, masking tape, and razor blades. Throughout the 1950s and 1960s, Smith's collage films became increasingly complex. He cut out pictures and meticulously filed them away in envelopes, building up an image archive which he used in later works such as *Film #12: Heaven and Earth Magic* (**1.20**).

After studying painting at Stanford, Robert Breer moved to Paris and became heavily influenced by the hard-edged geometric qualities of Neo-plasticism and the abstractions of the De Stijl and Blue Rider movements. Eventually, Breer felt restricted by the boundaries of the static canvas and produced a series of animations that attempted to preserve the formal aspects of his paintings. He also experimented with rapid montage by juxtaposing frames of images in quick succession.

Jan Švankmajer was one of the most remarkable European filmmakers of the 1960s. His innovative works have helped expand traditional animation beyond the concept of Disney cartoons. His bizarre, often grotesque Surrealist style aroused controversy after the 1968 Soviet invasion of Czechoslovakia, and his opportunities to work in Czech studios were restricted. Nevertheless, he employed a wide range of techniques, using man-made objects, animals, plants, insects, and bones to fuse object animation with live action. Švankmajer's love of

"I wanted to manipulate light to produce visual compositions in time continuity such as a musician manipulates sound to produce music . . . By turning knobs and switches on a control board I can 'draw' with a beam of light with as much freedom as with a brush."

—*Mary Ellen Bute*

1.19
Painting (untitled) by Harry Smith. Courtesy of the Harry Smith Archives and Anthology Film Archives.

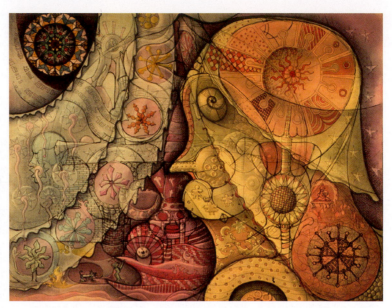

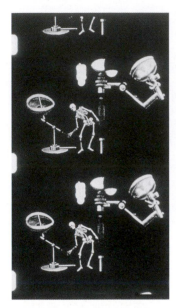

1.20
Frame from *Film #12: Heaven and Earth Magic* (1957–1962), by Harry Smith. Courtesy of the Harry Smith Archives and Anthology Film Archives.

"By simply limiting the viewer of a painting to 1/24th of a second I produce one unit of cinema and by adding several of these units together I produce a motion picture."

— Robert Breer

rapid montage, extreme close-ups, and Surrealism is characterized by his somber, haunting images of living creatures and inanimate objects that are thrust into worlds of ambiguity. The impact of his images often dominates the narrative, as people take on the appearance of robots, and objects engage in savage acts such as decapitation, suicide, and cannibalism. In *The Last Trick of Mr. Schwarcewalld and Mr. Edgar* (1964), a beetle crawls out of the main character's head. In *Jabberwocky* (1971), branches blossom and apples drop and burst open to reveal maggots. A jackknife dances on a table, falls flat, and its blade closes to produce a trickle of blood which oozes out of its body. In another scene, a tea party of dolls dine at a small table, consuming other dolls who have been crushed in a meat grinder and cooked on a miniature range.

Inspired by Švankmajer's films, twin brothers Stephen and Timothy Quay were among the most accomplished puppet animation artists to emerge during the 1970s. Their exquisite sense of detail and extreme close-ups enchanted audiences worldwide and contributed a sense of poetry to animated film. The Quay's miniature sets are worlds of repressed childhood dreams. Absurd and incomprehensible, antiquated-looking machinery, bones, and meat occupy chaotic, multilayered worlds where humans live at the mercy of insidious machines. Unexpected, irrational events distort space and time. The grimy atmosphere of decay, the ominous quality of chiaroscuro, the dazzling use of light and texture, and adept camera movements create an eerie, sublime quality.

During the 1970s, American animators Frank and Caroline Mouris developed the technique of collage animation in their Academy Award winning "Frank Film" (1973). In the 1990s, they created the short "Frankly Caroline" (1999). Both films portray an overabundance of images representing Western culture and iconography. The Mouris' animation style has appeared in music videos and television spots on the PBS, MTV, and Nickelodeon channels. Their films have also been featured on programs such as *Sesame Street* and *3-2-1 Contact*.

computer animation pioneers

Since the 1960s, advances in digital technology have exerted a tremendous influence on generations of animators and commercial motion graphic designers all over the world.

John Whitney hypothesized a future in which computers would be reduced to the size of a television for home use. His interest in film, electronic music, and photography was influenced by French and German avant-garde filmmakers of the 1920s. Whitney felt that music was part of the essence of life and attempted to elevate the status of the computer to a viable artistic medium to achieve a correlation between musical composition and abstract animation. In collaboration with his brother James, he devised a pendulum sound recorder that produced synthetic music for his animated compositions. During the 1950s, Whitney produced films for television and designed the title sequence for Alfred Hitchcock's *Vertigo* in partnership with Saul Bass. He also directed short musical films for CBS and in 1957 worked with Charles Eames to create a seven-screen presentation for the Fuller Dome in Moscow. In 1960, Whitney founded Motion Graphics Inc. and produced openings for *Dinah Shore* and *Bob Hope*. In 1974, John Whitney, Jr. and Gary Demos formed the Motion Picture Products group that led to the first use of computer graphics for film while working on the film *Westworld* (1973). This film employed *pixelization*—a technique that produces a computerized mosaic by dividing a picture into blocks and averaging each block's color to give a single color.

During the 1960s, Stan Vanderbeek became one of the most highly acclaimed underground filmmakers to experiment with computers and multiple screen projection. He produced films using collage, hand-drawn animation, live action, film loops, and computer-generated graphics. He also invented the Movie-Drome theatre, a 360°

"We really believe that with animation one can create an alternate universe, and what we want to achieve with our films is an 'objective' alternate universe, not a dream or a nightmare but an autonomous and self-sufficient world, with its particular laws and lucidity . . . The same type of logic is found in the ballet, where there is no dialogue and everything is based on the language of gestures, the music, the lighting, and sound."
—Stephen and Timothy Quay

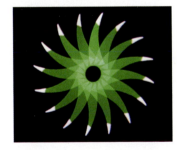

1.21
Frame from *Catalogue*, a compilation of analog computer effects by John Whitney. Courtesy of the Estate of John and James Whitney and the iotaCenter. All rights reserved.

"My computer program is like a piano. I could continue to use it creatively all my life."
—John Whitney

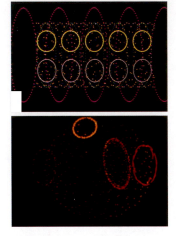

1.22
Frames from *Arabesque*, by John Whitney. Courtesy of the Estate of John and James Whitney and the iotaCenter. All rights reserved.

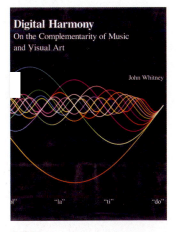

1.23
John Whitney's book, *Digital Harmony: On the Complementarity of Music and Visual Art,* explains the influence of historical figures such as Pythagoras and Arnold Schoenberg on his artistic process. It also provides insight into his groundbreaking work in computer animation and the integration of music and film-making. Courtesy of the Estate of John and James Whitney. All rights reserved.

overhead projection area that surrounded audiences with images as they lay on their backs around the dome's perimeter. This influenced the construction of "life theaters" and image libraries worldwide to advance international communication and global understanding.

During the time that Vanderbeek was producing collage films, Ken Knowlton, an employee of Bell Labs, was developing a BEFLIX programming language for the production of raster-based animation. He also investigated pattern perception and developed an algorithm that could fragment and reconstruct a picture using dot patterns. During the 1990s, he won several awards for his digital mosaics that, close up, depicted a complex array of objects, and from a distance, became a single, recognizable image.

In 1961, MIT student Ivan Sutherland created a vector-based drawing program called Sketchpad. Using a light pen with a photoelectric cell in its tip, shapes could be constructed without having to be drawn freehand. He also invented the first head-mounted display for viewing images in stereoscopic 3D. (Twenty years later, NASA put his technique to use to conduct virtual reality research.) Dave Evans, who was hired to establish a computer science program at the University of Utah, recruited Sutherland, and by the late 1960s the University of Utah had become a primary computer graphics research facility that attracted John Warnock (founder of Adobe Systems and inventor of the PostScript page description language) and Jim Clark (founder of Silicon Graphics).

A few years later in 1971, Robert Abel, who had originally produced films with Saul Bass, established the computer graphics studio Robert Abel & Associates with his friend Con Pederson. He was contracted by Disney to develop promotional materials and the opening sequence for *The Black Hole* (1979), and later to produce graphics for Disney's movie *Tron* (1982). Abel won multiple awards, including two Emmys and a Golden Globe, and his company became recognized for its ability to incorporate conventional cinematography and special effects techniques into the domain of CGI.

Chapter Summary

Optical devices that emerged throughout Europe during the late nineteenth century demonstrated *persistence of vision*—a phenomenon that involves our eye's ability to retain an image for a fraction of a second after it disappears. Eadward Muybridge's motion studies of animals and humans served as an aid to visual artists' understanding of movement. The Lumière brothers took these experiments further and invented the first camera-printer-projector in modern cinema.

At the beginning of the twentieth century, artists began to reject classical representation and express space in pure geometric terms. Swedish painter Viking Eggeling embraced the nihilistic tendencies of the Dadaist movement and described his theory of painting in terms of "instruments" and "orchestration." Fernand Léger's classic *Ballet mécanique* (1923) combined the energy of the machine with the elegance of classical ballet. Hans Richter produced geometric, abstract animations and Surrealistic films that explored fantasy by using special effects. During the 1930s and 1940s, Alexander Alexeieff and Claire Parker invented the pinscreen, a device that produced dramatic textural effects that resembled traditional etchings. Len Lye pioneered the technique of cameraless, direct-on-film animation by painting and scratching images onto 35 millimeter celluloid. Norman McLaren joined the National Film Board of Canada and produced experimental animated films that earned him worldwide recognition. Almost six decades before MTV, Oskar Fischinger's experiments with sound and image helped pioneer music videos. Harry Smith and Robert Breer became major forces in experimental fine art animation. In Eastern Europe, the films of the Brothers Quay and the bizarre images of Jan Švankmajer introduced a dark, multilayered approach to animation that involved a strong emphasis on light, texture, and adept camera motion.

In the 1970s, Frank and Caroline Mouris developed the technique of collage animation in their Academy Award winning short *Frank Film* (1973). Stan Vanderbeek became one of the most highly acclaimed underground filmmakers to experiment with computer graphics and explore multiple screen projection. John Whitney's balancing of science with aesthetics helped elevate the status of the computer as a viable artistic medium. Robert Abel was contracted by Disney to develop the opening sequence to *The Black Hole* (1979) and the graphics for the movie *Tron* (1982).

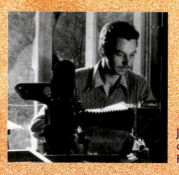

1.24
John Whitney. Photo courtesy of Anthology Film Archives.

2

motion graphics in film
an overview

"The title sequence of a film is like the frame around a painting; it should enhance and comment on what is 'inside,' alerting and sensitizing the viewer to the emotional tones, the story ideas, and the visual style which will be found in the work itself."
—*Walter Murch*

Since the 1950s, when legendary Saul Bass revolutionized the practice of film title design, the movie industry has integrated the language of traditional graphic design with the dynamic visual language of cinema. Motion designers have continued to be leading players in the creation of film titles.

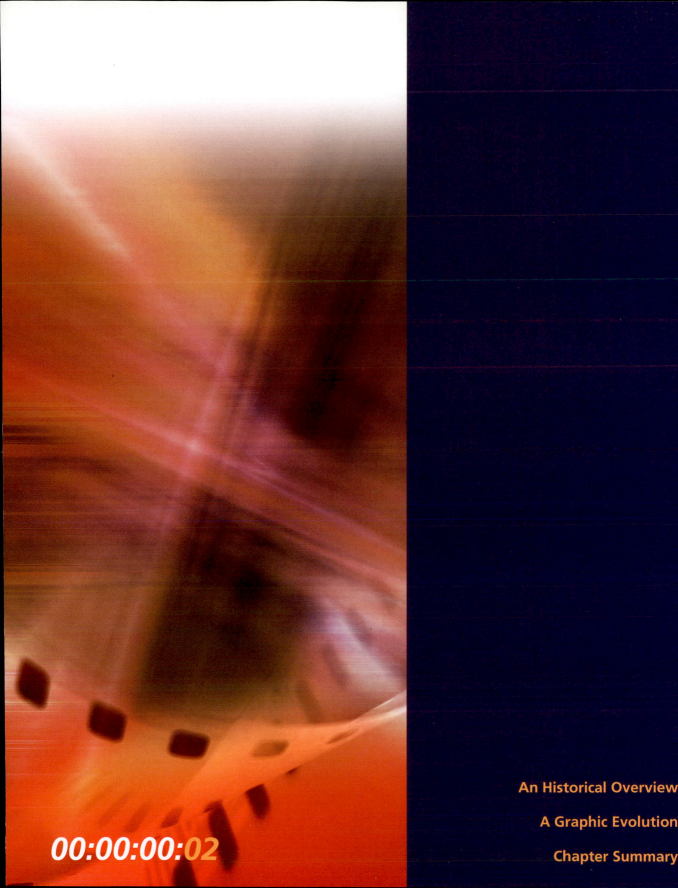

00:00:00:02

An Historical Overview

A Graphic Evolution

Chapter Summary

An Historical Overview

A film's opening titles are the first images that viewers experience once the lights are dimmed. Since the 1950s, title sequences have evolved as a form of experimental filmmaking in commercial motion pictures. A film's opening credits are designed to create the context of a film and establish expectations about its atmosphere and tone.

The origin of film titles can be traced back to the silent film era, where credit sequences were presented on title cards containing text. They were inserted throughout the film to maintain the flow of the story. (Ironically, they often interfered with the narrative's pacing.) Hand-drawn white lettering superimposed on a black background typically provided the title, the names of individuals involved (i.e., directors, technicians, cast), dialogue, and action for the scenes. At times the letters were embellished with decorative outlines, and usually the genre of the film dictated the style. Large, distressed block letters marked horror, while a fine, elegant script characterized romance. After the implementation of sound, film titles began to evolve into complete narratives and became elevated to an art form.

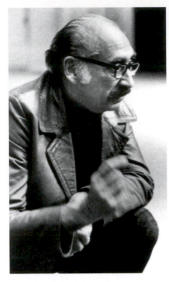

2.1
Saul Bass in his later years. Photo courtesy of Anthology Film Archives.

"We love doing titles. We do them in a nice, obsessive way—we futz with them until we're happy and do things that nobody else will notice but us . . . There's a Yiddish word for it, 'meshugas,' which is 'craziness.' I admire obsessiveness in others."

—Saul Bass

During the 1950s, American graphic design pioneer Saul Bass became the movie industry's leading film title innovator. His evocative opening credit sequences for directors such as Alfred Hitchcock, Martin Scorsese, Stanley Kubrick, and Otto Preminger garnered public attention and were considered to be miniature films in themselves.

Born in New York City in 1920, Bass developed a passion for art at a young age and became grounded in the aesthetics of Modernism through the influence of Gyorgy Kepes, a strong force in the establishment of the Bauhaus in Chicago. After working for several advertising agencies, Bass moved to Los Angeles and founded Saul Bass & Associates in 1946. His initial work in Hollywood consisted of print for movie advertisements and posters. In 1954, he created his first title sequence for the film *Carmen Jones* (1954). Bass viewed the credits as a logical extension of the film and as an opportunity to enhance the story. His subsequent animated openings for Otto Preminger's *The Man with the Golden Arm* (1955) and *Anatomy of a Murder* (1959) elevated the role of the movie title as a prelude to the film. They also represented a rebirth of abstract animation seen in the experimental avant-garde films of the 1920s. According to director Martin Scorsese, "Bass fashioned title sequences into an art, creating in some cases, like *Vertigo*, a mini-film within a film. His motion graphics compositions function as a prologue to the movie—setting the tone, providing the mood and foreshadowing the action."

During the 1960s, Friz Freleng, known for his work on the *Looney Tunes* and *Merrie Melodies* series of cartoons from Warner Bros, developed the opening cartoon animation for *The Pink Panther* (1963). This immediately became an icon of pop culture, appearing in numerous sequels and eventually its own television series. Freleng's cool, contemporary style, use of spinning letters, unscrambling words, and the distinctive theme music from Henry Mancini served as a complete departure from the cheaply made theatrical cartoons of the time.

In contrast, American designer Maurice Binder's openings for classic James Bond movies gained popularity for their abstract, erotic imagery. Beginning with *Dr. No* and ending with *License to Kill*, Binder's stylish credit sequences for fourteen 007 films became a trademark of the series and have been described as a visual "striptease" of nude figures against swirling, enveloping backgrounds of color. In a time when pop music and fashion permeated mainstream entertainment, these sensual openings were a perfect match for Bond's character. The classic gun-barrel opening that precedes the traditional precredit sequence in every 007 film was initially created by Binder for *Dr. No* (1962). Gunshots fired across the screen transform into the barrel of a gun that follows the movement of the silhouetted figure of Bond. The figure then turns toward the camera and fires, and a red wash flows down from the top of the screen as the gun barrel becomes reduced to a white dot. Binder achieved this effect by actually photographing through the barrel of a .38 revolver. This became a trademark of the 007 series and was used extensively throughout its promotion. (Each actor playing Bond had his own interpretation of the famous gun barrel walk-on—the first being stuntman Bob Simmons, then Sean Connery, George Lazenby, Roger Moore, Timothy Dalton, Pierce Brosnan, and finally Daniel Craig.)

Terry Gilliam's contribution to animation is manifested in a series of bizarre title sequences and animated shorts that he produced for Monty Python. Born in Minnesota, Gilliam became strongly influenced by *Help!* and *MAD Magazine* while studying at Occidental College in California. Gilliam joined *Fang*, the college's literary magazine, and sent copies of the magazine to Harvey Kurtzman, editor of *Help!* and co-founder of *MAD*. After receiving a positive response from Kurtzman,

Maurice Binder is known for his striking title designs in The Mouse That Roared *(1959),* Repulsion *(1964), and* The Last Emperor *(1989). A source of information on Binder is a short documentary included on the DVD* On Her Majesty's Secret Service.

he went to New York and was hired as Kurtzman's assistant editor. There, Gilliam met the British comedian John Cleese, and in 1969 he was asked to join the Monty Python group as animator for the show's opening credits. Gilliam's outrageous cutout animations worked well with the group's comedy routine. His ability to transform mundane objects into outrageous 'actors' entertained his audiences and demonstrated what stop-motion collage animation was capable of achieving. Gilliam also became involved in directing live action during the 1970s and 1980s. His quirky stage sets, bizarre costumes, and puzzling camera angles are seen in *Jabberwocky* (1977), *Time Bandits* (1981), *Brazil* (1985), *The Age of Reason* (1988), and *The Adventures of Baron Munchausen* (1989).

In 1977, Richard Alan Greenberg and his brother Robert founded the motion graphics studio R/Greenberg Associates. A traditionally schooled designer, Richard earned his reputation by "flying" the opening titles for the feature film *Superman* (1978). This early example of computer-assisted effects enabled the animation of three-dimensional typography. Throughout the 1980s and 1990s, Richard Greenberg designed credits for features such as *Family Business* (1989), *Flash Gordon* (1980), *Altered States* (1980), *Another You* (1991), *Death Becomes Her* (1992), *Executive Decision* (1996), and *Foxfire* (1996). Many of these titles are treated as visual metaphors that set the tone of the movie.

> *"What I do in film is the opposite of what is done with the print image.* Dracula *is a very good example of the process. There is very little information on the screen at any time, and you let the effect unfold slowly so the audience doesn't know what they're looking at until the very end. . .The audience is captive at a film—I can play with their minds."*
> —Richard Greenberg

For the past four decades, groundbreaking title sequences for classics such as *Dr. Strangelove* (1964), *The Thomas Crown Affair* (1968), and *A Clockwork Orange* (1971) earned Cuban-born filmmaker Pablo Ferro a reputation as a master of title design, alongside legendary designer Saul Bass. During his advertising career in the 1950s, Ferro introduced several techniques to the commercial film industry, including rapid-cut editing, hand-drawn animation, extreme close-ups, split-screen montage, overlays, and hand-drawn type. Many designers claim that his quick-cut technique, in particular, influenced what later became known in television as the "MTV style." In the opening sequence of the film *To Die For* (1995), Ferro developed the leading character through a montage of newspaper and magazine covers. (In the film, Nicole Kidman is so desperate to be a television newscaster that she convinces her lover to kill her husband so that she can pursue her career.) Pablo Ferro's revitalization of hand-lettered movie titles and classic broadcast animations, such as NBC's Peacock and Burlington Mills' "stitching" logo became his trademarks. Influenced by Pablo Ferro and Saul Bass, Kyle Cooper was one of the first graphic designers to reshape the conservative motion picture industry during the 1990s by applying trends in print design and incorporating the computer to combine conventional and digital processes. After studying under legendary designer Paul Rand at the Yale University School of Art, he worked at R/Greenberg Associates in New York and contributed to the title sequence for *True Lies* (1994). In 1995, his opening credit sequence for David Fincher's psychological thriller *Se7en*, which expressed the concept of a deranged, compulsive killer, immediately seized public attention. Today, it is regarded as a landmark in motion graphic design history.

After designing the opening for John Frankenheimer's interpretation of H.G. Wells's novel *The Island of Dr. Moreau* (1996), Kyle Cooper, Chip Houghton, and Peter Frankfurt founded the motion graphics studio Imaginary Forces in Los Angeles.

"Cooper's titles for Se7en transformed the written word into a performer. Cooper brought a new sensibility into the language of cinema— a taste for subtly deranged typographic details over large-scale special effects."
—Jean-Luc Godard

A Graphic Evolution

Since the 1950s, the evolution of film title design has introduced a wide range of revolutionary concepts and artistic approaches that continue to inspire motion graphic designers today.

Saul Bass' suggestive, metaphorical images served as storytelling devices for priming the audience. In *Anatomy of a Murder* (1959), he introduces a silhouette that disappears from view and reappears in disjointed parts that jump on and off the frame in concert with Duke Ellington's musical theme. A mood of betrayal and impending doom is established early on, keeping viewers on the edge of their seats. In *The Man with the Golden Arm* (1955), a jagged arm foreshadows the schizophrenic mindset of the main character. *The Seven Year Itch* (1955) uses abstract graphic shapes to form a sealed-off door that separates the main characters' apartments. In *North by Northwest* (1959), bars of text ascend and descend to emulate the motion of elevators. Anticipation grows as racing horizontal and vertical lines invade the frame and intersect to form the grid pattern of a skyscraper for the film's opening shot. Bass' humorous closing credits to *Around the World in 80 Days* (1956) show a frantic clock on legs journeying around the world, encountering symbols that represent various places (elephants in India, pyramids in Egypt, saloon doors in the American West). In Hitchcock's comedy–thriller *Psycho* (1960), parallel lines and type convey the dark side of the human psyche.

In the film Bass on Titles (1977), Bass discusses the evolution of his opening title sequences and addresses the method he uses to conceptualize motion pictures as graphic animation.

Bass' use of typography was also revolutionary at a time when motion pictures used plain, static text for their credits. In *West Side Story* (1961), the credits are treated as graffiti, and in *The Age of Innocence* (1993), as epistolary script. *Around the World in 80 Days* introduces the credits as fireworks that illuminate the scene when the clock encounters Paris. In the opening to *Cape Fear* (1991), Saul and Elaine Bass enlarged a sign reading "Cape Fear" on a Xerox machine. Using a kitty-litter box, Elaine put ink in the water to make it more reflective, submerged the sign in the water, and created ripples with a hair dryer. As the shimmering water settled, the words slowly appeared.

Maurice Binder's realistic and abstract images of undulating liquids and silhouettes of sensuous, female dancers created erotic, mysterious environments that characterized the 007 opening sequences during the 1960s. The titles to *For Your Eyes Only* (1981) show a nude female figure in a background consisting of a close-up of a fiber-optic lamp. In the opening sequence to *The Spy Who Loved Me* (1977), female figures move like belly dancers, as if conjuring up the vivid masses of background colors. After Bond jumps off a mountain slope and his parachute opens, a silhouette of a woman's hands rises from the bottom of the frame to cradle the parachute as the tune of "Nobody Does It Better" begins. In *You Only Live Twice* (1967), the opening credits begin with a close-up of a deceased 007 lying in a pool of blood that transforms into a Japanese fan. A solarized background of an erupting volcano fills the screen with red lava, and silhouetted parasols burst from the lava, giving way to the silhouette of a mountainside fading into a sunrise.

Kyle Cooper's groundbreaking opening credits to the movie *Se7en* (1995) incorporate scratched, hand-drawn letter forms that nervously jump around on the screen to the soundtrack by Trent Reznor (Nine Inch Nails), as close-up shots of instruments of torture (scissors, trays, and tape) flash before the audience's eyes. Profane words also appear in conjunction with biblical, nihilistic images to contribute to the mood of dementia and cold, calculated precision. When the negative was sent out for processing, the lab was told that pieces of film leader and twisted film were part of the finished product.

Cooper's titles to Guillermo Del Toro's *Mimic* (1997) introduced the crisis of a genetic experiment gone awry by displaying close-up images of moths and butterflies pinned to a wall. X-rays sporadically flash up on the screen, revealing the insects in menacing positions. These images are interchanged with pinned-up newspaper clippings featuring an insect-based epidemic and photographs of children affected by the disease. Torn headlines including the words "disaster" and "tragic" appear beneath the insects, and maps of the New York City subways convey the atmosphere of the subterranean underworld. Quick cuts display accompanying credits that jump around the frame to the sound of flapping wings and distant voices of screaming children. According to Kyle Cooper, "we did a temp sequence where we took a bunch of photographs, integrated them with graphics on a Mac-based Photoshop program, then dissolved back and forth and filmed it out."

Continuing the excellence of Cooper's legacy, Imaginary Forces' stylish titles for director Andrew Niccol's futuristic thriller *Gattaca* (1997) are based on the movie's concept of genetic modification and its possible use in human genetic engineering in the near future (**2.2**). Extreme close-ups of nail clippings fall to the ground with oppressive thuds and clatters, followed by hair and dead skin, all carriers of our genetic codes. These images are accompanied by the credits that display the letters A, T, C, and G—the four nucleobases of DNA (adenine, thymine, cytosine, and guanine)—in a bolder, semi-serif face font. This subtle introduction communicates the movie's premise of "perfect" humans being bred and trained for elite jobs, while imperfect "Godchildren" born the old-fashioned way are doomed to marginal lives.

"When we did Tron *there were four companies in the U.S.,"* says Rosebush. *"By the end of the decade there were 100 companies in New York alone. That opened up a tremendous amount of competition."*
—*Judson Rosebush*

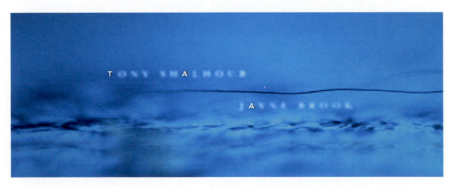

2.2
Frame from the opening title sequence to *Gattaca* (1997). Designed and produced by Imaginary Forces. © Jersey Films and Columbia TriStar.

Since the 1990s, motion graphics studios and designers have continued to experiment with new ways of expressing the premise behind movies and have produced award-winning titles for feature films.

The engaging title sequence to Nickelodeon Movies' feature film *Clockstoppers* (2002) is based on the idea of a wristwatch that has the power to slow down or accelerate time. Creative Director Karin Fong from Imaginary Forces conceived the idea of exploring the mechanics of a watch on a microscopic level to convey the theme of time travel. Footage of clock mechanisms, lights, and rich textures were composited and time-warped to symbolize the distortion of time in a virtual world. This futuristic sequence places us inside the watch so that we can observe its compelling mechanics while discovering the credits along the way, as lines of typography spin in 3D space to form the hands of a clock (**2.3**).

2.3
Frames from the opening titles to *Clockstoppers* (2002). Designed and produced by Imaginary Forces. © Nickelodeon Movies and Paramount Pictures.

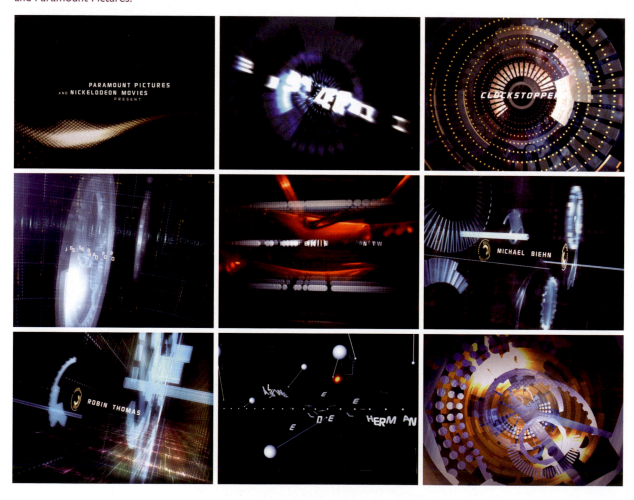

Joel Schumacher's psychological thriller *The Number 23* (2007) portrays an average man whose obsession with recurring instances of the number 23 in human history thrusts him into a nightmarish underworld of sex and death. Imaginary Forces' haunting title sequence introduces us to the cryptic enigma of the number 23 by showing us coincidental connections and catastrophes in history. For example, humans have 23 pairs of chromosomes; the Hiroshima bomb was dropped August 6, 1945 (8+6+1+9+4-5 = 23); 230 people died on TWA flight 800; blood pumps through the body every 23 seconds; the attack on the Twin Towers occurred on 9/11/2001 (9+11+2+0+0+1 = 23). Accompanied by unsettling music, the sequence is imbued with the color red, an obvious blood motif that also references the deep red color of the book which is prominent in the story. The interaction of vernacular typography with the movement of a typewriter and the blood seeping into the paper brings the composition to life and effectively expresses the downward spiral of the film's narrative (**2.4**).

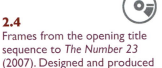

2.4
Frames from the opening title sequence to *The Number 23* (2007). Designed and produced by Imaginary Forces. © New Line Cinema.

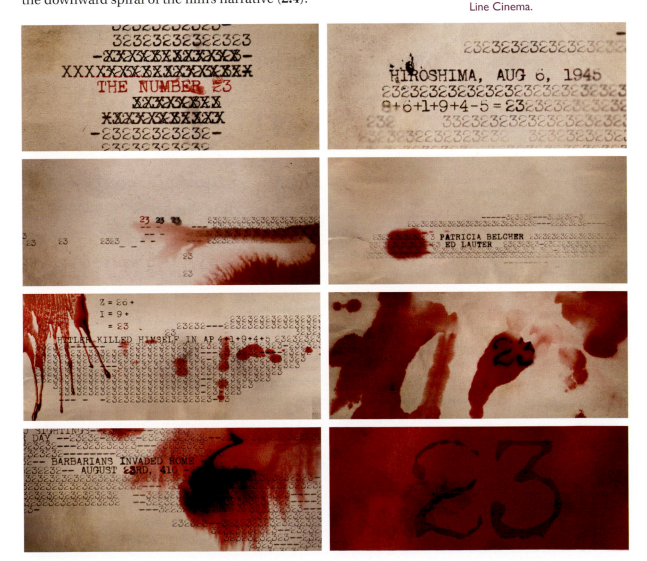

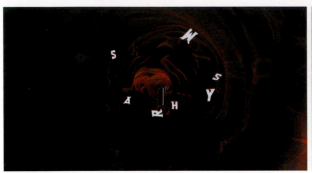 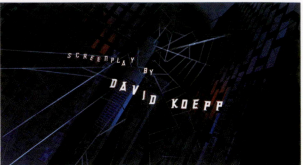

2.5
Kyle Cooper's stunning opening credits for *Spider-Man* (2002) reflect the sheer power of the film and build anticipation for it in a very memorable way. The vintage comic-style imagery by Alex Ross supports the credits, which get caught in the web as they are introduced. Designed and produced by Imaginary Forces. © Columbia Pictures.

The opening sequence of *Thank You For Smoking* (2006) borrows from an eclectic mix of cigarette package designs to give viewers a nostalgic spin on the movie's playful atmosphere. Shadowplay Studios turned the director's initial idea, which was to present a slide show of various package designs, into a rich, animated presentation that brings to life various brands of cigarettes (**2.6**).

In an experimental short film, Onesize, a motion graphics studio in the Netherlands created the opening and ending credits for *Genesis 3:19* (2007), a compelling independent movie directed by Dany Saadia. The film depicts a story of people that are bound together by coincidence. The title sequence shows a "journey through space in which we enter a '3D blue-print' of our galaxy the way God created it," according to Rogier Hendriks, the company's founder. "We see how everything in the galaxy is connected to a big clock mechanism. The film is all about how everything is connected" (**2.7**).

In addition to studios, individual designers have established worldwide reputations for their work. For the prologue to *A Thousand Suns* (2007), a documentary about the dangers of nuclear power, Dutch designer Joost Korngold was given several photographs and a written narrative from director Matthew Modin. He decided to place the photographs inside glass frames and film them falling to the ground and breaking. The event was played back slowly in reverse to create the effect of the broken images and frames becoming whole again. This concept served as a metaphor for turning back time in order to make things different for future generations. Typography was treated in a very subtle manner to give the appearance of melting—a second metaphor conveying the idea of nuclear meltdown: the strength of a thousand suns (**2.8**).

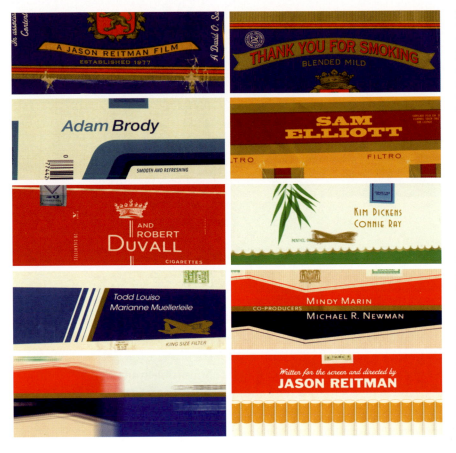

The clever title sequence to *Thank You For Smoking* (2006) borrows from an *eclectic* mix of cigarette package designs to give viewers a nostalgic spin on the movie's playful atmosphere. Courtesy of Shadowplay Studios.

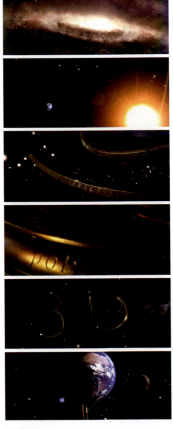

Deborah Ross's opener for Anthony Minghella's *The Talented Mr. Ripley* (1999) is one of the longest credit sequences (over eight minutes) to be produced on a Mac G4 desktop computer. Playing on the theme of jazz by referencing 1950s and 1960s album cover art from the Blue Note jazz label, the look is characterized by a liberal use of graphic shapes and typography. A distressed typewriter font fades in and out in concert with emerging, hard-edged shapes showing actor Matt Damon's face in profile in a contemplative pose. The letters of the title are compressed together with a rapid succession of adjectives that express Ripley's personality (**2.9**). Portions of the film were tinted with bars of color that served as masks to create transitions between the scenes. According to Deborah: "This underscored the dueling musical themes of jazz versus classical in the story, as well as the bohemian 'coolness' of the period. Sometimes, these bars echo playful piano keys; other times, they are jagged shapes that foretell the disturbing psychological aspects of the story."

2.7
Frames from the opening titles to *Genesis 3:19* (2007). Courtesy of Onesize.

2.8
A Thousand Suns (2007). prologue. Courtesy of Joost Korngold. © Renascent.

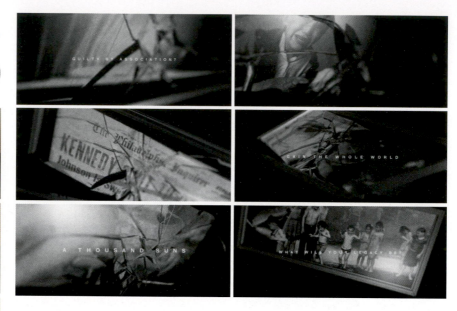

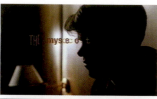

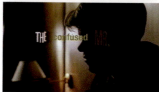

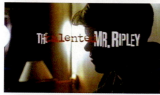

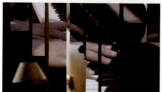

2.9
Frames from the titles to *The Talented Mr. Ripley* (1999). Deborah Ross Film Design. © Miramax.

Raised in LA, Deborah Ross assisted Dan Perri, who designed the opening credits for The Exorcist *(1973),* Close Encounters of the Third Kind *(1977), and* Platoon *(1986). In 1979, she established Deborah Ross Film Design and has developed titles for* The Little Mermaid *(1989),* The English Patient *(1996),* The Talented Mr. Ripley *(1999), and* Cold Mountain *(2003).*

The dark, fast-paced title sequence that French designer Kook Ewo created for Vincenzo Natali's sci-fi thriller, *Splice* (2006) is a visual masterpiece (**2.10**). In the film, two married scientists aim to push the boundaries of genetic engineering by combining animal and human DNA to create a superior humanoid creature. According to Ewo, Vincenzo's goal was to illustrate the concept of synthesizing different species by combining vegetable, animal, and human material. This mix of organic matter creates an unsettling ambiguity that prevents viewers from identifying the living material that partially depicts human flesh. Throughout the composition, the actors' names emerge as if they are tumor-like growths being pushed up from underneath the skin. To avoid graphic redundancy, each title was embedded in a different, anatomical way. An even more disturbing realism was achieved by compositing the visuals with footage of dense, poorly lit amniotic fluid. The murky environment that resulted helped avoid a slick, digitally-generated look and defined the atmosphere for the entire piece.

Ewo's atmospheric ending titles for *Silent Hill* (2006) effectively illustrate the eerie, psychological nature of the film, which is based on PlayStation's video game Silent Hill. In the game, the protagonist searches blindly for his daughter in a mysterious, alternate dimension while encountering various monsters in a desolate sea of darkness and fog. Inspired by pictures of abandoned hospitals and by the game's third-person view, Ewo proposed a simple idea—a subjective camera that passes over the

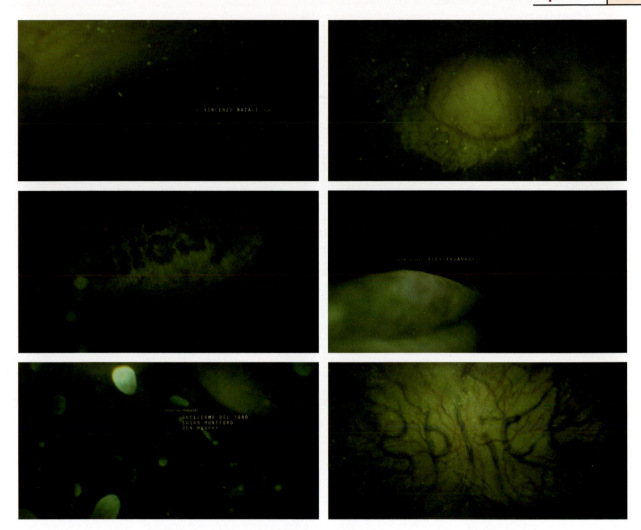

2.10
Frames from the opening credits to *Splice* (2006). Courtesy of Kook Ewo.

See also Chapter 7, figure 7.32 on p. 225, Chapter 10, figure 10.26 on p. 361, and Chapter 13, figure 13.23 on p. 466.

creatures from the film and torn, pinned-up photographs of the cast. Accompanied by handwritten, scrawly names that shake restlessly on the screen, black and white photographs of the actors which adorn the environment's walls appear almost holographic, similar to ghostly daguerrotype portraits peering out of the darkness (**2.11**).

Ewo's titles to Marc Silver's film *Who is Dayani Cristal?* (2012) are a groundbreaking mix of drama and documentary. His sequence unravels the mystery behind an anonymous body found in the Arizona desert bearing a tattoo reading 'Dayani Cristal.' The use of extreme close-up, black and white shots that recreate the tattoo evokes a disturbing, anxious atmosphere that immediately sets the film's tone (**2.12**).

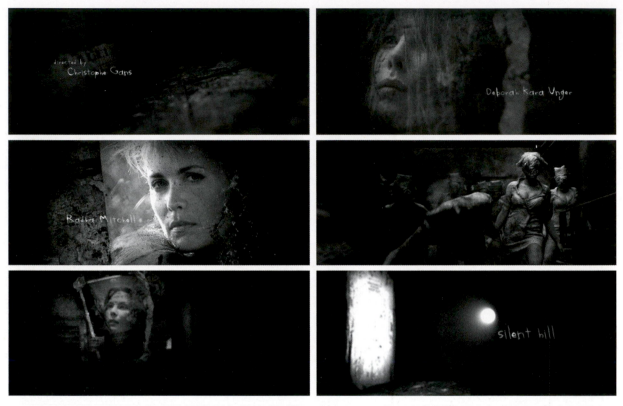

2.11
Frames from the opening credits
to *Silent Hill* (2006). Courtesy of
Kook Ewo.

2.12
Frames from the title sequence
for *Who is Dayani Cristal?* (2012).
Courtesy of Kook Ewo.

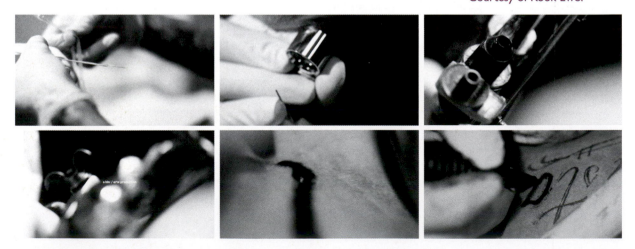

A Graphic Evolution

The delicate opener for Spanish director Kike Maíllo's film *Eva* (2012) is an intriguing masterpiece of mesmerizing 3D and photorealistic imagery. Set in the year 2041, this futuristic thriller tells the story of a young scientist who returns to his home town to complete the unfinished project of creating a boy robot with the help of his 10-year-old niece, Eva. Dvein studio in Barcelona conceived the "Hand Up," a holographic interface that allows the protagonist to configure the personality and emotions of the robot. This helped provide the foundation for the opening titles (**2.13**).

2.13
Frames from the opening title sequence to *Eva* (2012). Courtesy of Dvein.

See also Chapter 10, figure 10.2, on p. 342.

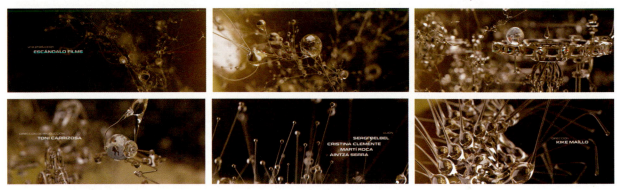

At Ringling College of Art + Design, Hunter Thompson's rich, emotive storyboard for a title treatment for *Black Butterflies* (2011) expresses the idea of racism in South Africa and the central character, Ingrid's opposition to the apartheid regime. Black ink falls across worn paper to form high-contrast images of apartheid crimes, giving an historical context. The images build into detailed butterfly wings that portray the suffering of South Africans, Ingrid's poetry, and the film's title (**2.14**).

2.14
Storyboard for *Black Butterflies* (2011) by Hunter Thompson. © 2012 Ringling College of Art + Design.

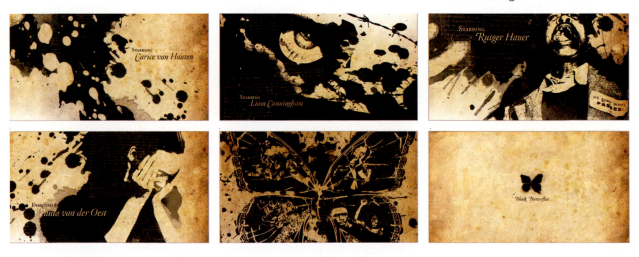

2.15
Title sequence frames for *When Life Gives You Lemons* (2010) by Andrew Schoneweis (above) and Sharon Correa (below). © 2012 Ringling College of Art + Design.

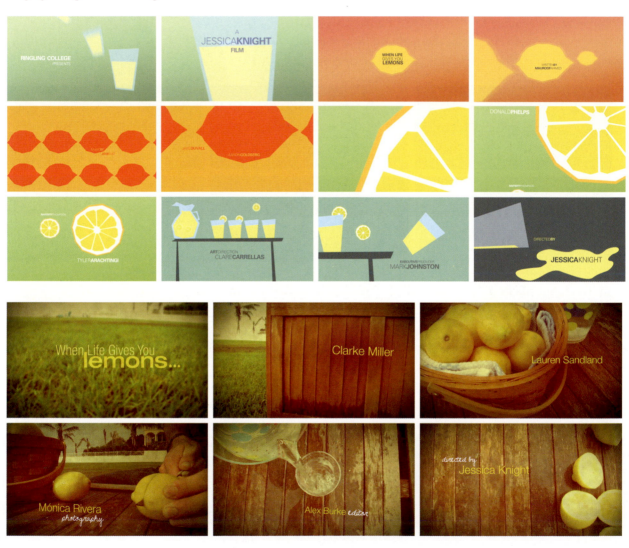

Andrew Schoneweis' opening title sequence (2.15, above) for *When Life Gives You Lemons* (2010) relies on a pure, graphic style that pays homage to Saul Bass. In contrast, Sharon Correa's intimate style (2.15, below) evokes nostalgic, childhood memories through a combination of live-action imagery, muted colors, and informal typography.

Chapter Summary

A film's opening credits are the first images that viewers experience once the lights are dimmed in the theater. Their purpose is to create the context of the film and establish expectations about its atmosphere and tone. Since the 1950s, movie title sequences have evolved as a form of experimental filmmaking.

The origin of film titles can be traced back to the silent film era, when opening credits were presented as static text on title cards. During the 1950s, Saul Bass became the movie industry's leading film title innovator. His evocative openings for directors Alfred Hitchcock and Otto Preminger garnered public attention as miniature films in their own right. Cuban-born filmmaker Pablo Ferro earned his reputation as a title designer from techniques including rapid-cut editing, hand-drawn animation, split-screen montage, and hand-drawn typography. His processes influenced what became known in television as the "MTV style."

The evolution of title sequences over the years has introduced a wide range of concepts and stylistic approaches that have shaped the visual landscape of film. During the 1960s, Friz Freleng's opening cartoon animation for *The Pink Panther* (1963) became an icon of pop culture. Freleng's use of spinning letters and unscrambling words was a complete departure from the cheaply made theatrical cartoons of the time. American designer Maurice Binder's titles for the classic James Bond movies gained popularity for

their abstract, erotic imagery. In Britian, Terry Gilliam's cutout animations for the Monty Python group entertained audiences and demonstrated what the technique of stop-motion collage was capable of achieving. During the 1970s, Richard and Robert Greenberg's title treatment for the feature *Superman* (1978) demonstrated the use of computer-assisted effects enabling three-dimensional animation.

Influenced by Ferro and Bass during the 1990s, Kyle Cooper was one of the first designers to apply trends in print to film titles and combine conventional and digital processes. His opening credit sequence for the psychological thriller *Se7en* (1995) is regarded as an historical landmark. More recent titles that have broken new ground include Imaginary Forces' haunting credits for Joel Schumacher's *The Number 23* (2007) and French designer Kook Ewo's dark, fast-paced titles for Vincenzo Natali's sci-fi thriller *Splice* (2006).

"Title sequences excite me because they're all about fitting into an existing universe. You have to bring a new note into a melody. I don't think I've one specific, very strong style (except some obsessions/gimmicks) and that's what helps me the most in this job. I'm not obsessed by showing beautiful looking things, I'm obsessed to stay in the melody; in the right mood. My work is all about that."

—*Kook Ewo*

3

motion graphics
in television
an overview

Early cinematic techniques used in experimental avant-garde film and movie title sequences were adopted in broadcast graphics when television became a new medium for animation. In today's competitive marketplace, the production of station identifications, show opens, network packages, advertisements, and music videos drives the need for more compelling on-air graphics, offering many creative opportunities to combine traditional graphic design with the visual language of cinema.

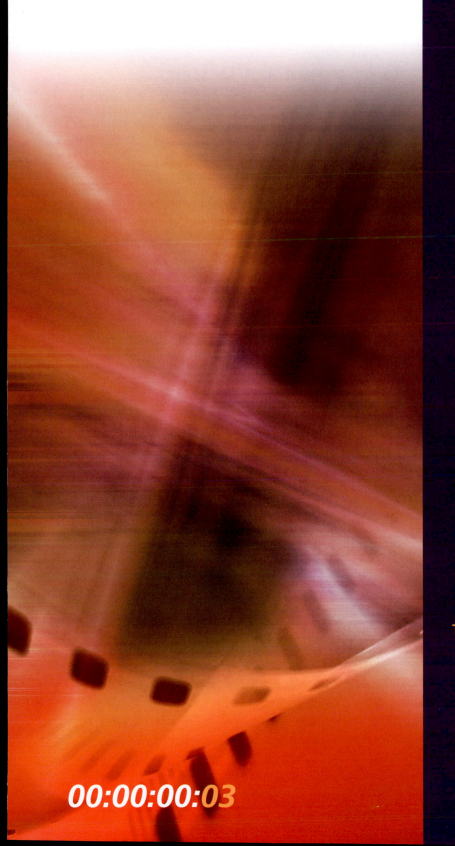

00:00:00:03

The Origin of Broadcast Design

During the 1960s, most prime-time television content was produced on color film. Tape-recording technology also became available and color videotape machines and tape cartridge systems were offered by RCA, providing stations with reliable playback. Broadcasters stretched the limits of portability with large cameras and recorders. Program relay by satellite also emerged, giving viewers live images from all over the world. When there were three television networks, brand identity was captured in three signature logos designed by Paul Rand: NBC's peacock, CBS's eye, and ABC's circle. During that time, Harry Marks, who was employed by ABC, conceived the prospect of the moving logo, and hired Douglas Trumbull, who pioneered the special effects for the film *2001: A Space Odyssey* (1968). Trumbull's slit-scan camera, developed as an extension of John Whitney's work, was mounted on a track and moved toward artwork that was illuminated on a table. In front of the art, an opaque screen with a thin vertical slit restricted the field of view of the camera to a narrow horizontal angle. Although this process was laborious and expensive, it introduced many graphic possibilities into the broadcast world. The opening sequence to ABC's *Movie of the Week* was a major accomplishment and captivated audiences nationwide. A precursor to modern digital animation techniques, it brought about a major graphic design revolution in the television industry (**3.1**).

In today's competitive marketplace, the need for station identifications, show openers, network packages, advertisements, and music videos drives the production of more compelling on-air graphics, offering many creative opportunities to combine traditional graphic design principles with the visual language of cinema.

As vice president and creative director at ABC and CBS, Harry Marks has been recognized throughout the United States and the rest of the world as the legendary father of broadcast motion graphics. Throughout his career, he pushed the envelope of digital technology and produced cutting-edge work that earned many awards, including an Emmy and the first Life Achievement Award from the Broadcast Design Association.

Network Branding

The average supermarket carries thousands of individual product lines. In order to get us to "tune in" to a particular product, its owner must gain our attention before we get to the market. Similarly, in today's multi-channel universe, branding is needed for a network to keep up with its competition. Television companies have become increasingly image conscious, investing large amounts of time in assessing their audiences and spending huge sums of money on developing their on-screen look.

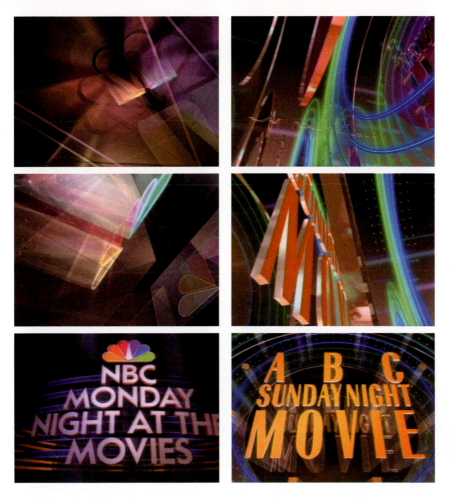

3.1
Frames from NBC's *Monday Night at the Movies* and ABC's *Sunday Night Movie* by Dale Herigstad (1989). Courtesy of Harry Marks/Pacific Data Images and NBC.

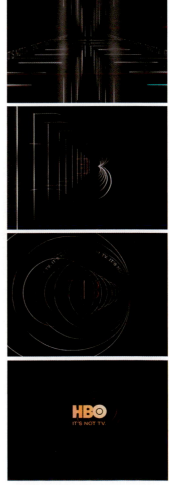

3.2
Station ID storyboard for HBO. Courtesy of Susan Detrie and New Wave Entertainment. © HBO.

station IDs

"Station identifications" (also called "stings" or "network IDs") identify the station or network being aired. Because of the number of signals that are available, the Federal Communications Commission (FCC) requires that all television and radio stations in the U.S. identify themselves on an hourly basis and at the beginning and end of each broadcast period. The station's call letters must be included, as well as its city of license and the channel number signifying its dial position (even though television sets do not come with dials anymore). Additionally, the communities that the station serves must appear on screen or be announced verbally. The FCC offers some flexibility so that stations can schedule around their programming and commercials. Many networks have their identifications programmed to play automatically during the

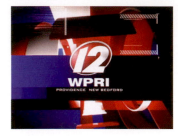

3.3
The call letters of this station ID are "WPRI," and the city is Providence. The channel "12" identifies the dial position. Courtesy of Giant Octopus.

period of five minutes before the hour. Many have also developed clever ways to utilize their station IDs as promotional tools. A pitch for an upcoming show or newscast can fulfill the identification requirements while building an audience by telling viewers to tune in to an event.

When animating a station ID, you must be able to apply the aesthetics of effective logo treatment to a time-based environment. Attention should be given to negative and positive shape relationships and to contextual design elements that contribute to the message the ID is sending. Additionally, you should consider how elements move, change, and interact with each other over time and across space. (Chapters 8 and 9 specifically discuss pictorial and sequential design criteria.) Although station IDs typically only last between 5 – 10 seconds, story structure should be explored to establish the tone and influence the audience's perception of the believability of the message.

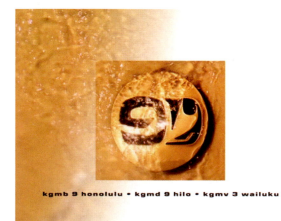

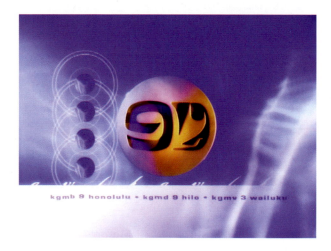

3.4
Station ID for KGMB-TV, the first TV station in Hawaii and a licensed broadcast affiliate of CBS. Courtesy of Giant Octopus.

Shilo, an award-winning design studio based on the East and West Coasts and in locations throughout Europe, designed a set of station IDs for AMC's twentieth anniversary celebration. Each is a short vignette depicting various genres. For example, "big-screen battles" are portrayed with iconic images of airplanes and parachutes, "great action movies" with police cars and headlights, and "romantic movies" with rose petals and jewelry (**see Chapter 8, figure 8.32 on page 279**).

During the late 1980s, world-renowned graphic designer April Greiman developed twelve IDs for Lifetime Television, using available low-end technology including Kodak disposable cameras, and 8 millimeter video shot without a tripod. Her goal was to produce an innovative use of the

Lifetime identity from hybridized footage elements (**3.5**). Imaginary Forces' recent identity package for Lifetime integrated handwritten images, Polaroid photographs, and free-floating natural images such as leaves and butterflies (**3.6**).

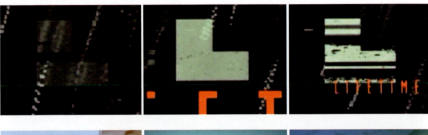

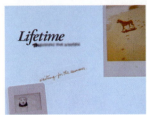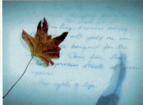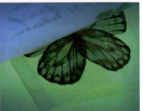

3.5
ID for Lifetime Television. Courtesy of April Greiman, Made In Space. © Lifetime Television.

3.6
ID for Lifetime Television. Courtesy of Imaginary Forces. © Lifetime Television.

Within the past few years, automated, real-time visualization has allowed a degree of customization in broadcast motion graphics. A groundbreaking example of interactive television branding is a series of IDs developed for the Wales-based bilingual channel S4C (**3.8**). Minivegas, a multidisciplinary design studio in London, explored the idea of delivering dynamically generated content within a traditional, photorealistic setting. The goal was to develop ten unique, audio-reactive scenarios depicting vignettes of Welsh life. Each time a spot is broadcast, the volume and frequency input from the announcer's voice causes certain elements in the scene to move or change unexpectedly, interrupting the normal flow of everyday life. For example, electric wires in a lighthouse warp and wave; painted signage on the ground springs to life in a car park; the lights in a store blink on and off while the shop proprietor climbs a ladder. Although each ID stands on its own merit without audio, the voice input breathes life into the composition. This automated approach allows each scene to be entirely unique each time it is screened. According to Minivegas' co-founder Luc Schurgers, lighting-based scenarios such as a lighting store and a welding shop involved turning hundreds of lights on and off to keep the background conditions as fixed as possible. Other IDs, including a lighthouse, floor-polisher cables in a museum, and a car park, involved

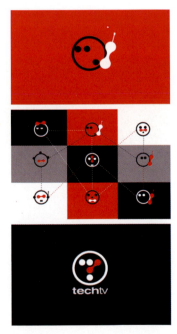

3.7
Frames from an ID for Tech TV, a cable channel in San Francisco (2001). Courtesy of Viewpoint Creative. © Tech TV.

3.8
Voice-reactive IDs for S4C, a Wales-based TV network. Motion responds to fluctuations in the television announcer's voice. Courtesy of Minivegas.

placing 3D elements in the scene to emphasize the subject's movements. Taking more then a year to develop, Minivegas created specialized software that integrated video decoding, compositing, and color correction, and built a piece of hardware that behaved like a digideck to synchronize the video and audio using broadcast-standard signals.

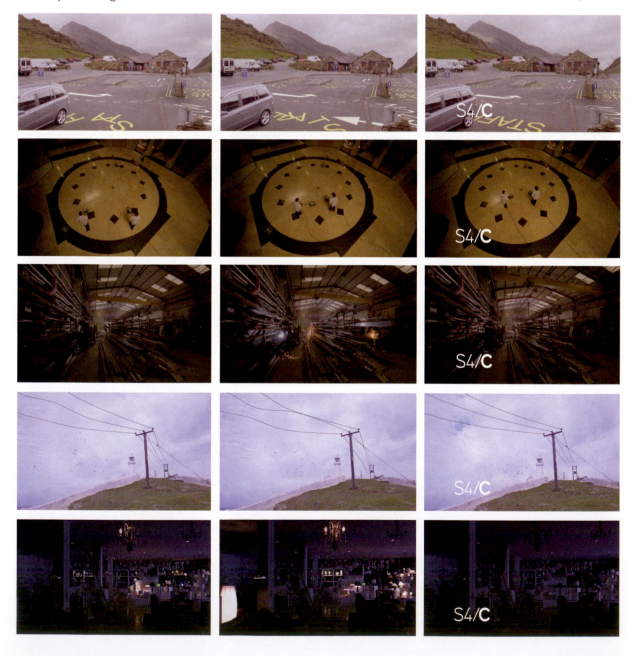

At Ringling College of Art + Design, Hunter Thompson explored the idea of combining photographs of people from the Tampa, Sarasota and St. Petersburg communities into mosaic views of the Gulf Coast in a WEDU network redesign. Using group and tag labeling on Flickr, images can be uploaded by people and stitched together to form a mosaic (**3.9**).

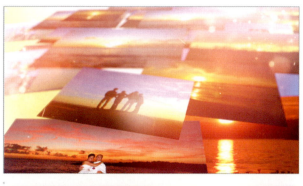 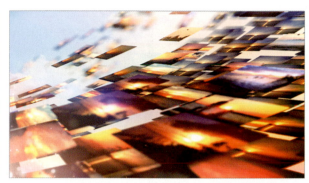

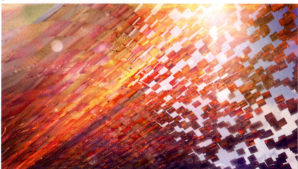 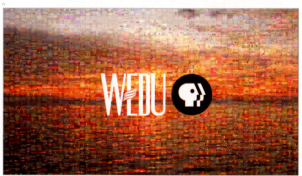

3.9
Frames from "Mosaic," a station ID redesign for WEDU by Hunter Thompson. © 2012 Ringling College of Art + Design.

show openers

Like a magazine cover or the introductory credits to a movie, a "show opener" sets the stage for the upcoming program. Imaginative show openers help to promote the network's identity and tone and can make the difference between captivating viewers and making them reach for the remote. Show openings typically last between 15 and 30 seconds.

In an opener to *Court TV Movies*, Court TV wanted a direct yet engaging means of promoting their movie block. Hatmaker, a broadcast design studio in Massachusetts, combined fresh takes of iconic cinematic imagery that suggested story snippets from original video footage and a rich theatrical palette. The graphics embrace the genre while conveying a sense of sheer entertainment (**3.11**).

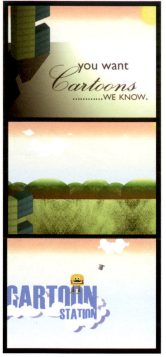

3.10
Justin Medas' Cartoon Network ID redesign plays on the nostalgia of late 1990s cartoons. Courtesy of Professor Jon Krasner, Fitchburg State University.

3.11
Frames from the show opener to *Court TV Movies*. Courtesy of Hatmaker and Court TV.

The opening to *The Hungry Detective*, a program on the Food Network hosted by Chris Cognac, was outsourced to four independent artists living in Chile. The underlying concept was based on a police investigator in search of the best off-the-beaten-path restaurants in the U.S. to write about. With a tight budget and a time frame of three weeks to deliver an entire package consisting of an open, lower thirds, and transitions, Matias Rivera, one of the artists, delivered an intriguing kinetic collage of objects from an investigator's desk. A magnifying glass communicated a "micro and macro" concept that allowed viewers to "fly" inside the elements almost microscopically (**3.12**).

ZDF (Zweites Deutsches Fernsehen, or "Second German Television") is a public service German television channel based in Mainz. Velvet, a motion design studio in Munich, designed an opener for ZDF's culture program *Aspekte* based on the concept of a mirror of culture and society. Combinations of photographic and live-action images showing various artistic and cultural events containing people with "mirrorheads" that awake illusions or open new perspectives. Dynamic typographic animations of letterforms move into empty blocks and spread out from a violin player, mimicking musical sounds or notes. This content is found in every element of the package including the logo containing a mirror as a means of self-reflection (**3.13**).

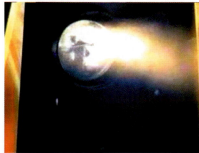

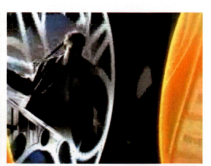

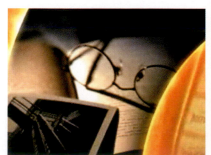

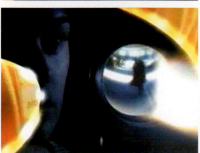

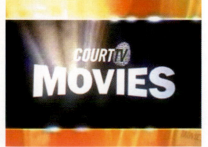

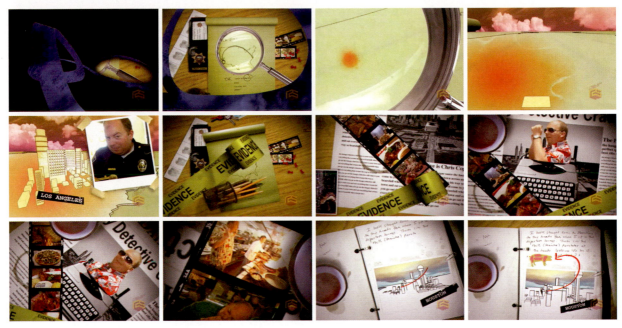

3.12
Frames from the show opener
for *The Hungry Detective*. Courtesy
of Reality Check Studios.

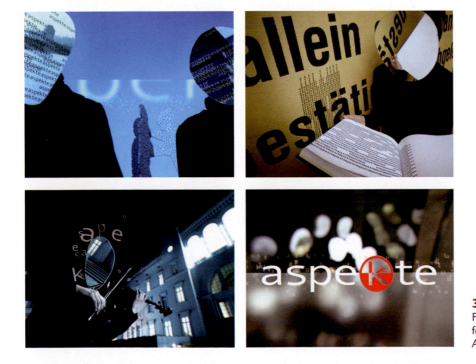

3.13
Frames from the show opener
for ZDF's culture program
Aspekte. Courtesy of Velvet.

3.14

In a show opener to *Destination Style*, typography was treated in a haiku-like way to complement the beauty and poetry of fashion and to express the global aspect of the show. Courtesy of Susan Detrie and The Travel Channel.

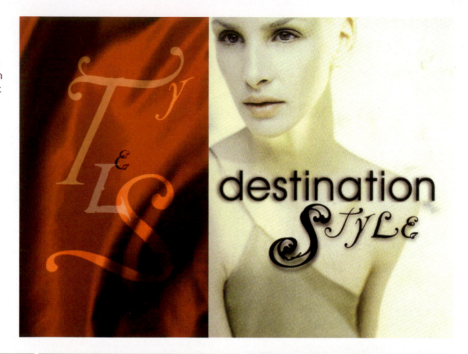

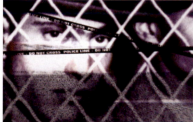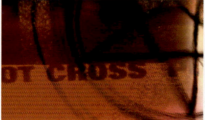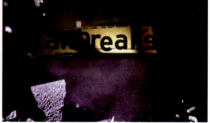

3.15

Frames from the opening titles to *Lawbreakers*. Courtesy of ZONA Design and The History Channel.

Combinations of live footage punctuated with shattered glass reflects the program's pacing and episodic quality.

On September 10 and 11, 2006, the two-part miniseries *The Path to 9/11*, was broadcast on ABC television. Written by Cyrus Nowrasteh and directed by David L. Cunningham, the film dramatized the 1993 and September 11, 2001 attacks on the World Trade Center in New York City. The opening sequence sets the tone of the film in a very poignant and beautiful way from the viewpoint of a New Yorker. Digital Kitchen, a Seattle-based motion graphics studio, aimed to portray this sensitive subject in a way that engaged the viewer, while setting the mood for the film (**3.16**). The concept began as a short piece that showed vignettes of New Yorkers involved in their mundane morning routines before leaving for work. This evolved into a longer sequence, beginning with a first person point-of-view shot looking out of a Brooklyn window, then moving on to activities centered around getting to work, and then to shots showing the city waking up, slowly migrating toward the Trade Center buildings. According to designer Lindsay Daniels, the goal of shooting the imagery in New York City over a period of two days was to capture interesting and unusual angles and voyeuristic viewpoints that would imply that someone was watching the city. Another conceptual element used throughout the composition is moiré patterns that become more prominent as the pace of the editing increases. They enforce the idea of the city being watched and serve as a natural transition into the architecture of the Trade Center buildings.

3.16
Frames from the opening titles to *The Path to 9/11*. Courtesy of Digital Kitchen.

See also Chapter 13, figure 13.32, on p. 474.

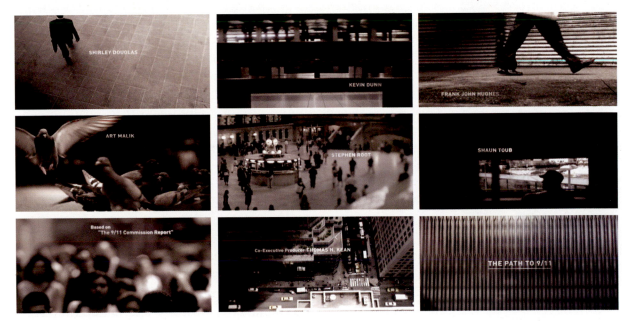

ZONA Design, a New York based design and branding studio, created the sexy and exciting opening titles for Orchard Films' *Indie Sex*, a four-part mini-series that aired on the Independent Film Channel (IFC) in August, 2007. The series investigated a vast range of highly controversial topics relating to how sex is presented to the public, from underage sex, to censorship, taboos, fetishism, and sexual extremes. Repetitive, stylistic depictions of teen sex, bondage, and homoerotica are infused with tactile patterns and a hot, fiery color palette to provide a tasteful yet bold approach, reflecting an attitude that captures the diversity of the series and expressing a sense of voyeurism. ZONA's creative director Zoa Martinez states: "The zipper on the black leather bustier opens to expose a series of sexually charged images—a sensual kiss, the interlocking of fingers while in the throes of passion, bondage, the graphic element of the condoms, which I wanted to represent the lights and neon of sex

It was reported before the airing of The Path to 9/11 *that the film misrepresented the Clinton administration as having neglected opportunities to capture or kill Osama bin Laden and did not acknowledge the George W. Bush administration's lack of pursuit of anti-terrorist activities.*

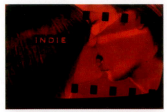

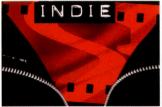

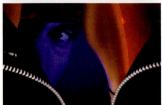

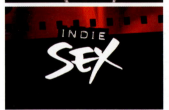

3.17
Opener to *Indie Sex.* Courtesy of ZONA Design.

3.18
Opener to *À la carte.* Courtesy of Studio Blanc.
See also Chapter 7, figure 7.81, on p. 255.

shops, but also to portray safe sex. The muscular male nude ("live boys live") and the repetition of his image is a stylistic representation of random sex. Lolita and her lollipop depict teen sex, and, of course, the suggestive opening and closing of a woman's gartered legs are as titillating as the move was in *Basic Instinct*. In addition, as sexuality infuses the sense, we wanted some of the graphics to have a tactile feel, so we added the leopard and red satin graphic patterns to the mix." With regard to the logo design, the graphic shape representing cut film was juxtaposed with gestural letterforms to create a contrast that generates "the energy of this thing we call sex" (**3.17**).

Studio Blanc, a Canadian graphic design agency, developed an opener for a television series on Radio-Canada Television about places around western Canada. The sequence, which portrays traveling through BC, Alberta, Saskatchewan, and Manitoba, is infused with iconography representing Canada's western provinces. Delivered in a modern style, the opening's kitsch, colorful journey leads you into Radio-Canada's *À la carte* program hosted by Jacky Essombe (**3.18**).

"Topical openings" are introductions to news programs that inform viewers of upcoming stories or events (**3.19**). They often integrate live-action video, still photography, typography, and graphics (including the station ID) to enhance their entertainment value. Design strategies and storytelling devices such as cropping, angle of view, and montage, are used to organize the clarity and readability of information and frame the veracity of the news by reinforcing the truth value of the coverage and the reputation of the station.

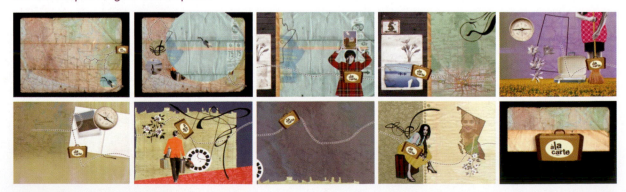

show packages

A "show package" is a "video information system" containing an assortment of design elements that are used to promote a program. These elements must demonstrate a visual synergy, although the vibe and pacing of them may be slightly different. For example, ZONA Design's branding package for NBC-TV's reality series *Lost* includes an opener, a series of bumpers, mortises, lower thirds, maps, and a logo for print and on-air design. The show, which has been described as a global adventure with unexpected twists and turns, follows six strangers who are paired off, blindfolded, and shipped to an undisclosed location to find their way back to the Statue of Liberty. ZONA devised a look that captures the sense of being confused and disoriented. A multilayered explosion of bold graphic elements and a fast editing pace exudes a heart-pounding kinetic energy. International signage, transportation symbols, and bold graphic icons such as grids, arrows, and numbers were incorporated as textural devices to express the feeling of billboards being peeled away. Throughout the piece, the words "lost," "north," "south," "east," and "west" appear in various languages, including Chinese, Russian, and Arabic (**3.20**). According to creative director Zoa Martinez: "Our design had to convey the excitement of the unknown, that envelops both the competitors and the audience. The contestants' starting points are strictly concealed. They are in a race against time and they must confront and conquer any barriers in their path." Zoa continued: "We designed a crisp, modular system from global, continent, country, and local-specific maps, complete with team comparisons and actual footage. We gave them a very stylized look in a neutral palette contrasted with vibrant colors for punctuation. There is nothing peaceful about the series and our designs are meant to keep the viewer on edge as well."

Kids' Choice Awards is an annual flagship awards show honoring the year's most popular television, movie, and music acts as voted for by children who watch Nickelodeon's cable channel. Each year the theme changes in order to appeal to Nickelodeon's teen audience. In 2006, Nickelodeon hired the motion graphics company Blur to develop a rock n' roll circus theme. The concept was inspired by psychedelic poster art and vernacular typography from the 1960s (**3.21**).

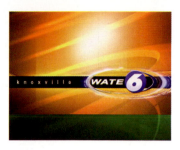

3.19
Topical news opening frames for ABC/Channel 9 and WATE/ Channel 6. Courtesy of Giant Octopus.

3.20
Frames from the branding package for NBC-TV's reality series *Lost*. Courtesy of ZONA Design.

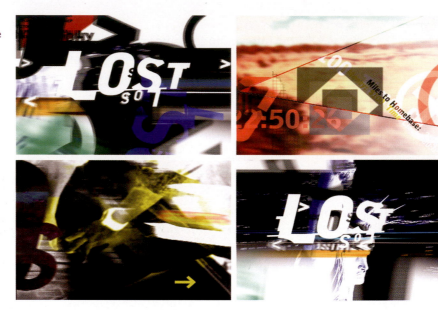

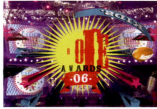

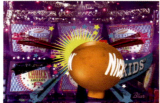

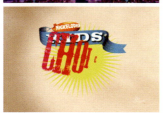

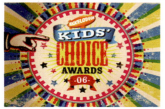

3.21
Frames from Nickelodeon's show package for the *Kids' Choice Awards*, 2006. Courtesy of Blur.

3.22
Frames from the opener for Fox's *Teen Choice Awards 2005* show package. Courtesy of Blur.

Blur's show package for FOX's *Teen Choice Awards 2005*, televised on Fox and on Global TV in Canada, was based on Venice, California's skateboard and surfboarding "dogtown" culture of the 1970s. The gritty, raw look of graffiti and spray paint was applied to combinations of gothic and hand-drawn elements. The theme behind the package depicted reggae and rock safari culture with a younger teen twist involving live-action shots of models surfing. The hand-made quality of the lettering, in the spirit of doodling, is effective in making the feel of the package accessible to the show's target teenage audience (**3.22**).

In Blur's awards show package for Black Entertainment Television, the graphics and rich color palette are intended to portray the luxury and expense of being a celebrity. An open mortise was used in the opening segment, and a keyable (versus a full screen) logo was placed over the live footage in the show opening and was also used in bumpers that were aired between commercial breaks. A combination of header and lower thirds is used to introduce artists (**3.23**).

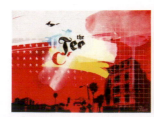

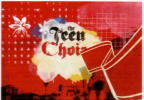

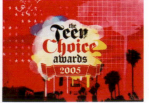

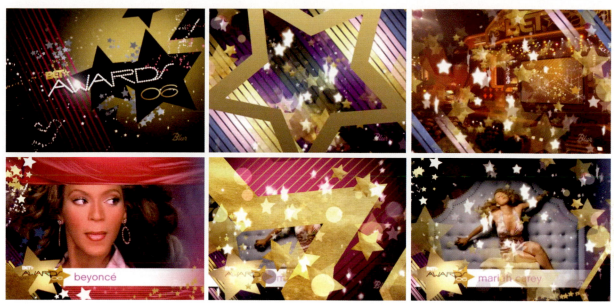

3.23
above:
Black Entertainment Television's awards show package, 2006. Courtesy of Blur.

3.24
below:

A distinctive redesign of Court TV's daytime show package features the image of Lady Justice blindfolded. Abstract typography and a sharp color palette adds depth and energy. Courtesy of ZONA Design.

See also Chapter 7, figure 7.56, on p. 240.

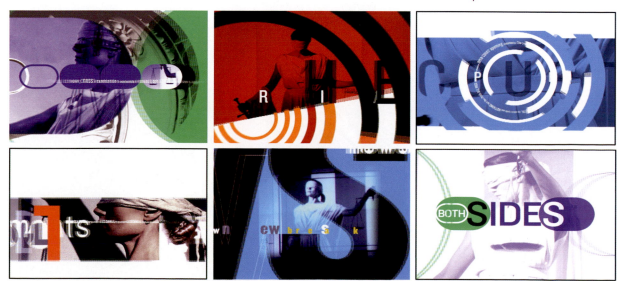

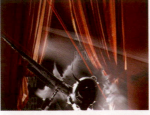
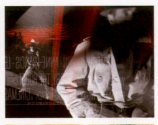
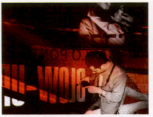
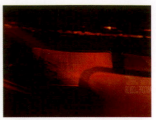
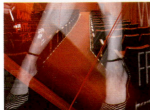
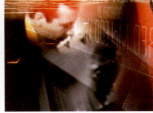
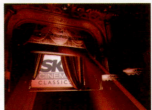
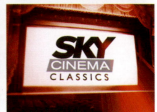

3.25

In the storyboard for *SKY Cinema Classics'* show opener, the doors of a darkened theatre open. We walk down the aisle to experience a mélange of cinematic, historical moments, including a World War II fighter plane and a figure in a trench coat occupying the space around us. As the curtains draw open and the flickering projector brings the screen to life, the logo blazes across the frame. Courtesy of Flying Machine.

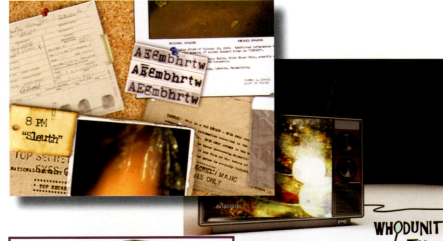

3.26

In Curtis Page's package for a murder-mystery-themed station, a cork board full of suspects, police documents, fingerprints, a magnifying glass, and a flashlight contribute to the old-fashioned feel he tried to convey. Courtesy of Professor Jon Krasner, Fitchburg State University.

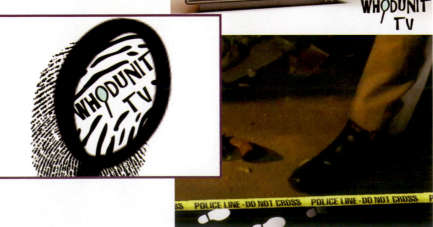

interstitials

"Interstitials" are 30 to 60-second mini-programs that appear between movies or other events, each having a specific objective. Some are designed to highlight key issues, people or events to establish a sense of context. Others function from a commercial standpoint to promote a network's brand by creating a link with an existing program. The character Squidley is used for Cartoon Network interstitials (**3.27**), and Noggin's interstitials are hosted by various characters such as Moose and Zee. Others feature hands-on demonstrations from star athletes on sports channels or interviews with actors on premium movie channels.

News interstitials are used to inform viewers that a top story is about to be featured or to suggest developing or continued coverage of a story. They also provide a transition from the anchorperson or studio into a live or prerecorded story. This form of interstitial is typically no more than 1 to 2 seconds in duration.

bumpers

A "bumper" (or "bump") is a brief presentation that transitions between a program and a commercial break. Lasting between 2 to 5 seconds, typically they display the show's name or logo and are accompanied by an announcement that states the program's title and network. Late-night bumpers are often quirky and amusing presentations that play on pop culture. For example, a bumper for an episode of *Late Night with Conan O'Brien* depicted Conan as Hermey the Elf in the televised Christmas special "Rudolph, the Red-Nosed Reindeer" (1964).

In children's television programming, it is a common practice for a bumper to distinguish between the program and a paid commercial because of the fact that children are not always able to discern the difference between the two. **Figure 3.28** features a bumper for *Flux Television*, a music television program that addressed digital culture, technology, and future culture music during the mid-1990s. A bright, highly saturated color palette, flat, stylized graphics, and looped live-action footage reflects the northern California aesthetic and technological flavor of the pre-dotcom era.

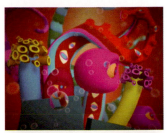
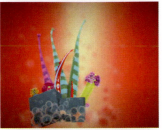
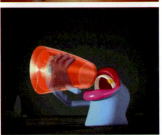
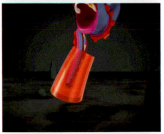
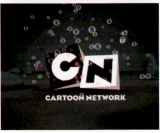

3.27
Frames from "Squidley," an interstitial for the Cartoon Network. Courtesy of Freestyle Collective. © Cartoon Network.

3.28
Flux Television bumper. Courtesy of twenty2product. © 1994 Flux Television.

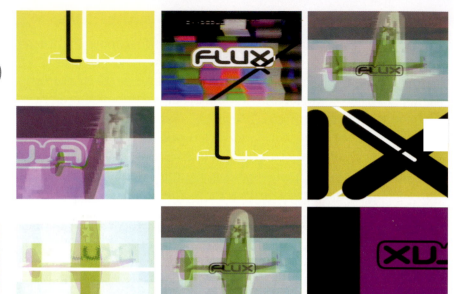

3.29
Bumper for Noggin (1999). Courtesy of Big Blue Dot and Nickelodeon.

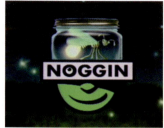

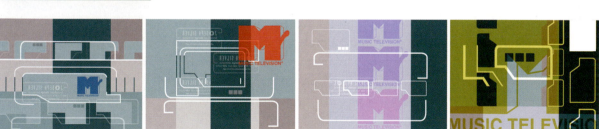

3.30
MTV bumper pitch. Courtesy of Joseph Silver.

lower thirds

"Lower thirds" are combinations of graphics and text that appear on the bottom portion of the screen to identify the station, the presenter(s), and the content being aired. They are most commonly found in news productions and documentaries. In most cases, they do not occupy a full third of the screen, especially when the only requirement is a name and title. In cases where the programming necessitates additional information, a side panel is usually added. Lower thirds can range from simple to complex graphical elements. Text and images often animate as they arrive on screen and then remain still. Sometimes animated backgrounds consisting of subtle shapes, colors, or patterns are designed to loop while the underlying video continues to play.

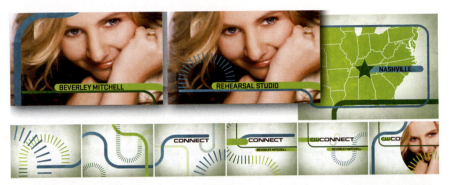

3.30
In a promotional package for "CW Connect: Beverley Mitchell," the lower thirds design complements the style of other insert elements, including a closing and map. Courtesy of Susan Detrie.

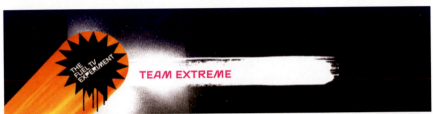

3.31
This lower third design for *The Fuel TV Experiment*, a two-year program that launched in May, 2004 to support up to ten aspiring action sports filmmakers. Courtesy of Fuel TV.

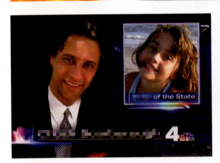 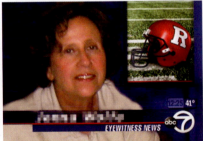 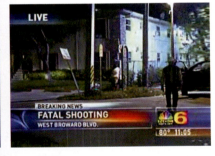

3.32
above:
Lower thirds are often arranged in tiers. In these news-related scenarios: one-tier identifies the presenter; two-tiers identify the person on the first line and the news program; three-tiers include a heading, sub-heading, and a locator identifying where the story is taking place. These also identify the channel and network. © 2012 Jon Krasner.

3.33
Lower thirds design for Black Entertainment Television's awards show package. Courtesy of Blur.

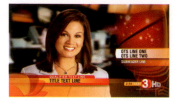

3.34
A lower thirds template for KTVK's news program. Courtesy of Reality Check Studios.

3.35
Mortise design for KTVK's news program. Courtesy of Reality Check Studios.

mortises

"Mortises"—full screen graphics that are used to frame live footage—are sometimes used in combination with lower thirds. In a mortise for KTVK (**3.35**), Phoenix's twenty-four hour news channel, the design maintains the graphic continuity of KTVK's end tag (**3.42**). Repeated three-dimensional structures from the channel's logo and live video footage of moving clouds appear again in the background, this time within a more compressed horizontal space. The color scheme, consisting of deep red, yellow, and magenta, is also carried over.

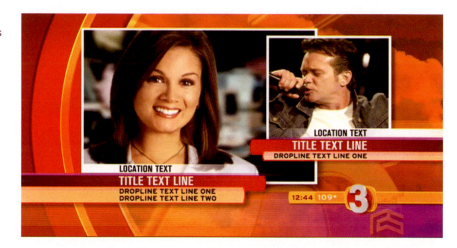

In most awards shows, mortises are used to showcase the individual talent being featured. In an awards show package for Black Entertainment Television, an open mortise was used in the opening segment (**3.36**). The design is effective in that all graphic elements carry over between the mortises representing different people, while at the same time, the general arrangement of the mortise's elements vary. In Blur's package for Nickelodeon's *Kids' Choice Awards*, the ending compilation of the show's best moments consists of a hybrid lower thirds mortise (**3.37**).

3.36
Mortise for Black Entertainment Television. Courtesy of Blur.

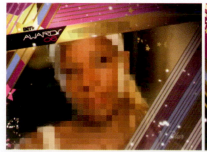
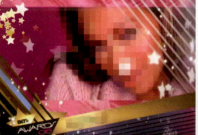
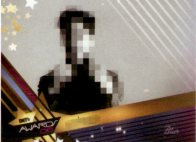

In **figure 3.38**, the mortise for Fox's *Action Sports Awards* was designed to work closely with the theme of the television show's opening that took viewers on an intense journey through a world of action sports iconography. The design package employed oversized background elements to create a whimsical 3D character animation context, departing from the typical grunge graphics that are associated with sports shows.

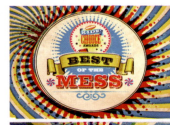
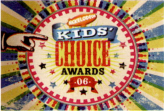

3.37
Mortise for Nickelodeon's *Kids' Choice Awards*. Courtesy of Blur.

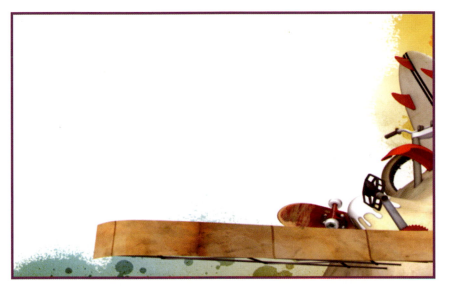

3.38
Mortise design for Fox's *Action Sports Awards*. Courtesy of Shilo and Fuel TV.

lineups and upfronts

A "lineup" is a full screen graphic that informs viewers about a network's upcoming program schedule by displaying the names of the shows, dates, and times. An "upfront" is a marketing piece that is designed to promote a network's shows to advertisers. Upfronts also unveil the following season's lineup to give viewers a first glimpse of what shows are returning, which have been cancelled, and what new series have been picked up. Similar to an awards show, they often involve stage presentations which may feature comedy routine and star walk-ons. Both lineups and upfronts have become more elaborate, dictating the need for eye-catching, supporting motion graphics.

3.39
Frames from an upfront for Country Music Television. Courtesy of NAILGUN*.

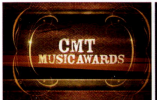
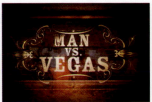
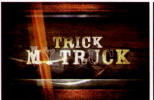
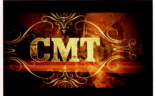

3.40
Frames from lineups for *Unprotected Sets* and *Stacked Sundays*. Courtesy of Fuel TV.

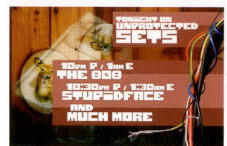 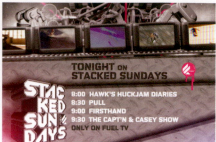

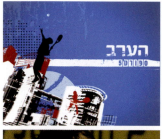

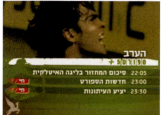

3.41
Frames from a lineup for Sports 5. Courtesy of Flying Machine.

3.42
End tag frame for KTVK, an independent news station in Phoenix. Courtesy of Reality Check Studios.

tags

A "tag" is a succinct, 3 to 4 second presentation that is shown at the beginning or end of a bumper, news opening, or commercial. For example, Fuel TV's wide variety of tag designs have been used to promote the unique personalities and epic moments in action sports (**3.44**). In commercials, tags are often customized to reinforce a particular brand of the product being described, recap its directive, or inform viewers where to go for additional information, such as a phone number or Web site address.

The end tag in a promotional spot for Verb—a youth campaign that helps teenagers lead healthier lifestyles by increasing physical activity—provides a URL in a colorful animation (**3.43**).

End tags can also function as a "legal IDs" or brief messages that are aired at the top and bottom of every hour. Legal IDs typically indicate the station's call letters and city of license.

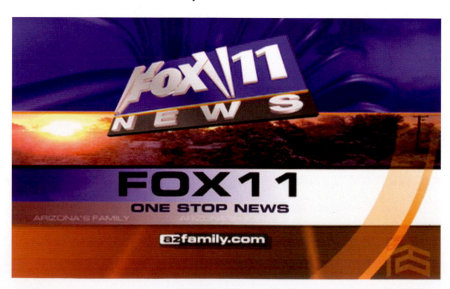

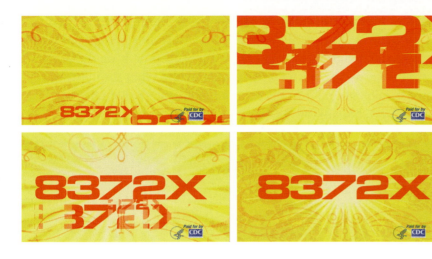

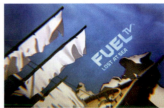

3.43
Frames from the end tag of a promotional spot for Verb. Courtesy of NAILGUN*.

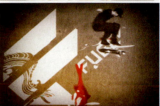

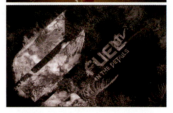

3.44
Network tags used by Fuel TV to promote personalities and epic moments of action sports. Courtesy of Fuel TV.

3.45
MTV K network package launch. Courtesy of Freestyle Collective.

network packages

Similar to a show package, a "network package" is a complete "video information system" that is comprised of promotional elements such as station identifiers, bumpers, lower thirds, and mortises.

MTV Ks network package helped launch the first premium channel in the MTV World family geared toward young Korean-Americans. Provocative combinations of live-action video, still photographs, and vibrant two-dimensional and three-dimensional animations evoke the young, cool lifestyle that has become synonymous with MTV culture. The commercial-free network features Korean music videos and is meant to speak to a diverse group of Korean-Americans between ages 13 and 30. Freestyle Collective's team rented a nightclub and karaoke bar in Manhattan's Koreatown and cast a variety of young talent. The resulting package covered different niches of Korean-American lifestyles (**3.45**).

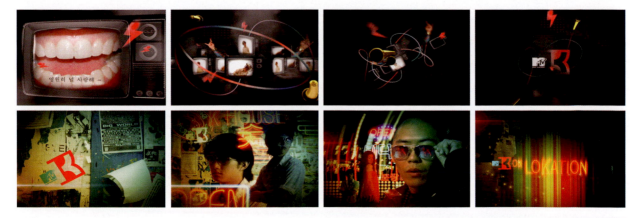

3.46
BET J relaunch. Courtesy of
Freestyle Collective.

See also Chapter 13, figure
13.17, on p. 462.

Freestyle Collective also created a full network rebrand for BET J—a
spin-off cable channel of Black Entertainment Television—to showcase
jazz music related programming. Drawing conceptually on the soul
and funk of jazz, the design conveyed all the ideas that the network
wanted to achieve and introduced a modular system that offered a
limitless set of possibilities (**3.46**).

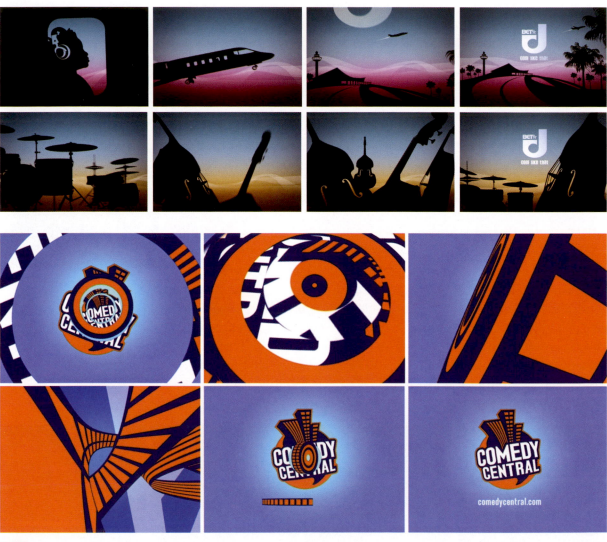

3.47
Frames from a network package
for Comedy Central. Designed
and produced by Imaginary
Forces. © Comedy Central.

Kemistry, a branding and communications agency in the United Kingdom, developed an identity package across all in-flight channels for KLM's Royal Dutch Airlines (**3.48**). (This Netherlands-based subsidiary of Air France is the oldest carrier in the world that continues to operate under its original name.) According to the company's Web site, the project demonstrated "a new spin on mile-high entertainment" by violating their own strict branding guidelines in deconstructing KLM's logo. Although the client was initially reluctant, it was eventually delighted with the final product.

Kemistry's branding, identity, on-air graphics, and news set design helped launch National TV, a TV station in Romania that features everything from live news bulletins to magazine shows, dating shows, horoscope programs, reality TV, and sports coverage. The channel was launched by Vorel Micula, a Romanian food and drinks businessman, whose most famous product is his Transylvanian Vodka. He harnessed the best Romanian talent using experts from the United Kingdom, and contracted with the on-air design company Kemistry to help him get the channel off the ground. In less than six months the television station was transformed into an on-air reality with its own offices, studios, and top-quality technical infrastructure (**3.49**).

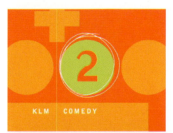

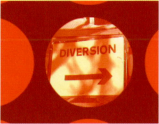

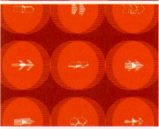

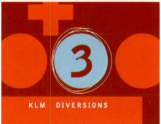

3.48
Frames from KLM network package. Courtesy of Kemistry.

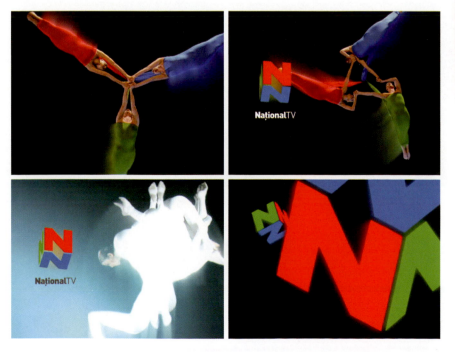

3.49
Frames from the network package launching National TV in Romania. Courtesy of Kemistry.

In 2006, NBC reinvented its on-air image across its prime time, daytime, news, sports, and online divisions, with a consistent new look for the 2006–07 season. This look would be based on the idea of convergence of digital and broadcast television and the presence of content on the Internet. After an intense competition between design and advertising firms, NBC's in-house design department, MAGIC, was hired. Its mission was to give the network a distinctive, interactive feel by using a single feather from the original "peacock logo" as a navigational device (similar to a cursor or a mouse pointer) to guide viewers through informational content pertaining to show names, dates, and air times. This concept speaks to the idea of rebranding the peacock network for the digital age. Additionally, their challenge was to make the identity flexible enough to be customized and paired with the tone and personality of different shows and genres and to adapt to changing schedules. Capacity TV was hired to implement their vision. "It was our challenge to figure out a way to bring personality to the peacock feather as it accessed information, selected characters, and navigated between shows," explained creative director Ellerey Gave. Capacity delivered hundreds of variations for the prime time motion graphics, and the final package consisted of show openers, bumpers, tags, identifications, transitions, and trailers (**3.50**).

3.50
Frames from the 2006 rebranding of the peacock network. Courtesy of Capacity™. Creative Director: Ellerey Gave; Executive Producer: Jennifer Gave; Producer: Jill Marklin; Designer/Animator: Ellerey Gave and Gene Sung; Editor: Benji Thiem; Music: Dave Hummel.

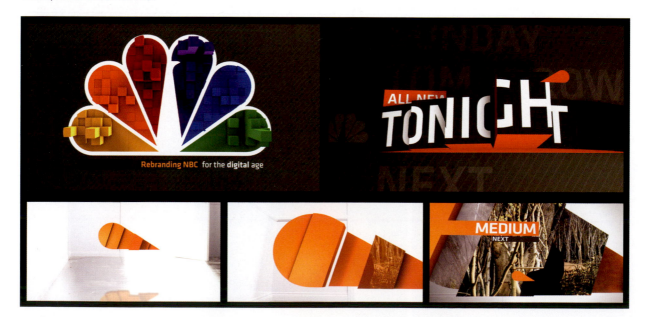

In 2006, award-winning design studios Onesize and yU+co collaborated to rebrand G4, a fast-growing Los Angeles-based network viewed in approximately 61 million homes (**3.51**). Onesize, based in Delft, the Netherlands, is internationally recognized for its work in design, animation, visual effects, and direction for commercials, broadcast, and film. yU+co, with offices in Los Angeles and Hong Kong, is also considered an industry leader in television show openers, network graphics packages, film titles, television trailers, theatrical logos, and commercials. As an entertainment-based network, G4 features shows about technology, gadgets, video games, and web culture to appeal to a demographic of males between the ages of 18 and 34. The concept involved an array of three-dimensional photo-realistic and abstract images, such as an iPod, a video game joystick, and a hip cell phone, floating around a silhouetted box containing G4's logo. A bold color palette is accented by a circular pattern that visually suggests a tornado of iconic images—complete with wires dangling everywhere—coming together inside the G4 logo and tagline "TV That's Plugged In."

This unique visual style offered a high degree of control over the design, empowering G4 to internally create their own specialized, program-specific animation sequences. The key to the design is that it never has to look the same way twice. Every aspect from background textures to images is customizable, allowing Onesize and yU+co to create hundreds of sequences that can be stacked in every way imaginable. According to Rogier Hendriks, co-founder of Onesize: "We wanted to create a look that would encapsulate all of the network's components into one iconic image, while at the same time giving them everything they needed to create their own specialized animations within the framework of our design . . . Basically the redesign is a big toolkit consisting of about 300 different animation sequences." Although it's unusual for two agencies, who might normally compete against each other, to collaborate so closely, Garson Yu, owner of yU+co, stated that this is the future for the global-minded design studio—"It helped us grow as a company to work with new people with different ideas and ways of communicating."

Sky, an Italian satellite platform in Milan and Rome, began in 2003 with over 130 television, interactive, and pay-per-view channels. Micha Riss, founder and creative director of New York design agency Flying Machine, attempted to give Sky's Cinema Classics movie channel a new look while maintaining the integrity of the network's programming. He developed a

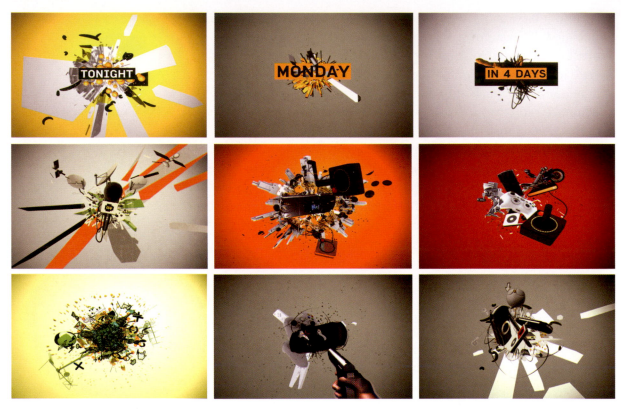

3.51
G4 network package redesign. Courtesy of Onesize and yU+co.

3.52
Sky's *Spazio Italia* network launch. Courtesy of Flying Machine.

concept that pays homage to stylized film posters of the 1930s through the 1980s. These cinematic elements were carefully crafted into a nostalgic presentation. In Milan and Rome, Sky Cinema Italia airs *Spazio Italia* ("Italian Space"), a block of classic Italian movies from the 1970s for native Italian audiences. Micha directed an extensive video shoot in Rome that tells a story of a man posting vintage film posters to the walls of a theatre (**3.52**). The scenes are intercut with real moments from famous movies, and written names of famous directors and actors that animate on the screen are deliberately flipped upside-down so that the viewer's attention will not be directed away from the main story.

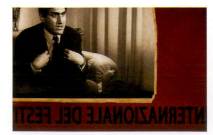
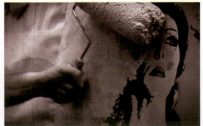
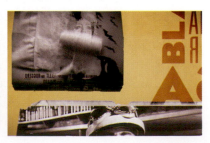

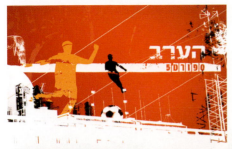

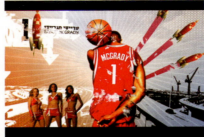

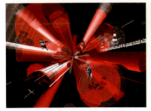

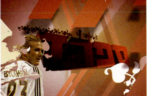

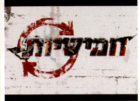

3.53
Frames from Sport 5's 2001 network launch. Courtesy of Flying Machine.

Sport5, Israel's premiere sportcaster, commissioned Flying Machine to execute the channel's first major rebrand in its seventeen-year history. This emotionally-driven package not only celebrates the glory of sports, but brings local fan culture to the forefront of the channel's branding.

Launched in 2003, Fuel TV is one of the first action sports networks dedicated to surfing, skateboarding, snowboarding, motocross, and wakeboarding. Within Fuel's series of channel IDs are Signature IDs that function to associate the channel with a well-known athlete, promote artistic endeavors, and inspire new artists in their art (**3.54 and 3.55**).

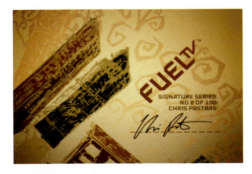

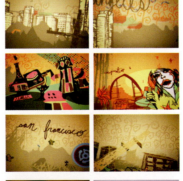

3.54
Frame from "Chris Pastras Signature Series." Produced by Brand New School, LA; Creative Director: Chris Pastras; Music: Echo Park. Courtesy of Fuel TV.

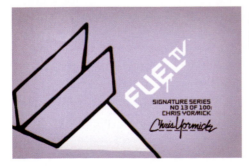

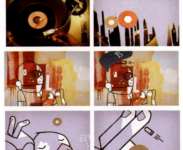

3.55
Frame from "Chris Yormick Signature Series." Produced by Todd Dever; Creative Director: Chris Yormick; Music: Barrington Levy. Courtesy of Fuel TV.

3.56
Elements from a show package for Nicktoona, a spin-off of Nicktoons featuring quirky, bizarre-style cartoons. Courtesy of Joost Korngold and Renascent.

This package includes a show opener, credit roll, lower thirds design, and "bug" (or station logo) that maintains the familiar Nickelodeon "Splat" that has been a Nick trademark since the network relaunched in 1984.

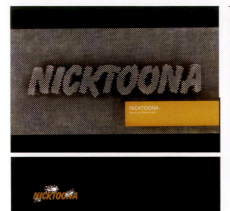
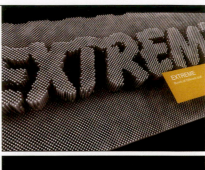
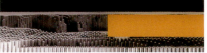

promotional campaigns

"Promotional campaigns" (sometimes referred to as "spots") are designed to make the public more aware of a particular product, brand, or service. Getting the right message across and making sure it is clear is vital to a campaign's success. This involves identifying and examining the intended target audience's gender, age, occupation, and lifestyle, and assessing marketing opportunities and communication channels such as personal sales presentations, print, radio, and television. Developing a promotional message usually requires a collaborative effort to create the content, appeal, structure, format, and source of the message.

Television promotional campaigns have been around since the 1970s and have opened up many artistic opportunities for broadcast designers. In 1977, ABC launched "Still the One," a campaign that was used on several networks around the world. The slogan was conceived by the American Broadcasting Company (ABC) and later adopted by the Nine Network in Australia, Channel 2 in New Zealand, and by Sky Television (now British Sky Broadcasting) in the United Kingdom. The spots featured a version of the 1976 song "Still The One" by the group Orleans.

In the Cartoon Network's campaign to mark Valentine's Day special promotions, Susan Detrie experimented with numerous found objects, from candy boxes to flowers, and arrived at the image of a cupid as the ultimate Valentine's Day symbol. Crayons on Color-aid paper were added to make the background look like a handmade valentine, and the cupids selected were from old Victorian cut-out books (**3.57**). A globe was then added to signify love around the world.

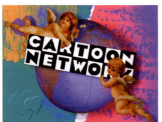
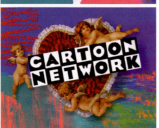
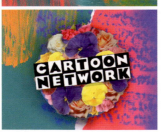

3.57
Frames from "Cupids," a promo for the Cartoon Network. Courtesy of Susan Detrie.

A dynamic promotion for the Independent Film Channel's *Cinema Red Mondays* involved building upon the concept of "pods" comprised of video-photographic collages. Each pod was designed to represent an aspect of Target and IFC's weekly indie film. The spot imitates the organic, textural depth of collage by layering 16-millimeter footage of subjects ranging from a cinema marquee to unfurling plant tendrils and photographs of nature (for example, blooming flowers, birds, ferns, and tree silhouettes). The spot also incorporates cinema-related graphics, including 16-millimeter film cameras and handwritten pages from a screenplay. Target's presence is branded through the use of red, white, and black—the colors of Target's bull's-eye logo. The logo appears in different forms: an old-fashioned film countdown, a rising sun, and a stream of floating bubbles (**3.58**)

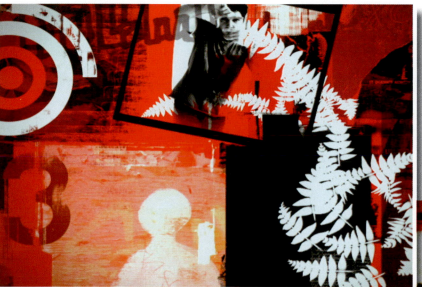

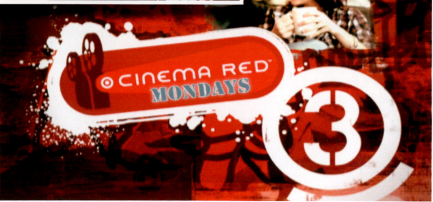

3.58
Frames from a spot promoting the Independent Film Channel's *Cinema Red Mondays*. Courtesy of Freestyle Collective.

Blur Studios in Venice, California developed a network campaign for Kids' WB, the Saturday morning cartoon portion of the CW Television Network's weekend programming. The campaign comprised of twenty-two spots, all of which were built around the quirky Kids' WB logo and studio water tower (the main elements of the network's previous brand). Blur's goal was to develop a novel, Japanese anime look that incorporated kids in a three-dimensional animated environment while retaining core elements of a brand that has been successful over many years. Each spot features a backlot or stage area and Pokémon-type characters that transform from the network's logo. The water tower graphic also transforms into an anime-type robot (**3.59**).

3.59
A promotional network spot for Kids' WB. Courtesy of Blur.

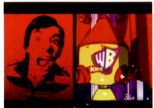
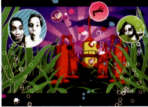
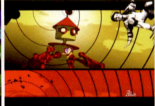
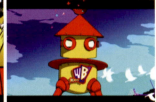

In 2004, Blur created an on-air promotional campaign for the movie *Lemony Snicket's A Series of Unfortunate Events* (2004), starring Jim Carrey. Aired on Nickelodeon, these promos humorously portrayed the dark, morbid, yet eccentric nature of the popular children's mystery book series written by Daniel Handler (under the pseudonym Lemony Snicket) and illustrated by Brett Helquist. The imagery reflects the woody nature of the books (**3.60**), and the mood is synonymous with that of the film.

3.60
An on-air campaign for *Lemony Snicket's A Series of Unfortunate Events.* Courtesy of Blur.

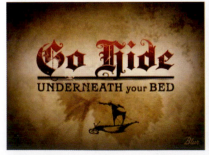
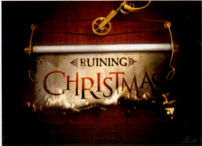
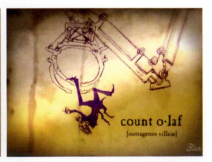

In 2005, Onesize was given the creative liberty to develop the format and style for a series of "cromos" (or commercial promos) for Kentucky Fried Chicken (**3.61**). Three spots aired on MTV Productions in the Netherlands over a period of three months. The first spot was a call for entries that invited the MTV audience to submit videos of what they can do best; the second displayed the video clips that were submitted and encouraged viewers to vote for the best video online; the third broadcast and rewarded the winner.

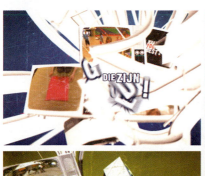
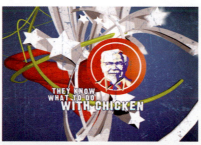
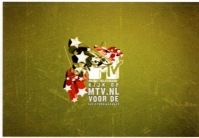
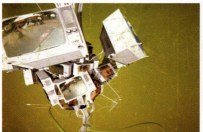
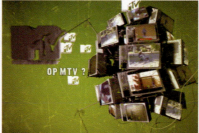
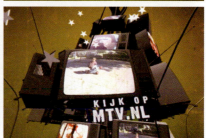

3.61
Frames from a series of KFC spots. Courtesy of Onesize.

Commercials

Television commercials are one of the most desired campaign vehicles and one of the most effective methods of generating brand recognition to facilitate sales. They can range from 5 to 10 seconds in length to hour-long infomercials. (Thirty-second commercials are also referred to as "spots.") The vast expenditures by television studios on advertising (according to Wikipedia, the average cost of a spot during the Super Bowl has reached approximately $2.6 million) has resulted in elaborate productions, many of which can be considered miniature movies.

In 2005, Stardust Studios, a creative design firm in New York, teamed up with McCann Erickson, a global advertising agency in San Francisco, to create the largest branding effort in the history of Microsoft Windows, reaching eleven countries over a period of fifteen months. The Windows

Since the 1960s, the gap has narrowed between programming and advertisements. Due to the introduction of digital video recorders, and services such as TiVo and On-demand, which allow users to skip advertisements, many media critics speculate that TV commercials will be replaced by the actual content of television programs.

"Start Something" campaign, a series of nine 30-second spots, was designed to support the global launch of Windows XP (**3.62**). Stardust Studios also designed a spot for Nokia in Singapore that aired in global broadcast outlets and in theaters. In the spot, a man and woman find inspiration from the phones of the Nokia L'Amour Collection (**3.63**).

3.62
Frames from the Windows "Start Something" campaign. Courtesy of Stardust Studios.

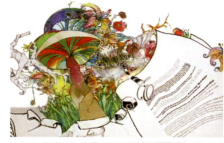
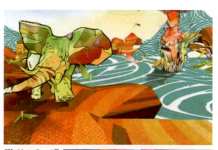
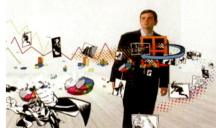
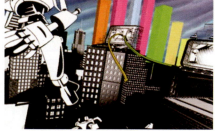

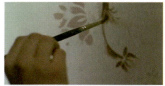
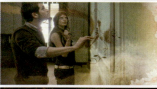
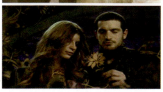

3.63
Frames from an ad for Nokia. Courtesy of Stardust Studios.

In a televised spot for KEXP, a Seattle-based radio station featuring musical styles ranging from bluegrass to electronica, Digital Kitchen developed a concept that involved translating a static print campaign for a band or solo artist into a time-based context. Low-tech graphic representations of bands and independent artists, which emulate the style of wheat-pasted posters displayed in the city, along with stop-motion, communicates the independent nature of the station's music. The words "from" and "to" continuously appear to show the range of artists represented (**3.64**).

The underlying goal of a commercial for Teri Lamp, a producer of lamps that use solar energy, was to emphasize education by encouraging children to read in the evening. Focusing on solar lamps that have been distributed to families in India who do not have access to electricity, Prague-based animation studio Eallin linked the theme of education to imagination and adventure. The shadow of a young boy and his book transforms into a series of fantastic, mythical creatures, landscapes, and images associated with space exploration that come to life as they are projected onto a wall (**3.65**).

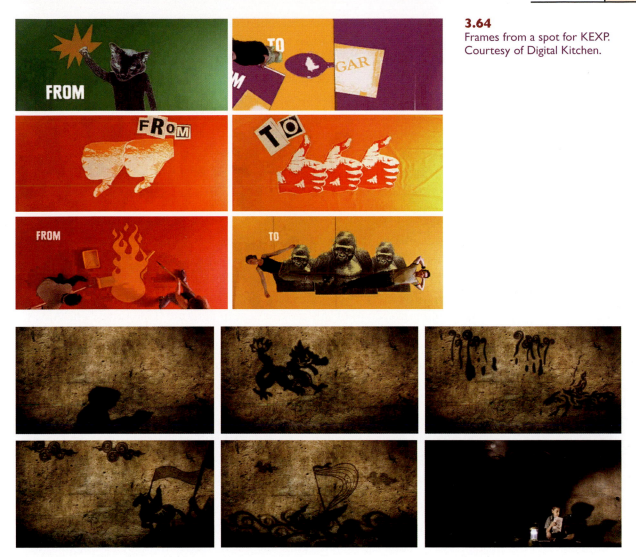

3.64
Frames from a spot for KEXP.
Courtesy of Digital Kitchen.

3.65
Frames from a spot for Teri Lamp.
Courtesy of Eallin.

Public Service Announcements

A "public service announcement (PSA)" is a noncommercial presentation that aims to raise public awareness about specific issues such as energy conservation, global warming, homelessness, and drunk driving. PSAs are also used to promote nonprofit organizations such as United Way, the Red Cross, and the American Cancer Society.

One of the most memorable PSAs of the 1970s was the "Crying Indian," sponsored by Keep America Beautiful, an environmental organization founded in 1953. Launched on Earth Day in 1971, it became an iconic symbol of environmental responsibility and has been deemed one of the most successful PSA campaigns in American history. Anti-smoking campaigns during the 1970s were also effective. (Smoking rates declined after 1971, when the tobacco industry withdrew cigarette advertising in response to Congress declaring it illegal.) Although cigarette consumption rose when the spots disappeared, public health professionals credit them with having saved millions of lives. Similarly, "This is Your Brain on Drugs" was a large anti-narcotics campaign launched in 1987 by Partnership for a Drug-Free America. Teenagers and young adults quickly popularized the phrase.

Since 1989, NBC Universal's "The More You Know" campaign has featured personalities from various NBC programs during its prime time, late night and Saturday morning programming. Topics have included anti-prejudice, HIV/AIDS, seat belts, and child abuse, to name just a few. Other examples of U.S. network campaigns are "CBS Cares" and ABC's "A Better Community."

Motion graphics have played an increasing role in television PSAs. David Carson's "Partnership for a Drug Free America" offers an example of how a powerful concept and effective motion graphics can persuade and educate parents on how to help their children cope with this critical social issue. According to Carson, "It was just a novel way to do a very 'tired' subject. It caused me to think about things in a different way and that's what made it good. Very clever solution."

The Diabetes Fonds in the Netherlands enlisted Addikt, a motion design company based in Amsterdam, to raise awareness about related health issues among diabetes patients. The advertisements were designed to encourage fundraising for further diabetes research (**3.66**).

Since 1942, the Ad Council has created some of our country's most memorable PSA slogans including "Friends Don't Let Friends Drive Drunk,""A Mind Is a Terrible Thing to Waste,""Only You Can Prevent Forest Fires" (personified by Smokey the Bear), and "Fight Cancer with a Checkup and a Check.""A Mind Is a Terrible Thing to Waste" raised millions for the United Negro College Fund, and the American Cancer Society's "Fight Cancer with a Checkup and a Check" raised public awareness and funding for research and patient services.

3.66
The Diabetes Fonds in the Netherlands enlisted Addikt, a motion graphics company based in Amsterdam, to raise help awareness about related health issues among diabetes patients. The PSAs were designed to encourage fundraising for further diabetes research.

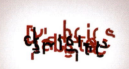
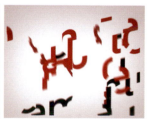

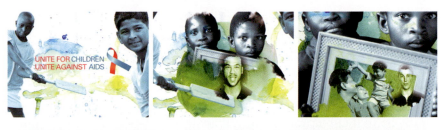

3.67
Frames from a PSA for Unicef to raise AIDS awareness. Courtesy of DesignOMotion.

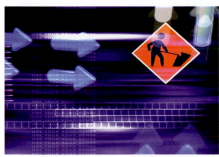
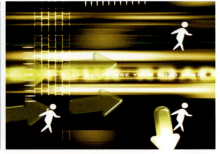

3.68
Frames from TV12's "ICBC Roadsense," a PSA promoting vehicle safety. Courtesy of Tiz Beretta and Erwin Chiong.

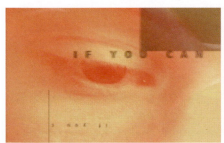
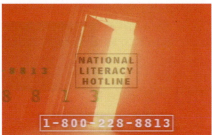

3.69
Frames from a PSA for the national literacy hotline. Courtesy of twenty2product.

Music Videos

Cinematic traditions that have been carried over from film into music videos have been enhanced by incorporating special effects and motion graphics. A live singing or dancing performance may be placed in a setting that is literally suggestive of the lyrics. On the other hand, music videos have deviated from narrative conventions. Traditional notions of past, present, and future can become lost in the flow of pictorial content, and contradictions in meaning between lyrics and image—along with the use of suggestive metaphors—have been created to provoke thought. When used well, this approach can produce a poetic experience. However, the larger the gap is between the lyrics and the imagery, the more challenging it becomes to discern the context. Other times, music videos are intended to function as pure "eye candy," creating a temporal experience where meaning is subject to interpretation.

During the 1980s, the music video became a cinematic art form that contributed to the transformation from narrative to nonnarrative film. Although music videos were predominantly filmic in nature, they broke the norms of traditional cinematic realism and allowed video artists to explore new visual possibilities for integrating animated and live-action imagery.

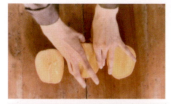

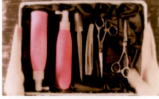

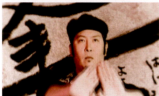

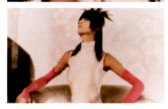

3.70
Frames from "Go Down" by The House Keepers. Courtesy of abstr^ct:Groove.

In 2004, abstr^ct:Groove, a design studio in Milan, Italy, produced the music video for "Go Down" by The House Keepers. This provocative composition portrays a sushi chef, a hair stylist, and a supermodel sharing a strange, surreal world composed of inanimate objects (**3.70**).

In 2004, Stardust Studios designed the "Megalomaniac" music video for the band Incubus and its Sony/Epic Records label. The footage for the debut single was shot over two days in downtown Los Angeles. Live video and animated sequences incorporate historical footage, barraging viewers with the song's powerful message. "Making a music video is tough on any level; to animate four minutes, tougher still," explained Jake Banks, Stardust's founder and creative director (**3.71**).

Acclaimed music video director Thomas Mignone commissioned the LA-based studio Heavenspot to create the motion graphics for the song "Dress Like A Target," by New Orleans metal/thrash band Superjoint Ritual. The raw footage, powerful graphics and pulsating editing style effectively portrays the heavy metal genre (**3.72**). This video was often aired on MTV's *Headbangers Ball* and Fuse Network.

The beautifully melodramatic video to "Love Said No" expresses the dark and tumultuous nature of H.I.M., the first Finnish rock band to sell a gold record in the United States. This epic performance-based piece blurred the line between fantasy and reality by seamlessly combining striking photography and animated type (**3.73**).

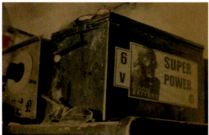

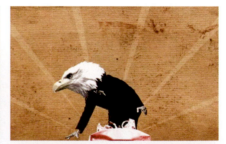

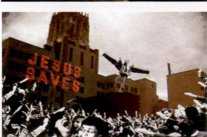

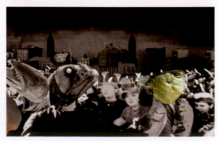

3.71
Frames from the music video for "Megalomaniac." Courtesy of Stardust Studios.

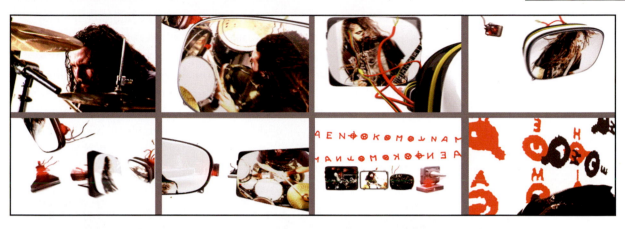

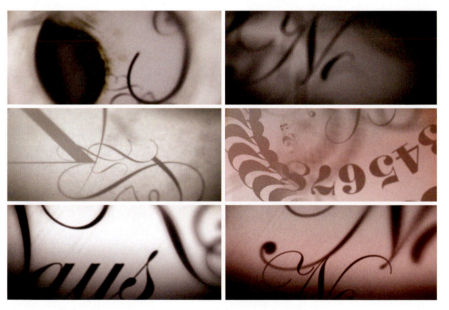

3.72
Frames from the music video for "Dress Like A Target" by Superjoint Ritual. Courtesy of Heavenspot.

3.73
Frames from the music video for "Love Said No" by H.I.M. Courtesy of Shilo.

The award-winning video for "Hibi No Neiro" ("Tone of Everyday"), by the Japanese indie band Sour, shows how motion graphics using simple web technology is helping the music video industry reach a wider target audience (**3.74**). A collaborative effort between the band and their international fan base, eighty "cast members" were recruited through social networking sites and blog posts, and filmed entirely on their own webcams. This approach enabled the band to work with a non-existent budget and overcame the problem that the band could not be filmed in person due to the distance between Tokyo and New York. Further, it provided an appropriate medium in which to visualize the song's poignant concept of embracing individuality in society.

Having been recognized internationally and gaining millions of views on YouTube, this video appeals to an audience that considers the webcam a standard means of global communication. It took three months to complete: the first two were spent storyboarding and planning, and the last organizing and filming the cast. Each sequence was carefully choreographed to display up to sixty-four people at a time. The movements inside the squares were planned according to their visual relationship to the surrounding grid. Detailed animatics served as "guide movies" for the cast to follow.

3.74
Frames from the "Hibi No Neiro" music video. Courtesy of Masashi Kawamura.

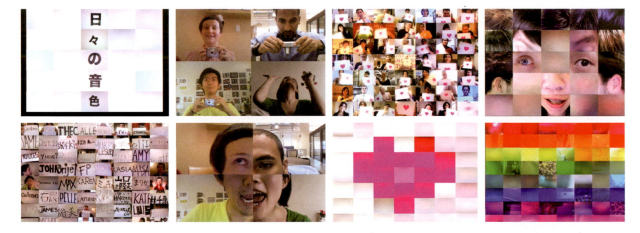

The music video for Sour's "Hangetsu" ("Half Moon") explored the concept of hand shadows while performing all the acting, directing, shooting, and editing. This provided an economical and aesthetically innovative solution to promoting the band's first feature track on a zero budget (**3.75**).

3.75
Hand shadows come to life in Sour's music video for "Hangetsu." Courtesy of Masashi Kawamura.

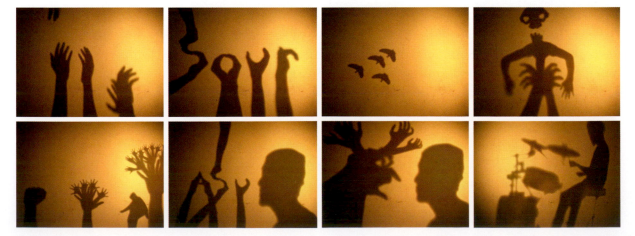

Chapter Summary

Television networks have become increasingly image conscious, and increased competition for viewers has driven the demand for more compelling motion graphics for station IDs, show openers, interstitials, network packages, television campaigns, public service announcements, commercials, and music videos.

A "station identification" (or ID) identifies a network's call letters, city of license, and channel number. Many television stations have developed clever ways of using their IDs as promotional tools to brand their networks. A promotion for an upcoming show or newscast can fulfill its identification requirements while building its audience by telling viewers to tune in to an event. Station IDs combine the aesthetics of logo design with other contextual visual elements and give consideration to story structure.

A "show opener" sets the stage for an upcoming program while promoting the network's identity. "Topical openers" for news programs are designed to inform viewers of upcoming stories or events, often integrating live-action footage and typographic elements (including the station ID) to enhance the entertainment value of the broadcast. A "show package" is a video information system containing an assortment of elements used to promote a particular program.

"Interstitials" are mini-programs that appear between shows or other events. Some are designed to highlight key issues, people, or events, while others function to promote a network's brand. News interstitials inform viewers that a top story is about to be featured or suggest continued coverage of a story. They are also used as transitions from the anchor or studio into a live or prerecorded story.

"Network packages" are comprised of promotional elements that meet the need for supporting, eye-catching motion graphics. "Bumpers," for example, are brief transitions between programs and commercial breaks. "Lower thirds" are combinations of graphics and text that appear on the bottom portion of the screen to identify the station, the presenter(s), and the content being featured. They can range from simple graphical elements to complex animations. "Mortises"— full screen graphics that are used to frame live video footage—are sometimes used in combination with lower thirds. "Lineups" inform viewers about upcoming programs, and upfronts are used to promote shows to advertisers and give viewers a glimpse of a network's upcoming schedule. "Tags" occur at the beginning or end of a spot, news opening, or commercial to inform viewers on how to find additional information.

"Promotional campaigns" have been around since the 1970s and have provided many artistic opportunities for broadcast designers. Television commercials are one of the most desired mediums for campaigns and are effective in generating brand recognition to facilitate product sales. The vast expenditure of production studios on advertising has resulted in elaborately produced commercials, many of which can be considered miniature movies.

"Public service announcements" (PSAs) are non-commercial spots that strive to raise public awareness about contemporary issues, such as global warming, drunk driving, and energy conservation.

Motion graphics have a considerable presence in music videos which are now considered multifaceted forms of art and popular culture.

motion graphics in interactive media
an overview

4

Late nineteenth-century optical inventions were the first to entertain audiences through the persistence of vision. These evolved into sophisticated devices that were capable of displaying animated figures over static backgrounds. This eventually gave way to the Lumière Brothers' contributions to modern cinema. Approximately one century later, advancements in computer processors, desktop video, and animation software have led to an repeated evolution from a slide-show format, to superimposed elements over static backgrounds, and finally to full-screen motion with the added dimension of interactivity—a complete reinvention of cinema.

"Once you made it, it stayed put. Great care was taken to get everything in just the right spot, just the right relationship. Now, increasingly, the output is a variable, not a constant."
—Chris Pullman

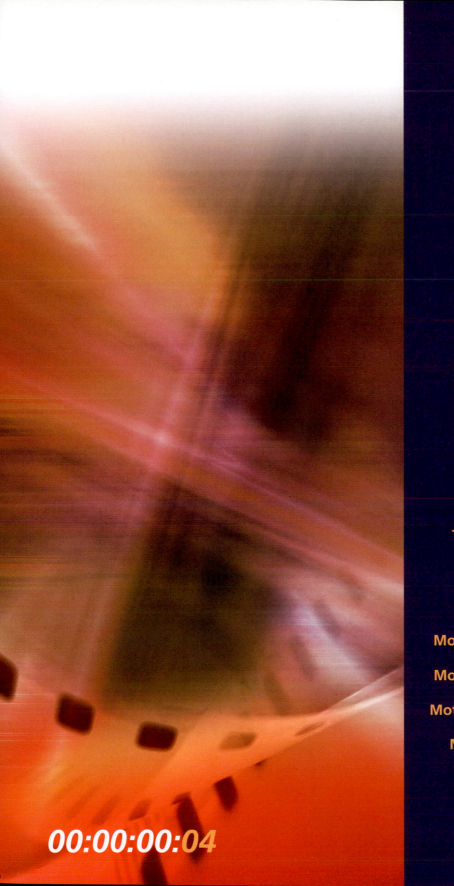

00:00:00:04

The Interactive Environment

During the nineties, CD-ROM training courses and digital reference books like almanacs and encyclopedias allowed users to access various informational formats about certain topics. Interactive training CDs challenged users to reach higher levels of performance by accumulating points or inputting correct answers. In the business sector, promotional CDs were used to advertise services or provide information to repeat customers.

For centuries, books have been used as linear information systems, delivering continuous content through a prescribed beginning, middle, and end. In contrast, interactive environments can organize information in a branching, nonsequential structure so that many paths can be taken through the material. As a result, the user's role shifts from passive viewer to active participant.

When interactivity plays a role, motion can be thought of in terms of behavior. A user-driven stimulus such as a mouse selection, a keystroke, a voice command, use of a controller, or a hand gesture in front of a webcam can trigger the behavior of elements in a given system, impacting the manner in which the content is displayed.

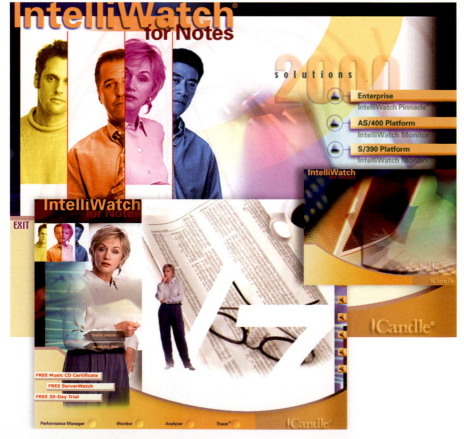

4.1
Candle Intelliwatch CD-ROM. Concept, graphic design, and motion graphics by Jon Krasner. © Candle Corporation and The Devereux Group.

In the 1990s, I designed a CD-ROM to advertise Candle Corporation's latest network management software. The primary navigation sports an administrator, an IT director, and small and large business managers. A selection enlarges a person while causing the navigation palette to shrink. Various figurative poses are juxtaposed with animated typography, graphic landscapes, and images depicting Candle's consulting services.

Motion over the Web

The advent of film and television allowed motion designers to deliver high-quality moving images and sound to their audiences. Due to the high cost of producing and showing films and videos, newer and less expensive technologies such as multiple projector slide shows were developed. On the computer, animation and interactivity began with applications such as HyperCard, SuperCard, and Director. This was followed by the infusion of animation into CD-DVD-ROM titles in the education, business, and entertainment industries. Today, the Web is the predominant medium for delivering dynamic, interactive content.

Facilitating real-time motion over the Web has faced technical challenges due to the limitations of connection speed and bandwidth, and the lack of an industry-standard animation format. Some types of animations have required browser plug-ins, while others can run on their own. Despite these limitations, designers have persisted in developing their artistic vision while waiting for the Web to mature. Today, higher bandwidth connections and video streaming has made the prospect of motion over the Web more enticing, allowing designers to push the artistic envelope beyond the movie and television screen and help shape our growing global visual language.

The incorporation of dynamic information into Web sites can enhance the user's experience if it is designed well and integrated logically into the interface. Many design studios that showcase their work online have used motion to heighten visual interest and enhance viewer longevity. Studio Dialog, a design agency in Calgary, Alberta, presents its multidisciplinary work in a professional "drawing board" format that integrates subtle types of motion (**see 4.44 on p. 117**). The animation of the site's elements, tempered by smooth, graphic transitions and a clear navigation system, demonstrate firm control over the presentation.

The online portfolio of Nessim Higson, IAAH ("I Am Always Hungry"), embraces various styles ranging from clean and contemporary to heavily layered, textured elements that appear distressed and worn. Images slide in smoothly from every edge, and the background's colors and content (including the site's identity) randomly changes, offering a multitude of compositional possibilities. This unique approach attests to the wide range of work that this award-winning Los Angeles-based designer from Birmingham, Alabama has produced. In a never-ending sea of

"There are no masters of Internet animation. Yet. But it's only a matter of time before people start to establish themselves as animators exclusive to the Internet. By coming up with new, mind-bending, Web-savvy ways to present its content and improve the medium as a whole, this new guard of animators will truly set itself apart."
—Anna McMillan

4.2
The unique online portfolio of of Taras Lesko at Kranestyle. com offers a rich palette of images that animate in response to horizontal mouse movements. Courtesy of LeskoMedia.

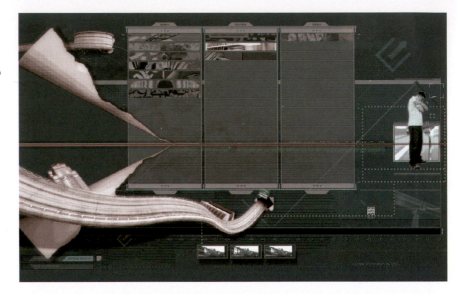

4.3
During the late 1990s, a group of independent filmmakers conceived of the idea of an online film festival site to showcase the work of independent filmmakers and video artists. Recognizing the potential of the Web for the online distribution of films, hillmancurtis, inc. developed the Manifestival, an online film festival Web site that features independent digital film and video shorts. This site was notable for its innovative use of Flash, which at the time was limited in its capacity to handle live-action video. Courtesy of hillmancurtis, inc.

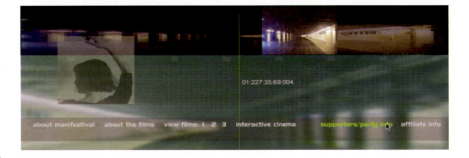

online portfolios, this dynamic website stands out as an island of graphic innovation. Its progressive yet intuitive interface runs the gamut of sophisticated print design, identity, and collages, as well as original typography that includes hand-drawn fonts (**4.4**).

A recent trend in many business-to-business sites has been a shift to simpler, more delicate graphic treatments. An example of this is April Greiman's design for RoTo Architects (**4.7**). This collaborative practice is engaged in the study of how natural and social conditions work together to form the spatial conditions of everyday life, providing opportunities for individuals who embrace architecture to share their work and ideas. Like a piece of architecture, this website is treated as a spatial medium that, through layering images and motion, reflects the

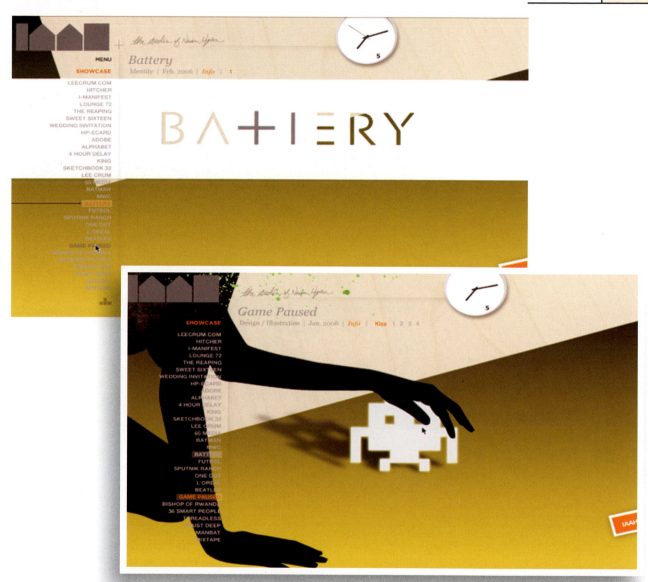

collaborative nature of the artistic process. A delicate balance of typography and collaborative graphics provides a visual landscape that viewers can travel through to access a large archive of sketches, notes, and snapshots. (This was one of the site's most important aspects because it shows the process of conceptualization.)

4.4
The Web site for IAAH ("I Am Always Hungry") represents the multidisciplinary design studio and portfolio of Nessim Higson As an advocate of converging media, Nessim claims "I am always hungry for life" and dedicates his work to New Orleans, which he describes as "The city that care forgot and the people that called it home."

4.5

An earlier version of *Made In Space* (www.madeinspace.la) featured the multidisciplinary design firm of world-renowned designer April Greiman. Referred to as "a visual, verbal think tank," her site's bold exploration of images, typography, animation, and color are rooted in an innovative fusion of technology and design. Courtesy of April Greiman.

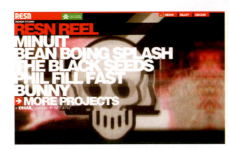
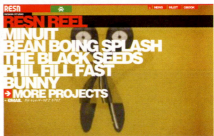

4.6

The interface for Resn—an interactive design agency in New Zealand—consists of large images from their show reel flickering behind a bold typographic navigation structure. Their use of animation won them the Business for Profit category at South by Southwest's 10th Annual SXSW Web Awards in Austin, Texas. Courtesy of Resn.

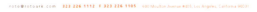

4.7

April Greiman's design for RoTo Architects showed a growing trend toward simplicity in Web design. The site's interface realizes April's vision of how ideas and images can be treated as objects in space. Courtesy of April Greiman.

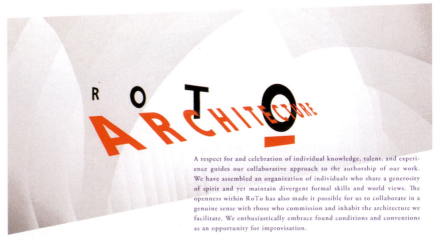
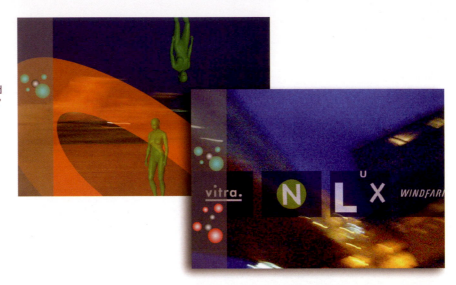

animation formats

animated GIF

Among the rapidly developing Web technologies, animated GIFs have been a popular low-tech option for adding motion to Web pages since the advent of the Gif89a format. Built into a single file, sequential images are displayed in succession like traditional animation frames. The GIF format is supported by all browsers and does not require special plug-ins for viewing. Specialized programming skills are not required to create animations, giving this format significant advantages over others. The size and bandwidth requirements of animated GIFs are smaller than those of noncompressed RGB images since they are color-indexed from an 8-bit (256 color) palette. This palette can be derived from Web-safe colors, the Macintosh or Windows color systems, or an adaptive palette. Reducing the number of colors can result in smaller file sizes and faster download times. The most effective GIF animations use colors that appear consistent on all displays.

GIF animations can play back a specified number of times at designated frame durations. Alternatively, looping offers an efficient way of holding a viewer's attention while waiting for material to download. Factors such as frame dimensions, number of frames, and color depth can also be specified to control file size and download time in order to improve playback efficiency. Looped GIF animations with small numbers of frames can maintain the illusion of motion. Since large shapes and horizontal patterns compress better than color blends, shadows, and vertical patterns, GIF animations typically consist of geometric shapes, horizontal lines, and single colors. They can be generated in any motion graphics program or in imaging software such as Photoshop.

Java

In the early 1990s, Sun Microsystems introduced Java to the Internet. This network-oriented programming language enabled Web developers to create small applications called "applets" that could be downloaded and applied to Web pages. Today, Java is still used to add motion to Web design. Java applets can generate successive images that play back at relatively high speeds. The advantage of Java's platform independence is that it can run on any supported operating system. However, many designers avoid Java as an animation format since it requires programming knowledge (Java derives much of its syntax from C and C++).

April Greiman has been acclaimed as a pioneer of digital design and has been internationally recognized as one of the most innovative and influential designers of the twentieth and twenty-first centuries. Since the early 1980s, she has been instrumental in embracing digital technology in her radical experiments with the Apple Macintosh and Quantel Paintbox.

April considers the computer to be a vital element in the design process. Her unique "Transmedia" approach considers successful design solutions to be capable of expression in any delivery format including Web sites, print, motion graphics, textiles, surfaces, video, and three-dimensional design. Presently she heads the Los Angeles based design firm Made in Space (http://www.madeinspace.la).

Animated GIFs "stream" in the sense that they begin to play before they fully download.

dHTML

During the release of HTML4.0 browsers, dynamic HTML (DHTML) was composed a combination of complex programming languages. It allowed the Netscape browser to display hierarchical layers and provided an improved method of handling text through Cascading Style Sheets (CSS). Although DHTML was not developed to provide animation, it has been used to animate HTML elements on a Web page. For example, a DHTML script can tell the browser to change the placement of an image to allow it to travel around the page. Like animated GIFs, DHTML was recognized by most browsers and did not require users to download extra components. However, its animation capabilities were limited, and it was challenging to code.

Flash

Since its inception in 1996, Flash has evolved from a simple, Web-deployed animation tool to a fully interactive media development tool for creating CD– and DVD–ROMs, interactive games, and Internet applications. Ironically, it has even been used for motion graphics in the broadcast and film industries.

Most of Flash's inherent animation capabilities can be accomplished today with a combination of CSS, JavaScript, and HTML5. In 2011, Adobe Edge was launched, allowing Web designers and developers to use these newer technologies in combination with Flash.

Over the years, Adobe Flash (formerly Macromedia Flash) has proved to be one of the most efficient animation tools for the Web. Two key advantages have been its ability to scale images without loss of resolution and its capacity to download content quickly if it is composed of vector graphics. Action Script, Flash's object-oriented programming language, offers endless possibilities for combining interactivity and motion. Flash's capacity to deliver full-screen playback on all display sizes and across multiple platforms still makes it an enticing Web distribution format.

Despite these advantages, Flash content is difficult to update and to index by search engines. For this reason, many e-commerce, business, and database sites have incorporated it into HTML pages rather than using Flash as the running platform. Since this format uses streaming to transfer data, animations that play smoothly on systems that are connected to the Internet through a DSL or cable modem may stutter when being received by slower methods. Using vector images takes advantage of Flash's low bandwidth requirements. Although Flash's integration of QuickTime has improved, video content on a website can impede download time. (A link to a movie clip or an alternative viewing method such as an animated GIF may be a better technical solution.) Another major disadvantage of Flash is that its content is not viewable on today's mobile devices such as tablets and smartphones.

Although Flash may remain a viable Web animation tool for some time, it is likely that newer technologies will become standards in the near future.

Cascading Style Sheets

Cascading Style Sheets is a language used to describe how an HTML document is formatted for Web presentation. Developed in 1996, it has provided Web designers and developers with more flexibility in the way elements such as layout, colors, and fonts are presented. In comparison to HTML tags (the rudimentary elements of the Web's markup language), CSS offers a range of properties that can be pre-defined and animated in response to an action such as a mouseover. For example, font and text properties include thickness or weight, family, size, style, spacing, alignment, and decoration. Box properties are used to define aspects like padding, borders, margins, and width to control the spacing in and around HTML elements. Color properties specify the color of text, and background properties control background colors and images. CSS3—the latest standard for CSS—offers a keyframe approach to animating most HTML elements without the need for JavaScript or Flash. Aspects such as the number of times an animated sequence can loop, whether it alternates between its beginning and end values, and whether it pauses can be controlled. CSS3's "transitions" are effects that allow elements to gradually change from one style to another. Figure **3.5 (on p. 41)** shows an example of how a transition effect is used to control the width of an object for a duration of five seconds.

CSS and CSS3 are supported by most browsers to date. Common tools that provide CSS3 animation include Sencha Animator, Adobe Edge, and Tumult Hype.

JavaScript

Originally called LiveScript, JavaScript is an object-oriented scripting language developed by Netscape in 1995 to offer nonprofessional programmers an alternative to using Java to code complex Web sites. JavaScript has become one of the most popular programming languages for creating enhanced user interfaces and dynamic Web sites. Common uses for JavaScript include expanding and collapsing panels, progress bars, and visual feedback elements, all of which can enrich the user experience and increase a Web site's usability. A key advantage of JavaScript is its potential for interactivity: viewers can control when and how animations occur. Additionally, most browsers support JavaScript without the need for additional software or plug-ins. JavaScript libraries such as Prototype, script.aculo.us, Ext Core, jsPHP,

> *Many designers are reluctant to embrace today's newer HTML5, CSS and JavaScript technologies because they do not deliver consistently across devices and browsers.*

MooTools and jQuery have been developed by major corporations such as Microsoft, Nokia, and Yahoo! to allow easier development for JavaScript applications. Released in 2006, jQuery is a cross-browser JavaScript library designed to simplify the client-side of HTML scripting, allowing developers to create plug-ins for web pages and applications.

HTML5

In response to the increasing popularity of mobile devices, HTML5 provides a decent solution to Flash's lack of support for touchscreen platforms. An improvement of native HTML, its multimedia capabilities allow you to display video, draw on the screen, and produce animations by incorporating JavaScript and CSS into HTML. Most animation tools for developing HTML5 content run on major browsers such as Firefox, IE, Opera, Safari and Chrome (as well as on mobile operating systems including Android, Windows Phone and iOS). Adobe's Edge, for example, provides an intuitive, timeline-based approach to creating animation without the need for specialized programming skills and is well-suited to developing content for mobile platforms. (It is thought of as Flash's counterpart for touchscreen devices.) Hippo Animator (from Hippo Studios) also uses a timeline approach and offers editing and effects capabilities. Its output can be exported to HTML5 for functionality in all major browsers and mobile devices. Hype (from Tumult Inc.) is a WYSIWYG animation tool built to run on Mac OS X, on tablet computers, and on Androids and iPhones. It offers a rich text editor and WebKit-based canvas for creating animated scenes.

video over the Web

The predominant video formats that are used over the Internet today are QuickTime, Windows Media Player, and RealPlayer. These formats allow data to be delivered through downloading or streaming. "Basic download" involves copying content from a server to a local computer and playing it from the hard drive. "Progressive download" places the most critical information at the beginning of the file structure. Since duration is no longer a determining factor for download time, the viewer only has to wait for the first portion of data to be copied. As this portion plays, the second portion downloads, and so forth. If the user's connection is within the animation's data rate, the piece plays smoothly from beginning to end. If the user's bandwidth is too slow, delays in playback may occur during download. Once a piece is downloaded, it can play back repeatedly without being hindered by a slow connection or network congestion. "Streaming" allows animations to be delivered almost immediately without the hassle of downloading. Since the user's computer stays in contact with a dedicated server running the movie, content begins playing as soon as the download process begins. New data continues to stream during playback while old data is discarded after it is viewed. If the client's connection is slow, or if there is network congestion, the data transfer rate is reduced and frames are dropped to preserve real-time playback. This method is best suited to situations where audience attention span is a factor or to animations that are over two minutes in length. Downloading, on the other hand, is a better solution for short works because it usually offers higher-quality video.

Connection speed and bandwidth are the critical factors that determine data transfer rate—the amount of data that can be delivered each second, which determines whether content will play back smoothly. Digital video is one of the most bandwidth-intensive assets. As data networks improve, it will be possible to deliver large-scale video content over the Web.

Data compression/decompression algorithms ("codecs") are often used to achieve reasonable download times. The demands of Web designers have caused the industry to develop lossless compression algorithms to achieve better quality video with lower bandwidth requirements and without the need of expensive hardware. If image details are of prime importance, a reduced frame rate may be a necessary trade-off to retain acceptable picture quality. (Standard frame rates are between eight and twelve frames per second. Lower rates are acceptable for collage and cutout animations that are intended to look disjointed and jerky.)

Codecs are capable of reducing video file size significantly by eliminating data redundancy, such as areas of the image that remain the same over time and large areas of similar colors or values. Most codecs are "lossy," resulting in some degree of image degradation. The type of content being animated, the speed at which elements move, and the size of the images relative to the frame can help determine which codec is most appropriate for your particular situation. Cross-platform QuickTime codecs differ with regard to how compression is performed, and some allow the degree of compression to be adjusted to provide control over balance between image and playback quality. The decreasing cost of storage capacity and network bandwidth may eventually obviate the need for lossy codecs in the future.

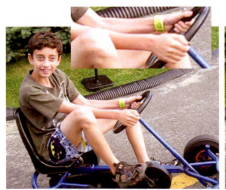 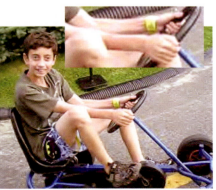

4.8
The left image shows the result Apple's Animation codec, a lossless algorithm. On the right, the image has been degraded due to Photo-JPEG compression. At high-quality settings, the result of the Photo-JPEG codec is almost indistinguishable from the original. However, since it is a "lossy" codec, it is not recommended for editing because image quality is reduced each time the file is updated.

splash animations

Splash animations (also referred to as "splash pages") are openers that appear before the main content of the site loads. Similar to traditional book covers, their purpose is to set a mood, reinforce a brand, intrigue visitors, and entice them into entering the site to learn more. They may also provide users with technical viewing requirements and give them a choice of how to enter the site. Splash pages that employ motion graphics are typically 5 to 10 seconds in length.

The popularity of splash pages has declined due to the complaints of users who experience unnecessary download time. Usability tests, focus groups, and Web analytics data have indicated that audiences respond negatively to splash pages; in particular, first-time visitors are often turned off because of the time commitment involved in waiting for the page to complete before the site's main content loads. Graphic appeal quickly drops when repeat users make subsequent visits to a site. Statistics show that splash pages can decrease search engine rankings. Most search engines rank Web pages according to their HTML code, text content, and links. Because splash pages typically lack body text and only provide a link to a site's home page, search engine spiders only recognize the home page or ignore the site entirely. Meta tags consisting of keywords can help spiders index splash pages, however the absence of links and content may be detrimental to a site's overall search engine ranking. Since search engine spiders usually only crawl through a Web site's first three levels when indexing and ranking, a splash page can hide valuable content by adding another level.

In some circumstances, however, splash pages can be used to present information quickly and ensure that viewers see that information at least once. Design studios and advertising agencies that sell creativity can benefit from a well-designed opening animation that demonstrates their design skills and levels of creativity. For example, *be-Designer* is a site for two Belgian interior architects who specialize in commercial and residential architecture, interior design, and furniture design. Its intriguing animated introduction begins with a single, large green number "4" which spins into view over a background of elegant grey patterns. The number fades to a dark grey as the title *be-Designer* animates in from the frame's right edge to its final position. Clicking the "enter" link generates a clever animated progress indicator consisting of a smaller version of the number "4" gradually filling up with a bright green color, similar to the way liquids fill a glass. Once the green color reaches the top of the number, the screen suddenly changes to display a series of horizontal wipes that introduce the site's main content (**4.9**).

Like motion picture title sequences, splash pages can establish mood and atmosphere. For example, the site opener for Salon de Fatima, a New England chain of hair salons and day spas, animates an elegant mix of typography and natural images such as water droplets, flower petals, and steam to convey the feel of a nurturing environment (**4.10**).

Depending on a site's demographics, viewers may be willing to tolerate the download time in exchange for being enticed and entertained.

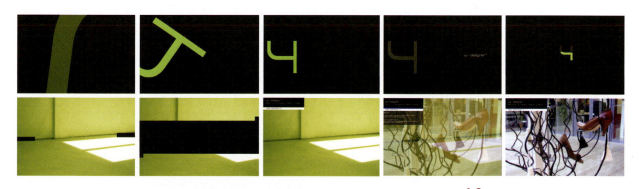

4.9
Frames from a Flash opener for *be-Designer*, a Web site for Belgian interior architects Stephanie Simov and Gilles Fostier. Courtesy of Dizynotip.

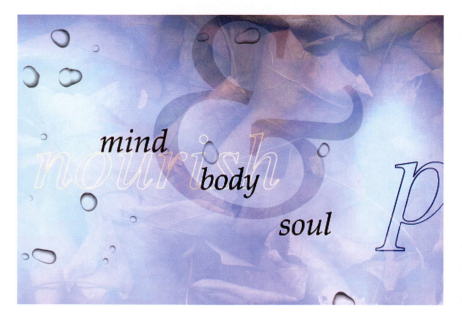

4.10
Frame from the splash page for Salon de Fatima, a New England chain of hair salons and day spas. © Jon Krasner 2007.

4.11
Storyboard pitch for a Web site opener for the Devereux Group. © Jon Krasner 2007.

The opening animation provides a natural transition into the site's home page.

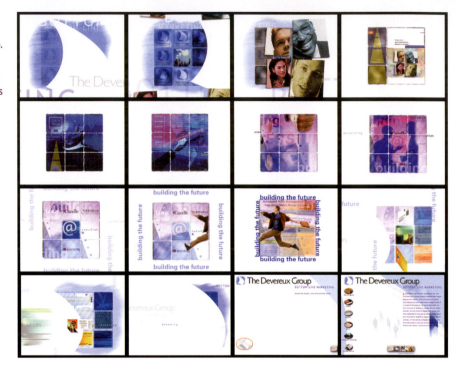

banners

Banners are often a key element of Internet advertising campaigns. As marketing devices, their strategy is to establish a strong, professional Web presence and create a favorable, lasting impression on viewers. A banner design that successfully brands a company's image can generate increased traffic to a Web site.

Banner design mandates a strong marketing approach that involves extensive research on the organization being advertised, including its benefits, features, competitors, and past campaigns. Designers must understand what the banner needs to accomplish its specific aims, deliver its key communication points, and influence its intended audience. They must be aware of the host sites that the banner will be running on and other banners that may be placed on the same page.

The dynamic application of motion graphics can help attract the attention of a site's users. Studies have shown that animated banners generate higher click-through rates (CTRs) than static banners.

The two principal animation formats used for animated banners are animated GIF and Flash. Although animated GIFs have been extensively used in advertisement banners, Flash-based banners have become quite popular due to Flash's ability to easily generate motion, along with its smooth playback rates and small file sizes. Further, Flash banners can be designed to be interactive, involving visitors directly. (Designers that submit a Flash banner for a banner ad campaign are often asked for the animated GIF version as well.)

Effective banner design can make or break a campaign. Studies have shown that typical Web surfers spend less than 10 seconds viewing the top portion of a Web page. Therefore banners that get the point across quickly through concise, direct communication are often the most successful in their advertising. Incorporating motion can be an effective way to draw users in; however, it should be kept simple and subtle. Its purpose is to attract visitors, not irritate them. Animations should blend in naturally and not clash with the design of the hosting page. They should be between 3 and 5 seconds, keeping in mind the differences in browser speeds. Since endless looping can be distracting, animations can be designed to repeat four or five times before displaying the main message on the last frame. Text should be clear and legible and should take no longer than two seconds to read. (On screen, serif fonts are often difficult to read at sizes below 14 points.) All of these criteria take into account the interest and patience of the viewers.

As a rule of thumb, standard "healthy" file sizes for banners that are 468×60 pixels in size are typically between 4 and 25K. Small button banner styles may range between 1.5 and 3K.

leaderboard
728 x 90 pixels

full banner
486 x 60 pixels

vertical banner
120 x 240 pixels

hald page ad
300 x 600 pixels

half banner
234 x 60 pixels

skyscraper
160 x 600 pixels

square
125 x 125 pixels

rectangle
180 x 150 pixels

4.12
These banner styles and sizes are some of the most accepted today, as outlined by the Standards and Practices Committee of the Internet Advertising Bureau.

Note: Image not shown at full size.

Businesses often require banner ads to go through a period of testing, which involves running the banner over a period of time and measuring the CTRs and resulting sales. They may slightly alter the design and run the banner again to measure the results. Unless the designer has conducted thorough research on audience preferences and behavior patterns, it is unlikely that a single banner is sufficient for an ad campaign. Since CTRs tend to drop significantly after two weeks, most designers start with six to ten banners, allowing the client to rotate them in order to measure the CTRs.

From a technical standpoint, file size is a critical factor. File sizes that are too "heavy" can result in slow downloads and choppy playback. File size depends on several factors, including the duration of the animation, the delivery method (Flash or animated GIF), and the image dimensions. GIF and JPEG optimization processes that involve data compression and color depth reduction can significantly reduce file size without changing the content's integrity. Once the animation is optimized, it is best to test it with different browsers, platforms, and connection speeds to ensure maximal and consistent results.

Some designers have expressed frustration with the limitations that banner design imposes, while others feel inspired to push the limits and make the content work in their favor. Taras Lesko of LeskoMedia designed and produced eye-catching motion graphics for a series of banner advertisements and surrounding header graphics for Anthrax's official reunion site (http://anthrax.com). Each banner was individually tailored to a theme corresponding to a different album cover. These designs, which were animated to bring life to the album cover art, could be accessed through the site's theme selection feature, giving viewers the option to customize the look of the Web site (**4.13**).

4.13
This series of Flash banners for the heavy metal band Anthrax was used to promote the band's official reunion site, anthrax.com. Courtesy of LeskoMedia.

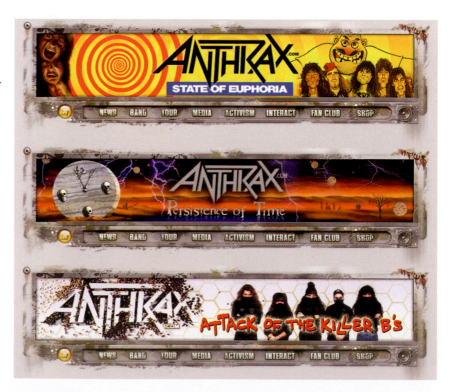

advertisements

Web advertisements, like television commercials, are designed to expose viewers to information that might be missed in a banner ad. They appear for approximately 5 to 10 seconds before the expected content page loads, or may appear between a main page and its secondary pages. Web advertisements typically display at sizes smaller than the destination page, and must be viewed in their entirety unless the user takes a step to remove them from view (many include a "Skip" option to accommodate viewers who choose not to wait).

Two principal types of Web ads are "PopUp" and "inline interstitials." PopUp advertisements appear as temporary windows in the foreground, while the destination page's content loads in the background. Inline interstitials, which occur in environments such as Shockwave, Java, or VRML, are usually interactive, with the intention of keeping users occupied during the download.

Due to the active participation that users engage in online (versus the passive role of television audiences), many Web advertisers have reduced the level of intrusiveness and disruption of online ads. Design formats such as interstitials and video-based ads are faced with the challenge of getting the message across to users as quickly as possible while maintaining their involvement with the experience. For example, Hillman Curtis's online advertisement for Lycos delivers the message quickly with only a few thin, green, vertical lines, six photographic images, and simple animated text (**4.14**). The letters of the word "discover" fade in one by one as they are introduced by two green lines that animate across the screen from left to right. The letters perform a 360-degree rotation, spinning into the word "fun," which then fades out to reveal "educate" and "share," as one of the empty frames at the bottom shows a young girl opening the lid of her laptop and turning to smile at the camera. Other words including "research," "inspire," "interact," "future," "headlines," and "global," follow in sequence, accompanied by other photos. In an interview by Susan Davis for Adobe's "Web Gallery," Hillman stated, "The emotional message is simply that Lycos has something for everyone, even your daughter."

Hillman's promotional spot for Roger Black's Interactive Bureau is also effective in quickly informing us that the Bureau combines the power of traditional graphic design with fluency in the latest technology

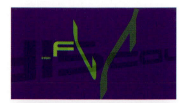
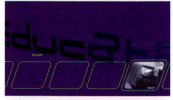
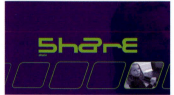
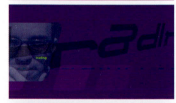
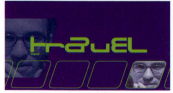

4.14
Frames from an online advertisement for Lycos. Courtesy of hillmancurtis, inc.

"I don't think any animation is worth a 30-second download."
—*Hillman Curtis*

(**see Chapter 13, figure 13.21 on p. 464**). His online interstitial for Softcom, a company specializing in e-business, also succeeds in describing it's process in a matter of seconds (**4.15**). Further, Hillman's straightforward approach is evident in his interstitial for Cysive, Inc., a provider of Interaction Server software. The objective of this animated, interactive piece was to promote the company's principal activities in building and developing Web, wireless, and voice-activated technologies (**4.16**).

4.15
Frames from an online advertisement for Softcom. Courtesy of hillmancurtis, inc.

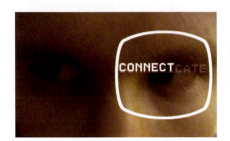
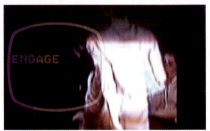

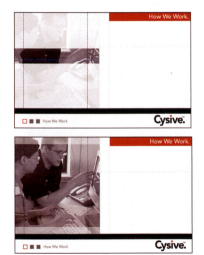

4.16
Screenshots from an online advertisement for Cysive. Courtesy of hillmancurtis, inc.

Many designers feel as the Internet continues to grow it will adopt more traditional television formats to make the future of online advertising more engaging. The appearance of Web-based commercials has already improved through the incorporation of motion graphics and high-quality sound, offering more effective ways for advertisers to get their messages across. For example, a clever online campaign for Subaru's 2012 Impreza car allowed the public to create custom automated animations based on memories of their first car, enabling consumers to recall and share their stories at FirstCarStory.com. Pioneering text-to-video technology has enabled the site to generate a considerable number of animations from a database of more than one thousand individuals (**4.17**). The animations are composed from a library of decorative doodles and key words and phrases. Users can set the visuals to music of their choice and narrate the story with their own voice. The videos can be shared through social media applications such as Facebook and Twitter or by email. Logging on to Subaru's homepage reveals a "car generator" accompanied by the sound of an engine starting up. You can choose a model (coupe, sedan, station wagon, SUV) or a silhouette that approximates the look of your first set of wheels, along with the color and condition your vehicle was in. After logging in through Facebook Connect you are prompted to agree with Subaru's terms and conditions, giving them the non-exclusive right to use your story and name for marketing.

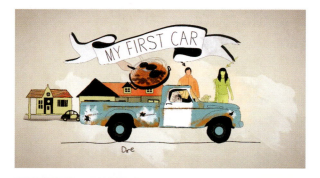

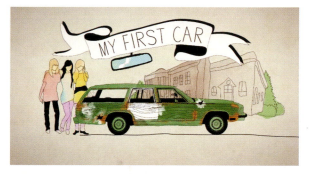

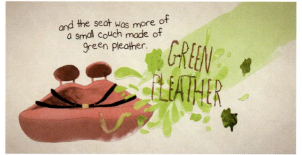

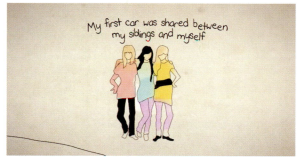

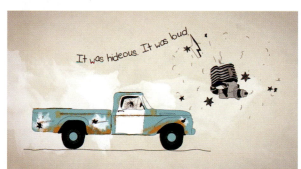

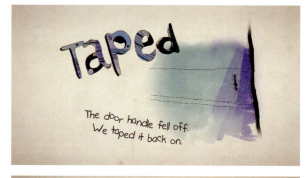

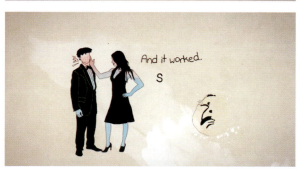

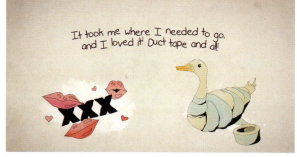

4.17
Frames from a group of Subaru Impreza spots. Courtesy of Minivegas.

music videos and online games

The presence of online music videos and games has grown due to the Web's capacity to combine motion and interactivity. Animations intended for entertainment can be user-controlled by inputting personal data. An example of this is the online music video for "Utsushi Kagami" ("Mirror") by the Japanese indie band Sour. After connecting to a webcam, the day-to-day sites that you visit (i.e., Facebook, Twitter, Google, and YouTube) are referenced and used as entertainment platforms (**4.18**). Viewing the video turns your desktop into a 'performance stage' that pulls in material from your webcam and social media accounts. Your own visual journey with the band members is personalized according to your unique social network status. Conceptually, this approach addresses the song's underlying theme about discovering who you are in the reflections of others.

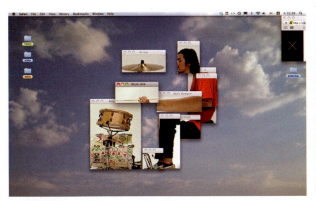
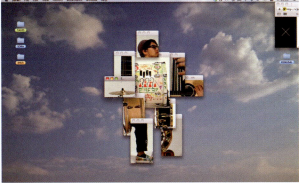
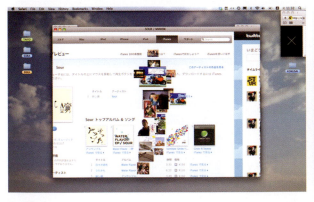
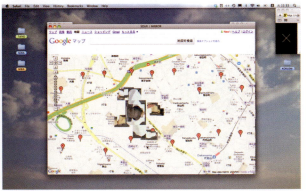

4.18
Viewing Sour's "Utsushi Kagami" turns your desktop into a "performance stage" that can reference video from your webcam and social media accounts.

Motion over the Web

In my Interface Design class at Fitchburg State University, students are challenged to design an alternative interface for an educational online game intended to help children learn about famous musical composers and their musical styles. I deliberately give them a written description of the game without any visual reference. The description contains playing instructions and a list of the game's components. For example: a portal presents an introductory animation that addresses the idea of time travel, bringing viewers to the present year. An informational text window contains quotes from individual composers and features major historical events that occurred during that person's lifetime. Navigational items include a graphic to allow users to access the game's instructions, an off/on audio switch and volume control mechanism. A "test" button to allow users to test the knowledge they have learned, and an "alert" graphic that warns the user to restart the game before the time machine falls into a wormhole. This approach challenges students to seek originality and exercise their imagination. They are asked to develop a method of choosing four musical genres or sub-genres, two composers from each category, and a graphic presentation of one of the composers that would appear if chosen. Students are expected to decide how the information will be presented graphically. There is no fixed number of screens, pages, or pop-up menus. They are told that all levels of the game must work together cohesively. Further, motion and transition should be treated as integral components of the interface.

Kristen Hogan's design is driven by a gear-like mechanism that rotates to feature various sub-genres of electronic music (**4.19**). According to Kristen, a selected sub-genre will "back-light on the wheel and information will scroll out of the right side of the gear spoke. The end spoke will lift upward and 'unlock' the gear. From there it splits in half and opens to reveal a 3D space behind it where the player will glide through the opening to the next scene." Garrick Kwan envisioned a mechanically-based time machine (**4.20**) with "a lot of steam pouring out, electricity zapping, controllers rattling and dials spinning." He states: "The process I had was for the user to spin the era dial having the composer pop up in the rectangular box. Now seeing the composer in that box, you would then select them to start up the time machine. Whistles go off, everything starts shaking and eventually the composer will appear in the circular frame with the information provided on the left side."

As a programmer, Masashi Kawamura entered the world of design when he became a member of the Masahiko Sato Laboratory in Tokyo. There he worked on the TV show 'Pythagora Switch', which is still one of the most popular kid's programs in Japan. He also served as Creative Director on global brands such as Nissan, PlayStation, Levi's, Adidas, Nokia, and Google. Masashi continues to push the boundaries of music videos, product design, and art installations and has won numerous international awards. His online music video "Utsushi Kagami" received a gold award for non-broadcast media at the Art Directors Club global awards in New York.

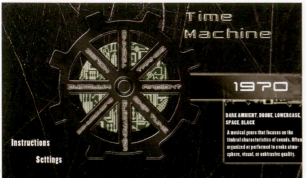

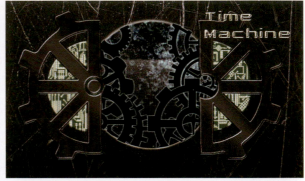

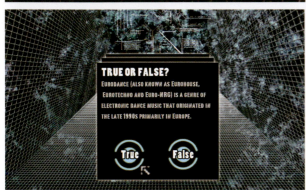

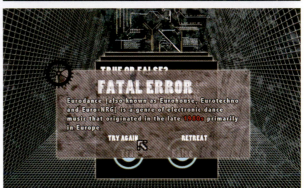

4.19

Style frames for *Musical Time Composer,*
by Kristen Hogan. Courtesy of Professor
Jon Krasner, Fitchburg State University.

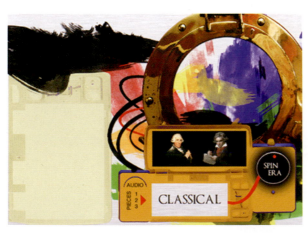

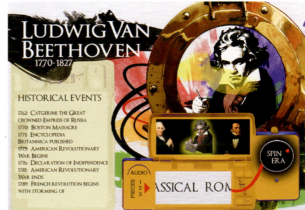

4.20

Style frames for *Musical Time Composer*
by Garrick Kwan. Courtesy of Professor
Jon Krasner, Fitchburg State University.

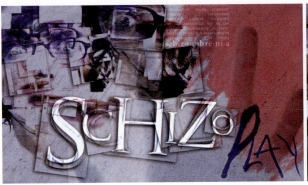
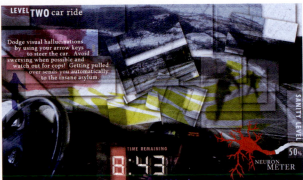

4.21
Style frames for a fictional game by
Hayley Carloni. Courtesy of Professor
Jon Krasner, Fitchburg State University.

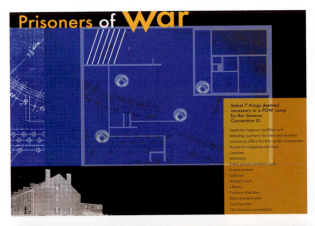
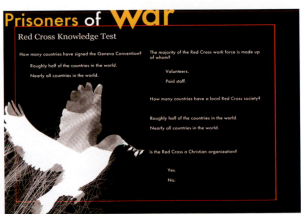
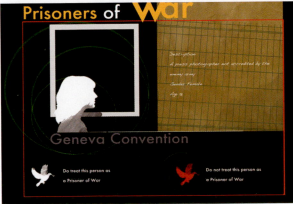
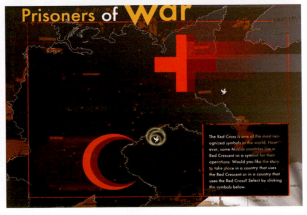

4.22
Style frames for a fictional game by
Hang Tran. Courtesy of Professor
Jon Krasner, Fitchburg State University.

Motion in Game Design

In the game industry, interactive experiences have become increasingly cinematic over the past decade. A multitude of portable video game consoles, such as Sega's Dreamcast, Nintendo's GameCube, Microsoft's Xbox, and Sony's PlayStation, have been developed to revolutionize home entertainment. In 1999, Sony Entertainment developed the PlayStation 2, the successor to the PlayStation (1994). The PS2 included a processor (the "Emotion Engine") that could perform complex calculations to support its graphics demands (**4.23**). Character movements were determined by events, rather than by the playback of prerecorded data. In *NBA ShootOut* (2003), for example, a player's lifelike movements are the result of dozens of NBA stars being motion-captured in dribbling, passing, shooting, and performing signature dunks.

The specialized field of game design requires a strong foundation in aesthetics, conceptual and imaginative thinking, programming, and motion design experience, an understanding of the dynamics of gameplay, and the ability to work in a team-based environment. More colleges and universities are developing programs in game design, most of which emphasize the artistry that is involved.

Sony's PlayStation 3—released in 2006 in Japan and North America—was part of the seventh generation of video game consoles that were considered to be the most commercially successful home video game systems at the time. The Cell Broadband Engine™ was a breakthrough processor that offered more evolved graphic expressions, live-action video, three-dimensional animation, and high-fidelity sound to produce a more vivid experience.

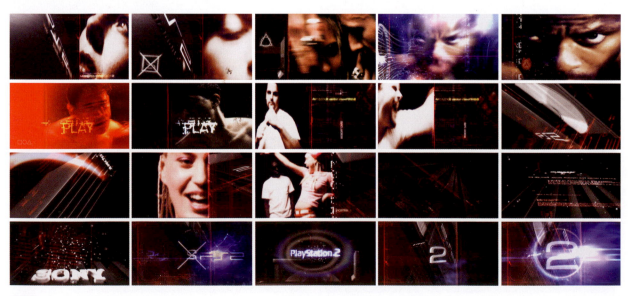

4.23
Opener for PlayStation 2, "Emotion."
Courtesy of Humunculus. © Sony
Computer Entertainment America Inc.

Motion in Informational Kiosks

Public informational facilities have become effective communication vehicles because of their ability to transmit messages in a nonlinear, multidimensional fashion. The education, entertainment, and advertising industries have made extensive investments in interactive display technologies. Kiosks, for example, can provide information to the public and retrieve data from individual users based on input devices that involve touch, voice, and body movement. Today's kiosk interfaces are capable of displaying high-resolution dynamic visual content. They can communicate in multiple languages, stream live video to consumers, and drive interactions between customers and sellers. Like mice, keyboards, pushbuttons, and trackballs, these stand-alone, touchscreen systems have assisted in the development of the PDA and cell phone industries, making these devices more advanced and user friendly.

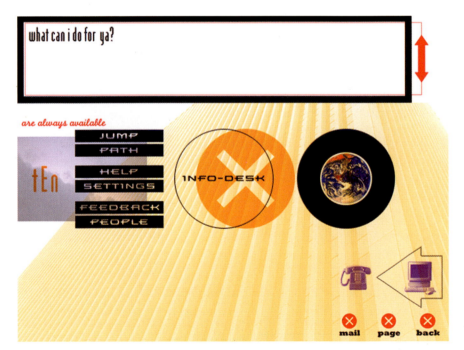

4.24
Concept sketch for an informational kiosk for the Total Entertainment Network. Courtesy of twenty2product.

Since Dr. Samuel C. Hurst's invention of the electronic touch interface in 1971, touchscreen technology has become commonplace in retail settings, on ATM machines, and on PDAs. The increased popularity of information appliances such as smartphones and portable game consoles is continuing to drive the demand for touchscreens.

Motion in Mobile Touchscreens

Today's overwhelming number of mobile device applications relating to lifestyle, entertainment, education, social networking, music, and travel (to name just a few categories) has led to more inclusive and generative combinations of digital technology and art. According to mobile analytics firm Flurry, there are over 500,000 applications for the iPhone and iPad, and thousands more for platforms such as iOS, Android, Blackberry, Windows Phone, Java ME and HTML5. Further, the number of consumers using mobile apps dwarfs those who watch prime-time television.

"For music's first 35,000 years it was interactive, people got together and created music together, and they taught music hands-on by doing. Then look at the 19th century, the app of the 19th century was sheet music. People would take the sheet music home and play with it: they could change the words or the notes, make the songs longer or shorter, perform on a piano or a violin. Music isn't meant to be one-way. We know that actors and musicians wouldn't put on a show without an audience, the two things interrelate."

—*Scott Snibbe*

The potential of animation for small screen interfaces is beginning to be realized in the music industry. As a collaborative medium, music has evolved from its integration with cinema, to music videos, to its recent infusion into interactive media. Today, the interactive possibilities of small screen apps challenge the way we think about music, providing more inclusive and generative experiences. During an interview with *Worldwide Interactive Design Guide*, media artist and filmmaker Scott Snibbe pointed out that the goal of musicians is not to create "a one-dimensional stream of notes" but rather "to create an emotional, sensory experience that often includes performance."

A noteworthy example of an innovative artist who has exploited the capabilities of mobile devices is the Icelandic musician Björk, who conceived of a suite of iPhone and iPad apps that would accompany the release of her album *Biophilia* in 2011. Originally conceptualized as a musical house with interactive spaces similar to an IMAX film experience, the goal was to allow people to explore and collaborate with the album's music. Intrigued by touchscreen technology, Björk ultimately envisioned a digital environment that would allow users to investigate the scientific and musical principles behind her songs. In an online interview, she said: "The interactiveness goes really to the core of the music, the structure of the song . . . It's not just something like an accessory. . . It is the song."

Created in collaboration with Scott Snibbe, M/M (Paris), and a handful of artists, scientists, writers, and software developers, *Biophilia*'s multi-layered suite of ten musical apps is considered to be a fully conceived artistic statement and has been described by Apple as an extraordinary exploration of the universe and various musical themes (**4.25**). Accompanied by the song "Cosmogony," the main program opens up into a three-dimensional galaxy with a compass as the main navigational structure (**4.26**). The voice of narrator David Attenborough says: "Just as we use music to express parts of us that would otherwise be hidden, so too can we use technology to make visible much of nature's invisible world. In *Biophilia*, you will experience how the three come together —nature, music, technology. Listen, learn and create." The apps are related to particular song tracks and are accessed by tapping on stars within particular constellations. Each app offers an intimate musical experience through educational games, essays, musical scores, concert footage, karaoke playback, album artwork, lyrics, and abstract journeys through time and space that accompany Björk's haunting voice. Together, these components investigate relationships between natural phenomena, humanity, and music. The animation for "Hollow" flies through a strand of DNA. "Virus" provides a strange narrative about a love that kills the object of its affection by showing a clump of cells being attacked by a virus. The inclusive game challenges you to stop the attack or allow the virus to run its natural course while watching the cells 'sing' along to the song's chorus. The emotional connection between the topic, Björk's music, and a strange love story inspires users to learn about microdiversity and biological processes.

Available in the iTunes App Store, "Biophilia" is one of the first "app albums" to be realized for the iPad. In concert with Björk's imaginative, colorful and bizarre costumes and hairstyles, this project was partially composed on a tablet computer using customized non-conventional instruments such as pendulums and a Tesla coil, which can be heard on the song "Thunderbolt."

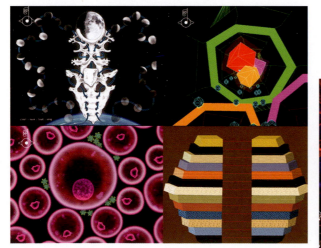

4.25
Biophilia, interface screenshots.
Courtesy of Scott Snibbe.

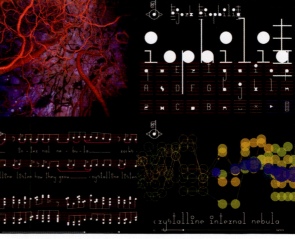

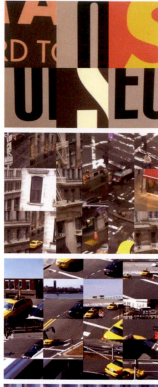

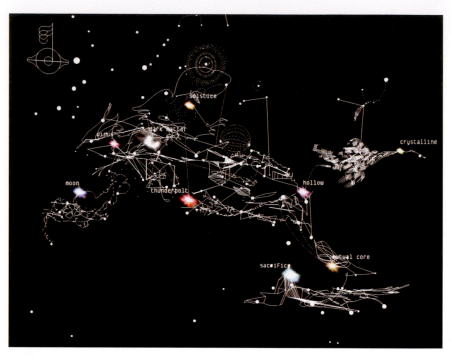

4.26
Biophilia, opening screen..
Courtesy of Scott Snibbe.

In July, 2011, New York based design studio Trollbäck + Company released the video app +loop. This program allows you to split your iPhone or iPad screen into a custom, definable grid of video players that can record and continuously play back small, juxtaposed loops of moving or static images (**4.27**). Content can be recorded and played back as a full-screen presentation or individually recorded and composed in separate squares. Once the idea for this app as a fixed grid originated, creative director Stephen Baker realized that it would be interesting to allow the grid to be customizable so that users could embrace the intuitive possibilities of motion in a new way. Factors such as grid size, frame offset, and playback speed can be modified to create a wide variety of compositions.

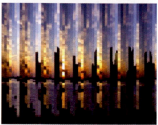

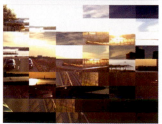

4.27
+loop screens. Video can be exported to your iPhone photo library.

Over the past few years, animated transitions have been developed specifically for mobile devices to enrich static visual content and enhance the user experience. Specific events can be emphasized to clarify a user's interaction and explain the content in a narrative way.

Motion in Desktop Applications

The potential for motion in digital interfaces has also been realized in desktop applications.

In my Interface Design course, I gave a project that involved redesigning a screen capture application named Copernicus. Students were told to consider how motion could enhance user interaction. Kyle DeStefano's idea was similar to that of a View-Master toy. Different navigational choices would rotate clockwise or counter-clockwise into the viewfinder in response to the user clicking the "Next" or "Back" items (**4.28**).

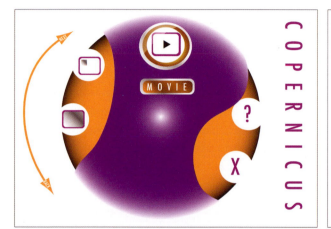
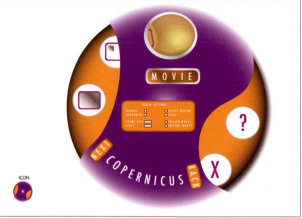

4.28
Interface design for the desktop application Copernicus by Kyle DeStefano. Courtesy of Professor Jon Krasner, Fitchburg State University.

Drawing on inspiration from the De Stijl movement, Jennifer Hanson envisioned a design with bright colors and bold lines, allowing the program to be easily visible against any background (**4.29, left**). She wrote: "When the user selects a specific feature, the bold lines would rise and fall from the various letterforms while the appropriate menu options slide down from the main program window." The movements of the elements would be fluid and quick.

Jennifer wanted her second design to express the idea of astronomy through an interface composed of celestial objects and serene, cool colors (**4.29, right**). With regard to the role motion would play, she wrote: "The galaxy on the interface is constantly swirling and moving at a leisurely pace, while the colorful background rings twist and turn in an atom-like motion. As the user selects a specific feature, the appropriate icon enlarges and moves to the foreground, the titles shoot in and out of the interface and the menu options fade into view."

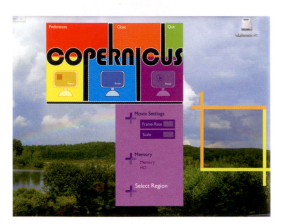

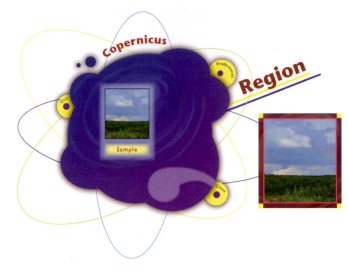

4.29
Interface designs for the desktop application Copernicus by Jennifer Hanson. Courtesy of Professor on Krasner, Fitchburg State University.

Cheri Zenoni's interface design was based on the notes and planetary diagrams of Nicolaus Copernicus (**4.30**). The background imagery was developed by rubbing coffee grounds into watercolor paper and adding faint lines and calligraphy. When the user hovers over the bottom menu of the editing screen, the selected option ("Save," "Copy," "Info," or "Print") would move upwards to indicate that the program is aware the user is about to make a choice.

4.30
Interface design for the desktop application Copernicus by Cheri Zenoni. Courtesy of Professor Jon Krasner, Fitchburg State University.

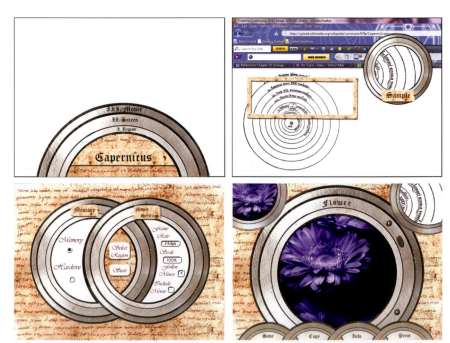

Motion in DVD-Video Menus

When DVD-video replaced the LaserDisc in the mid-1990s, the motion picture industry aimed to use digital media as a means of presenting full-length feature films. As compared to standard VHS, the image quality of DVD-video is superlative, and the content does not degrade over time. Like the Web, its nonlinear, interactive navigation structure can allow users to use a remote control or a joystick as a means to view individual scenes in a movie, access additional information, and customize settings such as multi-angle viewing, surround sound, and random shuffle playback to create a more engaging experience. P ersonal biographies, directors' commentaries, playlists, Web links, and interactive DVD-ROM content can be viewed.

Although some users only judge DVD titles on usability, others attribute their success to the design of the menus and consider attractive, stylish menus to be a large part of their initial visual appeal. Given the nature of DVD menu graphics for movie pictures, independent films, bands, documentaries, and training programs, most designers would agree that if the content on a DVD is worth watching, then the supporting menu structure should be equally engaging.

DVD titles typically consist of a background and a menu system. Background animations usually last between 15 and 30 seconds. Motion menus are typically short, lasting between 15 seconds and a minute. Motion can enhance the navigational process and add to the viewing experience, similar to how the opening titles of a film can set the mood beforehand. Many animated menus are designed to loop until the user makes a selection. This time limit is due partly to the DVD's storage capacity and partly to the length of the background animation or soundtrack.

Motion menus can be customized to incorporate animation or a moving preview of the DVD's contents. Special effects and video compositing techniques can be applied, and the video can be edited to a compilation of different scenes. Further, any type of interactive menu item can be blended into the background or designed to conform to a nonregular shape. These approaches can open up many intriguing design possibilities that break away from many of the template-based packages on the market.

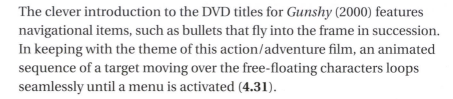

The clever introduction to the DVD titles for *Gunshy* (2000) features navigational items, such as bullets that fly into the frame in succession. In keeping with the theme of this action/adventure film, an animated sequence of a target moving over the free-floating characters loops seamlessly until a menu is activated (**4.31**).

4.31
Frames from the DVD titles for *Gunshy* (2000). Courtesy of Berretta Design.

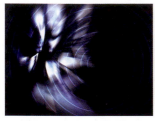 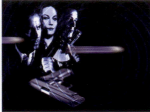 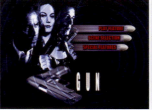 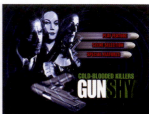

4.32
Motion DVD-video menus for *Macross II* (2000). Courtesy of Berretta Design.

These menus reflect the style of this Japanese anime cartoon. Seamless loops of dynamic character poses, animated sound levels, flying aircraft and spaceships are contained inside graphic shapes over a high-tech, futuristic background consisting of subtle kinetic shapes, lines, and bands of color.

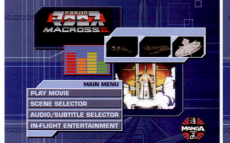 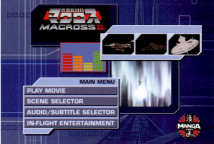

Figures 4.33 to **4.36** illustrate DVD-Video titles that were designed by undergraduate students in my Interface Design course. Daniel Dumont used a collection of visuals depicting his heritage in Lowell, Massachusetts. He deliberately chose to use a minimal amount of text, since representation through photographs, news clippings, and images of natural incidents (for example, the flooding of the Merrimack River over a bridge located down the street from where he was raised) would arouse enough curiosity to motivate users to dig through his family's past. Menu items would move slowly across the background of an old postcard mailed to a family member by Daniel's great-great-uncle who served in the military. When a user highlights a link, it would shake to generate a subtle earthquake effect to indicate what it might feel like to travel backward in time. Upon entering a scene, yellow silhouettes of birds would fly intermittently across the background. Each new scene would transition into the frame with a fade and exit the frame through a quick wipe when a new link is activated. Again, the new content would fade into the foreground.

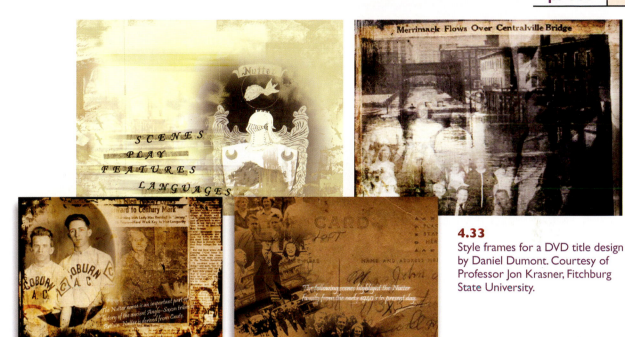

4.33
Style frames for a DVD title design
by Daniel Dumont. Courtesy of
Professor Jon Krasner, Fitchburg
State University.

John Brissette's *Cathedral* tells a fictional story about how a building's
existence shaped human lives around it. Each scene represents a
specific time period, from the cathedral's construction, to its inevitable
demise, and finally to its rebirth. The scenes also represent emotional
themes, from harmony, to chaos, to isolation and fear. The building
occupies the same position and is the same size in every frame, shifting
the viewer between time periods from a single vantage point. (John
envisions a narration by actors who would assume the role of a character living in each era.) Various static figures fade in and out to signify
time lapses. The cathedral's foundation in 600AD would be accompanied by laborers who haul and shape stones and cut lumber. 1225AD
sees the oath of a knight defending the cathedral from its enemies.
While he stands alert and vigilant in the foreground, knights patrolling
the building and worshippers enter and exit from the left, becoming
part of the visual landscape. "The Forgotten" (date unknown) reveals
the cathedral abandoned in the winter. Cloud cover would animate
in the background with drifts of snow occasionally blowing across the
frame. 1998AD depicts a working father whose stress level is elevated by
the unwelcome ringing of church bells. Images of him returning from
work and entering his home are accompanied by a flock of geese
migrating across the sky to symbolize the change that is needed.

4.34
Style frames from *Cathedral* by John Brissette. Courtesy of Professor Jon Krasner, Fitchburg State University.

2065AD shows a futuristic cityscape where an unknown enemy has wiped out most of the population. A resistance has been using the cathedral's underground chambers to seek refuge and coordinate efforts to defend themselves. Figures move in shadows across the middle-ground while an airship hovers in the sky looking for potential targets.

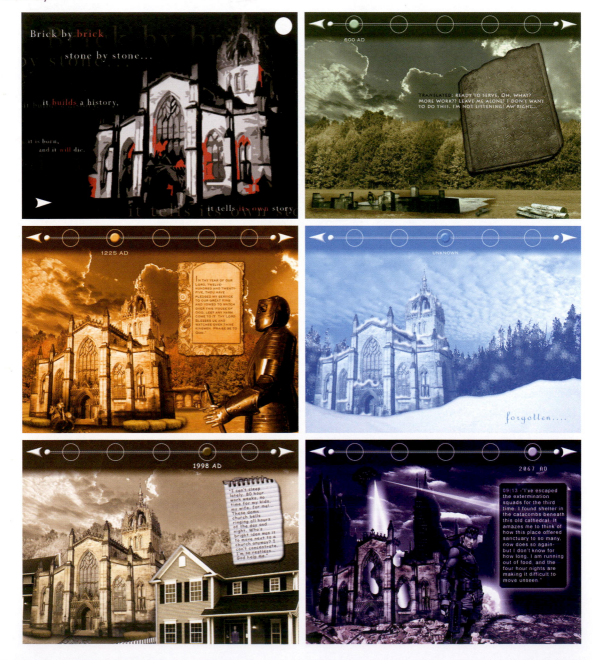

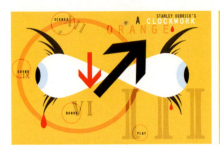
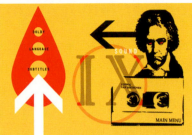
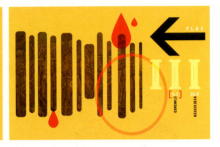

4.35
DVD menu style frames for *A Clockwork Orange* by Hayley Carloni. Courtesy of Professor Jon Krasner, Fitchburg State University.

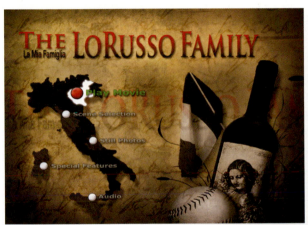
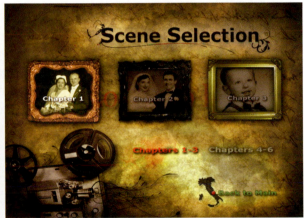
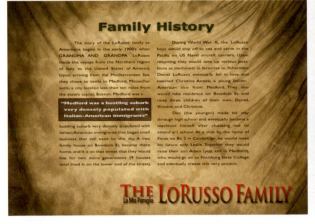
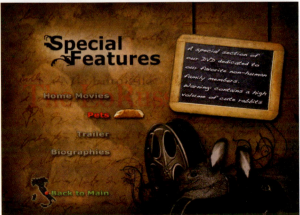

4.36
DVD menu style frames for a family history assignment by Adam LoRusso. Courtesy of Professor Jon Krasner, Fitchburg State University.

A Look at Navigation

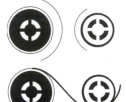

Successful navigation design provides an infrastructure that supports and directs users in a meaningful, logical way through the complexities of a Web site. It considers the interface—the intermediary between users and content—as well as the message, client, users, and medium.

Incorporating motion into the navigational structure of an interface can entertain and inform users. Animated icons, buttons, and text links can help place emphasis on items that users might otherwise overlook. Entire menus can be animated and accompanied by sounds to enhance a user's level of interactivity or simply to entertain.

A simple typographic menu in Nessim Higson's IAAH portfolio is accompanied by a subtle black arrow that moves in from the left edge of the frame, identifying the selected item (**4.4 on p. 83**). In Studio Dialog's site, mousing over a link moves the type in a slightly upward direction. This quick motion is accompanied by a change in the weight of an underlying bar from thick to thin (**4.45**). LeskoMedia's site for The Plumbing Joint uses motion to mimic the experience of turning on a faucet or pulling a stopper from a drain. In addition to activating menu items with a mouseover or click, the navigational graphics are designed to animate during the brief transitional periods between pages (**4.49**). A similar approach is Taras Lesko's award-winning site "Stickman On Fire," based on a bizarre yet clever concept of personified matchsticks that allow users to view intimate photographs of hand-made stick figures and movie clips of fire. As navigational elements, the matchsticks pop up and down when users mouse over them. A giant matchbook, serving as the main showcase, closes after a new menu item is selected and re-opens to feature updated content (**4.38**).

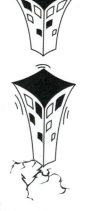

4.37
Navigation icons by Matthew Brunelle, John Brissette, and Chris Roux. Courtesy of Professor Jon Krasner, Fitchburg State University. This project involved creating navigational elements that would animate during a rollover state.

In Belgian movie director Philipo's Web site, the navigation system is a group of bound cards. When one is activated by a mouse click, it moves to the foreground and shifts its position and orientation to align with the frame's edges. Simultaneously, an extension of the "photos" or "videos" card slides out to reveal a group of thumbnail images. Activating one with a mouse click generates a window that slides out to display the selected photo or clip. Users can click any of the cards in the upper left corner or select the type items at the bottom of the frame (**4.39**). This navigation offers a straightforward approach to retrieving information.

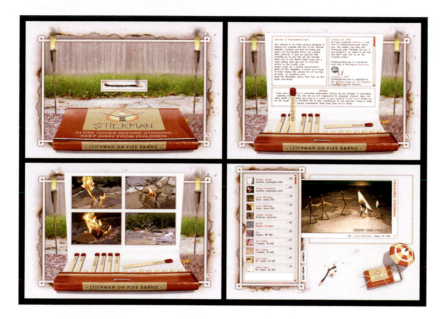

4.38
Web site for "Stickman On Fire." This Web site's innovative idea, conceived by Jenny Solima at Omar College of Design, won several prestigious industry awards for its bizarre content and originality. What began as a simple school project became an instant online hit, attracting over 70,000 unique visitors within one month of inception. Courtesy of LeskoMedia.

4.39
Web site for Philipo, a Belgian film director. Courtesy of Dizynotip.

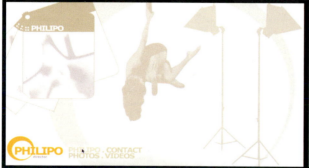
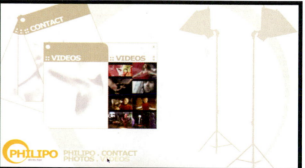

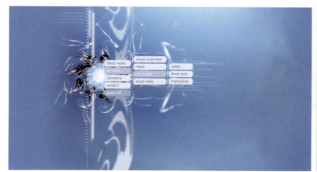
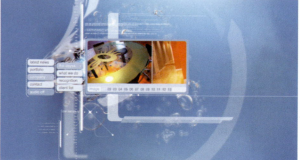

4.40
In Giant Octopus' Web site, floating menus move as if they are suspended in water when they are activated.

In a Web site re-design assignment, students considered how motion could contribute toward aesthetics and functionality. They were required to develop a navigation system that enhances user interactivity through animation. Cheri Zenoini's proposal for a crafts site was based on her own work area (**4.41**). She wrote: "When I do crafts I tend to either work on a desk or table for small projects and the floor for larger projects. The design is built off of the need for motion. In its rollover state, the ink holder would rattle to encourage users to select it. A mouse click will cause the ink to spill over and form the words for the navigation. A cleaning cloth would move up from the bottom of the screen, allowing users to wipe away the menu and display recent updates and outgoing links. Rolling over the desk would cause the paper and sticky notes to move upwards, indicating that they are separate choices. Clicking on the sticky notes triggers the drawer to open and release marbles that fly out to form a circle. The pad would then fly upward to the center of the marbles."

4.41
Style frames for a site redesign by Cheri Zenoni. Courtesy of Professor Jon Krasner, Fitchburg State University.

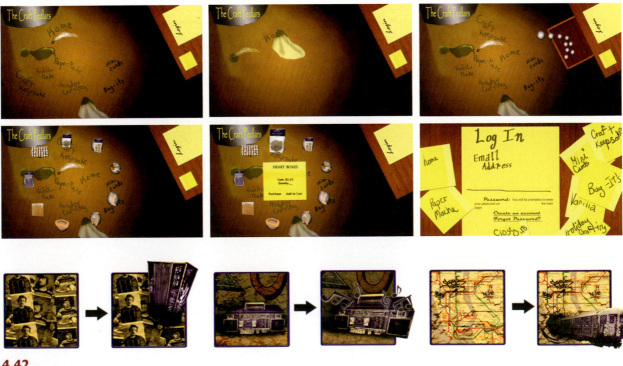

4.42
This navigation system, designed by Adam LoRusso, incorporates elements that would animate in a music-based site. Courtesy of Professor Jon Krasner, Fitchburg State University.

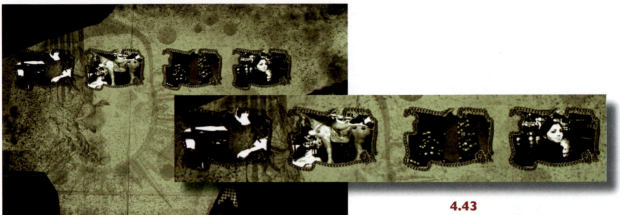

4.43
Heather Reno's navigation system was designed to function as video clips that would play in response to a mouse rollover. Professor Jon Krasner, Fitchburg State University.

A Look at Transitions

Digital interfaces are virtual spaces that consist of complex levels of information. Animated transitions can help move users between various levels of detail while maintaining an interface's original content. Brookfield Properties' site design for Bankers Court, for example, uses two-dimensional lines and simple geometric planes as architectural structures that rotate, change position, and slide open to reveal new content when a link is activated (**4.44**). The compositional possibilities that result from the framing of these transitions look similar to the paintings of Dutch De Stijl artist Piet Mondrian. The smooth, visual changes in layout and content that occur in this simple design solution make the site stand apart from other local office Web sites.

4.44
Brookfield Properties' Web site for Bankers Court, an office tower development for downtown Calgary, Alberta. Courtesy of Studio Dialog.

Studio Dialogue's site (**4.45**) begins with three pale orange, green, and blue horizontal bars moving across the screen from the right edge, leaving their "tail ends" visible on the left edge of the enclosed frame. The header simultaneously displays a succession of vertical rectangles that close from right to left in the manner of a window blind. As they close, the bars shift from a pale blue to an orange hue, then disappear to reveal one of the company's featured works. Thin blue lines animate to refresh page content in response to activating a link. The "window blind" effect in the heading's opening is echoed in the site's contact page, in which two sets of horizontal bars that close from top to bottom reveal a listing of clients and agencies. Activating a link triggers a pair of thin, horizontal blue lines that move vertically in opposite directions to the top and bottom of the screen. Once they reach their destination, new content is featured. A video wall simulation of the company's work features graphic transitions across the frames to display large images associated with particular mouseovers. In tandem with this transition, a blue rectangle slides out from the frame to identify the client, title of the work, and design category according to a simple legend.

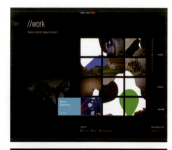

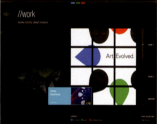

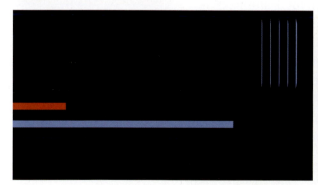

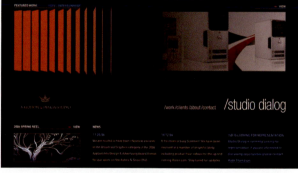

4.45
Frames from Studio Dialog's Web site. Courtesy of Studio Dialog.

Manuel Piton of DizyNotip, an interactive design studio in Brussels, used Flash's animation abilities to achieve subtle transitions in his Web designs for commercial arts studios in Belgium. His site for a film company specializing in independent shorts affirms that motion can enhance form and functionality (**4.45**). Aside from three simple text links that feature the writing, technical, and production aspects of filmmaking, an orange-highlighted "Choix du menu" allows you to choose upcoming events, achievements, filmmakers, and relevant links. A "Nos realisations" link generates an animation of Polaroid photos that move inward from the edges to fill the frame. A larger image featuring the short film "Le Sens De L'Orientation" (2006) rotates into position from the right to the left edge of the screen. Clicking anywhere triggers a shift in the position of background photos to accommodate scrollable text content and image, video, and music links. Choosing a different film from the interface's floating secondary navigation menu produces the same transition, with different Polaroid shots relating to the film.

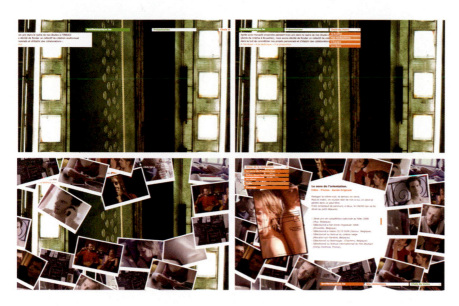

4.46
Web site design for LB.o lentillebioptique, a Belgian film production company specializing in independent, collaborative shorts. Courtesy of DizyNotip.

Resn's lush interface for the New Zealand band The Black Seeds (**4.47**) is an engaging kinetic collage of cheeky cutout photographs, flat, graphic images, and gold type superimposed on a black background. In response to selecting a navigation item, varieties of animals, plants, and props including musical instruments and disco balls move in and out of the frame to change the scenery, similar to how stage props might be changed to accommodate the scenes of a live play. The imagery and animation creates the feeling of a Pacific dance floor that suits the fun, laid-back nature of the band's music.

4.47
Web site design for The Black Seeds, a New Zealand band that blends reggae, funk, soul, and dub. Courtesy of Resn.

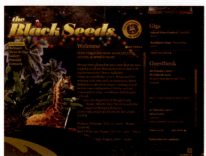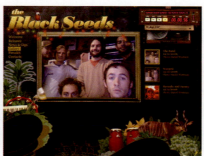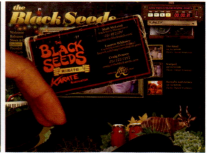

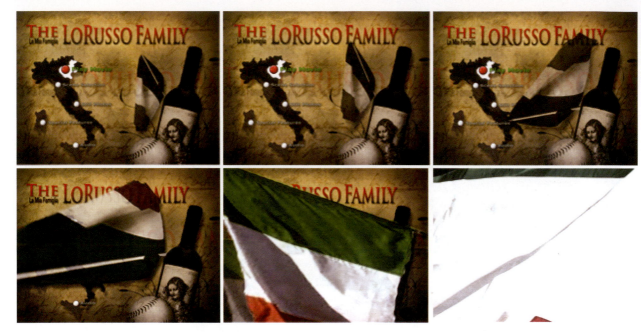

4.48

Adam Lo Russo's DVD menus for his family history show animated transitions between scenes. Courtesy of Professor Jon Krasner, Fitchburg State University.

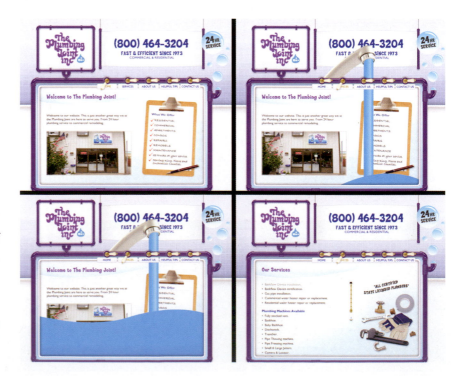

4.49

Web site for The Plumbing Joint, a privately owned plumbing business in Alabama. Courtesy of LeskoMedia.

The idea of water provided a clever design solution to transitioning between pages. Many graphic elements, including the site's navigational items, the main backdrop, and the header, were carefully choreographed to animate during the transitions.

A Look at Transitions

"Meaningful Transitions: Motion Graphics in the User Interface" is a thesis project developed by Johannes Tonnollo in 2011 for his Bachelor's Degree in Interface Design at the FH Potsdam in Germany. In it, Johannes demonstrates how the static design principles (scale and color contrast, proximity, alignment, positioning) that many interfaces rely on to enhance user interaction can be extended through motion. His research documents the cognitive benefits of six categories of animated transitions applicable to mobile devices and suggests how they can enhance meaning in otherwise static graphical environments. These categories are orientation, spatial extension, awakening controls, highlight, feedback, and feedforward. Taking into consideration how Disney's "Twelve Basic Principles of Animation" can portray realistic motion, Johannes created abstract visualizations of these transitions online (see http://www.ui-transitions.com/categories#home) to clarify their purposes. Each can be used to reinforce interaction and improve an interface's overall structure. Orientation transitions (**4.50**) can establish logical connections between objects and how the states of objects can be created and visualized. For example, directional motions

German designer Johannes Tonnollo recounted a story of an event that he witnessed in a subway station in Berlin. A little girl was playing what appeared to be a memory game on an iPad. At one point, she tried to cheat by looking underneath the device as if content existed below the screen. This experience led him to think about how movement, specifically transition, can create the illusion of a larger space beyond the screen. This could benefit people cognitively and emotionally by enriching content and providing clues to enhance interactivity and the storytelling experience.

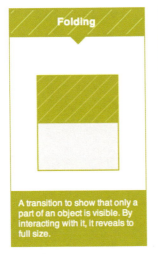 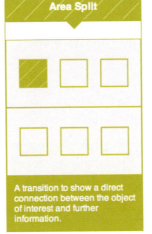 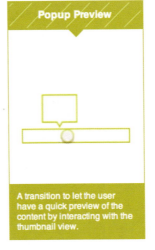 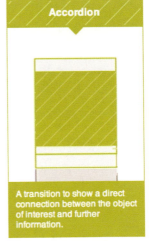

Folding A transition to show that only a part of an object is visible. By interacting with it, it reveals to full size.

Area Split A transition to show a direct connection between the object of interest and further information.

Popup Preview A transition to let the user have a quick preview of the content by interacting with the thumbnail view.

Accordion A transition to show a direct connection between the object of interest and further information.

describe the location and structure of information. Transitions such as slide, page turn, popup, and minimize can describe an object's environment and clarify a system's information architecture, inviting users to navigate through the interface. Spatial extension transitions can extend the virtual space by opening and closing it so that information is presented gradually rather than all at once. In Björk's *Biophilia* iPhone/iPad app (**4.25 and 4.26**), swiping and tapping the screen with your fingers

4.50
Orientation transitions are used to show the placement of objects. © Johannes Tonnollo.

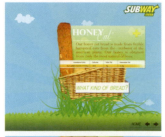

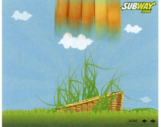

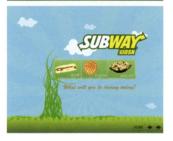

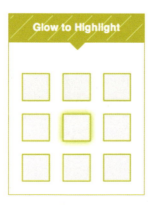

4.51
Style frames for a kiosk design by Justin Medas. This assignment involved the use of transitions between screens. Courtesy of Professor Jon Krasner, Fitchburg State University.

4.52
Highlighting transitions can direct a user's attention to specific elements and clarify changes in the interface that otherwise might be missed.
© Johannes Tonnollo.

makes the universe expand and turn as bits of music and songs emerge. Spatial extension transitions can save screen real estate while guiding users to focus more clearly on the most important elements. A common animation for spatial extension is turning a two-dimensional plane into a three-dimensional object that can be rotated to show different categories of information. This creates additional space while organizing information logically. Awakening controls allow users to focus on contextual items. They are present when needed and can disappear when they are no longer needed. Animations such as slide and fade can establish new methods of interaction when the user switches into certain modes or scenes. Highlighting transitions such as light and shade (**4.52**) can be used to direct a user's attention to specific elements and to clarify changes of states in the interface that otherwise might be missed. Feedback transitions are used to convey the outcome of a user's action visually. For example, they can denote a running process or indicate whether a particular action was successful or not. Two common types of feedback transitions are popups and progress-based animation. Progress-based animation can provide transitions that show the consequences of an action, making the resulting event more predictable and easier to follow. The user can anticipate the outcome more precisely and interpret it more reliably. At the same time animation can invite the user to interact and present new interaction mechanisms.

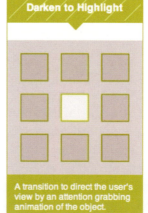

A transition to direct the user's view by an attention grabbing animation of the object.

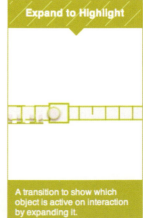

A transition to show which object is active on interaction by expanding it.

Chapter Summary

Interactive media organizes linear information into a branching, nonsequential structure, allowing users to assume more active roles. Motion graphics introduces new aesthetic possibilities and affords designers and animators opportunities to pursue their talents beyond the film and television screen. Basic design principles that interfaces rely on to enhance user interaction can be extended through motion.

Animation processes for the Web continue to improve in response to the demand for motion. Java applets have been used to produce interactive animations that can run in similar ways on various operating systems. Animated GIFs continue to be a popular low-tech option, since all browsers support the GIF format and programming skills are not required. During the release of HTML4.0 browsers, dynamic HTML (DHTML) offered an improved method of handling text through Cascading Style Sheets (CSS). Although it was recognized by most browsers and did not require extra components, its animation capabilities were limited. Flash has proven to be an efficient Web animation tool due to its capacity to scale vector-based images without sacrificing resolution. However, Flash content is difficult to update and index by search engines and is not viewable on today's mobile touchscreen devices. It is likely that newer technologies such as CSS and HTML5 will become Web standards in the near future. CSS provides designers control over properties that can be animated in response to an action or event. CSS3 gives a keyframe approach to animating HTML elements. JavaScript's object-oriented programming language is also appealing to designers, since most browsers support this format without the need for additional software or plug-ins. JavaScript libraries such as jQuery can simplify event handling and animation. Higher

bandwidth connections and video streaming has also made the prospect of motion over the Web enticing, and many designers have welcomed the opportunity to communicate beyond national boundaries.

Various forms of Web motion graphics have included splash pages as a form of advertising and to establish a company's or individual's Web presence. (Their use has, however, have declined due to download time and issues with search engine ranking.) Banners continue to be used in advertising, and more recently, Web or interstitials have become popular. Many designers hope that as the Internet continues to grow it will adopt traditional television formats to make online advertising more engaging. In entertainment, the demand for online music videos and games has increased due to the Web's capacity to integrate animation and interactivity.

The inclusion of motion graphics in portable games, kiosks, mobile devices, desktop applications, and DVD-video titles has also grown considerably. Interactive experiences have become increasingly cinematic in the game industry. The integration of touchscreen technology and the increased popularity of mobile devices and portable game consoles is continuing to drive the demand for motion designers. Further, the potential of animation in mobile interfaces is being realized in the music industry.

Successful navigation design supports and directs users through the complexities of an interface. Incorporating motion into a navigational structure can enhance the level of interactivity by placing emphasis on elements that might otherwise be overlooked. Additionally, transitions can help move users between levels of detail. The cognitive benefits of animated transitions enhance meaning in otherwise static graphical environments.

motion graphics in
public spaces

5

We live in a time and culture where all of our sensory experiences are challenged by the bombardment of information. The potential of motion graphics in our physical world has finally been realized and is helping to shape the landscape of environmental interior and exterior design. Public informational systems, performance art, memorial and donor recognition programs, and contemporary video installations are vehicles that have opened new doors for motion graphic designers.

"What made people stop painting frescoes and start painting on panels and stretched canvases anyway? And what if corporations moved away from fixed logo-type signage on the outside of their building facilities and put big video screens up there instead?"
—Terry Green, twenty2product

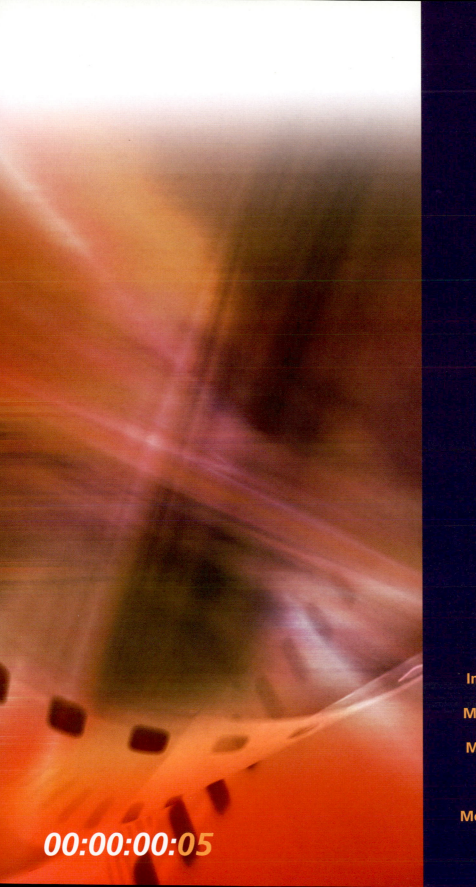

00:00:00:05

Immersive Environments

"Immersive environments" shape a sense of place by providing order, ambience, comfort, and insight in an existing physical space. They are unique confluences of architecture, imagery, and sound that operate holistically to provide aesthetic, meaningful experiences and enhance social interaction. They can also communicate products, services, and messages by merging interactive technologies with tangible spatial experiences. Today, immersive environments are capable of blending physical and imaginary worlds that respond to humans. The expressive qualities of motion are playing a greater role in shaping our visual landscape, as they make their appearances in hotel lobbies, retail spaces, museums, theme parks, and airports (to give just a few examples).

Historical Perspective

During the 1920s, French film director Abel Gance experimented with a three-screen version of Napoléon. In the 1960s, Cinemascope's elongated proportion was extended to a curved, concave screen to embrace audiences. The New York World's Fair of 1964 marked the apotheosis of the giant screen frenzy. Pavilions competed to create the most breathtaking displays: the circular Kodak theater, the GE "sky-dome spectacular," General Cigar's "Movie in the Round," and Charles and Rae Eames' "View from the People Wall"—a nine-screen projection on the ceiling of IBM's headquarters. These were the precursors of today's IMAX theaters.

Throughout the 1970s, slide projectors allowed dissolving images to be displayed in rapid succession. These slide shows relied heavily on film processing, glass mounting, and slide tray loading. When electronic imaging surfaced in the 1980s, slide screens were put aside for video wall displays. During the 1990s, digital signal processors and high-resolution projection cubes were developed to compete with brighter projectors. Virtual reality (VR) technology allowed viewers to enter a dimension that was set apart from their immediate surroundings, dissolving the boundary of the frame.

Emerging digital display technologies are thriving throughout the world in almost every arena, including shopping malls, nightclubs, retail stores, and sports arenas. Pier 39, located in Fisherman's Wharf in San Francisco, is visited by millions of consumers who experience a 9 × 15 foot video wall featuring headline news, sports programs, weather, and trivia for the Bay Area. A major benefit of video wall technology is that unlike projection systems it can display large images without sacrificing resolution, since the number of available pixels and brightness per square foot remains constant. It also allows many configurations. Large-scale video architecture also enables generative motion graphics to be created in real time based on the input of live data. In 2011, New York design studio Trollbäck + Company created a unique conference opener for the Association of Independent Commercial Producers (**5.1**) Rather than settling on a linear piece, the design team explored taking an input source—footage of the attendees arriving at Times Center—and creating something interesting on the spot. The video was shot against a lightbox to create a high contrast look, and a frame delay was added to offset the color channels, making the figures appear as silhouettes trailing a color array. The footage was organized into loops on a shifting grid, and the movements of the subjects triggered the audio. The incoming video's tonal values activated particular midi channels, and these factors enabled the soundtrack to be composed on the fly. According to Creative Director Stephen Baker: "You will never get the same result twice . . . With so many variables coming together, it was important that our underlying design principles were strong enough and the software smart enough to create beauty from a somewhat chaotic input."

The technology behind most video walls is similar. A video signal feeds into a processor that alters and splits a signal across multiple monitors to produce images from numerous sources. Depending on the sophistication of the software, separate data sources can be programmed to split a single image across all the screens, magnify a single image across the screens, or merge multiple images together.

5.1
Frames from AICP's 2011 conference opener. Courtesy of Trollbäck + Company.

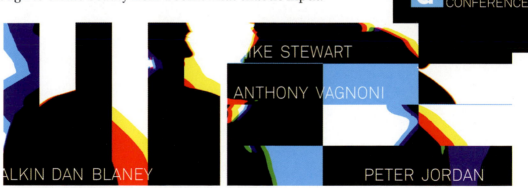

Digital signage is one of the fastest-growing marketing opportunities in the world today, ranging from sports scoreboards to giant video screens in large public spaces. As a "real-time" messaging medium, it is used to present many forms of content over high-speed networks on video displays in public venues. Interactive digital signage solutions such as touch-screen kiosks deliver dynamic, timely messages that can impart information or influence consumer behavior. In advertising, the marketing content can be crafted based on specific information that consumers provide or from the purchases that they make.

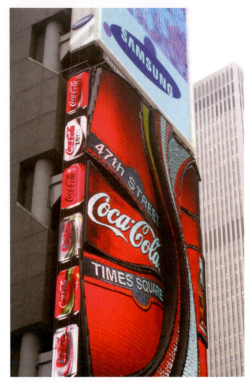

5.2
Coca-Cola display in Times
Square, New York City. Courtesy
of Daktronics Inc.

*NASDAQ, the largest U.S. electronic
stock market, presents the action
on Wall Street by displaying the
colorful company logos of its 5,600
securities, as well as live video,
news broadcasts, global market
information, and advertising on the
MarketSite Tower, the eight-story-
high video screen located in the
heart of Times Square.*

"Dynamic digital signage"—typically composed of a server,
monitor, and software—is emerging as a new generation
of sign technology in the advertising industry. It is capable
of delivering dynamic visual content to multiple locations,
making it possible for advertisers to communicate a brand
or send a message locally or worldwide from a central
location (**5.2**).

In response to demands from advertisers to reach more
audiences and to a decline in prices for projector displays,
the demand for digital signage has accelerated. Wal-Mart,
The Gap, and Foot Locker have adapted digital signage
technology to promote their brands nationwide. In 2006,
a partnership between Latin America's most dominant
companies, Grupo Televisa and Wal-Mart de Mexico (or
"Wal-Mex"), launched a network covering Wal-Mex stores
across Mexico. More than 5,000 LCD displays and kiosks
have enhanced the store's appeal to shoppers and assisted
them in making purchasing decisions. Shopping malls
have also embraced digital signage as a strategy to keep
consumers informed and entertained and to encourage
them to buy. The Adspace Mall Network—the largest
network of mall-based digital displays in the U.S.—consists of eight-
foot "smart screens" that feature specials, events, and commercials.

Digital Art Spots (DASs) are a core component of the Business Sponsored
Art Program™ developed by Billijam (http://www.billijam.com), a
cutting-edge visual design and digital art studio based in New York City.
With the mission of enhancing the aesthetic value of public spaces,
these original, digital artworks are sponsored by advertisers to support
their brand by displaying their logo or tagline. This in turn provides
the advertisers with PR buzz and public attention from pedestrians.
The artworks have been commissioned for in-store displays, shopping
malls, digital billboards, digital street networks, and large-scale displays
including wallscapes, spectaculars, and street and transit media. In
2005, Clear Channel partnered with Billijam to bring DAS to the streets
of Manhattan through its digital display network. Businesses could
sponsor original artwork to be displayed on 80 LED video screens
strategically placed at the entrances of major subway stations throughout
the city (**5.3**).

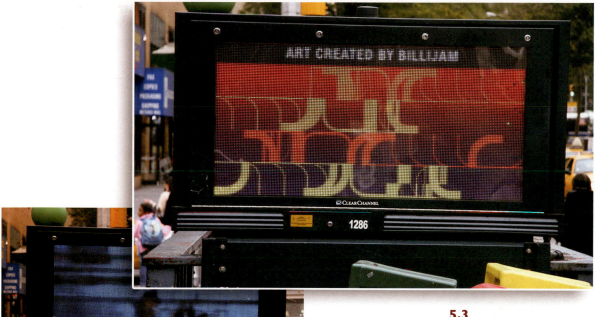

5.3
A Digital Art Spot in New York City, part of the Business Sponsored Art Program™. Courtesy of Billijam.

Other advanced display technologies have transformed public spaces by enabling the incorporation of motion. Companies like Daktronics—one of the world's biggest suppliers of large screens and electronic scoreboards—are trendsetting in the sphere of Light Emitting Diode (LED) technology. LED lighting has increasingly become the choice of architects and interior designers who want to enhance public spaces with "intelligent light." Unlike traditional, flat LCD or plasma screens, LED modules can be customized to any size and aspect ratio, to create various geometric configurations. Their square corners and lack of uninterupted seams allow for configurations of visuals. Further, they are bright enough to compete with sunlight, making content visible in front windows, and they can be viewed at distances of less than three feet, since the pixels are densely placed.

"Augmented space" (also referred to as "augmented reality") is physical space that is amplified with electronic, visual information to create an immersive environment. Many of the studies presented in this chapter are examples of augmented spaces. Larger and flatter screen displays, three-dimensional imaging, and improved network technologies have entered our world, presenting us with kinetic and context-specific

Billijam's founder Marya Triandafellos also founded the successful Web design and branding company MET Design, Inc., and has produced over 200 websites for corporate clients including IBM, McCann Erickson, and ABC News. Over a five-year period, she produced over 100 videos for a NYC local cable network; four of these were awarded production grants, and two were screened in film festivals. Since 2004, she has applied her entrepreneurial and artistic vision to introducing the concept of fine art to enhance the brand experience.

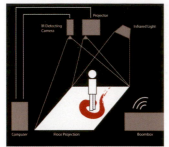

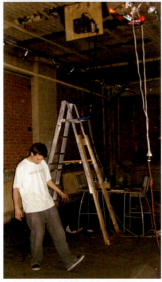

5.4
RhythmFlow by Karl Channell.

information that is continuously updated. Ubiquitous video surveillance systems can extract and deliver data to and from a given location. AR glasses can layer content over our own visual field. On a much smaller level, "cell space" can hold customizable data to aid users in checking in at a hotel or retrieving information about a product.

Unlike virtual reality, which removes content from real life, augmented reality reappropriates physical space through media, enabling us to acquire information and enrich social connections and self-expression in new ways. Created by Karl Channell, a Senior User Experience Designer at Apple Computer, *RhythmFlow* was a collaborative video system designed to encourage new ways of re-adapting to public spaces through body movement. This projection system was programmed to visualize rhythms in public dance recreation culture. Since dance typically exists in an open space that is unconstrained by walls, the system's architecture made use of the idea of "fat-free" design, reducing elements down to their essence in order to focus on human-centered approaches to problem solving. A projector mounted from the ceiling is pointed downwards onto a dance circle (**5.4**). Infrared lights are also projected downward onto the circle and reflected back to an infrared sensitive camera to detect a dancer's changing shadow. The history of the dancer's movements leaves trails of pixels behind. Fast movements produce thin lines, while slower movements leave thick blotches reminiscent of a pen being held to paper. As lines cross paths, they react by changing color and causing pixels to become more energized or agitated. As older patterns fade away, new ones appear. The style of the visuals can be altered, depending on which system the user selects. Karl states: "The focus remains on the dancers, but with a layer of virtual content and expressiveness on top of them and their surrounding dance territory."

Motion in Interior Spaces

Motion graphics have become a vital element in establishing mood and atmosphere in hotels, corporate lobbies, waiting rooms, casinos, and restaurants. They can reinforce a brand, update information, and define an ambience that might be unattainable with other mediums. In retail and event spaces, motion can provide drama in entranceways, attract outside traffic via display window content, stimulate guest interaction, and substitute mundane television programming with unique visuals.

Spanning across the lobby in Nielsen Media Research's head office in New York is a row of ten projection screens that play looped animations throughout the day (**5.5**). The architect who designed the lobby chose rear projection screens without frames to line up seamlessly. For projects of this nature, it is difficult to predict how the imagery will look at large scale, since the installation may not be implemented until after the content is designed. In this case, the wall was built just two weeks before the opening. Its massive scale made it challenging to gauge how it would look in the lobby with only a small preview movie available.

Nielsen Media Research analyzes the behavior of media audiences, including for television, radio, and newspapers. Since the 1950s, the Nielsen TV Ratings have statistically measured which programs are watched by different segments of the population.

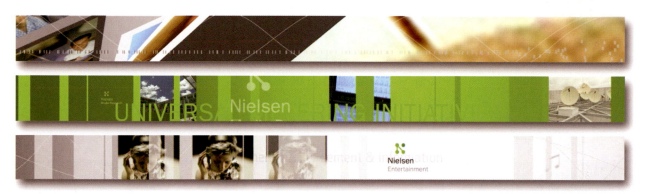

A video installation for John Levy, an international lighting design firm in Los Angeles, was used inside several casinos to provide ambience and entertain the patrons. Five 15-foot screens featured an animation entitled "Lava," an amalgamation of beach scenes including surfing, underwater imagery, and water sports (**5.7**).

5.5
Frames from a looped video installation for Nielsen Media Research's head office.

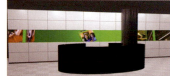

5.6
Computer-generated rendition of an installation for Nielsen Media Research's head office in New York. Concept and design by Dyske Suematsu and KSK:STUDIOS. Production by New Vision Comunications.

5.7
Frames from "Lava," a video installation for the John Levy lighting design firm. Courtesy of Reality Check Studios.

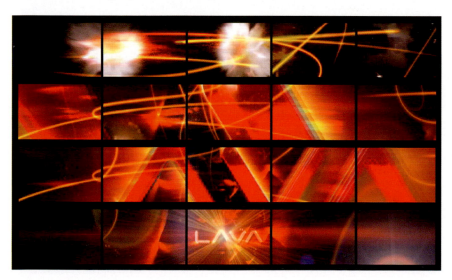

In 2004, Imaginary Forces designed a permanent video installation for the lobby of New York's Museum of Modern Art (MoMA). The installation randomly selects artworks from the museum's collection and animates them on nine 30-inch screens in tandem with changing content on events and exhibitions to provide both information and ambience. The system's architecture, consisting of high-definition LCD monitors and a network of ten computers, algorithmically selects from a repertoire of images and action sequences such as fast blurring, slow scaling, and cross-fading and applies them to the screens. The museum updates the system with text and new images from temporary exhibitions and the permanent collection on a regular basis, so that the content is always changing. According to Kurt Ralske, who designed and implemented the system and co-designed the image sequences, the original idea for the installation involved playing back video from a hard drive. Because of the amount of data needed to display the content at high resolution, the use of still images in motion could be created by transforming, scaling, and blending them in real time (**5.8**).

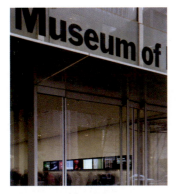

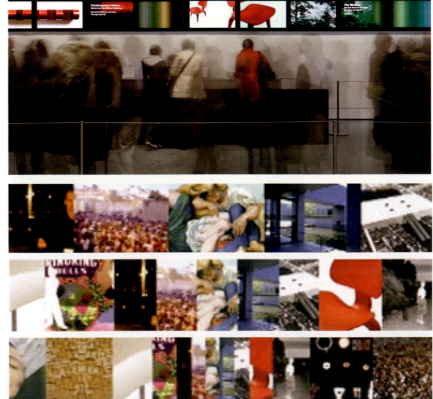

5.8
MoMA display screens, 2004.
Courtesy of Imaginary Forces.

In addition to using flat screens, many animated interior designs have utilized curved LED displays. Radio Shack's corporate headquarters in downtown Fort Worth, Texas uses a circular configuration of LED displays to line the 64-foot interior circumference of its rotunda (**5.9**). Each screen measures 4' high × 22 feet wide. A combination of vivid live-action and graphic content, theatrical lighting, and sound gives patrons a distinctive sensory experience and conveys Radio Shack's dominance in the consumer electronics market.

The Grand Court at the Mall at Millennia in Orlando, Florida houses a circle offreestanding LED displays that represent the Neolithic majesty of Stonehenge (**5.10**). Twelve screens are thrust 30 feet in the air, each measuring 10 feet high × 4 feet wide with a 40-degree arc. Since they can be viewed from behind, the cosmetic appearance of the rear surfaces had to be aesthetically pleasing and continuous. This grand scale celebration of American consumerism provides an entertaining, informative environment for the mall's patrons.

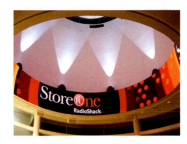

5.9
The rotunda at Radio Shack's corporate headquarters in Fort Worth, Texas. Photo courtesy of Daktronics, Inc.

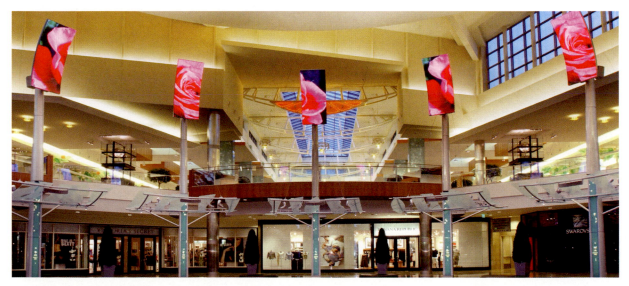

5.10
LED displays in the Grand Court at the Mall at Millennia in Orlando, Florida. Photo courtesy of Daktronics, Inc.

The cosmetic appearance of the Executive Suite at Goldman Sachs' global headquarters is enlivened with a digital media installation that features a rich display of live data reflecting the firm's visionary technological innovations, industry knowledge, and global insights. This compelling communication experience shares Goldman Sachs' position in world financial markets in an instantaneous and sophisticated way that engages their executive staff and impresses their visitors. Unified Field, a privately held media design company in New York City, implemented their Evolving Screen technology to transform this public space into "living architecture" by providing a self-evolving movie that interweaves the history, culture, and people of Goldman Sachs with current events, global financial data, and news in a virtual three-dimensional landscape. The information— which takes on many forms including live footage, text, images, real time news, data feeds, and data-driven four-dimensional models—continually changes in response to market and business activities, ranging from trading patterns of individual stocks to the decisions of personnel worldwide (**5.11**).

5.11
Screens in the Executive Suite of Goldman Sachs' global headquarters. Courtesy of Unified Field, Inc.

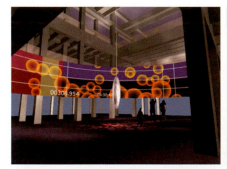
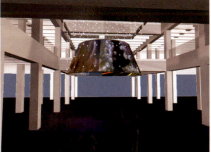
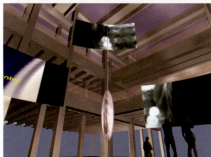
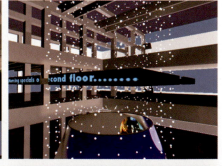
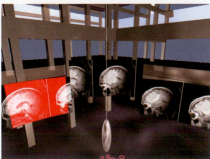
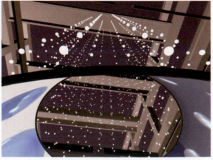

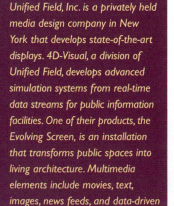

Unified Field, Inc. is a privately held media design company in New York that develops state-of-the-art displays. 4D-Visual, a division of Unified Field, develops advanced simulation systems from real-time data streams for public information facilities. One of their products, the Evolving Screen, is an installation that transforms public spaces into living architecture. Multimedia elements include movies, text, images, news feeds, and data-driven four-dimensional models.

The New York based video art company Billijam (also featured on p. 128 in relation to Digital Art Spots) specializes in creating distinctive animation sequences that bring life and culture to public spaces that need ambience enhancement (**5.12**). Founded by entrepreneurs Marya Triandafellos and Pat Lewis, the company has helped define brands in the hotel industry by providing immersive environments that can be displayed on plasma screens or projected onto almost any surface. Additionally, they can be timed to generate different ambiences for patrons throughout the day. Marya's captivating work has been displayed in the Times Square Hilton, the Marriott Marquis, the New York Barclay Hotel, Hotel 41, Club Avalon, and the Remote Lounge.

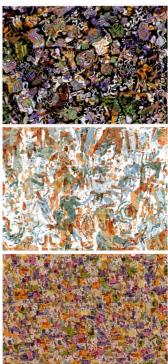

5.12
Marya Triandafelloss' dynamic animation sequences are imbued with colorful and textural video and graphic images to create ambient environments for public spaces. Courtesy of Billijam.

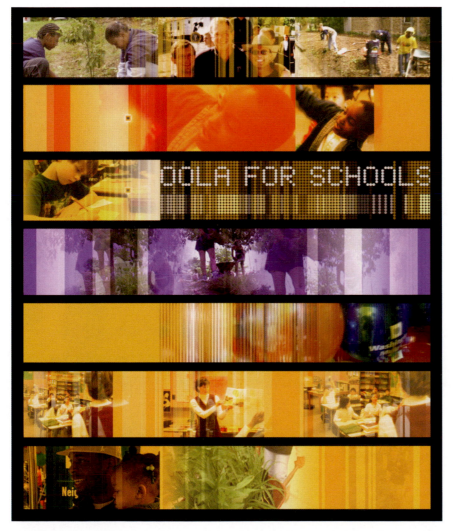

5.13
Frames from a community video wall for Washington Mutual's Manhattan retail space. Courtesy of twenty2product. © 2003 Washington Mutual. All rights reserved.

A stunning 36-foot motion-sensitive video installation at the University of Dayton's admission center provides a unique immersive experience that highlights the institution's achievements while encouraging active participation among prospective students and their families. Directed by Flightphase, an art and design studio based in Brooklyn, New York, the idea of a simple cube was used as a device to animate the screen. Cubes move around the display as small elements, at times changing size and congealing together to generate graphic patterns in response to the activity and positions of viewers in front of the wall (**5.14**). For example, the motion of a person passing by the system might be interpreted as sending energy into the field of cubes, pushing them in the direction that he or she is moving. A person's presence might also trigger the cubes to spin around to reveal segments of high-definition video portraying campus life. (Deliberate attention to lighting gave the footage a low-tech look, suggesting a first-person perspective.) The borders of the video may also change based on viewer presence.

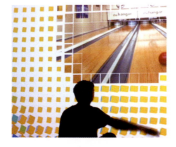

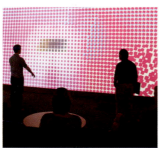

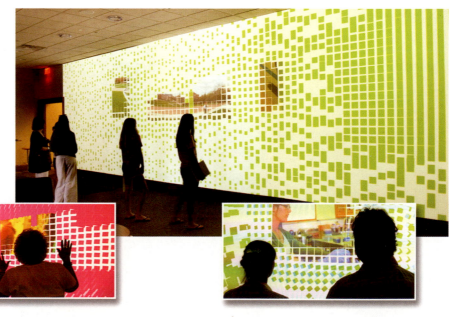

5.14
A mix of generative and user-driven animation gives the University of Dayton's video wall system "a life of its own." Courtesy of Flightphase.

Changes that occur in the installation are not entirely triggered by viewers in front of the wall. The cubes are also influenced by invisible forces called "affectors." These forces travel randomly through the space and affect the cubes' behavior by rotating, moving, or scaling those they pass. Two factors allow different interaction scenarios to occur. First, the longer a cube is stationed underneath an affector, the more it is influenced by it. Since the affectors were designed to begin small and scale to their final size during the course of their travels, many often combine together to act on the cubes simultaneously and generate different effects (**5.15**). When the application enters "idle mode," undulating patterns of cubes continue to move and transform, with changing color palettes, in coordination with typographic elements reflecting the University's values and mission (**5.16**). The system seems alive, like a living, breathing organism. One of the biggest challenges of this project was creating a balance between emergent behaviors and behaviors that were driven by visitors in the interaction area. Flightphase spent considerable time investigating various patterns of cubes that would look visually appealing in both scenarios. This curatorial process ensured a sense of constraint and established a design that was unexpected and emergent, yet to a certain degree controlled.

The interaction of University of Dayton's installation is driven by four overhead cameras that track the positions of visitors and map their contours onto the field of cubes. Running on two Mac Minis, the video tracking software was built from openFrameworks and a modified version of TSPS (Toolkit for Tracking People in Spaces).

5.15
The behavior of the cubes is partially influenced by "affectors." Courtesy of Flightphase.

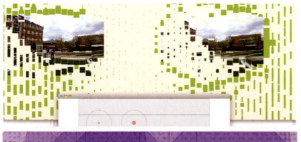
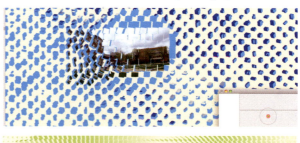
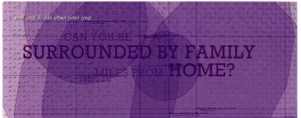
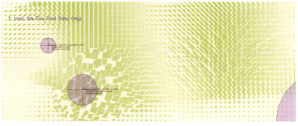
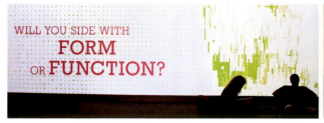
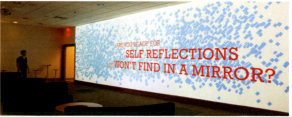

5.16
In "idle mode," patterns of cubes move in coordination with statements that express the school's mission. Courtesy of Flightphase.

An example of how motion graphics can place viewers into imaginary architectures or landscapes is a large-scale video installation entitled "Transit" above the arrivals waiting area in LAX airport's International Terminal (**5.17**). Designed by Scott Snibbe, this entertaining piece consisting of twenty-nine high-definition displays provides an artistic excursion from hectic, everyday life. The story begins with a little boy running across the expanse of monitors. You can see that he has escaped from his mother who follows behind, beckoning him to return. After rushing back to hold her hand, he again breaks free as crowds of travelers arrive. Appearing as silhouettes that move through the airport, they suddenly put down their bags and break into dance routines ranging from hip-hop, to salsa, to ballet, to punk—all reflecting the city's diversity. Eventually, the dancers stop, pick up their bags, and return to their anonymous advance. Halfway through the presentation, the story shatters into abstracted fragments showing multiple travelers walking across the screens. Duplicates sometimes appear on all the screens simultaneously. Moon-walking pedestrians float backwards to release new crowds of travelers. Among the crowd appears a non-silhouetted dancing lady in a red dress, ignored by the other pedestrians who seem oblivious to their surroundings. At the end of the story, two stragglers begin a romantic duet, and a lonely gentleman cuts through them. In close proximity to the overhead display is a rectangular 5 × 5-foot video wall that presents this same animation in a different configuration.

5.17
Photograph of LAX airport's installation "Transit." Courtesy of Scott Snibbe.

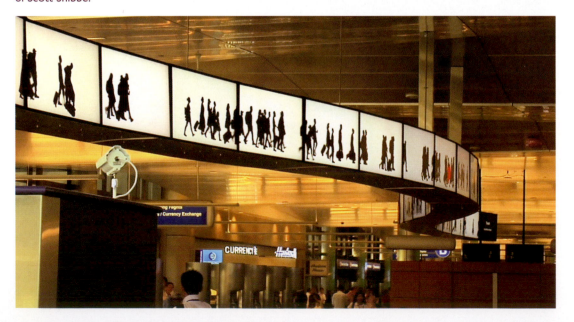

In retail spaces, immersive environments can create genuine, emotional branding experiences by putting shoppers in new, intuitive and exotic worlds.

In the HBO Shop in HBO's Manhattan headquarters, a large-scale installation transforms the store into an architectural canvas where large-format video projections, choreographed lighting, and audio work together to create a unique visual experience (**5.18**). Los Angeles design agency Imaginary Forces collaborated with the architectural design firm Gensler to convert this 750-foot retail space into an immersive interior and exterior design that features HBO's award-winning programming. From the outside, four parallel, large-format video displays appear to recede into an open, deep space, from the storefront window stretching to the back, leaving a lasting impression on nearby pedestrians. The store is encased in acid-etched, white glass walls that serve as a projection surface and soak up the changing colors of overhead lights. The LED screens, which appear to be suspended in mid-air, attract the attention of shoppers and entice them into the store. Inside the store, they are treated to themed environments that continually change, as the merchandise plays a secondary, supporting role. Behind the main displays are three high-resolution 65-inch plasma screens in portrait mode. In addition to the storefront displays, a 33-foot-long LED ribbon display is set back into the wall about 1½ feet to create an inlet that acts as a backdrop for props from the shows. The continuous animation displayed draws shoppers toward the back of the store. Further, two ceiling-mounted projectors throw 6-foot-high × 8-foot-wide video imagery onto facing walls. Lighting is used to make the store's 14-foot walls change color. (For example, when the displays feature scenes from *The Sopranos*, the walls turn blood red.) Lighting designer Michael Castelli and the design team experimented with various lighting fixtures to see how different types of glass would absorb colored light, and chose back-painted glass with an acid-etched surface that allowed for extreme color saturation to emulate the look of a high-resolution monitor.

As technology continues to advance, motion graphic designers will have more creative opportunities to design content for these types of public spaces.

5.18
As a clever marketing tool, the HBO Shop's audio, lighting, projection, LED, and plasma displays create multimedia-driven immersive environments. The content it displays is designed to lead shoppers to the store's checkout area.

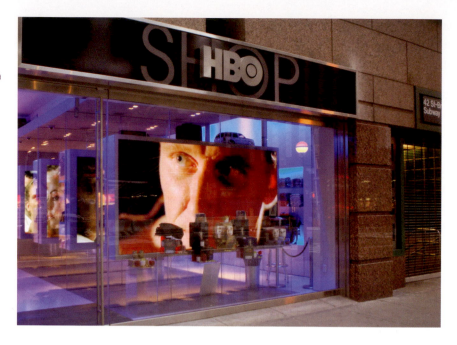

The field of exhibit design combines graphic design, interactive media, motion graphics, and product design. Exhibit designers must demonstrate strong creative skills and a sensitivity to aesthetic principles, along with a knowledge of materials, lighting, and architecture.

Motion in Exhibit Design

The inclusion of motion graphics in commercial, educational, art, and entertainment-based exhibits serves many purposes. Imaginative, well-designed exhibits create memorable, lasting impressions for viewers. Their success is judged by how the content meets a site's aesthetic and spatial requirements. Existing materials, lighting, and architecture are often factors that need to be considered . Further, the elements of color, typography, composition, and motion must work together cohesively to communicate information clearly, concisely, and consistently.

Located on the third floor of New York's Time Warner Center is the Samsung Experience—a 10,000-square-foot emporium of interactive virtual reality experiences that demonstrate to visitors how Samsung's brand and latest products can enrich their everyday life. Samsung's partners, including MIT Media Lab, Parsons School of Design, Napster, and Sprint PCS, are also featured. As an educational resource, this seamless world of sights, sounds, and sensations communicates the life-enhancing benefits of digital technology without the pressures of a sales environment. Giant rotating LCD screens feature interconnected virtual worlds. Interactive workstations allow users to create digital collages in real time. In the space outside of the Samsung Experience is an interactive map of Manhattan that can be viewed and manipulated with hand gestures, facilitating a user's experience of digital lifestyle in New York. Part of the Experience, the Cyber Brand Showcase, is a participatory Web site that blurs the boundary between real and virtual space by allowing visitor information to be exchanged between their physical surroundings and the online environment through cyber conduits.

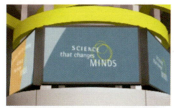

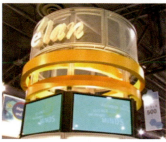

Elan was the premier sponsor of the 9th International Conference on Alzheimer's Disease at Philadelphia's Pennsylvania Convention Center. KSK:STUDIOS hired a environmental designer, Adrian Levin, to design the exhibition booth and hired a branding specialist, Anita Zeppetelli, to establish the visual identity for the convention. Video signage was presented on six plasma screens that were installed around the main tower. Instead of playing the same video on all six screens, a computer-based video device allowed six independent streams of video to be displayed in sync, so that elements could move across all the screens. The most challenging aspect of this project was that the screens were configured in a hexagonal arrangement, meaning that the video could have no discrete ends horizontally. Using a three-dimensional program, six cameras were aimed at the same objects from different angles (**5.19**).

5.19
Exhibit design for an International Conference on Alzheimer's Disease. Courtesy of Dyske Suematsu and KSK:STUDIOS.

BrainLAB, a German medical technology company, showcased their orthopedic products at a trade show convention using twelve plasma screens configured in a row, each screen representing a product (**5.20**). Rather than playing independent videos simultaneously, the company wanted certain elements to move across the screens. At KSK:STUDIOS, Dyske Suematsu designed the motion graphics and harnessed a computer-based video server to play twelve streams of video in sync. Since the screens had to act as one, the dimensions of the original design were enormous (10,368 × 486 pixels to be exact).

5.20
Installation for BrainLAB. Courtesy of Dyske Suematsu and KSK:STUDIOS.

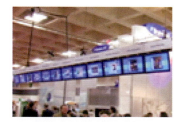

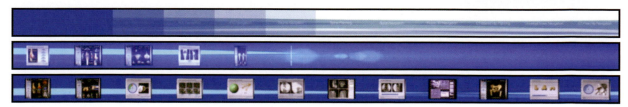

Educational exhibits have incorporated motion graphics to help shape the way we learn and reflect about the world and about ourselves. In the atrium of New Jersey's Liberty Science Center is an exhibition entitled "Vital Signs," which features an interactive, streaming media centerpiece that disseminates breaking news about our planet and the museum's themes of environment, health and invention. A mystical, wraparound display of LED screens is interspersed with projections of three-dimensional forms and interpretive text that move in space to produce a poetic and engaging blend of science, technology, and art. The installation delivers a rich sense of timelessness that inspires observation and inquiry by allowing visitors to select topics, upload information, and view streaming content from all sides of the atrium. Unified Field envisioned this "as a node in a knowledge network, where data from internal and external sources feed multidimensional representations to make the intangible visceral, while powerfully illustrating the ever-changing nature of science and technology." These "sculptural media" elements were designed to function as part of a digital narrowcast network, a digital sign system, a messaging system, and interactive exhibits. Visible from every location in the museum, they alert and inform visitors of the presence and wonder of science (**5.21**).

5.21
"Vital Signs," a media installation at the Liberty Science Center. Courtesy of Unified Field, Inc.

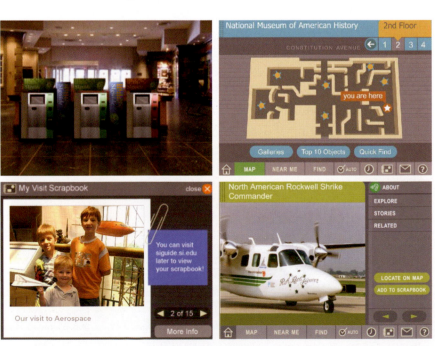

As a leader in global investment banking, Goldman Sachs wanted to evoke an inspirational learning environment that would reflect their commitment to building skills and encouraging new thought and behavioral patterns. In the Goldman Sachs' Learning Center in New York City, geometric animations play on four curved, frosted panels in response to people's traffic patterns. Advanced visualization software and an Intelligent Recognition Inference System (IRIS) simulates patterns and fluctuations that twenty-first century markets operate in. Information on stocks in the world's capital markets is layered with historical events, giving visitors a visceral experience and inviting them to extrapolate their own conclusions on investment banking (**5.22**).

The National Museum of American Jewish History in Philadelphia, Pennsylvania houses a remarkable moving exhibit that combines the storytelling power of film with the physical qualities of sculpture. "Dreams of Freedom: 1880–1945" is large wall installation chronicling the massive wave of European Jews who, motivated by persecution and the Holocaust, immigrated to America during the late nineteenth century (**5.23**). In 2010, New York design firm Local Projects collaborated with the museum's curatorial staff to determine how hundreds of archival letters and pages from diaries could be incorporated into films based on actual historical accounts. The concept of the mailed letter was used to portray the principle method by which relocation was discussed among families before making the journey. This poetic journey back in time touches upon the choices and challenges that one quarter of Europe's Jewish population confronted during World War II.

The development of the narrative was a product of considerable script-writing and research on Jewish architypes from different walks of life who were part of the wave of immigrants. An overwhelming amount of information was organized into chapters. A soldier in the Russian army, a social activist from Poland, a small child from Russia, and an orthodox Jew from Czechoslovakia all provided unique descriptions of life as it was experienced in Europe. These represented an important moment in time during which the Jewish people stood at a junction in history.

Instead of relying on flat projection, a signature display system was used to blend animated imagery onto a three-dimensional wall sculpture derived from actual aged and curved letters. This innovative approach offered unusual opportunities to mix the undulating form of the letter

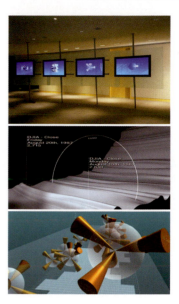

5.22
A dynamic media installation at the Goldman Sachs' Learning Center provides information on the history of stocks in the world's capital markets. Ten feet in front of the panels and embedded in the ceiling is a tracking video camera that monitors the motion of viewers and interfaces with a high-speed image processing board containing gesture recognition software. Courtesy of Unified Field, Inc.

Ariel Efron was one of the chief motion designers for "Dreams of Freedom." Growing up in Israel, he studied the art of photography and video at Bezalel Academy of Art and Design in Jerusalem. He began his career designing stages for dance companies and theater productions. Interested in how media could operate onstage with performance, his thesis project at New York University explored how media could provide an architectural context to connect story with place, as well as change mood, set an atmosphere, or describe a scene.

with projected illumination. The presentation's large scale and strong connection of narrative and physical qualities delivers a unique cinematic impact. The division of the canvas into handwritten letters enables one large story to be composed from many small, personal stories. Letters float and fall from the sky as people gather in villages, accompanied by the sound of a letter being read in English, Yiddish, and Hebrew. The voice discusses what the new world will bring, the good and bad that awaits the immigrants. Stylized animations of postcards, drawings, family photographs, and imagined landscapes play across the display, expressing what the Jews dreamt of and sacrificed. The motion of the elements was designed to portray fluid on a surface to reflect the thoughts of millions of people who traveled across two oceans.

5.23
In "Dreams of Freedom," the collaboration between content and form combines the storytelling power of film with the physical qualities of sculpture. Courtesy of Local Projects.

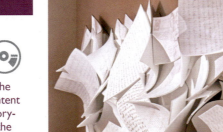

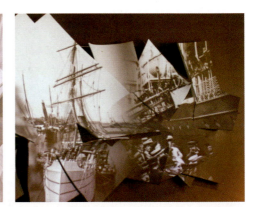

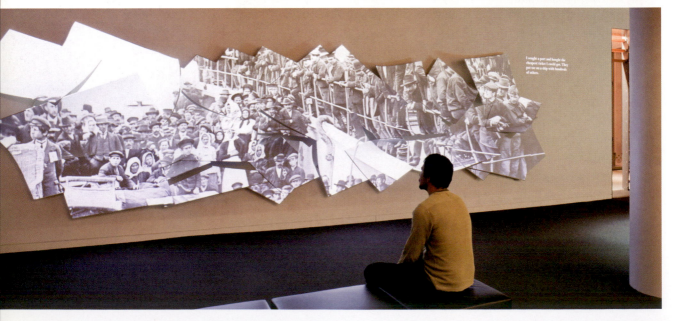

During the storyboarding phase of this project, Local Projects' design team attempted to choreograph a wide spectrum of events to occur across the composition. Crescendo moments in which the entire screen is overwhelmed with graphic information enhance the multiplicity of personal stories from events that happened simultaneously. At other times, moments of silence are accompanied by a single element (**5.24**).

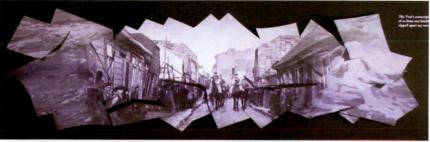

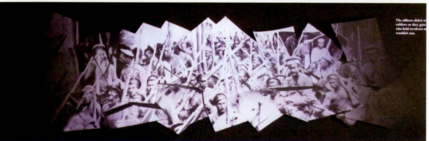

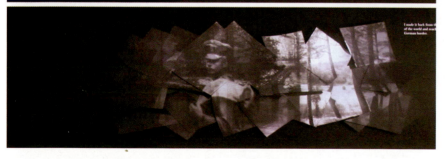

During the creation of "Dreams of Freedom," it took six months of testing to arrive at the best method of utilizing the sculpture's geometry. After attempting to model ocean waves algorithmically, designer Ariel Efron used paper models of cut paper stock soaked in water. The forms were fixed with a hardening material and digitized with a 3D scanner. The complex data were simplified into a digital polygon from which a polymer sculpture was fabricated. With a rig of three projectors, it took two days to map animations to all the individual pieces correctly. Careful attention had to be given to the differences between the original animations on the flat computer monitor and the projected footage, as determined by the three-dimensional surface and optics of the projector's lenses. In the end, the animations composed in After Effects were 85 percent accurate.

5.24
Scenes from "Dreams of Freedom."
Courtesy of Local Projects.

The National Museum of American Jewish History houses two other exhibitions designed by Local Projects: "Only in America" and "Innovation and Expansion." "Only in America" (**5.25**) consists of two wide, curved displays that stand upright in the center of the gallery. Both their size and non-conventional shape offers an immersive and inviting setting. In contrast to one-directional viewing of a flat film screen inside an enclosed theatre, the displays extend beyond a visitor's field of vision, allowing the content to be configured to address the space. This gives viewers the freedom to move around and become engaged in the installation's physical space while focusing attention on particular moments of impact. Careful consideration was given to how the breath of the screens could direct eye movement to lead viewers to specific points of interest. Semi-translucent overlays of rectangles help attract attention to particular events and provide transitions between images. At times, they move across both screens to encourage visitors to shift from one display to the other. Other times, sequences of photographs emulating stop-motion animation frames are revealed in lateral succession. By the time viewers track the buildup of images from left to right and land on the other side of the screen, they are met with a new image that continues the narrative. In a scene where Leonard Bernstein sings to the tune of "God Bless America," Bernstein's stage performance is presented as a succession of shots beginning with his figure crouched down low and ending in an upright position with arms fully extended. As the photographs reveal themselves horizontally, the audio of the actual performance plays in the background (**5.25, below**). This technique activates the viewing space by making the visitor turn from left to right. Another device used to foster interaction was dividing the

5.25
"Only in America." Courtesy of Local Projects.

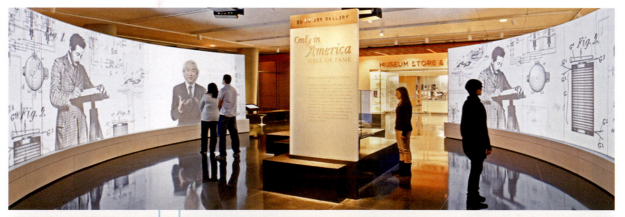

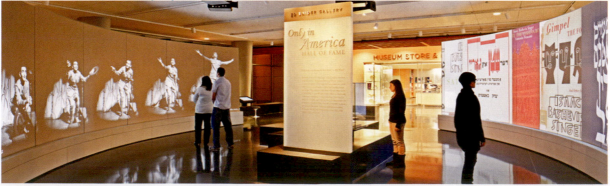

screen into sections highlighting particular events. In some cases, the screen is segmented into three or more spaces focusing on a specific subject. Many of the archival photographs of individuals being honored were brought to life using 3D layering to achieve a parallax effect.

The graphic treatment of the imagery and typography, color choices, audio location, and qualities of motion were all carefully orchestrated to achieve an architectural cohesion with the gallery and afford visitors an engaging experience from every angle.

"Innovation and Expansion" (**5.26 and 5.27**) describes historical events that led to the expansion of the Jewish community in America between 1820 and 1880. This exhibit consists of a large 16-foot × 12-foot display slightly elevated from the floor and a 32-inch touchscreen. Two films, "Industry and Invention" and "Rush to Riches," present the overall historical picture, serving as an introduction to additional information offered on the touchscreen. They narrate Jewish immigrants' attempts at colonization, their discoveries, and at the creation of the United States. Additionally, four short, biographical films focus on the lives of four Jewish pioneers of the period: Adolphus Sterne, Sigmund Heilner, Flora Spiegelberg, and Julius Ochs. In contrast to the main films, these are more localized; the animation zooms into a specific area and remains there while different images are displayed.

> *A critical lesson that was learned during the production of "Innovation and Expansion" was that the optical effect of speed is amplified when standing close to a screen of this magnitude. Objects that are viewed further away appear to move slower. Many of the animations needed to be slowed down considerably to counteract this effect.*

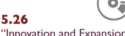

5.26
"Innovation and Expansion."
Courtesy of Local Projects.

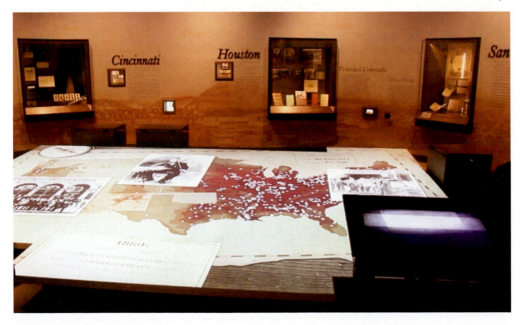

The touchscreen that projects a map of the United States functions as a control panel from which visitors can play films, retrieve data about specific images, or interact with map layers to display key points (for example, the expansion of travel routes across the country). The interface on the touchscreen replicates the visuals from the large display, making their relationship apparent to viewers. The action unfolds at different points on the surface without changing the framing so that the entire map is visible at all times. Elements fly rapidly in and out of the frame in response to the audio narration, creating natural transitions between stories. The chronological map choices at the bottom of the screen allow visitors to revisit key pieces of information that animate on top of the map. Population areas extend as a liquid; trails, paths, and railroads are drawn; icons representing resources (metals, cotton, oil, etc.) pop up. The animations move directionally from east to west, implying the direction of America's expansion.

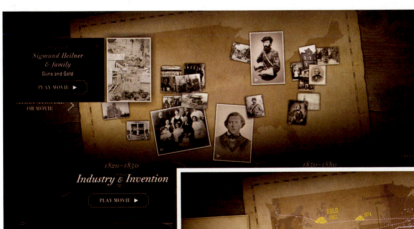

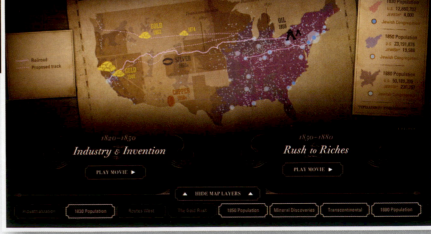

5.27
"Innovation and Expansion."
Courtesy of Local Projects.

To further enhance the experience, five independent channels of audio are streamed to a speaker hanging from the ceiling, and the room's lights shift between colors in response to events being narrated. In most cases, actions triggered by visitors from the touchscreen are replicated on the large surface. For instance, selecting a picture to see its caption enlarges it on the display. Likewise, the map on both the touchscreen and display will show or hide the same content according to a user's selection. If the program is not being used, it defaults to idle mode and presents items that appear later during the movies or on map layers. In interactive mode, the main view appears as the map with a few small pictures scattered across the top. These serve as navigational items viewing textual information or accessing the biographical movies represented by four larger portraits.

Design decisions regarding image style, color choice, and typography were inspired by the aesthetic of the period and are discussed in more detail in Chapter 8.

In the UK National Maritime Museum, "Voyagers" is a permanent exhibit that goes beyond the dogmatic approach that most museums take in presenting information (**5.28–5.30**). An archived collection of thematic images, typography, and video is transformed into an emotive audio-visual experience that evokes the sensation of the sea. Accompanied by a "soundscape" designed by Jude Greenaway, a 20-metre wave-shaped "canvas" composed of triangular facets and a spherical projector span the full width of the room. The installation comprises three conceptual layers of animation. The top layer, "Visual Journeys," features archival images based on the museum's themes. Underneath is the "Ebb and Flow" layer—a digital typographic ocean of keywords that wash across the wave-like surface. The text is based on archival metadata and interviews conducted with the public about their relationship to the sea.

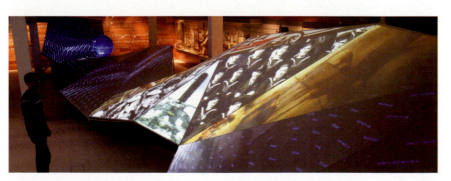

5.28
"Voyagers," National Maritime Museum, London. Courtesy of Flightphase.

5.29
"Voyagers," National Maritime Museum, London. In order to animate the surface, Flightphase subdivided the structure's facets into smaller triangles that fade and cascade based on their physical space. The temporal relationships between the facets were defined by assigning each a flow direction, a sequence position, and duration. Specialized software built with openFrameworks, an open source coding platform, was developed to implement the projection mapping, procedural animation, and spatial sound. Courtesy of Flightphase.

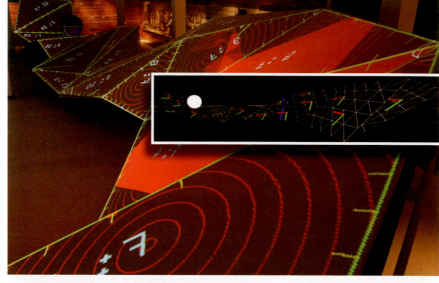

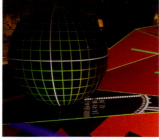

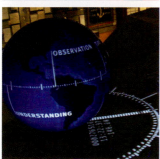

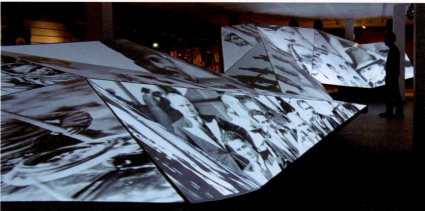

5.30
"Voyagers," National Maritime Museum, London. The "Puffersphere" required the images to be distorted in such a way that, when projected onto the globe, it appears spherical. Courtesy of Flightphase.

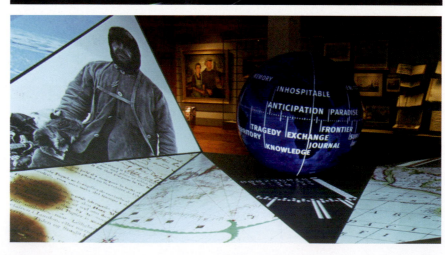

Inspired by the gyrocompasses and armillary spheres contained within the museum's archive, a globe-like object—the "Puffersphere"—is the third navigational layer, located at the end of the structure. Perceived to be floating atop the waves cascading underneath, it is lit from below with a stock projector and custom wide-angle lens, transforming an emulation of the earth into a canvas of free-flowing thematic words and video. Periodically, it assumes the image of the moon and constellations. All elements are choreographed to allow viewers to become immersed in a series of visual journeys that recall Britain's long maritime history.

5.31
"Overture," from the exhibition "Suite Fantastique." Courtesy of Imaginary Forces and the Wexner Center for the Arts.

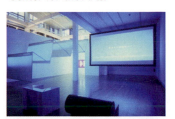

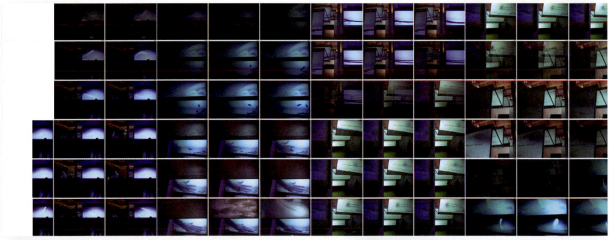

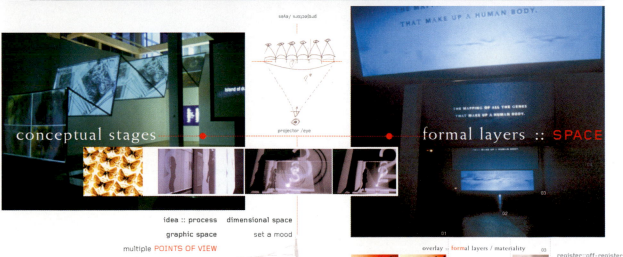

conceptual stages   projector /eye   formal layers :: SPACE

THAT MAKE UP A HUMAN BODY.

projectors /eyes

idea :: process   dimensional space
graphic space   set a mood
multiple POINTS OF VIEW
cinematic space   eruptive space
sequence   tension
narrative space
interwoven :: intersected

overlay :: formal layers / materiality   03   register::off-register
light :: shadow
transparency
scrims
patterning
imprinted screen surfaces

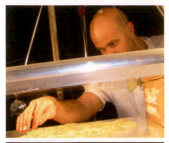

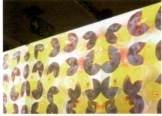

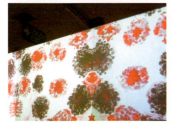

Nir Adar, a New York based food stylist, and artist, was commissioned to create a large-scale video installation for an annual dining design show at the Salone Internazionale del Mobile, a large restaurant in Milan, Italy (**5.32 and 5.33**). At the pavilion's entrance were two 24-foot × 7-foot screens of projected images that created a wallpaper of transforming food patterns. Across from the entrance was a 72-foot × 7-foot wall consisting of five screens, featuring photographs of Nir's food sculptures slowly morphing into each other in combination with video footage of foods getting squashed between sheets of glass. According to Nir, the footage expressed "a tension between beauty and repulsion." He adds: "When you look at it as mere abstraction, the colors, shapes, and motion are stunningly beautiful, but when you think of the fact that it is foodstuff being squashed, you feel repulsed by it." Some of images were time-reversed while others were flipped vertically or horizontally to produce a hypnotic, kaleidoscopic effect. This perfect alchemy of food, fashion, and design resulted in a visual odyssey of form, color, and texture that made the food seem touchable and engaging. Nir further explained: "My idea was to feature and reflect the synergy between food, architecture, design and fashion . . . The food sculptures symbolized architecture, and the food on plates represented the dining."

5.32
"Heat as Directed," a large-scale video installation by Nir Adar. Commissioned by Adam Tihany for his "Dining Design" show at the Salone Internazionale del Mobile in Milan. Courtesy of KSK: STUDIOS and Dyske Suematsu.

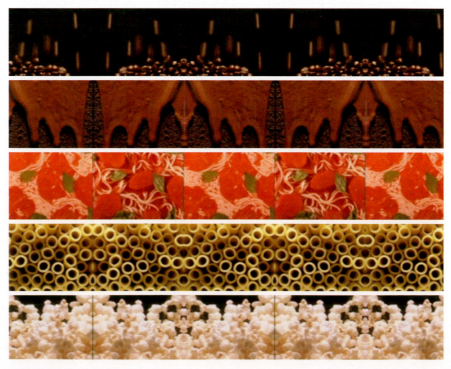

5.33
Frames from "Heat as Directed." Courtesy of KSK: STUDIOS and Dyske Suematsu.

Composed entirely from code, "Output" (**5.34**) is an animation for an art installation made for Future Shorts, a film festival targeting audiences worldwide. A physics engine generated the movements of elements based on audio mixed together from a library of classic movies. Muffled sounds and distorted graphics give the experience of watching a movie "from another side." Finding the right setting on the interface allows you to experience the "perfect image."

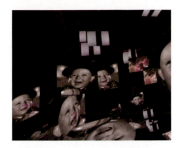

5.34
Frame from "Output" for Future Shorts. Courtesy of Minivegas.

In 2012, the Massachusetts Convention Center Authority sponsored "Art on the Marquee," a program that provided video artists with an opportunity to exhibit their work in a large-scale environment. The program featured a series of videos by six artists that were displayed in tandem with advertisements for local restaurants and television shows. This project posed the challenge of designing to the towering, 80-foot structure that wraps around the Convention and Exhibition Center in South Boston. Consisting of seven vertical and horizontal video screens, the structure assumes the shape of an open book. Interactive media artist Jeff Warmouth created a poetic video entitled "Fall" that portrayed multiple iterations of himself free-falling through the sky and landing in a pool of water. The figure's vertical descent, followed by the horizontal trajectory of him swimming around the sign, cleverly considers the juxtaposing vertical and horizontal screens of the marquee (**5.35**).

5.35
"Fall," a video for "Art on the Marquee," sponsored by the Massachusetts Convention Center Authority. Courtesy of Jeff Warmouth.

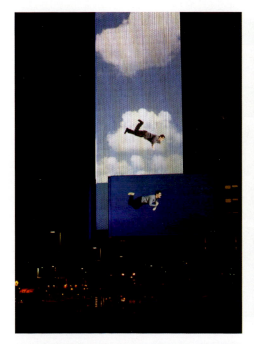
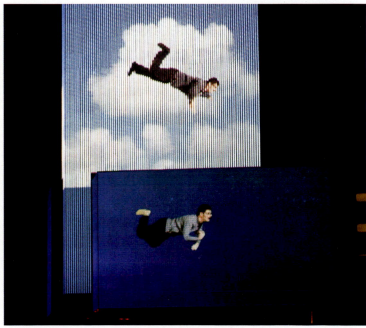

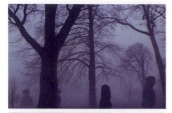

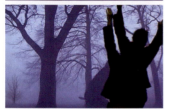

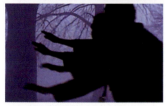

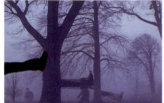

In entertainment, public exhibitions that incorporate animation are expanding the notion of cinema into a social, interactive experience. For example, Scott Snibbe's installation "Make Like a Tree" projects a dark, mystical forest that viewers can become immersed in. Their shadows are recorded and returned to the composition as eerie figures that move between trees in the foreground and background, disappearing suddenly or fading into the distance (**5.36**).

The potential for audio-responsive software and animation to work together in social entertainment venues is being realized. London-based design studio Minivegas developed their own proprietary software, Atlantis, to create sound-reactive visuals to be used for Red Bull Music Academy's 3D Soundclash at the Royal Albert Hall in 2010. This rare event encompassed a 180-degree arc of five large screens forming a virtual world around the perimeter of the club space. On the screens, generative, abstract animations played in response to audio generated by a 3D sound system. This system contained 16 powerful speakers arranged in two concentric rings to project sound effects from various locations. The goal was to deliver a highly cohesive, immersive experience by placing the audio-reactive animations in the same space as the sound. As a result, the audience was able to make strong connections between the music, the club space, and the content (**5.37**).

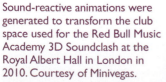

5.36
Frames from "Make Like A Tree."
Courtesy of Scott Snibbe.

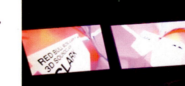

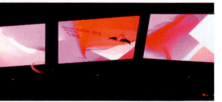

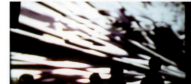

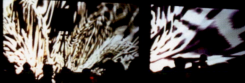

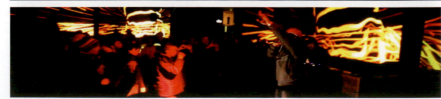

5.37
Sound-reactive animations were generated to transform the club space used for the Red Bull Music Academy 3D Soundclash at the Royal Albert Hall in London in 2010. Courtesy of Minivegas.

As part of an integrated campaign for Heineken, Minivegas created *Starvison*—an automated, interactive display system that helped launch the company's STR bottle in Milan, Italy. Originating as a stand-alone film that showcased abstract scenes from different cities, the content was redeveloped into customizable, looped animations that could be mixed by VJs in night clubs throughout the world. The animations were designed to respond to the movement of the audience. An ordinary club-goer can become a star for an evening by using his or her phone to tweet a picture or send an email to a large screen and watch it transform into an three-dimensional soundscape. Additionally, groups of up to six people can engage with the brand by assuming specific body poses that trigger predefined animations such as the Heineken star. The generative motion graphics created from audience participation have transformed the club scene into an active experience while promoting Heineken's identity with cohesive visuals that establish a sense of unity (**5.38**).

5.38
Through *Starvison*, animations that are generated from audience interaction enhance the nightclub experience. This system was distributed worldwide for platforms, events, festivals and parties to celebrate the launch of Heineken's award-winning STR bottle. Courtesy of Minivegas.

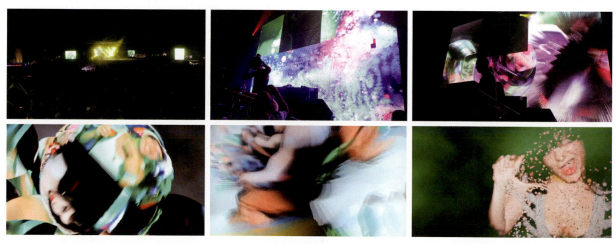

For the F5 festival in 2011, Minivegas conceived the idea of digitally simulated confetti portraying this event's celebratory theme. Similar to the University of Dayton's video wall, "Electric Confetti" combines traditional and generative animation. Shapes that mimic cut-out pieces of colored paper were designed to behave like large particles—dancing, floating, and flying around to trace the outline of the F5 logo and populate the screen with shifting patterns of bright, geometric shapes. At any given time, a person could tweet a text message to have it displayed as multicolored polygons. Festival-goers could also submit their pictures to the display, causing the software to deconstruct them into a mosaic of polygons (**5.39**).

F5 is a cutting-edge creativity festival exploring the intersection of art, design and entertainment. The two-day festival gathers filmmakers, digital artists, photographers, fashion designers, interactive and motion artists, graphic designers, agency executives, visual effects experts, musicians, industry visionaries, and many more.

5.39
Examples of generative motion graphics from Minivegas' "Twitter Visualizer." Courtesy of Minivegas.

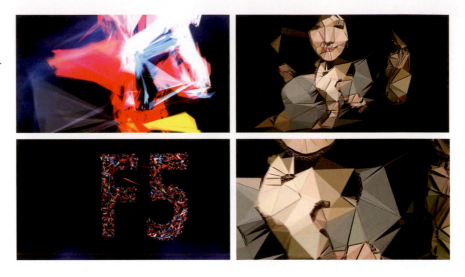

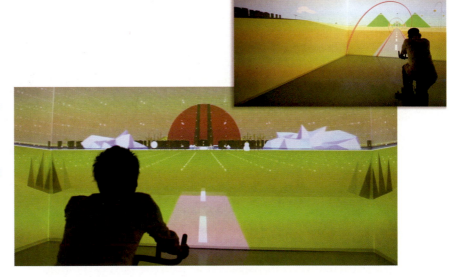

5.40
"Holiday Cycling" is an interactive bike ride through an imaginary landscape injected into a physical space through a triple projection system. Both the sound and the virtual "wallpaper" can be changed by viewers using their iPhones. Courtesy of Masashi Kawamura and TYMOTE.

Motion in Performance

The integration of motion graphics into live performances, including musical concerts, ceremonies, and awards shows, has increased substantially over the past decade. As staging becomes more extravagant, the possibilities offered by giant illuminated video screens and elaborate lighting facilities call for new methods of choreographing data to synchronize with changing scenery or music.

Motion in Performance

A performance of Blue Man Group in Las Vegas, Nevada's 1,800-seat theater at the Venetian Resort Hotel and Casino treated audiences to a dynamic, multisensory experience that merged artistic expression with technology. Accompanying a rectangular video screen in the center of the set were five circuit-board displays mounted on different levels of the stage. The performers could access the levels by running up a spiral staircase behind each platform. When lit, they conveyed animated typography and images, and backlit the performers with different colors to change the set's mood (**5.41**).

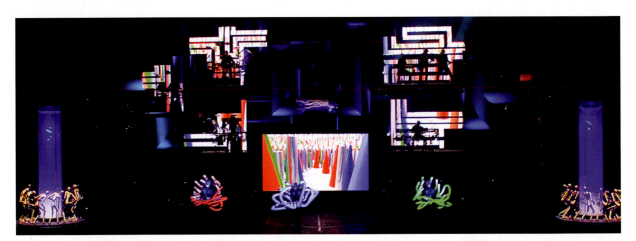

Each year, the Blip Festival in New York City celebrates the work of international artists who explore the musical potential of low-bit technology. Element Labs designed a series of fluctuating geometric patterns to accompany the rhythmic melodies of "small sounds at large scales pushed to the limit at high volumes" produced by ancient Nintendo and Atari video game consoles, Game Boys, Sega hardware, and Commodore computers (**5.42**).

5.41
Blue Man Group performance at the Venetian in Las Vegas, Nevada. Photo courtesy of Daktronics, Inc.

5.42
Blip Festival. Photo courtesy of Element Labs.

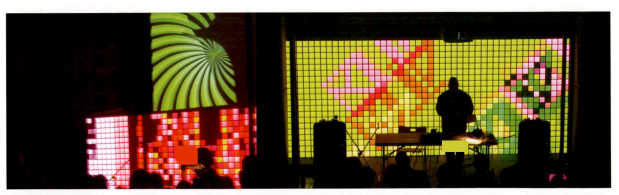

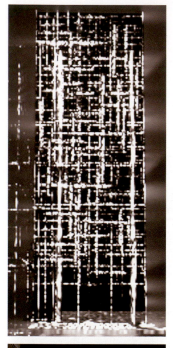

Motion in Exterior Spaces

Today, motion graphics are playing an important role in shaping our architectural, urban landscape due to advances in LED technology. Integrated software and hardware systems can stream and scale live video content from various media sources including servers, camcorders, and computers to accommodate to large-scale architectural installations.

Chanel Tokyo is a 10-story building in Japan's Ginza district, designed in 2004 by the Peter Marino architectural firm based in New York City. Part retail store and part giant electronic billboard, the building's edifice is covered with 700,000 computer-controlled LED units capable of flashing messages or patterns to portray the store's changing image. They can be programmed to emulate a giant swatch of Chanel's tweed fabric or display video from Chanel's fashion show. The facade also served as a screen for photographer Michal Rovner's video installation entitled "Tweed, Tokyo" which captured the perpetual motion of pedestrians outside the stores from a bird's-eye view (**5.43**).

The building at 745 Seventh Avenue in New York City demonstrates another symbiotic relationship between large-scale motion graphics and architecture. Three sides of the building are wrapped with long LED display bands that accentuate a 40-foot-high video monolith positioned at the west entrance. State-of-the-art technology and innovative, artistic vision make this building a showpiece for combining aesthetic form with practical function (**5.44**).

Since conventional, high-resolution video screens can be impractical due to their cost, low-resolution video grid systems have become more popular and affordable solutions for large-scale installations. A massive, 11,700-square-foot video screen wraps around Aspire Tower, the tallest building in Doha, Qatar (**5.45**). Color Kinetics, an innovator in LED lighting, created a suspended video display that curves with the tower's architecture. The facade's cylindrical screen was constructed from a wire mesh composed of approximately 156,500 nodes. The company's custom-engineered Chromasic microchip allows each node to function as a programmable pixel unit. Live coverage of the 2006 Asian Games was fed directly to the nodes through an integrated software/hardware system. The building's facade thus served as a real-time medium for sharing broadcast coverage of the Games and provides the public with a dynamic canvas for video content.

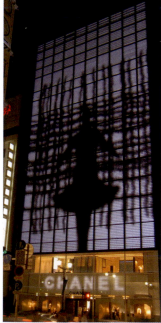

5.43
Chanel Tokyo building in Tokyo, Japan. Artist: Michal Rovner; Photographer: Takashi Orii; Architect: Peter Marino.

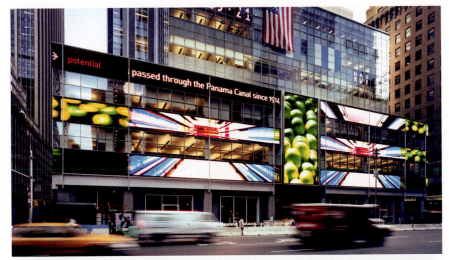

5.44
745 Seventh Ave, New York City.
Photo courtesy of Daktronics, Inc.

5.45
Aspire Tower, Doha, Qatar. Photo:
Lumasense. Courtesy of Color
Kinetics.

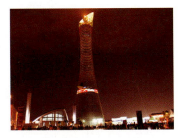

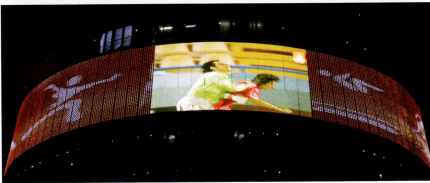

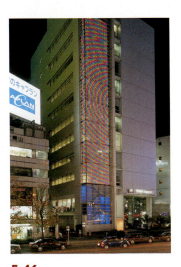

The Yoshikawa Building in Tokyo served as a perfect canvas for a stunning installation containing thousands of controllable, thimble-sized LED nodes behind an exterior glass wall running from the third to the tenth floors (**5.46**). Color Kinetics' highly developed control system (Light System Manager) showcased customized light show animations built in Adobe Flash. Onlookers were mesmerized by the building's holiday theme show of light as artistic expression. Animations included swirls of changing colors, geometric shapes, and rushes of color climbing up the facade.

Intricate, animated patterns on the tower of Harrah's Atlantic City Resort and Casino were generated from 4,100 aluminum bands of programmable LED lights that wrapped around each level of the building. Animated effects including color wipes, sunbursts, and simulations of graphic shapes changed the skyline of Atlantic City (**5.47**).

5.46
Yoshikawa Building, Tokyo. Photo:
Nacasa & Partners. Courtesy of
Color Kinetics Japan.

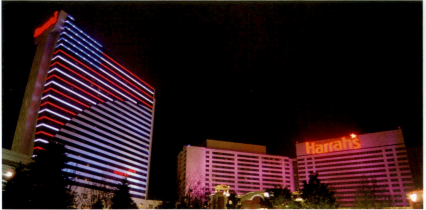
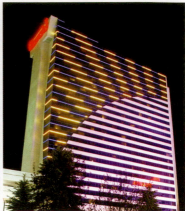

5.47
An LED lighting system creating an animated facade for Harrah's Atlantic City Resort and Casino. Photo: Stone Mountain Lighting Group. Courtesy of Color Kinetics.

Located next to Milan's famous cathedral is La Rinascente, Italy's largest department store, known for its stylish clothing and world-renowned former designer, Giorgio Armani. Its theme, "Shopping Requires Inspiration," was expressed through a sophisticated interior design and window display. The facade was transformed into a dazzling series of light patterns that inspired residents and visitors to shop. A lighting scheme consisting of 12,000 flexible LED strands spanning two exterior walls of the building contained nodes that were spaced in 12-inch increments. Each could be individually controlled to generate logos and images. Panels of frosted glass were mounted over the installation to magnify the appearance of each node (**5.48**).

5.48
An intelligent LED lighting system allows individually controllable points of light to form a unique window display for department store La Rinascente in Milan, Italy. Photo: Piero Comparotto, Arkilux.

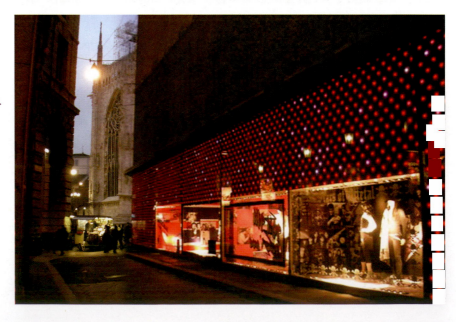

Chapter Summary

The potential of motion graphics in our physical world is helping to shape our public landscape.

Video walls capable of displaying large images at high resolutions are used throughout the world in trade shows, showrooms, nightclubs, retail stores, and sports arenas. Other display technologies have used light to transform public spaces, build brands, and fire the imagination by incorporating animation into the environment. Light Emitting Diodes (LED) displays can be built to accommodate various sizes and aspect ratios, allowing customized geometric configurations. These displays are are bright enough to compete with sunlight and can be viewed from short distances.

Motion graphics in interior spaces have become vital in setting mood and atmosphere. In corporate lobbies or waiting rooms they reinforce brands, change content to support messages, and define ambiences that might be unattainable with other mediums. In retail and event spaces, they can add a unique dimension, providing drama in entranceways, and attracting traffic by presenting content in display windows. Casinos, restaurants, and hotels have also used motion graphics to stimulate guest interaction and provide unique, animated content as a substitute for mundane television programming.

Immersive environments are designed to blend physical and imaginary worlds so that kinetic images, text, and audio can respond to human interaction. The artistic qualities of motion are being realized in educational exhibits, retail spaces, art installations, airports and theme parks. It is also playing a greater role in large-scale architectural installations and digital signage systems capable of delivering content to multiple locations.

The incorporation of motion graphics into live performance has increased considerably over the past decade. As staging becomes more extravagant, the possibilities offered by giant illuminated video screens and elaborate lighting facilities call for new methods of choreographing data to synchronize with changing scenery or music.

6 motion literacy
the language of movement

As a powerful storytelling device, motion can be choreographed to communicate information, convey emotions, and express pure aesthetic beauty.

"All of a sudden it hit me—if there was such a thing as composing music, there could be such a thing as composing motion. After all, if there are melodic figures, why can't there be figures of motion?"
—Len Lye

Early twentieth-century pioneers of experimental film and animation have proved that even with the most simple mundane shapes and images motion can deliver compelling and meaningful messages. Today, graphic designers regard motion as a fundamental component of their work.

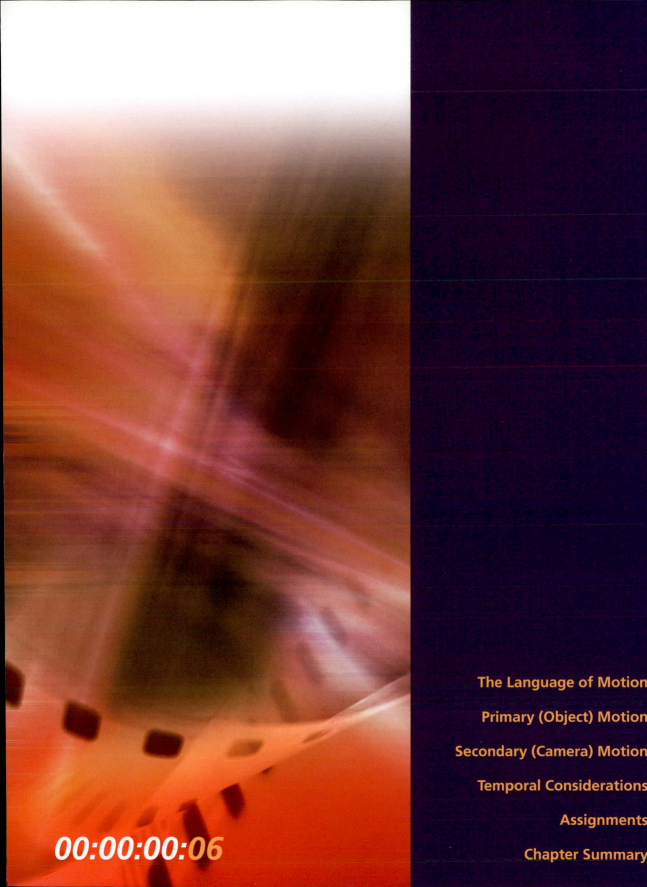

00:00:00:06

The Language of Motion

Motion is a universal language. It can have more impact than the actual content being animated. The method you use to move an element in the frame can enhance its meaning. For example, an object that slowly animates across the screen while fading in might provide a sense of mystery and calmness. If the same object flips over and whizzes across the frame, it may express a sense of playfulness, urgency, or even instability. The motion itself can be the message.

Motion can be traced back to the early days of character animation, experimental abstract film, and avant-garde cinema. Today, it continues to be one of the most fundamental storytelling devices.

The introduction of temporality into painting was brought about when painters attempted to suggest movement in their static works at the time of the invention of film. Leopold Survage, for example, produced hundreds of watercolor sketches that represented key ideas for choreographing the movement in abstract animation. Hans Richter named his paintings with titles such as Prelude, Fugue, *and* Rhythmus.

Motion Literacy

By Jan Kubasiewicz, in The Education of a Graphic Designer. Second Edition *by Steven Heller.*

Since motion is a constant in everyday life, then isn't motion integral to design? Of course motion has already been explored within different disciplines of art and science, but with the easy accessibility of kinetic tools, motion and communication design are more than ever integrated into one discipline. And since designers are becoming more concerned with injecting motion into their work, motion literacy—the act of trying to understand how motion can be used to communicate more effectively—is essential.

From a technical viewpoint, making type, an illustration, or a diagram move on a screen is a relatively easy task. However, achieving clarity of communication through the language of motion proved more challenging for many designers than achieving fluency in kinetic tools.

Communicating via motion involves issues of both "what" is moving across the screen— typographical, pictorial, or abstract elements— and "how" that something is moving.

The "how" question refers to the kinetic form and its grammar, defined by both space and time dimensions of motion such as velocity and amplitude.

Kinetic form itself may convey a broad spectrum of notions and emotions: from a sensible gesture, through a dramatic tension, to a violent collision. Of course, motion in combination with pictures and words (and sound, if available) multiplies those irresistible opportunities in making meaning.

The meaning of motion on a screen, similar to all other aspects of communication design, relies on conventions and artistic techniques. A cross-fade of two scenes conveying a lapse of time, or a split screen meaning simultaneous happenings, are just two examples adopted from the cinematic vocabulary—the source of inspiration for motion designers. The language of cinema in its century-old history evolved into a complex, universal system of communication, combining the visual, sonic, and kinetic aspects into a synchronized, multi-sensory experience, and that language now becomes a new realm of communication design.

While perceiving visual/sonic/kinetic information simultaneously through multiple channels and over a period of time, the mind attempts to organize these discrete messages into a story, however abstract that story might be. A story must have its beginning, middle and end, but a story does not necessarily need to be told in this order. Therefore, the designer's awareness of different timelines—the one of the story and another one of the storytelling—is essential. Equally essential is the designer's awareness of the "plasticity" of time, and consequently, the designer's ability of manipulating time—real time, its representation, and perception—through motion, sequentiality, and multiple-channel correspondence (multimediality). Time, as intertwined with motion, becomes the structural design element, as well as the subject of design.

One of the most spectacular historical examples of the design process for a multimedia structure is a post-production diagrammatic storyboard for *Alexander Nevsky*, a 1938 film by Sergei Eisentstein, a Russian film director and one of the first theorists of the medium. That storyboard is a timeline in which visual representation of the film components are precisely synchronized into a sequence of "audio-visual correspondences" including film shots, music score, a "diagram of pictorial composition," and a "diagram of movement." The "diagram of movement" represents specifically the camera work resulting in on-screen motion. Choreographed very precisely, in fact to a fraction of a musical measure, this "diagram of movement" attests to how essential on-screen motion and its meaningful integration with all other elements of his vocabulary was for the cinematographer. The same challenge of integrating motion as a meaningful component of communication design should remain the focus of research and practice for contemporary designers.

Currently, the integration of motion and typography is perhaps the most extensively exhibited practice of motion design. Kinetic logos and taglines very successfully "scream" their brand names and services, even from the muted TV screens. But a great potential of type in motion is not limited to TV commercials and film titles. Adding motion and time dimensions to typography is to add new possibilities to the imaging of verbal language. Kinetic typography complements traditional typography by exploring "real-time" visualization in a spirit of phonetic properties of spoken language, such as spontaneity, intonation, etc. The dynamic visualization of these properties, possibly codified at some point and customizable, would promote the user's personal preference of on-screen, typographical "behavior" of words and lines in such cases as closed captioning, for instance.

The concept of the kinetic "behavior" of an on-screen design object—such as typography, an illustration, or a diagram—especially the behavior triggered interactively by a user, is one of the central issues of motion literacy. For a user, such kinetic behavior may be perceived as a dynamic transformation of some spatial properties of the initial object, which occurred as a result of pointing,

dragging or clicking. For a designer to design a kinetic behavior means to define a matrix of specific dynamic parameters of transformation of that object mapped to specific variables of input. Injecting motion into interactive design means entering the environment of algorithmic thinking, and that is why suddenly the language describing it became very technical.

Integration of motion with information graphics has a tremendous potential of contributing, through interactive visualizations, to various disciplines of science, economy and education. Dynamic diagrams, charts, and timelines seem to be the only practical solutions for understanding complexity of large-scale information structures. However, translating complexity of data into clarity of visual information will not be easy on designers, since increasingly sophisticated computational imaging requires new conventions and strategies for dynamic visualization, and very often, the solutions adopted from traditional information design do not work successfully in interactive environments.

Interacting with complex data within hypertext structure is a special kind of motion involving the concept of multiple representation of information—dynamically linked text, image, audio, video, etc. Multiple representation of information is the real advantage for the user and a challenge for the designer, since in the context of interactive media, information is not fixed, but fluid. According to Lev Manovich, it is ". . . something that can exist in different, potentially infinite versions." Therefore, interaction is supposed to give the user a sense of the unique process of walking a personal path through databases to the most appropriate form of content delivery, according to the user's own individual preference or special needs. And since this unique path to knowledge is a result of action and reaction, a stimulus-response loop repeated ad infinitum, designers must always ask themselves how much motion is appropriate to their audience, to the content, and context. After all, motion is not the purpose for its own sake but a way of serving the purpose of communication, and since design requires equilibrium of nonmotion and motion, absence of motion is just a case of potential motion. And yes, motion is integral to design.

Jan Kubasiewicz is a professor of graphic design at the Massachusetts College of Art (massart.edu), Dynamic Media Institute (http://www.dmiboston.org).

Primary (Object) Motion

spatial properties

"Primary motion" (or "object motion") refers to the movement of one or more elements over time and across space. Choreographing primary motion mandates an awareness of an object's spatial properties including positioning, size, spatial orientation, and direction of travel.

Animating an object's position (referred to as "translation") involves moving it along predetermined horizontal (x) and vertical (y) axes in a two-dimensional environment and an x, y, and z axes in a three-dimensional environment (**6.1**). "Rotation" involves changing the angle that the object faces around a central point of origin. A wider circumference of rotation results when the anchor point is moved away from the object's center (**6.2**). Moving the origin point to the object's corner allows it to pivot like an arm.

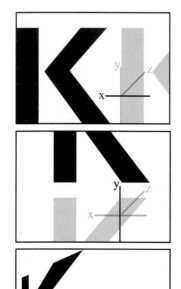

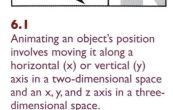

6.1
Animating an object's position involves moving it along a horizontal (x) or vertical (y) axis in a two-dimensional space and an x, y, and z axis in a three-dimensional space.

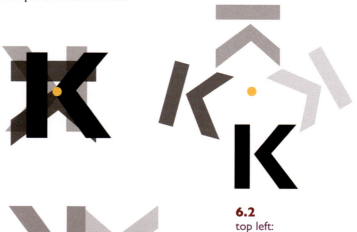

6.2
top left:
When an object's center of rotation is positioned directly over its center, the object rotates around itself like a wheel.

top right:
A wider circumference of rotation results when the anchor point is moved away from the object's center.

bottom left:
Positioning the rotation point on the object's corner allows it to pivot like an arm.

Primary (Object) Motion

In a kinetic typography assignment, students applied this principle to achieve different types of rotation. In **figure 6.3**, the letter "T" rotates 90° around its center to push the remaining letters off of the screen. In the bottom image, each object's point of origin was shifted to the left or right edge, allowing it to open like a hinge. "Scaling" involves resizing an object uniformly to maintain its proportions. Non-uniform scaling results in a vertical distortion of the letter "Z" in **figure 6.4**, producing the effect of squash and stretch as discussed on p. 169.

6.3
Frames from a 4D typography assignment by Brian Adair and Carolyn Kosinski (bottom).
Courtesy of Professor Jon Krasner, Fitchburg State University.

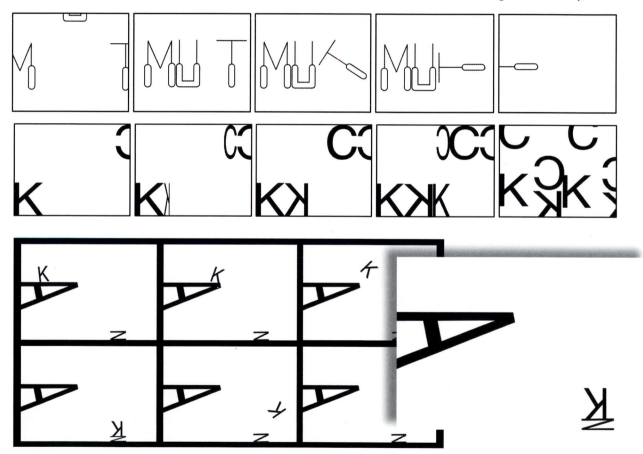

Spatial transformations can be combined, allowing you to animate an element's position, scale, and rotation simultaneously. At the Ringling College of Art + Design, Cielomar Cuevas designed several rotations of an identity, to be followed by individual rotations of the parts, meaning they close in to form a single unit, similar to the manner that the blades of a Swiss Army knife would fold in. The letterforms "tbs" then animate in vertically from the top edge of the frame to complete the logo (**6.5**).

6.4
Frames from a 4D typography assignment by Alex Kobbs.
Courtesy of Professor Jon Krasner, Fitchburg State University.

6.5
Frames from an assignment entitled "Branding Gymnastics" by Cielomar Cuevas. Ringling College of Art + Design, Courtesy of Professor Eddy Roberts.

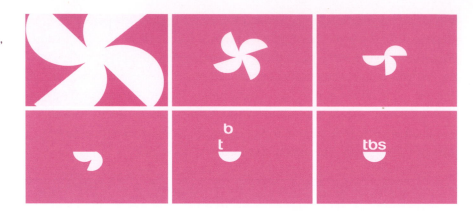

The direction or "route" that elements travel is important to consider. Two types of directions are "linear" and "non-linear"— a straight line or on a curve. Mechanical objects such as pendulums and wind-up toys travel in predictable, linear directions. On the other hand, living subjects and phenomena that are affected by natural forces (i.e, tree branches, water, grass blowing in the breeze) behave in more erratic ways. For example, a kite flying through the sky may change the direction it faces in response to alterations in the air current.

"Motion paths" are one of the most powerful devices that allow you to specify the courses of travel that elements in a composition take over a given time interval. They are represented as straight lines, curves, or a combination of lines and curves. Both linear and non-linear paths can be modified to control the direction that objects travel in a composition. In **figure 6.7**, the smaller letters were designed to follow a curved motion path to allow them to travel along the lines of the larger letter.

6.6
In Adobe After Effects, motion paths can be linear or non-linear. Both can be altered to change an object's course of travel.

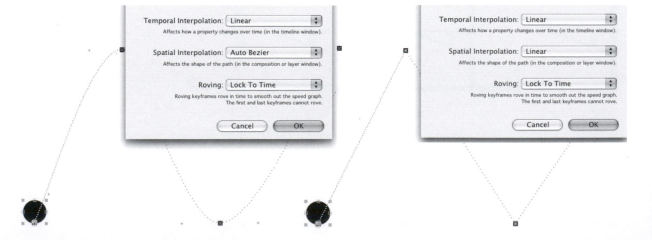

Primary (Object) Motion

With the exception of mechanical devices, most elements travel in "arcs"—slightly circular paths. Because the human body is composed of many joints that allow the limbs to rotate, a natural walk cycle shows a figure moving up, down, and forward to create an arc in space. Gravity is also accountable for this. When we move forward, our bodies are pulled down by gravity, creating a slight arc in our motion path. These principles of gravity and inertia can be used to support the quality of physical realism in animation.

birth, life, and death

When coordinating the primary motion, consideration should be given to the manner in which actions begin, the duration of the period in which they occur, and the manner in which they end. Elements can move into and out of the frame from any of its four edges, fade in or out, or grow larger or smaller. Additionally, they can be introduced by other elements, transformed through morphing, or constructed piece-by-piece.

basic animation principles

Understanding the linguistics of motion mandates an awareness of some of the earliest animation principles that were established back in the days of Disney. The concepts described here are derived from the book *The Illusion of Life* by Frank Thomas and Ollie Johnston.

squash and stretch

In the physical world, most objects deform as they move. For example, when a rubber ball hits the ground, it becomes temporarily squashed, then bounces back into the air while being stretched. When a figure crouches down, it appears to be squashed; when it leaps into the air, it looks stretched. Before diving off a cliff, a diver looks around, and as her arms swing up, her knees bend. As she springs up, she raises her arms and her knees straighten to commence the action.

The technique of "squash and stretch" can help establish the physical basis of objects that have mass, giving their motions the illusion of weight and volume through distortion. The distortion can range from subtle to extreme. In traditional character animation, squash and stretch has been useful for animating dialogue and mimicking facial expressions. **Figures 6.4** and **6.8** illustrate how this principle can be used to personify objects and breathe life into their actions.

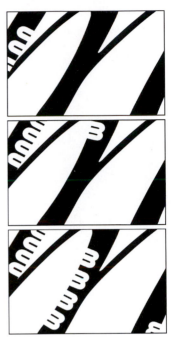

6.7
Frames from a kinetic typography assignment, by Nicole Mercado. Courtesy of Professor Jon Krasner, Fitchburg State University.

anticipation

Most lifelike actions have an opposite preceding action. Before leaping off the floor, the dancer executes a downward motion before moving upward. Before swinging a golf club, the golfer twists his body into a coil, bringing the club over his head. Before throwing a ball, a pitcher pulls his arm back to allow for a more forceful throw. In all these cases, the word "before" is key; it denotes the idea of "pre-action" or implied action. Anticipation creates a sense of natural motion while indicating to the viewer that an action is about to occur. In **figure 6.9**, a commercial for Asics footwear illustrates the virtues of strength, agility, and speed. Anticipation is applied to the snake just before it lunges at the story's main character.

6.8

Frames from an assignment involving the personification of letterforms, by Alex Wall. Courtesy of Professor Jon Krasner, Fitchburg State University.

Principles of anticipation and squash and stretch convey natural, lifelike movements.

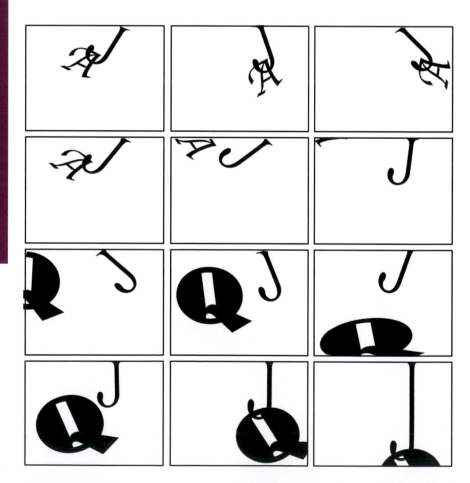

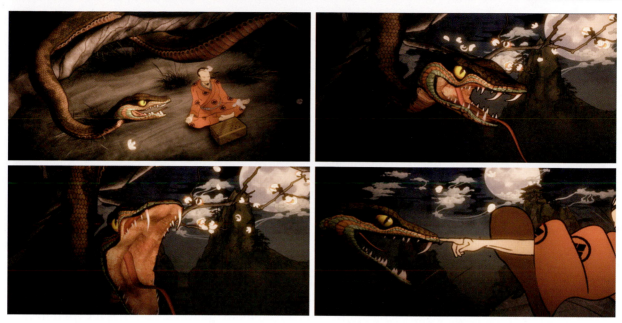

6.9
Frames from a commercial for Asics footwear advertising the Onitsuka Tiger brand of sports shoes. Courtesy of Belief.

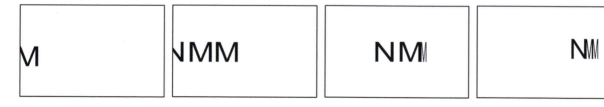

follow through and overlapping

Follow through and overlapping actions enable the flow between actions to be carried smoothly. These subtle techniques can be used to make an element's motion more believable by adding a little detail.

"Follow through" involves the continuation of an action past its termination point. For example, when a woman swings her head, her hair continues moving after the main head movement ceases. In the case of a complex object that consists of different moving parts, each of those parts may move at different times and at different velocities in relation to the object's main mass. When an object's motion comes to an abrupt halt, its parts continue to catch up to the object's main mass. In character animation, for example, the hip region of a moving figure

6.10
Frames from an assignment involving the personification of the student's first and last initials, by Nicole Mayou. Courtesy of Professor Jon Krasner, Fitchburg State University.

Principles of anticipation and squash and stretch were applied to breathe life into the action.

leads and is followed by the leg and then the foot. Lighter elements such as the arms, hair, tail, and parts of the clothing also follow through.

"Overlapping" occurs when an element changes its direction when it is in motion, and its smaller parts assume the new direction of motion a few frames later. In the case of a complex object consisting of multiple moving parts, slightly varying the timing and speed of those parts when the object's main mass changes direction maintains a continuous flow between the actions, making the movements seem more natural.

Timing is critical to the effectiveness of follow through and overlapping action. If it is too slow, it may appear too obvious, making the primary action look awkward. If it is too fast, it may not be obvious enough.

pause

The "pause" can be a powerful communication tool when it is properly used. In jazz, pauses between riffs are often used as an important part of phrasing during improvisation. In grammar, commas are used to prompt readers to pause between phrases, and semicolons are used to allow them to compare two related ideas. In the natural world, a pause occurs when a person stops walking and changes direction. This is like a semicolon in grammar, while a definite stop is like a period. With a swing, there is approximately a half-second pause at the top of each arc. In animation, pauses can prevent movements from appearing too frenetic or mechanical, allowing viewers to catch their breath between actions. Further, they can create expectation and tension.

timing

In animation, "timing" involves choreographing how actions are spaced according to the sizes and "personalities" of elements. Timing can affect how we perceive an object's size or mass. For example, a large object that moves at a slower pace than a small object may take more time to accelerate or decelerate. In frame-by-frame animation, timing is achieved by controlling the number of frames between motions. The more drawings there are, the slower and smoother the action will be. Fewer drawings produce faster and clearer movements.

Timing can also contribute toward a composition's atmosphere or mood. Fast movements typically produce snappy, energetic effects, while longer movements can feel more deliberate and dignified.

acceleration and deceleration

The principles of acceleration and deceleration (discussed earlier in relation to squash and stretch, on p. 169) can help to soften movements, making them appear more natural and lifelike.

In frame-by-frame animation, emulating natural movements may involve creating a large number of drawings near an object's starting pose, fewer drawings in the middle, and more drawings near the next pose. This will mean that as the object approaches the middle phase, it begins to accelerate, and each calibrated distance it travels is further than the previous one. As an action begins, fewer drawings at the starting point and more drawings near the end of the action produces a sudden burst of acceleration, which gives way to a gradual slowing down toward the end. In digital interpolation, velocity changes that create the effects of acceleration and deceleration are established through using key frames.

6.11
Frames from an opener for Marlboro Manufacturing's Web site. © 2012 Jon Krasner.

"Manufacturing" rotates from its left edge downward prior to accelerating upward to hit the word "Marlboro," creating an impact when knocking the letter "O" off the frame.

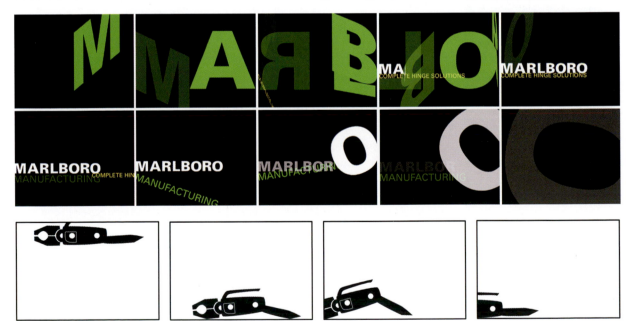

6.12
In this object-personification assignment by David DiPinto, impact is established through acceleration and to emulate an inchworm slithering out of the frame. Courtesy of Professor Jon Krasner, Fitchburg State University.

secondary action

Most movements in the physical world are the result of cause and effect. For example, when a basketball hits the edge of the backboard, it wobbles back and forth. Human figures typically swing their arms back and forth while walking. These actions work together in support of one another. With this in mind, the secondary actions of the backboard and the swinging arms result directly from the primary action.

Secondary actions can be used to heighten interest or add realistic complexity by supplementing and reinforcing the primary action. Keep in mind that an element's secondary action should subordinate or compete with its primary action.

exaggeration

The origin of exaggeration as an animation concept lies at the heart of traditional figurative animation, where character movements and facial expressions are distorted to create a more lifelike appeal.

In rotoscoped graphics which are accurately traced from live footage, exaggeration can be used to make the movements appear less stiff and mechanical. Canadian animators Carol Beecher and Kevin Kurytnik employed the techniques of exaggeration to express "the uneasy coexistence between life and Mr. Death" in their award-winning figurative animation entitled *Mr. Reaper's Really Bad Morning*. This is apparent in the movements of the figures as they chase after their prey. Additionally, anticipation is evident in the movements of the animal prior to running and in the backward motion of the hunter preparing to throw his weapon (**6.13**).

Exaggeration can help communicate ideas more effectively while making the content enjoyable to watch. On the other hand, excessive use of this device can make actions appear theatrical or contrived. Determining the degree of exaggeration to apply to movement relies on intuition, experimentation, and patience.

coordinating relative motion

No color stands alone; the way we perceive a color is affected by the presence of another color. Likewise, motion is relative. Our perception of an object's movement can be influenced by a different movement from the same or from another object. Coordinating movements between objects in a composition is like being a musical conductor.

In a typography assignment involving storytelling through motion, students were challenged to personify the first and last initials of their name and create a narrative by choreographing the relative movements of the letterforms. Jillian Bailey was inspired by motions typical of Nintendo video games (**6.14**). According to Jillian: "I wanted there to be a quarrel between the 'J' and the 'B.' When the 'B' squashes the 'J' I wanted the 'J' to react by pushing the 'B' off screen."

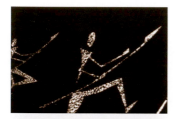
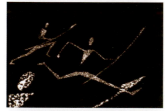
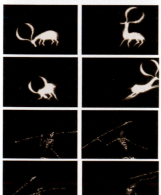

6.13

Frames from *Mr. Reaper's Really Bad Morning* (2003). Courtesy of Carol Beecher and Kevin D.A. Kurytnik. © Fifteen Pound Pink Productions.

Exaggeration is applied to the movements of the figures as they chase after the animal.

At the Ringling College of Art + Design, Diana Han demonstrated a mastery of motion in a lighthearted composition called "Organic." Her careful observation of non-linear, figurative motion was applied to groups of leaves in a way that makes her subject matter spring to life. Diana's tasteful use of earthy textures and subtle color combinations contributes toward the natural yet upbeat tone of this piece (**6.15**).

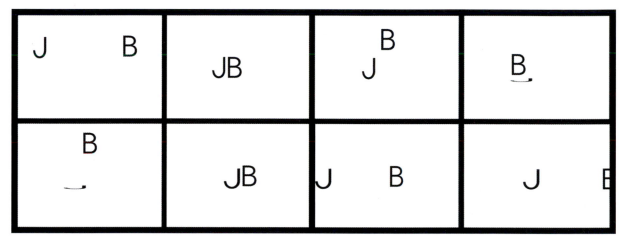

6.14
Frames from a kinetic typography assignment by Jillian Bailey. Courtesy of Professor Jon Krasner, Fitchburg State University.

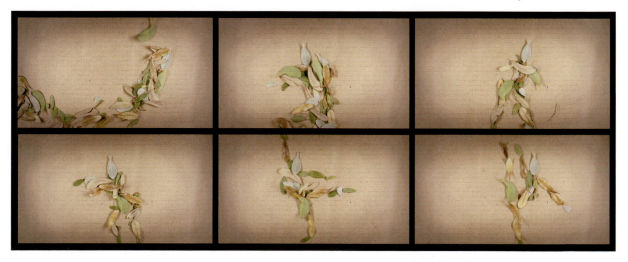

6.15
Frames from "Organic" by Diana Han. © 2012 Ringling College of Art + Design.

The University of Dayton's video wall installation (also discussed in Chapter 5) provides a wonderful example of how relative movements between objects can be programmed to occur in realtime. The effect that the cubes have on each other is organic, in that the movement of a single cube slightly influences the motion of others. Invisible forces called "affectors" were programmed to travel randomly through the animation space and affect the behaviors of cubes they pass over, moving, rotating, or scaling them. When the installation enters "idle mode," the cubes continue moving and changing. At times, there is an intuitive connection between the cubes' behavior and the presence of visitors. For example, a person walking across the width of the display may cause a visible trace of patterns to be generated, interrupting the cubes' normal flow of movement. These different scenarios produce motion as an expression of being alive and having an agency.

In **figure 6.16,** two Web site concepts for Sky Bridge (an interactive broadband communication company) suggest possible relationships between the movements of live video imagery and those of simple, graphic lines and shapes. The graphic elements could assume non-linear, progressive movements that complement the footage. Alternatively, they could be choreographed to move mechanically, in a linear fashion, to conflict with the video. The movements of graphics and type might be designed to make the interface look controllable, letting viewers know that they have the option of zooming in or panning into off-screen space. The row of small circles near the bottom could be interactive, causing a transition to feature updated video content when highlighted with a mouseover. Lines or shapes could also move in a manner that implies an upcoming change in the interface, triggering a transition such as a wipe or a fade. Lines might animate in from the frame's edges, pause at a point of intersection, then slide across the field in opposite directions to reveal updated video. The box encompassing the video might move to either side in counterpoint to the screen to signal a change in scenery. All of these scenarios suggest carefully designed motions that would create strategic relationships between the elements.

Isadora Williams' animated poster assignment at the Massachusetts College of Art effectively integrated non-linear and linear movements to create a believable race car scenario. The green, white, and red arrows from Max Huber's Swiss poster for the Monza races were animated in precise synchronization with the accompanying soundtrack. The piece

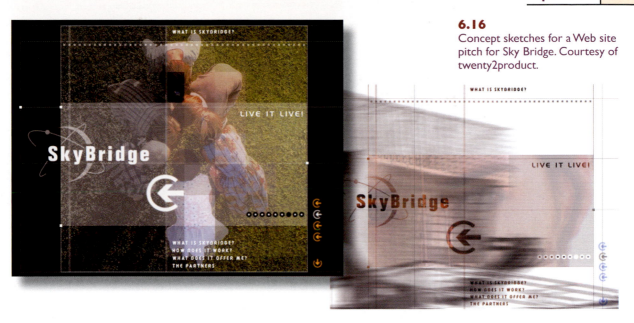

6.16
Concept sketches for a Web site pitch for Sky Bridge. Courtesy of twenty2product.

begins with the three arrows being introduced into the frame, where they shake to the trumpet of the soundtrack like turbo engines being revved. After accelerating off of the bottom edge of the frame one by one, a blue arrow is displayed in three incremental sizes to the accents of timed musical notes. The original arrows reappear from the right edge of the frame and move mechanically from right to left in a linear fashion. After reaching the center of the frame, they suddenly change course and accelerate around a bend, then speed up once again to disappear off the bottom edge of the frame (**6.17**).

6.17
Animated poster "Monza Milano" by Isadora Williams, Courtesy of Professor Jan Kubasiewicz, Massachusetts College of Art.

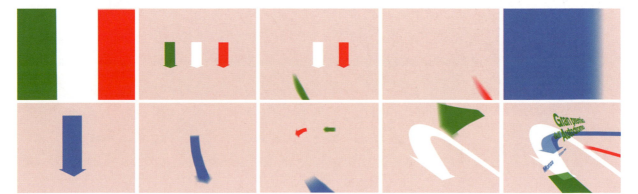

At the Iceland Academy of Art, Helga Arnalds had been experimenting with images connected to prehistoric figures. Influenced by the style of animator Len Lye, she created a mesmerizing musical journey in which elements move to a carefully choreographed "dance." Stylistically, the simple, abstract nature of her imagery allows us to pay considerable attention to variations of movement that occur throughout the animation as the images sway, undulate, and twist to a rhythmic, hypnotic melody of percussive instruments (**6.18**).

6.18
Frames from "ORGI," by Helga Arnalds, Iceland Academy of Art, Professor Kristín Ingimarsdóttir.

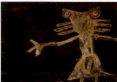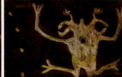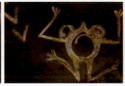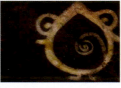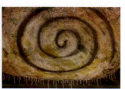

Likewise, the structure of Tavo Ponce's promotional spot for Music One Classic in Madrid, Spain lies in the personification of form through motion. Clusters of colorful, abstract shapes swim and jump around like schools of fish as they pass across the frame to form the typographic content (**6.19**). In a group of station identifications and bumpers for The Voice, a Scandinavian music television network based in Denmark, hard-edged, geometric ribbon structures also move in a lifelike manner. As forms move and unfold erratically against a patterned backdrop of stripes, their movements are echoed in an abrupt change of the background pattern at the very end of the composition, creating an explosive and edgy visual language (**6.20**).

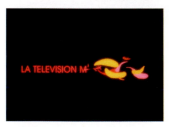

6.19
Frame from a spot for Music One Classic. Courtesy of Tavo Ponce and Monkey Revolution.

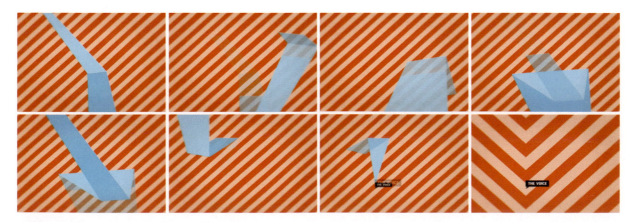

6.20
Station ID for The Voice, a Scandinavian music network in Denmark. Courtesy of Daniel Jennett.

An exercise that I give to students at the beginning of the semester involves animating simple dots and lines—two basic elements of composition—to express meaning. The rudimentary subject matter deliberately allows motion to become the central focus. Students begin by choosing a word from a list (such as order, increase, congested, tension) and experiment with a single dot inside the frame to see if they can convey the word's meaning. They are asked to explore the possibilities for movement by considering the dot's course of travel, its overall velocity, and how nonlinear motion produced from acceleration and deceleration can give it life and personality. Students then choose a second word and attempt to convey its meaning with two dots. They are told to consider how they can interact with each other and with the edges of the frame and the manner they enter and leave the frame. The exercise is repeated with lines of the same thickness and length. Cheri Zenoni's interpretation of "tension" is based on the strain that builds up in an exercise band that shakes as it is stretched out (**6.23**). She writes: "The implications of tension for this are not only for the tension that builds up in the line but the relief of tension from the invisible person tugging on the line." In her study for the word "playful," "the dot became the embodiment of many children and friends as well as assimilating the expression of bouncing off the walls. It only waits the briefest of moments before bouncing up and down to express its wish to play and be payed attention to before leaving the screen." "Increase" is expressed through three lines that imply stairs moving upward. They then shrink to display increase in another fashion, as the middle line increases in size and moves to the top to create a graphic very similar to the "increase volume" symbol. For the word "congested," two dots compete for space and become steadily larger on the screen. When the space becomes too small for them to fit, they shudder from the strain.

Klarissa Marie Parduba's cut-out animation for a SyFy channel bumper was designed to match the motion of elements with the timing and beats of a prescribed audio track. Based on the concept of transformation, the goal was to have a dragon become interested in a dangling lamp and hit the object to try and break it open (**6.24**). This was accomplished by choreographing a joint motion of the arm (called a '"hit"). Klarissa states: "I was trying to convey the dragon's emotions and frustration over the object, determined to break it open and reveal the logo. The motion helps the creature interact with the SyFy theme of transformation on the lamp exploding into the logo after the final hit."

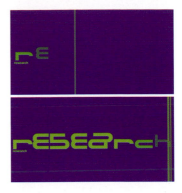

6.21
In this online advertisement for Lycos, groups of vertical lines animate horizontally across the screen to introduce each heading. Courtesy of hillmancurtis, inc.

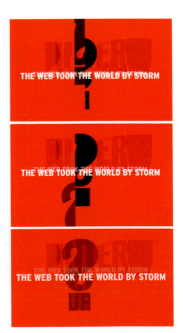

6.22
In this an online advertment for Roger Black Interactive Bureau, several geometric structures come together from opposite edges of the frame to form symbols that eventually fade out. Courtesy of hillmancurtis, inc.

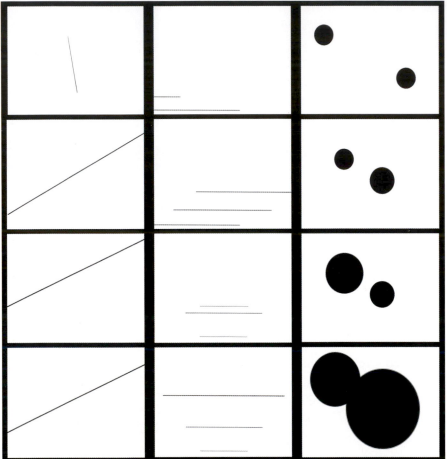

6.23
Frames from a word association exercise by Cheri Zenoni. From left to right: "tension," "playful," "increase." Courtesy of Professor Jon Krasner, Fitchburg State University.

6.24
Frame from a potential SyFy channel animation by Klarissa Marie Parduba. © 2012 Ringling College of Art + Design.

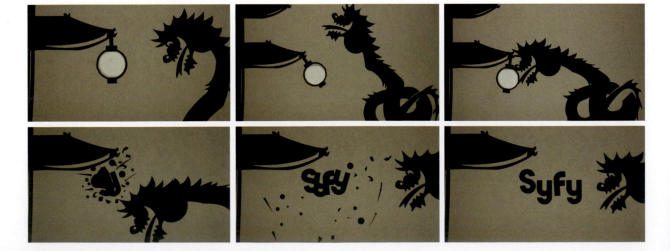

Secondary (Camera) Motion

Character animation, whether it is 2D or 3D, conventional or digitally generated, requires careful observation of nature and attention to detail in order to coordinate the movements of elements and create realism. In a short video celebrating the 100th issue of the design magazine *IdN*, the motions of a colorful character named Morbidus were carefully constructed to make the creature seem cute and friendly, while at the same time having a disgusting or negative connotation (**6.25**). Life becomes more difficult with every step he takes. As colorful balloons grow all over his body, walking and breathing become challenging. The design team at Dvein motion and interactive studio in Barcelona wanted the character's movements to feel organic and natural, and developed a special "rig" of bones and cloth dynamics for reference. According to Anna Dvein, the goal was to create "a colorful drama, an inflatable thought about the weight of creativity on individuals."

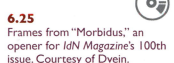

6.25
Frames from "Morbidus," an opener for *IdN Magazine*'s 100th issue. Courtesy of Dvein.

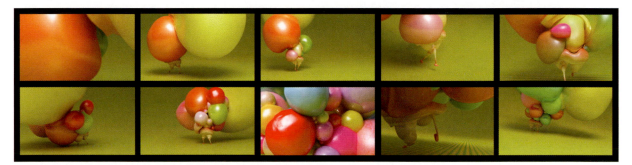

Secondary (Camera) Motion

The study of movement is not just confined to how objects travel inside the composition; it also involves "secondary motion"—the perceived motion of the viewer that dictates how the content is framed over time. The technique of "frame mobility" (also discussed in Chapter 13) can be applied through actual or simulated camera movement to breathe life into scenes and achieve various compositional framings. When used judiciously, the basic types of camera movements described here can be used to alter an audience's mood and perception of space.

Panning is one of the most common camera techniques. It involves moving the camera horizontally to create the impression of a subject being scanned. A slow pan of a panoramic scene can approximate the motion of moving one's head from side to side to take in the view.

Historical Perspective

After World War I, French Impressionist filmmakers developed innovative ways of portraying psychological states of mind through mobile framing. These included using awkward camera movements to depict characters in drunken or ill states. They even went as far as fastening their cameras to moving vehicles, amusement park rides, and machines that could move through space. Surrealist and Dadaist filmmakers also experimented with camera techniques to emphasize abstraction and create shock value. The camera's position would often change to provide a new outlook on subsequent portrayals of a subject to intensify the audience's curiosity. In the late 1950s, bumpy camera movement became a common practice in documentary filmmaking. In the film *Vertigo*, Alfred Hitchcock popularized what is known as the vertigo shot which involved synchronizing the motion of the subject with a zoom. The subject stays the same size while the background changes.

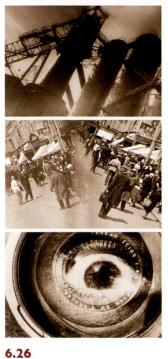

6.26
Dziga Vertov's film *Man With The Movie Camera* (1929) features a spectrum of camera moves that transform reality and break away from traditional narrative cinema.

A "whip pan" (also called a "flick," "zip," or "swish pan") is a brisk side-to-side movement that produces the effect of blurred, horizontal motion. This simulates the action of your eye moving abruptly from one subject to another. (Whip pans were commonly used in action genres such as kung-fu movies during the 1970s.) "Tilting" produces the effect of scanning an object or a space vertically from top to bottom or vice versa. It can enhance an image's height and depth by showing it in small increments. A long, slow tilt in an upward direction can express the sheer bulk of a subject. Tilting can also change the angle of framing in order to gradually reveal offscreen space. It can produce suspense or anticipation as the camera motion forces our attention in a precise direction without knowing when it will cease or what will be revealed. "Tracking" (also referred to as "dollying") involves changing the camera's position in relation to a subject so that it travels forwards, backwards, diagonally, in a circle, or from side to side in the frame. This action can bring viewers physically closer to or further away from a subject or make it appear as though it is being followed. The movement of foreground and background in the periphery of a shot can create tension or excitement. "Crane shots," such as helicopter and airplane shots, allow the camera to travel up and down. "Zooming" increases or decreases the camera's field of view, magnifying a portion of the scene without moving the camera. (Zooming is fundamentally different from camera movement, because the optical properties of the lens change.)

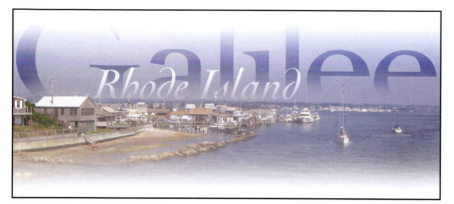

6.27
Panning is used to emphasize the sheer vastness of this scene and the grandeur of the type.

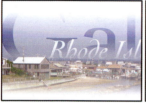 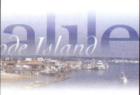 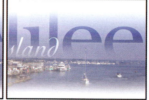

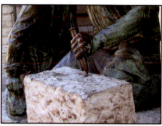

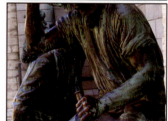

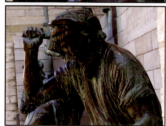

Mimicking natural head and eye movements can involve an audience, giving them a sense of motion through space, as if they are physically transported from their world into the one displayed on the screen. At Rochester Institute of Technology, Kim Miller takes us on a visual journey in an assignment involving the creation of a personal, abstract video diary. A combination of zooms, tilts, and pans, accompanied by graphic transitions, contributes to the formal and emotional language of the piece, making us feel as if we are experiencing her inner world from a subjective point of view (**6.29**).

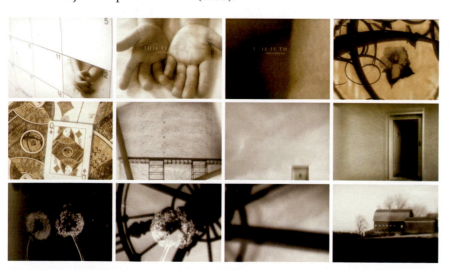

6.28
Tilting is used to enhance the subject's height by showing it in small increments.

6.29
Frames from a personal video diary, by Kim Miller, Rochester Institute of Technology. Courtesy of Professor Jason Arena.

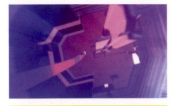

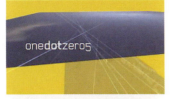

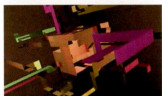

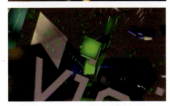

6.30
Frames from a series of trailers.
Courtesy of onedotzero.

Figure 6.30 illustrates how incorporating the device of perspective into mobile framing can generate tension and excitement. A series of trailers takes us on a dynamic journey as if we were in a sci-fi action movie or on a Disney ride, twisting, turning, and plummeting on various trajectories in a multidimensional world. **Figure 6.31** shows how frame mobility can build intensity. Several sequences of camera movements showing various angles and spatial distances are linked together to take us on an adventure through a complex, three-dimensional environment where we can experience the multi-faceted nature of the television industry.

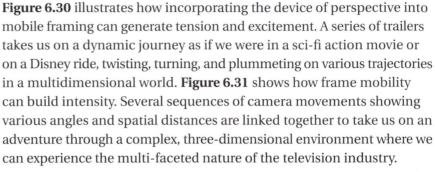

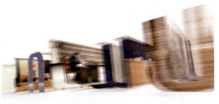

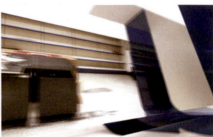

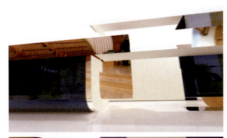

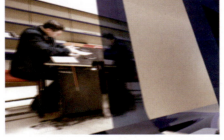

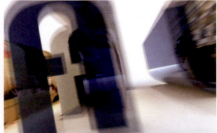

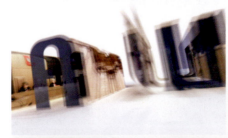

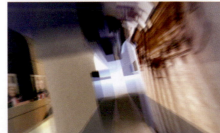

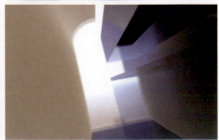

6.31
Frames from TVN Unwaga,
a German television network.
Courtesy of Velvet.

Secondary (Camera) Motion

In a worldwide television ad campaign for Hugo Boss Green, Jake Banks of Stardust Studios designed a series of advertisements introducing this new cologne for men. His blending of live-action and 3D animation allowed him to construct impossible environments that we travel through as observers (**6.32**).

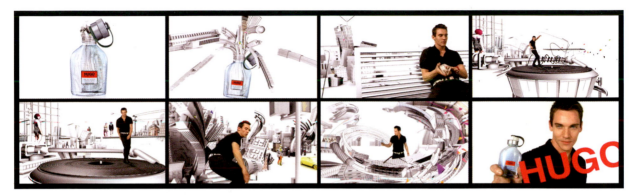

6.32
Frames from a TV campaign for Hugo Boss Green. Courtesy of Stardust Studios.

Mobile framing can influence how we perceive object motion. The pivoting motions of panning and tilting, for example, can change how we react to an image moving across the field of view. Like music, mobile framing can have expressive qualities ranging from fluid (legato) to shaky (staccato). These qualities can generate visual patterns of motion that evolve and repeat over time to complement the rhythmic possibilities of music videos and other types of presentations that embrace rhythm. An example of this was Fuel TV's show opener to *Cutmasters*, a series where contestants raced against the clock to edit the best video segment featuring sports professionals. Combinations of zooms and pans varying in speed and direction emphasized the sporadic motion of images. These moves were organized incrementally in synchronization with the percussive, steady rhythm of the soundtrack (**6.33**).

6.33
Frames from the show opener for *Cutmasters*. Courtesy of Fuel TV.

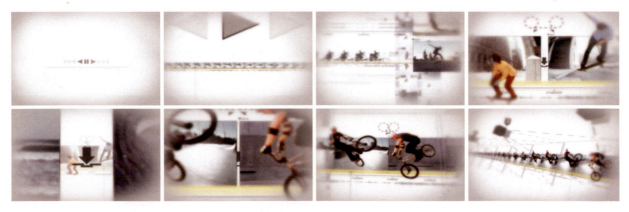

Another example is Kevin Passmore's "Falln'Love," a potential Fox network ID that takes us on a visual journey through a "lovescape" of delectable hearts and rose petals (**6.34**). The deliberate camerawork helps showcase the personified movement of the letterforms as they cleverly play upon the "OX" of the identity. The camera movement also enhances the influence of gravity on the objects as they shift from being weightless to free falling, visually reinforcing the composition's theme of falling in love. Kevin states: "Within the piece I focused on illustrating attraction, gravity, the pulse of a beating heart. I started with camera perspectives that placed the viewer falling along with the petals and candies instantly helped put the audience in the scene. I used simple horizontal sweeping pans along the letterforms while they bounce in rhythm and ended by flipping the camera perspective for the payoff. I tried to correlate my camera movements with the action that was going on within the scene and help guide the viewer to create anticipation for the Fox logo reveal."

6.34
Frames from a network ID assignment by Kevin Passmore. © 2012 Ringling College of Art + Design.

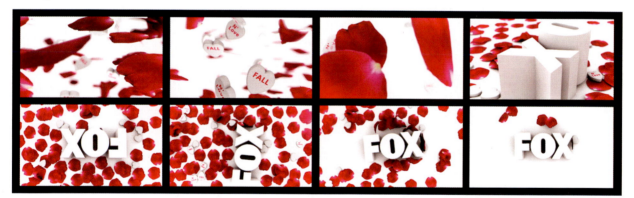

The device of frame mobility can be used to set a mood and arouse feelings that support a story's narrative structure. In an opener to *Arte Metropolis*, a political evening program on Franco-German culture, shaky camera movements reinforce the concept of political entanglement and depict the show's disjointed, fragmentary nature. Disturbing, unstable camera motions are used in coordination with unusual camera angles, abrupt jump cuts, and tempo changes to accompany a range of gestures made by actors to symbolize their dual role as both puppets on strings and the masters who are pulling the strings (**6.36**). Similarly, the frenetic camera motions that were used in David Carson's music video for Nine Inch Nails support the fleeting, multilayered imagery to convey the energetic, rebellious nature of the song (**6.37**).

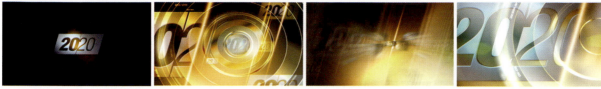

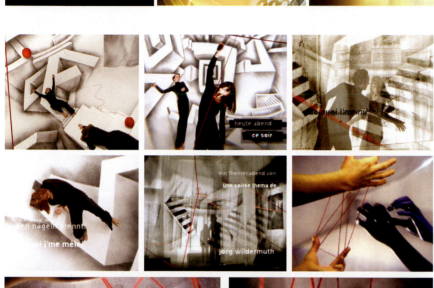

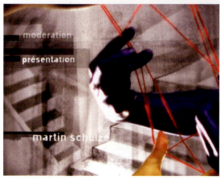

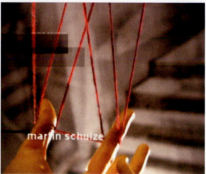

6.35
In a show package for ABC News' *20/20*, a series of zooms were choreographed to match the beat of the music. Courtesy of Nailgun*.

6.36
Frames from *Arte Metropolis*, a European culture magazine program. Courtesy of Velvet.

In the opener for the Indian television program *Ghe bharari* (**Chapter 10, figure 10.12 on p. 350**), the camera slowly moves left to right as individual elements animate in sucession. Director and designer Varun Chawla stated in an interview with *PrintMag.com*: "I wanted the motion of the camera to be slow, smooth, and linear, without any cuts." This subtle, almost invisible camera motion allows viewers to carefully take in the actions which unfold in an imaginary, dreamlike space.

Camera movements can also express a subjective point of view, as in Shilo's station IDs for AMC's twentieth anniversary. One particular vignette entitled "Twenty Years of Scary Movies" transforms an iconic

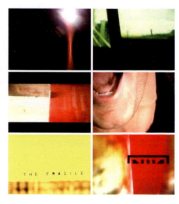

6.37
Frames from a music video for Nine Inch Nails' "The Fragile." Courtesy of David Carson.

scene from a horror movie into a graphic sequence shown from a first person perspective. The "camera's" implied viewpoint depicts a heart-stomping race in which we run through a moonlit cemetery and fall into a ditch, only to be met by an open coffin, its door slamming closed upon us. Another segment based on "killer thrillers" casts us in the role of a voyeur who suddenly realizes that he has been caught in the act (**6.38**). In a broadcast commercial for the Tour de France, Digital Kitchen's use of camera movements and subjective camera angles make us feel as if we are a participant in the race (**6.39**).

6.38
Frames from station IDs for AMC's twentieth anniversary. Courtesy of Shilo.

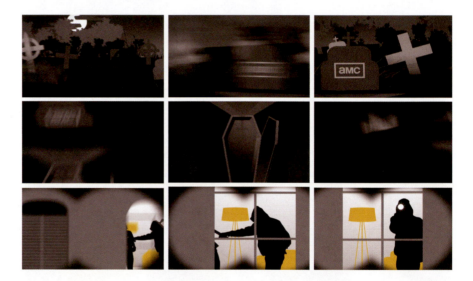

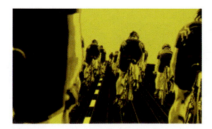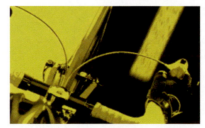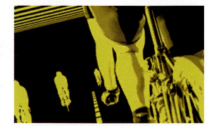

6.39
Frames from a commercial for the Tour De France. Courtesy of Digital Kitchen.

On the other hand, mobile framing can be used from a purely aesthetic point of view with the objective of exploring compositional possibilities. This may occur with or without consideration of the story's content and narrative structure.

Finally, frame mobility can be used as an alternative to editing in constructing the sequential composition, as discussed in Chapter 13.

Temporal Considerations

time

Choreographing object and camera motion requires a fundamental understanding of how time is measured. Depending on whether you are designing for film, video, or digital media, each format has its own standard for measuring time.

time standards in film and video

In film and video, time is described numerically as frames per second (fps). This frame rate describes the maximum speed that animations can play at to create the illusion of continuous, believable motion.

Film has a frame rate of 24 fps, which, today, continues to be standard for commercial motion pictures. In 1953, the National Television Standards Committee (NTSC) designated a frame rate of 29.97 fps for broadcast video in the United States. The EBU (European Broadcasting Union) standard is used throughout Europe and Australia, where color televisions are based on PAL and SECAM systems.

In 1967, the U.S. Society of Motion Picture and Television Engineers (SMPTE) adopted a rate of 30 fps and introduced "timecode," a method by which time is calculated in the form of an eight-digit, 24-hour clock consisting of 0 to 23 hours, 0 to 59 minutes, and 0 to 59 seconds. Seconds are subdivided into frames, and the number of frames varies depending upon the specified frame rate. (For example, 00:02:23:15 means 0 hours, 2 minutes, 23 seconds, and 15 frames). Time code is encoded onto videotape to enable precision in editing and in the synchronization of audio and images. This efficient system continues to be used today in identifying frames for video editing, enabling you to coordinate the timing of elements from different video sources.

Video that is produced by SMPTE standards applies a drop-frame method in order to match the footage of NTSC time code. The first two frames are reassigned a number after every minute except for every tenth minute. For example, at 1:06:59:29 (one hour, six minutes, fifty-nine seconds and the twenty-ninth frame), the next frame will be 1:07:00:02.

The frame rates mentioned above are sufficient to achieve believable motion for film and animation, although frame-by-frame animations have been produced at much lower speeds (between 6 and 15 fps), usually resulting in less detail. However, if the frame rate is too slow, an animation can appear choppy. If the playback rate is set to a higher value than the rate at which the original material was created or captured, frames will be duplicated, and a slow motion effect will result. If the playback rate is set to a lower value than the original, the result will be choppy, as frames will be skipped or dropped out.

time standards in digital media

Frame rates for multimedia (CD-ROM and DVD-ROM) and Web delivery can vary between 8 and 30 fps due to technical factors associated with playback performance, such as processing speed and storage requirements. Today, a frame rate of 12 to 15 fps usually yields adequate results over the Web, enabling smooth and consistent playback across various platforms.

velocity

"Velocity" is the speed at which elements move or change over time and space. This is a considerable determining factor in achieving dynamic, lifelike animation. Like direction, velocity can be linear or non-linear.

If the velocity of an element's motion is linear, it proceeds at a steady, uniform rate. Devices such as clocks, CD players, gears, and electric fans all display a constant rate of motion. Although linear velocity does not lend itself to lifelike animation, it may be applicable to the subject matter or to your conceptual message.

Linear velocity can be applied to motion graphics presentations that are intended to look fluid or mechanical. An example of this is Velvet's ID design for Kabel 1 News, one of Germany's most popular commercial television channels. The mechanical movements of the circular, ribbon-like structures that are layered at varying opacities appropriately reflect the corporate, clean atmosphere and soundtrack. The faster motions of short vertical and horizontal lines surrounding the logo complement the slower, revolving motions of the larger structures (**6.40**). Another example is a series of motion studies that twenty2product created for Adobe's Expert Support trade show, which focused on Adobe's technical support services. Fluid, linear motions were used to express the synthetic nature of digital technology, and supported the look and feel of how Adobe's logo and titling could be animated in an orthographic space with a flattened perspective (**6.41**).

Linear velocity also works well with objects that travel in straight lines on linear motion paths. If an element follows a complex path that changes direction dramatically, maintaining a constant speed from one key frame to the next can be challenging. In **figure 6.42**, the distances between key frames vary abruptly due to the path's sudden shift.

Studies have shown that the human optical system can capture images 18–20 times per second. The higher frame rates of motion picture film and broadcast video were developed to provide a more convincing illusion of motion.

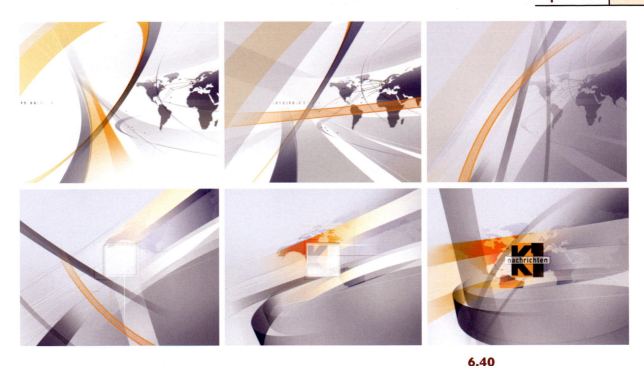

This is indicated by the uneven distances between key frames on the animation's timeline. The dots along the path indicate an abrupt change in the speed in the object's course of travel.

It is seldom that living things in the natural world move at a constant, linear pace. Natural movements typically begin slowly, speed up, and slow down unless an obstacle interrupts them. Human and animal motion, as well as motion caused by natural forces, can be very erratic and unpredictable, involving acceleration and deceleration. It is highly unusual for things to start or stop instantaneously. Inexperienced animators may overlook this fact and produce motion that feels too "linear." In contrast, some of the most sophisticated animations contain subtle, less predictable changes in the way things move. The result is more gradual, fluid-looking imagery that conveys a more dynamic, realistic persona.

The motion profiles in **figure 6.44** illustrate how non-linear velocity can vary. A straight line climbing upward represents a sudden change from a static state to an active state (an abrupt acceleration) and an abrupt halt at the end of the motion. A curved motion profile, however, represents a more gradual, realistic change in speed from start to finish.

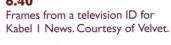

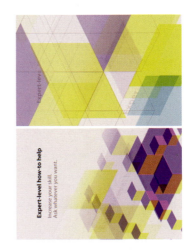

6.41
Frames from Adobe's Expert Support trade show. Courtesy of twenty2product. © 2004 Adobe Systems. All rights reserved.

6.42
The linear velocity of the object's motion occurs in constant time increments, as indicated by the uneven distances between the dots along the motion path.

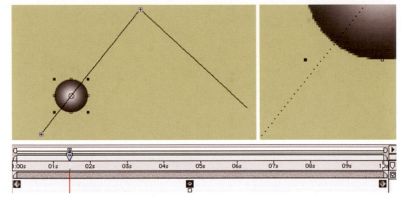

6.43
The dots along this motion path indicate that the object's speed changes abruptly.

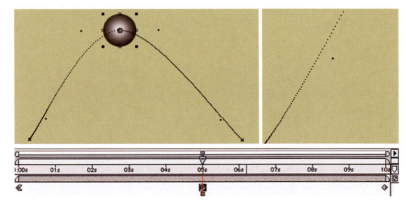

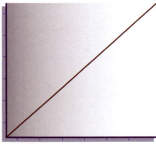

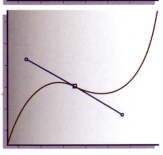

6.44
Motion profiles of acceleration and deceleration.

Applying non-linear movements to objects requires a careful analysis of living subjects and knowledge of how to apply these observations by analog or digital means. In a television spot promoting the Brazilian bank, Banco Real, collections of colorful images are brought to life through the use of non-linear motion. Groupings of abstract, graphic shapes mimic cellular organisms with lively, natural movements as they playfully spring up and down and dance around. At one point, a pair of wireframe shoes walk briskly across the screen, emulating the variation in the way that human feet naturally move (**6.45**).

Throughout the history of cinema, altering the speed of filmed events has been a powerful method of moving audiences. In Kurosawa's *Seven Samurai* (1954), slow motion is used to contrast the emotional rescue of a child with the death of the man who kidnapped him. Dziga Vertov's film *Man with a Movie Camera* (1929) pushed the envelope of the optical printer's capabilities and utilized "overcranking" or "undercranking" to render sports events in slow motion. The invention of time-lapse cinematography allowed lengthy events such as a sun setting or a flower

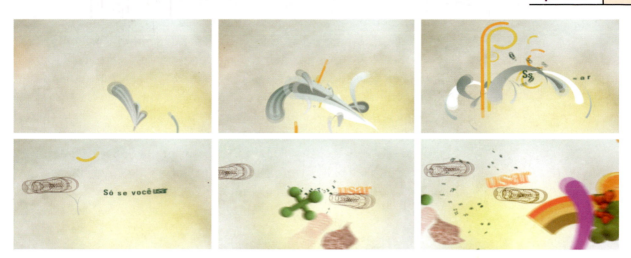

6.45
Frames from "Esteria." Courtesy
of The Ebeling Group.

blooming to be condensed into short sequences. High-speed cinema-tography has been used to slow down events, such as a sequence of ripples from a water droplet or a bullet shattering a piece of glass.

Techniques such as slow and fast motion, reverse playback, and freeze-frame can help emphasize or exaggerate actions. They also support a composition's underlying rhythm, enhance mood, and alter our sense of objective and subjective time. Introducing slow motion has the effect of interrupting a composition's flow, because it presents a close-up of time. Perceptually, it can provide a clearer view of the content, allowing us to appreciate subtle, visual details. Because it violates physical laws, motion is intensified, making the appearance of actions more powerful than normal. In **figure 6.46**, a promotional television spot for the Middle Eastern network Al Jazeera Sport demonstrates this effect. METAphrenie, an award-winning design firm based in Berlin, integrated actual athletes into unique, dream-like visual landscapes. The spots depict a duality between player and landscape, giving a unique perspective on the "beautiful game." The playback is slowed down to emphasize the body movements and the dynamic impact of the players' actions. According to Andrea Dionisio, one of the company's founders: "Our strategy was to take sports and the athletes that play them, and isolate these two elements, stripping things down to the bare essentials."

In contrast to slow motion, fast motion yields an aesthetic effect that seems to accelerate objects forward in time. Their movements are shown faster than normal, at times resulting in an erratic, jumpy appearance that is known to induce laughter or create drama. In the

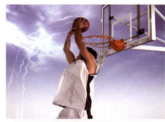

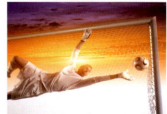

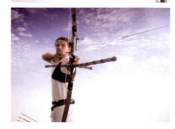

6.46
Frames from television spots for Al Jazeera Sport. Courtesy of METAphrenie.

opener to *Arte Metropolis* (**see page 186**), velocity changes occur in the introductory sequence featuring a pair of hands spinning an illuminated globe (**6.47**). Abrupt increments of accelerated motion are accompanied by echoed whispers on the soundtrack, both of which contribute toward the program's theme of political entanglement. This effect is consistent with the wide range of body movements and gestures from the actors that occur throughout the composition. In a later sequence, a series of shots reveal various pairs of hands restlessly interacting with the strings from an implied ball of yarn. Their abrupt, accelerated movements further accentuate the effect of panic and anxiety.

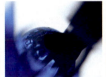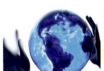

6.47
Frames from the show opener for Arte Metropolis. Courtesy of Velvet.

See also Chapter 10, figure 10.15, on p. 351.

The technique of "freeze-frame" can be used to show arrested motion or a pause in an object's movement, versus no motion. Like slow motion, it interrupts a composition's flow, presenting a close-up of time while providing a clearer view of the content's subtle details. This effect is exemplified in "In the Details," a captivating network ID created for Fuel TV (**6.48**). The illusion of a slow-moving freeze-frame creates a surreal, hyperreality in which events that would normally go unnoticed as they take place in the flash of an eye are emphasized. By combining static images and camera mobility, the ID tells a simple story of a skateboarder performing a trick on a flight of stairs. As the world slows down to a snail's pace, the resulting distortion of time allows us to hone in on the "Details" of the scene. We navigate through three-dimensional space, taking in scenic details that would normally be ignored, including the reflection in the skateboarder's mask, a close-up of the sole of his sneaker, and his exhalation in the winter's cold evening air. This all magically occurs during the few seconds that his trick takes.

Whether the effects of velocity change are created during capture or creation, they can be applied to the motions of one or more elements, entire animated sequences, and live-action content that contains real movement. In a sting for DNACreative, a design studio in Dublin, Ireland, a synthesis of fast and slow motion, reverse playback, and accelerated transitions is consistent with the somewhat disturbing yet hilarious nature of the content (**6.49**).

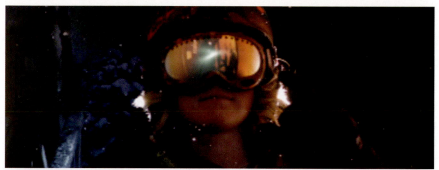

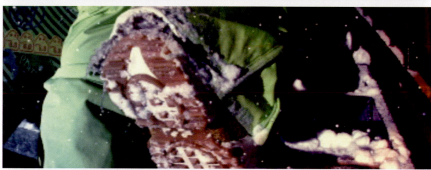

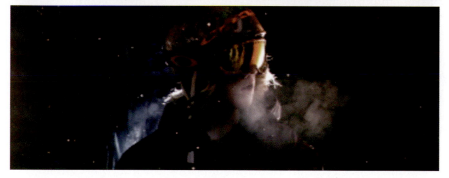

6.48
Frames from "In the Details,"
a network ID created for Fuel
TV. Produced by Shilo. Courtesy
of Fuel TV.

6.49
Frames from "Experience."
Courtesy of G'Raffe.

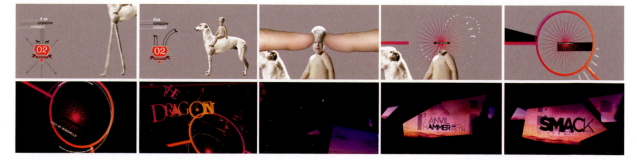

6.50
Frames from "Bubbles" and "Hair," by Chelsy Ann Hulet (http://www.chelsyannphotography.com).

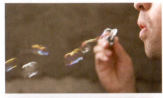

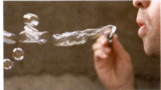

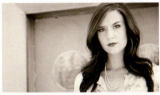

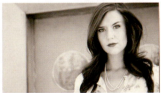

The term "cinemagraph" was coined in 2011 by Jamie Beck and Kevin Burg, two New York based photographers who have been developing animated fashion and news photographs. They describe their work as "something more than a photo but less than a video." They claim to have created a "new form of digital photography" even though many photographers have been experimenting with this process for years. Beck and Burg have refused to contribute their work to this chapter.

Last, an image's motion can be emphasized by being isolated and juxtaposed with static elements in the same composition. The technique of seamlessly blending movement with freeze-frame is evident in a recent trend in animated photography that has led to new forms of storytelling over the Web and on mobile devices, and which has provided unique ways of combining still photography and cinema. Deriving creative inspiration from simple observation, Utah-based photographer Chelsy Ann Hulet reinvents the subtleties of the natural world by capturing a subject's actions and integrating them with elements that are frozen in time (**6.50**). Her animated photographs are incorporated in a product for her wedding clients as part of a photography package.

Having been interested in motion since childhood, visual effects artist and photographer Kert Gartner recalls creating stop-motion animations with transformers and an old VHS camcorder. After working at a television station, he began experimenting with "cinemagraphs"—photographs that add subtle motion to an isolated part of an otherwise static image. Specific movements in a scene loop continuously, in contrast to the stillness of the remaining imagery. A figure's moving eyes or the reflection of a taxi in a restaurant window may be the only kinetic components of a scene. As an extension of traditional photography, these images—which at first glance appear to be still photos, but then suddenly catch your eye with a glimmer of movement—have an uncanny ability to draw viewers in due to their subtle emotional power. Gartner's composition "Moulin Rouge" captures the spirit and activity of the famous night club in Paris (**6.51**). According to Gartner: "I just set the camera up with the framing I liked, and let it roll for about 10 minutes, and just let people walk by and into frame. Once I saw that little moment with the man and woman, I knew I had the right moment, and I just lucked out that it was close to being in focus." Rather than combining a sequence of still images, piecing together video clips can allow happy accidents to occur, such as the bird flying overhead in the animated photograph entitled "Patricia Beach" (**6.52**). This mundane detail might be overlooked in real life, but showcasing it in an otherwise static picture suddenly makes it engaging. Gartner states: "I had the idea to do something with the waves at the beach, but needed a good foreground subject. I tried some plants, some trees, and nothing was really working until my friend's daughter started playing in the sand next to me. I set up the camera, and just let it roll for about a minute, and that seemed like it did the trick."

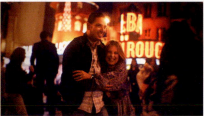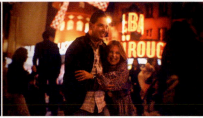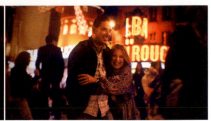

6.51
Frames from "Moulin Rouge," by
Kert Gartner. © Kert Gartner
2012 (http://kertgartner.com).

German photographer Marcel Meyer prefers to display his quiet, animated photographs at their small original sizes on iPads that he disguises as handmade wooden frames. His series entitled "My Favorite Childhood Nightmares" portrays intimate subjects that unfold with a magical yet haunting melancholy (**6.53**). The infinite, subtle movements of the images pull you into the scenes, inviting you to relive your own childhood fears and dreams, depending on your personal experiences and perceptions. The motion is subtle but fluid, providing delicate, fleeting moments that seamlessly repeat. According to Marcel: "My animated photographs seem to get stuck on their way forward, they are looking for release in some sort of infinite loop—and that's where they unfold their very own melancholy, their magic."

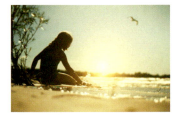

6.52
Frames from "Patricia Beach," by
Kert Gartner. © Kert Gartner
2012 (http://kertgartner.com).

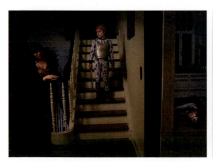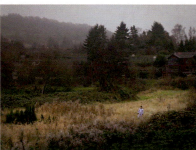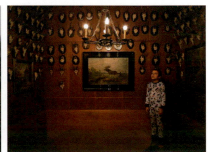

6.53
Frames from "My Favorite
Childhood Nightmares."
Courtesy of Marcel Meyer.

Assignments

The following assignments are intended to help you develop a better understanding of motion literacy. Share your work with others and discuss the subtleties of motion with respect to spatial and temporal considerations, tempo, rhythm, and the basic animation principles in Frank Thomas and Ollie Johnston's *The Illusion of Life*.

natural motion: study #1

You are to create a rotoscoped animation based on a motion study of Eadward Muybridge. The objective is to develop an increased awareness of natural, lifelike movement.

Download one of Muybridge's photographic motion studies from *The Human Figure in Motion* or *Complete Human and Animal Locomotion* (Dover Publications). In Photoshop, separate the images and save them as separate files, naming them with sequential numbers. Import the images into a program that offers onion skinning. Create a sequence of line drawings from the frames, and play it back. (Alternatively, you can draw over the images with a pencil and tracing paper, scan in the artwork, and play the frames back digitally.) Observe and discuss the presence of Disney's animation principles in the finished sequence.

natural motion: study #2

Human motion, animal motion, and motion in nature is erratic and unpredictable. Create a rotoscoped animation from video footage that demonstrates natural movement. The goal is to explore how natural movement can be enhanced through animation.

Download from the Web a 3 to 4 second video clip of one of the following:
- plant growth (time lapse)
- a butterfly opening and closing its wings
- a person or an animal walking or running

Render the footage with a frame rate between 6 and 8 fps. Note that 4 seconds will need 24–32 frames. The movie's dimensions should be 720 x 480 pixels. From the footage, develop a set of line drawings in pencil that capture the subject's basic movements. You may digitize and enhance the drawings in Photoshop. Consider Disney's animation principles.

natural motion: study #3

Hands are unique, and the way people express themselves with their hands can offer insight into their personality.

Choose a 3–4 second excerpt of music and choreograph a dance for your hands. After listening to the excerpt several times, experiment with various movements that express your interpretation of the music. Be imaginative and daring! Plan and practice your sequence several times, and then videotape it. Digitize the footage and render it as a QuickTime movie with a frame rate between 6 and 8 fps. (Note that 4 seconds will need 24–32 frames.) From the footage, develop a sequence of simple line drawings that capture the basic movements. Your objective is to translate human movements into animation.

motion and gravity: study #1

Create a rotoscoped animation from a short segment of video that demonstrates the effect of gravity on movement. Your goal is to develop an awareness of how motion is affected by natural gravitational forces.

Download from the Web a 3–4 second clip of one of the following:
- a ball bouncing down a slide
- a ball bouncing down a staircase
- a ball in a racquetball court

Render the footage with a frame rate between 6 and 8 fps. (Note that 4 seconds will need 24–32 frames.) Develop a sequence consisting of simple line drawings.

motion and gravity: study #2

Create a rotoscoped sequence that demonstrates the effect of gravity on movement based on one of the following:
- a feather falling to the ground
- a paper clip falling and bouncing off of a hard surface
- a rubber eraser falling and bouncing off of a hard surface

Share your work with others and discuss what animation principles from Frank Thomas and Ollie Johnston's *The Illusion of Life* apply.

relative motion

The way we perceive an element's motion can be influenced by another element's motion, just as our perception of a color can be affected by the presence of another color. Your goal is to develop a sensitivity to relative motion by exploring how two or more animated elements can be choreographed to create meaning.

Create two simple graphic images. These may be lines, abstract or geometric shapes, or a combination of lines and shapes. In a 10–15 second animation, coordinate their movements so that they complement each other. Create a second animation, this time choreographing the movements of the elements so that they conflict with each other. Consider how supporting and contradictory motions influence your overall perception of the animation. How can both scenarios potentially communicate a concept with further development? How might they work together to heighten the viewer's interest?

kinetic typography: letter personification

Develop an animation based on the first and last initials of your name. The objective is personify the letters by assigning them non-linear, lifelike movements that are consistent with the laws of gravity.

Stick with only one sans serif typeface and use only black and white. Colors, shades of gray, drop shadows, and special effects are prohibited so that you can focus on the kinetic aspects of the type. The duration of the composition should be 10 seconds. It is critical that you are able to tell your story within this specified time frame.

Begin by creating a rough storyboard showing the chronological order of events. Critique this sketch as you would critique a film script, and develop a tighter iteration that conveys the story's events more clearly. You may want to develop an animatic to resolve some of the movements ahead of time. Be aware that you are not just presenting an animated slideshow of the initial sketches; you are clarifying the types of motion, camera angles, and transitions that will occur in the final production. Keep an open mind and be prepared to deviate from your original ideas. You may decide to go back to your initial sketches if you are not satisfied with the results or if you wish to explore other possibilities.

Consider the letters' relative directions of travel and velocity. Varying speed, direction, linear and non-linear movements can add interest and create dynamic visual relationships. The manner in which the letters appear, live, and disappear in the frame (birth, life, and death) should also be given close attention. Last, consider pictorial aspects such as scale, orientation, positive and negative shape, and the association and possible interaction of the letterforms with the frame's edges.

from print and motion

The pictorial aspects of composition can impact how messages are communicated. The kinetic aspects of composition can also shape the way messages are constructed.

Animate a poster of your choice. Your goal is to investigate how the static aspects of composition can be conveyed through movement.

Create a rough storyboard that demonstrates how the piece could be animated according to its pictorial and spatial qualities. Critique the sketch, and develop a revised version that clarifies the sequence of events and the types of movements and transitions that will occur. Do not hesitate to develop a new set of sketches if you are not satisfied or if you wish to explore other possibilities. If you decide to develop an animatic, be willing to deviate from it, to an extent, during production.

Digitize the piece, and separate its elements or recreate them digitally. Import the components into an application of your choice and animate them. Use every element from the design that you chose. Additional images and type are prohibited. The duration of the composition should be between 15 and 20 seconds.

The style of the motion should complement the design that you chose. Be experimental and innovative, yet consistent with the original style, purpose, and target audience. Be sure to give attention to the birth and death of the elements and to their relative durations in the frame. Consider how the device of frame mobility might be used to add interest and create visual hierarchy.

Attention should also be given to how the relative scale of elements, as well as their spatial orientations and directions of travel, relates to the frame's edges as they move throughout the composition.

visual poetry: sound and motion

Sound can play a considerable role in shaping the way motion is choreographed. Motion graphic designers are often faced with the challenge of animating their content to sound.

Create an animation based on three 30-second excerpts of music. Your objectives are to use sound as an inspiration for visual expression and to develop explicit relationships between sound and movement.

Listen to each excerpt several times, and imagine how each could be translated into simple, animated lines or geometric shapes. Starting with the first excerpt, write a simple script describing the types of motions that elements might have in response to the music. Digitize the music and begin animating the elements according to your script. Over time, you may find yourself wanting to deviate from the script as you develop a stronger connection to the music. This is perfectly acceptable.

Create a second animation consisting of two lines or two shapes. Try to develop an interplay between the movements of the elements. Play the animations back several times without the sound and observe how movement alone can trigger the emotions that the music produced. Consider how the qualities of your music can apply to movement. Some sounds may be linear, repeating at regular intervals, while others may feel sporadic or random. Other variables, such as tempo, pitch, texture, and distance, should play an important role. For example, pitch might be conveyed through velocity, while distance might be illustrated through secondary or camera motion. Consider how all of these variables might be conveyed through movement.

typeface and motion

Animate the name of a font in a manner that describes the personality of the typeface based on its classification, history, and visual characteristics. Your goal is to describe the quality of typographic form and the personality of the typeface through motion.

Visit Adobe's type library on the Web (http://www.adobe.com), and research a typeface of your choice. Note its classification (Old Style, Transitional, Modern, etc.), and become familiar with its history.

Chapter Summary

Motion literacy is a fundamental to effective storytelling in motion graphics. "Primary motion" involves animating an element's spatial properties, such as its position, scale, and spatial orientation. Coordinating primary motion requires that attention be given to how actions begin and end and their duration in the frame. It also requires a knowledge of early animation principles that were established by Disney. "Squash and stretch," for example, can establish the physical basis of objects that have mass, giving their movements the illusion of weight and volume. "Anticipation" creates a sense of natural motion by indicating that an upcoming action is about to occur. "Acceleration" and "deceleration" can soften movements, giving non-representational content the appearance of living subject matter.

Since primary motion is relative, the way we perceive an object's motion can be influenced by other movements of the same object or of different objects. Coordinating the relative movements of objects is like being a musical conductor.

"Secondary motion"—the perceived motion of the viewer that dictates how content is framed—is achieved through camera movement. The technique of "frame mobility" can control our perception of space by allowing the framing of objects to change over time. Mimicking natural head and eye movements can give audiences a sense of movement through space or a sense of omnipresence. Incorporating the device of perspective into mobile framing allows you to construct environments that viewers can travel through as observers, or become active participants. Frame mobility can impart information by establishing a visual hierarchy and can connect elements to each other and to their surroundings.

Temporal considerations play a considerable role in shaping primary and secondary motion. Linear movements that proceed at steady, uniform rates mimic mechanical devices, while non-linear movements that are produced from acceleration and deceleration can convey more natural qualities. Techniques such as slow motion, fast motion, reverse playback, freeze-frame, and isolating movement by juxtaposing it with static content can emphasize actions and alter our sense of objective and subjective time.

7

kinetic images
and typography
design considerations

The visual power of images, the connotative power of typography, and the union between these elements are the foundations of effective graphic design. These dynamic elements function as a visual language when they are combined on the printed page or in a time-based environment. In contrast to static designs, which can imply or inspire stories, imbuing visual and verbal information with the dimensions of motion and time can tell stories with expression, clarity, and meaning.

"When type meets image, there is automatically a dialogue between them, and each can pull the other in many different directions."
—Nancy Skolos and Tom Wedell (Type, Image, Message: A Graphic Design Layout Workshop)

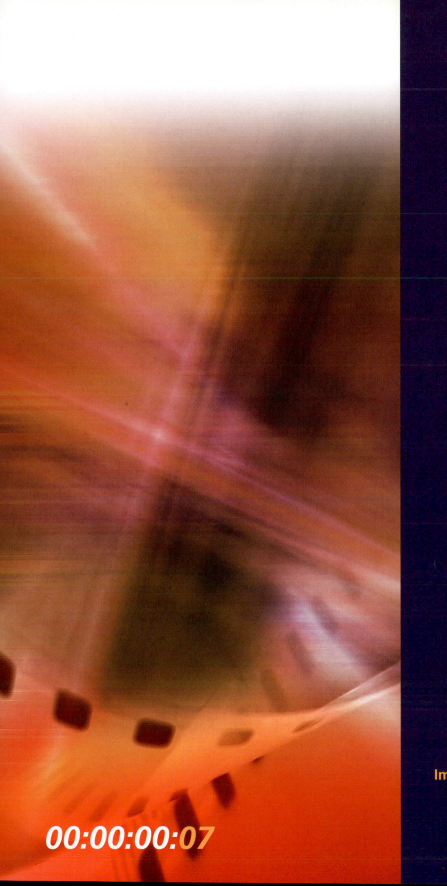

00:00:00:07

Visual Properties of Images

It is critical that motion graphic designers understand the symbolic language of aesthetics as it applies to images and typography.

form

Form is a basic element of graphic communication, in addition to point and line. Two-dimensional, three-dimensional, photographic, and typographic form can be used to suggest ideas and convey moods or emotions. Form can also imply spatial depth, provide emphasis, and help organize information by directing the viewer's eye through the frame.

Linear geometric forms have always fascinated designers because of their identifiable qualities and mathematically defined parameters. Structures such as honeycombs and crystals display the qualities of symmetry and pattern. Culturally derived symbols such as the octagon that communicates "stop" or a starburst that signifies something new or powerful have been used to represent literal objects or ideas. Images such as a vertical rectangle with a folded corner or a hollow circle with a diagonal line running through it have become universally recognized. Curvilinear forms derived from organic elements such as water droplets, plants, and microbial organisms offer a sense of freedom and spontaneity and can be seen in Chinese calligraphic writing and in art movements such as Ukiyo-e, Art Nouveau, Surrealism, and Abstract Expressionism.

Modern art was founded on the exploration of geometric, abstract form, and the basis of visual experience as the perceptual effect of shape and color on the viewer. Form became the content, and its expressive qualities were often developed from intuition. In animation, an emphasis on two-dimensional form is evident in German avant-garde films from the 1920s that made the transition from nonrepresentational painting to animation. Artists like Hans Richter and Walter Ruttmann saw abstraction as the basis of film and explored the linguistics of rhythm and motion through geometric form. Richter's *Rhythmus 21* explored the manipulation of elemental square and rectangular shapes. *Rhythmus 23* experimented with negative reversals and crisscross patterns (**7.1**). Walter Ruttmann's *Opus* series investigated how converging abstract shapes could exhibit playful, kinetic qualities. His film *Opus IV* (c. 1924) expressed a minimal graphic style characteristic of the Bauhaus period (**7.3**). Viking Eggeling's films (discussed in **Chapter 1**) demonstrated a painstaking analysis

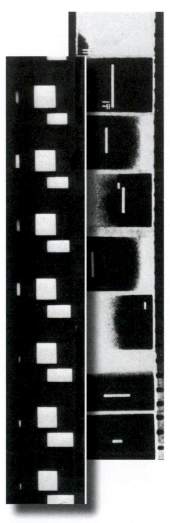

7.1
Filmstrips from *Rhythmus 21* (1921) and *Rhythmus 23* (1923) by Hans Richter. Courtesy of Cecile Starr.

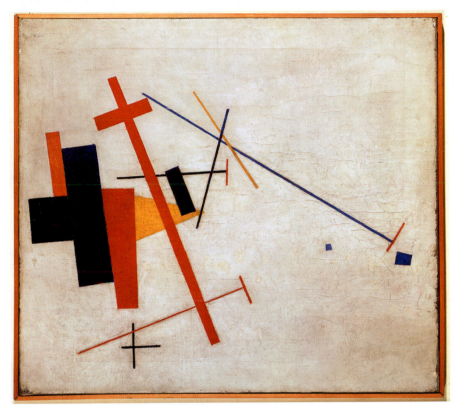

7.2
Suprematist Composition, (1915) by
Kazmir Malevich. Wilhelm Hack
Museum, Ludwigshafen © Erich
Lessing/ Art Resource, NY.

Malevich's style was founded on
the extreme reduction of images
to elemental geometric shapes.

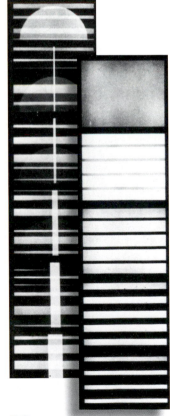

of linear forms and their positive–negative interplay. Animators who
followed in the footsteps of these experimental film pioneers continued
the tradition of two-dimensional abstraction, applying a variety of
artistic processes including drawing, painting, stop-motion, cut-out,
and direct-on-film. Stan Brakhage's film *Mothlight* (1963) was produced
by randomly adhering the wings of moths to a strip of clear film and
duplicating the results on a negative. When projected on the screen, the
positions of the wings change between frames, and a flickering effect of
the changing shapes is produced. Although these images came from a
real source, the end result is semi-abstract (**7.4**).

Three-dimensional animation has been used since the 1970s in opening
movie credits and station identifications. Desktop applications that offer
3D modeling, rendering, object animation, and camera animation have
become more affordable and more intuitive. Today, they are capable of
allowing you to see the results in real time and make adjustments during
playback without having to render.

7.3
Filmstrips from *Opus IV*
(c.1924) by Walter Ruttmann.
From *Experimental Animation*.
Courtesy of Cecile Starr.

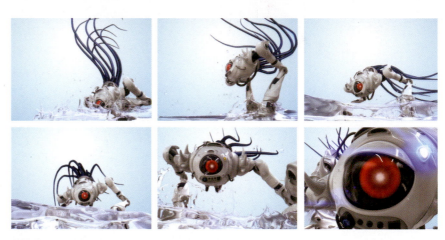

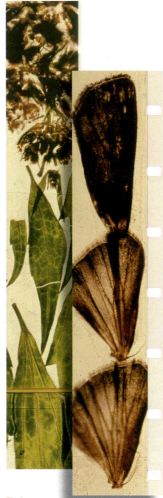

7.5
Frames from the Web site of Giant Octopus, a broadcast motion graphics studio in Clearwater, Florida. This entertaining 3D animation was used in 2007 to introduce the company's news reel. Courtesy of Giant Octopus.

7.4
Frames from *Mothlight* (1963), by Stan Brakhage. Courtesy of the Estate of Stan Brakhage and Fred Camper (www.fredcamper.com).

7.6
Frames from an animated ID for Karl Storz Endoscopy, a leading manufacturer of medical instruments. Courtesy of Reality Check Studios.

This well-crafted animation derives an endoscope from the letter "O," giving us an entertaining, exploded view of the contents of the instrument.

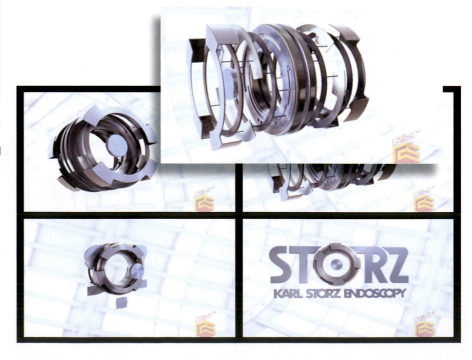

At Kent State University, Ben Dansby's disparate mix of superimposed three-dimensional objects and text in his animation "Rethinking Measurements" (**7.7**) conveys a chaotic environment symbolic of the imperial measurement system. The volumetric, three-dimensional aspect of the imagery introduces attributes such as length, width, mass, and volume to emphasize "the endless and absurd nature of the imperial system," according to Ben. It also complements the calmer two-dimensional layering of typography and vector art in the video's second half which touts the metric system.

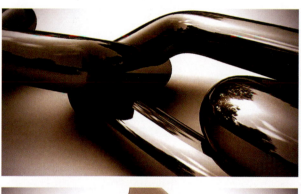

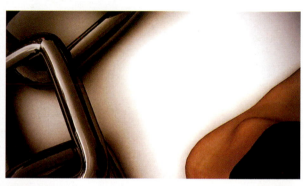

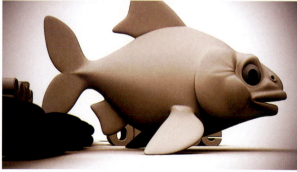

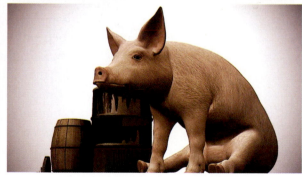

In 2012, Time Warner Cable's Primetime On Demand campaign gave the network's rounded typeface the characteristics of liquid and plastic (**7.8**). According to Creative Director Jakob Trollbäck, computer-generated, 3D images allowed "an ethos of precision and clarity, which is apt for a cable provider." He further states: "Extruding the type provided a catalyst and organizing principle for the package while staying on brand. This enabled us to build a rich 3D environment in which the materials, palette, and movement were specific to each of the subbrands. The type itself was filled with volumetric light, creating a stroboscopic effect as the letterforms move past camera."

7.7
Frames from "Rethinking Measurements" by Ben Dansby. © 2012 Kent State University. Courtesy of Professor Gretchen Rinnert.

See also Chapter 13, figure 13.25, p. 148.

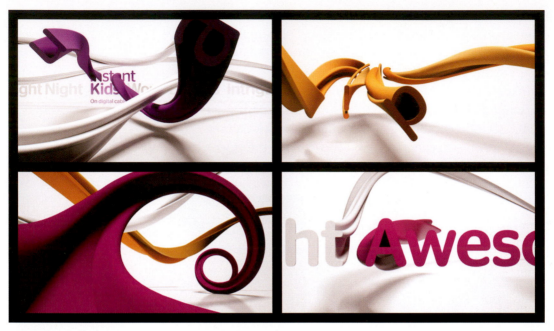

7.8
Frames from Time Warner
Cable's Primetime On Demand
campaign, 2012. Courtesy of
Trollbäck + Company.

Psyop's whimsical, dreamy pitch for Cadbury used 3D imagery to
metaphorically suggest the iconic swirl of chocolate from Cadbury's
logo and branding (**7.9**). The design team strived to convey a sense
of irreverence and playfulness by creating a massive apparatus that
looked as if an artist might have crafted it over a lifetime. The look of
this sophisticated, magical device had to inspire the imagination of an
adult audience and appear to exist in an outdoor setting, so that wind,
rain, and other natural elements could interact with it. Similar to a Rube
Goldberg machine or an elaborate mobile, every mechanical structure
had to have a purpose. This required considerable attention to form
and lighting to convey the realism of the structure's details. According
to Anh Vu, the project's lead designer, the initial thought process was to
use actual objects and avoid building a scene in 3D. However, the time
constraint of two days to develop the pitch necessitated the use of CG
images. The modeling and lighting was used as a sculptural base to
generate the forms; texture details were later added in Photoshop.

In a campaign for A FLAVA—the first cigarette in Indonesia to combine
two flavors—Dvein's design team modeled a series of fluids and
splashing liquids that mimicked the behavior of paint meeting water.
These stunning visuals provoke a sense of curiousness while expressing
the concept of two flavors in one (**7.10**).

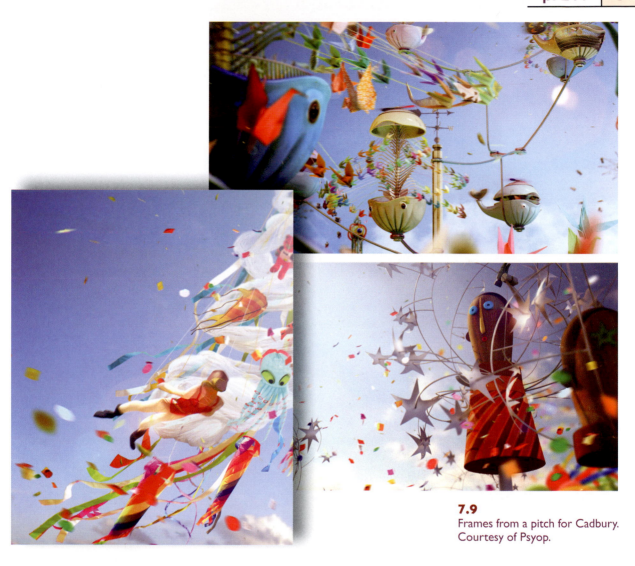

7.9
Frames from a pitch for Cadbury.
Courtesy of Psyop.

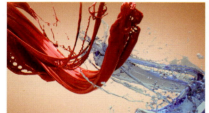
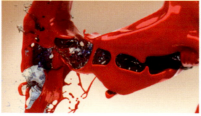
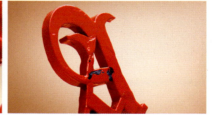

7.10
Frames from the 2011 campaign
for A FLAVA. Courtesy of Dvein.

TED's mission statement begins: "We believe passionately in the power of ideas to change attitudes, lives and ultimately, the world. So we're building here a clearinghouse that offers free knowledge and inspiration from the world's most inspired thinkers, and also a community of curious souls to engage with ideas and each other."

The beauty of three-dimensional form is expressed in the 2011 opening titles for TED (Technology, Entertainment and Design), a global set of conferences set up to disseminate "ideas worth spreading." (Founded in 1984, the conferences address a wide range of topics within the research and practice of science and culture. Past presenters include Bill Clinton, Al Gore, Gordon Brown, Richard Dawkins, Bill Gates, and many Nobel Prize winners.) The conference opener entitled "The Stuff of Life" explores the relationship between nature and science by dissecting a variety of man-made and organic objects to reveal their complex beauty. The decision to use a monochromatic color palette contributes to the purity of the imagery and allows us to view the subject matter in a way that is not photorealistic, but that is more artistic and expressive. Further, the absence of texture and strong attention to lighting heightens the beauty of the forms, making them appear very stylized and reflective, as if from another world (**7.11**).

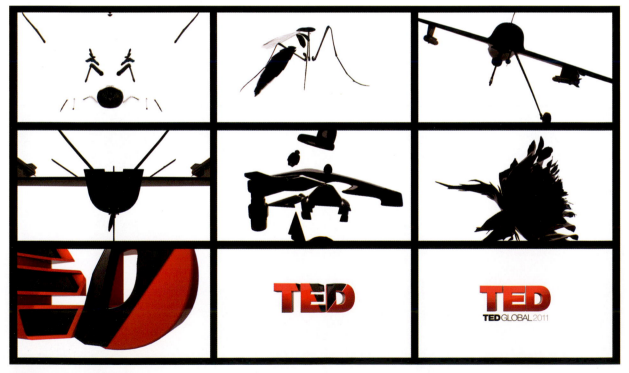

7.11
Frames from the opening titles for the TED Global 2011 conference. Courtesy of Trollbäck + Company.

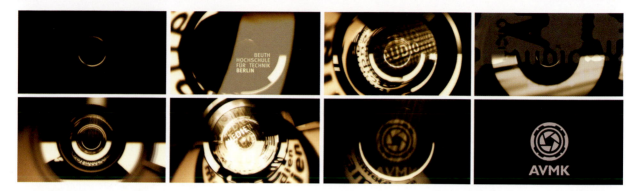

value and color

Value, one of the strongest determinants of visual contrast, measures the lightness or darkness of an image's tones or colors. It can be used to enrich visual messages and create focal points in a composition. Color has the ability to create mood, symbolize ideas, and express emotions to produce a desired audience response. Studies have indicated that most human beings make a subconscious assessment about what they see within 90 seconds of initial viewing, and that their evaluation is based on color alone.

Managing color can be complex in its technical application, and its conceptual and aesthetic direction. As graphic messages are often designed for global audiences, color selection and coordination takes on a special challenge with respect to psychological and social contexts. Familiarity with basic color principles and the psychological and cultural aspects of color can help you simplify color decisions and make color choices that foster a desired audience response.

the components of color

Color can be divided into three components: hue, saturation, and value. "Hue" denotes colors with regard to their identification (e.g, orange, green, red, cyan). "Saturation" (or "chroma") measures a hue's purity or intensity. Reducing a color's saturation by adding gray or by mixing a complementary hue from the opposite side of the color wheel has the effect of muting or subduing it (**7.15**). "Value" (also referred to as "tone" or "brightness") describes a color's lightness or darkness. Decreasing value is like adding black pigment, while increasing its value is like adding white. Every hue has a different value range. Yellow, for example, has a lighter tonal range than blue.

7.12
Frames from an opener for a film screening in the Audiovisual Media Camera (AVMK) program at Beuth Hochschule, Berlin. Courtesy of Johannes Tonnollo, Potsdam University of Applied Sciences.

This opener relies on 3D form and the interplay between light and shadow to reflect the work behind the camera.

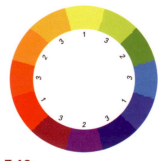

7.13
In traditional analog color theory, hues are referenced by their angle on a color wheel.

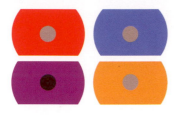

7.14
The top two hues share the same brightness but differ in saturation. The bottom hues share the same saturation but differ in brightness.

7.15
Decreasing a hue's saturation level reduces its "purity," bringing it closer to a muted gray value.

emotional, gender, and cultural associations

Psychological reactions to color vary, depending on the demographics of the target audience. Understanding how color can evoke different emotional responses can help with the color decisions we make. For example, universally, light red is commonly associated with cheerfulness; however, bright or dark red can induce irritability. We commonly associate yellow-green with freshness and youth while sometimes associating a dark shade of olive with death and decay. A light blue sky can produce tranquility, while a deep indigo can induce melancholy.

Color preferences and perceptions also vary with respect to gender and culture. Studies have shown that men are attracted to dark, saturated colors, while women prefer cool colors and softer tints. North American mainstream culture associates red with urgency, heat, love, blood, and danger, and green with nature, health, money, and abundance. Chinese culture represents death with white, while Brazilian culture depicts death with purple. Greek culture often interprets yellow as sadness, while the French associate it with jealousy.

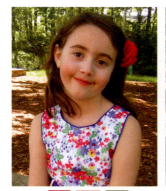
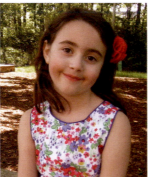
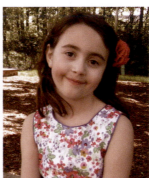
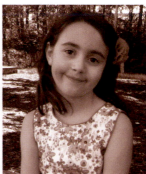
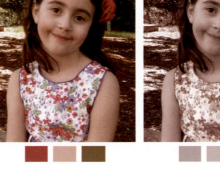

The color palette used for the male-oriented entertainment network MOJO was carefully selected to reflect the program's upscale nature. Deep crimson, black, and white serve as signature hues, while subdued variants of blue and orange function as secondary colors (**7.16**). In a show package for Black Entertainment Television, a rich color palette of gold, royal blue, and magenta portrays the luxury of being a celebrity (**Chapter 3, 3.23 on p. 51**). In the music video for "Decent Days and Nights" by The Futureheads, fluorescent colors were used to express the band's part vintage rock and part progressive nature. "Analog" color washes were used to give it a late '70s, early '80s appeal (**7.17**).

The National Museum of American Jewish History's installation "Only in America" strategically references a palette of sky blue, gold, and subdued tints of beige and silver to provide cohesion between elements and reinforce the contemplative and celebratory tone of the subject (**Chapter 5, figure 5.25 on p. 146**). The majority of visuals came from an asset pool of historic archival documents and images, many of which were originally black and white photographs. The main color palette for the museum's exhibit "Innovation and Expansion" consists of brown and red. Combinations of old etchings, sepia-tone photographs and drawings capture the the historical aspects and spirit of the era and relate visually to the exhibition's other elements, such as display boxes made of wood that tell stories about people living in the period (**Chapter 5, figures 5.26 and 5.27 on p. 147 and on p. 148**).

Although color choices are often subjective, designers must exercise appropriate color usage according to certain established conventions. Within those conventions, however, they should be willing to experiment and take risks.

texture and pattern

In addition to value and color, surface texture and pattern can add contrast and depth to a composition while providing viewers with the sensory experience of touch. Since the days of cartoon marker renderings, film animators have scratched, painted, and chemically altered the surface of film to achieve rich, tactile-looking content.

Motion graphic designers have also simulated textural effects to add richness and depth to their compositions. For example, Susan Detrie's bumper for TBS Network (**7.18**) incorporates a rich palette of digitally generated 3D textures into the letters of the identity. In a promotional animation for an experimental project called "Promsite in Motion," Ritxi Ostariz, a young digital designer from Bilbao, Euskal Herria, employed colorful patterns to add a sense of texture to his animation (**7.19**).

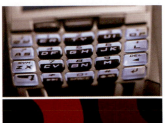
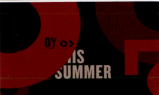
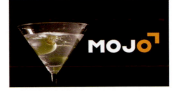

7.16
Frames from MOJO. Courtesy of Flying Machine.

See also Chapter 9, figure 9.34, on p. 328.

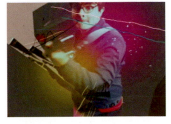

7.17
Frame from the music video for "Decent Days and Nights." Courtesy of Stardust Studios.

7.18
Frames from "The Big Screen." Courtesy of Susan Detrie.

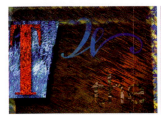
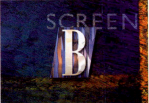
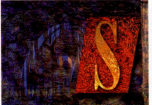
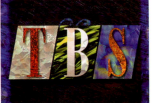

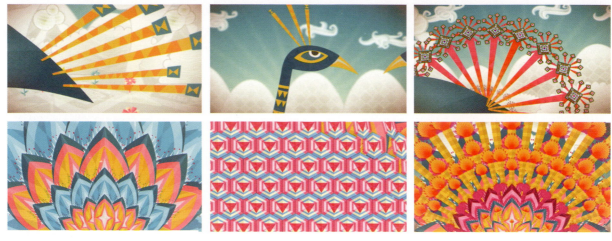

7.19
Frames from "Promsite in Motion"
by Ritxi Ostariz.

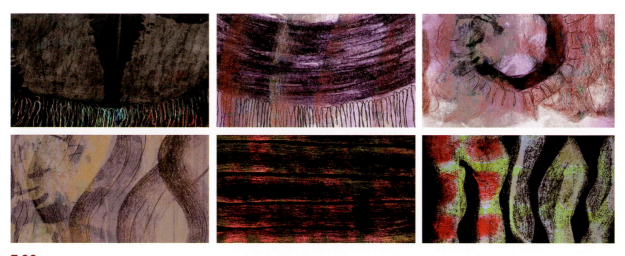

7.20
Frames from "ORG1" by Helga
Arnalds, Iceland Academy of Art.
Courtesy of Professor Kristín
María Ingimarsdóttir.

Richly textured images dance
passionately to a percussive
rhythm.

Graphic Style

Choosing the appropriate graphic style is critical to supporting your
concept, message, or mood. Two-dimensional, three-dimensional, or
live-action images can take on characteristics, ranging from textural,
sketchy, photographic, whimsical, realistic, abstract, to heavily layered.
Processes such as cropping, distortion, color alteration, and deconstruction can enhance their expressive properties. Both simplification

and exaggeration can translate the most dominant forms of an image into pure, elemental structures. The resulting slightly abstract, graphic depiction of the subject yields a very different feel than a detailed illustration or photographic representation.

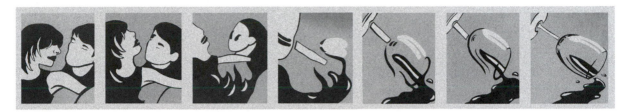

7.21
above: "Metamorphosis" by Donna Tappin. Courtesy of Professor Jon Krasner, Fitchburg State University.

This assignment involved creating a graphic interpretation of two subjects and choreographing smooth transitions between them in a storyboard.

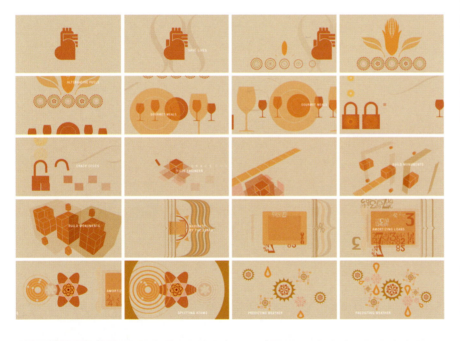

7.22
left: Frames from JWT "CET relaunch." Courtesy of L.inc Design and JWT Worldwide.

Historical Perspective

German Expressionist films shared many of the qualities of Expressionist painting, the most common one being stylized imagery. Many of the images' details were reduced through extreme tonal contrast, allowing viewers to focus on to the main forms that were distorted. The actors often wore heavy make-up and moved with exaggerated gestures to enhance the film's expressive quality.

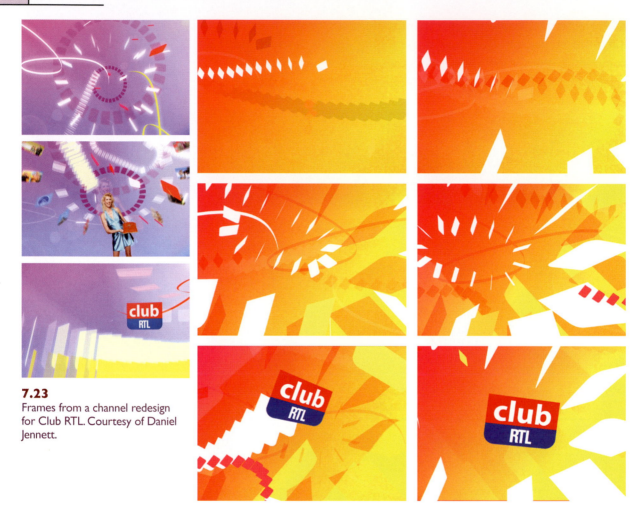

7.23
Frames from a channel redesign for Club RTL. Courtesy of Daniel Jennett.

Hatmaker, a Boston-based broadcast design studio, created a realm of cinematic splendor by combining highly stylized 2D images, halftone dot patterns, lush colors, and dimensional lighting to reflect the grandeur of "the event." In a spot for Cinemax's prime movie slot, Hatmaker put a fresh spin of the concept of the film projector lens by showing the emergence of light and color from darkness (**7.24**).

7.24
Frames from Cinemax's "See It Sunday." Courtesy of Hatmaker.

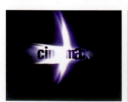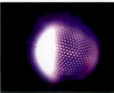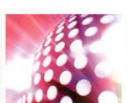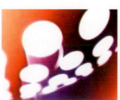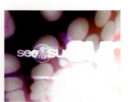

Nate Johnson's stop-motion animation "Censorship" demonstrates how graphic style can create meaning and enhance a message (**7.25**). According to Nate: "I was trying to convey a subtle message, that when literature, art, speech, or other media is censored, the whole message can be unclear, or lost entirely, which is ultimately a loss for the artist and the viewer. With my design elements, I wanted them to be confusing, skewing the message in a way the viewer would understand only after watching the entire video, much like a viewer would after seeing censored material. Also, I wanted the viewer to understand that we may not always receive the whole message from the media, and it is important to always get all the information as the sender intended, not a distorted or biased message." He adds: "I wanted to use multiple elements and techniques to obscure the message as much as possible, because censorship takes many forms. This gave rise to such elements as the circle and the bars but also inspired the use of type in silhouette and 'projected' on a piece of vellum. Each element added a different layer to the meaning of censorship, and hopefully a new understanding for the viewer." Bold letterforms melt into each other while being scrambled around inside the circle. This adds an element of deceit, conveying the idea that although a message can be strong, its clarity can be flawed. The rough, circular composition and black bars deliberately hide some of the typography by constricting the view and concealing letterforms.

7.25
Frames from "Censorship" by Nate Johnson. © 2012, Kent State University. Courtesy of Professor Gretchen Rinnert.

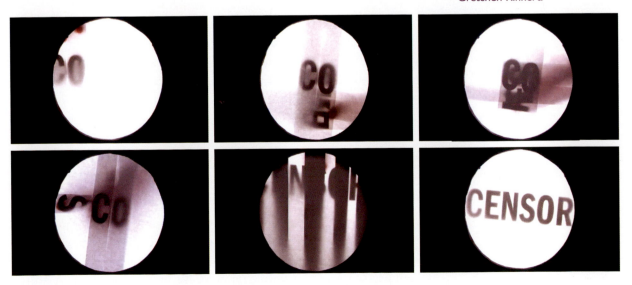

In an opener for the Sarasota Film Festival, Cory Fanjoy created an abstract visual style that suited a soundtrack of electronic music. Ink drops were used to mimic the free-flowing synths that are heard throughout the piece (**7.26**). According to Cory: "Instead of going with film and live action, we decided to take a different route. The goal was to create an immersive journey that represented the music we were animating to. We chose to experiment with it by challenging ourselves to only use background color, morphing geometric forms, and keyed ink drops in water. We were trying to build a sense of excitement in our audience by using strictly abstract visuals and a driving audio track."

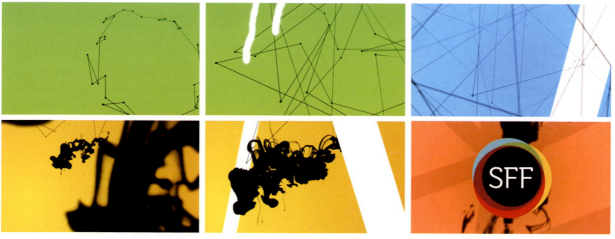

7.26
Frames from an opener for the Sarasota Film Festival by Cory Fanjoy. © 2012 Ringling College of Art + Design.

The hand-drawn quality of Alexis Copeland's end tag for Ringling College of Art + Design's ART Network Channel (**7.27**) evokes a feeling of process, invention, and aspiration to new ideas. Giving consideration to the demographic of the channel—Ringling students who are learning the principles of art and design—Alexis' inspiration came from the students themselves and their working artistic process. She wrote: "It all starts with a sketch, hand drawn. This style seamlessly fit within the development of the students and conveyed a message of development in the beginnings of the ART Network Channel."

A recent PSA for the American Red Cross entitled "Stuff" demonstrates how a simple idea and spare design approach can effectively express a concept and move an audience (**7.28**). Although the client's initial concept was to develop a simple typographic animation, director Andy Hall of Elastic design studio felt that was important to use humanity to

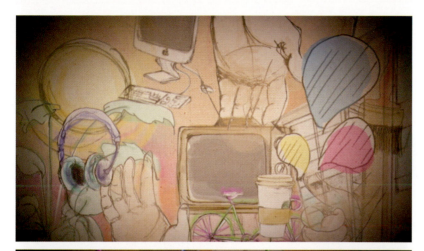

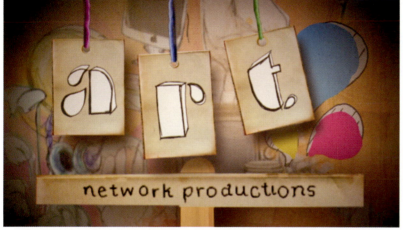

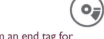

7.27
Frames from an end tag for
Ringling College of Art + Design's
ART Network Channel by Alexis
Copeland. © 2012 Ringling
College of Art + Design.

convey the message of giving donations in lieu of gifts. He pitched the idea of a digitally simulated claymation adventure featuring a character named Fred who becomes overwhelmed by the events of the holiday season. Flustered by the stress of receiving and giving so many gifts, he hauls the "stuff" between stores and his home, jamming it into boxes and closets. Suddenly, the idea hits him to pack "hope," "help," and "compassion" into a box to be shipped off to a person in need. The world that this character inhabits is very graphic, consisting of a red and white color palette and a simple backdrop. Considerable attention was given to the staging of the scenes which were composed and lit to feel sparing and theatrical. The simplicity of the figure and background imagery helps focus our attention on the stop-motion quality of the character's lifelike movements and childlike facial expressions, adding to the piece's charm and overall emotional impact.

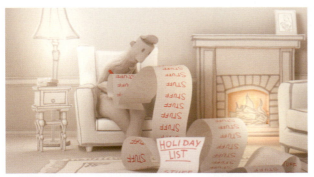

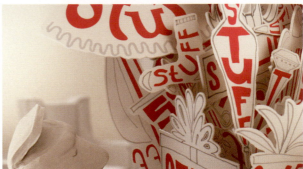

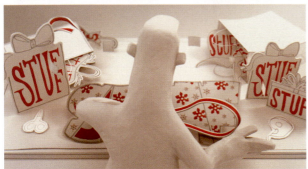

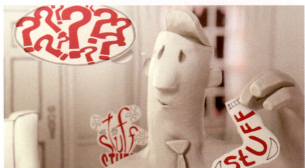

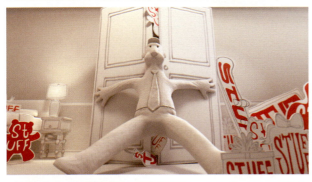

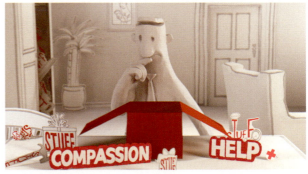

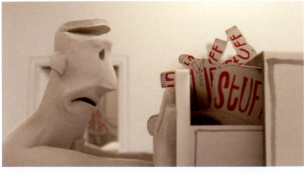

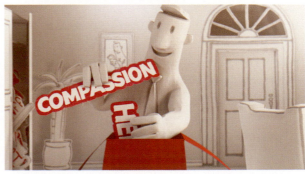

7.28
Frames from "Stuff," a PSA for the American Red Cross. Courtesy of Elastic.

The epic stop-motion masterpieces of Terry Gilliam and Tim Burton helped Elastic's director Andy Hall conceptualize the theatrical opening titles for the tenth annual Newport Beach Film Festival. Envisioning a celebration of movie studio fanfare, he aimed to create a narrative, referential journey that cleverly deconstructed and connected many of the classic animated studio preludes. According to Andy, "After much thought, it felt right to give the work a sense of style that tipped its hat to those opening fanfares—but in a whimsical way . . . and getting back to my roots in animation, I really wanted to create a unique vision that would make the opening something special in its own right." As a result, he achieved a hand-crafted style and stage-like quality in the scenes. Painted backgrounds and layers of scanned paint, wood, and fabric textures give detail to 3D models, replacing the veneer of CG images with a more organic and tactile quality that breathes nostalgia into the piece. Additionally, close attention to lighting ensures a new experience for viewers every time it is watched (**7.29**).

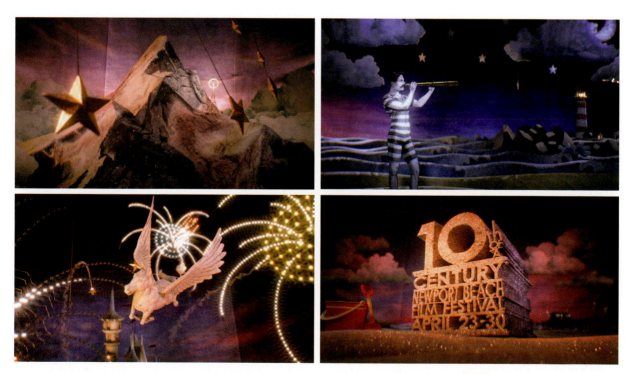

7.29
Frames from the opening titles for the tenth annual Newport Beach Film Festival. Courtesy of Elastic.

In Psyop's pitch for Glenmorangie, the hand-drawn quality of the storyboard imagery provides a highly impressionable tone within a loose narrative framework (**7.30**). John Saunders, one of Psyop's lead designers, worked in pencil and charcoal from photographs of a model in a variety of poses (i.e., marching up a hill, leaning against tree, holding up a glass). The goal was to express the idea of a master artist documenting the process of refining the taste of malt whisky.

7.30
Style frames from a pitch for Glenmorangie. Courtesy of Psyop.

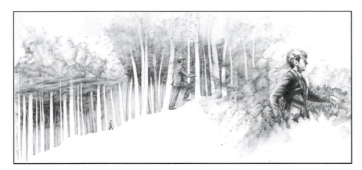
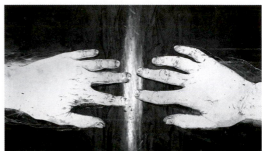
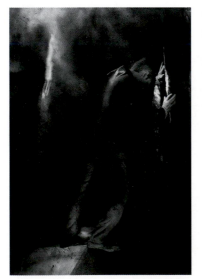
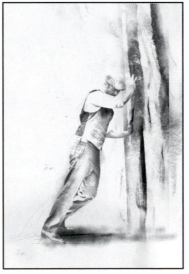
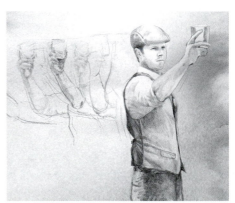

Each year, Blur Studios produces an in-house opening animation for its demo reel. On a trip to Venice, Italy, the design team was awed by structures such as St. Marks Cathedral and by the two-dimensional feel of Italian woodblock prints. They hired motion designer Adam Schwaab to model and animate elements, such as a lion, gondolas, and the Rialto Bridge. The final production is a stunning graphic interpretation of Venice, California and Venice, Italy (**7.31**).

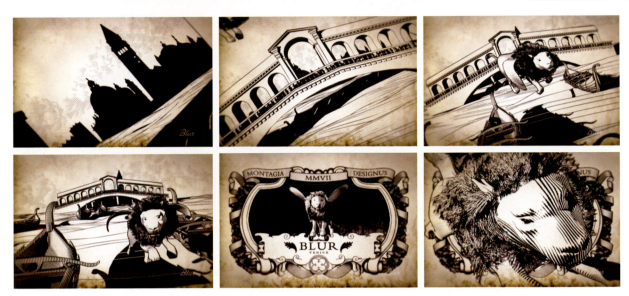

In the opening titles for the film *Splice* (2006), a photorealistic 3D rendering was achieved by combining texture mapping, particle effects, and digital compositing to emulate a mix of organic vegetable, animal, and human material (**7.32**). It took considerable planning to control the manner in which the actors' names would emerge like growths underneath the skin, since the goal was to make each title anatomically different to avoid redundancy. A specialist was hired to create complex particle effects. It took approximately five months for the 3D fabrication, due to the technical challenge of maintaining the quality of the particles at large and small scale, depending on the camera view and angle. It took another ten days to develop "skin tests" to master the desired level of ambiguity and convince the producers of the imagery's realism.

7.31
Frames from "Design Intro: Blur Venice." Courtesy of Blur Studios.

7.32
Frames from the making of the opening titles to *Splice* (2006). Courtesy of Kook Ewo.

See also Chapter 2, figure 2.10 on p. 31, Chapter 10, figure 10.26 on p. 361, and Chapter 13, figure 13.23 on p. 466.

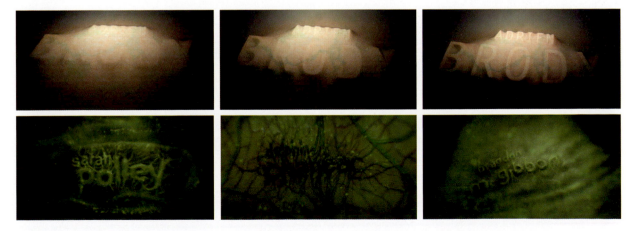

In 2010, four televised spots were aired as part of Honda's national campaign for its Accord Crosstour during ABC's Bowl Championship Series and CBS's Super Bowl. A spare design approach reflects this generation of sporty, crossover vehicles. The faceted 3D forms create a striking, stripped-down graphical language echoing the accompanying vibrant, rhythmic music. The stylish feel of the vignettes conjures up a personality that, without the trappings of photorealistic detail, reveals how modern lifestyles can fit conveniently with the Crosstour (**7.33 and 7.34**). The spot "Instruments" began with a few pencil drawings that established the retro, polygonal tone. The animation's vibrant colors and angular figures reflect the play between music and imagery that is intrinsic to the campaign. "Boxes" builds on this lively minimalism, linking the scenes with transitions driven by neon squares.

7.33
Frames from "Instruments" and "Boxes," two televised spots for Honda's 2010 Accord Crosstour campaign. Courtesy of Elastic.

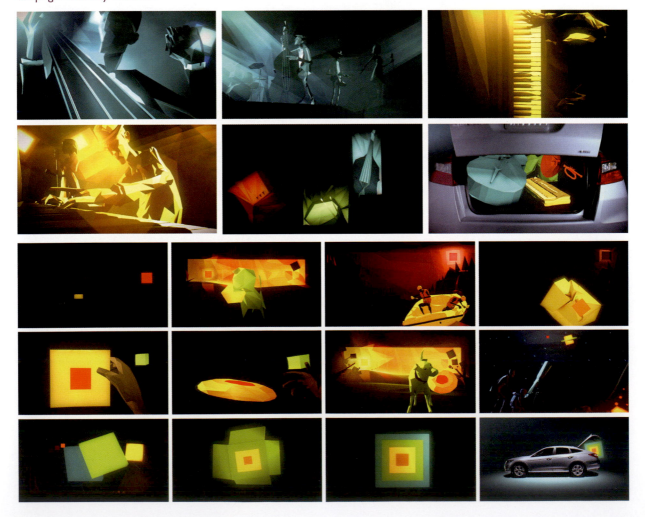

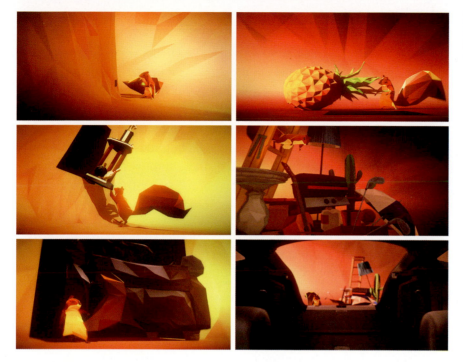

7.34
Frames from "Squirrel," a TV spot for Honda's 2010 Accord Crosstour campaign. Courtesy of Elastic.

A unique combination of 2D and 3D imagery was used in a fantastical opener for Raha Fit (**7.35**), a health program that has been featured on Star Majha's 24-hour news channel in Mumbai, India. This program offers helpful tips and advice on the topics of health and fitness. Rather than showing the program's scientific aspects, Varun Chawla built a dreamlike landscape composed of essential parts of the human body. The 3D models were texture-mapped from imagery derived from hand-created drawings. Only ambient lights were used to create a soft effect that a spotlight could not achieve. These decisions were made purely from an artistic standpoint to achieve a look that was somewhat two-dimensional and organic.

7.35
Frames from the show opener for Raha Fit, a health program in India. Courtesy of Varun Chawla.

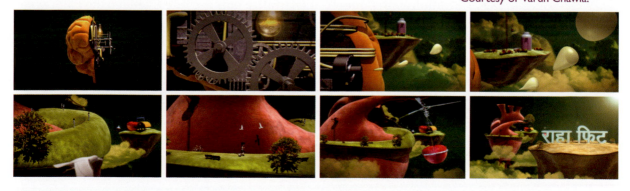

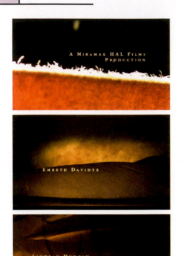

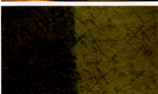

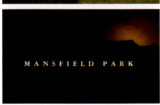

7.36
Frames from the opening title
sequence to *Mansfield Park* (1999).
Courtesy of Kemistry.

Live-Action Images

Over the past decade, live-action imagery has had a stronger presence in motion graphics due in part to the growing cinematic vocabulary of designers, and also to technical advancements in digital compositing. Today, graphic designers are expected to have a basic understanding of cinematic principles as they relate to film and video. Whether live-action content is appropriated or filmed, its qualities must contribute to the concept being communicated. Visually, it must work aesthetically with other graphic elements, regardless of the space that it occupies in the frame.

Factors that should be considered when working with live-action image content include the context of the project, filmic form, and cinematic properties such as tone, contrast, lighting, depth of field, focus, camera angle, shot size, and mobile framing.

Most film scholars consider the narrative, the documentary, and the experimental film to be the three major forms of filmmaking. Typically, the majority of of motion graphics presentations are narrative. For example, public service announcements address topics such as global warming, homelessness, and energy conservation to modify public attitudes and raise social awareness. Title sequences establish the context and tone of a movie or television program.

The narrative use of filmic images in motion graphics can be realistic or abstract. For example, Kemistry, a branding and communications agency in the UK, filmed eighteenth-century writing tools for the opening credits to *Mansfield Park* to express the distance between two sisters who exchange letters (**7.36**). In contrast, the abstract qualities of David Carson's television advertisement for Nike (**Chapter 9, figure 9.18 on p. 314**) fulfills the commercial's narrative purpose by enhancing the emotional impact of ideas of power and speed. The formal devices of shape, color, and texture serve as a basis for the composition's form.

Being aware of the form of your project is critical in determining the type of live-action content that will be used, how the content will be treated, and how it will fit into the larger motion graphics composition.

Historical Perspective

Narrative films tell stories. Fictional narrative films have been around since the invention of modern cinema.

The documentary is a continually evolving film form that attempts to capture reality. Biographies, live performances, interviews of footage compilations from government sources, and spoofs (or "mockumentaries") qualify as non-fictional documentary film. Early documentaries by the Lumière Brothers portrayed images of life such as a train entering a station or factory workers leaving a plant. Modern day documentaries include *A Brief History of Time* (1992),

Madonna: Truth or Dare (1991), *This is Spinal Tap* (1984), and *Best in Show* (2000).

Experimental films have been a significant part of the history of motion graphics. Often characterized by the absence of a linear narrative, they prioritize formal design aesthetics over story. One of the earliest examples is Man Ray's Surrealist film, *Emak Bakia* (1926). This lyrical piece interwove bizarre fragments, such as dancing legs, swimming figures, and electric turntables with out-of-focus light forms, silhouettes, and revolving type.

filmic properties

tone and contrast

"Tonality" and "contrast" are filmic properties that affect the reception of the image. "Tone" refers to the full range of values between extreme dark and light. "Contrast" refers specifically to the ratio of dark to light values. For example, high-contrast films that utilize low-key lighting are used in genres such as the horror film and the film noir, while many motion picture films use low contrast to achieve naturalistic lighting.

Like still photography, exposure, lighting, image processing, and digital manipulation can control tone and contrast. Exposure can be manipulated by widening or narrowing the lens aperture to govern the degree of light that passes onto the film. Narrow apertures that allow less light produce underexposed images, while wider apertures can result in overexposure. Lighting can also control tone, as described in the next section. In film processing, the chemicals used, the manipulation of the optical printer, and techniques such as tinting and hand-coloring can also change the tonal and chromatic appearance of black-and-white and color film stocks. Further, the range of tools and techniques for digital alteration offer endless visual possibilities.

Traditional filmmakers have altered exposure to achieve atmospheric effects. In the American film noirs of the 1940s, images were often underexposed to express darkness. Glass and gelatin filters on the camera lens or printer have also been used to manipulate the range of values and colors. Hollywood films of the 1930s often employed diffusion filters in glamour shots of women. The speed of the film stock also offers different tonal possibilities. Slow black-and-white film produces a wide range of mid-tone detail and soft contrasts, while faster film speeds yield greater image contrast, resulting in a reduced range of mid-tones.

7.37
In a public service spot for safe sex, the quality of low-resolution video footage has a dark undertone and graininess that conveys the urgency of the topic at hand. Courtesy of twenty2product.

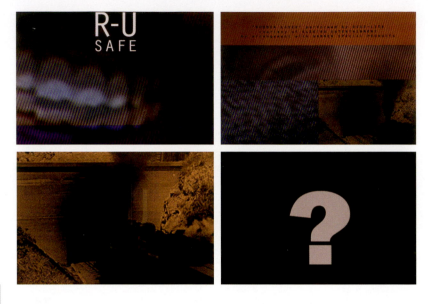

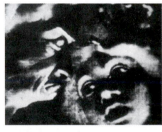

7.38
Alexander Alexeieff and Claire Parker's pinboard animation technique produced dramatic tonal and textural effects that resembled traditional etchings. In their film *Night on Bald Mountain* (1933), the forms have 3D, chiaroscuro-like qualities as they dissolve out of and back into space. Courtesy of Cecile Starr.

lighting

Lighting is one of the most important aspects of visual storytelling in cinematography. It must serve the story or concept, and in some cases, it can even become the story.

Although lighting can be subjective (some film directors prefer to shoot in natural light, others depend upon the effects of artificial lighting), over-lit scenes or deficient lighting can be blatantly obvious and detract from the story. Effective lighting, by comparison, is "invisible" to viewers, since it melds with the story.

Lighting is usually established at the time of capture, although lighting effects can be applied digitally during production and post-production. "Key lights" establish a subject's main illumination. High-key and low-key lighting can vary the emotional impact of the subject considerably. "Fill lights" are used to soften the contrast of the key light and provide illumination of the areas of an image that are in shadows to bring out subtle details (**see 7.39**). A fill light that is at least half the intensity of the key light will produce flat, low-contrast tonalities, while lower intensities can produce high-contrast images.

Key-to-fill ratios can be varied to give different effects. Low key-to-fill ratios, for example, are sometimes used for interior scenes with white or highly reflective surfaces, as well as overcast or snowy outdoor scenes. High key-to-fill ratios are used in night scenes to produce dramatic, suspenseful effects. Experimenting with the positioning of the key and fill lights can accentuate shadows to create the illusion of depth and texture. "Back lights" are used to illuminate foreground elements from the rear to visually separate them from the background. This technique often creates defining edges between the element and the background and sometimes causes these edges to glow (**see 7.40**).

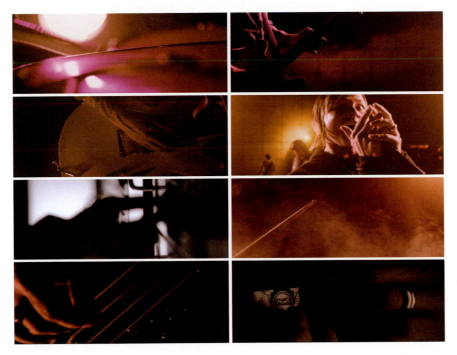

7.39
The sensuous low-key lighting in the music video for "Do It For Me Now" by Angels and Airwaves contributes to the emotional mood of the song. Fill lights are used to soften and extend the key light's illumination in order to bring out subtle image details. Courtesy of Shilo.

Traditional "three-point lighting" (or "portraiture-style lighting") positions a key light overhead at 90° downward and 45° to the side of the subject. The fill light is typically eye level and is angled about 45° toward the subject's opposite side. A back light is positioned between the subject and the background at a 45° angle to the subject's shoulder (**7.41**).

depth of field and focus
The devices of depth of field and focus can be used to enhance the emotional nature of an image or scene.

"Depth of field" is the distance in front of and behind a scene that appears to be in sharp focus. This property can be controlled by lighting, lens aperture, and "focal distance"—the distance between the lens and the object that is in focus. High-key lighting and wide-angle lenses tend to produce images with very large depths of field, while close-up shooting

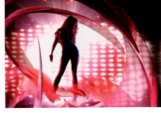

7.40
Frame from *ZOOM*, a network package for Times India's Zoom Channel. Back lighting is used to provide a separation between the subject and the background. Courtesy of Belief.

See also figure 7.80, on p. 254.

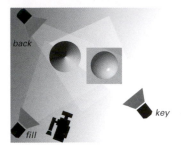

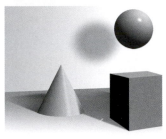

7.41
Traditional three-point lighting.

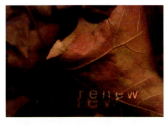

7.42
Shallow depth of field can be achieved by shooting close-up in low lighting conditions.

7.43
The technique of racking focus can create psychological links between elements.

in low light conditions often produces a shallow depths of field. As an alternative to cutting, restricting depth of field can focus an audience's attention on a particular aspect of a scene.

"Focus" refers to the "sharpness" of an image as it is registered in a scene. It is directly connected to, but not to be confused with depth of field, which involves the extent to which the space represented is in focus.

Giving elements at very different spatial depths or planes the same degree of focus produces "deep focus." Restricting the depth of field to keep only one plane in sharp focus produces "shallow focus." Shallow focus can direct the viewer's attention to a particular element of a scene and is quite commonly used in close-up shots to suggest psychological introspection, where the actions or thoughts of a character prevail over everything else. "Racking focus" involves changing the focus of a lens so that an element occupying one plane goes out of focus and an element in another plane comes into focus. This technique can steer audiences through a scene or link two subjects or spaces. It is often used to mimic a brief, fleeting glance from one subject to the other (**7.43**).

camera angle and shot size
Changing a camera's angle can affect the appearance of a shot and help determine the audience's point of view. A "bird's-eye view," for example, provides an aerial perspective of a scene, allowing us to feel as if we are hovering above a subject. High camera angles can make elements appear smaller, younger, weak, or harmless. Eye-level shots from five to six feet off the ground provide a frame of reference and capture the clearest view of a subject. Frontal angles tend to flatten elements, while three-quarter or profile angles reveal a greater three-dimensionality. Placing a camera below eye level and angling it upward establishes a low-angle shot. This effect is typically used to exaggerate the impression of height and inspire awe or excitement, making subjects appear larger, stronger, or nobler.

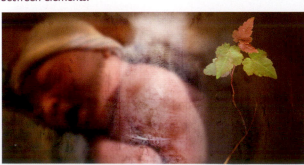

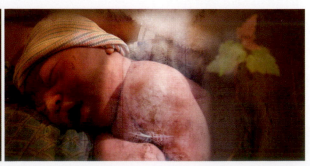

"Shot size" (or "camera distance") identifies how large an area is visible in the frame. An "establishing shot," such as a bird's-eye view, is taken from a great distance to establish an overall context. A "long shot" portrays a subject from a lesser distance to reveal aspects of the environment, such as architectural details. "Medium shots" typically frame people from the waist up and are used to focus attention on the interaction between two people or objects. "Medium-wide shots" are wide enough to show the physical setting where the action takes place, yet close enough to reveal facial expressions. "Over-the-shoulder shots" are used to focus the viewer's attention on one actor at the time during interaction. "Close-up shots" are designed to direct the audience's attention to facial expressions or object details, and are among the most powerful storytelling devices. An extreme close-up fills the screen with the detail of the subject.

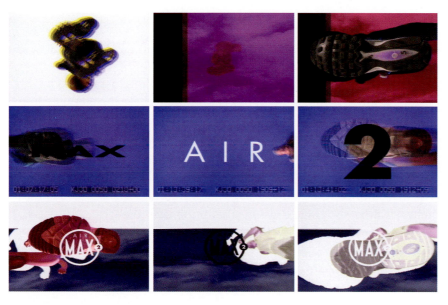

7.44
In an in-store video for Nike, an unusual low camera angle was used, with a runner shot from below to express the power and endurance of the Air Max shoe. Courtesy of twenty2product. © 1994 Nike.

See also Chapter 10, figure 10.35, on p. 367.

integrating live-action footage

Whether live-action content occupies the full frame or is incorporated as a smaller element into a larger frame, its presence can accentuate the message and mood being communicated.

At Massachusetts College of Art, Karolina Novitska created a cinematic visualization of Alzheimer's disease by revealing video content through layers of torn paper and fabric that are peeled away. The partially concealed quality of the footage accentuates the dreamlike, disoriented feel associated with this disease (**7.46**).

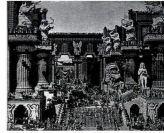

7.45
In D.W. Griffith's film *Intolerance* (1961), slow crane shots were employed to create a feeling of majesty and monumentality.

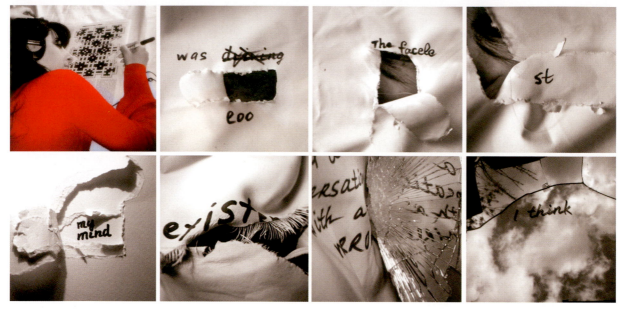

7.46
Frames from "Crossword" by Karolina Novitska, Massachusetts College of Art. Courtesy of Professor Jan Kubasiewicz. (Winner of 2006 Adobe Design Achievement Award).

"Videographers must be prepared to learn the language that film shooters have built over the last 100 years. It's a language made up of camera movements, filtering techniques, subtleties of focus, and depth of field. And it's a language coming into the video world through the gateway of HDTV."

—*Pierre de Lespinois*

In her other short film, "Sound Inside Out," Karolina takes us on a visual, 3D journey inside a pair of headphones where the elements of sound are broken down, translated into human dance, and displayed in different spaces. In this experimental approach to visualizing music, the treatment of the live-action image sequences is critical. Content is contained inside windows which we, the viewers, can travel between. Unusual color combinations, image negatives, and mirrored body parts create strange, surrealistic visions that punctuate the style and mood. Additionally, Karolina played with accelerated time, carefully synchronizing the movements to the beat of the music. At the end of the experience, we are pulled outside the headphones, from a colorful world of fantasy into a darker, sepia-toned reality (**7.47**).

The humorous title sequence for a music video competition called "Handle the Jandal" demonstrates a seamless integration of live-action figures into compositional spaces that contain a rich, eclectic mix of graphic information achieved by shooting them against a green screen (**7.49**). In contrast, combinations of small, free-floating, and contained live-action elements were seamlessly integrated with photography, illustration, and 3D graphics in the television show opener for *The Hungry Detective* (**Chapter 3, figure 3.12, on p. 45**). The idea of containing live-action images inside specific shapes is also evident in Kemistry's identity package for KLM Royal Dutch Airlines in-flight channels, (**Chapter 3, figure 3.48, on p. 61**) and in Onesize's commercial promos for Kentucky Fried Chicken aired on MTV (**Chapter 3, figure 3.61 on p. 69**). Corey Hankey's approach to integrating live-action in the design of a video diary assignment also restricted the images to "living" inside specific shapes (**7.48**).

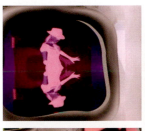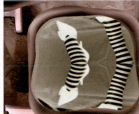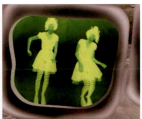

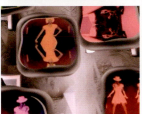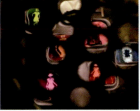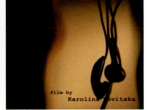

7.47
Frames from "Sound Inside Out." Written, performed, filmed, directed, and edited by Karolina Novitska, Massachusetts College of Art. Courtesy of Professor Jan Kubasiewicz.

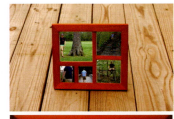

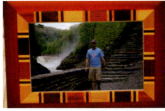

7.48
Video diary assignment by Corey Hankey. Rochester Institute of Technology. Courtesy of Professor Jason Arena.

A very different type of live-action treatment is seen in the captivating opening sequence to *Voxtours*, a German travel program that is known for reporting authentic and cultural aspects of holiday destinations (**7.51**). Velvet, a German broadcast and film design firm, effectively integrated video footage elements with stunning graphic visuals and type. The scale of the video clips varies as they animate inside the frame, establishing visual hierarchy. Some of the clips play in real time, while others have been slowed down to emphasize the romantic quality of the subject matter.

Nori-zso Tolson of twenty2product expressed the importance of live-action and graphic elements looking like they belong together visually. In the concept sketches for a Web site, Sky Bridge (**Chapter 6, figure 6.16 on p. 177**), the video and graphics were designed to perform a "dance." If this project had been carried to production, the movements in the video and graphic content would have been coordinated. For example, the translucent rectangle in the first sketch (on the left of **figure 6.16**) might be treated as a sliding window that moves across the footage, revealing or obscuring it. It becomes part of an overall pattern, like a tapestry that weaves the elements together, rather than just a box on top of a picture. The half-grayscale, half-color aspect of

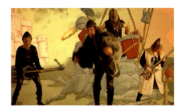

7.49
Frame from "Handle the Jandal." Courtesy of Krafthaus.

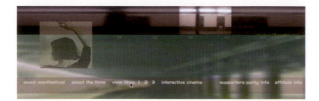

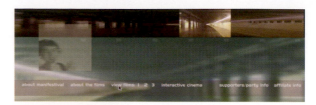

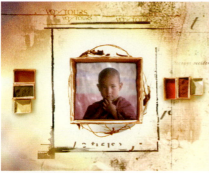

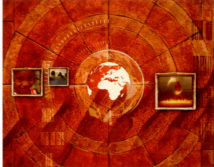

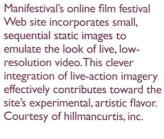

7.50

Manifestival's online film festival Web site incorporates small, sequential static images to emulate the look of live, low-resolution video. This clever integration of live-action imagery effectively contributes toward the site's experimental, artistic flavor. Courtesy of hillmancurtis, inc.

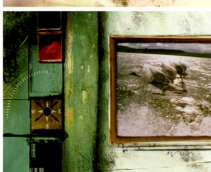

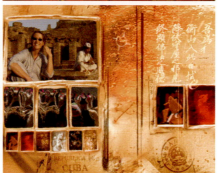

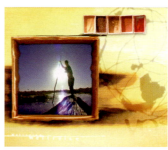

7.51

Frames from the show opener to *Voxtours*, a German travel program. Courtesy of Velvet.

the video adds diversity and interest to the composition. In the other sketch (on the right of **figure 6.16**), a larger, screened-back clip occupies the background space behind the rectangle which contains the more recognizable footage. The duality between these elements could suggest the same image shown from a different point of view or two juxtaposed images that deliberately conflict.

In the collaborative film entitled "Feelm," Javier Aparicio and Yahira Hernandez at Ringling College of Art + Design mixed non-objective graphic images with live-action footage. The flock of birds in the composition provides a smooth transition into the unexpected eye that peeps through a paint splotch. This footage introduces the element of surprise, keeping the viewer fully engaged (**7.52**).

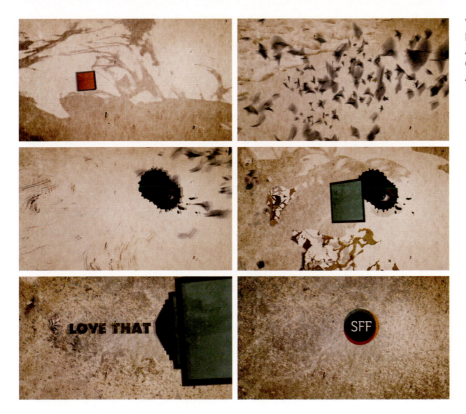

7.52
Frames from "Feelm" by Javier
Aparicio and Yahira Hernandez.
Courtesy of Ringling College of
Art + Design.

Typographic Style

Type is one of the principal means of constructing messages in graphic design. The meticulous craft of typography lives on in our digital millennium, and experimental forms of type design have leapt off the page and onto the screen. Numerous examples of typography in print, film, television, and digital media have demonstrated that the expressive treatment of letterforms can enrich visual messages.

Today, text is no longer limited to static, spatial forms of communication; it can make use of time and motion. These added dimensions further enhance its communicative power.

The typographic milestones that have been reached in print design have led to new innovations and forms of expression in the area of motion graphics. During the 1980s and 1990s, the impact of film titles helped kinetic typography become mainstream in the eyes of the public. The opening credits to the Warner Brothers film *Altered States* (1980) used a simple transformation of the two words of the title to express the film's

*"Graphic design is painting
with typography."*
—Paul Rand

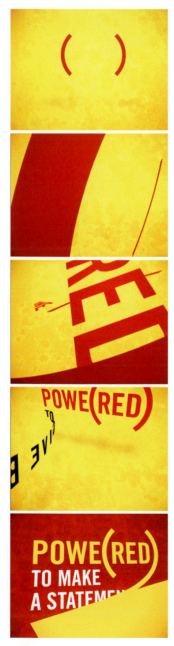

7.53
Storyboard design for Sprint's (RED) campaign to raise awareness and money for the fight against AIDS in Africa, by Chris Swenson, California Institute of the Arts.

theme. The sequence begins with a transparent pattern, the title words slowly overlapping each other as they move across the screen. Superimposed on them, the film's credits appear in white. The letterforms become smaller against the dark background, as if the camera is pulling away. Finally, the complete title, "Altered States," sits alone against a vast, black background. In the opening credits to the film *True Lies* (1994), four faint blue streaks of light begin rotating in space, revealing the letterforms of the word "true." These letters continue rotating in space as four individual, three-dimensional cubes, revealing the word "lies," which is reversed on black on the adjacent face of each cube. Such a simple effect succeeds in illustrating the title's oxymoron. Kyle Cooper deliberately manipulated the text in David Fincher's psychopath serial killer thriller *Se7en* (1995) to make it look scratchy and carelessly handwritten. In addition, the type moves in and out of focus with a play of camera angles (see also **Chapter 2, p. 24**).

Distinctive handwriting became a trademark of Cuban-born filmmaker Pablo Ferro, who earned his reputation as a master of title design, alongside Kyle Cooper and legendary designer Saul Bass. Ferro is best known for his revitalization of hand-lettered film titles. For the classic *Dr. Strangelove* (1964), he conceived the idea of filling the frame with letters of different sizes and weights. Ferro's elongated lettering is also apparent in his contemporary film titles, such as *Stop Making Sense* (1984), *Beetlejuice* (1988), *Good Will Hunting* (1997), *Men in Black II* (2003), *For Love of the Game* (1999), and *My Big Fat Greek Wedding* (2002).

The role of expressive kinetic typography is to represent a concept in a visual format. Rather than being literal, it can convey an intended emotion through its unique graphic impact and its movement in space. In many cases, it no longer reads as text but is perceived as physical shapes that create complex semiotic experiences through metaphor and motion. An example of this is the opening animation to *Black Day to Freedom* (2005), a 100-page book and short film released by Beyond, a company that aims to raise greater awareness of social issues through design, illustration, and motion. The motivation behind this project was to educate people and raise awareness of the global displacement of people and the challenges they encounter in obtaining their freedom. Shown at animation festivals worldwide, the film portrays the displacement of refugees, asylum seekers, and immigration detainees by showing a city in turmoil and the tragedy of a young family. Dutch graphic designer Joost Korngold of Renascent created an emotionally charged film that combines typography and motion to express the tension and discomfort associated with the content (**7.58**). The words "liberty" and "beauty" race across the frame, as if determined to escape from a prison-like background of dark lines and shapes that loop with abrupt back-and-forth movements. An emulated camera zoom then brings us closer to the words "darkness," "violence," and "kill," which fade into the foreground space and animate off the left edge of the frame in succession. As we zoom back out, the red letterforms "l," "a," and "c" fly off of the word "black" in the title, and portions of the title are intercepted with stuttering, nervous movements. The composition's dark, underlying tone, coupled with the deconstructed treatment of the type, serve as a metaphor for the frustration and despair that displaced people encounter as a result of unfair and discriminatory practices.

In a graduate assignment that involved memory and recollection, Eddy Roberts' projected typography addresses childhood games and their deeper meaning. His piece entitled "Axis and Allies" leads the viewer into a shifting interior psychological space that recalls games of youth and the emotions associated with them. The text examines the underlying power structures inherent in many children's games and their implications in the adult world—dominance and submission, aggression and passiveness, winning and losing (**7.55**).

In her film "Crossword," Karolina Novitska expresses the mental and emotional state of Alzheimer's disease by manipulating handwritten text in an environment consisting of images of shattered glass, poured liquids, and layers of fabric and torn paper. At times, words are crossed out and appear partially concealed, with overlying images and textures to portray the conceptual element of confusion. This is enhanced by a soundtrack that plays in reverse during the film's "dream" sequence. Variations of scale, orientation, transparency, and the speed with which the type animates are well choreographed to interact with the moving and changing images (**7.46, on p. 234**).

Apart from communication, typographic form and motion can be explored on a purely formal, aesthetic basis. For example, a distinctive combination of clear and abstracted letterforms and a bold color palette helped position Court TV's daytime show branding by adding depth and energy to the composition (**7.56**).

"Typographic communication today is not a tutorial, not a how-to. It's a critical review of twentieth century typographic design. It aims to open eyes and minds to the potential power of typography..."

—*I-Hsuan Wang*

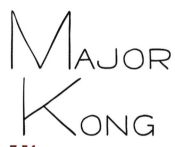

7.54
Inspired by the hand lettering of film title designer Pablo Ferro, Yuji Adachi developed a font called Major Kong.

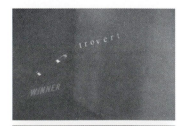

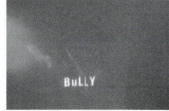

7.55
Frames from "Axis and Allies" by Eddy Roberts, University of Houston. Courtesy of Professor Beckham Dossett.

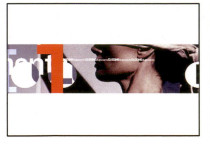 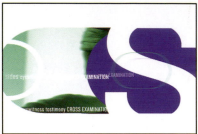 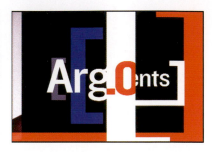

7.56
Frames from Court TV's daytime show package. Courtesy of ZONA Design.

See also Chapter 3, figure 3.24, on p. 51.

7.57
Opening title to *Lawbreakers* on the History Channel. Courtesy of ZONA Design.

The type echoes the shattered glass and sepia-tone photos.

We have been conditioned to view typography as distinct from images. One of the keys to innovative type design is to consider text elements as pure forms that consist of positive and negative shapes. For example, letters such as "d," "g," and "o" contain closed shapes, while others such as "s," "f," and "w" are open shapes. Closed and open spaces emerge when letterforms are juxtaposed or superimposed. Further, letterforms that are in close proximity create negative shapes between them, sometimes referred to as "counterforms."

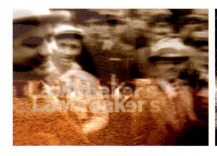 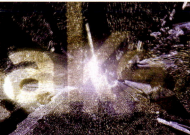 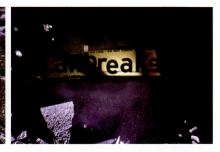

7.58
Frames from the opener to "Black Day to Freedom." Courtesy of Renascent.

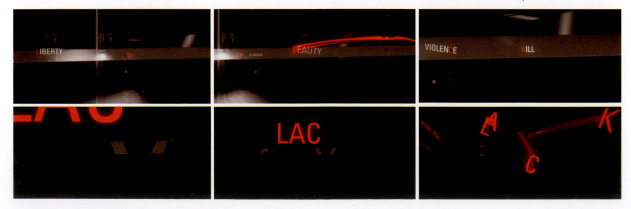

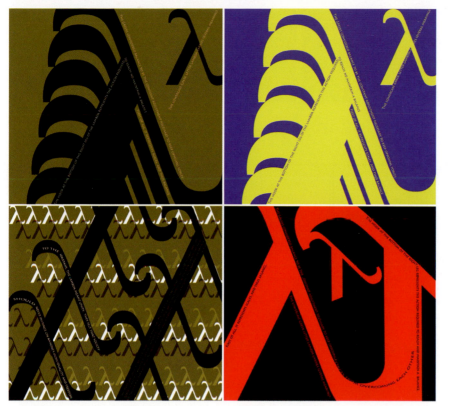

7.59
In a beginning-level typography assignment, students investigated the aesthetic qualities of form by developing studies that integrated display type, body text, and a symbol from the Greek alphabet. Design by Michael Michaelides. Courtesy of Professor Jon Krasner, Fitchburg State University.

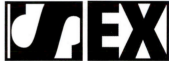

7.60
Closed and open spaces emerge from the positive and negative shapes and spaces of letterforms. Letterforms that are in close proximity create negative shapes or "counterforms."

In my beginning motion graphic design class, students animate their first, middle, and last initials while keeping in mind pictorial aspects of composition, including positive and negative form, asymmetry, relative scale and orientation, and figure–ground (**7.61–7.63**).

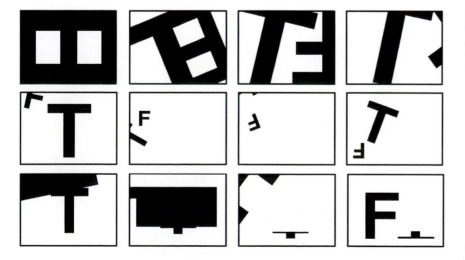

7.61
Frames from a kinetic typography assignment by Takafumi Fujimura. Courtesy of Professor Jon Krasner, Fitchburg State University.

7.62
Frames from a 4D type project by Kathy Beck. Courtesy of Professor Jon Krasner, Fitchburg State University.

Accelerated movements of the small letterforms appear to be trampling down the larger letter.

7.63
In a dynamic type assignment, students were challenged to convey a word's intrinsic meaning in print through implied motion. Courtesy of Professor Jon Krasner, Fitchburg State University.

7.64
Frames from a "self referential type" assignment by Ryan Hammond. Courtesy of Professor Eddy Roberts. Ringling College of Art + Design.

7.65
Frames from a "self referential type" assignment by Jonah Page, Ringling College of Art + Design, Professor Eddy Roberts.

7.66
Frame from an animated creative writing project by Amanda Woodward. Courtesy of Professor Eddy Roberts. Ringling College of Art + Design.

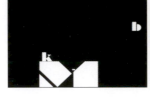
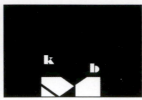
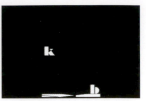

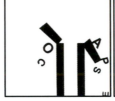
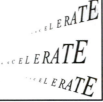
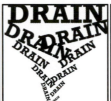

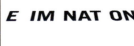
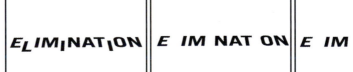

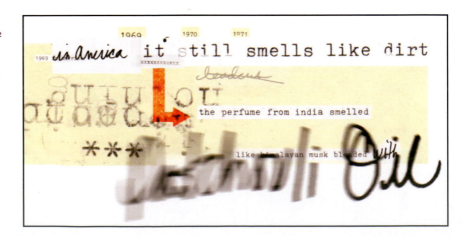

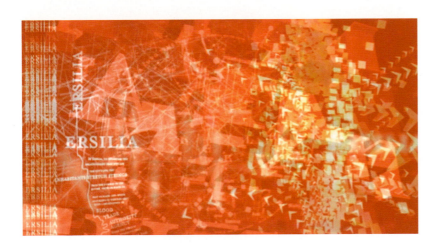

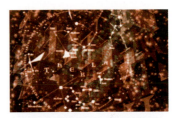

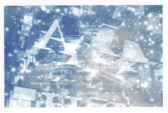

7.67
"Invisible Cities" by Ryan Duda. Courtesy of Professor Jan Kubasiewicz, Dynamic Typography (2003), Massachusetts College of Art.

The use of deconstructed type here heightens spatial depth and creates a highly textured graphic style.

Typography played a significant role in a design conference opener for the Munich-based agency TOCA ME. The team at Dvein studio in Barcelona worked closely with type designer Alex Trochut to develop a series of monograms that would represent each of the artists who attended. Known for conducting experiments that push the limits of typography to the extreme, Trochut sculpted monograms from what appears to be styrofoam. The use of real, three-dimensional letterforms with stick-on type and images of melting materials achieves a powerful abstract representation of artistic growth (**7.68 and 7.69**).

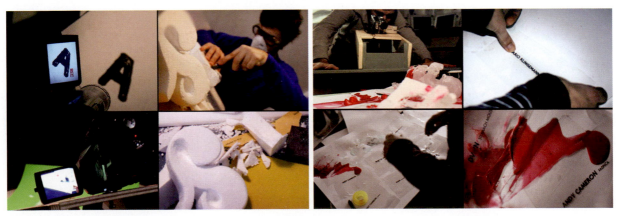

7.68
Photos showing the making of the opener for TOCA ME design agency's 2008 annual conference. Courtesy of Dvein.

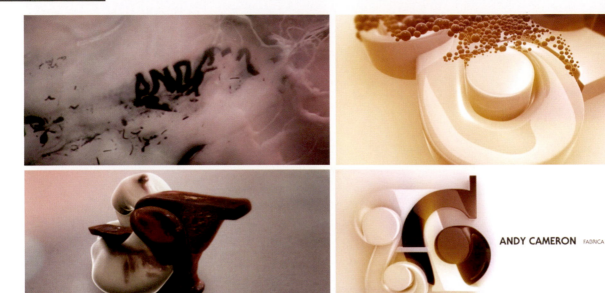

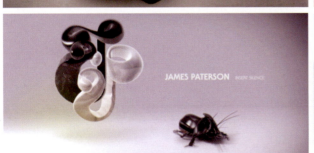

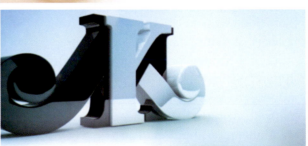

7.69
Frames from "Beyond Surface,"
the opener for TOCA ME design
agency's 2008 annual conference.
Courtesy of Dvein.

See also Chapter 12, figure 12.3,
on p. 418.

7.70
Frames from an animation based
on a poem by the Nigerian poet
and novelist Ben Okri. Layers of
copy mimic the voiceover that
sometimes echoes as if in a large
chamber, creating a sense of
deep audio space. At times, the
type remains static to emphasize
camera movement. Courtesy of
Kook Ewo.

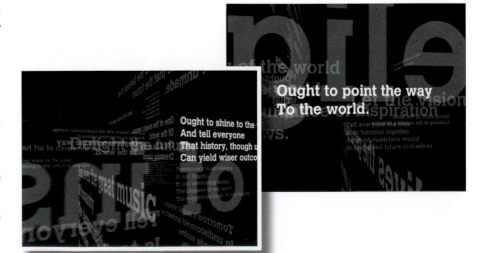

expression through typeface

In addition to a font's ability to look good and move smoothly, it has the ability to express the tone of the imagery in a composition. For example, Dutch motion graphic designer Joost Korngold is consistent in his preference for using simple, sans serif fonts such as Univers Condensed to complement the graphic style of his images (**7.71**).

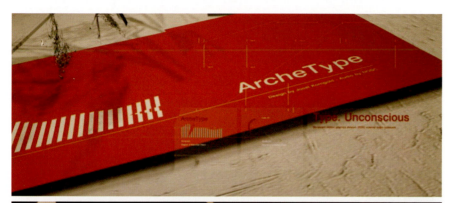

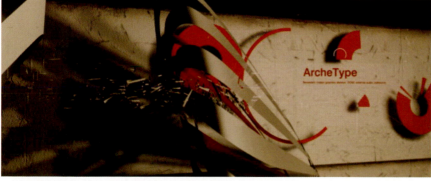

7.71
Frames from *ArcheType*, "an inherited pattern of thought or symbolic imagery derived from the past collective experience and present in the individual unconscious." Courtesy of Joost Korngold. © Renascent.

"Type is like actors to me. It takes on characteristics of its own. When I was younger, I used to pick a word from the dictionary and then try to design it so that I could make the word do what it meant."
—*Kyle Cooper*

On a conceptual level, choosing fonts that appropriately express your message is key to achieving effective communication. In 2006's rebranding of the peacock network, NBC Magic's font choice was Klavikac (**Chapter 3, figure 3.50, on p. 62**).

In 2007, Viewpoint Creative design agency designed a new and unusual typographic treatment for the opener for the third season of Discovery Channel's *Deadliest Catch* series (**7.72**). This documentary-style program depicts the incredibly brutal conditions and lifestyle that commercial crab fishermen experience aboard their fishing boats in the Bering Sea during the Alaskan and Opilio crab fishing seasons. Discovery requested a bold and crisp look that conveyed the content of the program from a human perspective. After experimenting with at least ten different typefaces, styles, weights and lowercase and a mixture of lowercase and capitals, Viewpoint decided that an uppercase typeface would yield a more powerful cinematic experience. The distressed, eroded quality of the letterforms, along with their traditional looking old-style serifs, gives the typeface a physical, tactile quality that reflects the hardships the fishermen encounter out at sea. The type's centered alignment and positioning is straightforward and in accordance with the visuals. Its partial transparency allows the background images of sky and sea to show through. This treatment effectively conveys the ominous, mysterious atmosphere of the series.

7.72
Frame from the title sequence to *Deadliest Catch. Deadliest Catch* is a trademark owned by Discovery Communications, LLC. Image courtesy of Viewpoint Creative and Discovery Communications, LLC and used by permission of Discovery Communications, LLC.

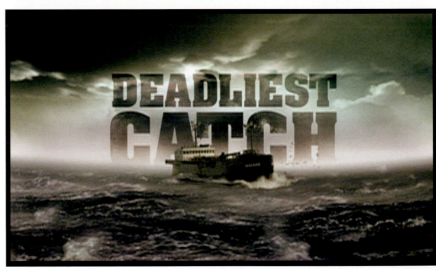

"I have seen beautiful commercials where the photography is unbelievable, but then some graphic designer comes in and throws on some cheesy animation or bad type. They've taken this wonderful series of images and made it pedestrian."

—Kyle Cooper

Directed by Michael J. Bassett, the epic film *Solomon Kane* (2009) tells the story of an English mercenary who owes his soul to The Devil's Reaper and redeems himself by fighting evil. The concept behind the title sequence is to express a character—represented by the camera—who is sometimes turned upside down, always stretched between good and evil. In the storyboard for the film's ending titles, the fonts at the beginning of the sequence begin as hieroglyphs that represent evil and gradually shift to the Latin font, Poetica, to symbolize redemption (**7.73**). Additionally, the subtle outer glow of the letterforms and the use of extreme 3D perspective, cropping, and distortion complement the menacing black, white, and red color scheme.

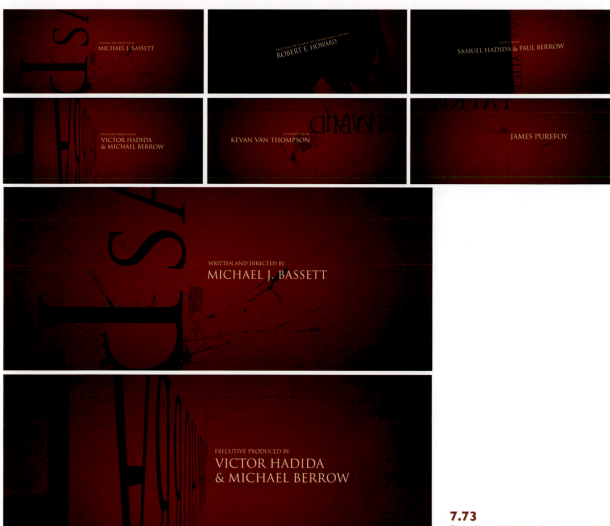

7.73
Storyboard frames for the ending titles to the film *Solomon Kane* (2009). Courtesy of Kook Ewo.

For the opening credits for *Fracture* (2010), French title designer Kook Ewo chose the commercial typeface Dinengrschift 1451, a sans serif font used for road signage in Germany. The structure of the letters, especially when set in uppercase, portrays the only seemingly perfect world of the film's main character, who feels "oppressed by an invisible evil which eats away at him" (http://www.imdb.com). The stylized, thin structure and generous tracking between letterforms further conveys the tension of the plot and reinforces the minimalist underwater backdrop which shows the killer's point of view (**7.74**).

"I sincerely love typography. It's the simplest way to express complex, subtle ideas. And of course a good title sequence can be based only on typography."
—*Kook Ewo*

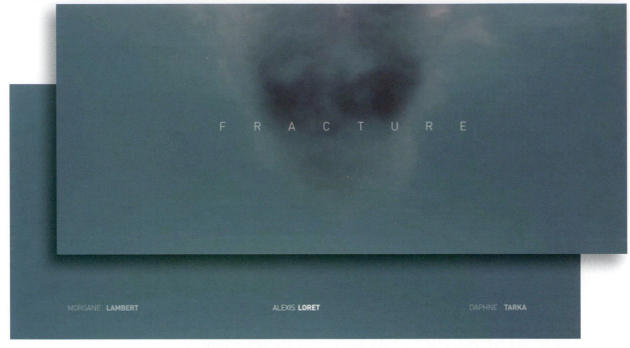

7.74
Frames from the opening credits to *Fracture* (2010).

The opening titles for Bassett's *The Horde* (2009) also rely heavily on typographic impact. Kook Ewo explains: "This is a zombie movie and the directors asked me to make a title logo with an urban feeling." Incorporating dust and debris into the background and foreground letterforms helps imply the film's action-packed violence. Hiragino, a basic Apple font, is the typeface used (**7.75**).

7.75
Frame from the titles to *The Horde* (2009). Courtesy of Kook Ewo.

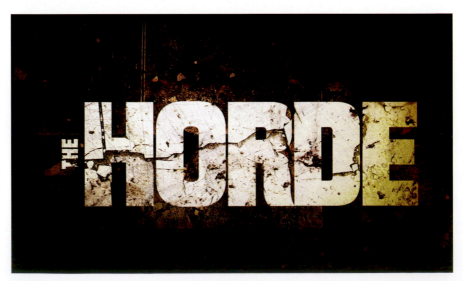

The typography in the National Museum of American Jewish History's installation "Innovation and Expansion" is contextual, strongly inspired by the calligraphy of the nineteenth century. Versions of Bodoni (Old Face and Book) are used for the body text on the exhibit's surrounding walls and for the ornaments on its map. The sans serif typeface Univers Condensed is used for the labels and subtitles. Specific details are highlighted with the slab serif font Constructa (**7.76**).

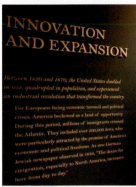 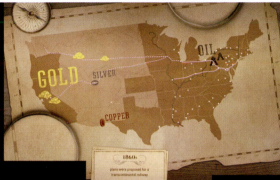

7.76
"Innovation and Expansion," an installation containing motion graphics at the National Museum of American Jewish History. Courtesy of Local Projects.

See also Chapter 5, figures 5.26 and 5.27 on p. 147 and p. 148.

type anatomy 101

The basic anatomy of today's letterforms originated over 500 years ago, when monks were hunched over in scriptoriums engaged in the painstaking process of hand-lettering Bibles. Understanding the "anatomy" of letters gives you an appreciation for the integrity of typeface design and makes it easier for you to identify and select a given font as part of purposeful design decisions.

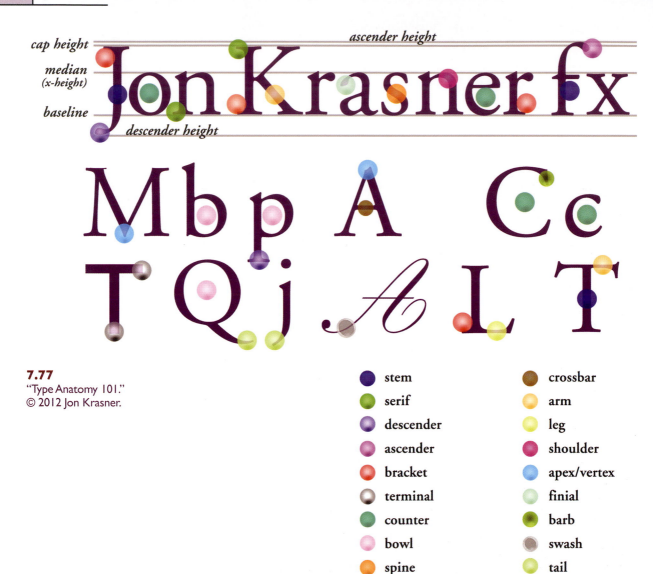

7.77
"Type Anatomy 101."
© 2012 Jon Krasner.

- stem
- serif
- descender
- ascender
- bracket
- terminal
- counter
- bowl
- spine
- crossbar
- arm
- leg
- shoulder
- apex/vertex
- finial
- barb
- swash
- tail

typeface classifications

A well-combined variety of fonts can contribute to your overall message or story, set emotional tone, and bring expression and harmony to your design. Since every font has distinct qualities with regard to proportions, line weights, widths, directional slants, and so forth, it is important to recognize the basic classifications of fonts. The classifications described here demonstrate responses to advances in technology, changing commercial needs, and aesthetic trends. Within these classifications, each typeface has its own expressive personality.

Blackletter:

Blackletter typefaces are derived from the handwritten manuscripts Medieval Europe. The Gutenberg Bible, the first book to be printed with movable type, was set in a Blackletter face to emulate the look of these illuminated manuscripts. Examples include Cloister Black and Goudy Text. Approximate date: 1450.

Oldstyle:

Oldstyle typefaces were developed during the Italian Renaissance to replace the heavy gothic feel of the Blackletter style. Based on Roman inscriptions and lowercase letterforms used by humanist scholars for book copying, they are characterized by bracketed serifs and a low contrast between thick and thin strokes. Examples include Bembo, Garamond, Caslon, Jenson, and Palatino. Approximate date: 1475.

Italic:

Italic typefaces mimic the look of Italian handwriting. This classification has unique features not found in upright roman faces. Venetian printer Aldus Manutius and his type designer Francesco Griffo are credited with creating the first italic typeface. From a practical standpoint, this condensed style allowed more words per page. Approximate date: 1500.

Script:

Script typefaces have been designed to replicate engraved calligraphy. Due to their high degree of embellishment, they are not recommended for lengthy body texts. Examples include Kuenstler Script, Mistral, and Snell Roundhand. Approximate date: 1550.

Transitional:

Transitional typefaces were designed to refine Oldstyle letterforms, as a response to advances in casting and printing. Thick-to-thin relationships are exaggerated, and bracketing between the stem stroke and the serif is lightened. Examples include Cloister Black, Goudy Baskerville, Bulmer, Century, and Times Roman. Approximate date: 1750.

Modern:

Modern typefaces were developed in the late eighteenth century as a further rationalization of Oldstyle fonts, and continued in use through most of the nineteenth century. They are characterized by extreme contrasts between thick and thin strokes. Examples include Bodoni, Didot, Bell, and Walbaum. Approximate date: 1775.

"Letters are things, they are not pictures of things. While the generic letter 'A' may indicate a variety of sounds, the lowercase 'a' as rendered in Bembo is a specific character, different in form and sensibility from the lowercase 'a' rendered in Bauer Bodoni, Serifa 55, Helvetica, or Futura. All five convey the idea of 'A'; each presents a unique esthetic."

—Eric Gill

The following type foundries can be used as a resource for learning more about and purchasing typefaces:

Adobe Type Library
http://store.adobe.com/type

Bitstream
http://www.bitstream.com

Linotype
http://www.linotype.com

Castletype
http://www.castletype.com

Identifont
http://www.identifont.com

Square and Slab Serif:

In response to the needs of advertising in commercial printing, Square Serif fonts were designed with heavy bracketed serifs and minimal variation between thick and thin strokes. When the brackets were eventually eliminated, this style became known as Slab Serif. Examples of Square and Slab Serif fonts include Clarendon, Memphis, Rockwell, and Serifa. Approximate date: 1825.

Sans Serif:

First introduced by William Caslon IV in 1816, Sans Serif typefaces became widespread, beginning in the twentieth century. These fonts are described in five classifications: Grotesque, Neo-Grotesque, Geometric, Humanist, and Informal. Within each classification, fonts share similarities in stroke thickness, weight, and basic geometry. Examples include Helvetica, Arial, Futura, Univers, Frutiger, Gill Sans, Meta, and Akzidenz-Grotesk. Approximate date: 1900.

Serif/Sans Serif:

Serif/Sans Serif typefaces are the most recent development, based on the notion that a family of fonts can be designed with and without serifs. Examples include Rotis, Stone, and Scala. Approximate date: 1990.

Images, Live Action, and Type

The possibilities that exist when graphics, live-action footage, and type are combined are endless. They can push the limits of artistic experimentation and expression. In a Sunday morning show package for *Breakfast with the Arts*, ZONA Design moved away from a classical mindset toward a younger demographic by integrating video, images, and expressive typography (**7.78**). The piece begins with a coffee mug that is lifted from a table, leaving a ring on the surface. Director Zoa Martinez states: "The exhilaration, the caffeine syndrome begins. Typography evolves and comes jetting out from under and behind the mug enumerating the many subjects covered in the programming; music, performance, the Arts. The combination of this typography and images of performers juxtaposed with arrangements of flowers, film strips, unusual perspectives, action painting, an architectural stage, and a DJ spinning wax, provide the color and texture that give the package its youthful exuberance."

In **figure 7.79,** Blur's show package for Nickelodeon's *Kids' Choice Awards* 2006 combines 3D imagery, such as ribbons and smoke trails, with 2D graphics. These elements were carefully choreographed and composited to create a rock n' roll circus theme that embraced psychedelic poster art from the Fillmore neighborhood of San Francisco in the 1960s. This piece was geared toward kids between the ages of 8 and 13.

"ZOOM," Belief's network package for Times India's Zoom Channel is another example of how live-action images can be integrated with three-dimensional graphics and type. A cross between E! and Fine Living, this example of India's expanding broadcasting industry offers a behind-the-scenes look at celebrity lifestyles. A surreal discotheque environment, combined with slick, exotic images of glamour and glitz, conveys the sexy feel of this new Indian network (**7.80**). In the first sequence, Belief shot a car on a black stage to avoid any reflection or spill problems. Next, they filmed various types of moving foreground and background elements to provide flexibility for the compositing stage. The studio was split into three areas to obtain all of the shots

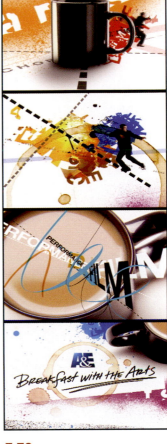

7.78
Frames from a show package for *Breakfast with the Arts.* Courtesy of ZONA Design.

7.79
Frames from a graphics package for Nickelodeon's *Kids' Choice Awards* 2006. Courtesy of Blur.

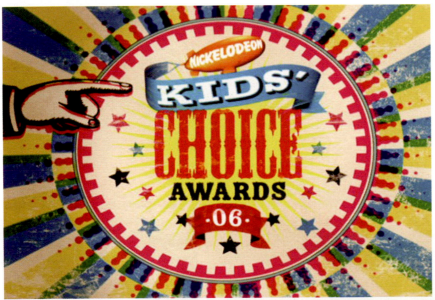

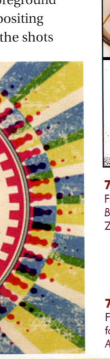

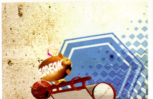

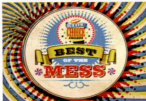

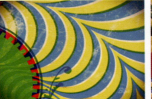

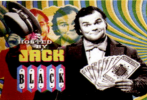

needed: a green screen area on rises to get low camera angles, an enclosed area covered in black that allowed the team to wet the floors and control the smoke while shooting the cars, and an interior night-club set where they suspended large metal sheets on revolving motors. According to Mike Goedecke, Belief's founder and executive creative director: "What's really unique about Zoom is the fact that it's an Indian network, but the execs there wanted it to evoke a very western sensibility in style and design. We definitely achieved this with our upscale night-club/lounge setting." Richard Gledhill, Belief's creative director, stated: "It was imperative that the look of this new channel be glossy and exclusive, yet mysterious. By shooting the talent in a dark environment with lots of hard edge lighting, we were able to achieve that effect. The exotic car and limousine really helped to pull off the exclusive, VIP nature of this new channel."

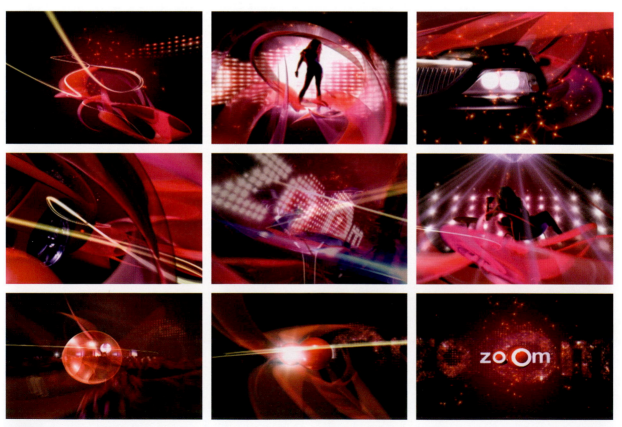

7.80
Frames from "ZOOM," a network package for Times India's Zoom Channel. Courtesy of Belief.

In the opener for TV Prima's *PARTIE* (**Chapter 8, figure 8.37, on p. 282**), video footage is combined with strong typographic elements against a stark, white background. The uppercase sans serif font portrays the strength of the formally-dressed talk show's moderators as they enter the studio to prepare for a live broadcast. The elemental nature of this modern-style typeface echoes the simplicity of the composition and allows enlarged parts of the letterforms to interact with the imagery. For example, part of a letter may act as a mask to reveal a portion of the moderator, or serve as a ground that defines the space he occupies.

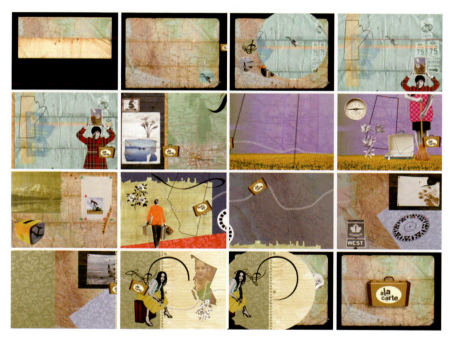

7.81
Frames from the show opener to *À la carte*, a television series on Radio-Canada Television about places around Western Canada.

Two-dimensional graphics and type were animated and then composited with live-action video clips that run throughout the piece. Courtesy of Studio Blanc.

See also Chapter 3, figure 3.18, on p. 48.

Assignments

image and motion #1

overview
Visual style and movement can work together to enhance the message that images can convey.

Create an animated self-portrait based on your shoes. Try to plan the motion according to the subject's visual style. Your goal is to create a dynamic interplay between the style of the image and its movement.

stages

Begin by creating a rough storyboard in pencil that demonstrates how motion will reflect the graphic style of the image. Critique the sketches, and develop revised editions that clarify the types of movements and transitions that will occur. Recreate the shoes conventionally through drawing, painting, or collage. Animate the image using any combination of frame-by-frame and interpolation processes. If you decide to develop an animatic first, be open to new ideas. You can go back to your initial sketches if you wish to explore other possibilities.

specifications

Background elements or supplemental images and type are prohibited, since your goal is to focus on the style and movement of the image alone. The duration of the composition should be between 15 and 20 seconds. It is critical that you are able to tell a story within a specified time frame, so be sure to adhere to this limit.

considerations

Consider how movement complements the image's visual style. Lifelike, non-linear motions that accelerate and decelerate generate a different feeling than mechanical, uniform motions. Be sure to give attention to the birth and death of the image. Consider possible interaction of the image with the frame's edges as it moves.

image and motion #2

overview

Create an animation based on a group of objects that have personal, sentimental value for you.

stages

Collect 5–8 small artifacts that describe your past, present, or future. Write a short 30–50 word explanation for each item. Be descriptive, yet open to interpretation, allowing readers to use their imagination. Your description can be literal or metaphorical. Consider the role of language, gender, inflection, and mood. Next, recreate the artifacts using any combination of conventional and digital processes. Keep in mind that the graphic style of the content will set the mood. Images can be symbolic, metaphorical, or iconic, ranging from realistic to abstract or any form in between. Animate the imagery using a combination of frame-by-frame processes and interpolation.

specifications

The content should be created and scanned at a size that is large enough to ensure stable quality if it is to be scaled up in the animation.

considerations

Consider how visual style and movement together can support and enhance your message. Be imaginative and expressive!

animation and live-action

overview

Investigate and develop purposeful relationships between animated images and live-action content.

stages

Film 10–15 seconds of a figure moving in space. Import the footage into a program of your choice, and create 2–3 additional images consisting of lines, geometric shapes, or a combination of lines and shapes.

In a composition integrating the live action and graphics, animate the graphic elements in a way that relates to the movements of the live-action footage. Create a second study, this time choreographing the animation to complement the live-action motion.

considerations

Consider how supporting and contradictory motions influence your overall perception of the animation. How might the relationships between animation and live-action imagery work together?

type as kinetic form

overview

Animate the first, middle, and last initials of your name.

specifications

Use one sans serif typeface and black and white only. Your goal is to focus strictly on form and motion. The duration should be 10 seconds. It is critical that you are able to tell a story within the specified time frame.

stages

Develop a rough storyboard and critique it as you would critique a film script. Create an edited iteration that conveys the events more clearly.

If you decide to create an animatic, be sure to clarify the types of motion, camera angles, and transitions that will occur. Keep an open mind and be prepared to deviate from your original ideas. You may decide to go back to your initial sketches and explore other possibilities.

considerations

Consider how positive and negative form changes through motion and transition. Give attention to the manner that elements appear and leave the frame. Consider the interaction of the letters with the frame's edges.

typographic fortunes

overview

Create a self-portrait based on a message in a fortune cookie, using only letterforms, numbers, and punctuation marks.

stages

First, enjoy a good meal at your favorite Chinese restaurant. Be sure to get a fortune cookie on your way out! Recreate the fortune by cutting out letters from printed sources such as newspapers and magazines and scanning them. Animate the type using frame-by-frame or interpolation processes.

specifications

All elements should be appropriated from books, newspapers, magazines, and other printed materials.

considerations

Consider the relationships between the geometric qualities of the type and its movement in space. Be deliberate in choosing typefaces that best express your message.

metamorphosis: form and transition

overview

Develop a metamorphosis based on two images that express different meanings to create a third meaning (or "tertium quid").

stages

Begin by creating two graphic interpretations of two different objects using black marker or cut pieces of construction paper. Both images should show a high level of graphic refinement achieved by reducing detail and simplifying form. Then create a five-step metamorphosis that illustrates a smooth transition between the beginning and end images. The fourth image should be a fifty-fifty synthesis of the first and last image. This project requires careful planning through the development of concept sketches.

specifications

Each step of the metamorphosis should be the same size and no larger than 10 inches vertically or horizontally. Use only black, white, and two gray tones since the focus is on pure form and implied motion.

considerations

Allow your imagination to run wild, and don't be afraid to inject humor. Consider implied primary (object) and secondary (camera) movement. Think about how figure and ground will be treated, and give attention to the background. Background shapes can be made to look static or dynamic by implying motion.

Chapter Summary

The union of images and typography functions as a visual language in a time-based environment.

Form can symbolize or suggest ideas, imply depth, and help establish hierarchy. Value and color can elicit mood and express emotions to ellicit a desired audience response. Understanding color contrast and how color can evoke emotional responses according to individual, gender, and cultural factors can help you make sound color decisions. Texture and pattern can also add contrast and depth while providing viewers with the sensory experience of touch.

Live-action video has a strong presence in motion graphics due to the growing cinematic vocabulary of designers and technical advancements in compositing. Filmic properties such as tone and contrast, and cinematic properties such as lighting, depth of field, focus, camera angle, shot size, and mobile framing can serve the story, and in some cases become the story.

Kinetic typography can also express concepts and convey emotions. In many cases, type can be perceived as physical shapes that create complex semiotic experiences through metaphor and motion. Choosing fonts that appropriately express a message is also critical to achieving effective communication. Understanding the basic anatomy of letters and general classifications of fonts gives you an appreciation of the integrity of typeface design and makes it easier to identify and select fonts as part of purposeful design decisions.

The unusual creative possibilities that exist when animated images, live-action footage, and typography are combined can push the limits of artistic experimentation and personal expression.

8

the pictorial composition
designing in space

There are many ways that pictorial compositional space has been interpreted, constructed, and deployed in motion graphics compositions. Innovative creative strategies have given designers the potential to overcome the homogeny of the fixed rectangular frame that has been associated with conventional film and television production.

"The painter's canvas was too limited for me. I have treated canvas and wooden board as a building site, which placed the fewest restrictions on my constructional ideas."
—*El Lissitzky*

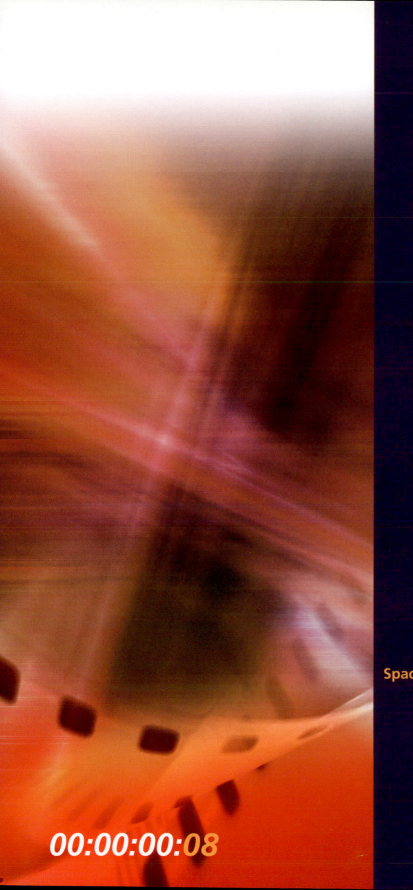

00:00:00:08

Space and Composition: An Overview

Space is interpreted through the prism of composition—in this case, pictorially (as opposed to sequentially). Spatial composition is the blueprint from which elements are organized. In painting, it describes the two-dimensional canvas. In graphic design, it is the viewing area of a poster or an interface. In motion graphics, it describes the environment containing the action—the frame.

Through history, artists have explored different types of space because of its affinity with the content they are trying to express. "Primitive space" (or "flat space"), for example, is characterized by a flat surface that has little or no depth or perspective; it does not have three dimensions. Utilized by many early and untrained artists, it often has a decorative quality, emphasizing pure design, flat colors, and repetitive patterns. During the late nineteenth century, many French painters and poster designers were influenced by Japanese prints and began an evolution toward using primitive space in western painting, a tradition that continues today. "Illusionistic space" (also referred to as "Renaissance space" or "traditional space") was developed during the Italian Renaissance by painters such as Piero della Francesca, Filippo Brunelleschi, and Leonardo da Vinci, who used the devices of linear and atmospheric perspective to depict forms receding into space. (Brunelleschi is credited with inventing linear perspective.) "Modern space" was developed by the Post-Impressionist painter Paul Cézanne during the early twentieth century. His unique method of comparing and contrasting planes of color resulted in a combination of primitive and illusionistic space, which had a major impact on twentieth-century art. Modern space was further developed by Jackson Pollock, whose drip paintings resemble an infinite or all-over space.

Compositional styles have differed across various cultures and art movements throughout history. Japanese painting, for example, delights in the generous use of negative space and intuitive placement of elements within an asymmetrical layout. Art Nouveau, Arts and Crafts, and Vienna Secessionist artists were characterized by their use of arbitrary compositional arrangements. De Stijl and Constructivist painters carried abstraction to its furthest limits in their quest for rational, geometric order.

Experimental film pioneers of the 1920s gave close attention to how pictorial space was organized. Hans Richter, for example, saw animation as a logical step in expressing the kinetic interplay between positive and negative forms, and considered the film frame as a space that could be divided and "orchestrated" in time. In films like *Rhythmus 21* and *Rhythmus 23*, motion is choreographed in horizontal and vertical directions and through scale changes of the forms to establish depth. Non-objective lines and rectangles move in alignment, as figure–ground is disrupted due to the changing interplay between positive and negative space. Taken out of context, individual frames from Richter's *Rhythmus* series demonstrate a liberal use of negative space, an interplay between figure and ground, and a purposeful alignment of shapes to the frame's edges (**see Chapter 1, figure 1.12, on p.9**).

Principles of Composition

Today, designers continue to explore how compositional principles can be used to express concepts and emotions and to establish clear and effective communication.

unity

Most of us seek unity in our day-to-day experiences, creating order of "the big picture." In design, unity is an underlying principle that refers to the coherence of the whole—the sense that all of the parts are working together to achieve an overall harmony. It creates a sense of cohesiveness within a composition and is one of the primary ways designers create stability.

gestalt theory

Originating in Germany around 1912, the Gestalt school of psychology explored how elements in a composition could comprise an integrated "whole," achieving a sense of harmony. The conviction of this theory is that the whole is greater than the summation of its parts. For example, a guitar is made up of strings, a body, a neck, tuning knobs, and so forth. Each of these components is unique and can be examined individually. The guitar as a single unit, however, has a greater presence than its parts. This overall perception gives a sense of purpose and completeness to an object or to a composition and is communicated through certain visual cues such as balance, proportion, and proximity.

Theorists have indicated that humans have a propensity to group things together unconsciously by formulating connections and relationships among and between elements in a design.

case studies

Pictorial unity in a motion-based environment can be established through consistency in the the visual properties of elements, such as value, color, and texture. Additionally, it is achieved in the treatment of elements with regard to their relative scale, positioning, orientation, and proximity in the frame.

In a teaser for Artevo, the largest fine art collection in North America, the shapes of the logo are cleverly repeated and animated according to various themes that recur throughout the composition. Each theme creates a different mood and ambience through changing backgrounds, colors, and typography. The consistency in the use of the logo and similarity of background imagery, as well as the repetition and variation of both background and foreground elements and colors, maintain a sense of order and unity (**8.1**).

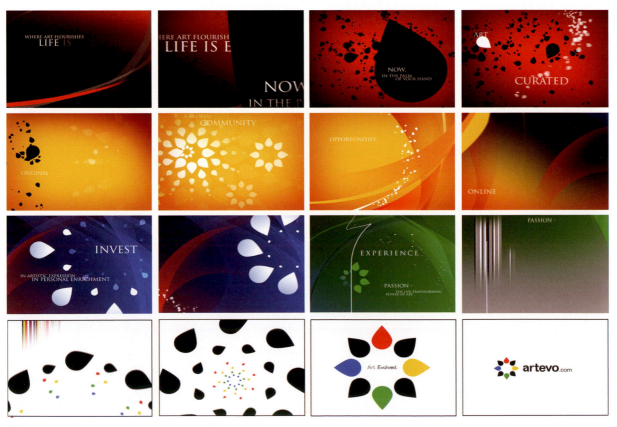

8.1
Frames from a teaser for Artevo.
Courtesy of Studio Dialog.

The program opener for *Entertainment Weekly*'s "The Biggest Little Things of 2004" (**8.2**) achieves unity through repeating patterns of stripes that are interwoven between graphic silhouettes of figures. Between each transition there is consistency in the relationships between the colors, patterns, and subjects presented in each scene.

8.2
Frames from the show opener to *Entertainment Weekly*'s "The Biggest Little Things of 2004." Courtesy of NAILGUN*.

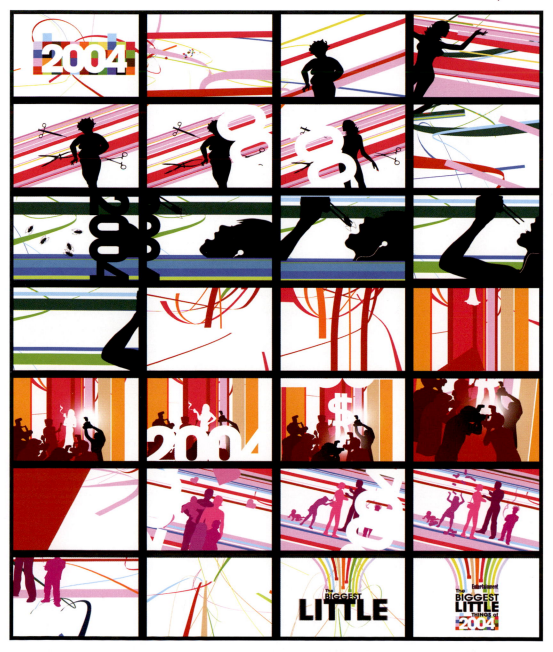

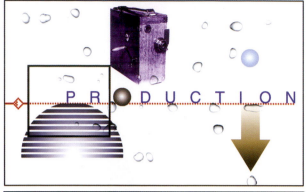

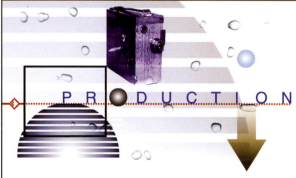

In **figure 8.3**, various images ranging in graphic style, shape, color, size, and spatial proximity are unified by a large screened object in the background. This solution is commonly used in complex compositions containing multiple levels of information.

balance

Balance is a primary component of our day-to-day lives and one of the primary methods of achieving unity. We seek balance in our experiences to create a sense of order in our work and play, finances, family life, and so forth. Within the frame, balance suggests a sense of cohesiveness. It is one of the primary devices that designers use to create stability or instability.

"Symmetrical balance" is the division of a space into parts that are equal in size and weight. Human beings are symmetrically balanced by a vertical plane. Synthetic objects such as cars, tables, and chairs also exhibit symmetry. In the early days of film, titles were usually placed symmetrically in the center of the frame. "Radial balance" is a type of symmetrical balance in which images are emitted from a central focal point (for example, ripples from a stone thrown into water). "Crystallographic balance" (also referred to as "all over balance") contains numerous focal points that are strategically arranged into a repeating pattern. Quilts, for example, consist of crystallographic patterns that are organized into gridlike designs. The random effect of scattered confetti also produces a sense of crystallographic balance. However, there is too much uniformity without enough variety.

Balance does not always necessitate symmetry. For instance, a small object that is visually engaging in color, texture, or shape can balance a much larger object that is visually less exciting. "Asymmetrical balance" is an informal type of balance that achieves a dynamic division of space. It can be used to create a more dynamic sense of organization and to establish emphasis. Asymmetrical compositions allow better use of negative space, giving designers greater compositional freedom.

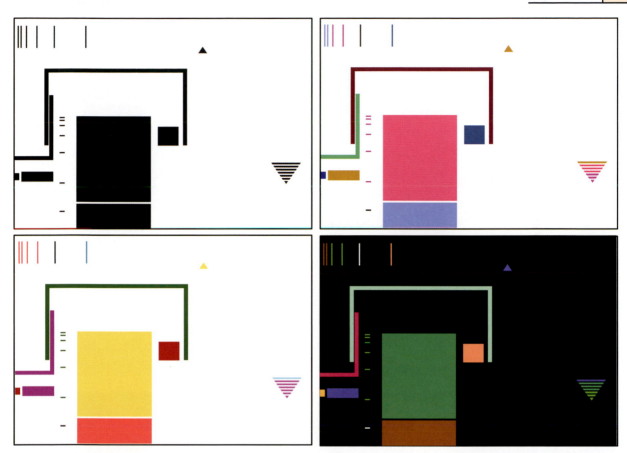

figure and ground

"Ground" (also known as the "picture plane") defines the surface area of a composition; "figure" refers to the subjects that occupy the foreground space. Throughout history, works of art have ranged from clearly defined delineations of foreground and background elements (for example, a figure posing in a landscape) to the complete eradication of figure and ground, where space becomes ambiguous to the viewer. Abstract Expressionist and Cubist paintings have continuous two-dimensional space, where negative and positive forms are inter-changeable (**8.5**). In motion graphics, figure and ground relationships can change as the positioning, orientation, and sizes of elements vary over time. For example, the compositions in **figures 8.6** through **8.8** emphasize the structural and dynamic use of positive and negative shape interaction. As the elements shift in the frame, foreground and background spaces become interchangeable.

8.4
In this asymmetrical composition, varying shapes and spaces are unevenly dispersed, creating an active and energetic picture plane. Color is used to counteract the dissimilarity of shapes, sizes, and positions to achieve balance.
© 2012 Jon Krasner.

8.5

left: *Eketete and Erbeybuy* by Bruce P.O. Onobrakpeya.

top right: *Igbo and His People.* by Jacob Afolabu.

bottom right: *Chaos* by Amir Ibrahim Mohed Nour.

Courtesy of the Harmon Foundation Collection and NARA.

These contemporay African artworks range from a clear interpretation of figure–ground in which foreground and background relationships are clearly defined to the obliteration of figure–ground through the use of heavily layered visuals varying in color, texture, and opacity.

8.6

Frames from a network relaunch of the SCI FI Channel. Courtesy of Flying Machine.

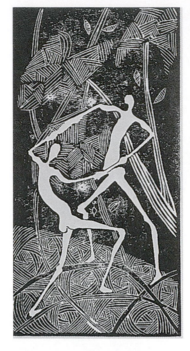

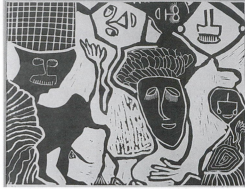

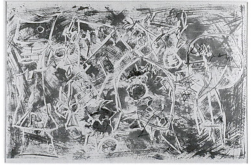

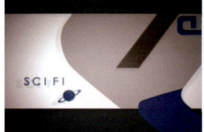

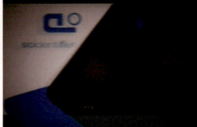

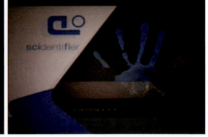

8.7

Frames from a fictional station ID assignment by Jim Reynolds. Courtesy of Professor Jon Krasner, Fitchburg State University.

The black shape on the red ground becomes the ground that holds the red shapes.

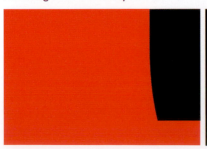

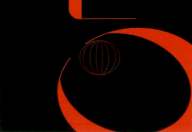

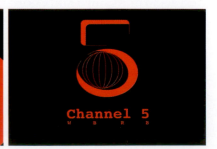

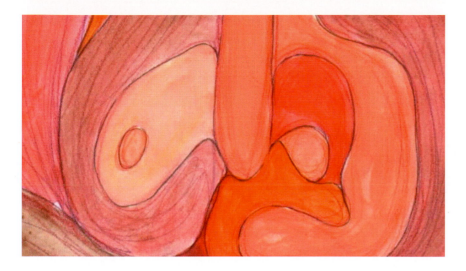

8.8
Frame from "Mijn wit plafond en ik" ("My White Ceiling and I") (2002) by Violette Belzer.

An interchangeability between foreground and background forms eliminates the sense of figure and ground. © il Luster Productions.

negative space

Related to figure and ground is the concept of positive and negative space. Positive spaces are areas that are occupied in a composition; negative spaces are areas that are unoccupied or empty. Negative space (also referred to as ground) is analogous to white space in print design and is evaluated using the same criteria that applies to the rest of the elements in a design—unity, balance, contrast, etc. Negative space can add to or detract from a composition's overall balance and rhythm and can provide visual emphasis and eye movement.

Dramatic or subtle, negative space can affect the viewer visually and emotionally. In the series of network identifications for the Middle Eastern network Al Jazeera Sport, live footage of athletes are isolated from their natural environment and integrated into minimal, dream-like landscapes to depict duality between figure and space, allowing us to focus on the subject's "bare essentials" (**Chapter 6, figure 6.46, on p. 193**). Designers often use extensive negative space to create a feeling of sophistication and elegance for upscale brands of clothing, shoes, and cosmetics to express their high level of quality to viewers. An example of this is German designer Daniel Jennett's in-store video presentation for ESCADA, an international luxury fashion group specializing in women's fashion (**Chapter 10, figures 10.39-10.40, on p. 369**).

From an aesthetic standpoint, negative space provides breathing room for the eye, making the composition feel less dense, confusing, or over-whelming. It is important to realize that negative space is not just

"One can furnish a room very luxuriously by taking out furniture rather than putting it in."
—*Francis Jourdain*

Foundation drawing classes often disregard the fundamental principle of composition. Although students are taught to master proportion, to model with light and shadow, and to be expressive with the medium, they are seldom provided with adequate information on how to plan their picture space. As a result, negative space is poorly planned and does little to contribute toward the expression of the piece.

empty space that serves as a ground for positive components; rather, it has weight and mass and should be deliberately planned. In a series of program IDs for *Unsolved History*, a show on Discovery Channel that investigates mysteries of the past, negative space is strategically constructed to organize free-floating photographic images, graphic images and symbols, and typographic information (**8.9**).

8.9

Frames from a series of program IDs for *Unsolved History* (2002–2003). Courtesy of Discovery Channel and Viewpoint Creative.

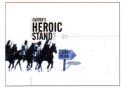
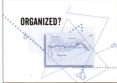
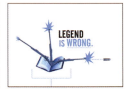
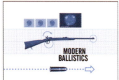
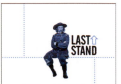
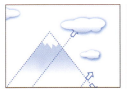
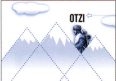
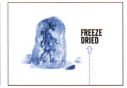
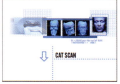
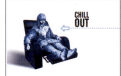

size and scale

Many compositional possibilities can be derived from manipulating size and scale. "Size" relates to the format (or the frame) that elements are placed in; "scale" describes the relative relationships that exist between elements. Objects that are in scale give the appearance of belonging together; objects that are out of scale exhibit a visual imbalance. Whether objects are static or moving, both devices play a major role in composition. Size can contribute conceptually to the message being communicated by establishing weight or mass. For example, an object may appear "heavier" or "lighter" depending on the dimensions of the frame it occupies (**see figure 8.10**). Size can also help improve composition. The use of large elements gives you the opportunity to divide the frame into positive and negative structures. These, in turn, can establish a more active sense of "architecture" in which other elements can be positioned and directed to move.

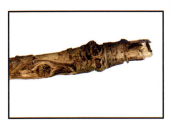

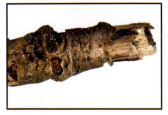

8.10

An image can appear "heavy" or "light" depending on the dimensions of the frame it occupies.

edge

Throughout art history, edge relationships have been a fundamental component of design. They define a composition's parameters and play a critical role in guiding eye movement and establishing hierarchy. Early Egyptian manuscripts, which had consistent design formats with rigid sets of compositional rules, strongly emphasized the relationship of visuals to the borders of the picture plane. Edges were given considerable attention, determining the placement of illustrations and hieroglyphics. Horizontal bands containing small illustrations were often placed across the top, while larger illustrations and adjacent hieroglyphic text columns hung from the top border (**8.11**).

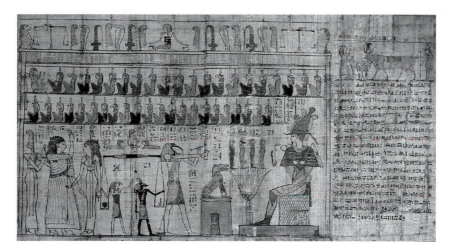

8.11
"Psychostasia" ("Weighing of the Souls"). *Book of the Dead of Tsekhons*. Ptolemaic period. Museo Egizio, Turin © Erich Lessing/Art Resource, NY.

In motion graphics, the frame's edges provide you with four possible points of entry and exit. For example, an object can touch an edge, and its movement can be strategically aligned to it, reinforcing the vertical or horizontal nature of the frame. In a television commercial for Citibank, David Carson's alignment of elements to the edges of the frame emphasizes its horizontal and vertical structure (**8.12**).

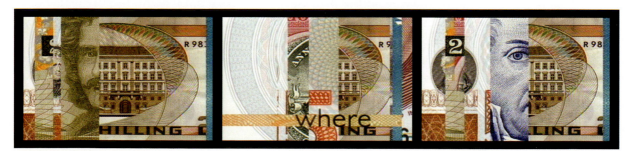

direction

8.12
Frames from a commercial for Citibank. Courtesy of David Carson.

Direction has powerful control over how a viewer's eye moves within a space. It helps establish a composition's sense of purpose by providing a point of entry and exit for the viewer, and in complex compositions it can be used to organize, connect, or separate dominant and subordinate elements. Direction can also be used as a means of counteracting motion in order to stabilize eye movement within the frame. For example, the movement of a figure in one direction can be neutralized by another figure's movement in the opposite direction. In **figure 8.13**, the horizontal motion of an element is stabilized with a vertical wipe that introduces a new background image. In **figure 8.14**, a large letterform animates from the bottom left corner toward the top right edge of the frame. A series of smaller typographic items, aligned parallel to the image's path of motion, animate into the frame from the left edge, drawing the eye diagonally upward.

8.13
A horizontal movement across the frame is counteracted by a vertical transitional wipe.

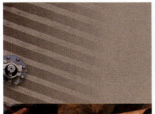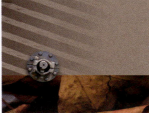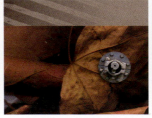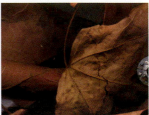

contrast

Visual contrast is one of the most important principles of graphic communication and expression. It can introduce variety into composition, clarify or simplify information, intensify meaning, or refine the message being communicated. Standard types of contrast are scale, value, color, shape, surface, proximity, and orientation.

Scale is the most elemental and widely used form of contrast. Along with value and color, it can emphasize a point of interest or create the illusion of spatial depth. In visual perception, smaller objects naturally appear to recede into the background, while larger objects appear closer. Extreme scale differences can capture the imagination of the viewer. For example, taking an object out of its original context and juxtaposing it with other objects that have been altered in size can dramatize its impact, as evidenced in **figures 8.15** through **8.17**. In these compositions, scale differences create the illusion of depth, accentuate the impact of the subject, and enhance the visual impact of the frame. In the opener for *Arte Kurzschluss*, a weekly TV program that features short experimental films on the Franco-German TV network, the extreme scale differences between human figures and film equipment fracture our logical sense of space (**8.15**). The opening to a teen-targeted identity package for Cosmopolitan Television also employs scale contrast in the juxtaposing of spirited, joyful young women and iconic objects to suggest a playful, liberating atmosphere (**8.16**).

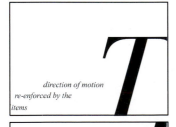

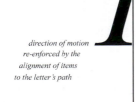

on of motion

direction of motion re-enforced by the items

direction of motion re-enforced by the alignment of items to the letter's path

8.14
The alignment and repetition of structures take the eye toward the top right edge of the frame.

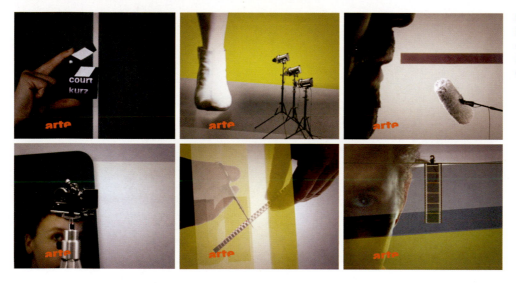

8.15
Frames from the opener for *Arte Kurzschlus*. Courtesy of Velvet

Value, which measures the lightness or darkness of an image's tones or colors, is also a widely practiced form of contrast. (As newborns, we first distinguish objects in black and white.) It can enrich visual messages and can be used to create focal points in a composition. In the title sequence to the film *Magnolia* (1999), an image of a blooming magnolia flower is superimposed on street maps and content from the film, producing a dynamic blending of tonal ranges. This interplay between light and dark helps express the concept of people's lives overlapping and intersecting. On an aesthetic level, it helps clearly differentiate the elements in the frame (**8.17**).

Color contrasts can be used to create mood, symbolize ideas, and express emotions to produce a desired audience response. It is important to understand that color is relative to its surroundings; a color that stands alone in a visual field is perceived differently than a color that is surrounded by other colors. For example, "value contrast" between light and dark is the strongest method of distinguishing colors. Generally, colors more disparate in value produce more contrast than those that are close in value. "Temperature contrast" between warm and cool hues has been used to suggest spatial proximity and depth (see figure **8.18**). The recessive qualities in the cool blue-green spectrum can indicate distance, while warm ranges in the red-yellow spectrum can express closeness. "Complementary contrast" occurs when colors that are opposite one another on the color wheel are placed in close proximity, producing dramatic or shocking effects.

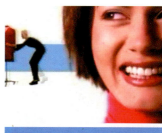

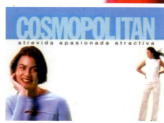

8.16
Cosmo Fun Zone. Courtesy of Cosmopolitan TV and Hearst Entertainment and Syndication.

French chemist Chevreul discovered that color inconsistencies in dyed fabrics were the result of viewing conditions. Areas of cloth of similar color appeared different from one another depending upon the colors that surrounded them.

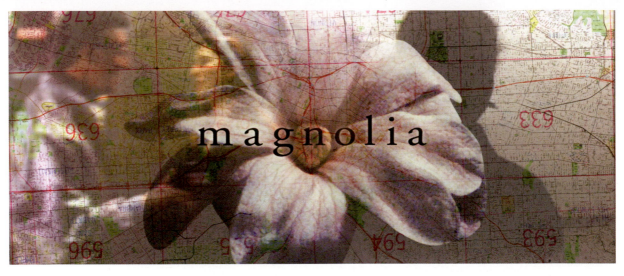

8.17
Title frame from *Magnolia* (1999). © MXMXCIX Fine Line Features. All rights reserved. Photo by Peter Sorel. Photo appears courtesy of New Line Productions, Inc.

In **figures 8.19** and **8.20**, the program opener for Hallmark Channel's, *Crown Cinema* and a television spot for Esprit Kids both demonstrate complementary color contrast. "Simultaneous contrast" occurs when a neutral gray tone assumes the complementary hue of a color that is in close proximity. For example, if a gray tone is next to a green hue, a neutralization process makes it appear as warm, reddish gray (**8.21**).

8.18
Temperature contrast is evident in an animated banner ad for Washington Mutual. Courtesy of twenty2product.

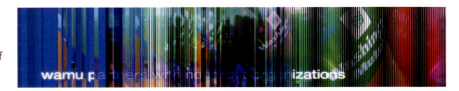

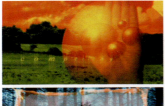

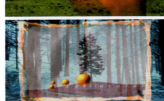

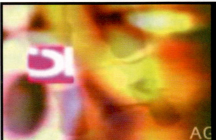

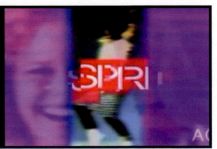

8.19
Frames from *Crown Cinema* (2001). Courtesy of Viewpoint Creative. © Hallmark Channel.

8.20
Esprit Kids was aired throughout Japan and in several boutiques. Courtesy of April Greiman, Made In Space. © Esprit.

Contrast in the graphic representation of texture and pattern can also add spatial depth and emphasis. In **figure 8.22**, Stephen Seeley, creative director of Studio Dialog, has employed a unique background texture that makes the images look as if they have been silkscreened or stamped in ink. This quality heightens the impact of the contrasting polished shapes and lines that are characteristic of the foreground images animating on top of the background.

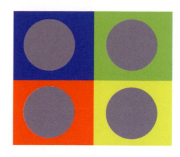

8.21
An example of simultaneous color contrast.

"All colors are the friends of their neighbors and the lovers of their opposites."
—*Marc Chagall*

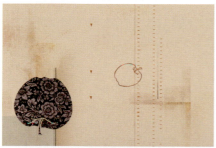
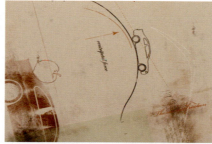
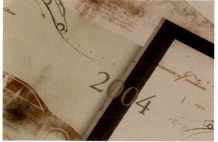
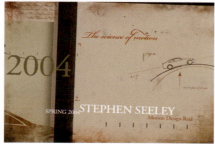

8.22
Frames from Stephen Seeley's motion design reel. Courtesy of Stephen Seeley and Studio Dialog.

Fuel TV's signature network identity in **figure 8.23** incorporates images of aged fabric as fills for the background and foreground elements. The unique, tactile characteristics of the patterns create an aesthetically engaging contrast with the flat, graphic imagery and typography.

Shape contrasts can be deliberately arranged in a composition to create visual conflict in the frame. In a "Visual Music" assignment at the Massachusetts College of Art, students created mesmerizing landscapes of live-action images to represent sound. Ted Roberts' composition entitled "Organic Unit" combined the natural, abstract forms of filmed liquids with the hard-edged forms of buildings in cityscapes (**8.24**). In an opening for the Travel Channel's *Destination Style*, a program that features a behind-the-scenes look at the people who work on fashion photography shoots around the globe, dissimilar shapes create interest by introducing visual conflict (**8.25**).

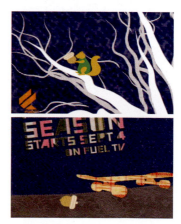

8.23
Frames from Fuel TV's signature network identity for its fall season. Courtesy of Fuel TV.

8.24
Frames from "Organic Unit" from an assignment entitled "Visual Music" by Ted Roberts. Courtesy of Professor Jan Kubasiewicz, Dynamic Typography (2003), Massachusetts College of Art.

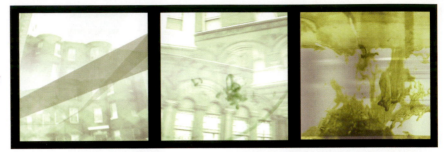

8.25
Frames from the show opener for *Destination Style* for the Travel Channel. Courtesy of Susan Detrie Design.

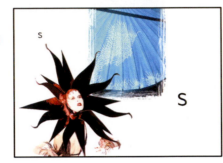
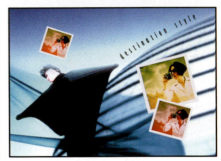

Variation in the proximity between objects and their positioning relative to the frame's edges can also increase contrast. Further, the direction that objects point can be varied to distinguish different types of graphic information and to create emphasis (**8.26**).

8.26
Varying the orientation of objects throughout the frame draws our eye in different directions.

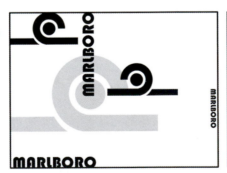
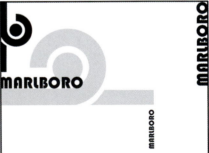

In addition to these standard forms of visual contrast, others can be considered: line versus mass; symmetry versus asymmetry; ornamental versus simple; representational versus non-objective; premeditated versus spontaneous; deliberate versus chance; ordered versus random; cerebral versus emotional; duplicated versus varied; cohesion versus disparity; clarity versus ambiguity; and open versus closed. Graphic designers who are starting out in the field should explore all of these methods to find out what suits their temperament and sensibility.

hierarchy

A principle related to contrast is hierarchy. In fact, it is usually dependent upon contrast. Most viewers rely upon visual clues to direct their attention. "Visual hierarchy" is a product of their need for direction. It allows you to organize complex information and direct a viewer's attention through the frame on an informational and a visual level.

The most artistically innovative designs can function on an aesthetic level but fail to communicate the information. In contrast, compositions that demonstrate effective hierarchy are organized in a clear, systematic, and easily understood manner by differentiating elements by their order of importance. In a publication design, headings, subheadings, paragraphs, and side notes are clearly differentiated by their typeface, size, spacing, color, and so forth. In motion graphics, the primary, secondary, and tertiary elements form the basis of the visual communication. The primary, most important elements in the frame must capture the immediate attention of viewers and lead them into the design. They should offer the most important information and create a mood or emotional response based on what is being communicated. Viewers should then be drawn to the secondary components, which should reinforce the overall message and enhance the impact of the design. Finally, tertiary elements should also support the primary and secondary elements and overall message.

Visual hierarchy can be achieved by establishing contrasts in shape, scale, value, weight, positioning, orientation, color, and proximity. In **figure 8.27**, for example, shape is used to establish visual hierarchy by connecting or separating visual information. The most dominant shapes act as directional tangents to help our eye move through the frame, while smaller graphics function as accents to contribute to the composition's secondary hierarchy.

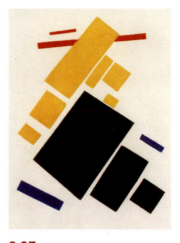

8.27
"Suprematist Painting: Aeroplane Flying" 1915 by Kazmir Malevich.

The Russian Suprematist art movement gave size and scale considerable attention in establishing spatial relationships and hierarchy.

repetition and variety

"Repetition" is the recurrence of one or more elements in a composition. With subtle variations, repetition can inject a provocative, visual beat. Pop artist Andy Warhol's paintings, for example, demonstrate a monotonous repetition of images to convey the idea of consumerism. In furniture design, the articulation of surfaces through decoration and ornamentation can be visually engaging because the repetition of

8.28

Prototype splash page design for Salon de Fatima by Jon Krasner. © Jon Krasner.

A large semicircular background shape is used to help organize the most important information while balancing and unifying the composition. Smaller graphics function as accents to contribute toward the composition's secondary hierarchy.

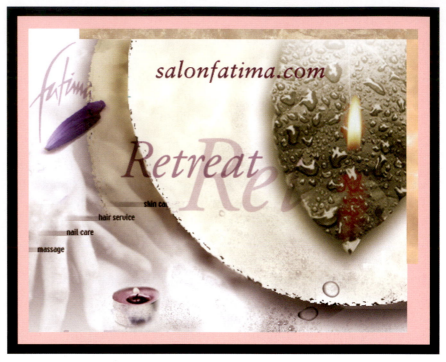

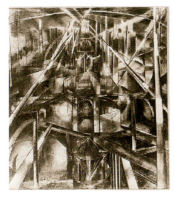

8.29

Cubist painting of the Brooklyn Bridge (c.1917–1918), artist unknown. Courtesy of NARA.

8.30

Composition study by Mike Cena. Courtesy of Professor Jon Krasner, Fitchburg State University.

forms and textures. In painting and static design, repetition can be achieved through the spacing of elements. In a Cubist painting of the Brooklyn Bridge, for example, a rhythmic vocabulary of architectural, volumetric forms is established by the manner in which the image is fragmented into overlapping geometric planes (**8.29**).

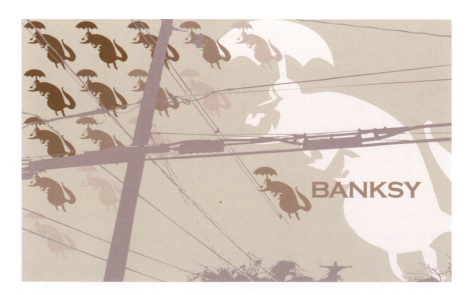

The pictorial recurrence of elements can also create spatial rhythm, as seen in a show opener for Fine Living Network (**8.31**). AMC's twentieth anniversary station IDs employ repetitive geometric forms to emphasize the concept of "twenty years of big-screen battles." In "twenty years of romantic movies," the repetition of similar patterns provides rhythm, pictorial continuity, and compositional balance (**8.32**).

Within repetition, predictability can be disrupted by introducing change. Repeating shapes that differ in scale, color, orientation, or proximity can enhance visual interest by adding variety to what might otherwise be monotonous or boring design. Together, repetition and variation can contribute to a composition's pictorial rhythm. In "Loop" (2003), a short, animated film that expresses a romantic view of alternative energy, pictorial rhythm is established through repeating images that vary in shape, texture, and pattern of motion (**8.33**).

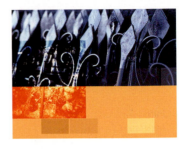

8.31
Frame from *Live Like You Mean It* for Fine Living Network. Courtesy of Detrie Design and Another Large Production.

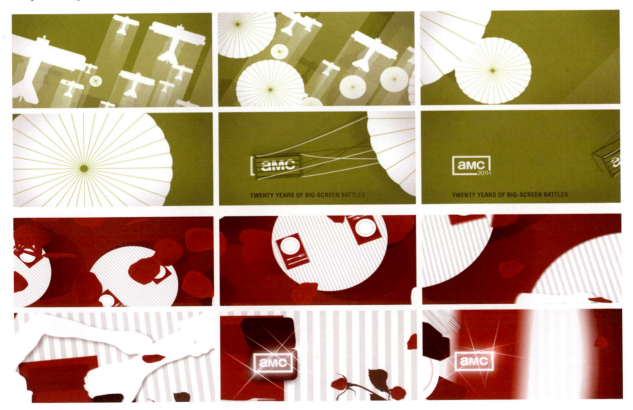

8.32
Frames from station IDs promoting AMC's twentieth anniversary. Courtesy of Shilo.

See also Chapter 6, figure 6.38, on p. 188.

8.33
Frames from "Loop" (2003), by Terry Green and Nori-Zso Tolson. Courtesy of twenty-2product.

This animation was inspired by a cover design for *Hemispheres*, a United Airlines in-flight magazine. Live-action footage of wind farms, sunsets, and cityscapes were combined with 2D graphics to communicate about alternative energy and to reinforce the composition's overall continuity.

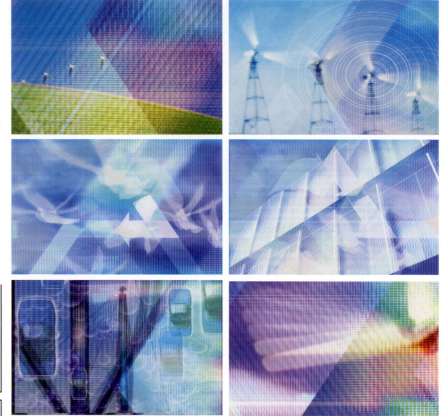

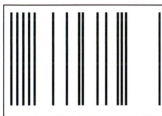

8.34
Evenly spaced lines on a ground establish a repetitious rhythm. Varying their proximity produces a more dynamic rhythm.

Pictorial rhythm can range from monotony to chaos, depending on the degree of variation introduced. It is important to recognize the distinction between pictorial rhythm and sequential rhythm. Pictorial rhythm considers the distances at which elements are repeated in the space of the frame; sequential rhythm considers the continuity and recurrence of elements *between* frames.

juxtaposition and superimposition

Two methods of constructing images in space are juxtaposition and superimposition. "Spatial juxtaposition" is the placement of two or more elements that are related or unrelated in meaning in close proximity to suggest a new meaning. For example, the bilingual show opener for *DW Euromaxx* consists of juxtaposed images, for example of female figures, violins, shoes, and chairs which are arranged into animated patterns of geometric shapes (**Chapter 13, figure 13.38, on p. 481**). In American Movie Classics' show opener for *Tough Guys*, New York

Principles of Composition

design firm ZONA created a mélange of typographic and live-action elements such as nails, fists, tattoos, fire, a chain, and a Harley-Davidson motorcycle. The juxtaposition of these elements with horizontal and vertical bands of bold colors expresses the adrenaline-fueled toughness of AMC's weekly program, which aims to showcase Hollywood's leading males in their grittiest roles (**8.35**). ZONA Design also created the opening title sequence for Orchard Films' *Indie Sex*, a four-part mini-series that aired on the Independent Film Channel (IFC) in August, 2007. Juxtapositions that occur throughout the composition include male nude figures, women wearing leather attire, red satin graphic patterns, and type printed on handheld labelers (**8.36**). The relationships between elements reinforce the controversial and rebellious nature of extreme topics about sex.

During the Modernist era, the Surrealist movement employed bizarre juxtapositions of objects in unusual settings and in absurd situations. Pop artists juxtaposed fragments of popular culture in painting.

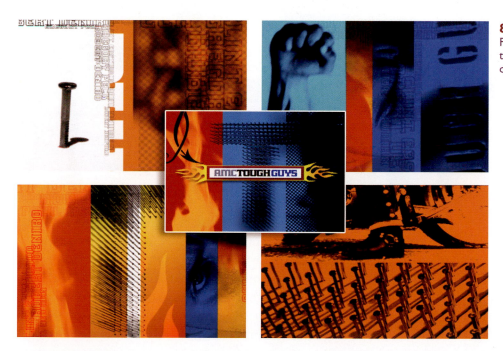

8.35
Frames from the opener to *Tough Guys*. Courtesy of ZONA Design.

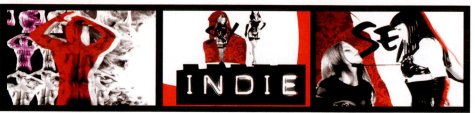

8.36
Frames from the opener to *Indie Sex*. Courtesy of ZONA Design.

See also Chapter 3, figure 3.17, on p. 48.

The graphic power of juxtaposition is also exemplified in the opening titles for *PARTIE*, a talk show on TV Prima ("cool television"), one of the Czech Republic's most watched prime-time stations (**8.37**). The show presents discussions and debates on a broad range of topics including politics, art, and music. The visual relationship between the male, foreground figure and the large typographic background structures mimics a chess game and echoes the clash of opinions between the show's moderator and its guests. A deliberate black-and-white palette and austere image treatment helps distinguish the background and foreground elements, logically reinforcing the theme.

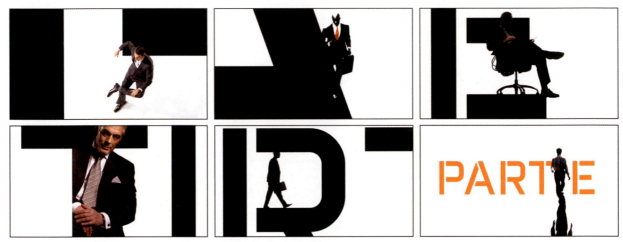

8.37
Frames from the opener for TV Prima's *PARTIE*. Courtesy of Eallin.

"Superimposition" involves laying one or more elements on top of others. For example, the opening title sequence for *Boogeyman* (2005) consists of superimposed words that fade in and out to set the film's mood (**8.38**). Freestyle Collective's promotional spot for IFC's *Cinema Red Mondays* is a textural video collage of superimposed imagery from nature (**Chapter 3, figure 3.58, on p. 67**). In a multilayered ad for explore.org, collections of photographs, geometric forms, and brushstrokes are superimposed to achieve a rich, tactile palette of visuals to entice viewers to visit the Web site (**8.39**). Last, the spot "Standing Up for Freedom" for Amnesty International—the world's largest human rights organization—demonstrates the graphic power of superimposition. Throughout the animation, superimposed images on a dark prison wall feature a young boy who takes us on a metaphorical journey representing mankind's struggle for freedom over the last half century (**8.40**).

In broadcast production, titles are "supered" over live background footage. In collage, superimposition allows the original identity of found objects to be maintained in tandem with the new meaning that each takes on in association with other objects. In photomontage, it provides a method of combining two or more images to create a new image or scene.

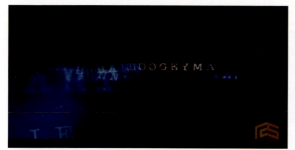
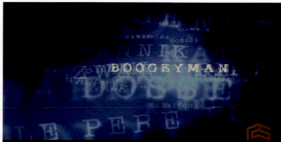
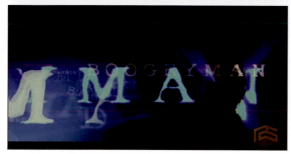
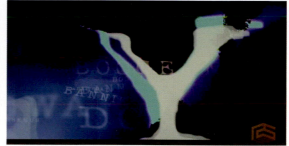

8.38
Frames from the opening titles to *Boogeyman* (2005). Courtesy of Reality Check Studios.

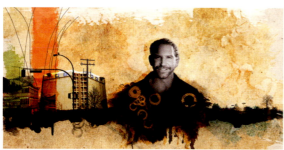
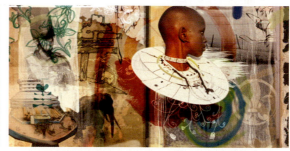
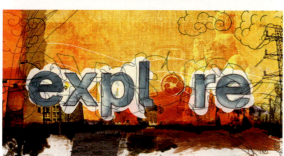
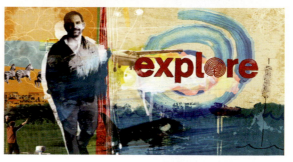

8.39
Frames from an ad for http://www.explore.org. Courtesy of Belief.

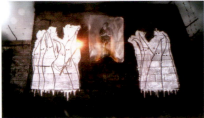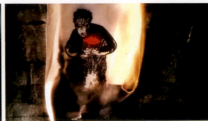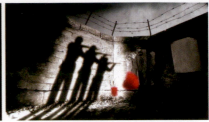

8.40
Frames from the television spot "Standing Up for Freedom" for Amnesty International. Courtesy of Eallin.

See also Chapter 13, figure 13.1, on p. 452.

Inspired by Cubism, Dutch De Stijl painter Piet Mondrian broke down his subjects into scaffoldings of interlocking lines and flat planes of color. Over time, he became increasingly interested in the formal interplay of geometric forms and moved toward greater abstraction, rejecting diagonal lines and relying less on objective subjects. He embraced the principles of stability and spirituality through balancing horizontal and vertical lines, shapes, and spaces. The work of De Stijl painters such as Piet Mondrian and Theo van Doesburg in turn inspired Swiss designer Josef Muller-Brockmann, whose reductivist style was also derived from mathematics and rationalism. Along with sans serif typefaces, the use of the grid provided him with a unified sense of compositional balance and proportion. Muller-Brockmann's book, Grid Systems in Graphic Design, *has been highly influential on generations of graphic designers.*

Chapter 12 discusses how digital compositing has allowed designers to create unique compositions through juxtaposition and superimposition.

Grid Systems

A "grid" is a formal underlying structure that can serve as a guide to making purposeful design decisions regarding the placement, size, and proportions of elements in a composition in order to maintain a sense of organized unity.

Today, grids are used more casually in print to provide consistency in column widths, margin sizes, the space surrounding images, and the placement of repeating elements such as body text, headers, and footers from page to page. Web designers have also embraced the grid as an alignment tool for graphics and type positioned inside tables or layers. In presentations tailored for interactivity (on the Web, mobile devices, kiosks, DVD titles), grids can be used to align elements in the frame and provide consistency between pages or scenes by ensuring continuity in the positioning of elements. When used in conjunction with aesthetic intuition, they can help organize complex information and achieve balance between visuals to allow for clear communication.

The modern grid is the result of an evolutionary process that can be traced back to the inception of graphic design in Mesopotamia 4,000 years ago. Consisting of horizontal and vertical lines, grids have long been used as a reliable method of organizing information into logical, coherent arrangements of text and images.

Should you decide to use a grid, it is best to sketch it out on paper first and then implement it in the application that you are using. Most motion graphics applications provide guides that can be adjusted and locked to position elements using vertical or horizontal alignment.

Once a grid system has been established, you can deviate from it to add visual interest or emphasize particular elements. While certain objects may be aligned to specific regions of the grid, others may break away.

A grid system should be guided by the design concept and the content. It should only act as a guide, not as a substitute for creative intuition.

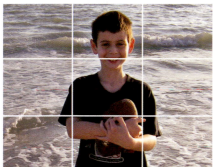 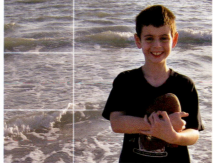

8.41
The "Rule of Thirds" uses a grid system that divides a space into three equal segments vertically and horizontally. Points of focus occur at the intersections of the lines. This strategy can prevent elements from being placed in the dead center of the space in order to achieve asymmetry. © 2012 Jon Krasner.

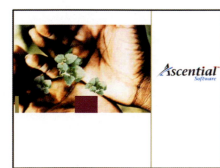 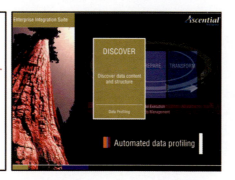

8.42
A CD-ROM presentation for Ascential Software suggests the use of an underlying grid to ensure continuity in the alignment and placement of images and text. Courtesy of Corporate Graphics. © Ascential Software.

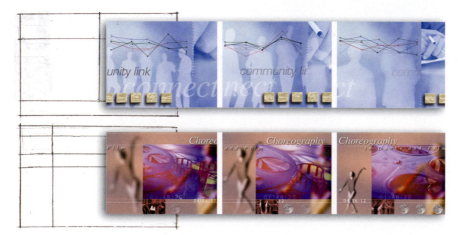

8.43
Underlying grid structures used in print and Web design can be applied to motion graphics to provide pictorial order to a kinetic composition.

Breaking Spatial Conventions

As we struggle to find new opportunities for creative expression on the screen, it is critical to identify with the imposed rectilinear parameters that the frame—which remains the basis of traditional cinematic composition—prescribes. As new, non-conventional approaches to composition involve spatial, rather than framed, arrangements, the frame has moved to a subsidiary position, and restrictions that have been imposed by spatial norms of film and video have been eliminated.

The fact that film and television screens are rectangular does not imply that your work must conform to the frame's rectangular format! In fact, many interactive motion graphic artists feel confined by the fixed aspect ratios and zoning laws of film and television screens.

"Photography is all right . . . if you don't mind looking at the world from the point of view of a paralyzed cyclops— for a split second."

—*David Hockney*

Historical Perspective

Since the beginning of the twentieth century, artists have challenged classical assumptions of space in order to break the homogeny of the rectangular frame. Throughout the modern era, Cubist and Constructivist painters gravitated toward nontraditional approaches to composition by investigating multiple viewpoints, asymmetry, and diagonal eye movement. During this period, graphic designers also began to deviate from popular spatial conventions. Russian Constructivist painters and designers broke away from vertical and horizontal arrangements in favor of diagonal layouts. Later, Swiss and Dutch postmodern designers began pushing scale contrasts, angular forms, and dramatic camera angles in their compositions.

Attempts to break the rectangular format were striking during the early twentieth century. Modern artists such as Robert Delaunay, Piet Mondrian, and Giorgio de Chirico were among the first to introduce circular, diamond, and triangular compositions. Eventually, painters began to investigate ways to extend their content beyond the confines of the frame. Many negated the idea of enclosure and considered borders as virtually nonexistent (or self-defining) visual devices. Frank Stella's mixed media, decorative abstractions of the 1970s broke the deadlock of the pictorial surface by leaping off the wall onto the gallery floor. His book *Working Space* (1986) has challenged artists to rethink how space can be manipulated. Influenced by Cubist aesthetics, American photographer David Hockney brought to the late twentieth century an increased desire for spatial exploration. His photocollages, constructed from 35 millimeter prints, were compiled to create a "complete" picture by eliminating the idea of a fixed field.

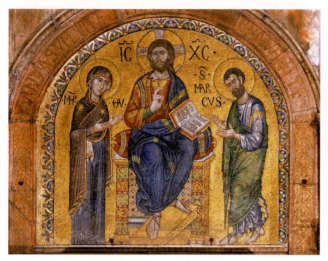

8.44
Byzantine painting (476–1453).
© Erich Lessing/Art Resource, NY.

Since paintings during the early Renaissance were created strictly for religious purposes, artists took into consideration the structures that existed in churches (**see figure 8.44**). When the context shifted from religious to the secular, canvases were needed to display artwork. As a result, the rectangle became the most widely accepted picture format. Despite this fact, designers can become liberated and "think outside the box." Although the viewing area may be fixed inside the frame, non-rectangular structures can serve as compositions within a composition. In **figure 8.45**, the animations were designed to conform to non-conventional shapes within the frames rather than to the frame boundaries. The client Candle requested a design that would promote their information management software while holding the viewer's attention. Wanting to push the envelope, I became intrigued with the possibility of using masks to frame animations that were part of the interface. Members of the production team, who had little regard for experimentation, were grounded on the supposition that video images should *always* be presented in a 4:3 aspect ratio format. I politely ignored their beliefs, and with a little client convincing, I finally arrived at an idea that worked!

8.45
Frames from Candle's Intelliwatch CD-ROM by Jon Krasner. Courtesy of Candle Corporation and the Devereux Group.

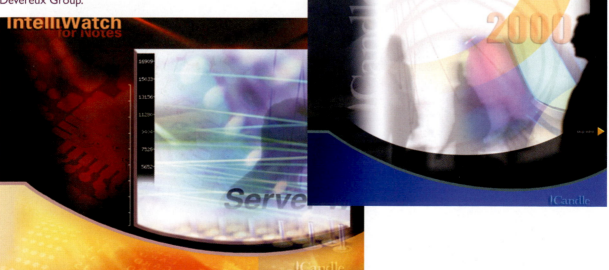

In motion graphics, space can also be suggested, rather than defined by the hard-edged physical boundaries that the screen imposes. This allows the viewer to consider the possibility of an infinite, undefined viewing area that continues in all directions. For example, the background of the inner city playground in **figure 8.46** abandons the idea of a fixed frame. The figures leap out of the circle, providing a feeling of continuous space without borders.

8.46
Mural painting in Hell's Kitchen, Manhattan, New York. Courtesy of the EPA and NARA.

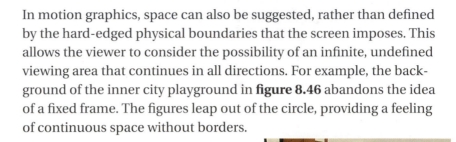

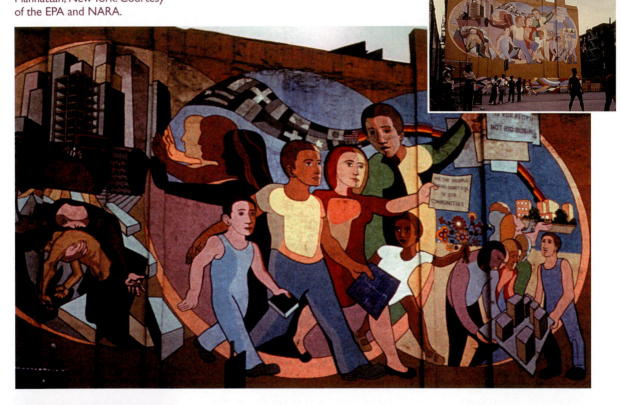

Los Angeles Pop artist David Hockney, one of the most influential artists of the twentieth century, invented an alternative way of constructing space by combining Polaroid photographs to show multiple viewpoints of an image or an event. His work suggests an absence of boundaries that might be imposed by traditional framing.

In the opening titles to a fast-paced top-ten countdown for *ZeD*, a CBC Television program that showcases Canadian films and music, the majority of the action is composed to occur within or break out of the skewed image of an index card, which serves as the backdrop. Free-floating cutout silhouettes and abstract symbols demonstrate a complete disregard for the frame (**8.47**). The dark and edgy motion graphics for *ZeD*'s third season ignores the frame's rectangular format by giving us a "slice" of the action inside a narrow, horizontal strip (**8.48**). In a rich, action-packed trailer for the Slamdance Film Festival, America's most prominent festival "by filmmakers for filmmakers," the frame only serves the purpose of "housing" an open compositional format. Similar to **figure 8.47**, images seem unbounded by the frame's rectangular constraints (**8.49**).

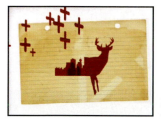 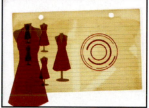 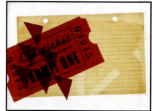 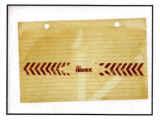

8.47
Opener to *ZeD*, season 4, CBC Television. Courtesy of Studio Blanc.

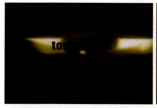 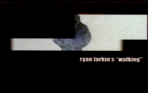 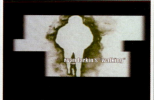 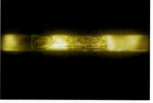

8.48
Show opener to *ZeD*, season 3, CBC Television. Courtesy of Studio Blanc.

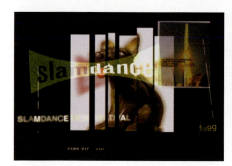 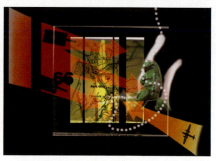

8.49
Frames from a trailer for Slamdance. Designed by Brumby Boylston and Elizabeth Rovnick. Courtesy of Humunculus.

Dividing up the frame can fracture time and space, allowing viewers to use their peripheral vision to observe several actions and perspectives simultaneously. In the opener for *Movie Magic*, a television show that gives audiences a behind-the-scenes look at how films are made, segments of live-action footage of physically constructed letterforms and intimate close-up shots of silkscreening, welding, carving, and sandblasting are duplicated in the frame as multiple video windows. The relative positions and scale relationships of the windows changes in each scene, emphasizing the sensitivity and complexity of these artistic processes used to handcraft the three-dimensional letters of

Immersive virtual reality environments naturally eradicate the familiar compositional devices that a rectilinear border provides. The boundary of the frame is completely eliminated as viewers enter into the action and become totally involved in an all-enveloping experience.

Pablo Ferro's title sequence for The Thomas Crown Affair was the first to introduce the concept of screen division in motion pictures. This helped define a cinematic style during the late 1960s.

the title "Movie Magic" (**8.50**). Susan Detrie's pitch for ESPN expresses the concept of a runner who pre-visualizes himself crossing the finish line. Splitting the composition recalls sports footage, which is often presented in a divided frame format to give viewers a chance to observe the action from multiple viewpoints. The type, which reads "small is beautiful," refers to the fact that a tiny fraction of a second can separate winning from losing (**8.51**).

Historical Perspective

The concept of the divided frame was explored in the 1880s during the English Arts and Crafts movement by graphic designers such as Selwyn Image, who used this device to organize his compositions, which were packed with graphic detail.

In the motion picture industry, the divided screen was one of the oldest effects to be used during the silent film era to depict telephone conversations between people. Filmmakers that subscribed to this formal modernist aesthetics also entertained its concept. Abel Gance's three-screen classic titled *Napoleon* (1927) used a process that he called "Polyvision." Gance suggested that the ability of the viewer to navigate through multiple images was a result of an increasingly shortened attention span. During the 1960s, underground filmmakers such as Jordan Belson and the Eames Brothers projected multiple images in light shows in galleries, planetariums, and public settings. Their technique of superimposing images using as many as seventy individual projectors became known as the "expanded cinema" (a quintessential method used for expressing the effect of a hallucinogenic drug trip). Pop artist Andy Warhol also applied a split-screen technique in *Chelsea Girls* (1966), the first double-screen film to be commercially released.

During the 1970s, multi-image slide projection allowed numerous dissolving images to be displayed in unison with sound. Video wall technology during the 1980s elaborated on this idea by offering modular, multi-screen systems that could display large images without sacrificing picture resolution. Exciting compositional possibilities could be realized as signals from different sources could appear across adjacent monitors or be divided up, repeated, and shown separately in various shape and size configurations.

Today, prime-time television shows and motion pictures have embraced split-screen juxtaposition. Mike Figgis' film *Timecode* (2000) employs four panels depicting four interconnected personal experiences that unfold in real-time. Stephen Hopkins' television drama *24* also used the technique to present various viewpoints and camera angles in as many as six simultaneous scenes.

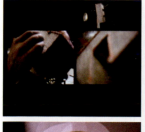
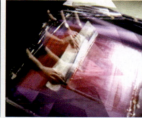
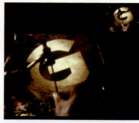
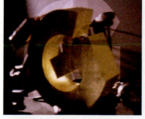
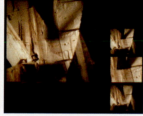
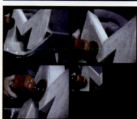
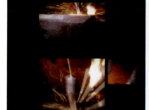
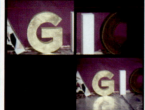
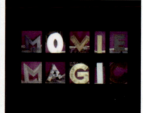

8.50
Frames from the opener for *Movie Magic*. Courtesy of Velvet.

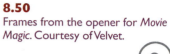
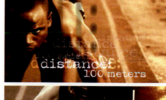
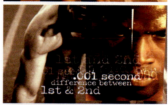
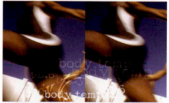
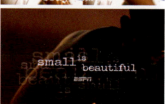

8.51
Frames from a pitch for a spot for ESPN. Courtesy of Susan Detrie.

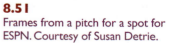

8.52
The motion in Rockshox's 2000 Web site was composed to work within a split-screen format. Courtesy of twenty2product.

In my Motion Graphic Design course, the cinematic practice of screen division allowed Nick Moreau to show different events occurring simultaneously in a PSA addressing light pollution (**8.53**). He cleverly chooses to show us the cause of the problem but holds back the explanation until the very end. Nick writes: "I used video (most of which I personally took) to show a number of bright lights and electric signs—the causes of light pollution. I started with just one or two light switches, but it quickly multiplies as the piece goes on, showing that every light is part of a larger issue." He adds: "The reason I decided to use a lot of split screen in the piece is to show that all of these lights are being turned on—and remain on—simultaneously. One or two lights do not cause light pollution—thousands and thousands of lights do. By showing multiple lights on simultaneously, I wanted to give a sense that lights are everywhere all the time. The appearance of each of the lights is also timed with the clicks from the song 'Twinkle Twinkle Little Star,' making it appear that these lights are each being turned on all around the world."

8.53
Frames from a PSA on light pollution by Nick Moreau. Courtesy of Professor Jon Krasner, Fitchburg State University.

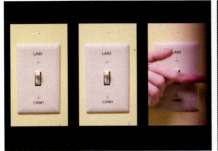
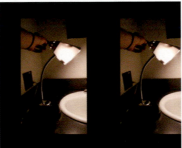
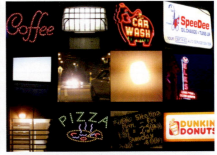

8.54
At Kent State University, Catherine Zedell's promo for the film *City of God* (2002) combines repetition and frame division to convey the vibrant, fast-paced energy of the movie without revealing the plot. © 2012, Kent State University. Courtesy of Professor Gretchen Rinnert.

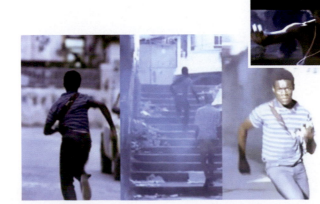

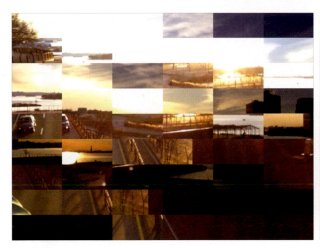

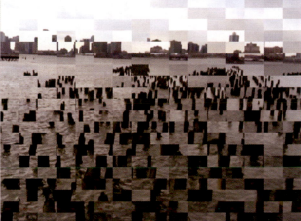

8.55
The iPhone and iPad application +loop can divide the screen into a customized grid of video players. This offers infinite amount of intuitive compositional possibilities. Courtesy of Trollbäck + Company.

mobile framing

Changing the framing of a composition by simulating camera motion can guide our perception of onscreen and offscreen space. It can give a sense of mystery, as important elements that were concealed gradually become visible within the frame. For example, for an assignment that challenges students to animate a famous poster from the history of graphic design, Mike Sokol investigated several compositional possibilities using various camera angles and movements that reveal the components of a typographic poster. We travel on various trajectories through a graphic landscape of two-dimensional planes and letterforms. At the very end, all the elements of the poster are presented in the frame (**8.57**).

"Frame mobility" can link elements and emphasize relationships between elements and their environment. For example, zooming in or tracking forward moves elements off the edges of the screen, while images and overlooked clues that exist beyond the frame's boundaries are revealed. This alternative to cutting or transitioning between views arouses our curiosity about the story, since we anticipate what the result of the zoom will be. Camera motion can also function to keep our attention focused on a moving element by following it. For example, a tracking shot may follow a bird in flight, or a crane shot may follow an object plummeting to earth.

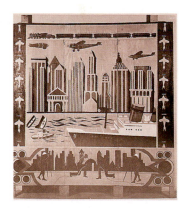

8.56
Mural for the Harlem Art workshop. Courtesy of the Harmon Foundation Collection and NARA.

Here, the concept of frame division functions as a means of showing multiple views of Harlem.

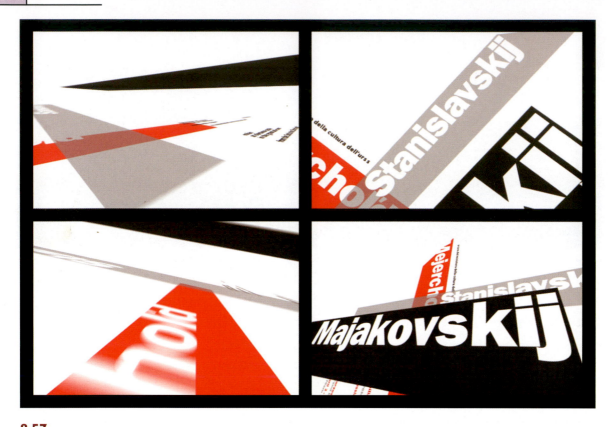

8.57
Frames from "Monguzzi Poster," an animated poster by Mike Sokol. Courtesy of Professor Jan Kubasiewicz, Dynamic Typography (2005), Massachusetts College of Art.

In the short film "About Face," animator Marilyn Cherenko employed the cinematic techniques of dollying and zooming to enable viewers to follow a subject from room to room at spatial distances ranging from wide shots to extreme close-ups (**8.58**). In Stephen's Seeley's composition in **figure 8.22 on p. 275**, we are led through space by a graphic of an apple that moves in coordination with a long camera tilt downward. The apple fades out, and a –90-degree frame rotation shifts our viewpoint so that we follow the movement of the type off the frame's right edge. In both cases, reframing accommodated the subject when it changed its spatial positioning and maintained an overall compositional balance.

Frame mobility can also be used to impart information by establishing visual hierarchy and providing emphasis. An example of this is a PSA designed to engage private companies to help in the fight against AIDS in Africa (**8.59**). Here, Ryan Leonard, a student at the Art Institute of Philadelphia, relied on camera movement to establish clear legibility and logical sequencing of information.

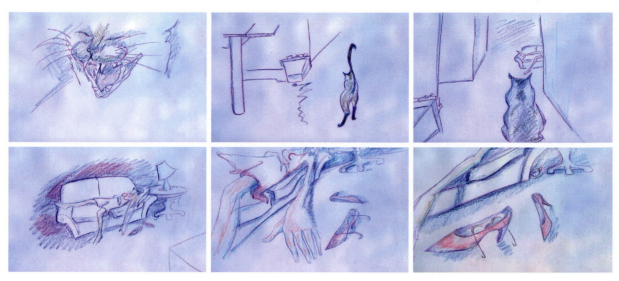

8.58
Frames from "About Face" (2000) by Marilyn Cherenko.

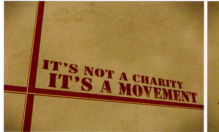 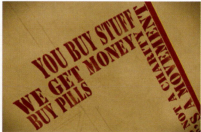 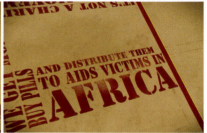

8.59
Frames from a PSA promoting joinred.com, by Ryan Leonard Art Institute of Philadelphia. Courtesy of Professor Genevieve Okupniak.

3D space

Three-dimensional space can move our eye into a realm that is less constricting than the frame's fixed two-dimensional parameters. Visual advance or recession, frontal views, and oblique views from any location, along with the device of perspective achieved through the use of lines and angles, allow you to create the illusion of three dimensions within a two-dimensional framework.

In Reality Check Studios' 2007 show reel, overlapping, transparent square shapes from the company's logo emphasize the illusion of depth. Two-dimensional lines, planes, and typographic elements are positioned at various angles in a digital 3D space to create a sense of deep perspective. Further, the use of mobile framing enhances their positioning as they animate on different spatial trajectories (**8.61**).

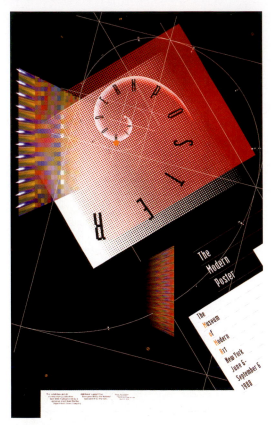

New York motion graphics firm Flying Machine created a show package for *CNET News.com* and *CNET TV.com.* CNET, Inc., a San Francisco based company specializing in the Internet and computers, wanted to express a human connection to technology. The graphic design incorporated a variety of live-action content and computer-generated backgrounds while picking up on the yellow and red color scheme from CNET's branded network. In a spot for CNET's television news program, three people engage in a playful journey along the information superhighway. They interact with hand-held devices, video displays, and touchscreens in a 3D space, conveying the effect of technology in the work-place, at home, and in daily life (**8.62**).

In **figure 8.63,** a branding video for Harman Industries Inc. combines perspective and camera motion to emphasize interconnectivity between Harman's brands. The broadcast design firm Humunculus produced a spot that expressed Harman's technological ability to provide information and entertainment in the twenty-first century through a single delivery system. The concept involved a pixel becoming the source of the universe with the company's logo in the center of the "big bang," which creates a vast, 3D universe containing communications technologies (email, satellite, voice activation). The use of mobile framing helps create a complex, multitiered message in a visually stunning way.

8.60
"The Modern Poster" (1985) by April Greiman provides a great example of how the illusion of three-dimensional space can take the viewer's eye beyond the restricting borders of the frames' fixed, two-dimensional viewing plane.

The Museum of Modern Art Collection. Courtesy of April Greiman, Made in Space.

8.61
Frames from Reality Check Studios' show reel. Courtesy of Reality Check Studios.

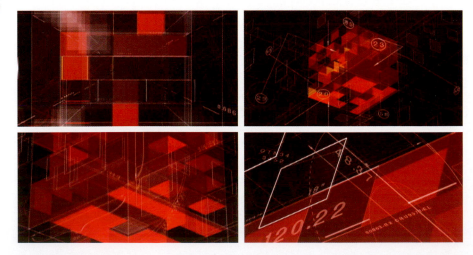

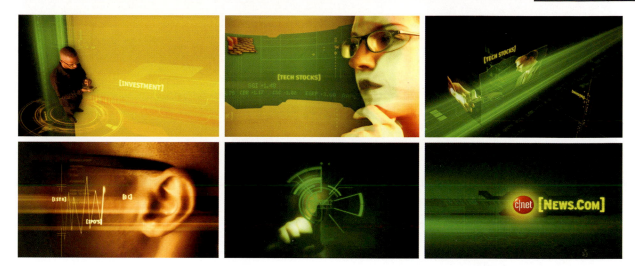

8.62
A spot for CNET's news network and television program. Courtesy of Flying Machine.

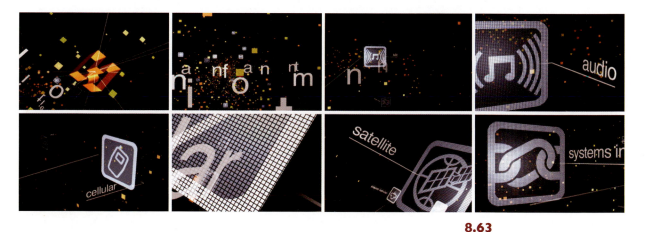

8.63
"Infotainment," a branding video for Harman Industries. Courtesy of Humunculus.

Assignments

line, plane, asymmetry, balance

overview

The objective of modern, asymmetrical composition is to encourage the viewer's eyes to move about the frame. You will create a series of studies that demonstrate how the elements of line and plane can be used to choreograph an asymmetrical, changing space over time.

stages

Create two square compositions measuring 500 × 500 pixels. Then create a black, 400 × 400 pixel square and animate its position and rotation properties over 10 seconds, keeping it away from the center of the composition. Your goal is to maintain an asymmetrical, changing space.

Incorporate this animation into another 500 × 500 pixel composition, and place a black line measuring 200 pixels in length. Animate the line over 10 seconds, keeping it away from the center of the composition. Again, your objective is to maintain a dynamic sense of asymmetrical space. Be deliberate in how the line's positioning, spatial orientation, and direction of travel changes in relation to the changing space of the first study. Consider how you can emphasize asymmetry but at the same time maintain balance.

Incorporate your animation into a third 500 × 500 pixel, 10-second composition, and animate a second line, keeping it away from the center of the composition. Think carefully about how this third element can contribute to asymmetrical balance.

specifications

Avoid using any three-dimensional transformations that involve a z-axis, since the illusion of depth can detract from the assignment's purpose—to choreograph two-dimensional, asymmetrical space.

considerations

Consider the relationships between positive and negative space. As space changes over time, consider how the supporting element of line can be used to achieve compositional balance. How can balance and imbalance potentially work together to heighten the viewer's interest? Last, consider how elements can interact with the frame's edges.

animated space: figure and ground #1

overview

Develop an animated space that changes over time with respect to its figure and ground relationships. Your objectives are to develop a sensitivity to positive and negative structure and to explore the interchangeability of figure and ground.

Assignments

stages

Create three 10–15–second compositions based on the formats below:

- square: 480 × 480 pixels
- horizontal rectangle: 720 × 480 pixels
- vertical rectangle: 480 × 720 pixels

In each composition, create a square measuring 720 × 720 pixels and animate its position and rotation properties.

specifications

Use only black and white. Colors, grays, and effects are prohibited. The duration of each composition should be 10–15 seconds.

considerations

Your goal is to establish interchangeability between figure and ground. Consider how dividing positive and negative space within the frame can establish new figure and ground relationships. Give attention to the positioning of shapes and their relationship to the frame's edges.

animated space: figure and ground #2

In this assignment, you are to substitute the square from the last assignment with a simple graphic of a mechanical object that has an interesting combination of shapes that vary in geometry and size. Give careful consideration to establishing interchangeability between figure and ground over the given time period. Consider the positioning of the shapes and their relationship to the edges of the frame.

typographic hierarchy: early letterform

overview

Develop three typographic animations based on a letterform from the Phoenician or Greek alphabet.

stages

Research a symbol from the Phoenician or Greek alphabet and find three to four phrases that describe its history. Create three compositions based on the symbol, its display type (i.e., phi, sigma, delta), and the copy. In the first, the symbol should be the primary focus. In the second, the display type will be the most dominant element. In the third, the copy should be given the most emphasis.

specifications

The dimensions of each composition will be 720 × 480 pixels. Images are prohibited. You may make alterations through traditional and/or digital processes. However, legibility of the type must be maintained.

Use no more than two typefaces that complement each other. You may duplicate the elements as many times as you wish and vary their sizes, spatial orientation, colors, shades, transparency, and letter spacing values to establish visual hierarchy.

considerations

Consider how the relative positioning, scale, orientation, and spatial proximity of elements contribute to creating an hierarchy.

PSA: juxtaposition and superimposition

overview

Compose an animated PSA that combines disparate images to convey a message. The objective is to explore how juxtaposition and superimposition can help create meaning between unrelated images.

stages

Choose one of the following topics: global warming, drunk driving, domestic violence, or depression. Find a minimum of three images. You are encouraged to use your own photos or found objects.

The following categories of text should be included:

- title and subtitle
- word list (for example, statistics relating to drunk driving)
- two quotes associated with your topic

continuity through the grid: storyboard design

overview

Choreographing the motion and change of objects over time and space requires careful planning during the early phase of storyboarding.

You are to design a storyboard to be used for a potential television bumper based on a theme of your choice (such as sports or religion). Your goal is to explore how the use of a grid can help organize visual content clearly and systematically.

stages

After you have appropriated or created the image and type elements, develop an initial storyboard that demonstrates the major events and transitions that will occur. Observe the relative placement of elements in the frames and their directions of travel, also their alignment to each other and to the edges of the frame. Create a grid structure on paper that shows your observations.

In Photoshop, implement your grid system using guides. Keep an open mind and be prepared to deviate from the grid to add visual interest or emphasize particular elements. While certain objects may be aligned to specific regions of the grid, others may break away.

specifications

The story should consist of eight frames, each measuring 4 × 5 inches. All eight frames can fit into one tabloid (11 × 17 inches) size document. The frames can then be cut and pasted onto a scored, two-fold piece of Bristol board.

considerations

Consider how the positioning and alignment of objects and their relationship to the frame's edges are influenced by the structure of your grid. Also consider how the directions that elements move in can adhere to or deviate from this structure.

Chapter Summary

Through history, the artistic approach to space and composition has differed across cultures and various art movements. Today, designers continue to explore how compositional principles can be used to express concepts and emotions and to establish clear and effective communication.

Design principles such as unity, figure and ground, negative space, visual contrast, hierarchy, juxtaposition, and superimposition can all be used to construct space. Non-conventional approaches to composition involve spatial, rather than framed, arrangements. Space can be suggested rather than defined by the boundaries that the screen imposes. The technique of frame division can fracture time and space, allowing viewers to use their peripheral vision to observe several actions and perspectives simultaneously. Mobile framing, or camera movement, can also guide our perception of onscreen and offscreen space.

Emphasizing spatial depth moves our eye into a realm that is less constricting than the frame's fixed two-dimensional borders. Visual advance or recession, frontal views, and oblique views from any location, as well as the device of perspective, allow us to create the illusion of three dimensions within a two-dimensional framework.

9

the sequential composition
designing with time

Every story has a beginning, middle, and end. The visual and sonic experience of images, actions, and sounds over time allows a story to unfold in its natural, chronological order. The same story can be expressed artistically according to a different timeline. Similar to the way musical conductors orchestrate sounds, motion designers orchestrate sequences of events. They choreograph the manner in which elements move and change over time, appear and disappear, and transition from one event into the next.

"Animation's ability to instantly dissolve the representational into the abstract, to leap associatively with ease, and to render simultaneously a flood of images, perceptions, and perspectives, makes it an unparalleled form of cinema."
—Tom McSorley

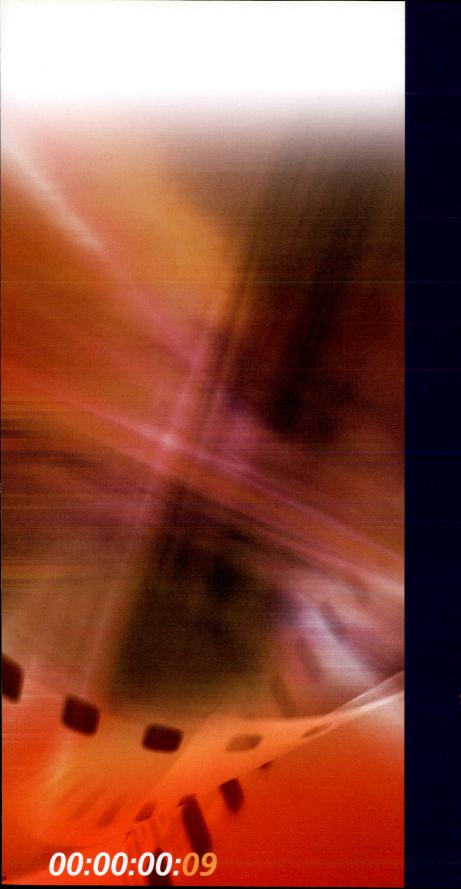

00:00:00:09

Sequencing: An Overview

The mind compartmentalizes visual information, motion, and sound into units. For example, in musical compositions, we structure sounds into predefined arrangements. In dance, we organize patterns of movement into highly refined sequences. The same is true in motion graphics: we "orchestrate" events into units or sequences that unfold over time and across space through movement and transition. This allows us to create order, build excitement, or arouse anticipation.

"Sequential composing" is a developmental process that, with dedicated thought and adequate planning, can enhance artistic expression and conceptual impact. The language of cinema can be used to tell stories in effective, meaningful ways.

Forms of Continuity

Continuity throughout a composition generates the feeling that space and time are fluid and continuous. During the 1930s and 1940s, many narrative American films were produced and edited according to the classical continuity editing style. The approach was guided by explicit rules to maintain a clear, logical narration, and relied heavily on spatial and temporal relationships between shots. Later films, such as *Singin' in the Rain* (1952) and *Persona* (1966), demonstrate a strict adherence to these continuity standards.

The application of continuity editing to motion graphics can allow you to be clear in your storytelling and delivery of information.

9.1
Frames from a Flash-based Web interstitial for SquarePig TV. This composition demonstrates an effective use of traditional cinematic continuity principles. Courtesy of hillmancurtis, inc.

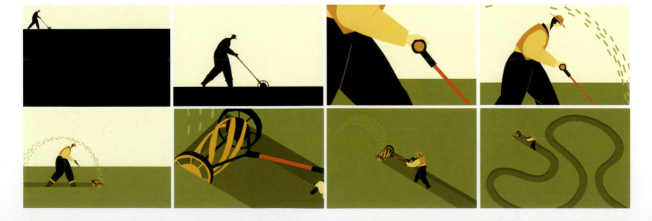

spatial continuity

Continuity can be used to structure both onscreen and offscreen space in a way that preserves the viewer's cognitive map. This means, simply, that the viewer's sense of where things are in the frame and outside of the frame is coherent and consistent throughout the composition. There should be a common space between consecutive sequences so that the viewer's flow of attention is maintained without disruptions.

establishing context

Establishing a context prior to cutting between elements facilitates the preservation of spatial continuity. For example, if you establish a context of two people looking in the same direction, subsequent frontal close-up shots should allow to us to perceive the direction of their gaze as continuing into offscreen space (**9.2**). In **figure 9.3**, frontal close-ups of two people looking at each other continue the converging vectors (discussed on p. 306) established in a prior medium shot. When the context establishes diverging vectors, subsequent frontal close-ups continue our perception of these vectors (**9.4**). In the title sequence shown in **figure 9.5,** a humorous shot of two figures combating a fictional monster cuts to a frontal, close-up shot of one of the figures, revealing his expression of dread. The context established in the first scene allows us to interpret his gaze as being directed toward the monster, and not at the viewer.

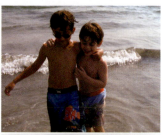
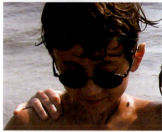
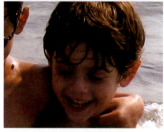

9.2
Spatial continuity of continuing vectors in subsequent close-ups.

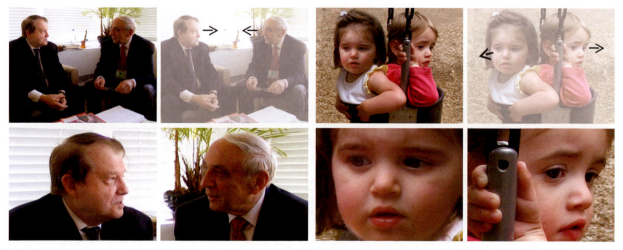

9.3
Spatial continuity of converging vectors in subsequent close-ups.

9.4
Spatial continuity of diverging vectors in subsequent close-ups.

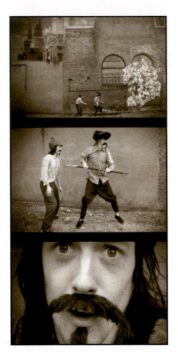

9.5
Frames from "Handle The Jandal," an opening title sequence for DIY NZ music video awards. Courtesy of Krafthaus Films (New Zealand).

index and motion vectors

"Index vectors" are powerful structural elements that provide stability in a composition. In the sequential composition, they can preserve our sense of spatial continuity between consecutive images, actions, or events. The application of a continuing index vector in **figure 9.6** is shown in a medium shot of a person looking to the right followed by a close-up in which the direction of her glance is maintained.

In traditional continuity editing in live-action film, scenes are constructed along an imaginary "axis of action" (also commonly referred to as the "vector line" or "line of conversation"), where the subjects are recorded from one side of a 180° line. The goal: to stabilize space. Although the cuts can vary between long shots and over-the-shoulder shots, they ensure a consistent screen direction in which viewers can predict where the subjects are.

The axis of action can also be used to establish relationships between two interacting subjects, for example a speaker and an audience. Cutting between two views on the same side of the 180° line establishes a "converging index vector" that creates the sense that the speaker and the audience are looking at each other. Cutting between views from opposite sides of the line, however, would produce a "continuing index vector" that make them appear to be looking at a third party. In a motion graphics environment, this principle is illustrated in the music video for the song "Megalomaniac" by the band Incubus. This dark piece, barraging us with historical live footage and animated sequences, makes use of both converging and continuing index vectors to complement the song's powerful message (**9.7**).

As a general rule, maintaining the positions of major elements in the frame between shots preserves the viewer's cognitive spatial "map." Maintaining the directions that elements move from scene to scene also preserves continuity of onscreen and offscreen space. **Figure 9.8** illustrates this principle as it is used in Velvet's recent design package for Nova TV, the first Croatian commercial television network. A male figure is shown on the right, while a female figure is located on the left. Their positioning is maintained in subsequent views, preserving a sense of spatial continuity. This partially compensates for abrupt transitions between shots. A quick cut to a close-up of the male figure's feet followed by a zoom out and a quick 360° rotation shows the male

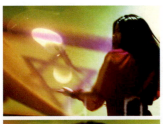
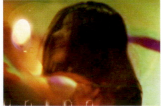

9.6
Frames from "Heritage (Phase 3)" by Jon Krasner. © Jon Krasner..

figure floating away from the woman. The direction is preserved in the diverging motion vector created by his movement. **Figure 9.9** shows another humorous sequence in which a donkey's position is fixed on the left side of the frame, while the woman's remains fixed on right. When we cut to a close-up of the donkey resisting its owner, the motion vector continues toward the right edge of the frame and into the offscreen space that we presume the woman occupies.

9.7
Frames from the music video to "Megalomaniac" by Incubus. Courtesy of Stardust Studios.

See also Chapter 3, figure 3.71, on p. 74.

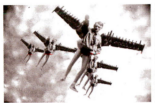
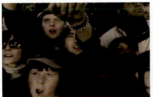
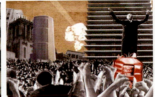
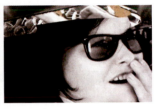

9.8
Frames from a package redesign for Nova TV, the first Croatian commercial television network. Courtesy of Velvet.

Spatial continuity is maintained in the consistent diverging motion vector of the male figure.

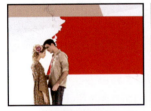
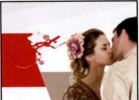
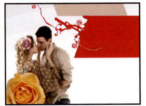

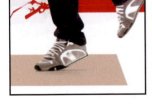
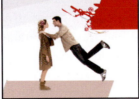
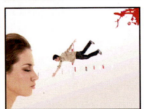

9.9
Frames from a package redesign for Nova TV. Courtesy of Velvet.

In this humorous sequence, spatial continuity is maintained in the continuing motion vector between the woman and her donkey.

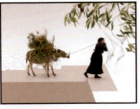
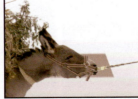
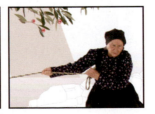

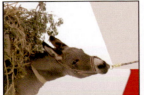
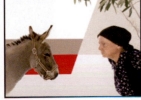
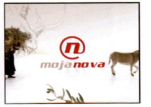

Figure 9.10 illustrates a different example of how continuing motion vectors can achieve spatial continuity. The bottom of the uppercase "E" in "innovate" extends outward to the right, leading our eye into the next scene. The view is then zoomed and rotated to feature the detective character. The wide tracking between the letters "NHANCE" guides our eye to the right, in concert with the camera's pan to the next scene.

9.10
Frames from "Adobe." Courtesy of IAAH.

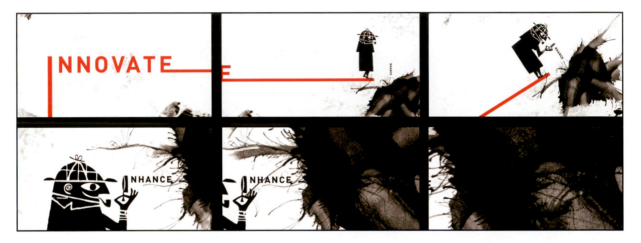

In the Pink Panther-style opener for *The Man Who Knew Too Little* (1997), a motion vector is established from the character's flick of an image to the left. After a cut to the next scene, the image's motion continues toward the left before bouncing off of the rim of the trash receptacle. The next scene features the character's hand unrolling a blueprint toward the right-hand edge of the frame. The motion of the image established by the impact with the trashcan enters the frame from the left and continues off the right edge of the screen (**9.11**).

9.11
Frames from the opening titles for *The Man Who Knew Too Little* (1997), a comic film starring Bill Murray. Courtesy of Kemistry.

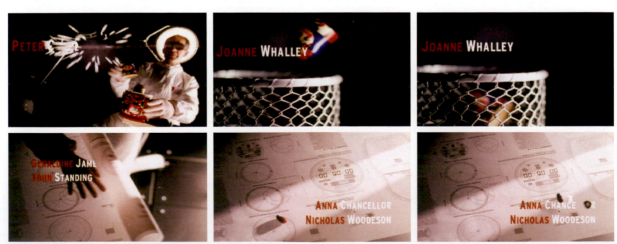

frame mobility

The effect of "mobile framing" (or "camera motion") on the sequential aspects of a composition can preserve spatial continuity. An example of this is the Web "teaser" for Artevo (**Chapter 8, figure 8.1, on p. 264**). Different scenes are presented through several emulated camera moves. A pause or a deceleration between each move is used to emphasize the most important aspects of the concept shown in words or phrases such as "a global community," "opportunities," "artists," and "invest in artists of the world." In **figure 9.12**, a single continuous pan is used in an in-store motion graphics sequence for Telecom, maintaining the viewer's cognitive spatial map.

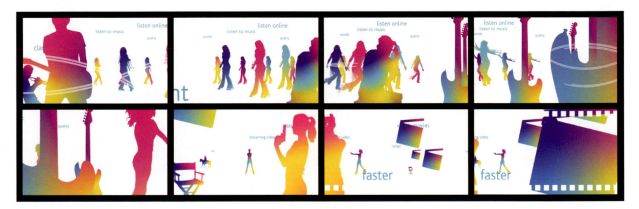

9.12
Frames from an in-store looped animation for Telecom, based on Xtra Broadband's new communications technologies. Courtesy of Gareth O'Brien of Graffe.

In a TV ad for Miller Genuine Draft, constant camera motion is employed throughout the composition to maintain both spatial and motion spatial continuity between segments (**9.13**). As we follow the movement of the soccer ball in the opening sequence, we cut to the next scene to observe its continued motion from a different perspective. In another instance, frame mobility gives us a sense of omnipresence as we are shifted in space from a straight-on, medium view, to a bird's-eye view of a drummer. As the frame continues to pull us in an upward direction, the flying drumsticks provide a natural transition into the next scene of a flying suitcase that closes on the sticks in midair. The framing of the last sequence of the composition makes us feel as if we are riding the waves with the surfer.

graphic continuity

"Graphic continuity" considers the inherent visual properties of line, form, value, color, and texture. For example, instead of employing a fade to link two segments, you might decide to zoom into a shape that matches a shape in the next segment.

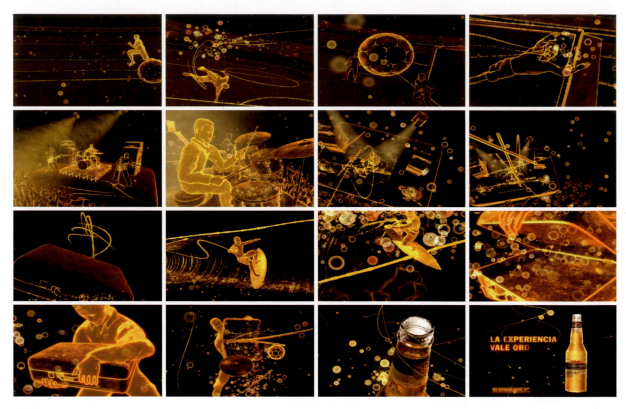

9.13
Frames from "Collector," an ad for Miller Genuine Draft. Courtesy of The Ebeling Group.

9.14
Frames from a film festival trailer. Courtesy of onedotzero.

In **figure 9.14**, the graphical sequences in a trailer for an annual digital film festival are linked together with straight cuts to match the soundtrack. As similar mechanical structures are repeated, variations of forms, values, colors, textures, and movements maintain our interest. The trailer's smooth, fluid sense of pictorial continuity feels similar to a piece of well-constructed classical music.

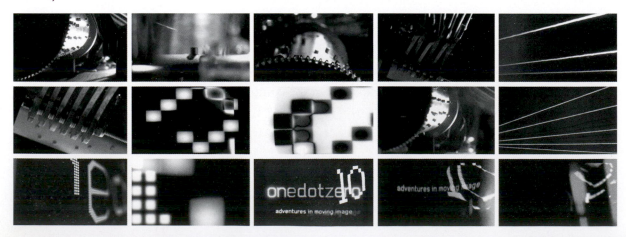

Graphic continuity can also function to provide natural transitions to move you between motion graphic sequences. In Hillman Curtis' online advertisement for Craig Frasier/Squarepig.tv (**Chapter 13. figure 13.19, on p. 463**), zooming into a portion of a scene allows us to focus on a simple geometric shape. We then cut to a similar shape and zoom out to show the same event from a different viewpoint. This transitional effect creates a smooth linkage between the two scenes.

temporal continuity

"Temporal continuity" controls the timing of an action and contributes to a plot's manipulation of story time—the way the order of events is presented. Events can be organized in chronological order or, through editing, can depart from temporal succession to take the viewer into the past, present, or future. This can achieve a sense of cause and effect, suspense, or surprise. "Classical continuity editing" presents sequences of actions in their logical order, and each action is displayed only once. Occasionally, "flashbacks" and "flash-forwards" are used to enhance the viewer's awareness of prior events and their relationship to the present. "Cutaways" are also sometimes used to show events related to the main action. In *Strike* (1924), Sergei Eisenstein made frequent use of temporal expansion through overlapping shots to prolong the action and reinforce the drama of the event. In *October* (1927), he combined overlapping shots of rising bridges to demonstrate the event's impact.

Using "dissolves" (as opposed to "cuts") aids continuity because temporally they act as a time bridge, producing thematic or structural relationships between events. For example, dissolving between a long shot of the wind blowing through trees, a close-up of leaves blowing on the ground, and wind blowing through a woman's hair creates a thematic relationship. Dissolving between tree branches blowing in the wind and a woman's hair blowing in the breeze represents a structural relationship.

"Temporal ellipsis" can condense small or large quantities of time, with the purpose of omitting unnecessary pieces of information that would normally divert the viewer's attention from the main story. Typical examples of temporal ellipsis from the 1930s and 1940s include displaying newspaper headlines, book pages fluttering, and clock hands dissolving. In Stanley Kubrick's film *2001* (1968), a sequence of a bone flying through the air cuts directly to a graphic match of a sequence showing a nuclear weapon orbiting the earth. Millennia are

In video editing, dissolves are often discouraged, because they tend to be overused to cushion discrepancies between shots, serving as a quick fix to sloppy editing.

eliminated in less than a second. Many times, dissolves, fades, or wipes are used to indicate temporal ellipsis so that viewers can recognize that time has passed. Brief portions of footage are able to be linked to compress a lengthy series of actions into a few moments.

action continuity

Animated graphic elements and live-action images can be carried smoothly across cuts and transitions to preserve both spatial and temporal continuity.

The following tips can help preserve action continuity:

1. Cutting just before or after an action will emphasize the beginning or end of the action, rather than the "flow of the action" between sequences. Cutting from a sequence containing a static element to a sequence where the element is in motion will create the effect of the element suddenly accelerating awkwardly. On the other hand, if you cut from a sequence that contains a moving element to one where the element is static, the element appears to come to an abrupt halt. Therefore, it is better to avoid the above scenarios and cut *during* an action to ensure maximum continuity. **Figure 9.15** illustrates this principle in a sequence of shots that show different views of a tennis player. Employing cuts during the action preserves continuity.

2. Cutting between different types of actions that move in the same direction will preserve continuity.

3. When cutting during a camera move, such as a pan or zoom, continue the same motion in the following sequence.

4. If you are panning with a moving element, continue the pan in the same direction and at the same velocity in the following sequence. This will maintain the camera movement *through* the cut, as opposed to interrupting the cut. Otherwise, there will be a sudden disruption to the flow of movement, and this might appear to be a mistake rather than an intentional decision.

Examples of temporal ellipsis in cinema can be seen in the opening montage in the film 9 to 5, which depicts three women on their journey to the office and in Jaws, where various shots of vacationers at the beach are linked together to portray a time shift covering the beginning of the tourist season.

9.15
Frames from Flying Machine's Sci-Fi reel. Courtesy of Flying Machine.

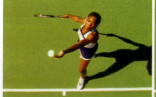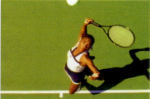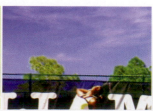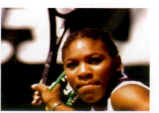

Forms of Discontinuity

"Discontinuity editing" offers an alternative approach to editing, one that uses techniques considered unacceptable, according to traditional continuity principles. Although the classical continuity system has been the most popular historically, violating this system can produce aesthetic effects that may weaken the narrative but intensify its context. In fact, discontinuity editing is guided more by emotion than story. It can be used to enhance anticipation or arouse anxiety. David Carson's music video for Nine Inch Nails is composed entirely of fleeting, disjointed images that convey the energetic, rebellious nature of the song. This abandonment of space or time lends itself to what appears to be the band's underlying themes of rage, self-loathing, and technological hype. Similarly, a montage for a title sequence, illustrated in **figure 9.16**, demonstrates how mismatching spatial and temporal relationships can be deliberately, in this case, used to express the dynamism and power of the Formula 3 race car. In **figure 9.17**, the motion graphics sequence for the Kia Magentis Web site also uses discontinuous space and time to establish the mood.

narrative and non-narrative forms

Discontinuity has been explored in both narrative and non-narrative forms of cinema and motion graphics. In traditional cinema, alternatives to continuity editing have created unusual ways of telling stories and have become integrated into mainstream culture and practice. "Accelerated editing," for instance, has been used to create tension when a story builds to an emotional climax. "Crosscutting" between simultaneous actions that occur in different locations was considered a radical innovation at the time and is still used frequently today.

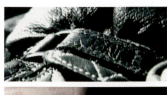
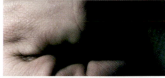
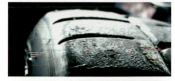
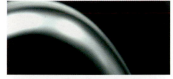
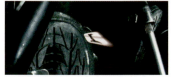

9.16
Frames from titles for *Formula 3*. Courtesy of Krafthaus Films.

9.17
Frames from the Kia Magentis Web site. Courtesy of Tavo Ponce.

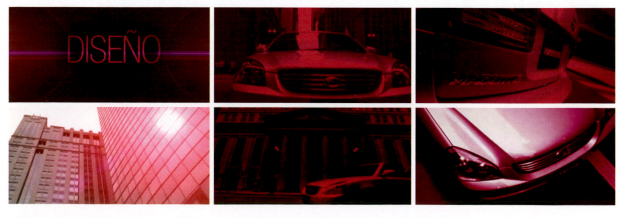

During the 1920s, many European avant-garde painters became the pioneers of avant-garde cinema, and took the most daring steps in establishing alternatives to continuity editing. Non-narrative forms of discontinuity allow motion graphic designers to focus not on content, but rather on aesthetic form and process.

graphic considerations

A myriad of graphic and rhythmic possibilities exist when you break away from the limitations of spatial, graphic, temporal, and action continuity. Images, actions, and sequences of events can be joined together by virtue of their formal graphic and rhythmic qualities.

In cinema, Bruce Conner's experimental films, such as *Cosmic Ray, A Movie*, and *Report*, for example, joined segments of found newsreel footage, film leader, and old clips according to their graphic qualities and patterns of movement.

Many discontinuity practices in early twentieth-century cinema have inspired generations of filmmakers and motion graphic designers. David Carson's intuitive use of kinetic images and typography is similar to his print work, in that it is expressive, experimental, and multilayered. He reinforces content with form, and his use of subtle shape and color contrasts effectively communicates the feel of the subject matter, often eliciting an emotional response from the viewer (**9.18**).

9.18
Frames from a TV commercial for Nike. Courtesy of David Carson.

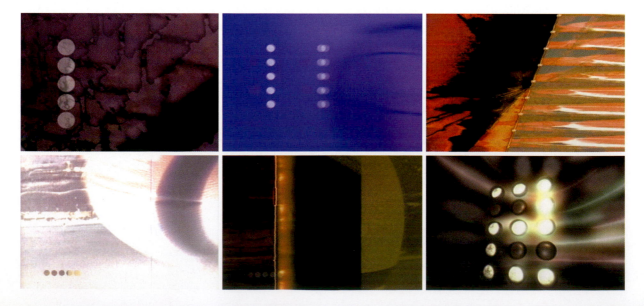

Historical Perspective

Modern art movements, such as German Expressionism, Dadaism and Surrealism, have employed various forms of discontinuity in film to engage audiences on a purely visceral level. Erich Pommer's German Expressionist film, *The Cabinet of Dr. Caligari* (1919), was groundbreaking in that it merged avant-garde techniques with conventional storytelling. Throughout the film, continuity was often sacrificed to make viewers aware that the irrational environment depicted a world of insanity experienced by the main character.

Surrealist filmmakers after World War I attempted to express dreams and the subconscious by juxtaposing and superimposing ordinary images and events that occur in daily life in unusual combinations. Their spontaneous and undirected approach to editing allowed them to arrive at far-fetched analogies and bizarre personal fetishes. Many of these films continue to be highly regarded as works of art. Luis Buñuel's *Belle de Jour* (1968) provides a voyeuristic view into the subconscious mind of a troubled heroine. Buñuel and Salvador Dali's *An Andalusian Dog* (1928) presents several disturbing events that are intentionally unrelated at a conceptual level. Hans Richter's *Ghosts Before Breakfast* (1927) presents an actor wearing a hat in one shot, immediately followed by a bareheaded shot of the same actor. Similar changes throughout the film shatter the illusion of graphic and pictorial continuity.

In Russia during the 1920s, Soviet filmmakers such as Sergei Eisenstein and Dziga Vertov also experimented with spatial and temporal discontinuity, with the objective of shocking their audiences out of passive spectatorship, inviting them to make their own conceptual connections between events.

Although narrative can take a back seat when priority is given to visual and conceptual criteria, a composition's graphic possibilities can help enforce its underlying theme. The ending title sequence to *Stranger than Fiction* (2006) is an example of this. The theme of the film is how life might play out like a story. The monotonous existence of an IRS agent is disrupted when he hears the voice of an esteemed author inside his head, ominously narrating his life. When the author narrates that he is going to die, he becomes anxiously determined to find her and convince her to change the story. In the credit sequence, quick camera movements and rapid, restless movements of elements entering and leaving the frame completely throw our sense of space and time. Unrelated spaces and events are shown with different color

When you watch a film that does not obey classical continuity, turn off the sound in order to develop an increased awareness of its underlying editing patterns. Observe one editing aspect at a time, such as the time between shots, or the manner in which space is constructed and broken up.

tints or at unusual angles (sometimes upside down). They appear to occur simultaneously as they are juxtaposed temporally through frame mobility or spatially through superimposition (**9.19**).

Without having seen the film, we see what appears to be a kinetic collage of unrelated images and events. We are forced to appreciate it from a purely formal perspective in terms of its shapes, layering, color, and movement. After hearing about the film's concept, it becomes apparent that this stylistic approach reinforces the underlying theme. The way in which the composition is sequenced gives us an insight into the world of the character of the author (or of authors in general). When writing a fictional story, authors often "pull" disparate ideas "out of a hat" and experiment with ways that they could fit together. The disjointed feel of "possibilities" is expressed in the discontinuity of image, time, and space, illustrating the struggle of the author.

9.19
Frames from the ending titles to *Stranger than Fiction*. Courtesy of the Ebeling Group. Producer: Keith Bryant; Director: MK12.

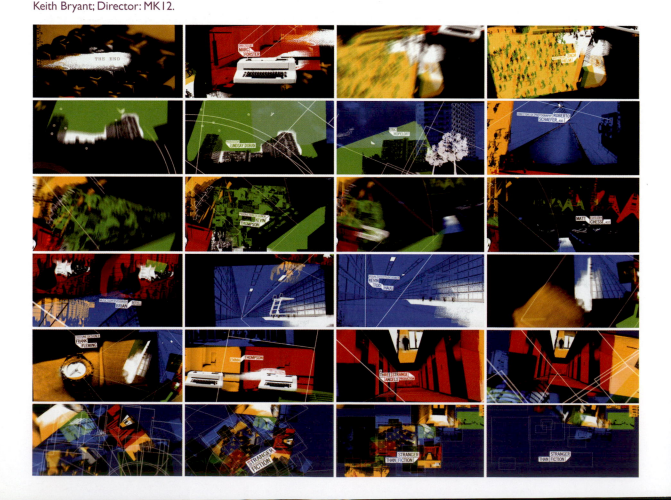

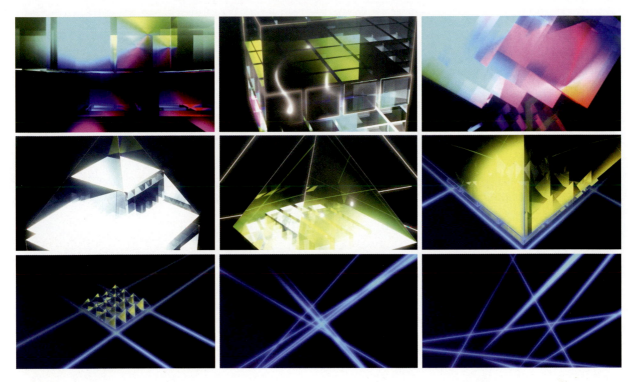

subjectivity

The use of subjectivity through "point-of-view editing" can enhance a story's narrative structure by representing the viewpoint of one or more characters. This approach tends to evolve through developing psychological connections that violate the believable space and time inherent to traditional continuity editing.

In Stanley Kubrick's *2001: A Space Odyssey* (1968), the Star Gate scene representing Dave Bowman's (Keir Dullea's) cosmic journey through time and space is historically one of the most conceptually imaginative sequences in narrative cinema. It confounds our expectations of character point of view by breaking free from the conventions of linear time and space, inviting us to engage with the mysteries of human life and the universe on a deeper level than an average narrative film could.

In motion graphics, many popular film title designs utilize the device of "montage" to create an emotional environment that allows audiences to connect or identify with the main character. For example, in David Fincher's crime film *Se7en* (1995), Kyle Cooper's renowned opening credit sequence recreates a particular state of mind, with unusual camera angles and manic, unstable movements of typography and

9.20
Frames from Addikt's promotional film leader, 2007. Courtesy of Addikt.

Discontinuity between sequences of lines and shapes enhances this composition's aesthetic impact.

Historical Perspective

After World War I, point-of-view editing allowed French Impressionist filmmakers to portray states of mind. Out-of-focus and filtered shots with awkward camera movements and unusual angles were used to depict the state of mind of characters who were drunk or ill. They also invented ways of fastening their cameras to moving vehicles, amusement rides, and machines that could move. Experimentation with editing patterns, lenses, masks, and superimpositions allowed a character's inner consciousness to be expressed. The use of flashbacks was also quite common, and sometimes the majority of the film was a flashback.

In Abel Gance's romantic melodrama, *La Roue* (1923), techniques such as rapid cut montage, extreme and low-angled close-ups, tracking, and superimposition establish a rich psychological portrayal of the film's main character. In the French silent film, *La Souriante Madame Beudet* (1923), director Germaine Dulac paints his character's emotional feelings of anxiety, entrapment, and disillusionment through slow motion, distortion, and metaphorical juxtapositioning of images (8.21). Scholars and theorists regard this psychological narrative as one of the first "feminist" films. It influenced Hollywood directors such as Alfred Hitchcock, as well as popular American genres and styles.

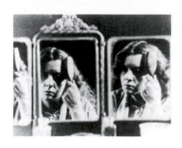

9.21
Frame from Germaine Dulac's *La Souriante Madame Beudet* (1923).

live-action elements mimicking the psychology of a character driven by obsession. The imagery appears as if it "were attacked with razor blades and bleach," according to Kyle (interviewed in "David Fincher: Postmodern Showoff," by Renee Sutter). In another interview, he stated that somebody told him "I don't know what that [film] was about, but I felt like I was watching somebody being killed."

In an animated identity for Film4Extreme's channel launch in the UK, "stylized shots of things that make you squirm" are combined with the themes of "sex, drugs, and tattooing." Particular portions of the sequence feel similar to the opening titles in *Se7en* with respect to seeing through the eyes of a character. Abrupt cuts and disjointed, disturbing images of the tattooing process allow us to connect with the bizarre female figure who appears at the very end of the sequence (**9.22**).

spatial discontinuity

Breaking spatial continuity allows you to reconstruct an environment that partially relies on the viewer's imagination. This can establish a character's viewpoint or intensify the emotional impact of the concept.

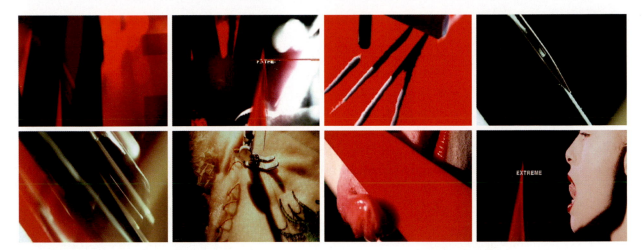

9.22
Frames from an animated identity for Film4Extreme. Courtesy of Kemistry.

In Sergei Eisenstein's film *October* (1927), a scene of crouching soldiers precedes a shot of a falling cannon. This juxtaposition creates a violation of space, forcing us to see the figures as if their government was crushing them. A shot of a cannon hitting the ground gives way to an image of starving women and children. Once the cannon's wheels hit the ground, we cut to a shot of a woman's feet in the snow. The repetitive use of cannon imagery makes it difficult to tell whether multiple cannons are being lowered or if one is shown several times. Again, we have no choice but to formulate our own interpretation of the event, in contrast to being fed the narrative.

Violating the 180° rule can be used to intentionally disorient viewers, throwing off their cognitive spatial map to weaken their impression of an objective world. In Surrealist filmmaking, the 180° principle was often abandoned in favor of cutting between opposite sides of a subject's index vector. This allowed filmmakers to create fantasy worlds that expressed the irrational thoughts of the subconscious mind. The opposing screen directions could effectively portray a character's troubled condition. In **figure 9.23**, this strategy adds visual interest to a scene that might have been too predictable if edited in traditional Hollywood-style. Giant Octopus' promotional interstitial for the Sundance film channel, which portrays a female figure posing next to a movie screen with the channel's identity projected onto it, commences with a medium-close-up shot of the figure seductively pulling her glasses downward. This subtle motion is accompanied by an abrupt frame stutter effect that lasts for a few frames. An abrupt shift to a long shot and a zoom into the figure gives us a cognitive spatial map of the environment. Our logical sense of the space is,

The internationally acclaimed Japanese film director Yasujiro Ozu was known for constructing a 360° space and filming the action was filmed in the center. Film cameras could be moved around to any point on the circle's circumference to achieve various spatial distances and camera angles in relation to the subject. The resulting violation of spatial continuity can be seen in films such as An Autumn Afternoon, Floating Weeds, *and* Late Autumn.

however, interrupted as another frame stutter is followed by a bird's-eye view of the scene. A rotating film reel occupies the foreground plane, and a line of type moves across the frame. Another cut leads into a camera tilt upward from the figure's waist to her face. This motion is intercepted by another long shot in which an animated filmstrip plays next to the figure in the foreground. A cut to a close-up of the projected channel identity is followed by a final long shot that shows the movie screen from a side angle. The varied scene duration contributes to the composition's overall sense of discontinuity.

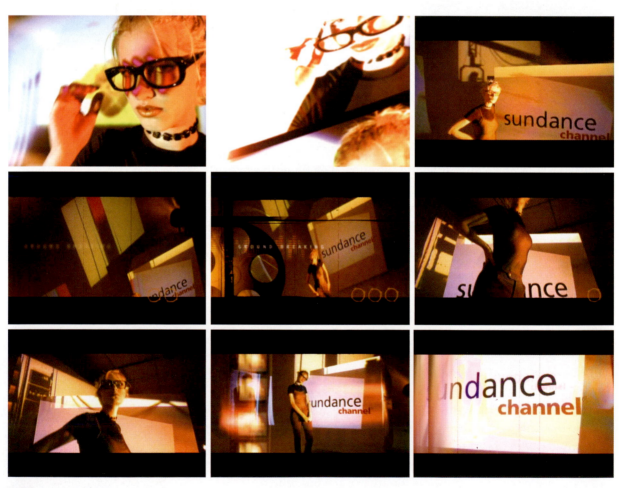

9.23
Frames from an interstitial for the Sundance film channel. Courtesy of Giant Octopus.

In Velvet's show package for the Franco-German culture *Arte Metropolis* (**Chapter 6, figure 6.36, on p. 187**), the theme of political entanglement is symbolized by a labyrinth and a ball of yarn, and expressed through the deliberate spatial discontinuity between shots. The backdrop of the labyrinth—similar to an Escher drawing where space defies the laws of physics—reinforces this concept. Throughout the composition, discontinuity is created by mixing camera angles in coordination with the actor's chaotic body and hand movements. In contrast, the rebranding of a German children's television program in **figure 9.24** illustrates how spatial discontinuity between scenes is used to express the feeling of haphazard, spontaneous play. The goal of the package was to appeal to children between the ages of 3 and 14 years.

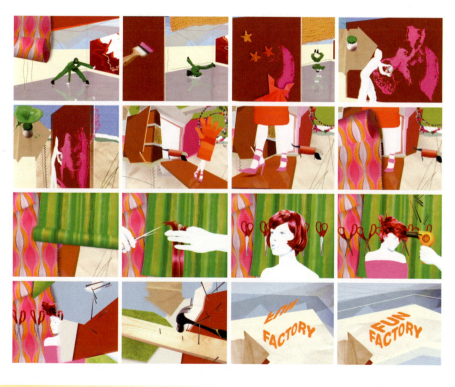

9.24
Frames from the rebranding of *ZDF-TIVI*, a German national television program for children. Courtesy of Velvet.

temporal discontinuity

Breaking temporal continuity also allows you to deliberately create ambiguity, build tension, and intensify emotional impact.

Sergei Eisenstein conceived of film as a vehicle for experimental editing, and he aimed to alter the viewer's consciousness by refusing to present a story's events in their correct, logical order. Likewise, Hans Richter strove to alter our sense of chronological time in his *Ghosts*

Before Breakfast (1927). Mismatched cuts and unexpected transitions present shots of men with and without beards, with the effect that their beards magically appear and disappear in the frame. Teacups fill by themselves, hats fly around, and a man's head detaches itself and floats in the air. At times, characters even move in reverse.

jump cuts and flash cuts

In classical continuity–style editing, "jump cuts" and "flash cuts" are considered technical flaws since they violate temporal continuity. However, they have become part of today's cinematic vocabulary because of their ability to show an ellipsis of time, arouse tension, or create disorientation by breaking the flow of events. For example, the promos for *Chappelle's Show* employ jump cuts to illustrate the sharp, defiant humor of the series (**Chapter 13, figure 13.7, on p. 456**).

9.25
Frames from "Melting Point," a fictional television show opener by Corey Hankey, Rochester Institute of Technology. Courtesy of Professor Jason Arena.

Jump cuts are used with choppy camera movements and abrupt transitions to create the hip atmosphere of a reality TV show.

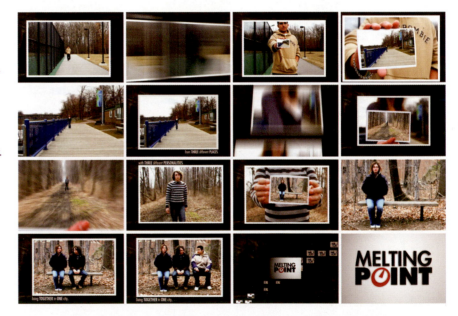

The captivating opening titles to the FearMakers film *Death4Told* (2004) combines jump cuts and flash cuts to provide an insight into the mind of a voyeur whose presence is only suggested. Fear and anxiety are induced in viewers as they witness startling evidence of the character's madness in the form of a trail of items that he has obsessively collected. In one particular segment, a pan of a brick wall containing various crime scene paraphernalia is followed by a flash cut to the dark face of a woman emerging from the background as the first credits begin to appear. Another cut presents an eerie image of a doll's face that connects to one of the piece's vignettes, "The Doll's House" (**9.26**).

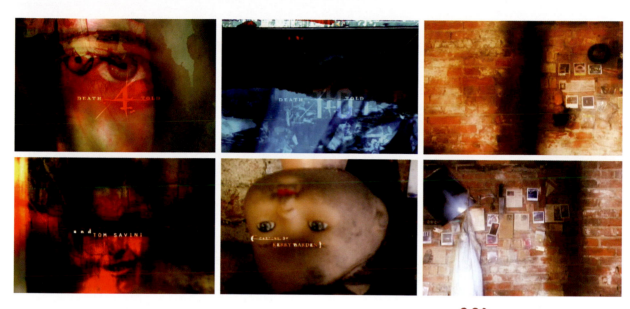

9.26
Frames from the opening titles
for *Death4Told* (2004). Courtesy
of Steelcoast Creative.

9.27
Frames from *Box,* a Surrealist
film. Directed by the Toronto-
based company Nakd. Courtesy
of The Ebeling Group. Executive
Producer: Mick Ebeling; Producer:
Susan Lee.

Jump cuts and use of camera
angles, distances, and movements
of the figure create a sense of
drama and urgency.

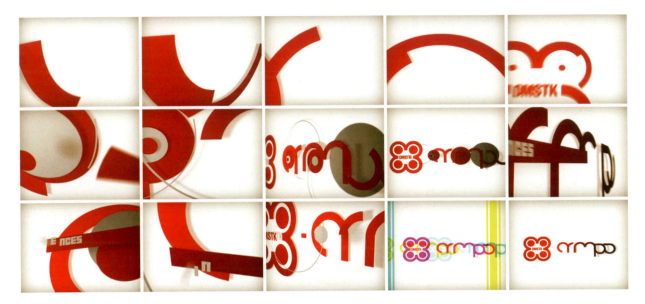

9.28
In an identity for Domestika, a community that fosters sharing among artistic disciplines, jump cuts and frame stutters were choreographed to match the rap-like beat of the soundtrack. Courtesy of Tavo Ponce.

parallel editing

"Parallel editing" is a common way of exploring discontinuous spatial and temporal possibilities. Achieved through the technique of cross-cutting, it can be used to create the illusion that different events are interwoven in time or in space. D.W. Griffith's film *Intolerance* (1916), for example, interweaves events from different eras and distant countries based on their logical (as opposed to spatial or temporal) relationships. At one point, he cuts from a setting in ancient Babylon to Gethsemane, and at another from France in 1772 to America in 1916. In *Schindler's List* (1993), director Steven Spielberg used parallel editing to contrast the hardships faced by the Jews with the comfortable lifestyle of Schindler and the Nazis.

Music videos have used crosscutting to create impossible worlds in which, for example, a character magically appears in different sets or locations "at the same time." In a television commercial promoting Bombay Sapphire gin, Stardust Studios presented various women, all representing the same heroine, walking along while pieces of the environment attach to them. The use of parallel editing allows the heroine to be transported between different worlds, from a grim, black-and-white cityscape into an exotic dream, lush with vegetation and wildlife. After diving into a body of water and swimming with a school of translucent jellyfish, she appears to be free and revived, and is again transported this time into a newly transformed sapphire blue city to make her way home in the evening's clear moonlight (**9.29**).

In a public awareness advertisement for Japan Railways, parallel editing was used to create a dual existence connecting a young musical performer who passionately plays the violin with a group of kinder-garteners. In a second ad, shots of the performer are crosscut with shots of a service manager in a subway station directing commuters to their destinations (**9.30**).

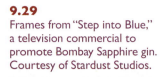

9.29
Frames from "Step into Blue," a television commercial to promote Bombay Sapphire gin. Courtesy of Stardust Studios.

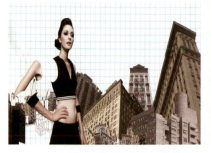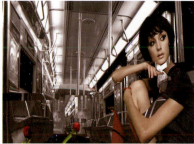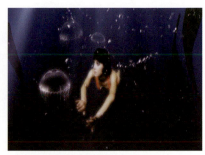

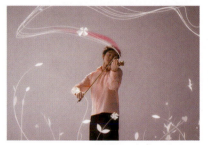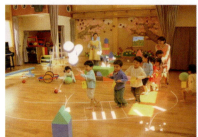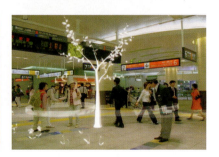

event duration and repetition

Controlling the "life" of onscreen events allows you to differentiate actual story time from screen time (or storytelling time). You can take liberties with the duration of events; events can be stretched out to make screen time longer than story time, or they can be consolidated in order to emphasize the principal actions. For example, an event that would normally last five hours could be reduced down to a few minutes or seconds to deliver the main point. Additionally, events can be repeated, and each repetition can be shown from different camera angles, spatial distances, and heights, as well as at a different speed or frame duration.

In a television segment for Times Now, a cable network based in India, the movement of the graphic flying toward the camera is repeated five times, each time with a slightly different speed and a different angle and positioning in the frame. This break with temporal continuity effectively conveys a sense of urgency that depicts the fast pace of the

9.30
Frames from "Service Manager" and "Kindergarten," ads from a public awareness campaign for Japan Railways. Courtesy of the Ebeling Group. Executive Producer: Mick Ebeling; Producer: Susan Lee; Director: Nakd.

broadcast news industry (**9.31**). In a bumper for the Golf Channel cable network, the action of a figure swinging a golf club is repeated in tiny silhouettes that are juxtaposed in the lower portion of the frame. Their similar, repeated motions alter our perception of time to emphasize the swing (**9.32**).

9.31
Frames from *6 Minutes*, a segment from Times Now, a cable network based in India. Courtesy of Giant Octopus.

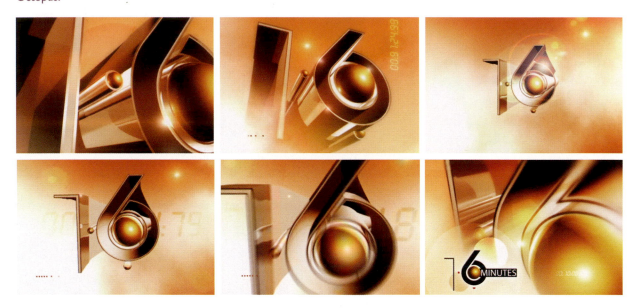

Montage

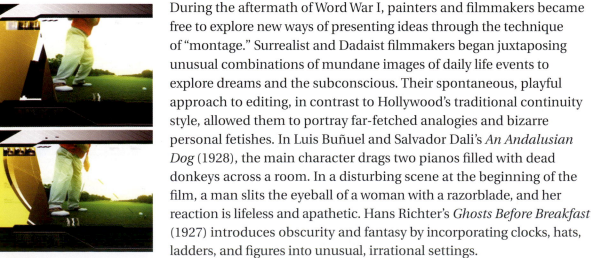

During the aftermath of Word War I, painters and filmmakers became free to explore new ways of presenting ideas through the technique of "montage." Surrealist and Dadaist filmmakers began juxtaposing unusual combinations of mundane images of daily life events to explore dreams and the subconscious. Their spontaneous, playful approach to editing, in contrast to Hollywood's traditional continuity style, allowed them to portray far-fetched analogies and bizarre personal fetishes. In Luis Buñuel and Salvador Dali's *An Andalusian Dog* (1928), the main character drags two pianos filled with dead donkeys across a room. In a disturbing scene at the beginning of the film, a man slits the eyeball of a woman with a razorblade, and her reaction is lifeless and apathetic. Hans Richter's *Ghosts Before Breakfast* (1927) introduces obscurity and fantasy by incorporating clocks, hats, ladders, and figures into unusual, irrational settings.

9.32
A bumper for the Golf Channel. Courtesy of Giant Octopus.

conceptual forms

"Conceptual montage" (also referred to as "idea-associative montage") involves juxtaposing two different ideas to formulate a third concept or "tertium quid." This allows you to communicate complex messages to an audience in a short period of time.

One form of conceptual montage is the "comparison montage," which involves juxtaposing two thematically similar events to reinforce a basic idea. For example, an image of a lighted cigarette on the ground followed by an image of a burning forest conveys the idea of environmental awareness. The "collision montage" involves juxtaposing two thematically unrelated events. The resulting idea is the result of the dualistic conflict between the two original ideas.

Flying Machine's design package for MOJO, a high-definition, male-oriented entertainment network, demonstrates a combination of comparison and collision montage. The goal was to create an edgy, suggestive design that had "attitude." Many of the themes, ranging from beer and cooking to exotic cars, exotic women, music, and travel adventure, allowed creative director Micha Riss to take liberties in comparing and contrasting images. For example, a shot of twisting and turning kitchen utensils precedes a slow pan of a sensuous female torso in the foreground and the sleek body of a car in the background. The juxtaposition between human and machine (or organic and synthetic) challenges us to make a connection. Another segment featuring extreme close-up shots of a guitar neck and a microphone moving in opposite vertical directions also invites us to construct a tertium quid through comparison and contrast. The composition ends with a medium shot of a female figure erotically blowing the smoke from the barrel of a gun with her lips (**9.34**).

Sergei Eisenstein discovered that if a film was edited to synchronize with the human heartbeat it could have a tremendous psychological effect on his audiences. In his essay "A Dialectic Approach to Film Form," he compares conflict in history to editing in film. In *Strike* (1924), he juxtaposes a workers' rebellion being put down with a nondiegetic insert of cattle being slaughtered. Eisenstein's use of parallel editing synthesizes two ideas to produce a third idea, that the workers are cattle. In the "Odessa Steps" sequence in *The Battleship Potempkin* (1925), Eisenstein juxtaposed images of innocence with images of violence. He also mixed contrasting long shots and low-angle

Clearly, Surrealist painting directly influenced the Surrealist use of cinematic montage. The stark city squares in director Germaine Dulac's The Seashell and the Clergyman (1927) were inspired by the paintings of Giorgio de Chirico. The ants appearing in Luis Buñuel and Salvador Dali's An Andalusian Dog (1928) come directly from his paintings.

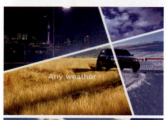
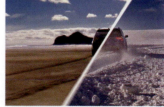
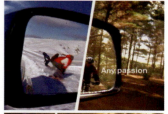
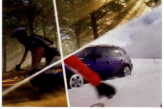

9.33
This commercial for BMW employs an animated split screen to tie together various driving conditions governed by weather and terrain. Courtesy of Stardust Studios.

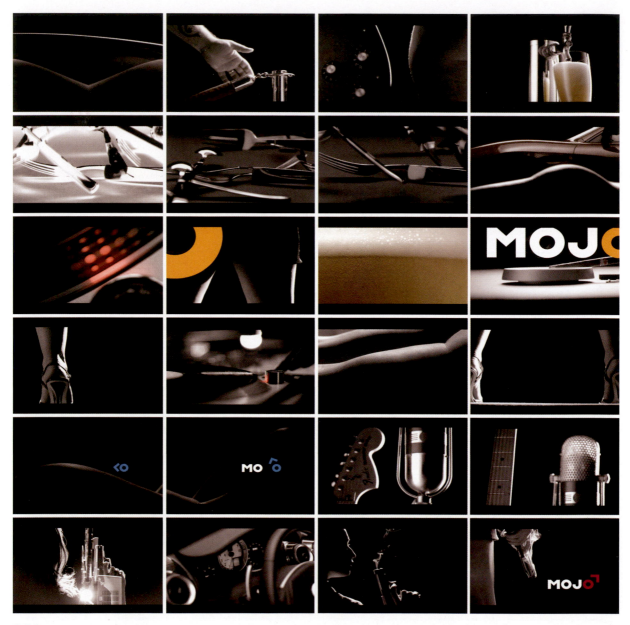

9.34

A network package for MOJO, a male-oriented, high-definition TV channel featuring a block of original prime-time shows. Courtesy of Flying Machine.

See also Chapter 7, figure 7.16, on p. 215.

shots of the soldiers with close-ups of the citizens to depict their fear and panic. In *October* (1927), Eisenstein forces us to actively interpret the events by confronting us with disorienting sequences of images of the protagonist—the Russian people—and the antagonist—the Provisional Government, which continued to support its allies after the Revolution. Shots of soldiers socializing with their German enemies are followed by a shot of a bombardment in which they run to their trenches.

Another scene of the soldiers on the battlefield follows a shot of a cannon being lowered from an assembly line. Shots of a tank are crosscut with scenes of hungry women and children standing in breadlines in the snow. As a result, the narrative is sacrificed in favor of a rhythmically striking composition that invites us to connect with the theme emotionally.

Since the late 1980s, many music videos have employed Eisenstein's theories of montage.

analytical forms of montage

Analytical forms of montage can be used to indicate the passage of time or condense or expand time within a narrative context. It can also be used to synthesize the different "time zones" of one or more related events into a single event. Although the content is critical and must be considered in terms of its thematic attributes, analytical montages often violate continuity to focus on the emotional aspects of the subject.

The early cinematic technique of "sequential montage" (also referred to as "cause-and-effect montage" or "narrative montage") has been used to tell stories in shorthand by condensing events down into their primary components and presenting them in their original cause-and-effect order.

Historical Perspective

In early avant-garde filmmaking, sequential montage often involved deconstructing the content by cutting up the film and editing it back into a condensed series of events. It often relied on devices such as repetition, close-ups, rapid cuts, and dissolves to capture and hold the audience's attention. Walter Ruttman's *Berlin: Symphony of a Big City* (1927) is an extraordinary documentary that provides an intimate portrait of urbanization by juxtaposing sequences of images of horses, trains, bustling crowds, and machines to express the dynamism of Berlin. Associations between the everyday lifestyle of the working class and that of the wealthy elite suggest a basic similarity, rather than a class struggle. The linking of these scenes unifies the content of the film by showing a cross section of a city in motion, the interaction of its parts contributing to the whole.

In Russia, Sergei Eisenstein and Dziga Vertov utilized sequential montage to express ideas about popular culture. Influenced by the Soviet avant-garde, Eisenstein rejected conventional documentaries that linked scenes in a smooth, logical manner. His films made complex, visual statements by shocking his audiences with totally unexpected scenes composed of numerous different shots.

Although the presentation is linear, spatial continuity rules are often broken to emphasize the story's highlights and shift viewers through time to suggest a fleeting passage of events.

In Krafthaus Films' opener for a New Zealand music video competition, sequential montage was employed to showcase "the ultimate sexy rock chick" in "a virtual world where she moves from heavy rock hardware into a more zen-like space after her climax," according to David Stubbs, the video's producer, writer, and director (**9.35**).

9.35
Frames from the opening titles for a New Zealand music video competition. Produced, written, and directed by David Stubbs and Gareth O'Brien for Radio Active 89FM. Courtesy of Krafthaus Films.

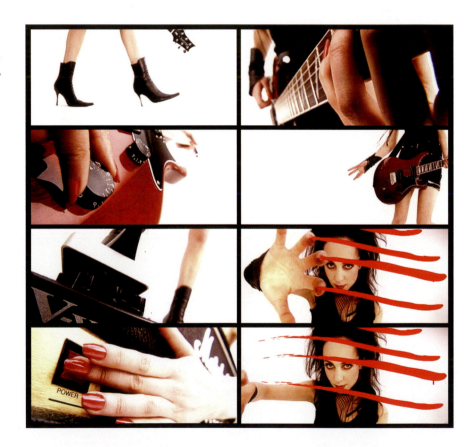

Sequential montages do not usually show the main event; rather, they imply it. This forces viewers to participate in the story by making their own personal connections. A boxing sequence, for example, may begin with a medium shot of one fighter gearing up to throw a punch. We then cut to a bird's-eye view of both fighters during the action of the punch. A shot of the crowd immediately follows, and then we cut to a final close-up of the second fighter down on the ground. The action of

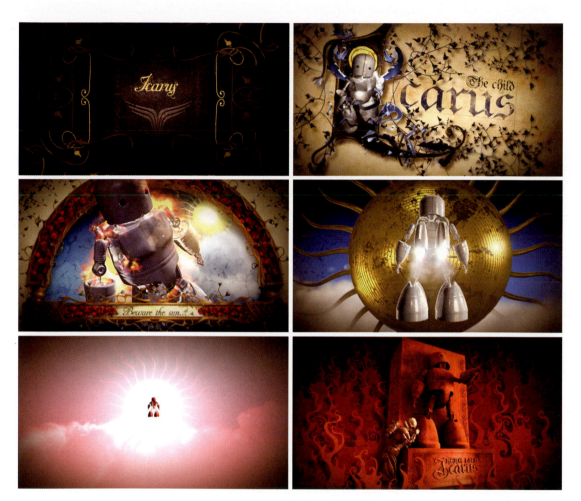

9.36
Adam Swaab's animation based on the Greek legend of Icarus is consolidated into a sequential montage that lasts a little over a minute. © 2005 Adam Swaab.

the second fighter receiving the punch is never actually shown. We are also forced to perceive space and time as continuous, even though continuity rules are broken. In a simple motion graphics scenario, a shot of an object moving across the screen is followed by a shot of another object crossing its path. These are the *cause* aspects of the montage. The next shot reveals the object's effect after the impact. The actual event in which they interact is only implied. We are expected to apply closure to realize the full event, rather than being hand-fed all aspects of the story. Although time has been condensed to intensify the emotional feel, the original order of events has been preserved.

In a Sundance Film Festival bumper, Digital Kitchen conceived the idea of using pop-up imagery from children's books. Their animated version of the story of Icarus begins with a long shot of the main character poised on a balcony. An abrupt cut reveals a close-up of his legs standing at the edge and then leaving the balcony as he begins his journey toward the sun. After a quick cut to a circular, radiating image of the sun (a desk lamp), the sequence ends with feathers floating down behind the main title to the bottom of the frame. Instead of experiencing the entire event, we are treated to its aftermath (**9.37**).

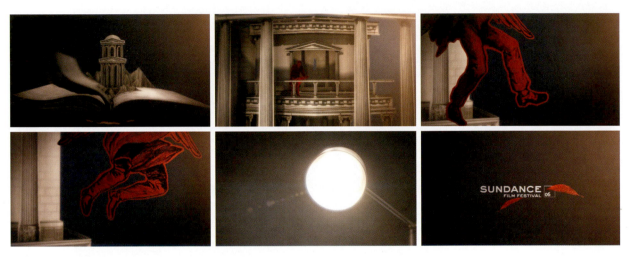

9.37
Frames from an animated bumper for the Sundance Film Festival 2006. Courtesy of Digital Kitchen.

Unlike sequential montage, "sectional montage" interrupts the flow of time by bringing the progression of events to a halt in order to focus on an isolated action. Events are not presented in their original cause-and-effect sequence, but rather, in a nonlinear fashion, allowing us to construct a new meaning, separate from the larger context they belong to.

Herbert Zettl offers a terrific analogy in his book, *Sight, Sound, Motion*: "The sectional montage acts more like a musical chord in which the three notes compose a gestalt that is quite different from playing them one by one." As an alternative to cuts, events can be juxtaposed in a split-screen display or across multiple screens to show them happening concurrently. Sports telecasts and news presentations often rely on the split screen to reveal specific moments from various points of view.

Assignments

The following assignments will help you strengthen your approach to the sequential aspects of composition. Share your work with others and discuss which devices (motion vectors, frame mobility, event duration, repetition, subjectivity, etc.) create continuity or discontinuity.

spatial continuity: primary motion #1

overview

You are to construct and edit three animated sequences of a moving object shown from multiple viewpoints. Your objective is to explore how continuity editing can create a logical interpretation of a space shown from multiple perspectives.

stages

Create a 10-second animation of a 2D shape or letterform moving in 3D space. Nest the animation into three 5-second compositions, and incorporate a camera into each composition. Adjust the camera's position and settings to show different perspectives. Nest these into a fourth 5-second composition, and vary their in and out points to show only a portion of each. Edit them using straight cuts.

specifications

Be sure to stay within the 10-second time limit. Use only straight cuts, since transitions occupy time.

considerations

Consider how spatial continuity can be preserved from onscreen into offscreen space by maintaining the direction that the element moves between the segments. Employ the 180° rule. (Placing all cameras on one side of an imaginary axis of action will help maintain continuity.)

spatial continuity: primary motion #2

overview

You will construct and edit animated sequences of two interacting objects shown from multiple viewpoints. Your goal is to explore how continuity editing can create a logical interpretation of an animation in a space shown from multiple perspectives.

A few of these assignments require recording live-action footage. If you do not own or cannot afford a camcorder, use a cellular phone that has video capabilities. (Alternatively, disposable video cameras are inexpensive and can be purchased at most convenience stores.)

Many of these projects involve the technique of nesting, as described in Chapter 12. Be sure that you are familiar with how this technique is used in the application that you are using. For example, Adobe After Effects uses precomps, while Flash uses symbols.

stages

Begin by developing a simple 10-second animation of two shapes or letterforms interacting in 3D space using an application that has 3D capabilities. Nest the animation into four 10-second compositions, and incorporate a camera into each. Adjust the camera's position and settings in each to show different perspectives of the action. Nest these compositions into a fifth composition, and vary their in and out points to show only a portion of each. Edit them using straight cuts.

specifications

Be sure to stay within the 10-second time limit. Use only straight cuts, since transitions occupy time.

considerations

To establish spatial continuity in the scenario of two people having a conversation or engaging in a game or physical activity, all cameras are placed on one side of a 180° line. The same principle should be applied to this assignment. Consider using an imaginary axis of action to determine the correct camera viewpoints. Additionally, consider how spatial continuity can be preserved from onscreen into offscreen space by maintaining the direction that elements move between scenes.

spatial continuity: secondary motion

overview

You are to construct and edit a series of animations that show an object from multiple camera angles and spatial distances, and using mobile framings. Your goal is to explore how continuity editing can create a logical interpretation of an object in a space through camera animation.

stages

Create a simple shape in a 3D space. Create five 5-second compositions that contain the static shape. Incorporate a camera into each and adjust its position to reveal different perspectives of the shape. Animate the camera in each to create a different type of mobile framing. (One animation might show a zoom-in from a bird's eye view, while another might employ a tilt upward from a frontal, close-up view.) Nest the animations into a new 5-second composition, and vary their in and out points to show only a portion of each. Edit them using straight cuts.

specifications

You are to stay within the 10-second time limit and use only straight cuts.

considerations

Consider how frame mobility preserves spatial continuity. Consider employing the 180° rule. (Placing all cameras on one side of an imaginary axis of action will help maintain spatial continuity.)

primary and secondary motion #1

overview

You will construct a live-action sequence of two figures interacting based on a series of shots that involve multiple camera angles, spatial distances, and mobile framings. Your goal is to explore how continuity editing can create a logical interpretation of an event shown from various perspectives and using mobile framings.

stages

Choreograph a 10-second performance involving two people interacting in a conversation or physical activity. Have them rehearse the motions so they are consistent. Videotape the event five times, each time from a different camera angle and distance. Frame mobility can be employed during shooting or on the computer after the footage has been digitized. Each clip should be approximately 10 seconds long.

Digitize and import the clips into a motion graphics application of your choice. Vary the in and out points of each clip to show only a portion of each. Edit them together using straight cuts.

specifications

Be sure to stay within the 10-second time limit. Use only straight cuts, since transitions occupy time.

considerations

Consider how frame mobility preserves spatial continuity. Consider employing the 180° rule. (Placing all cameras on one side of an imaginary axis of action will help maintain spatial continuity.)

primary and secondary motion #2

overview

You are to record and edit a live-action scene using multiple camera angles, spatial distances, and mobile framings. Your objective is to explore how continuity editing can create a logical interpretation of an event shown from various perspectives and with secondary movements.

stages

With the help of three people, film a short live-action sequence from four different camera angles and spatial distances. Frame mobility can be employed during shooting or created digitally after the footage has ben captured. Each clip should be approximately 10 seconds long.

specifications

Stay within the 10-second limit. Use straight cuts since transitions occupy time.

considerations

Consider how frame mobility and the 180° rule can be used to preserve spatial continuity.

breaking spatial continuity

overview

Reconstruct the first four assignments to deliberately break continuity. Your objective is to investigate how violating continuity can strategically disorient viewers and evoke a sense of mystery or induce emotion.

specifications

You may duplicate objects and camera movements and present them out of their original sequence. Use only straight cuts in order to stay within the specified 10-second time limit.

considerations

Observe how deviating from the 180° rule and cutting before or after object or camera actions makes space discontinuous.

"In the creative state, a man is taken out of himself. He lets down, as it were, a bucket into his subconscious, and draws up something that is normally beyond his reach. He mixes this thing with his normal experience, and out of the mixture he makes his work of art."

—E.M. Forster (1879–1970)

Chapter Summary

Sequential composition considers the manner in which a story's events occur over time. Cinematic language and traditional editing techniques can be used to tell stories in meaningful ways.

Continuity editing practices have been used to create a logical sense of space and time. The use of index and motion vectors can preserve the viewer's logical sense of space between scenes. Both graphic and temporal continuity can be used to create smooth linkages between scenes and to contribute toward a plot's manipulation of story time. The device of temporal ellipsis can condense time in order to omit unnecessary information that might divert an audience's attention from the story.

Discontinuity can be used to enhance anticipation or arouse anxiety. The use of subjectivity through point-of-view editing can enhance a story's narrative structure by representing the viewpoints of one or more characters. Breaking spatial continuity can reconstruct an environment in a way that partially relies on the imagination of the viewer. Varying event duration and repetition allows you to break temporal continuity in order to differentiate actual story time from screen time. Events can be stretched out, consolidated, or repeated from various viewpoints.

The technique of montage can be used to help audiences connect or identify with the subject matter. Conceptual montage involves juxtaposing two different ideas to formulate a third idea, or tertium quid. Sequential montage tells stories in shorthand by condensing events into their primary components in their original cause-and-effect order. The main event is typically implied, forcing viewers to make their own personal connections. The sectional montage interrupts the flow of time by bringing the story to a halt in order to focus on an isolated action or event.

10

conceptualization
ideation and design

Regardless of tools and delivery format, concept development is critical to all forms of graphic communication. Since the beginning of the twentieth century, artists have expressed their ideas through the medium of animation. In more recent years, graphic designers have harnessed the potential of time and motion to convey their ideas in movie titles, network identities, Web sites, multimedia presentations, and environmental graphics. In the past, developing concepts to communicate ideas was the first challenge. Their current challenge is developing *unique* concepts and communicating them by storytelling.

"Creation is the artist's true function. But it would be a mistake to ascribe creative power to an inborn talent. Creation begins with vision. The artist has to look at everything as though seeing it for the first time, like a child."
—Henri Matisse

"The greatest art is achieved by adding a little Science to the creative imagination. The greatest scientific discoveries occur by adding a little creative imagination to the Science."
—James Elliott

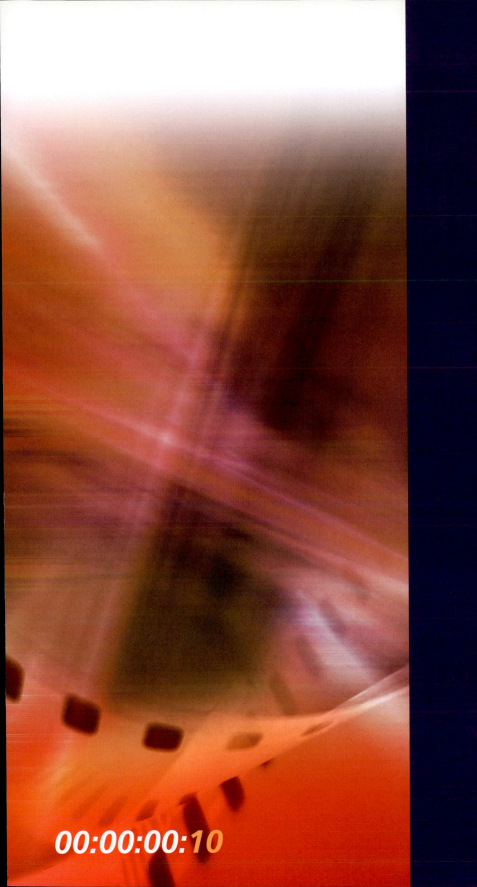

00:00:00:10

Assessment

defining the objective

Every design begins with an objective. Without a clear objective, your ideas can become lost in an ocean of right-brained activity. Before plunging into the creative waters, it is best to clearly define your objective on paper, without a lengthy narrative.

Coming to terms with a project's objective may take time. Once it is established, it should be kept in mind from conceptualization through design to the final execution.

conducting the research

Research is key to effective communication. Great design may not be enough to express an idea or convey information if adequate research is not conducted ahead of time. Diving into the creative waters too soon carries the danger of time and energy being wasted on concepts that may be irrelevant or inappropriate to your project's objectives. Therefore, thorough research of your target audience and subject matter must occur before you begin putting the pencil to paper.

Since the goal of visual communication is to elicit a reaction from an audience, this audience should be clearly defined.

Clients can mistakenly assume that the designers are well informed about the topic being considered. This assumption can be dangerous for both parties. Therefore, it is wise to step up to the plate and educate yourself about the subject at hand. A wide range of resources are available to aid you in your investigation. Many people consider the Internet to be the quickest method of finding information. Others find the library to be the most efficient resource. Setting up a meeting to discuss the material with your client first-hand can be beneficial—he or she will be the most valuable source of information.

After director Carlos Lascano wrote the short film that commemorated human rights organization Amnesty International's fiftieth anniversary, he and the design team at Prague-based motion graphics studio Eallin investigated episodes in which basic human rights, including freedom of conscience, speech, and religion, have been attacked or suppressed during the past 50 years of world history. Their research showed that many of the countless examples were followed by a positive outcome.

To define your target audience, ask yourself the following questions:

1. What are the demographics (cultural, social, economic) of my target audience?

2. What does my audience already know about the subject?

3. What do they need to know?

4. How has this information been communicated before?

5. What single message should people walk away with?

6. What type of response should be expected from my viewers?

In the industry, clients often think they know what they want but change their mind in the middle of a project. It is wise to review with the client a clear articulation of the project's objective before the creative process commences.

The fact that human rights always seemed to prevail led to the idea of turning the reawakening of freedom into the narrative thread of the story. One particular event—the Carnation Revolution that took place in Portugal in the 1970s—led to the idea of using the red carnation flower in the film to represent freedom. Serving as a powerful symbol of hope, this metaphor appears across a moving storyline demonstrating mankind's struggle for freedom throughout history. (**Figure 10.6** shows some of the original sketches that were used to formulate the storyline of "Standing Up for Freedom." These provide a written description of events that occur in different episodes and a breakdown of animation techniques to be used in each scene. Actual frames from the completed production are shown in **Chapter 13, figure 13.1, on p. 452.**

At Kent State University, Renee Volchko's spot for Big Brothers Big Sisters involved considerable research. According to Renee: "I wrote up a project scope along with a creative brief. Then, I became involved with the program by volunteering at a festival, getting to know some of the 'bigs' and 'littles' while learning more about this company. Then, I began software tutorials to refine my skills and devised a plan as to how I could obtain the direction I wanted. To make the project more unique and to give the ad spots a more modern feeling, I started a slight identity re-brand. Afterward, I comped up some rough pitch boards to solidify decisions and establish the look I was aiming for. About a week later, I scheduled interviews with the kids and began filming. During this whole process I blogged about my work." Renee's decision to combine live-action imagery and simple cartoons resulted in a fresh style of storytelling that caters to the theme of childlike innocence (**10.1**).

In Kike Maíllo's film *Eva* (2012), researching the topic of neural interconnectivity helped formulate the concept for the holographic interface in the movie which gives the main character the ability to control his robot's consciousness. The goal was to represent the behavior of interconnected elements in a neural network, similar to thought processes or emotions inside the brain. The interface's detailed, crystalline structures were also inspired by the presence of snow in many of the film's scenes and from the romantic feel of outdated laboratory equipment waiting to be used for experimentation and discovery. These ideas also served to provide the main imagery for the film's title design (**10.2**).

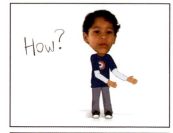

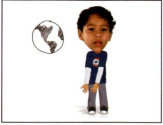

10.1
Frames from a spot for Big Brothers Big Sisters, by Renee Volchko. © 2012 Kent State University. Courtesy of Professor Gretchen Rinnert.

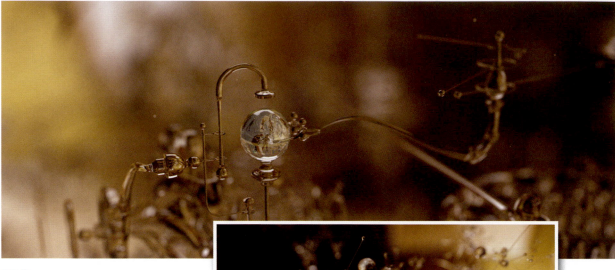

10.2
Frames from the opening title sequence to *Eva* (2012). Courtesy of Dvein.

See also Chapter 2, figure 2.13, on p. 33.

10.3
Concept sketches for a trade show video by Jon Krasner. Courtesy of Syncra Systems, Inc. and Corporate Graphics.

The metaphors used here came as a result of educating myself about supply chain management.

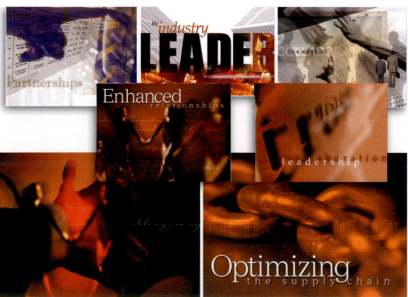

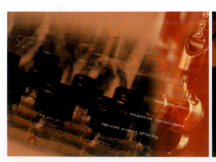

understanding the restrictions

Successful artists aspire to exceed their own potential. Passion drives them to become better at what they do. Artists create not because they want to, but because they have to in order to feel personally rewarded. However, the design industry imposes certain restrictions that artists need to observe in the commercial world. Budgetary constraints can limit the use of materials, equipment, and reliable technical support, and prohibit hiring outside photographers or purchasing larger numbers of images or video clips. Regardless of how unreasonable deadlines may appear, designers are forced to be realistic about what can and cannot be accomplished within the given window of time that is available. For example, E! Networks declared the need for a show opening for *Style Court* less than three weeks before airing (after spending many weeks looking through hundreds of static logo designs to choose the show's identity). Designer Susan Detrie was put to the test, with a time frame of under forty-eight hours for developing a storyboard. A combination of quick thinking and late evening hours resulted in an engaging board that presents a variety of images that reflect the show's entertaining nature and wide age range. Humorous "style crime" icons, such as a bad hairdo, a leopard-skin suit, and an evidence bag consisting of 1970s platform shoes, create a feel similar to that of a police show such as *NYPD Blue* (**10.4**).

"With creative freedom, time, money, and reliable technical support, the potential here is limitless. Just imagine the possibilities!"
—Jon Krasner

"Better to have the creative reins pulled back than to be kicked in the flanks for more!"
—Meagan Krasner

10.4
Storyboard for a show opener to *Style Court.* Courtesy of E! Networks and Susan Detrie.

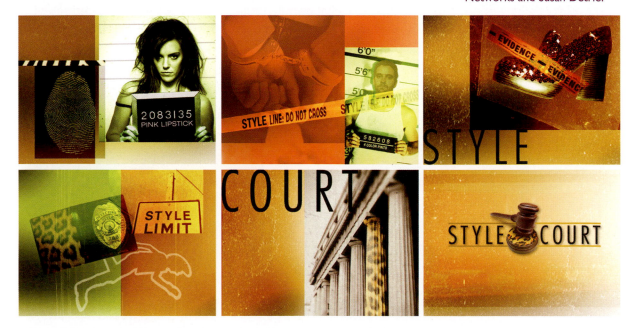

Addressing the client's needs up front will avoid frustrations down the road. Miscommunication is prone to happen when an intermediary intervenes between you and the client. If the opportunity presents itself, try to establish a one-on-one rapport with the "head honcho." A relationship based on mutual respect and trust provides you the opportunity to unlock the client's mind and convince him or her that your idea will work.

With a combination of professionalism, assertiveness, and respect, clients can be convinced on an idea, provided that trust has been built.

Client opinions and biases can also be creatively restricting. Clients are not always open to new ideas, even if they say they are. It is seldom that designers are given complete artistic freedom. Some clients may seem utterly inflexible and closed-minded, while others may attempt to play the role of art director or "creativity gatekeeper." Because the client controls the paycheck, and to an extent your reputation, pride built on years of educational training may have to be swallowed in order to keep your client satisfied.

These restrictions should not be perceived as limitations to creativity, but rather, as guidelines to help give your ideas direction.

imagery and graphic style

There are many types of images to choose from: photographic, typographic, illustrative, abstract, and so forth. As discussed in **Chapter 7**, images can take on different graphic styles—blended or textural, whimsical, or sketchy, to name just a few. Techniques such as cropping, lighting, distortion, color manipulation, layering, deconstruction, and masking can enhance the expressive properties of your content prior to production. The style of the visuals depends on your underlying theme or message, whether it is marine, sports, rock n' roll, theatre, or country. A figurative interpretation of an idea may require metaphorical images, while other types of visuals may be suited to a literal interpretation. Your imagery's graphic style should reflect the demographics of your target audience, whether they are artists, yuppies, teenagers, or working professionals. These factors need to be determined as early as possible.

10.5
Frames from "Planted," a motion identity for Capacity motion design studio.

The metaphor of seeds being planted to grow into something beautiful expresses the concept of running a creative business.

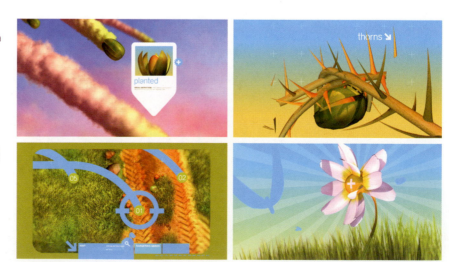

Formulation

Once the objective, target audience, and restrictions have been defined and the subject has been thoroughly investigated, the floodgates of creativity can be opened to allow imaginative ideas to pour forth.

"An idea is a point of departure only. As soon as you elaborate it, it becomes transformed by thought."
—*Pablo Picasso*

brainstorming

Brainstorming is the first step to generating ideas and works best in an environment that is conducive to creative thought without annoyances such as junk email, uncooperative technology, and telephone sales calls. Scheduling a continuous block of time to think quietly without distractions is recommended. Some people react well to background music while others require complete silence in order to concentrate.

All concepts begin in the imagination. As they emerge, they should be recorded immediately. It is wise to have a sketchbook handy to capture the spontaneous flow of ideas. Putting pencil to paper is an invaluable process that, like music improvisation, keeps ideas fresh and moving. Sketches (or "thumbnails," as they are referred to in print design) should be small and loose, allowing a quick generation of ideas. Spending too much time polishing a sketch can break creative momentum. Some designers prefer to work out their concepts in a more polished, digital format because the results more closely resemble the final product.

Every new project is a growing experience, and the fruits of your labor do not have to be wasted. Ideas do not have to be discarded; they can be jotted down, drawn on paper, voice recorded, and filed away for future use. Sometimes new ideas are abandoned and replaced with old ones.

10.6
Concept sketches with episode descriptions for the film "Standing Up for Freedom" for Amnesty International. Courtesy of Eallin.

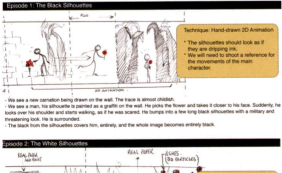

Episode 1: The Black Silhouettes

Technique: Hand-drawn 2D Animation
• The silhouettes should look as if they are dripping ink.
• We will need to shoot a reference for the movements of the main character.

- We see a new carnation being drawn on the wall. The trace is almost childish.
- We see a man, his silhouette is painted as a graffiti on the wall. He picks the flower and takes it closer to his face. Suddenly, he looks over his shoulder and starts walking, as if he was scared. He bumps into a few long black silhouettes with a military and threatening look. He is surrounded.
- The black from the silhouettes covers him, entirely, and the whole image becomes entirely black.

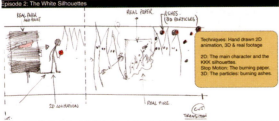

Episode 2: The White Silhouettes

Techniques: Hand drawn 2D animation, 3D & real footage
2D: The main character and the KKK silhouettes.
Stop Motion: The burning paper.
3D: The particles: burning ashes.

We see that the black texture is, actually, black paint censuring a poster in which we still can see the drawing of a red flower.

- From the poster, a black silhouette of a man walks out. He carries a red carnation on his hand. After a few steps, he enters another poster, a blank one. The man is surrounded by silhouettes with pointy hoods. When they open their eyes, we realize what they really are: members of the KKK, that rise their torches and set the blank poster with the man in it on fire. The poster is burnt in a stop motion effect, and it turns into dozens of little pieces of burnt paper that peel off from the wall and are blown away by the wind. The poster is gone but in the place where it was, on the wall, we now see the silhouette of the carnation, made of ashes and paper, that still burns, stuck to the wall.

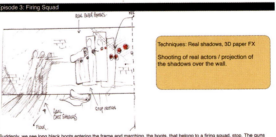

Episode 3: Firing Squad

Techniques: Real shadows, 3D paper FX
Shooting of real actors / projection of the shadows over the wall.

Suddenly, we see long black boots entering the frame and marching, the boots, that belong to a firing squad, stop. The guns rise, the camera pans to the side and shows several posters, each one with a silhouette, as if each one was a person against the firing wall. The guns fire, making holes on the wall, as the posters peel off from the wall and fall to the ground as executed people. In some of the wholes made on the wall, red flowers grow with a stop motion effect. They all form the large silhouette of the red carnation.

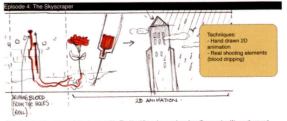

Episode 4: The Skyscraper

Techniques:
- Hand drawn 2D animation
- Real shooting elements (blood dripping)

From the bullet holes on the wall, blood starts to drip. The blood flows downwards and ramifies as veins. We see these red vessels nourishing the roots of a big, red, bright flower.
Suddenly, a huge syringe sinks in the ground and starts to suck up the red sap. The petals fall off and the flower withers quickly, and dies. The camera pans up and we see the syringe growing as it sucks up the liquid, and becomes... a huge black skyscraper.

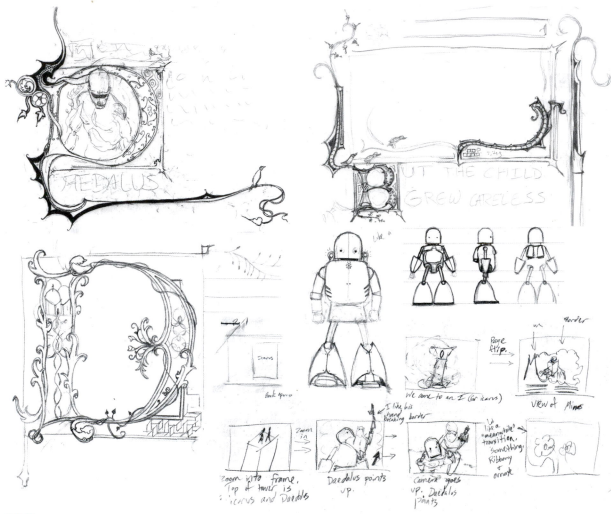

10.7
Concept sketches for "Icarus."
Courtesy of Adam Swaab.

See also figure 10.32 and
Chapter 9, figure 9.36, on p. 331.

In a pitch for Cadbury (**10.8**), the design team at Psyop wanted to induce a child-like wonder in its adult audience while reinforcing the company's visual brand. Anh Vu, the project's lead designer, conceptualized an apparatus that would operate like an elaborate Rube Goldberg machine to suggest Cadbury's iconic swirl of chocolate. He envisioned this device (which he refers to as the "twirly gig") being triggered by birds and began working out the mechanics on paper while hand-crafting sculptures of paper cranes. He states: "I decided to hand fold 80 plus flying paper birds and hang them, creating a spiral vortex of paper cranes. I liked the idea of paper cranes because it felt tactile, playful, and magical. The birds would fly and trigger a reaction to the twirly gig, creating a domino effect to the structure, essentially adding some functionality to it."

He further explains: "In order to finish the pitch on time, we quickly mocked up a sketch of a whale cage that would contain trapped paper birds. As the twirly gig starts to rotate, it would open the cage contraption and spin the vertebrae of the whale which at each end had a paper bird attached on strings. Everything would be spinning and each detail of the piece would have a meaningful functionality to the main structure."

10.8
Style frame and concept sketches from a Cadbury pitch.

See also Chapter 7, figure 7.9, on p. 211. Courtesy of Pysop.

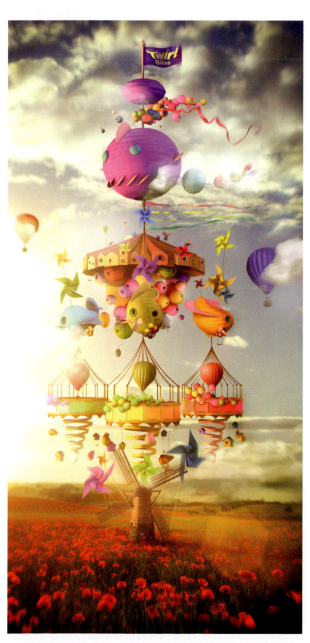

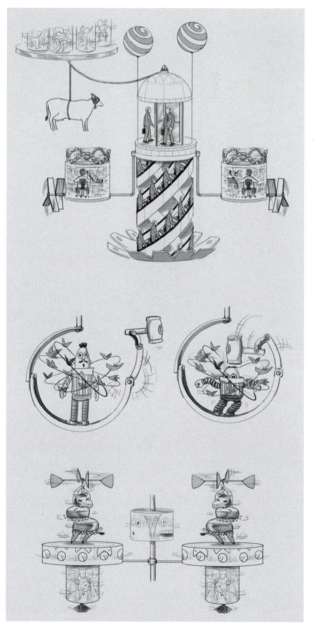

p. 348

10.9

Concept sketches from "The Princess and the Sub-Prime Variable Rate Mortgage," a PSA animation by Ken Cadieux. Courtesy of Professor Jon Krasner, Fitchburg State University.

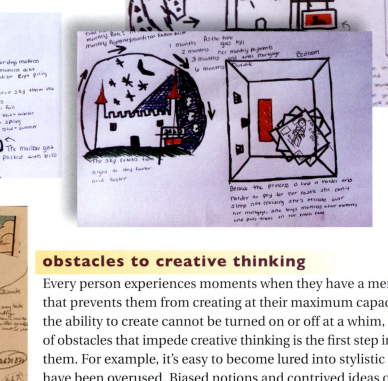

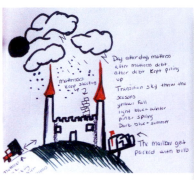

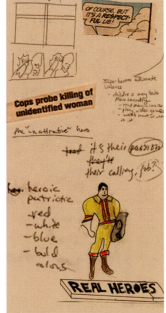

10.10

Sketches for a sting entitled *Hero Stereotype* by Megan Mock, University of San Francisco. Courtesy of Professor Ravinder Basra.

obstacles to creative thinking

Every person experiences moments when they have a mental block that prevents them from creating at their maximum capacity. Although the ability to create cannot be turned on or off at a whim, being aware of obstacles that impede creative thinking is the first step in avoiding them. For example, it's easy to become lured into stylistic trends that have been overused. Biased notions and contrived ideas of what's "hot" can limit the range of creative opportunities and prevent you from being original. Being aware of trends in the industry is healthy, as long as your design does not become reliant on them. The range of digital effects that are available can also intrude on creative thinking, since they require minimal artistic skill or sophistication. Although they can be beneficial when used intentionally, they lack ingenuity, and their ease of use can impede imaginative thinking and obscure aesthetic judgment. The abundance of stock photography, illustration, fonts, and clip art makes it easy for designers to rely on ideas relating to popular culture rather than on their own capacity to conceptualize.

Last, the demand for maintaining technical proficiency can impede creativity. Be sure not to lose sight of your primary goal as a designer.

Formulation

pathways to creative thinking

Creativity can be mistaken for originality, when in fact very few original ideas exist. Many designers merge previous concepts in their own personal way. *Creative* designers, like laboratory scientists, trust their intuitions and are not afraid to face new challenges. Yet, the creative process can be elusive. Ideas sometimes spring up when we least expect them to. Inspiration, risk taking, and experimentation can foster innovative thinking and allow ideas to develop naturally.

inspiration

Inspiration is the motivating force behind innovation. Unlike a job that ends when the shift is complete, seeking out inspiration is a continuous process of searching for new angles and directions in an attempt to smuggle your ideas into each new assignment.

In India, *Ghe bharari* ("Fly" in English) is a women's show that features topics such as yoga, diet recipes, and ayurvedic tips. The concept behind the program is to focus on women from different walks of life who have had the courage to fight against extreme consequences and reach their goals. Inspired by the Surrealist painter Salvador Dali, creative director Varun Chawla used metaphors in the show opener to portray the innermost qualities of females in contemporary Indian culture rather than showing a literal depiction of women. For example, the oyster reflects inner beauty, a bird expresses freedom and transformation, a pair of wings depict escaping society's constraints, and two hands express the act of giving. The painterly quality of the imagery, exquisite attention to detail, and subtle camerawork allows us to derive our own interpretation of the inner beauty of a woman (**10.12**).

Artists often find inspiration by identifying with their subject. A student of mine once expressed the idea of violence through her experience in working with victims of domestic abuse. Able to connect with the psychological consequences they faced, her emotional identification inspired her to develop genuine ideas. In creating an opener for a CD-ROM mailer, the themes of panic and disaster inspired me to develop an entertaining animation that marketed software designed to protect data from the possibility of a hard drive crash. Panic was expressed from a physiological standpoint with images pertaining to physical responses to stress or fear. Disaster was conveyed through images of tornadoes, earthquakes, and floods (**10.13**).

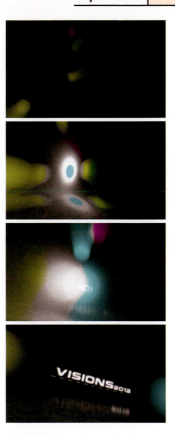

10.11
In a bumper for *Visions*, an annual student honors exhibition at Fitchburg State University, Justin Medas used the theme of light to depict various technology-based artistic media to represent the concentrations of the Communications Media department. Dynamic balls of vibrant, colored light rush to a common spot in the frame and explode to reveal the title "Visions 2012." Courtesy of Professor Jon Krasner, Fitchburg State University.

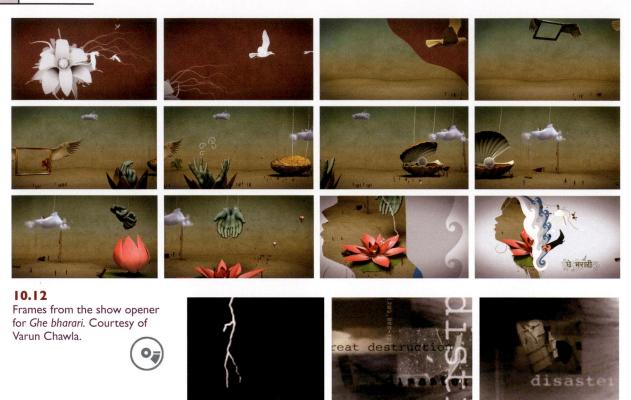

10.12
Frames from the show opener for *Ghe bharari.* Courtesy of Varun Chawla.

10.13
Frames from an opener to a CD-ROM mailer for Accurate Data. Concept and design by Jon Krasner. Courtesy of Belden-Frenz-Lehman, Inc.

"I have ideas floating around everywhere and it has become routine for me to jot them down on whatever I have at the time. . . my phone, a napkin, the back of my hand."
—Renee Volchko, Kent State University student

The ability to identify with your subject, however, does not always come naturally. In most cases, it occurs after conducting adequate research. In 2000, twenty2product was asked by RockShox, a leading company in the global cycling community, to develop concepts for a Web site and trade show video. After becoming familiar with the cycling industry, twenty-2product developed an appreciation for the mechanical know-how involved in designing bicycle parts. Technical machine drawings became a source of inspiration and were used to inform the look and feel of the graphics. Complex diagrams, abstract graphic patterns, typography, and live-action footage were integrated into a highly compelling series of sketches that conveyed forward thinking and the millennium and all of the things that it implied (**10.14**).

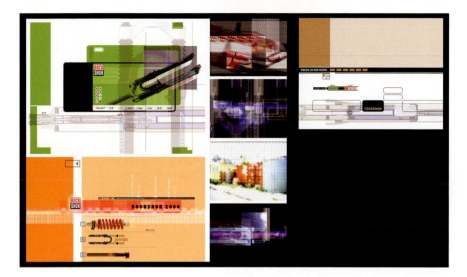

10.14
Style frame for RockShox's
Web site for. Courtesy of
twenty2product.

For the opening to a political Franco-German evening program *Arte Metropolis*, the antique Greek drama of Ariadne and Theseus served as an inspiration for the central theme. Two elements from the story—a labyrinth and a ball of yarn—establish the context of political entanglement. The body movements and gestures of the actors symbolize puppets on strings and the masters who pull the strings (**10.15**).

In my beginning Motion Graphics course, students are challenged to create PSA animations that draw inspiration from a children's story. Ken Cadieux addressed financial debt by creating a parody of Hans Christian Andersen's fairytale "The Princess and the Pea." He writes: "I have a part time job that has me find properties that banks have foreclosed on, and I take pictures that show the condition of the house in question. One day I thought to myself that I was profiting off the misfortune of others. This really bothered me so I asked my boss why these homes were empty. He explained that the banks had thrown caution and common sense to the wind and were allowing unqualified families to buy these homes without money down, credit, or proof of employment. However, the families that walked in knew that there was no way they could afford the payments. I decided I wanted to show a story from the point of someone self-entitled like a princess that buys a castle and goes through the real life stresses of debt." "The Princessand the Sub-Prime Variable Rate Mortgage," shows the princess being kept awake at night by the stress of her debt (rather than the pea in the original story). She continues to buy more mattresses, adding to the financial mess (**10.16**).

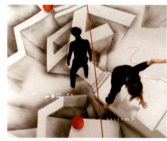

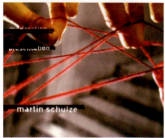

10.15
Frames from a Franco–German political evening program *Arte Metropolis*. Courtesy of Velvet.

See also Chapter 6, figure 6.36, on p. 187.

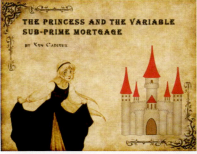
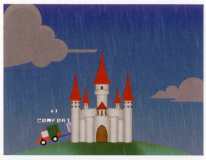
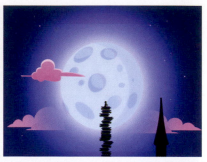

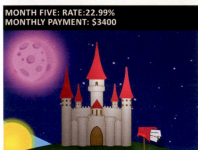
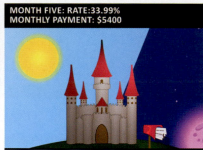
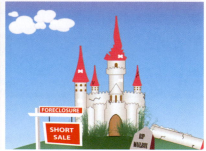

10.16

Frames from "The Princess and the Sub-Prime Variable Rate Mortgage," by Ken Cadieux. Courtesy of Professor Jon Krasner, Fitchburg State University.

Jillian Bailey chose to connect global warming with the traditional nursery rhyme "London Bridge." Her animation features scenes such as a bridge and a house falling apart due to a continuously moving hurricane which produces extreme weather and creates transitions between the images. In the last scene, the "fair lady" is represented as Mother Nature with a thermometer that shows the earth's rising temperatures (**10.17**).

Be open to ideas from almost any source—magazines, books, films, etc. Involving the client may reveal that you are not an incredible walking idea factory; however, ideas formulated through collaboration may be more beneficial than those that are generated in isolation. Observing the work of other designers and design movements can also help foster new ideas. This should be pursued with moderation, however, since relying too greatly on other styles can be dangerous.

10.17

Frames from a PSA animation, by Jillian Bailey. Courtesy of Professor Jon Krasner, Fitchburg State University.

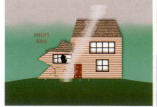
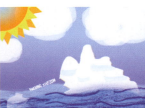
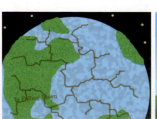
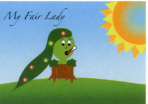

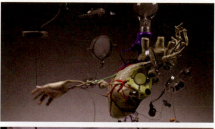

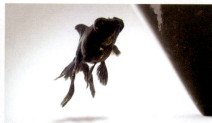

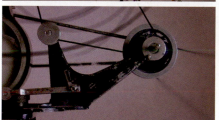

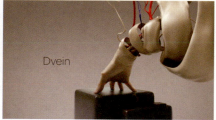

10.18

Frames from the titles for F5's 2009 creativity festival in New York City. Courtesy of Dvein.

The goal of this annual festival was to foster collaboration between artists, designers, and storytellers and break new ground in media and design. Intent on portraying the eclectic spirit of the conference, the design team asked each speaker to name five objects that have inspired his or her work. A wide variety of objects, including wind turbines, microscopes, lights, and smoke, provided a starting point for the story. The final titles present a rich mix of ideas from "different universes," infusing unknown facts about each speaker.

See also Chapter 13, figure 13.31, on p. 473.

10.19

Pride in workmanship and family traditions served as inspirations for these HTML and Flash-based website designs. Concept, design, and animation by Jon Krasner. © AML Moving & Storage.

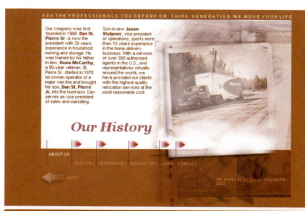

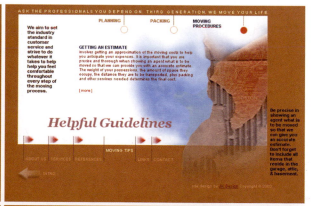

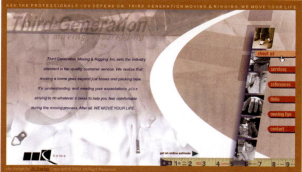

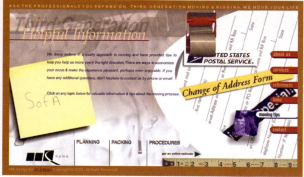

risk taking

Throughout history, art and design movements have manifested from groundbreaking visionaries who deviated from the norm. Early twentieth-century fauvist painters were frowned upon and referred to as "wild beasts" because of their garish color combinations and harsh, visible brush strokes. American graphic designer David Carson ignored the conventions of print and introduced a broad spectrum of innovative design experiments in *Ray Gun* magazine. Although his style was rejected at first, it became a milestone and gained popularity among a fast growing audience. The rebellious nature of designers who were hired by MTV challenged the conventions of corporate identity by introducing a new edgy style that spawned new approaches to broadcast motion graphics for channels such as CNN, VH1, and Nickelodeon. These individuals did not gain artistic satisfaction from following the design recipes. They broke out of their safe, cozy territories and kept an open mind to unexpected ideas.

Taking risks means venturing into new, unfamiliar territory. This may feel uncomfortable because of the potential dismissal of an idea by your client or audience. (Realize that you can always fall back on alternative, perhaps less radical, approaches.) Despite the level of discomfort, applying the same formula time after time can become intellectually dull, and your creative resources can become stale if you remain on a plateau for too long. The consequences of not being accepted by the mainstream are worth your chance of discovery.

experimentation

Like science, artistic concepts are based on an evolution of discovery through experimentation. Experimentation contributes to ideation by opening up your thought processes and eliminating contrived or trendy solutions. It relies on the element of play and embraces the unexpected, allowing accidents to become possibilities. New discoveries can lead to better approaches to problem solving. Experimentation gives you the opportunity to attain individuality. Since risk taking is involved, it is not intended to produce mediocrity. Its goal is to make life less predictable.

A colleague of mine once defined art as "studied playtime." In order to keep the pathways to creativity open, allow your mind to take the "scenic route." Stay alert to the possibility of serendipity. If you come back to an idea that lacks ingenuity, revisit it later from a fresh perspective.

The experimental, rebellious nature of MTV challenged the conventions of corporate identity by introducing a new edgy style that spawned new approaches to broadcast design.

Cultivation

Once ideas have been formulated, they must be cultivated in order to mature properly, just as a garden must be cultivated by fertilizing, weeding, and watering to produce a successful harvest.

evaluation

Once your concepts have been generated through brainstorming, evaluating them objectively helps you decide what to keep and what to discard before plunging into production. This involves reconsidering the concept's appropriateness with respect to the project's goals. Questions to ask youself at this stage are:

1. *Will my concept capture and hold my audience's attention?*

2. *Is this idea based strictly on technique or trend?*

3. *Is this concept different enough from what has already been done?*

4. *Is this concept realistic enough to implement technically?*

5. *Will the means needed to implement my idea fit within the budget?*

My six-year-old son, Harris, is often lost in experimentation when collecting discarded objects for a "garden party" or preparing for his trip to the Arctic Circle. To him, time magically folds in on itself, and the surrounding world comes to a screeching halt. In many cases, his original idea becomes secondary to the exciting possibilities that he discovers along the way. Later in his life, Harris will become exposed to rules and conventions. I will always be there to celebrate and help him embrace his imagination, creative spark, and individuality.

selection

Once evaluation has taken place, the process of selection can begin. On a positive note, you get to make the first cut before the client begins the jurying process. Although it can be painful to let go of invigorating ideas that may be more appropriate for another project, presenting too many concepts can be counterproductive. The client can develop the expectation that you will always provide numerous concepts for every project. Relinquishing too much creative control can result in the client choosing a concept that you do not support. In your absence, bits and pieces of your ideas may be mixed in a way that is not in line with your thinking. Further, the opinions of co-workers not involved in the project may be considered. Such uninformed input can be harmful to what you are trying to accomplish. Therefore, it is in your interest to be discriminating and submit only the concepts that, in your opinion, are the best.

"In traditional design you learn from accidents: You spill paint and come up with something better than what you intended. The same thing happens on the Mac: You go into Fat Bits, see a pattern, and say, 'Ah, that looks better than the original!'"

—April Greiman

clarification and refinement

Depending on your clients and test audience's responses, your ideas will most likely need further clarification. Pencil sketches may not adequately represent your ideas in visual terms. Refined sketches may be needed to clarify image style, typographic choices, compositional treatment, and motion strategies. Natural media including brush, marker, and colored pencil—in addition to techniques such as collage and photocopying—can bring clarity to your concept. Digital refinements (or "style frames") offer an even greater degree of polish, giving your concept the look and feel of a final production.

10.20
These digitally executed style frames explore how Adobe's multidimensional logo could be animated. Courtesy of twenty-2product.

See also animatic, figure 10.37.

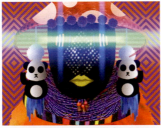

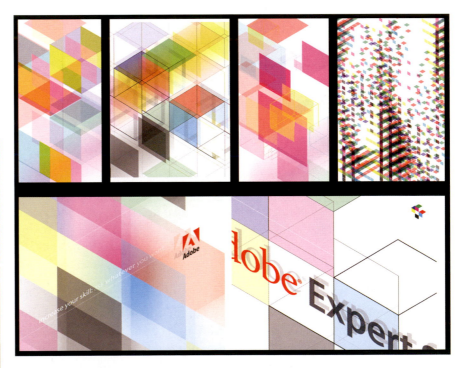

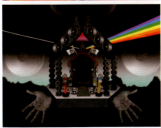

10.21
These style frames for Fuel TV's signature network ID are based on the fictional character 'Poopa-Ooba,' a demigod who invented "Skatism" as a culture and religion for skateboarders. Courtesy of Fuel TV.

See also Chapter 11, figure 11.15, on p. 382.

At Ringling College of Art + Design, José Díaz pitched the concept of embracing learning for his senior thesis project. **Figure 10.22** was one out of three style frames that was chosen to be developed into a storyboard. José writes: "Education is your right, but learning is your responsibility. Sometimes distractions take our focus away from things that benefit us, like an education. An education can help us achieve so many things in life, but many do not take advantage of the opportunity to truly learn. If you find yourself in the middle of a bad situation, you can always find your way out through education."

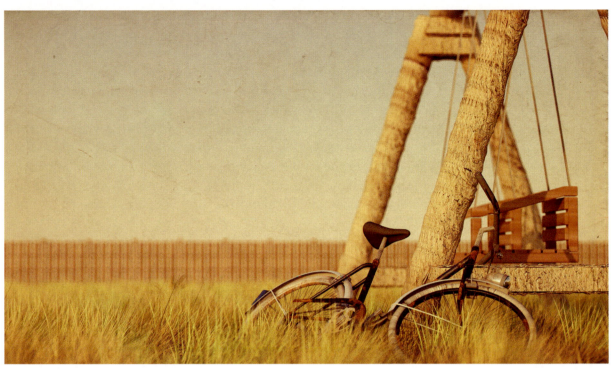

10.22
Style frame for pre-production of a senior thesis project, "The Way Out," by José Díaz. © 2012 Ringling College of Art + Design.

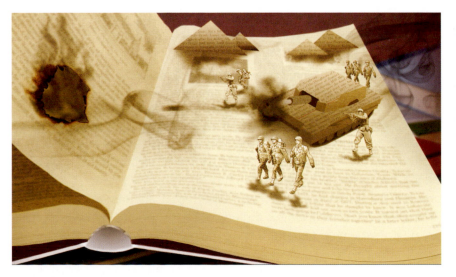

10.23
Style frame for "Peace in History," by Justin Timmons. © 2012 Ringling College of Art + Design.

Justin used the device of a history book to portray how violence has been part of our culture and to show that working together could lead to a day of peace.

See also figure 10.41.

The abstract, three-dimensional quality of Sharon Correa's style frame set the tone for a personal story about her childhood (**10.24**). According to Sharon: "I used to be a very shy and quiet young girl; which led me to this concept of Beauty." She adds: "If you recognize you were made beautifully, you can inspire others to see their own beauty. Once they recognize it, they will inspire others to discover their own. People want to see themselves reflected through others, missing the whole point of life. We all have something unique to share with others. And this will remain untouched until someone discovers it." Once Sharon's concept was approved, she began developing a comprehensive storyboard and additional style frames to solidify the story's graphic quality.

10.24
Style frame for "Beauty," by Sharon Correa. © 2012, Ringling College of Art + Design.

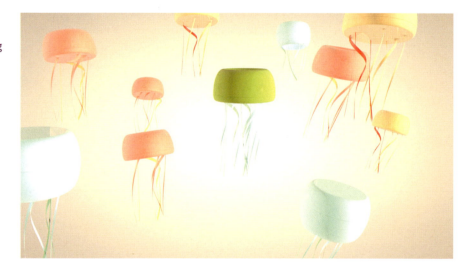

Storyboards

Once your concept has been clarified, refined, and has received client approval, storyboarding is usually the final phase of conceptualization.

A "storyboard" is a cohesive succession of "frames" that provides a visual map of how events will unfold over time. It identifies key transitions between the events. Sometimes accompanied by supporting text, it establishes the basic narrative structure of your story. **Figure 10.25** presents the storyboard for *Nefertiti Resurrected*, aired on the Discovery Channel in 2003. According to director Michael Middeleer of Viewpoint Creative, "We sought to demonstrate the beauty, drama and mystery surrounding Nefertiti and show how the Discovery Channel resurrects one of ancient Egypt's most famous and powerful queens."

Scientific studies have demonstrated that thinking in images is a natural process of receiving and deciphering information. Evidence suggests that learning and retention levels are enhanced when images are used rather than words. The earliest forms of graphic communication were purely visual. Today, words are more commonly used to support graphic information, in contrast to traditional advertising and copywriting practices that used images to support written information.

Storyboards

Storyboarding requires preparatory mental visualization since many factors need to be determined. Unless your assignment calls for improvisation, this process requires strategic planning.

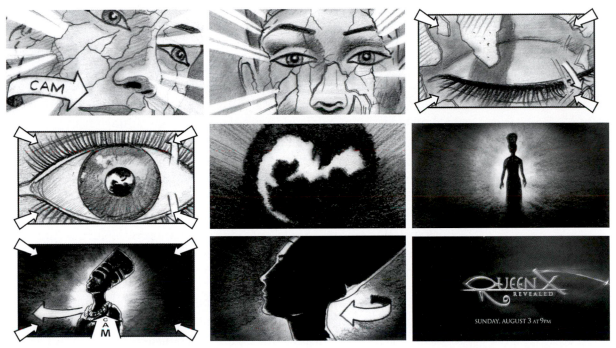

10.25
Storyboard frames for *Nefertiti Resurrected* (2003). Courtesy of Viewpoint Creative and the Discovery Channel.

visual content and style

Many traditional and digital artistic processes, including drawing, painting, collage, and montage, can support the graphic style that you choose. Images that are created in raster-based applications yield a certain hand-executed or photographic look, while vector graphics achieve a flatter, more stylized quality.

Environmental or atmospheric conditions should also be considered. The background provides the setting or stage where events take place, and at this point, the background should be developed and treated as an integral part of the piece. Background images can be moved or changed over time, or they can serve as unchanging backdrops against which the animations of foreground elements take place. In a 3D environment, lighting, environmental effects (such as fog, movement of water, and smoke), and camera views should be planned during storyboarding, since all play a significant role in establishing the atmosphere and perspective of a scene.

pictorial and sequential considerations

The single most important measure of a storyboard's effectiveness is its continuity. "Pictorial continuity" across the frames should be acheived with regard to the style of images and type, color scheme, and overall treatment of space. An organized pictorial space may require object movements to adhere to an underlying grid. On the other hand, the motion of objects in a loose, free-flowing composition may be more random. Establishing a clear distinction between background and foreground elements can achieve a strong sense of spatial depth, while breaking traditional figure–ground relationships through heavy layering will flatten the space. "Sequential" or "progressive continuity" should convey a comprehensible and logical flow of events from one frame to the next. For example, the sequence of events in the storyboard for the opening credits to the film *Splice* was carefully worked out with clearly defined camera movements. The transitions successfully captured French title designer Kook Ewo's idea of a fast-paced sequence that takes viewers on an anatomical journey through a part-human, part-animal organism (**10.26**).

I recently gave students an assignment that involved designing a storyboard for a potential television station bumper based on a theme from the Bible. They were challenged to establish pictorial continuity across the frames and sequential continuity between frames, giving consideration to the birth and death of elements, their duration in the frame, and visual transitions. Choosing the classic story of David and Goliath and giving it a darker twist (David holds a rocket launcher), Paulo Viera conveyed the bizarre, quirky sense of humor and unorthodox content of the [Adult Swim] network (**10.27**). He states in his written account of the events: "The first scene would be similar to an old western stare down. The camera would zoom in on their eyes, David's would be more serious while Goliath's eyes make it look like he is enjoying the tension. It then cuts to David's sling swinging around. The camera would be fixed but the weapon would come in and out of the shot. The part where Goliath laughs at David, I imagine the "Ha-Ha's" to be wiggling and fading out as they move away from Goliath's head and the sound would be multiple laugh tracks going out as this happens. The scene cuts to David no longer swinging the sling but holding a rocket launcher. You hear the cock of a gun, the rocket launcher moving up and down as it's being aimed, and David fires the weapon. A flaming

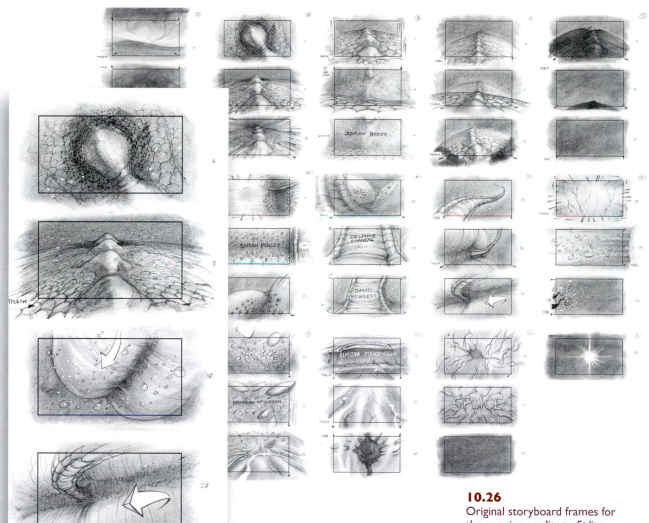

10.26
Original storyboard frames for the opening credits to *Splice* (2006). Courtesy of Kook Ewo.

See also Chapter 2, figure 2.10 on p. 31, Chapter 7, figure 7.32, on p. 225, and Chapter 13, figure 13.23 on p. 466.

stone would shoot out of the gun with a loud explosion. The camera would follow the stone out of the camera from a POV shot with added camera shake and rocket noises and as it approaches Goliath his jaw drops as he realizes what is about to happen. That's when he brings up the "Yipe!" sign like in a Roadrunner and Coyote cartoon. It cuts to black right before the stone hits Goliath and you hear the "Ting" of rock against metal. After a few seconds the last scene fades in without the helmet. The helmet falls in from the right with a huge dent. The logo fades in over the scene. The audience is to infer what happened to Goliath."

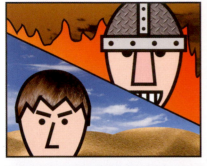
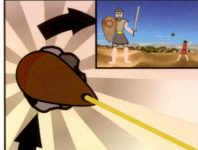
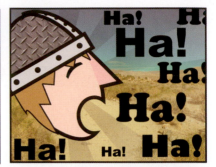
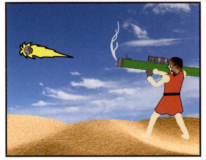
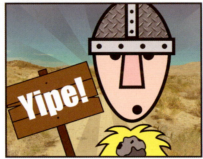
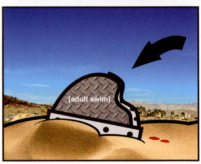

10.27
Frames from a proposed bumper for the [Adult Swim] network by Paulo Viera. Courtesy of Professor Jon Krasner, Fitchburg State University.

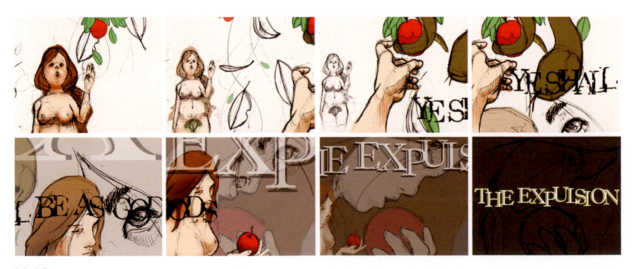

10.28
Storyboard design based on the biblical theme of Adam and Eve, by Mike Cena. Courtesy of Professor Jon Krasner, Fitchburg State University.

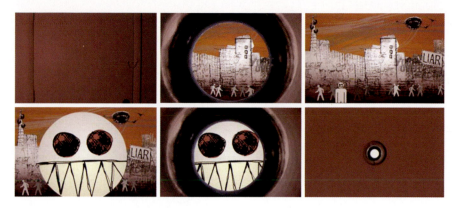

10.29
This storyboard illustrates the concept of sociophobia—the fear of people or society. As the viewer looks out, he sees a highly abstracted cityscape with personified symbols walking by. The city's buildings are layered with various words and phrases.

By Justin Ruggieri, Kansas City Art Institute. Courtesy of Professor Jeff Miller.

stages of development

early development

As seen in the examples provided in this chapter, storyboards can range from groups of quick sketches to a series of highly developed style frames. Depending upon your working process, the client's demands, and other factors such as budget and time, most storyboards go through several iterations before production of the animation begins.

An "initial comprehensive" is a series of quick, sequential drawings that have a 4:3 (conventional) or 16.9 (widescreen television or film) aspect ratio. Here, the story is broken down into its major components. These sketches will save you time later since they can be individually worked out on separate pieces of paper, rearranged, and discarded once they have been analyzed. The quality of the drawings is not as critical as the flow of action between the frames. In fact, dedicating too much time to making each image look realistic can take attention away from the most critical factor—continuity. At this stage, careful attention should be paid to the logical order of events from scene to scene as well as the methods of transition between scenes.

This stage offers tremendous creative freedom, allowing you to deviate from your original ideas. Elements can be simplified, exaggerated, added, or deleted. Be open to serendipity; "happy accidents" offer creative opportunities. Do not get too far down the road with a concept before submitting it. The client should be kept in the loop to avoid too much time being spent on perfecting ideas, only to have them rejected later. Unless your idea has been approved in writing, proceed with caution! Posting frames to the Web for client approval can save valuable time.

In the past, "comping" involved drawing out the details by hand on tissue or tracing paper with markers. This type of quick, visual thinking was considered a highly evolved skill. During the late 1980s and early 1990s, "paint systems" such as Quantel Paintbox were used by storyboard artists for pre-production. Today, common applications such as Photoshop and Illustrator can quickly generate, manipulate, and composite images and type.

Although there are cases when an initial comprehensive may look much like the final storyboard, the client may never see it. Keep in mind that there is room for improvement and that several drafts may be necessary before arriving at the final storyboard. Evolution is key; creative ideas are meant to build upon one another over time.

10.30
Initial comprehensive sketch for SKY Cinema Italia's *Spazio Italia*. Courtesy of Flying Machine.

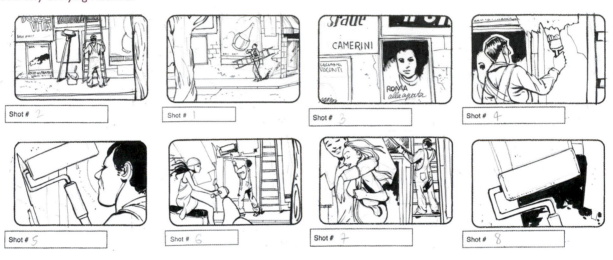

10.31
Initial comprehensive storyboard for Nestlé's Wonka Egg Hunt. Courtesy of Shadowplay Studios.

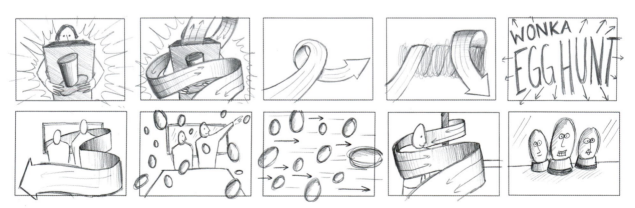

the final comprehensive

Once your sketches have been revised, they should be reworked and edited down into a "final comprehensive"—a more refined series of frames showing major events, transitions, framing, and camera moves. Six to ten frames are typical for a 30-second spot, while a one- or two-minute movie trailer might require up to 20 frames. Station IDs are typically presented in no more than eight frames.

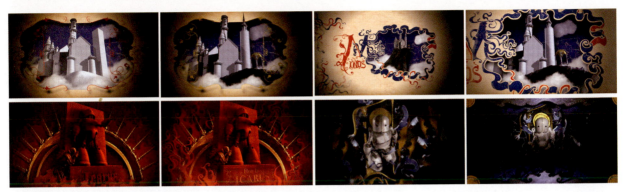

10.32
Final comprehensive storyboard for "Icarus." © Adam Swaab.

See also figure 10.7 and Chapter 9, figure 9.36, on p. 33.

Professionalism is key to convincing your client (and yourself) to settle on an idea. Sloppy execution or ambiguity can create a negative impression. Although hand-drawn artwork is sometimes used today, digital execution is most favored since it is quicker and more appropriate in situations where the visuals will be photographic. If time is critical, stock images are available from numerous suppliers. (Be sure to read the terms and conditions to avoid using material illegally.) The most impressive boards are assembled from high-quality prints that are pasted onto poster or Bristol board. Supporting text can be added as a supplement but should not be used as a substitute for clarity.

Last, your storyboard should serve as a basis from which additional creative opportunities can be pursued. Although major decisions may have been worked out, there is still room for continued experimentation during production, provided the client has some flexibility.

10.33
Storyboards from "Cowboy" and "Smoke" IDs for SKY Cinema. Courtesy of Flying Machine.

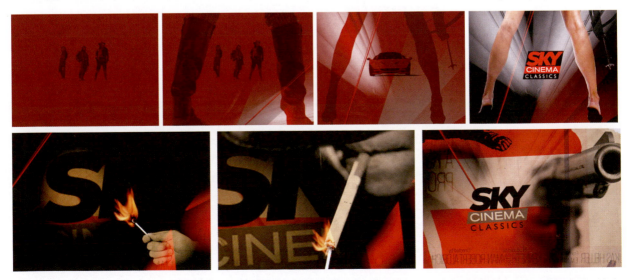

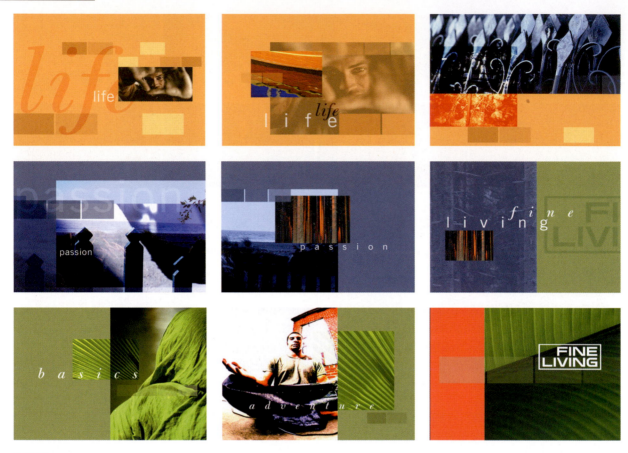

10.34
Storyboard for a Fine Living Network bumper. Courtesy of Another Large Production and Susan Detrie.

Animatics

Since storyboards describe motion in a static manner, "animatics" (or animated storyboards) are sometimes needed to pre-visualize and resolve the motion and timing of events. They take the art of storytelling one step further by breathing life into the images and synchronizing their movements and transitions with sound. (Animatics are typically produced after the soundtrack has been created.) In some cases, the storyboard and soundtrack may be modified, and a new animatic may be generated, if necessary, until the storyboard is perfected.

Animatics have proven to be time and cost effective, since editing during this stage can prevent you from dedicating unnecessary time and labor to generating content that is later eliminated.

Animatics

Animatics bring projects closer to final production, allowing potential problems with lighting, cinematography, and sound to be pinpointed. This means fewer iterations during implementation, since the major changes that need to be made have already been detected.

Animatics can range from crude animated sketches and improvised video footage to polished 2D and 3D animations containing hand-drawn and digital illustration. It is important to keep in mind that you are not just presenting an animated slideshow of your storyboard; rather, you are presenting the types of motions, changes, and camera angles that you envision for the final production.

In an animatic for an in-store video showcasing Nike's Air Max 2, Terry Green, director and co-founder of twenty2product, was presented with several live footage assets and asked to develop a scheme that would tie them together and integrate them with text and graphics. He quickly composited stock images and video footage to provide a clear idea of how the final piece would be animated and sequenced. This allowed twenty2product and the client to assess potential problems, develop solutions, and rethink the entire approach at an early stage, prior to production (**10.35**).

The first person to be credited with using animatics was George Lucas. The documentary Empire of Dreams, *aired on the Arts and Entertainment Network, contains a segment featuring Lucas' conversion from storyboard to animatic. A story about the animatic from* Star Wars Episode I *has been posted at http://starwars.com). The animatic for* Raiders of the Lost Ark, *can be found on YouTube.*

In television, animatics have been used as preliminary versions of commercials before they are made into full spots. They have also been used for marketing, video game animation templates, and actual bumpers and show openers.

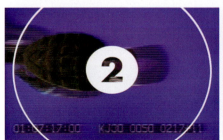
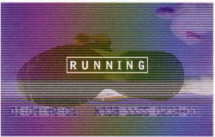

10.35
Frames from an animatic for Nike's Air Max 2 in-store video. Courtesy of twenty2product.

Twenty2product also developed an animatic for a looped opener to "My Favorite Conference," a large-scale trade show in Singapore (**10.36**). This event was sponsored by *IdN*, an international publication for the design community in Asia-Pacific. Similar to Macworld, the event was dedicated to the merging of different graphic design disciplines to give rise to unique creative and contemporary insights. The goal of the opener was to introduce the topics to be presented and acknowledge individual speakers and corporate sponsors. Director Terry Green refers to these segments as "artefacts" of their working process that may or may not appear as a layer in the final composition. Working in this manner helped move ideas forward.

10.36
Frames from an animatic for "My Favorite Conference." Courtesy of twenty2product.© 2004 IdN. All rights reserved.

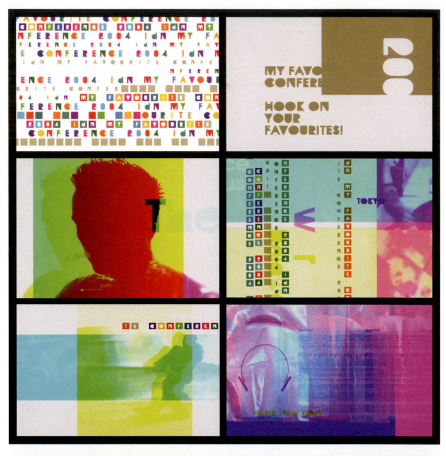

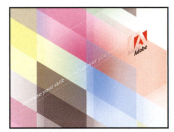

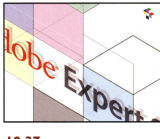

10.37
Animatics for Adobe's Expert Support trade show offered ways that the components of Adobe's logo and titling could be animated in an orthographic space with a flattened perspective. Courtesy of twenty2product. © 2004 Adobe Systems.

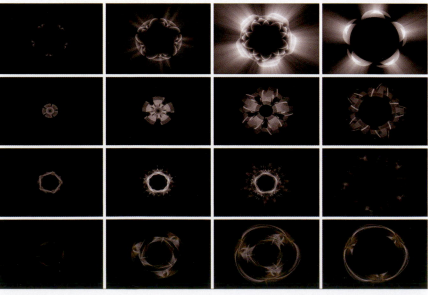

10.38
This set of animatics were used in a music video for Susumu Hirasawa, a Japanese electropop artist known in Western cultures for his anime soundtracks. They were also used in a promotional spot for Santana Row, a premier retail and entertainment complex in San Jose, California. Courtesy of twenty2product.

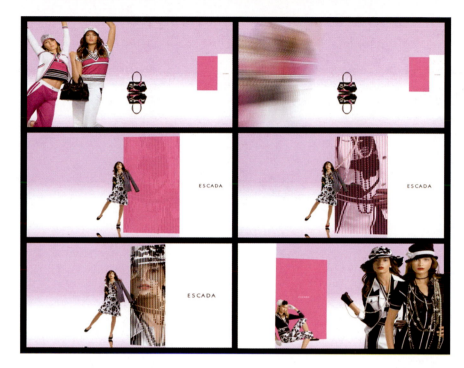

10.39
This animatic was used in a pitch for the worldwide in-store presentations of the German fashion brands ESCADA and ESCADA Sport. Courtesy of Daniel Jenett.

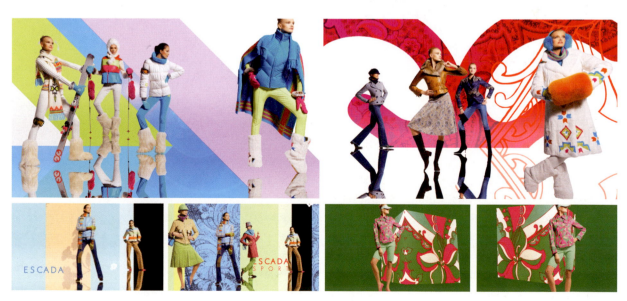

10.40
Frames from the final in-store presentation for ESCADA. Courtesy of Daniel Jenett.

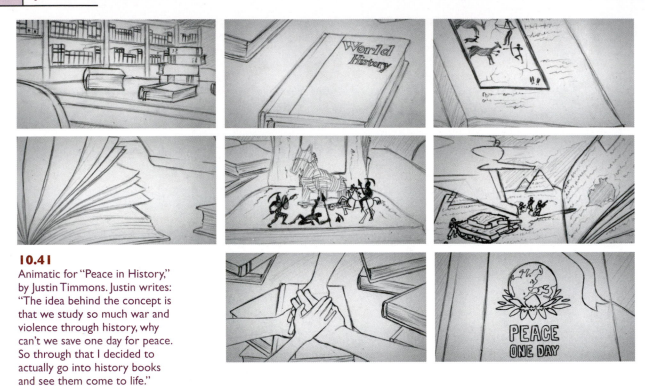

10.41
Animatic for "Peace in History," by Justin Timmons. Justin writes: "The idea behind the concept is that we study so much war and violence through history, why can't we save one day for peace. So through that I decided to actually go into history books and see them come to life."
© 2012 Ringling College of Art + Design.

See also figure 10.23.

Chapter Summary

Planning and conceptualization is necessary in all forms of graphic communication. Assessment, the first step in planning, begins with defining a goal before plunging headfirst into the creative waters. Attention must be given to the demographics of the target audience and their prior knowledge of the subject being addressed. Research is key to being well informed about your topic, and thorough analysis of the subject must be conducted before the process of ideation takes place.

Motion graphic designers who are working in the industry must understand budgetary constraints, deadlines, and the degree of client flexibility with regard to new ideas. These parameters should not be perceived as limitations to creativity, but rather as creative guidelines that can help give ideas direction. Direct, one-to-one communication with clients can help avoid frustrations down the road. Clients can be convinced of an idea provided that a relationship of mutual trust and respect has been established.

Once the project's objective and target audience have been defined and the subject matter thoroughly investigated, the floodgates of creativity can then be opened for brainstorming to occur in an environment that is conducive to creative thought. Ideas should be recorded immediately by writing, sketching, or generating images digitally.

Motion designers should be aware of obstacles that can impede creative thinking and obscure artistic judgment. These obstacles include overused stylistic trends, effects that lack ingenuity, the over-abundance of stock images and fonts, and the pace of software development. Designers must find ways to embrace pathways to creative thinking. Inspiration can be achieved by establishing personal connections with the subject, conducting adequate research, looking at the work of other designers and design movements, and involving the client. Risk taking and experimentation can also be liberating by preventing reliance on safe, mainstream design solutions.

Once ideas have been formulated, they must be cultivated through evaluation, selection, clarification, and refinement.

A *storyboard* is a cohesive succession of frames that establishes a concept's basic narrative structure. It shows how events will unfold over time and identifies key transitions between the events. The single most important measure of a storyboard is its continuity. *Pictorial continuity* indicates a cohesion in the content and style of visuals. *Sequential continuity* communicates a comprehensible and logical flow of events between frames. A storyboard typically goes through several revisions before it is refined and presented as a final comprehensive.

Since storyboards describe movement in a static manner, *animatics* (or animated storyboards) are sometimes needed to resolve issues pertaining to motion and timing. Animatics can be time and cost effective, since they can allow clients to pinpoint potential problems ahead of time. Animatics can range from crude, animated sketches to polished motion graphics sequences that combine 2D and 3D content with hand-drawn and digital illustration.

11

animation processes
creating motion

"The ability to deconstruct a movement and reassemble it in a new or convincing way is the animator's territory. Many artists have realized their visions using animation as a means to externalize their inner thoughts and unique points of view. Animation gives the viewer the opportunity to gaze at a frozen moment of thought and to experience another person's rhythms."
—*Christine Panushka*

The human eye has the capacity to assemble slightly different consecutive images that are presented at a fast enough rate and interpret them as continuous movement. This phenomenon, called persistence of vision, allows motion graphic designers to convey their messages and move their audiences by means of frame-by-frame animation, interpolation, and compositing. The unusual creative possibilities that exist in merging diverse types of content are pushing the limits of artistic experimentation and expression.

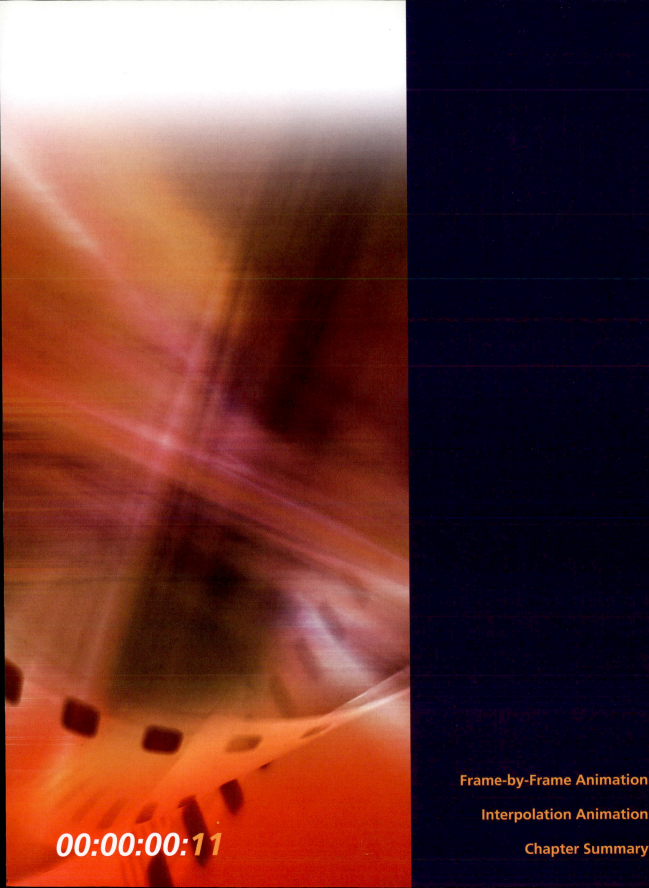

00:00:00:11

Historical Perspective

In the early 1880s, British photographer Eadward Muybridge pioneered a body of experiments in motion photography that analyzed the movement of live subjects. His research proved that a maximum of 10 to 12 images depicting incremental movement can give a convincing illusion of motion when viewed in sequence. This spawned the birth of classical frame-by-frame animation for film, a method that continues to be employed by artists and motion graphic designers today.

Frame-by-Frame Animation

The term "frame-by-frame animation" defines itself: a sequence of images that created on a frame-by-frame basis. Flip-books were one of the earliest frame-by-frame animation techniques. Each piece of paper in a book contained a unique drawing, and the illusion of motion was produced when the drawings were displayed one after the other by flipping the pages quickly. The more drawings (or frames) that were displayed each second, the smoother and more believable the motion was when they were flipped in sequence.

Frame-by-frame animation includes two types of frames: "key frames" and "in-between frames." Key frames (or "extremes") are nonadjacent frames that identify the major events in a scene. These are used as guides for constructing the intermediate or in-between frames, which complete the transitions between the key frames. The number of in-between frames can vary, depending on the degree of motion or change that is needed. Generally, small numbers of frames per second produce quick changes and abrupt transitions, while greater numbers produce smoother transitions. Depending on the subject matter, it is not always necessary for an animation to contain large numbers of frames. In fact, four or five key images may be adequate for a looped sequence intended to produce a continuous repetition of events.

Frame-by-frame animations are well suited to situations that involve changing the physical appearance of images. For example, a figure's eyes may bulge out of their sockets, or a creature's feet may grow into a tail or set of flippers, or a letterform may change its surface texture.

Over the last two decades, digital technology has streamlined animation production. The versatility of software can mimic traditional processes without the need for a film camera. The cost of materials has decreased, although there are other expenses such as software, hardware, and a more highly trained and highly paid staff. The reduction of time, labor, and cost justifies the industry's eager embrace of digital production.

Whether your content is generated by conventional or digital means, animating on a frame-by-frame basis can be a time-consuming undertaking. Its great advantage, however, is having ultimate control over every mark, line, and brush stroke to develop your vision. Professional experience or a fine arts degree is not necessary to create meaningful compositions. In fact, the most primitive drawings can be provocative or humorous when played back in sequence. However, some degree of drawing or painting experience is beneficial, along with creativity, patience, and a familiarity with the techniques described here.

classical "old-school" animation

During the 1930s and 1940s, classical or "old-school" animation for film was a labor-intensive undertaking that involved generating artwork on a frame-by-frame basis. Since film runs at a rate of 24 frames per second, a single minute of film required 1,440 individual drawings. These drawings were executed on paper or on semi-transparent sheets of vellum or onionskin to allow previous frames to show through the frame on which the artist drew. This technique was known as "onion skinning." In later years, it involved placing a light source beneath a drawing on a translucent page. The animator referenced the positioning of elements in the prior frame to draw the elements in slightly different positions.

cel animation

Cel animation, invented by Earl Hurd in 1914, reduced the time and labor of classical animation. Celluloid film sheets were used to layer foreground, middleground, and background elements. Background images were usually executed on paper, and the cels containing the elements that changed would be superimposed in front of a camera. Cel animation was a laborious task, since 24 drawings were needed for each second of film. Senior-level animators focused on establishing the key actions, while "cleanup artists" were hired to refine the images by erasing and smoothing the pencil lines. The responsibility of generating the intermediate drawings was delegated to the "in-betweeners."

Digital production does not require computer-generated imagery; it can embrace any combination of hand-rendered techniques, or be as simple as scanning consecutive frames and playing them back on a computer or optimizing them for playback over the Web.

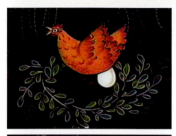
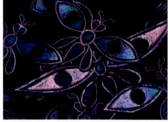

11.1
Frames from *Madan and the Miracle Leaves*, by Frederic Back. © Trees for Life, Inc.

This animation is intended to promote the drumstick tree, a rich source of vitamin A, in villages in India that face vitamin deficiencies.

Before cel animation was invented, many productions created from drawings on paper combined foreground and background images on a single sheet. Every element had to be recreated for every frame.

Historical Perspective

Hand inking and xerography were two common techniques used for transferring hand-created artwork from paper to animation cells. Both practices are still practiced today. *Hand inking* involved tracing drawings onto clear acetate cells with quill pens and brushes (similar to those used by monks during the Middle Ages, who spent hours hunched over in scriptoriums to produce illuminated bibles). An example is Disney's *Fantasia*. Hand-inked cells from the 1950s are popular collector's items and can be seen in art galleries. In the 1930s, Disney Studios developed a photographic process that could reproduce drawings photographically on animation cells. This technique was first utilized in *Snow White and the Seven Dwarfs* and continued throughout the early 1950s. *Xerography,* also created by Disney, involved photocopying pencil drawings onto celluloid. It yielded a truer depiction of the original artwork and enabled greater spontaneity. The Xerox technique also made it possible to simulate camera zooms by reducing or enlarging images.

direct-on-film

The term "direct-on-film" refers to the "cameraless" animation technique of creating images directly on a filmstrip. This method allows an endless variety of effects to be created with traditional media, chemical compounds, and processes such as scratching, burning, and rubbing. The emulsion of black film can easily be altered or removed chemically.

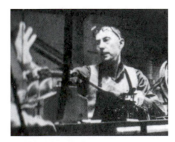

11.2
Len Lye, c.1957. Courtesy of Cecile Starr.

American animator Len Lye was a major figure in avant-garde cinema, and pioneered the process of painting and scratching images directly onto the celluloid surface of film leader. Living in Samoa between 1922 and 1923, he became inspired by Aboriginal motifs and produced his first animated silent film, *Tusalava* (1929), which he created to express "the beginnings of organic life." (The film's title in Samoan means "things go full cycle." British censors believed that it was about sex!) Grub-like images suggest a life cycle by coming together, dividing, and morphing into what Lye described as "a cross between a spider and an octopus with blood circulating through its arms" (**11.3**). This film took two years to complete, each frame hand-painted and individually photographed.

Intrigued by the occult, Harry Smith spoke of his art in alchemical and cosmological terms. He combined painting onto 35 millimeter stock with stop-motion and collage. Similar to his life and personality, his art was complex and mysterious and has often been interpreted as an exploration of unconscious mental processes. In his first animation, he placed adhesive gum dots on the surface of the film, wet the film with a brush, and sprayed it with a dye. After the film dried, he greased it with Vaseline, pulled the dots off with a pair of tweezers, and sprayed color onto the unprotected areas occupied by the dots. In another film, he used masking tape and a razor blade to generate the image content (**11.4**).

In American animator Stephanie Maxwell's film *Driving Abstractions* (1997), the experience of driving at night is conveyed in an abstraction of colorful, energetic bursts and patterns of light in a three-dimensional darkness. The imagery was drawn, painted, and etched onto the emulsion of clear and black 35mm film stock with markers, paints, and dilutions of nitric acid (**11.5**).

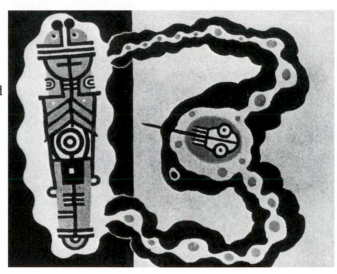

11.3
Frame from *Tusalava* (1929) by Len Lye. Courtesy of Cecile Starr.

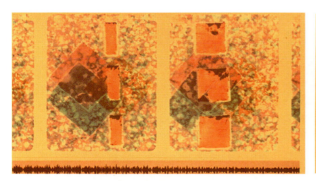

11.4
Film strips from *Early Abstractions* by Harry Smith. Courtesy of Harry Smith Archives and Anthology Film Archives.

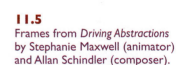

11.5
Frames from *Driving Abstractions* by Stephanie Maxwell (animator) and Allan Schindler (composer).

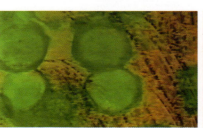
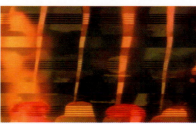
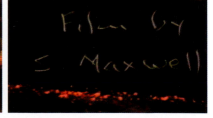

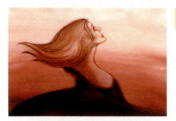

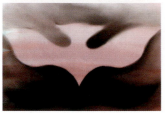

11.6
Dutch animator Chris de Deugd used pastels, ecoline, watercolors, and colored pencils on paper and frosted cels in her debut film *Daedalus' Daughter* (2001).

According to Chris, this poetic film is a "sad refrain about mortality, sung in burnt sienna and sepia, the colors of the earth." © il Luster.

freehand animation

Today, the process of freehand animation, whether it's produced direct-on-film, on paper, or on the computer, covers a wide range of styles and genres, from traditional figurative animation to expressive abstract painting and spontaneous gesture drawing.

Many substrates are available for freehand animation. The advantages of paper are affordability, availability, and its acceptance of a wide range of media. However, its density makes it difficult to view previous frames while creating new frames. Since papers vary in opacity, a minimal amount of transparency may be enough to create an onionskin effect. Nonabsorbent substrates such as glass, Plexiglass, and ceramic tiles allow paint or ink to be wiped away easily and allow spontaneity and improvisation, since images are in a constant state of evolution.

Throughout history, animators have experimented with media and substrates. J. Stuart Blackton produced one of the earliest American animations, entitled *Humorous Phases of Funny Faces,* on a blackboard with chalk. After each frame was filmed, part of the image was erased and redrawn with a slight alteration (**11.7**).

11.7
Frames from *Humorous Phases of Funny Faces* (1906). © Vitagraph.

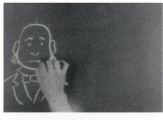

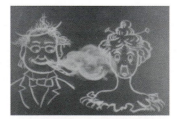

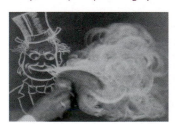

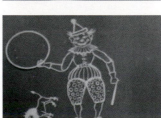

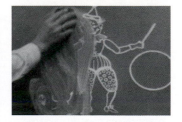

Contemporary Polish animator Piotr Dumala etched images on plaster and recorded each subtle alteration onto film (**11.8**). The more obscure stop-motion technique of "sand animation" involved drawing images into sand with brushes, wooden sticks, stencils, strainers, and fingers. After a frame was photographed onto film, portions of the image were wiped away, updated, and photographed again. This freeform approach, which is still used today, keeps the artistic process fresh and spontaneous (**11.9**). "Pinboard animation" was another eccentric process. It was invented in the early 1930s by Russian filmmaker Alexander Alexeieff and his American wife Claire Parker. A contraption consisting of closely spaced pins that could be set to varying heights was used to cast shadows to produce dramatic expressionistic effects when subjected to light. The resulting forms had a soft, chiaroscuro effect that resembled charcoal drawings or etchings.

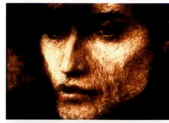

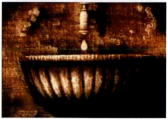

11.8
Frames from *Crime and Punishment* (2000) by Piotr Dumala. © Acme Filmworks.

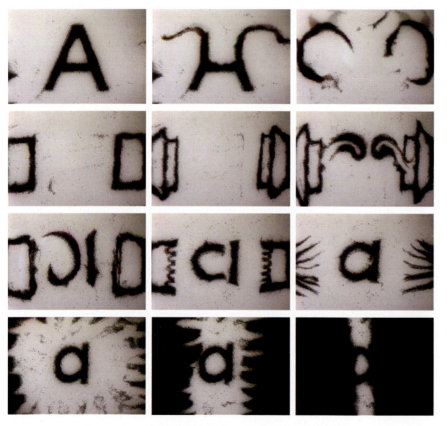

11.9
Frames from a sand animation for the letter "A" by Eliot Noyes. Courtesy of Sesame Workshop.

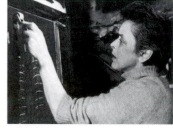

11.10
Claire Parker moving pins with a roller into a perforated screen that is lit to create areas of light and dark. From *Experimental Animation*, courtesy of Cecile Starr.

The depth of the pins affects the degree and distribution of light and shadows.

The development of desktop applications has made available a more affordable range of "natural media" tools designed to imitate traditional media such as acrylic, oil, and watercolor paint, charcoal, crayon, chalk, and fountain pens, to name just a few. Freehand drawing can be done on a frame-by-frame basis. In fact, you can emulate the direct-on-film technique by painting on or altering multiple frames simultaneously, rather than working on one frame at a time. Brushes can be customized with regard to their shape, size, and degree of softness.

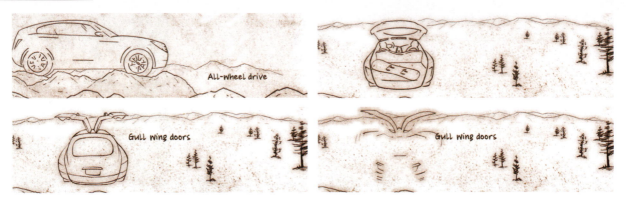

11.11

Frames from a spot for Infiniti Triant. Courtesy of Nissan North America, Inc. and Humunculus.

Original drawings were created freehand on animation cels.

Graphics tablets can enhance the process of drawing and painting in the digital environment. Lines can be drawn with increased sensitivity to pressure to produce more natural results. Depending upon the speed and pressure that is applied, lines can become lighter, darker, thinner, or fatter. For these reasons, in addition to preventing carpal tunnel syndrome, they are wise long-term investments.

I often have students create PSA animation, by drawing or painting with conventional media. Since this assignment is open to many stylistic possibilities, students are encouraged to be experimental and are told to consider how the artistic style can help express the concept.

The concept behind Ryan Houle's PSA (**11.12**) was to poke fun at the mass hysteria over microwave radiation. Ryan's technical processes involved using a MacBook camera to film the footage and a Wacom tablet to draw out the frames. The scratchy style of the characters and the exaggerated movements and expressions of the figures enhances the comical spirit of the animation. The quality of the contour lines evolved from thin and smooth into bold, more aggressive and less predictable strokes as the subject's exposure to radiation increased. Ryan writes: "I had my brother and his friend act ridiculously as if they were burning with radiation after putting their faces right up to the microwave door. I varied the weight of the rotoscope lines around the subjects. I got more and more aggressive with lines weights as the video progressed until the subjects melted." To help push the mood of the piece further, approximately half of the frames were eliminated to create instant jump cuts between the scenes in order to show the effect of the radiation on the subjects. This generated the effect of "an old film reel gone wrong"—especially due to the speed the subjects were moving at the time of the cut.

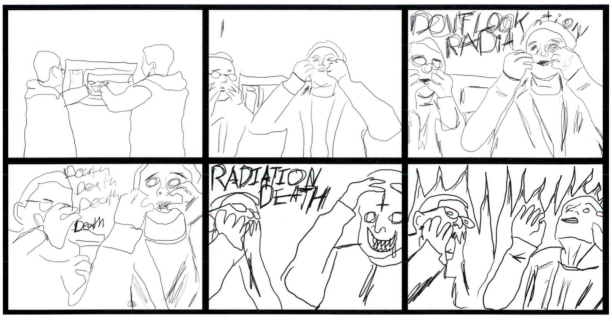

11.12
Frames from a PSA by Ryan Houle.
Courtesy of Professor Jon Krasner,
Fitchburg State University.

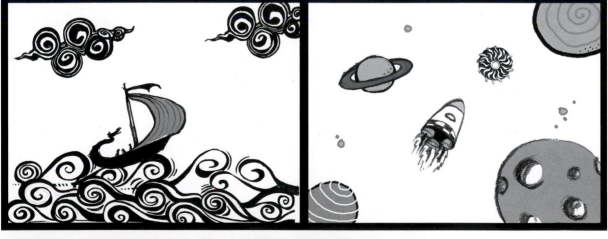

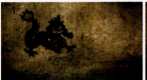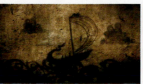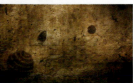

11.13
In a TV spot for Teri Lamp, the foreground elements were hand drawn,
projected on a wall, and then filmed.
Courtesy of Eallin.

See also Chapter 3, figure 3.65, on
p. 71.

stop-motion

11.14

In a television spot for Nestlé Wonka Egg Hunt products, stop-motion photographs of children create a playful mood expressing the enjoyment and curiosity of a child participating in a scavenger hunt for chocolate. Courtesy of Shadowplay Studio.

"Stop-motion animation" involves moving a subject in space, capturing each variation one frame at a time, and stringing the frames together into a sequence that mimics movement when played back. The popularity of stop-motion has grown considerably in on-air commercials, ad campaigns, and music videos, and more recently on Web sites such as YouTube and Vimeo. Its strong psychological effects have been capitalized on through the use of various artistic media.

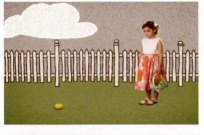
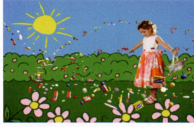
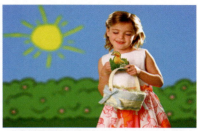
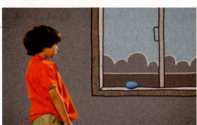
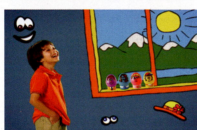
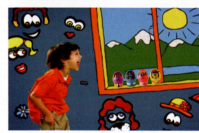

11.15

Frames from a set of network IDs. Courtesy of Fuel TV.

See also Chapter 10, figure 10.21, on p. 356.

Fuel TV developed a series of entertainingly bizarre stop-motion IDs depicting a fictional demigod, inventor of "Skatism," and a clan of stuffed panda bears (**11.15**). The objective was to create a feeling of "intercepted communications from some distant planet whose daily realities defy human comprehension." Another series of IDs for Fuel's Pinto network involved using a digital camera to shoot frames of Pinto, a stuffed sports action figure who finds himself in dangerous situations while skating, snowboarding, or riding his motocross bike (**11.16**).

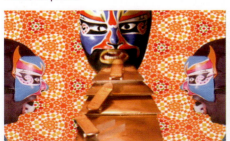
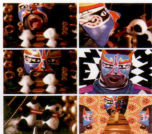
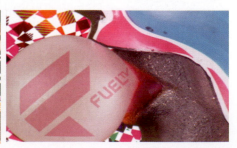

In June, 2012, Kia Motors of Korea launched what they claimed to be the first online "nail art" commercial to promote its 2012 Picanto car. During a period of 25 days and nights, Kia's crew of artists used 900 artificial acrylic nails and 1200 bottles of nail polish to produce a stop-motion piece that expresses the concept of "small." Targeting an urban female audience who can identify with manicures and sporty vehicles, this fashion statement serves as a metaphor for packing things into a small, compact vehicle. Approximately two hours of painstaking work went into decorating each nail in order to show a level of detail that would achieve the stylish yet practical aspects of the Picanto as it zipped along the fingernails of a model's hand (**11.17**).

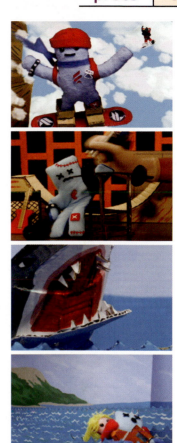

11.16
Frames from the Pinto network series of IDs for Fuel TV. Produced by Brand New School. Courtesy of Fuel TV.

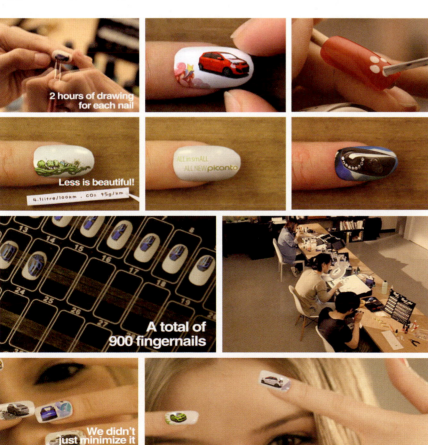

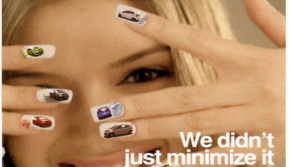

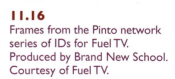

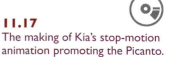

11.17
The making of Kia's stop-motion animation promoting the Picanto.

"Stop motion removes limitations. It makes anything possible. Stop motion makes it your responsibility to stretch your imagination to do those things that you wouldn't even think of if you were using a different technique. You HAVE to think without limits. It is a lovely exercise."

—Kohler and Griffiths

Responsible for developing many of Amazon's Kindle commercials, Angela Kohler and Ithyle Griffiths—a directing team from Los Angeles, California—are at the forefront of the stop-motion genre and are known for their homemade techniques in advertising. The ethereal, short film "Lost Things" that they wrote and directed creates a world in which inanimate objects found around their home and in local flea markets propel the heroine between scenes (**11.18**). According to the artists, the objects become a "haven for memories and dreams that harkens back to another time. They add: "Stop motion gives us the ability to create magical transitions; an orange causes her hair to grow into a tree that sprouts a flower that becomes a teacup that grows wings and flies away and saves her from being locked in a birdcage. With stop motion we can (and should) defy gravity."

At Kent State University, Ben Dansby's animation entitled "How to Make a Quiche" shows how stop-motion can emphasize the step-by-step nature of an activity by eliminating the agent—in this case the chef (**11.20**). This allows viewers to focus on the most important elements of the process. Based on a series of photographs played sequentially, the live footage was manipulated by desaturating the background elements to highlight the main objects. Large, bold typography and sound effects were added to accentuate the key actions and keep them fluid, to ensure that viewers are able to keep up with the fast pace. For example, the word "wait" appears after the quiche has popped out of the oven, implicitly telling the viewer when and why to wait.

Amy Peck's stop-motion study "Stitch" allowed her to personify a needle and thread with a level of energy that would not have been possible to achieve through interpolation or live-action (**11.21**). This process allowed Amy to trick the viewer into thinking that the needle was alive, bringing life to the message by showing something unexpected. Amy writes: "I knew that this was going to be tricky as I didn't want my hand to be in the scene at all. I wanted it to look as if the needle was working on its own, so the point of view and angle it was shot was going to be incredibly important. I used a bike repair stand to support the embroidery hoop that held the fabric. A piece of foam core was taped to the back of the stand so that no background was showing and the bike stand allowed me to access the fabric from above and below. I was also able to light the fabric from underneath. Once I had everything set up it was just a matter of moving the needle and thread along the word while taking lots of pictures."

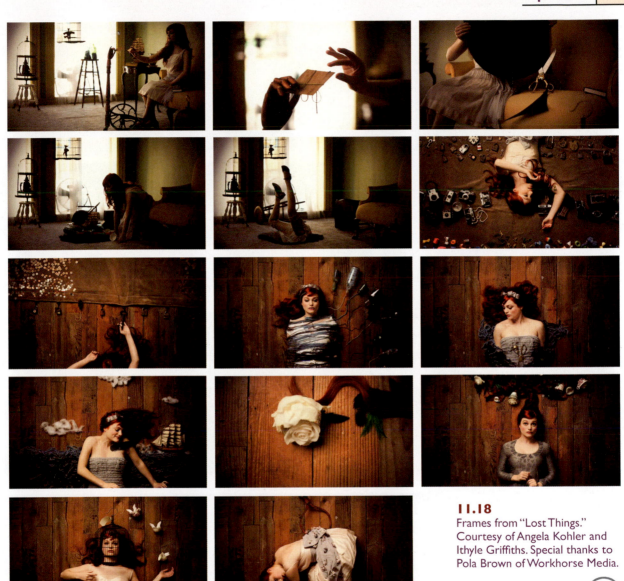

11.18
Frames from "Lost Things."
Courtesy of Angela Kohler and
Ithyle Griffiths. Special thanks to
Pola Brown of Workhorse Media.

Nate Johnson's stop-motion PSA entitled "Censorship" (**Chapter 7, figure 7.25**) creates a sense of deception. Nate writes: "I wanted the video to give the impression of a magician's quick sleight-of-hand, fooling the eye with distraction and trickery. The stop action technique gave the feeling that information could be concealed, missing, or changed, helping to convey a powerful message of censorship. That could not have been achieved as effectively without the 'covert' element of stop-motion."

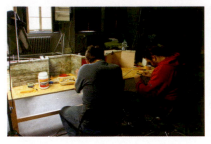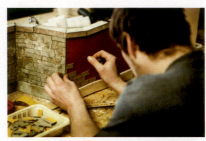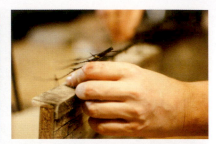

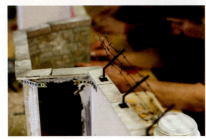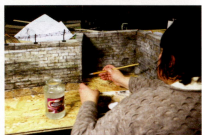

11.19
Photos from the making of the stop-motion set for "Standing Up for Freedom" for Amnesty International. Courtesy of Eallin.

See also Chapter 8, figure 8.40, on p. 284 and Chapter 13, figure 13.1, on p. 452.

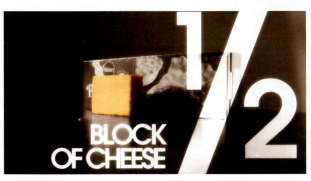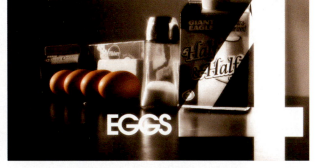

11.20
Frames from "How to Make a Quiche" by Ben Dansby. © 2012 Kent State University. Courtesy of Professor Gretchen Rinnert.

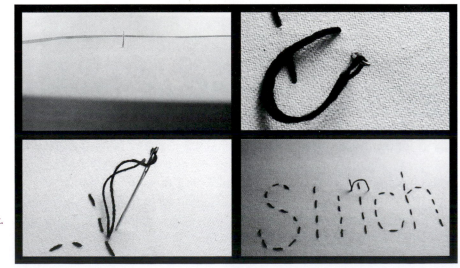

11.21
Frames from "Stitch" by Amy Peck. © 2012, Kent State University. Courtesy of Professor Gretchen Rinnert.

Ari Torbin's PSA entitled "Candy" uses simple word play to relate to younger children. Ari states: "I find it funny to use incorrect words or pronunciations to make things different. Growing up I had a speech impediment, so I constantly hear in my head the correct and incorrect pronunciations of words all the time." His process involved taking photographs of pieces of candy moved around by hand. The frames were imported into Adobe Photoshop and reconfigured to control the timing of the animation (**11.23**).

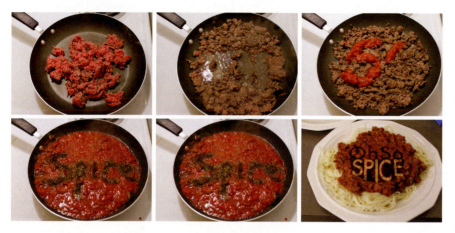

11.22
Frames from a PSA by Kristen Hogan. Courtesy of Professor Jon Krasner, Fitchburg State University.

Kristen's whimsical stop-motion animation for a fictional "Oh So Spice" network involved taking photographs "while cooking on a stove, creating the words in the meat, sauce, and spices" then compiling them together frame by frame in Photoshop. This very basic idea and process gets the point across in a slightly entertaining and appetizing way.

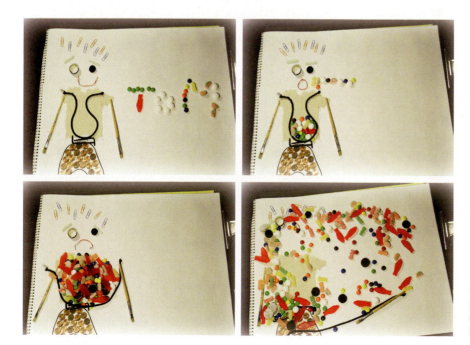

11.23
Frames from a PSA by Ari Torbin. Courtesy of Professor Jon Krasner, Fitchburg State University.

"Collage animation" relies on stop-motion to assemble printed and found materials on a frame-by-frame basis. It provided early twentieth-century painters a heightened sense of spontaneous, artistic freedom. In many cases, surface texture and pattern was the dominant feature, rather than the clarity of the subject matter. Animator and director Terry Gilliam popularized the technique of stop-motion collage in his work for *Monty Python's Flying Circus*. Independent filmmakers Frank and Caroline Mouris pushed the envelope of mixed media collage in their classic short "Frank Film" (1973). Their innovative process has been featured in commercials, documentaries, music videos, and shows including *Sesame Street* and *3-2-1 Contact*. Filmmakers have continued developing a broad range of styles, ranging from heavily layered non-objective compositions to conceptual, representational animations.

The beauty of collage in motion graphics is that images and type can be integrated in ways that would be difficult to achieve in the physical world. Digital layering can mimic the feel of collage or cutout animation with the added components of transparency and blending.

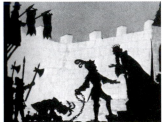

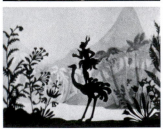

11.24
Frames from *The Adventures of Prince Achmed*. This film took almost three years to complete. The characters were black cardboard marionettes that were cut out with scissors and photographed frame by frame. Courtesy of Cecile Starr.

"Cutout animation" is a type of collage animation that was developed by Lotte Reiniger during the sound-on-film era of the 1930s. Her unique, silhouette style is evident in *The Adventures of Prince Achmed* (1926), one of the first animated motion pictures to be produced (**11.24**).

At Kent State University, Ruth Turner used cut paper, colored pencil, black marker, and tissue paper to create "Graft." The goal of the project was to express the meaning of a word by animating its letterforms. The letter "f" lifts from the 'g' and then occupies the space between the "a" and "t," similar to how a skin graft is performed, according to Ruth. Stop-motion helped create the illusion of the letters floating and allowed them to be edited out to create a seamless effect (**11.25**). Ruth writes: "The process of skin grafting is very meticulous and the preparation is slow and steady, much like the process of stop-motion animation. I didn't have that in mind when I was ready to shoot the animation. It was only after my experience with the process that I drew the conceptual connection to my piece and the word's definition." She adds: "At the time I made "Graft" I was really into the work of Jan Svankmajer and in particular to this project his short animation "Et Cetera" (1966). That's probably why I also chose such an unusual word to animate. He tends to pick obscure themes and tales to animate and film."

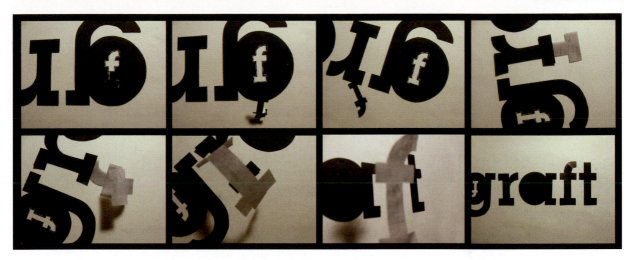

11.25
Frames from "Graft," a cutout animation by Ruth Turner. © 2012 Kent State University. Courtesy of Professor Gretchen Rinnert.

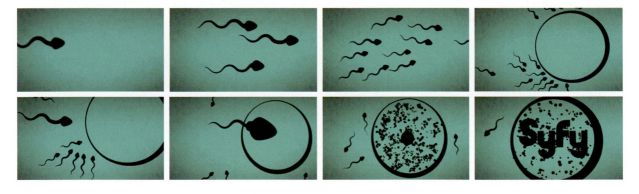

11.26
Frames from "Fertilization," a cutout animation assignment for SyFy network, by Kevin Passmore. © 2012 Ringling College of Art + Design.

In a playful bumper for *Visions 2012*, a screening of student work from Fitchburg State University, Jillian Bailey employed cutout animation, using images created from construction paper to convey different genres of movies (**11.27**). She writes: "First, I started with a storyboard that showed the story going through the different genres. It also helped me create transitions between the different genres. Next, I created the objects with construction paper. Using my desk, I taped the scenes up and then used the camera on my laptop to take the pictures."

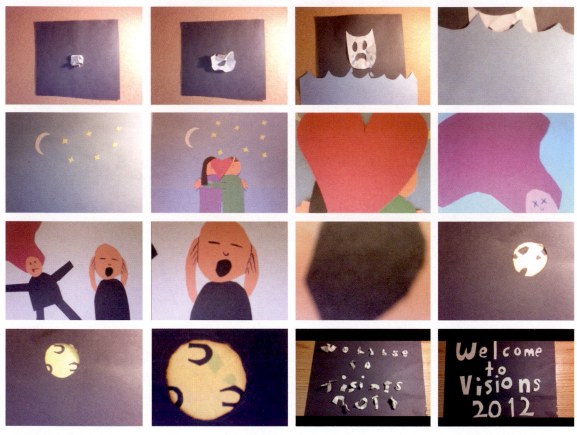

11.27
Frames from a bumper for
Visions 2012 by Jillian Bailey.
Courtesy of Professor Jon
Krasner, Fitchburg State
University.

rotoscoping

Live-action imagery can serve as the basis for animation. The practice of "rotoscoping"—drawing or painting over live footage—enables a wide range of animation approaches, including freehand, image alteration, and compositing. Today's digital technology can automate color and tonal adjustments, special effects, and standard operations such as blurring, dodging, burning, and tinting individual frames or ranges of adjacent frames. This "painting on movies" allows you seamlessly combine live-action images with animated content.

Rotoscoping can be a labor-intensive undertaking that requires time and patience. However, if your goal is to achieve realism, the results are extremely rewarding. Plan on creating a comfortable environment for yourself, and schedule adequate time so that you can work efficiently and at a steady pace.

Historical Perspective

Rotoscoping was developed in 1917 by Max Fleischer during the silent film era. It involved tracing stages of movement of live human and animal subjects from film one frame at a time. Used as a learning aid for animators to become better acquainted with motion and timing, this practice held up over the years and soon became a cornerstone of Walt Disney's in-house training. According to American catoonist and animator Walter Lantz, "I would take the old Charlie Chaplin films and project them one frame at a time, make a drawing over Chaplin's action, and flip the drawings to see how he moved. That's how most of us learned to animate."

Max Fleischer's use of the rotoscope can be seen in his early *Out of the Inkwell* films such as *Koko the Clown* and the 1940s *Superman* series. There were limitations, such as lengthy production time, cost, and trends, which were set mainly by Disney.

Rotoscoped animation looks only as mechanical as you make it. Simply tracing the outlines of filmed images can make a subject look lifeless and boring. Choreographing movements and physical attributes beforehand, however, can help determine the amount of exaggeration needed to make it appear more lively and animated. Devices such as acceleration and squash and stretch can heighten artistic expression and naturalize the subject, keeping it from clashing with other elements in the composition.

Using the right tools can help streamline your activity. A graphics tablet and a pressure-sensitive stylus can expedite workflow while protecting your carpal tunnels.

Frame rate is also a consideration, and experimentation may be needed to find a compromise between smooth playback and the amount of drawing time needed to generate the content. High rates between 15 and 30 fps provide smooth playback but require more frames. Lower frame rates will require fewer frames but produce choppier movements. Frame rates between 6 and 12 fps can achieve adequate, believable results. If you are stranded on a desert island or are serving a long prison sentence, rotoscoping at a frame rate of 24 or 30 fps might make you famous if you are rescued or released!

A fond memory from the 1980s is A-ha's music video "Take On Me." Its integration of line drawings and live-action color images is still refreshing to this day.

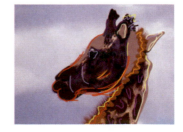

11.28
Loose gesture drawing over a live-action figure heightens the artistic expression of the image.

11.29
Adobe Photoshop's animation palette allows you to paint on indivudal frames of video. Gesture drawing was performed on a transparent layer above the video clip layer, frame by frame. The video, used as a reference, was then deleted, leaving the artwork.

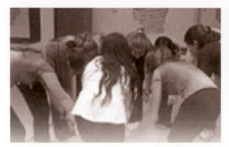
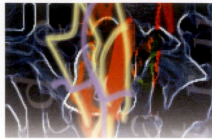

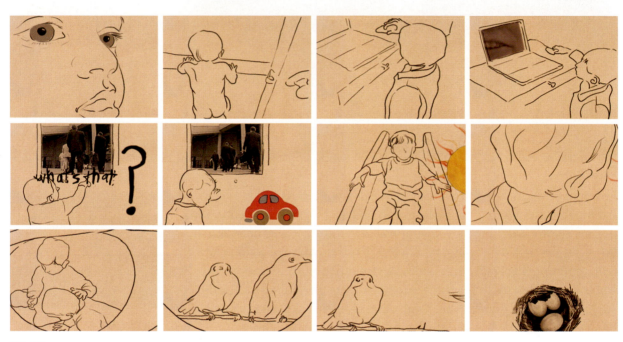

11.30
Frames from *Siblings* (2005). © 2012 Jon Krasner.

Generating simple line drawings from live footage of my children allowed me to express the idea of pure childhood experience in a society that can restrict personal expression and individuality.

In the groundbreaking spot "Standing Up for Freedom" for Amnesty International (also discussed in Chapters 8, 10, 12, and 13), rotoscoping was used to depict the tragedy of a mother losing her child (**11.31**). The description of events provided in the script reads: "We see a baby in the arms of his mother. The baby withers as a flower and disintegrates, dispersing in the air in the form of black ashes. The mother looks up to the camera, as a white headscarf surrounds her head. We start to see, behind her, many other mothers, wearing the same white headscarf. Their faces vanish, as the headscarfs remain. . . becoming doves that fly away when the tank appears."

Kyle Goines' PSA entitled "The Choice" (**11.32**) revolves around a casual "no thank you" to an offer of a cigarette. The cartoon-like aspect of the

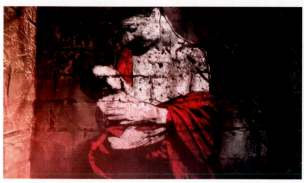

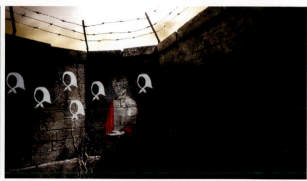

11.31
Frames from "Standing Up for Freedom" for Amnesty International. Courtesy of Eallin.

See also Chapter 13, figure 13.1, on p. 452.

nondescript characters helps convey the message about simple choices that people make every day. Challenged with the workflow issue of having to rotoscope over 600 frames of video, Kyle developed a process that allowed him to organize the components (i.e., shirts, pants, hands, feet, and faces) into layers to outline and fill separately with a set of custom colors. He was also able to work quickly using a Wacom tablet to capture the line style. Rendering the video as a series of JPEGs provided an easy and readable naming convention for the frames.

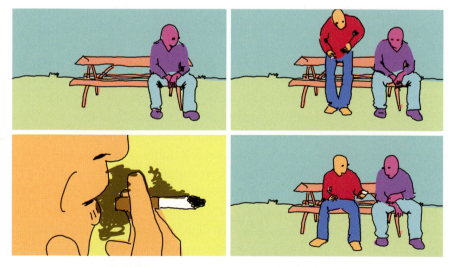

11.32
Frames from a PSA by Kyle Goines. Courtesy of Professor Jon Krasner, Fitchburg State University.

11.33
A rotoscoping exercise involving painting over live-action footage by Justin Bonitz. Courtesy of Professor Jon Krasner, Fitchburg State University.

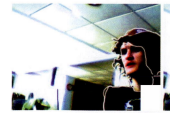
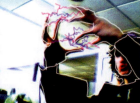
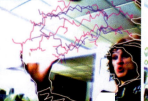
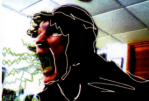

film capture

The rich, soft quality of motion film is attributed to its light-sensitive emulsion which is capable of capturing high-resolution images photographically (unlike video, which records images as electronic signals). Additionally, film cameras have the inherent ability to capture material one frame at a time, which is critical for any form of stop-motion animation. For these reasons, film continues to be a preferred medium by many independent and commercial animators.

Since most independent designers cannot afford 16 millimeter film, Super 8 millimeter is still considered to be an acceptable format. Companies such as MovieStuff (http://www.moviestuff.tv) specialize in transferring Super 8 footage to mini-DV tape, which then can be digitized using a DV camcorder and a computer.

digital capture

The advantages of capturing frames on a computer are instantaneous playback, preservation, and affordability. Instantaneous playback enables you to get the feel of the motion as it progresses without having to wait for a lab to develop. Digital storage preserves the quality of the work, unlike film or videotape which degrades over the years. Finally, there are no developing costs.

The most efficient methods of digital capture are DV cameras, digital still cameras, scanners, and single-frame capturing software. Unlike film cameras, the majority of consumer camcorders do not have a built-in single-frame capture mechanism. Standard analog and digital video camcorders are made to shoot several frames each time the button is pressed. However, an analog or digital camcorder can be used as an input device to record frames into the computer (rather than onto videotape). Alternatively, you can invest in software that allows for single-frame capture. Today, digital cameras are remarkably inexpensive, and most frame capture programs accept USB or FireWire connections. An alternative method to a camcorder or digital camera is to create your production on a piece of glass placed directly on a scanner. Each manipulation can then be digitized and saved as a frame.

There are a few important considerations that apply to digital capture. First, the input resolution should be determined in advance. Since the quality of raster-based images decreases when they are scaled up, be sure to digitize the artwork at a resolution that will accommodate scaling. Here is a standard formula to use: screen resolution × degree of scaling = input resolution. For example, if your images will be enlarged to twice their original size, scan them at 144 dpi (72 × 2 = 144).

When planning a project, be careful not to underestimate the amount of available disk space that will be needed; prepare for large storage requirements. FireWire devices have the best chance of playing the frames back smoothly, due to their high data transfer rates.

To streamline your process, keep different animation sequences in separate folders. Because frames are usually imported into applications in numerical order, name them with "padded" numbers (**11.34**).

tips

Depending on the length and complexity of your animation, all of the techniques discussed here require substantial time and patience. Here are a few additional tips to help streamline your process.

1. Start by creating thumbnails.
Loose drawings (or quick digital mockups on the computer) can go a long way in helping you resolve the basic motions of elements ahead of time. They can also help determine how your scenes will fit into the visual flow of the composition before you create a storyboard.

2. Work smart.
Since key frames depict the most important changes, create them first, and then generate the intermediate frames. Non-changing elements such as backdrops and static images should be developed only once, since they can be used repeatedly. Objects that change their physical appearance should also be developed independently.

3. Enlist the photocopier.
The photocopier can be a wonderful production tool. The sketchy appearance of xeroxed images can be a satisfying alternative to the time needed to create individual frames by hand. Photocopying can yield camera effects, such as zooming, by reducing or enlarging the images.

In collage or cutout-style animations, photocopying actual objects onto transparencies can eliminate the laborious task of tearing out images from magazines or other sources. (Unless you are using a surgeon's

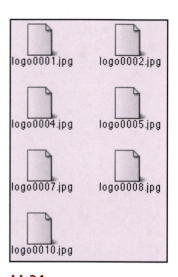

11.34
Sequences of frames from different segments of an animation are saved in separate folders and named with "padded" numbers.

scalpel and a magnifying glass, the results are also much cleaner.)
The raw, high-contrast look of xeroxed images can add to the conceptual
and aesthetic aspects of your design. Be sure to read the photocopier's
manual; extraordinary effects can be achieved by experimenting with
its brightness and color settings.

4. Plan the duration of motions individually.

Choreographing simultaneous movements can be challenging, and
establishing a game plan ahead of time will pay off in the long run.
As a general rule, longer actions require more frames than shorter
actions. Fifteen or more frames may be necessary for a walk cycle, while
only two to three frames may be needed to animate a blinking eye.

5. Layer.

If you envision your animation having various levels of foreground
and background elements, create them on overhead transparencies
or on actual celluloid sheets. Overlaying them allows you the freedom
and flexibility of adding depth to the frame. As an alternative, consider
photocopying opaque artwork onto transparencies. Your local Kinko's,
OfficeMax, or Staples are affordable options for accomplishing this.

6. Let the camera do the work.

Camera movements, such as pans, tilts, and zooms, can easily be
achieved by changing the camera's position in relation to the artwork
in small steps, as opposed to having to emulate these effects by hand-
executed means. Alternatively, you can move the imagery. Repetitive
motions, such as rolling, vibrating, or lifting the base, can produce the
effect of waves at sea, walking, or experiencing an earthquake.

7. Loosen up and push the media!

Be expressive and experimental in your artistic style. (You do not have
to be a cartoonist!) There is a wide range of possible drawing approaches,
and content can be executed with any combination of media.

8. Sacrifice detail for pictorial continuity.

Complex textures and details can lead to inconsistencies that become
eyesores when your frames are played in sequence. Moving foreground
characters in traditional cel animations are usually painted with flat
colors, in contrast to background scenery, which is often more detailed
and complex.

9. Combine media and techniques.
Frame-by-frame animation does not need to rely on any one technique. Combinations of traditional and digital media and techniques can contribute toward a richness of content and personalize your style. Investigate what feels natural; there is no "right" or "wrong" formula.

10. Consider lighting.
Lighting is one of the most vital aspects of filming. Bad lighting can cause unwanted shadows or overexposure. Be sure that you have plenty of light to work with. Studio lights are designed to match the color balance of film. If you cannot afford them, desk lamps or halogen lights can suffice with filters or manual white balance on digital cameras.

11. Shoot "on twos," "on threes," etc.
Animations that do not require seamless motion can be shot on every other or every third frame. This works particularly well for collage or cutout animations that are meant to look choppy.

Interpolation Animation

Interpolation is the process by which an element's spatial or visual characteristics are animated between two or more instances in time. Theses instances are known as "key frames." Key frames designate where the most extreme changes occur on a timeline and contain data about an element such as its position, size, orientation, transparency, or color. Unlike frame-by-frame animation, intermediate data between key frames are automatically calculated without having to create the in-between frames one at a time. For this reason, interpolation can generate animations much quicker, with less effort, and with greater control over how motion and change are choreographed.

Interpolation can be applied to the primary motion of elements in a composition, or to the secondary motion of a camera to achieve mobile framing. In **figure 11.36**, beginning, middle, and end key frame values describe an object's spatial location at three different points in time. The data between key frames are automatically interpolated to produce animation when the sequence is played back. This frame range marks the beginning and the end of the interpolation. The last key frame denotes the beginning key frame of the next, adjacent frame range.

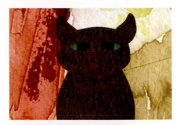
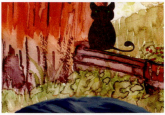
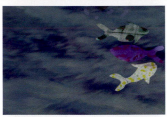
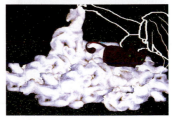

11.35
Alex Wall combined her original watercolor paintings with digitally generated textures in a visually stunning animation. Courtesy of Professor Jon Krasner, Fitchburg State University.

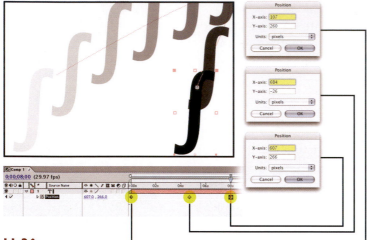

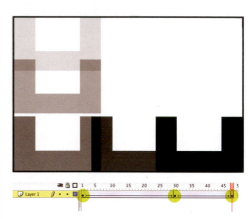

11.36
Adobe After Effects and Flash use key frame event markers. A beginning and an end key frame value describe an object's spatial location at two different frames or points in time. The last key frame of a frame range denotes the starting key frame of the next frame range.

"Linear interpolation" produces mechanical, uniform motion or change. Differences in the velocity values of the intermediate frames occur in steady time increments. The rate of motion progresses at a consistent pace until a new interpolation occurs at a new key frame. "Non-linear interpolation" (or "Bezier interpolation") produces less predictable, more lifelike results, and smoother transitions between interpolations. "Spatial interpolation" refers to the direction that objects travel. "Visual interpolation" refers to visual properties, such as color, texture, opacity, and shape geometry. "Temporal interpolation" refers to the rate at which objects travel, taking into account factors such as acceleration and deceleration.

Creating effective animation requires substantial focus and aesthetic sensitivity. Beginning animators often create too many keys, resulting in jerky movements and painstaking editing. Others allow the software to perform too much of the work, resulting in unnatural movements.

spatial interpolation

Spatial interpolation (also referred to as "path animation") involves animating an object's position, orientation, or scale. In timeline-based applications such as Adobe After Effects, spatial interpolation is achieved by establishing key frame values on a timeline (**11.37**). The property of position defines the horizontal and vertical direction that elements travel along a predetermined "route" or motion path. "Linear spatial interpolation" occurs on straight motion paths; "non-linear spatial interpolation" occurs on curved motion paths. The geometry of a motion path can be modified to change an element's course of travel (**11.38**).

Most applications offer "motion tracking"—a process that enables you to monitor an element's movement and generate a motion path from the movement. The resulting path can then be applied to different objects

Interpolation Animation

to make them move in the same direction. Through this technique, objects can be choreographed to mimic the movement of other objects in space. In **figure 11.39**, the *x*- and *y*-coordinates of groups of pixels that pertain to live-action elements in a video clip are tracked, and the resulting data are used to generate motion paths. The paths can then be applied to other layers containing typography and graphics.

👁 🔊 ○ 🔒	🔳 #	Source Name	Mode	T	TrkMat	0:00f	05f	10f
👁	▽ 🔲 1	⬛ circle.tif	Normal ▼		⬜			
	▷ Masks							
	▷ Effects							
	▽ Transform	Reset						
	○ Anchor Point	324.5 , 324.5						
◀ ✓	▷ ○ Position	104.0 , 53.0				◆	◆	
◀ ☐	▷ ○ Scale	41.0 %					◆	◆
	○ Rotation	0 × +0.0 °						

11.37
In Adobe After Effects, spatial interpolation is established by key-framing an object's position, rotation, and scale properties on a timeline.

11.38
below: Motion paths can be straight lines, curves, or a combination of lines and curves, and can be modified to change an object's course of travel.

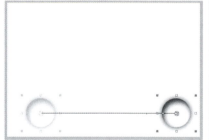

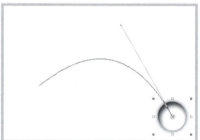

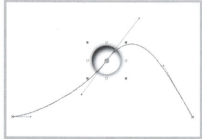

11.39
Motion tracking of a group of pixels is used to generate a motion path. The path's data can then be applied to another image to make it appear to be following the movement of the hand.

visual interpolation

Visual interpolation involves animating an object's visual appearance by changing its geometry, color, transparency, or surface texture.

interpolating form

Animating changes in geometry can be achieved by the technique of morphing or by applying distortion effects. "Morphing" produces seamless intermediate changes between two images. "Cross-dissolving" and "warping" are the two most common digital morphing procedures. Cross-dissolving involves interpolating the colors from the pixels of a source image to those in a corresponding destination image. Although this method does not alter shape geometry, it is effective when the initial images have similar structures. Warping, in contrast, shifts the physical locations of pixels between images without transforming their colors. "Point warping" uses control points to govern how pixels shift their positions in space (**11.40**). Combining these techniques can produce effective results.

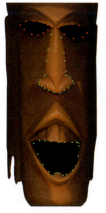 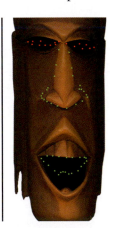 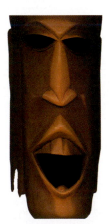 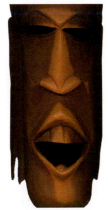 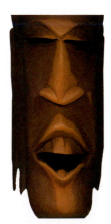

source   *destination*

11.40
Point warping shifts the locations of an image's pixels in space to distort its geometric appearance.

In Adobe Flash, the technique of "shape tweening" interpolates the vertex points of two vector-based shapes. Flash's "shape hints" can be used to achieve increased precision when animating complex shape changes, since they identify points that are matched between starting and ending shapes (**11.41**). For example, in morphing a graphic of one animal into another, shape hints instruct the software to morph the legs, head, and tail regions of the start and finish images independently, giving you more control over each animation.

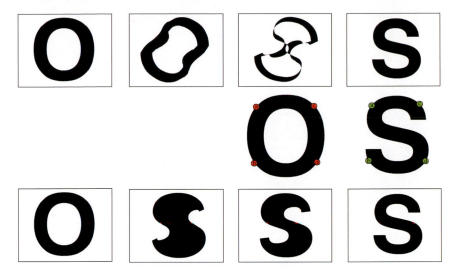

To achieve the best results, it is best to morph objects that are similar in size, shape, resolution, and background content. For example, if the starting image is a close-up of a face, a close-up of a different face would be a more appropriate choice than a full body shot of another person. Matching the face's general size and shape can also improve the morph's transitional quality. If the source and destination images have uniform or matching backgrounds, the effect will be focused on the subject, not on the background.

As an alternative to morphing, distortion filters can produce incremental changes in 2D or 3D forms. 3D modeling and animation applications offer mathematical processes such as free-form deformation (FFD), a process commonly used to twist, bend, and stretch 3D models in computer-aided design (CAD). In 2D environments, warping effects can shift an image's pixels by altering sets of vertex points. This can correct unwanted distortions or to emulate the effects of wind or water (**11.42**).

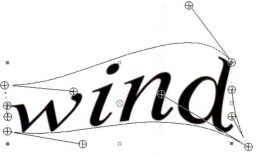

11.42
After Effects' Bezier Warp filter can reshape an image by altering a set of vertex points. Interpolating this operation creates the effect of the image blowing in the wind.

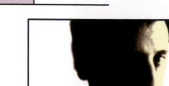
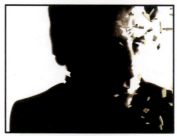
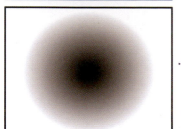
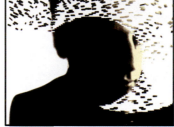
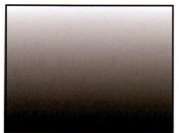
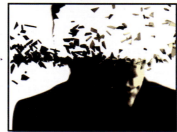
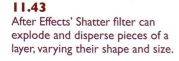

interpolating surface

Properties such as value, color, opacity, and effects can be interpolated through key frames. Standard operations such as Levels and Curves can animate an image's tonal effects by remapping its distribution of shadows, mid-tones, and highlights. Common color operations allow you to alter hue, brightness, or intensity level or add a color tint to a monochromatic image. More advanced operations such as After Effects' Channel Mixer provide specific control over an image's separate red, green, and blue color components (**11.46**).

In addition to the multitude of filters that come bundled with software, third-party developers continue to distribute compatible plug-ins that are intricate enough to serve as standalone applications. Some can generate textures and volumetric simulations that imitate natural phenomena like fire and smoke. Others are capable of photographic effects like solarizations, lens flares, and video malfunctions.

11.43
After Effects' Shatter filter can explode and disperse pieces of a layer, varying their shape and size.

11.44
Interpolation of a tint applied to a grayscale image.

11.45
Hue/saturation is interpolated to increase the image's saturation levels and shift its color cast.

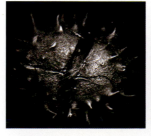
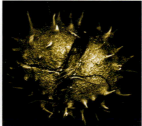
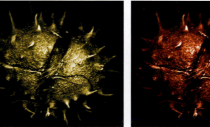

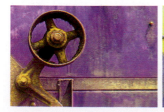
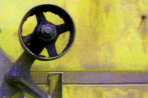
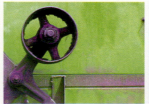
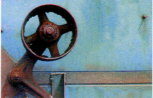

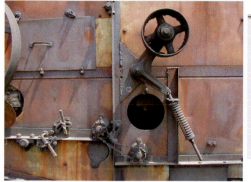

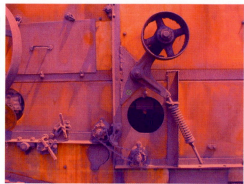

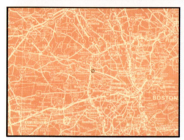

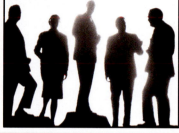

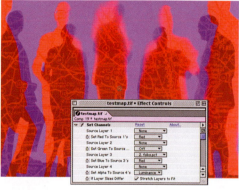

11.46

After Effects' Channel Mixer is used to blend the red, green, and blue data for an image. Entering different percentage values can create astonishing effects, such as sepia tones. A Set Channels control can also create a variety of provocative color effects. Here, it is used to replace the luminance values of one image layer with the values from another layer.

11.47

The use of an adjustment layer in After Effects allows you to apply multiple tonal and color effects to all layers that appear underneath it in the timeline. Altering an adjustment layer's opacity controls the degree to which the effects apply to the underlying layers. After Effects' Blend with Original parameter can be interpolated to animate the progression of an adjustment layer's effect.

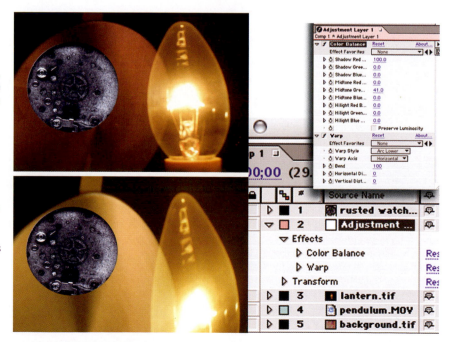

temporal interpolation

"Temporal interpolation" describes the manner in which elements move through time. While controlling the direction of an object on a motion path affects its spatial interpolation, controlling the speed that the object moves affects its temporal interpolation.

"Linear temporal interpolation" produces mechanical, uniform motions and is represented by a straight line on a speed graph. Differences in velocity values between key frames occur in even increments, and the rate of motion or change progresses at a consistent pace. "Non-linear" (or "Bezier") temporal interpolation involves changes in acceleration or deceleration, resulting in less predictable, more natural motions. Smoother transitions between frame ranges produce more realistic results.

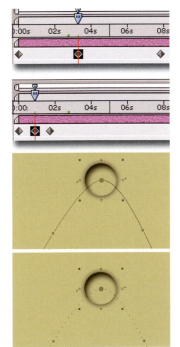

duration and velocity

Velocity is a temporal property that can be governed by controlling the distance between key frames. Closing down or opening up the space between key frames on a timeline shortens or lengthens the duration of events (**11.48**). You can also control velocity by modifying the degree of interpolation. For example, After Effects allows you to change, numerically or manually, the start or end values for an element's position, scale, or rotation.

In most applications, velocity curves can be altered to accelerate or decelerate an incoming or outgoing velocity. For example, an object can slow as it approaches the key frame and then speed up as it leaves it (**11.49**). Once an element's velocity between key frames has been calculated, it can be adjusted so that elements play back at their normal rate, speed up, or slow down.

11.48
The distance between key frames on the timeline determines the motion's velocity. Compressing the distance increases velocity, since the duration of the action is shortened. The spacing between the dots on the motion path is wider, indicating a greater velocity.

The technique of "time stretching" allows you to control and change how fast the content in a layer moves by manipulating the layer's duration. For example, stretching a layer to 200 percent doubles the frame length so that the animation plays back at half speed; shortening the length to 50 percent doubles the speed (**11.50**). Time stretching can be applied to an entire animation sequence or to its individual segments to introduce speed changes. For example, you can play a portion of a sequence in slow motion, while the remainder plays back at normal speed.

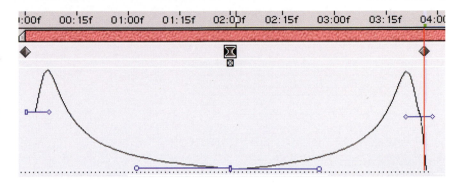

11.49
Using a velocity graph, you can adjust the rate of motion to control how fast or slow changes occur between key frames. In this case, the velocity curve was manipulated to create the effect of the motion gradually stopping and then starting again.

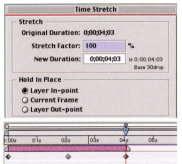
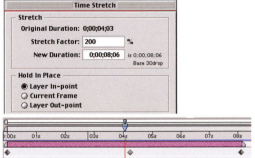
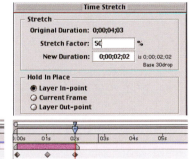

11.50
After Effects' Time Stretch function allows you to speed up or slow down playback.

Most applications also offer built-in algorithms that can produce acceleration or deceleration. Flash's "ease in" and "ease out" feature, for example, uses a standard velocity curve. In **figure 11.51**, After Effects' Easy Ease function is applied to the last position key frame, producing a gradual deceleration of an object as it approaches its final position. Acceleration in the velocity at the beginning of the interpolation results when Easy Ease Out is applied to the first position key frame. When it is applied to both key frames, the incoming and outgoing velocities are affected. The spacing between the dots on the motion path is uniform before each effect is applied. Initially, the graph displays a straight line, indicating a constant speed of motion along the path. After each algorithm is applied, the spacing changes to represent acceleration and deceleration.

parenting
Multiple transformations can be interpolated on a timeline, allowing you to animate an object's positioning, scale, and spatial orientation simultaneously. Advanced techniques such as "parenting" and "nesting" provide more control in coordinating the different types of movements

11.51
Adobe After Effects' Easy Ease operation.

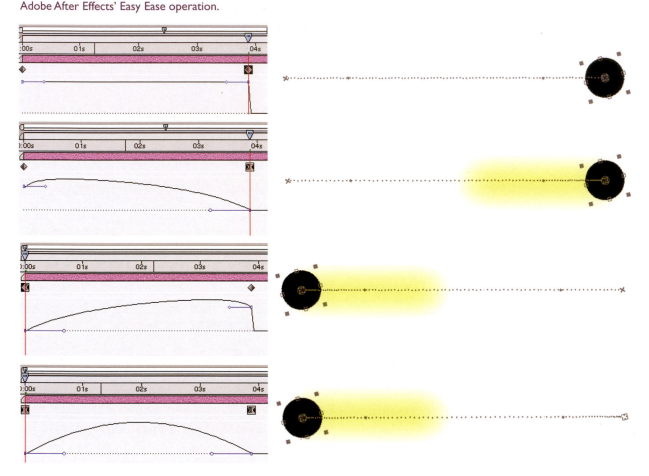

between elements. For example, a figure's hands, arms, head, and legs can be animated separately, and these animations can be combined into one. The entire subject, consisting of its different moving parts, can then be animated to walk across the screen.

Parenting in animation allows you to create relative (no pun intended) movements between elements by setting up hierarchical relationships. For example, a clock's hands can rotate independently while following the position of their parent—the clock—moving across the screen. This concept is easy to understand if you apply this simple analogy: When parents hold their child's hand to keep him or her from straying away, the child naturally moves with the parent and follows wherever the parent goes. The child maintains the freedom to turn or move freely within his or her own space; however, those motions are not transferred back to the parent. The parent's main actions are automatically passed on to its children, but a child's action does not necessarily affect the parent. A parent can have an infinite amount of children. (Having three of my own, I would suggest stopping there!) However, a child in this instance can only have one parent. Children can be parents to other children, and there is no limit to the number of levels of hierarchy that you can build.

11.52
In After Effects, a parental hierarchy is built to coordinate the motions of the main "body" and its smaller parts.

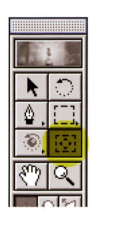

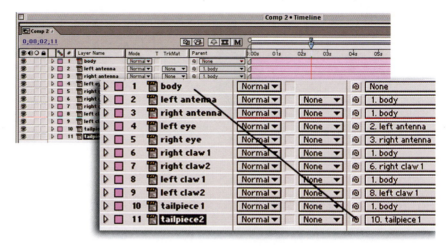

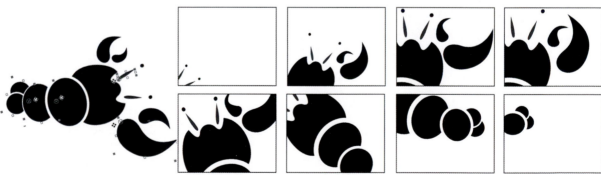

nesting

Complex animations may consist of many different types of motions among elements. The technique of "nesting" (also referred to as "precomping" in Adobe After Effects) allows you to organize individual movements into separate animations that can later be combined. In **figure 11.53**, symbol nesting in Flash is used to combine and coordinate individual movements. In Symbol 1, the graphic's rotation is animated across a series of key frames. Symbol 1 is brought into Symbol 2.

Inside Symbol 2, Symbol 1 is looped 4 times, and its opacity is interpolated to fade out at the end of the last sequence. Symbol 2 is then animated in the scene to a motion guide layer. Each individual component of the animation can be refined inside its original symbol.

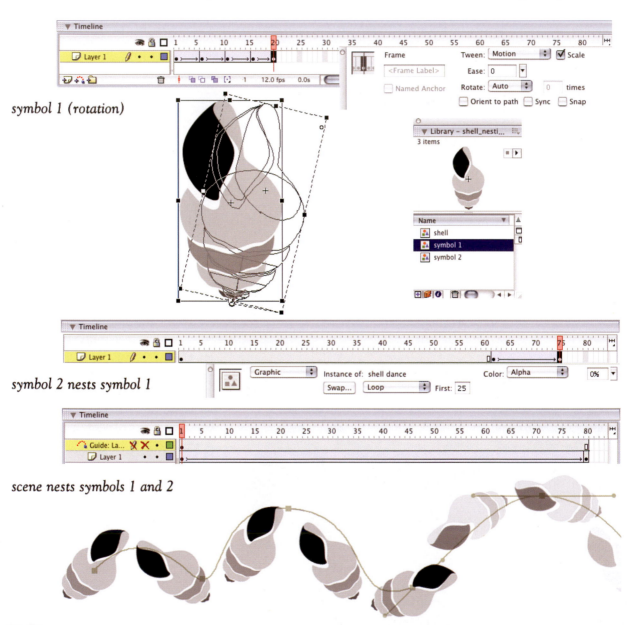

symbol 1 (rotation)

symbol 2 nests symbol 1

scene nests symbols 1 and 2

11.53
Symbol nesting in Adobe Flash.

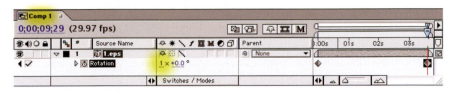

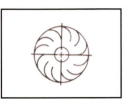

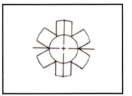

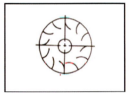

*Each image is animated in its own Comp
with varying speeds of rotation.*

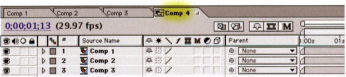

*Comps 1, 2, and 3 are nested inside of Comp 4
to group the animated images together.*

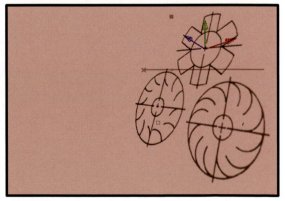

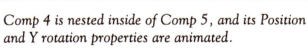

*Comp 4 is nested inside of Comp 5, and its Position
and Y rotation properties are animated.*

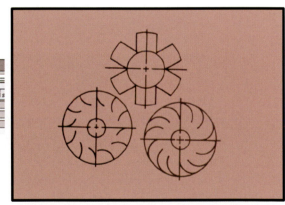

11.54
Precomping is used in After Effects to combine and
coordinate layers that animate at different speeds.

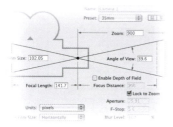

11.55
After Effects provides camera presets that simulate the capabilities of common lenses and 35 millimeter film.

11.56
After Effects' multiple-view layout allows you to view a scene from different angles.

mobile framing

Today, 2D and 3D motion graphics packages give designers considerable control and flexibility, allowing them to experiment with mobile framing. Inserting "camera objects" into a composition can provide various perspectives and viewpoints. Adobe After Effects, for example, provides several camera presets, all of which simulate the capabilities of common lenses and 35 millimeter film. These are named according to focal length, which describes the distance between the image displayed and the viewer's perspective (**11.55**). Editing between different camera views can show an action unfolding from different angles and spatial distances.

Basic camera motions that are used in traditional filmmaking can be emulated through interpolation. Panning and tilting, for example, can be achieved by moving an image that is wider than its visual field across the frame. Zooming can be achieved by changing the camera distance in relation to a subject or by scaling the subject up over time.

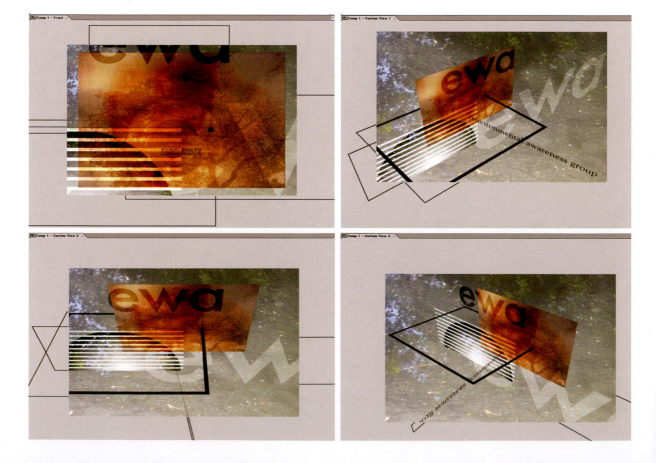

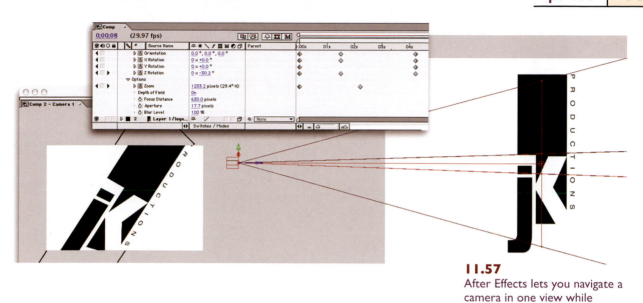

11.57
After Effects lets you navigate a camera in one view while observing the result in another.

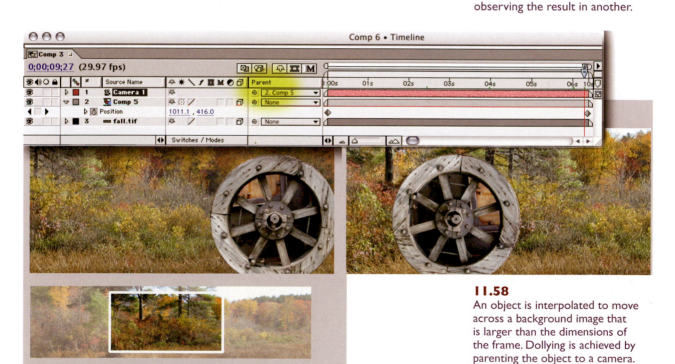

Size of background image relative to frame.

Comp 5, which contains an animation of the wheel rotating 360°, is nested inside of Comp 6 and assigned as a parent to the camera, as seen in the Timeline above.

11.58
An object is interpolated to move across a background image that is larger than the dimensions of the frame. Dollying is achieved by parenting the object to a camera. As a result, the camera (that is our point of view) moves horizontally with the object.

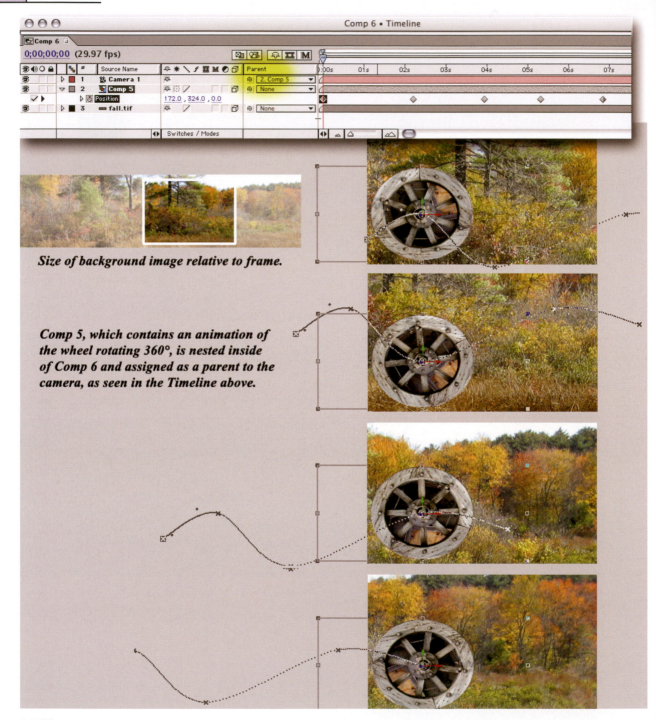

Size of background image relative to frame.

Comp 5, which contains an animation of the wheel rotating 360°, is nested inside of Comp 6 and assigned as a parent to the camera, as seen in the Timeline above.

11.59
The object's motion is interpolated to animate across a background that is larger than the frame. A "child" camera object follows its motion path.

Chapter Summary

Frame-by-frame animation involves creating individual images and displaying them in quick succession to create "persistence of vision"—the illusion of continuous motion. Key frames identify major changes in a scene and are used as guides for constructing the in-between or intermediate frames that complete the transitions between them.

During the 1930s and 1940s, "classical frame-by-frame animation" for film was labor-intensive, involving the creation of drawings on paper or on semi-transparent sheets of vellum. "Cel animation" reduced the labor of classical animation by layering foreground, middle-ground and background elements onto sheets of celluloid film. Experimental film pioneers such as Len Lye popularized the "direct-on-film" or "cameraless" technique that involved creating images on filmstrips with traditional media, chemical compounds, or processes such as scratching, burning, rubbing, collage, and stop-motion. Today, digital, "natural media" tools offer motion designers a heightened sense of freedom.

Unlike frame-by-frame animation, "interpolation" software can calculate intermediate data between "key frames" to produce linear or non-linear uniform motions. "Spatial interpolation" (or "path animation") involves animating an object's position, orientation, or scale, while "visual interpolation" involves animating geometry, color, opacity and surface properties. "Temporal interpolation" describes how elements move over time. Velocity is a temporal property that can be controlled by changing the distance between key frames as well as through the technique of "time stretching."

Advanced animation techniques such as "parenting" and "nesting" allow you to coordinate and preserve types of motions and modify them independently. Further, most motion graphics applications allow you to work with "cameras" to portray various perspectives and viewpoints. Basic camera motions that are used in traditional cinematography can be emulated digitally through interpolation.

12

motion graphics compositing
synthesizing the content

"Human life itself may be almost pure chaos, but the work of the artist is to take these handfuls of confusion and disparate things, things that seem to be irreconcilable, and put them together in a frame to give them some kind of shape and meaning."
—Katherine Anne Porter

Motion graphics compositing techniques allow for the seamless integration of 2D and 3D images, typography, and live-action content. "Thinking in layers" has become a standard trend. The unusual creative possibilities that exist for merging diverse imagery are pushing the limits of artistic experimentation and expression.

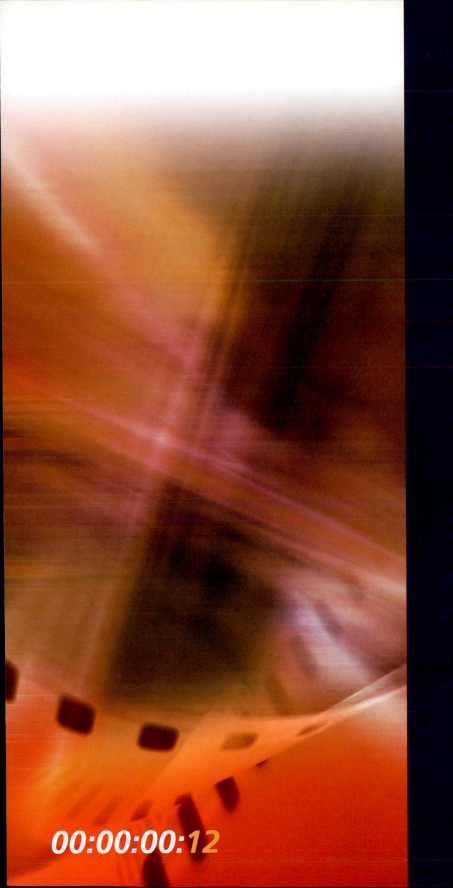

00:00:00:12

Compositing: An Overview

"Digital compositing" involves merging various types of elements into a uniform, seamless compositional space. It allows you to create unusual relationships that are impossible to achieve in the real, physical world by combining live-action, graphics, hand-drawn elements, and typography.

Historical Perspective

In the early twentieth century, Dadaist and Futurist artists were among the first to liberate ideas through the techniques of collage and photomontage. The German Dadaist movement at the end of World War I prompted painters and graphic designers to explore collage, and photographers to experiment with multiple exposures, combination printing, and assembling cutout pieces of photographs. The works of John Heartfield, Herbert Matter, and Kurt Schwitters were among the most influential of this period, demonstrating a heavy reliance on experimentation, playfulness, and spontaneity.

The role of the compositor used to be unique and specialized. When digital editing processes replaced traditional video editing tools, the distinction between compositors, editors, and CGI artists became blurred. The gap between video editing and motion graphics software has also narrowed, since live-action footage has become an integral component of motion graphic design. Further, the processes of animation and compositing are often performed at the same time and with the same software.

Amnesty International's television spot "Standing Up for Freedom" (**Chapter 13, figure 13.1, on p. 452**) combined processes ranging from stop-motion and traditional cel to CGI and models and miniatures. Live-action footage of shadows and 3D paper effects were used to express the impact of the "Firing Squad" scene. The "Skyscraper" episode conveys the negative effect of industrial growth on freedom by combining live video footage of blood dripping from bullet holes in the wall with freehand animation of a syringe sucking up the blood, depriving the flower's roots of nourishment. The ending scene mixes 3D animation with video footage of debris, dust, and smoke to achieve the positive, climactic effect of the wall crumbling down to reveal the sunlight through the dust. Maintaining a visual cohesion between these techniques was technically challenging.

The Fuel TV ID in **figure 12.1** shows a seamlessly layered magical world where eagles fly over ancient landscapes, bikes leave trails of rainbow-colored paint, unicorns gallop over fire-engulfed swords, and skaters ride the edge of a rainbow. Inspired by seventies airbrush art on surfboards and rock album covers, director Jonathan Notaro synthesized live footage, 3D images, and digitally airbrushed graphics.

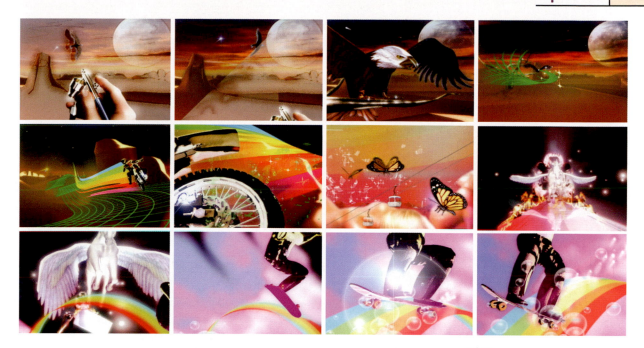

A variety of animated 2D and 3D graphics interact with one another in an instructional video for the music channel Fuse. Buck, a motion graphics design company in Los Angeles, aimed to make the content reflect the humorous nature of Fuse. Ryan Honey, creative director/co-owner of Buck, based his concept on how to make things out of brands that are related to music in some way. The "Fuse Shoe Box" theme, for example, shows how to make a speaker out of a Puma shoe box; "Winterfuse Fronts" shows how to make metal teeth fronts of the word 'Fuse' out of a stick of Winterfresh gum (**12.2**).

12.1
Frames from *Fantasy*, an ID for Fuel TV produced by Brand New School (Los Angeles). Courtesy of Fuel TV.

12.2
Frames from "Winterfuse Fronts" and "Fuse Shoe Box" IDs. Courtesy of Buck.

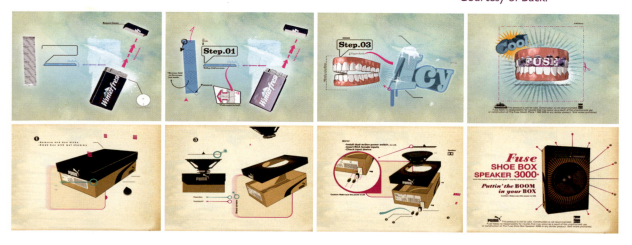

In 2008, the Munich-based design agency TOCA ME commissioned Dvein studio in Barcelona to create the provocative opening titles for their annual conference. Dvein's goal was to feature the thought processes of the artists who were invited to attend by expressing the idea of looking deep into the meaning of things. The techniques that were used to create the imagery evolved with considerable research and experimentation. Using an industrial hair dryer to melt plastic, the design team learned that the reaction of certain materials to very high temperatures could emulate the effect of growing organic tissues and textures. The imperceptible combination of computer graphics and live footage gave the titles a scientific, under-the-skin feeling (**12.3**).

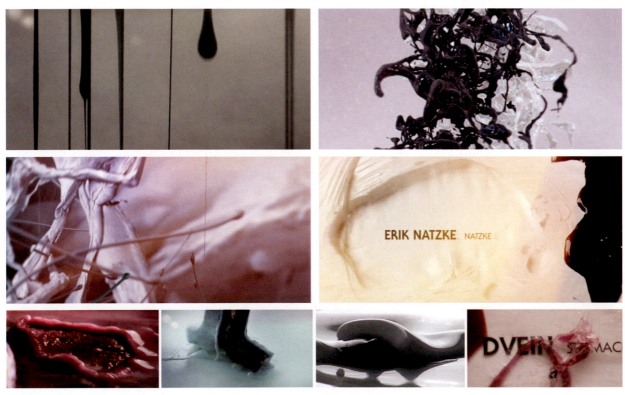

12.3
Frames from "Beyond Surface," an opener for TOCA ME design agency's annual conference. Courtesy of Dvein.

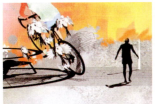
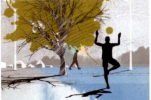
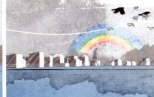
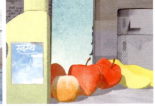

12.4
Layers of 2D sketches, paintings, and drawings were composited in a show package for Apna Khyal Rakhiyega, a health program in India. Courtesy of Varun Chawla.

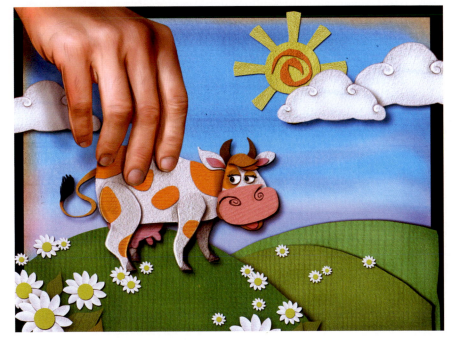

12.5
This spot for the multinational food packaging and processing company Tetra Pak combines graphic cut-out elements made from cardboard with live-action footage of hands to tell the story of ultra-pasteurization. Courtesy of Eallin.

Blend Operations

The most basic compositing techniques involve controlling the transparency of multilayered images and the manner in which their colors "mix" visually.

Degrees of transparency between static and moving elements in a composition can be established by specifying a layer's opacity value. Similar to interpolating an element's positioning, scale, or rotation over time, opacity is an attribute that can be animated to emulate semi-opaque materials, such as water or glass, or to create simple dissolves between key frames.

During the mid-1990s, Fractal Design Painter and Specular Collage were among the first raster-based programs to introduce the concept of layering. Over a decade has passed since Adobe Systems featured layers as a major advancement in Photoshop. Photoshop continues to reign as having the most superior layering facilities, while After Effects is still recognized as a leader for its intuitive layering processes in motion graphics compositing.

"Blend operations" (also referred to as "composite modes" or "layer modes") allow you to mix the hues, saturation, and brightness values of superimposed images (**12.7**). "Multiply" references the color and brightness values of an image's color channels and multiplies the values with those of an underlying image, producing a blend of darker colors. Multiplying any color with black produces black; multiplying it with white leaves the color unchanged. Values between black and white produce progressively darker colors. "Screen" multiplies the inverse of each image's pixel values to produce lighter colors, similar to projecting photographic transparencies over each other. "Overlay" multiplies or screens an image's values depending on the color and brightness data of the underlying layer. "Darken" overlays an image's pixels that are darker than those of the layer(s) below. "Lighten" produces the opposite effect, overlaying the top layer's pixels that are lighter than those of the layer below. "Difference" subtracts an image's pixel values from those of the bottom layer or vice versa, depending on which has the greater value. "Exclusion" produces a similar effect with lower contrast. "Hue" generates a result based on the brightness and saturation levels of the bottom layer's pixels and the hue of the top layer's pixels. "Saturation" considers the luminance and hue of the top layer's pixels and the saturation of those of the underlying layer. "Luminosity" considers the hue and saturation values of the bottom layer and the luminance values of the top layer.

Figure 12.6 illustrates a rich arrangement of 2D and 3D information. This was made possible by varying the opacity levels and blend modes of the layers. In **figure 12.8**, a multilayered, tactile palette of photos, graphic shapes, and brush strokes was achieved by using the blend operations described in a promotional spot for explore.org.

12.6
Frames from Giant Octopus' motion graphics newsreel.

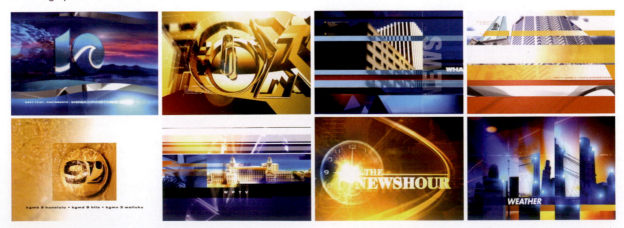

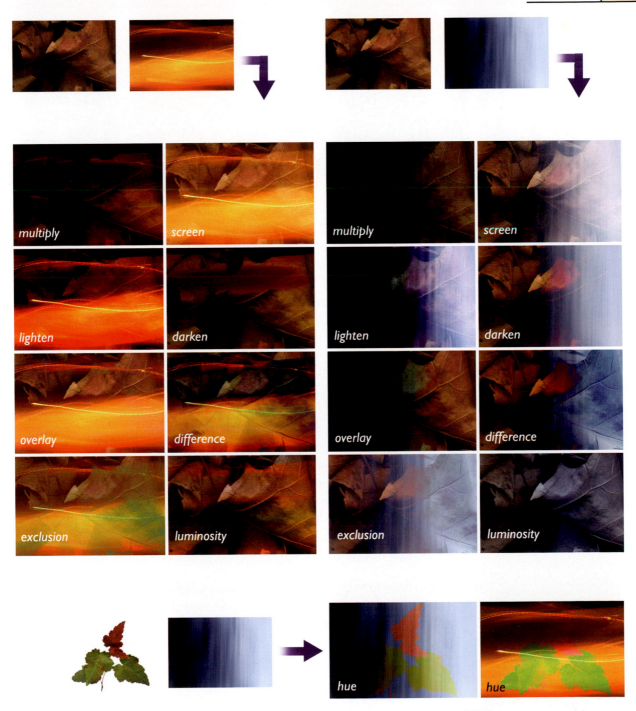

12.7
Standard blend operations used for layer compositing.

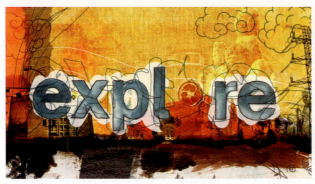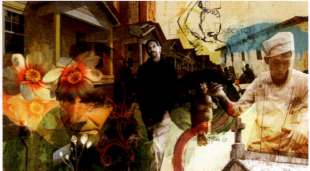

12.8
In this composition, After Effects' layer modes were used to achieve a richness of color and texture of images photographed in various world locations. Courtesy of Belief.

See also Chapter 8, figure 8.39, on p. 283.

Keying

"Keying" is a technique that eliminates a selected range of colors to create areas of transparency. It is often used to place actors or scale models shot against a solid green or blue screen into imaginary situations. For example, the classic *Sgt. Pepper Party* (1967) filmed an elephant against a green screen that was replaced with a "background plate" of the Adelphi Hotel. For *Spider-Man* (2002), the hero was filmed leaping around a room painted with a flat color that was then substituted with footage of a cityscape. *The Matrix* (1999) involved placing multiple cameras in a 360° room painted green or blue. Computer-generated images were "keyed" into the scene to produce a seamless composite.

"Chroma keys" are single colors that are used to substitute parts of a scene with new data. The most well-known implementations of chroma keying in television occur in the local news. A talent who appears to be speaking in front of an animated weather map is most likely sitting in front of a blue backdrop. The blue hue is keyed out in the production room, and the animated map footage is inserted into the broadcast.

In the titles for a music video competition held in New Zealand, live subjects were filmed against a green screen and composited with illustrations ranging from a half-fish half-drill, Jandal plants, a skill saw ocean, and animal builders. This unique mix of imagery conveyed the theme of "do it yourself" for a target audience of young artists (**12.9**).

"Luma keys" are brightness keys that enable a range of tones to become transparent. The technique of luma keying works best with high-contrast footage in which the tonal ranges of the background elements are significantly different than those of the foreground elements.

The term keying is derived from the word "keyhole" and is interpreted as cutting a hole into an image and filled with another image.

The term "chroma key" is often used in the video industry, whereas in film, the term "matte" is more common. Both processes are related in that mattes are often generated from keys. When a subject is filmed against a blue screen, the blue hue is removed, and a matte is left behind from the foreground image (similar to a cookie cutter).

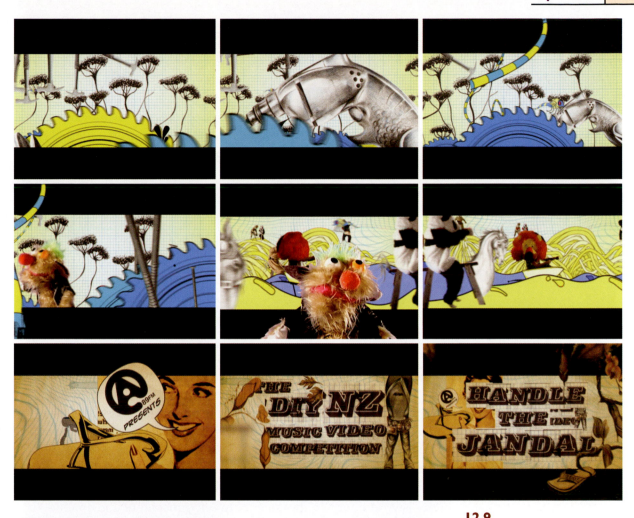

12.9
Frames from "Handle the Jandal" (2005). Courtesy of G'Raffe.

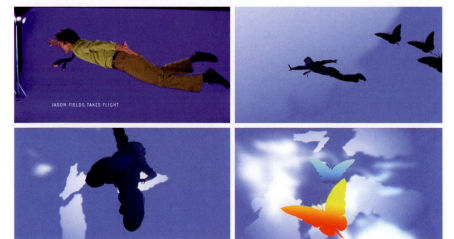

12.10
In the narrative short film "Untitled 003: Embryo" (2007), Santa Monica studio Belief filmed the main character, a neurotic man stricken with agoraphobia, in front of a blue screen to create the illusion of him flying through the sky. Courtesy of Belief.

Bright blue and green are considered to be the standards for chroma keying in the broadcast television industry.

In the past, keying tools were out of the price league of most designers and could only be found in professional television studios. Today, they are well integrated into most compositing applications. Adobe After Effects, for example, contains versatile tools for refining mattes created from luma and color keys. In **figure 12.11**, a threshold value is asigned to a luma key to determine the pixels to become transparent according to their brightness levels. A color key operation can knock out evenly lit backgrounds that have minimal or no variation in color (**12.12**).

12.11
After Effects' luma key operation.

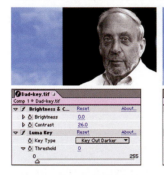
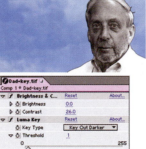
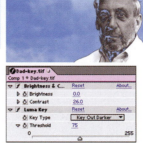
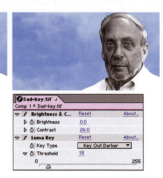

In **figure 12.13,** an edge thin operation helps eliminate edge pixels that contain the key, and an edge feather option is used to soften the foreground-to-background transition. If a background contains subtle color fluctuations due to uneven lighting, a color tolerance function can knock out unwanted pixels (**12.14**). After Effects' color range operation defines a matte that allows you to select a range of colors to key out. The matte can be refined, expanded, and "painted" over, to achieve a better key. Additionally, the edges between transparent and opaque areas of the matte can be feathered to soften the transition (**12.15**).

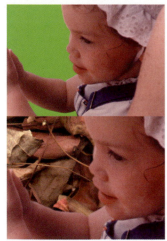

12.12
After Effects' color key operation.

12.13
After Effects' edge thin operation was used here to eliminate residual pixels containing the luma key. It was also used to feather the transition from the foreground to the background.

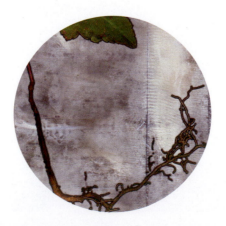
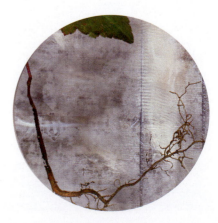

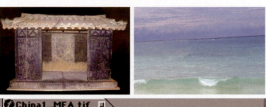

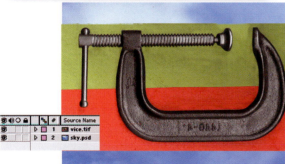

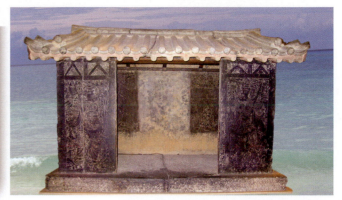

12.14
After Effects' color tolerance function can help knock out backgrounds that contain subtle fluctuations in color.

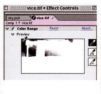

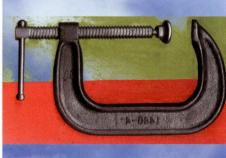

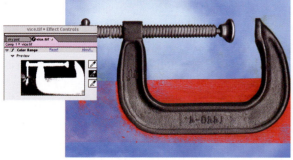

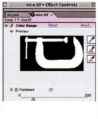

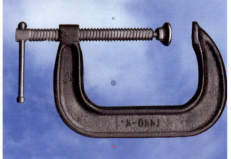

12.15
After Effects' color range option defines a matte that can be refined.

Since fine details can be difficult to key out, After Effects provides "choking" methods that can refine a key. For hard edges, a "simple" choker is ideal for cleaning or tightening up a key, while a "matte" choker's detailed settings can blur the area between the subject and the background, providing a softer transition (**12.16**).

Historical Perspective

In the 1970s, Petro Vlahos invented the *Ultimatte*—an analog video processor that performed soft edge matting. In the mid-1990s, the term "Ultimatte" had denoted a closer association with chroma keying. During the 1990s, Ultimatte Corporation's high-end Ultimatte system was used by broadcasting and film studios around the world. When a subject was placed in front of a blue screen, the Ultimatte activated the background image and allowed it to appear in proportion to the amount of blue that it recognized in the camera's blue channel. Areas containing the brightest and most saturated blues were replaced with the background source, while darker blue areas meant less of the background showed through.

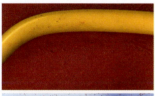

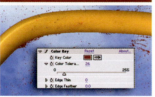

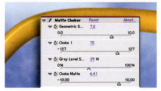

12.16
After Effects' choking options.

"Cyc walls" (or "infinity walls") are two walls and a floor that curve into each other. Seamless transitions between wall and floor produce the illusion of infinite background space. Cyc walls can be rented along with lighting equipment.

tips

The process of keying takes time, patience, and the right tools if it is to be accomplished successfully. Here are a few general guidelines.

1. Avoid the key color, and choose the right color.

Be sure the subject that you are shooting or creating does not contain values or colors that are similar to the type of key being used. If it has bright values, luma keying it against a white background may result in "dropout." You may need to reshoot or recreate the subject on a background that is more suitable for keying.

Be sure that the background is different from the colors or brightness levels of your subject. Red is difficult to key because of the high constant of red in many color variations. Even the most subtle movements or changes in lighting can cause a red key to bleed into the image. In **figure 12.17**, red was not a wise choice because of the amount of red found in the subject's skin tones. Green proved to be a more effective key color.

A backdrop can be any color, as long as it is uniform and not part of the foreground subject. Green and blue are the most widely used in video, since they are built from red, green, and blue (or in some cases YUV) signals. Skin pigments vary; some work well with a blue screen, while others are better with green. If you are keying live footage, the DV format prioritizes luminance over chroma. Since green has a higher luma content than blue, green usually yields a better result.

2. Research your materials.

Your local hardware or home improvement store can provide you with affordable paint to be mixed at 100 percent purity at your request. As an alternative, blue or green fabric can be used, as long as it is smooth and free of wrinkles. Muslin, which can be purchased at any art supply store, can be stretched over a wooden frame and painted to make the fabric tight. Bulletin board paper from any local school or office supply store can also be handy and allow you to extend the screen onto the floor. Rolls of green or blue photographers' paper can also be used. Try to prevent wrinkling or crumpling, which can cause fluctuations in value.

3. Light wisely!

Lighting is a factor in keying. Color uniformity is critical, and the backdrop should be evenly lit with several bright, diffuse light sources. Lighting inconsistencies can be caused by unwanted shadows from backgrounds that are not uniformly lit or from subjects placed in close proximity to the backdrop. Because of subtle fluctuations in tone, the color of shadows may not be uniform enough for your software to produce an accurate key. A handheld meter can confirm that light distribution is consistent. Place your subject as far away from the background as possible to prevent shadows from falling onto the screen.

Measures can taken prevent or minimize the effect of *spillover*, which occurs when background light reflects onto the subject. An overhead ambient light with an amber or yellow gel can wash out color that might spill over into hair detail. A backlight with a color gel that is complementary to the key color also can neutralize the effect. (Try using a magenta gel against a green screen or an orange gel against a blue screen.) Be sure that light falling onto the subject is not falling onto the background. Separate the subject from the background by a substantial distance. Further, imitating the lighting of the environment that will be keyed in behind the subject adds a sense of realism. And cheap floor fans can come in handy if you can't afford a wind machine!

4. Use high-quality footage.

Despite the superior quality of digital video over analog video formats, its compression codec is prone to producing video artefacts, blockiness, and noticeable aliasing along curved and diagonal edges when keying. Therefore, high-end analog video formats, such as Beta-SP, are recommended over DV when capturing footage to be keyed in the studio.

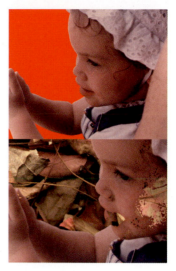

12.17
If a subject contains color or brightness values that are similar to the key, dropout may result.

"If you were to set up a luma key shot of a TV personality in front of a white backdrop, things might go fine, right up until the talent starts perspiring. When his shiny forehead catches the key light and reflects back a 100 percent luma level to the video camera—whoops. Your expert suddenly has a hole in his head. This is a bad thing."

—*Bill Davis*

5. Experiment.

Spend considerable time experimenting with lighting, camera settings, and the positions of your subject and backdrop. Planning in advance will save time and labor in the long run.

6. Work closely.

Zoom in closely to the composite to make sure that the edges of your foreground elements look clean.

7. Soften the transition.

Effective keys avoid the harsh look of hard-edged foreground elements that appear to be cut out with a pair of scissors. Softening a key with a slight feather or edge blur can help fuse foreground and background images naturally, giving the appearance of the two being indistinguishable. Edge blurring works especially well with moving images as the eye is more focused on the action. After Effects' luma and color key effects allow you to soften transitions between subject and background by controlling the opacity of edge pixels. In **figure 12.13**, the edge thin operation was used to constrict the matte, and the edge feather setting was used to increase the foreground edge transparency.

8. Be patient.

Shadows and fine details can be difficult to work with, even with the most sophisticated software. Therefore, plan to dedicate considerable time to testing your key and cleaning up your mattes, if necessary.

Alpha Channels

Alpha channels should not be confused with an image's red, green, and blue color channels. Unlike a 24-bit color (or RGB color) image which contains three channels of information, a 32-bit image carries a fourth alpha channel that stores transparency (or alpha) data. The alpha channel's 8-bit data are reserved giving an image or video clip shape and transparency when composited in a motion graphics environment.

Alpha channels are one of the most powerful compositing devices for combining static and kinetic content. The term "alpha channel" is based on a 32-bit file architecture. Unlike a 24-bit color (or RGB color) image which contains three channels of information, a 32-bit image carries a fourth alpha channel that functions to store transparency information. That data is used to determine image visibility when imported into a time-based animation or video environment. Like color, transparency is based on 8 bits or 256 levels of data that dictate areas of an image will be concealed, which will remain visible, and which will be semi-visible or partially concealed. Alpha channels can contain any type of visual data, including simple graphic shapes, type, gradient blends, and elaborate continuous-tone images.

Alpha Channels

The secret behind alpha is often best understood in the context of a static compositing program such as Photoshop. (Alpha channels have been one of Photoshop's most powerful features since its inception in the 1980s.) Transparency data stored inside an alpha channel can be applied to an image as a mask (or a selection), or can be imported into a motion graphics environment (**12.18**).

When a 32-bit image is brought into a time-based environment, its visibility conforms to its alpha channel, meaning that it is only displayed where white or gray levels are present in the alpha channel. Areas that correspond to black are cropped (or "keyed") out (**12.19**).

Adobe Illustrator and Photoshop content created on transparent backgrounds retain their background transparency when imported into a motion graphics application. This is because an alpha channel matte is automatically generated.

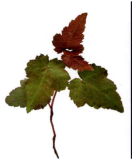
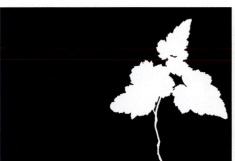
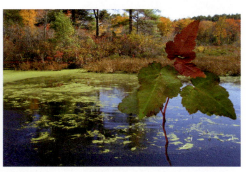

12.18
Transparency data stored inside an alpha channel can be applied to an image as a mask (or a selection), or can be imported into a animation compositing environment.

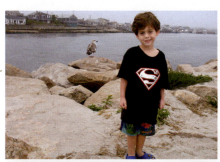
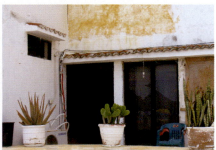

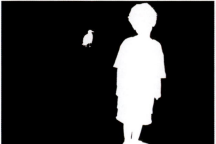
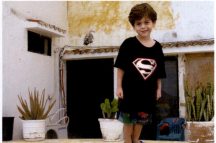

12.19
When a 32-bit image is brought into a time-based environment, its visibility conforms to the data stored in the image's alpha channel. Portions of the image that correspond to black areas remain invisible. When composited with a background image, the underlying image appears through the transparent or alpha portion.

Mattes

A "matte" is a static or moving image, which, like a stencil, can be used to govern the visibility of another image. In compositing, mattes provide unlimited creative possibilities.

Generating hand-executed mattes for moving images on a frame-by-frame basis is traditional rotoscoping in its true form—laborious hours spent on meticulously reproducing detail! The development of keys, alpha channels and spline-based masks has automated this process by enabling automatic matte extraction.

Historical Perspective

Hand-executed mattes have been used to create a variety of illusions since the beginning of motion pictures. One of the oldest special-effects techniques involved using a double-exposure matte. A cameraman would film a group of actors cautiously walking across a bridge, and a piece of black paper or tape would cover a portion of the lens corresponding to the sky, leaving that area unexposed. The film was rewound, and black paper or tape was placed on the lens to cover the exposed portion of the film. A menacing thunderstorm scene was then shot at a slow film speed, so that when played back normally the clouds appear to be quickly rolled in across the sky. Both scenes might be shot separately on separate pieces of film, and through optical compositing, projected onto a third piece of film one frame at a time. Alternatively, both sequences might be scanned, digitally composited, and written back out to a third piece of film with a film printer.

luma mattes

A "luminance matte" (or "RGB matte") is an external image used to make portions of another image transparent based on its combination of RGB brightness values.

Luminance mattes should not be confused with alpha mattes, which are internal mattes derived from alpha channels. Alpha mattes are attached to images; the data residing in of an alpha channel are used to control what parts of the image will be visible. (They also determine how visible the parts will be, according to the brightness levels.)

Luminance mattes are external to images and are needed when an alpha channel is not present (for example, in QuickTime video). Alpha mattes are 8-bit, grayscale images, and luminance mattes are 8-bit or 24-bit images consisting of three RGB channels. Luminance mattes can be static or moving, while alpha channel mattes are only static.

In **figure 12.21**, the brightness levels of an external luminance matte govern the visibility of an image superimposed on a background. Black areas function as the mask; white areas permit the background to pass through at 100 percent opacity, like paint being pushed through the holes of a stencil. Intermediate gray values represent varying levels of transparency, allowing the image to pass through partially, depending on how light or dark the gray levels are. (The lighter the gray, the more opaque the image will be; the darker the gray, the more transparent it will be. Note this is not physically possible with traditional stenciling.)

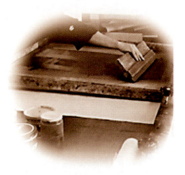

12.20
Traditional silkscreen printing offers an analogy for how mattes are created digitally. Ink is pushed through the unprotected areas of a screen to form a positive image. The areas of the screen that are covered with emulsion act as a matte, preventing the ink from being transferred to the paper.

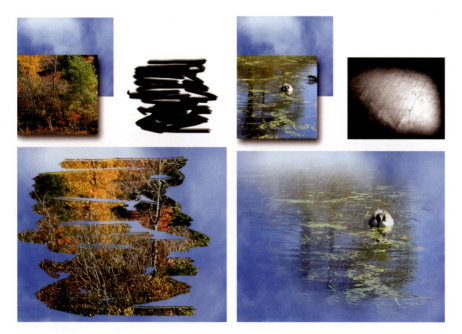

12.21
A luminance matte is used to govern the visibility of an image superimposed on a background.

Figure 12.22 shows After Effects' track matte feature involving the use of luminance and alpha mattes. The difference between them has to do with where the information determining visibility resides—in an image's RGB channels or in its alpha channel (if it has one).

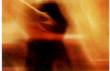
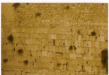

video layer   background layer

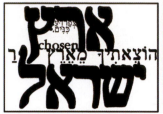

luminance matte

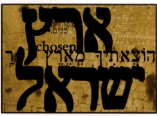

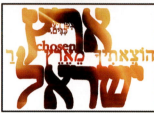

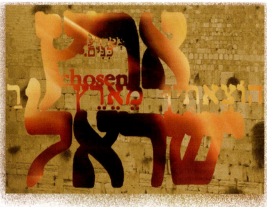

composite

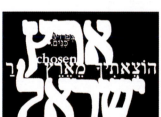

luminance matte
(inverted)

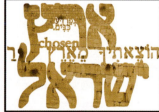

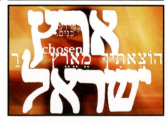

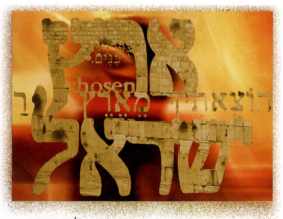

composite

12.22

A track matte consisting of black type on white combines a static background with a superimposed video layer. The video referencing the matte is sandwiched between the matte and background layers. Dark areas of the matte clip the video to the letterforms, allowing the background to show through regions outside the type.

matte styles

Both alpha channel mattes and luminance mattes can be composed of solid shapes, feathered shapes, gradients, typography, and entire images. Additionally, they can be "painted" digitally using black, white, and gray values and brushes varying in size and softness.

solid mattes

High-contrast black-and-white mattes mimic conventional stenciling or silkscreening in that they confine images to shapes. In **figure 12.23**, an image appears through a white shape on a black background. The image is clipped to the areas of the matte containing the brightest luminosity values, while the background image appears at full opacity through the regions of the matte that are black.

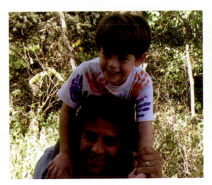
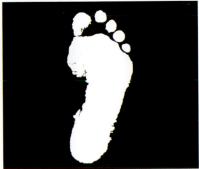
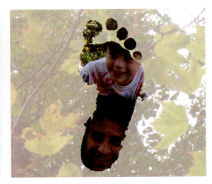

12.23
A solid, high-contrast black-and-white matte confines an overlying image to a specific shape.

continuous tone mattes

Unlike traditional mattes that act like cookie cutters, digital mattes can be composed of feathered edges, paint strokes, gradients, and images that have intermediate levels of gray. Values between black and white allow superimpositions to occur at varying degrees. For example, portions of a matte containing pixel values of 128 (halfway between black and white or 0 and 255) allow superimposition to occur at 50 percent opacity. . This prospect of semi-permeability can lead to many exciting layering possibilities (**see figures 12.24–12.26**).

12.24
A matte containing a shape with feathered edges is used to create a vignette effect. As values become lighter in the transition from edge to background, the image fades out accordingly.

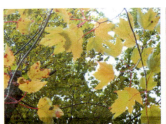
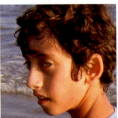

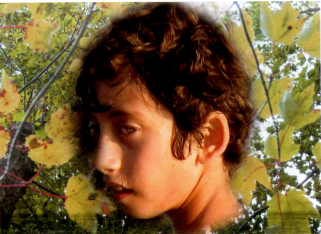

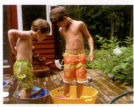
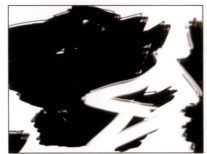
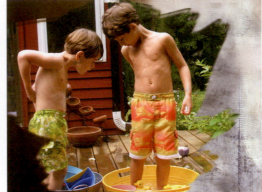

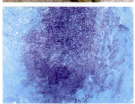
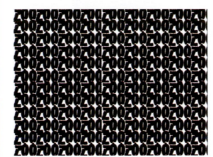
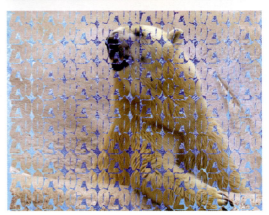
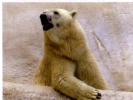

12.25
Mattes consisting of complex brush strokes, shapes, or patterns offer a variety of artistic effects.

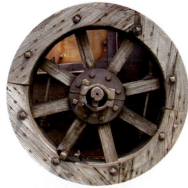
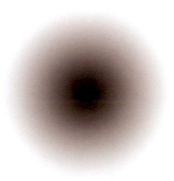
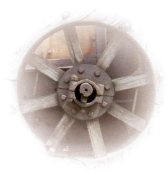
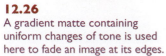

12.26
A gradient matte containing uniform changes of tone is used here to fade an image at its edges.

traveling mattes

A "traveling matte" is a matte that changes its appearance or position each frame in cases where the subject moves or changes. In **figure 12.27**, four different elements are composited: a magnifying glass, a luma matte based on the shape of the lens, background text, and a fill layer containing larger text. The order of the layers on the timeline from bottom to top is: background text, the magnifying glass image, the large text, and the matte. The visibility of the fill layer containing the large text is restricted to the circular shape of the luma matte. The matte layer is registered into position with the lens and is parented to the lens layer so that they both move together as one unit. The lens' position property is key-framed, and the matte pans along, revealing portions of the fill layer. At the same time, scale key frames are created for the fill layer to simulate the effect of zooming.

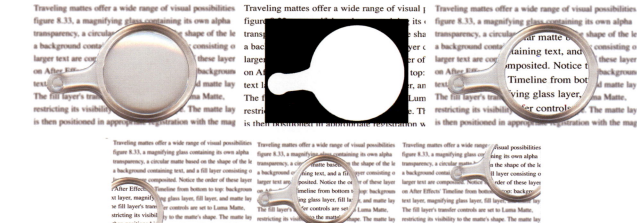

12.27
A matte conforming to the shape of the magnifying lens is moved into registration. The visibility of the layer containing clear text is set to reference the matte. The lens layer is parented to the matte layer, allowing them to move as a unit. The matte layer's position property is key-framed.

Spline Masks

Unlike keys, alpha channels, and luminosity mattes that establish transparency through brightness data, "splines"— paths that consist of interconnected points that form line segments or curves—generate transparency mathematically. **Figure 12.28** compares type used as an alpha channel matte to type used as a Bezier spline. In the matte, a video clip appears through the white areas (the alpha portion). In the spline mask, the clip appears inside the paths. The splines are then are manipulated to change their geometric appearance over time.

12.28
top row:
The image appears through the matte's white areas (the letters).

bottom row:
Text outlines are converted into splines, and their geometry is animated through interpolation.

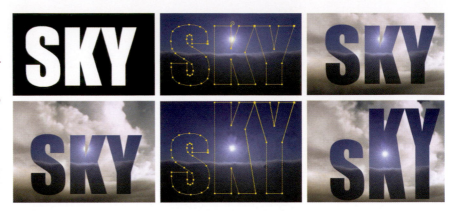

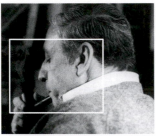

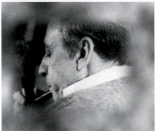

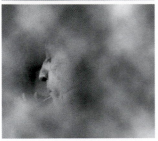

12.29
A spline-based mask can be expanded, contracted, or feathered to soften transitions from foreground to background.

rotoscoping and animated masks

The technique of interpolating the changing geometry of a spline mask can automate the process of generating mattes for moving images frame by frame.

In the film *Titanic* (1997), puffs of human breath were used to depict the chilled environment of the North Atlantic. A large portion of the film was shot in the warm waters of the Pacific. Several breath sequences were filmed and combined with the original footage. Masks were created to protect foreground elements such as heads and shoulders so that a superimposed breath appearing to come from an actor's mouth would disappear behind them. Each mask was animated with extreme precision to follow the motions of those foreground elements. At points where registration was inaccurate, the compositor manually refined the mask's shape and position at key frames.

Most motion graphics packages allow mask properties to be key framed to change over time. In **figure 12.30**, a mask is created on a layer containing a live-action video clip of a book's pages being flipped by a gust of air generated by a fan. Key frames are established every ten frames for the spline's shape, feathering, and expansion properties. New key frames are then generated at every fifth frame in between, allowing the mask to more closely adhere to the changing image.

Viewer attention is immediately drawn to elements that appear to be unnatural in the way that they move or change. Professional "roto artists" give serious attention to maintaining visual consistency, since

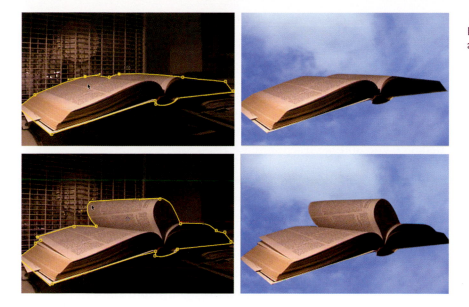

12.30
Rotoscoping is used here to achieve mask interpolation.

their goal is to minimize distractions that are obvious to scrutinizing eyes. Even with today's advanced tools, "roto-masking" can be a tricky and laborious process. Here are several tips:

1. Analyze the subject.
Rotoscoping requires careful analysis of the subject. This means identifying the frames that represent the most extreme changes. Once these frames have been established, alteration can be made at these points to conform to the image, and the software's ability to calculate in-between key frames saves a great deal of time and labor.

2. Zoom into your work.
Working close up is critical for achieving precision, especially along complex edges.

3. Minimize the number of vertices.
An undesirable effect of sloppy compositing is "edge chatter"—a phenomenon that occurs when a mask's outline changes irregularly from one frame to the next. This is usually a result of using too many vertex points and moving those points inconsistently between frames. Creating a mask on the frame where an element's shape is intricate allows you to determine the minimum number of vertices needed to adequately mask it over the frames being rotoscoped.

In addition to the most common motion graphics packages, expensive high-end programs such as Matador Paint, Flame, Cineon, and Domino offer advanced masking tools that are specifically designed for rotoscoping live-action footage.

4. Break down complex images into multiple masks.

Consider breaking parts of a complex image down into separate masks and animating those masks individually. This will help establish accuracy and consistency and will help maintain the integrity of the paths. Some masks will only require interpolation of position or scale, while others may need shape alteration by repositioning the vertex points. Mattes that conform to different parts of a subject can be articulated and animated separately.

5. Weigh the options of masking, matting, and keying.

In compositing video images, there are advantages of masking over keying, such as the elimination of spillover caused by poor lighting conditions and the ease of performing in a natural setting versus on a synthetic blue-screen set. On the other hand, keying elements that move against a uniform background can be easier than animating a mask's position and shape frame by frame. If only a mask's position changes, a luma matte or an alpha channel may be a better solution.

Nesting

Nesting is another powerful and convenient compositing technique that involves implementing an organized hierarchy of actions or events to make the editing process more effective. This is accomplished by building a layered composition then consolidating it into a single layer to be brought inside another composition.

Most professional non-linear editing tools leverage the ability to nest. The Avid Xpress system, for example, allows you to combine multiple video layers into a single track. In Apple's Final Cut Pro, any number of clips can be nested into a sequence, and audio tracks belonging to the original clips are automatically consolidated into a single track. Applications such as Adobe After Effects and Flash are also capable of this. After Effects refers to an intermediate (as opposed to a final) composition as a "precomp." Precomps were used to integrate layers of complex visual information in "First Stop for the News," a television commercial for NY1's 24-hour cable news channel (**12.31**). Belief, a motion graphics firm based in Los Angeles, created an impressionistic version of NYC based on NY1's campaign to purchase the billboards showcased on the city's buses. This concept spawned the concept of a traveling bus that brings the city to life. After taking numerous photographs of iconic intersections around the city, storyboard artists were hired to create hand-drawn sketches of the printed photographs with tracing paper. In After Effects, a precomp was built from the original photos, and various camera motions were incorporated. The precomp was duplicated, and in the duplicate, the photographic images were replaced with the pencil sketches. In a third composition, the second precomp containing the pencil sketches was layered on top of the original composition containing the photographs. (Since precomps 1 and 2 shared the same key frames, both sets of images and camera movements were perfectly syncronized.) A layer containing images of ink bleeding into paper was sandwiched between precomps 1 and 2 to allow transitions to be made between photographic and hand-drawn elements. The results were rendered out as QuickTime movies, and the movie files were imported back into After Effects to be layered over a paper-textured background. This fostered experimentation by reducing the amount of time it would normally take to render all the precomps and their respective layers.

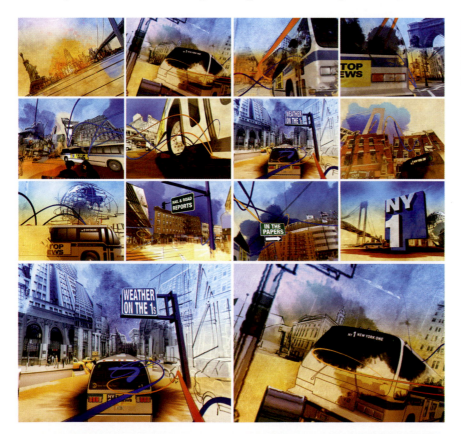

12.31
Frames from "First Stop for the News," a television commercial for NY1. Concept and motion graphics by Belief.

In **figure 12.32**, several QuickTime video clips have been arranged to create the effect of an animated video wall. The precomp is brought into a new composition, and its position, scale, Y-rotation, and X-rotation is interpolated. Additionally, a color tint is applied. This is an example of how nesting allows you to efficiently organize your composites. Rather than having to apply a transformation or an effect to each layer individually, nesting gives you the ability to apply it only once. If, at any point, the layers in the original composite are tweaked, those changes are automatically updated in the nested composition.

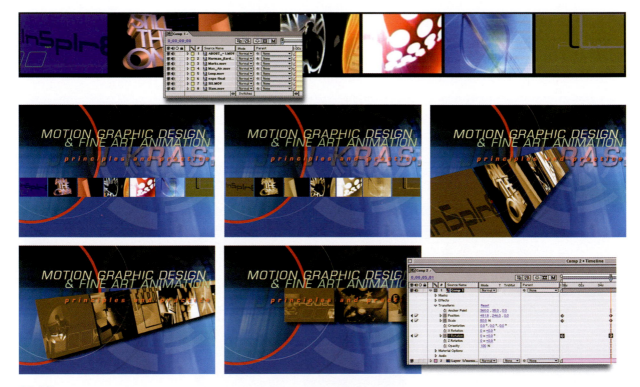

12.32
Nesting two levels in Adobe After Effects is used to create an animated video wall effect. Comp 1, consisting of multiple live-action video layers, is nested into a second composition, Comp 2. As a single layer in the nested comp, a color effect is applied, and its position, scale, and Y-rotation properties are interpolated as each clip plays separately.

In the television show opener to *The Hungry Detective* (**Chapter 3, figure 3.12, on p. 45**), After Effects was used to connect multiple precomps. Each precomp consisted of its own internal camera moving in 3D space. Bezier masks, keying, and alpha channels were also used to composite live-action footage, photography, illustration, and 3D graphics. The magnifying glass at the beginning of the sequence communicates a "micro and macro" concept that allows us to "fly" inside the elements.

Color Correction

Representing color accurately and consistently is a critical part of compositing. Color correction and enhancement operations can rectify mismatched colors from different sources, enhance color, or alter color to achieve certain effects or consistency between visuals. Insufficient lighting conditions due to poor capture, inadequate scanning, or mismatched sources are all variables that may mandate color correction.

Since no two people will ever agree on what looks right (including your clients), it is best to trust your own eyes when color correcting your work, especially when attempting to match colors from diferent sources.

improving luminance

Since color is highly dependent upon luminosity, improving luminance or brightness information is the first step to establishing color accuracy.

assessing tonal range

Assessing an image's tonal range can be achieved by referencing its histogram to identify its distribution of brightness values. **Figure 12.33** compares the histograms of "healthy" and "unhealthy" video clips. The healthy version utilizes most of the available values between 0 (black) and 255 (white), unlike the unhealthy version, which lacks detail in the shadow areas. Additionally, gaps in the central region of its histogram indicate that the footage is deprived of subtle mid-tone levels.

Once tonal range has been assessed, measures can be taken to improve tonal contrast and detail. The ideal remedy would be to acquire a better original or improve its quality by reshooting or rescanning it. Of course, this is not always possible due to financial and time restrictions. The next and most often the more pragmatic option would be to improve the element's luminance.

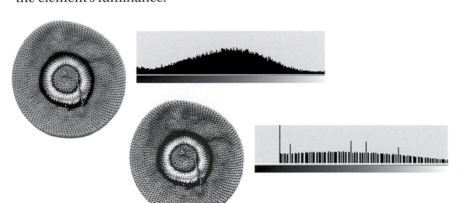

12.33
These histograms demonstrate a "healthy" and an "unhealthy" use of an image's brightness levels.

luminance operations

Standard brightness/contrast operations can serve as a quick fix for content that lacks shadow or highlight detail by producing linear shifts in luminosity levels. Darkening shifts shadow details to black, eliminating highlights, while brightening maps highlight details to white, eliminating shadows. Increasing contrast reduces mid-tone levels, causing subtle highlights to be mapped to white and shadows to black. The result, however, can deprive an image of its subtle mid-tone details. The process of "equalization" can produce a more uniform distribution of luminance by mapping the darkest values to black and lightest values to white while redistributing intermediate gray levels more evenly. It can, however, be detrimental to shadow and highlight details. In comparison, the technique of "unsharp masking" produces the most effective results, because shadow and highlight subtleties are accentuated (**12.34**).

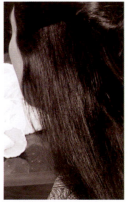 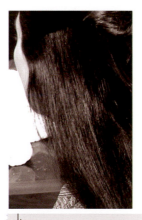 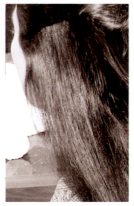 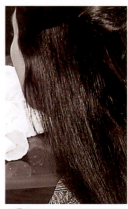

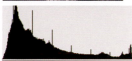 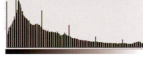 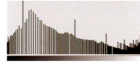 

original image with a "healthy" histogram | *value deprivation caused by standard brightness and contrast adjustments* | *more extreme value deprivation caused by equalization.* | *best improvement of contrast through unsharp masking*

12.34
Best improvement of tonal contrast is achieved through the process of unsharp masking.

"Levels" and "curves" operations offer more precise control over how values are dispersed. For example, if shadows are too dark, they can be shifted to higher values without affecting an image's mid-tones and highlights. This process can increase an image's contrast while removing unwanted color casts (this is described in the next section). Cropping the histogram incorporates values on the extreme lower and upper ends of the scale, resulting in accentuated shadow and highlight detail (**12.35**).

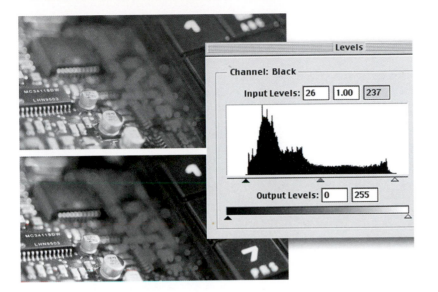

12.35
Cropping the histogram extends the image's tonal range to include darker shadows and lighter highlight details.

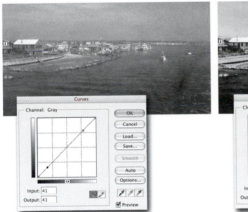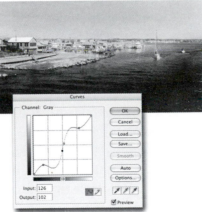

12.36
Redistribution of tonal values on a gamma curve is achieved by shifting the points corresponding to the image's input levels. In this case, only the mid-tone ranges were modified, while shadow and highlight details were maintained.

Mid-tone ranges are difficult to target, unlike black and white points. Although mid-tone levels can be set by selecting a neutral region of an image, the results can be unpredictable. A "healthy" scan should include mid-tone detail in its histogram. Color correcting poor scans wastes time and further reduces brightness detail.

The most effective approach to improving an image's color luminance is remapping its original brightness levels to the full 8-bit (256-level) range by setting its black and white points. Levels and curves controls allow you to set black and white points by permitting darks or lights above or below a specified threshold level to be remapped to black or white. In the curves operation in **figure 12.36**, the eyedropper on the left, corresponding to black, is used to select a pixel with a value of 25. All pixels between 0 and 25 are remapped to 0 (black). The right eyedropper, corresponding to white, selects a pixel with a value of 220, and all pixels between 220 and 255 are remapped to 255 (white).

12.37
Improving an image's tonal detail is accomplished by remapping the darkest and lightest pixels to pure black and white, a process referred to as "setting the black and white points."

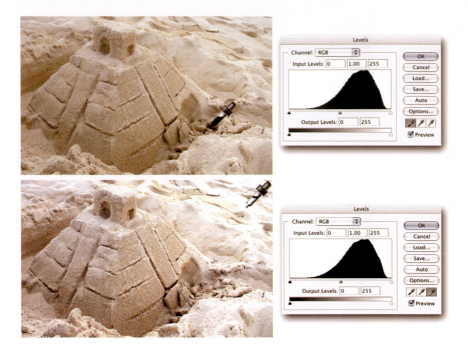

value alteration

Alteration of luminosity values can be used to enhance images or to experiment with tonal effects. "Posterization," for example, reduces the number of brightness levels that are used, producing a flatter and more graphic-looking image. "Inversion" produces a negative image as luminosity values or colors are reversed. Black becomes white, and a light gray with a value of 30 becomes a dark gray of 225. Mid-tone levels are changed the least (128, or 50 percent gray, is unchanged).

removing color casts

Once tonal range has been improved, adjustments can be made to remove "color casts"—unwanted colors that result when an element's red, green, and blue channels are not properly balanced. Color casts can occur universally or can be limited to specific highlight, shadow, or mid-tone details.

Color balancing provides a quick method of removing casts by shifting specific color polarities simultaneously. The results are best if shadows, mid-tones and highlights are balanced separately. Entire ranges of hues are shifted on the color wheel, producing changes ranging from subtle to dramatic. Applying a levels operation to an image's RGB channels can also improve color across its tonal range. Altering the individual distributions of red, green, and blue may be time consuming, but enables greater precision in enhancing color and identifying unwanted casts. Cropping the histogram can improve contrast and color depth because it redistributes the value mapping to the full 8-bit (256- color) spectrum. This approach can also neutralize problematic casts. Curves, in conjunction with levels, allow precise modifications to be applied to an entire color range, to any one color channel or to any combination of color channels. For example, the red channel of the image in **figure 12.38** has the poorest tonal quality, as seen in its histogram. There is also a slight green cast evident in the image's highlights. Extending the value range of the red channel by cropping the histogram and decreasing the intensity of highlights in the green channel by altering the tonal curve resolves this issue.

Most motion graphics programs are capable of color correction. After Effects' color balance operation provides individual controls for the red, green, and blue channels for shadows, mid-tones, and highlights. Its hue/saturation operation lets you shift a layer's hues while controlling its saturation and brightness levels. A "colorize" option eliminates the existing colors and adds an overall tint to create effects such as an old sepia look.

color manipulation

Any combination of the techniques that have been discussed can be applied experimentally to individual elements or entire animation sequences. Color alteration can also be performed on grayscale images that have been converted to RGB color space prior to compositing. For example, colorization techniques can emulate the effect of a hand-tinted photograph. Grayscale images that have been converted to 8-bit duotones, tritones, and quadtones also lend themselves to dynamic

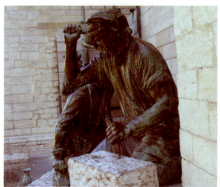

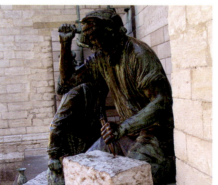

12.38
Color correction is performed here through levels and curves operations in the image's red and green color channels.

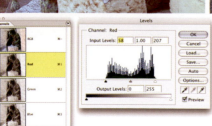

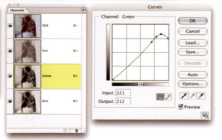

If your work is intended for television display, it is best to view your color alterations on an NTSC monitor as you create them to be sure that they are "broadcast safe." Green and overly saturated colors can be especially problematic in video color space.

color effects, and these can later be translated back into RGB color space. In **figure 12.39**, Photoshop's duotone features was used to assign specific hues to the shadow, mid-tone, and highlight regions of the histogram. Once a desired color effect is achieved, the image was converted back to RGB color to be imported into a compositing program.

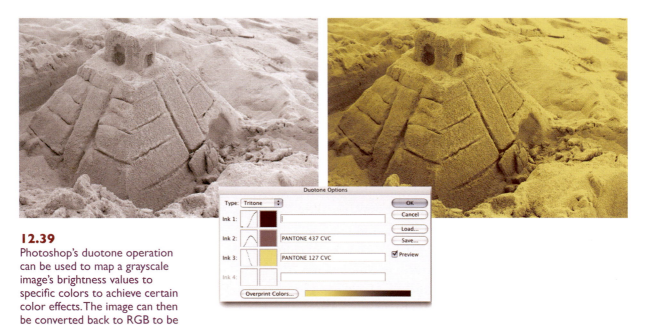

12.39
Photoshop's duotone operation can be used to map a grayscale image's brightness values to specific colors to achieve certain color effects. The image can then be converted back to RGB to be imported into a motion graphics environment.

12.40
After Effects' Channel Mixer can mix and match brightness values from different color channels to achieve compelling effects.

Mixing brightness data between an image's color channels is another powerful and intuitive way of enhancing color intensities. Brightness percentages from multiple channels can be combined and added to a specified target channel. In **figure 12.40**, values within the red channel are mixed with those from the image's green and blue components.

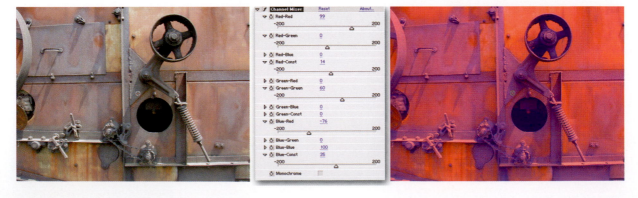

Chapter Summary

Motion graphics compositing allows you to seamlessly integrate many types of content into a uniform, multi-layered space to create unusual visual relationships.

"Blend operations" allow you to determine how the pixel information in superimposed images blends to create intriguing effects. "Keying" involves eliminating a selected range of colors or brightness levels to produce areas of transparency. "Alpha channels," which rely on 32-bit color architecture, can also combine different types of content by using transparency data to determine an element's visibility. "Splines" offer an alternative method of compositing—masking. The practice of "nesting" can be used to construct complex animation sequences by building an organized hierarchy of compositions in order to make the editing process easier and more effective. Most non-linear editing tools leverage the ability to nest animations in their timelines.

Representing color accurately and consistently is critical to achieving successful compositing. Color correction and enhancement can rectify mismatched colors from different sources as well as enhance or alter color. Assessing an image's tonal range by identifying its brightness values on a histogram is an important step in establishing color accuracy.

13

motion graphics sequencing
synthesizing the content

The process of sequencing in motion graphics can provide visual rhythm, enhance narrative, create emotions, and enable you to construct and restructure time and space. Time can be dramatically condensed from a period of several weeks into minutes or seconds. Space can be radically altered, jolting viewers between different environments to empower them and give them a sense of omnipresence. Further, sequencing can lend new meaning to the subject being portrayed, making it more memorable and perhaps even life changing.

"The essence of cinema is editing. It's the combination of what can be extraordinary images of people during emotional moments, or images in a general sense, put together in a kind of alchemy."
—Francis Ford Coppola

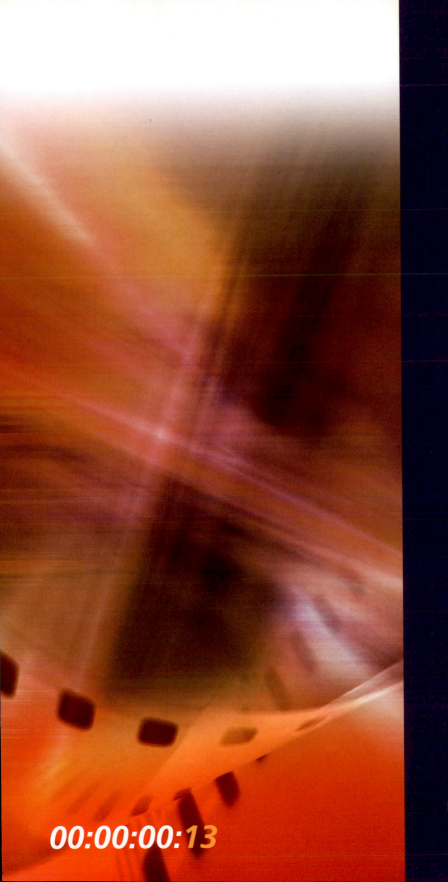

00:00:00:13

Editing: An Overview

The technique of editing has been alive for years, giving much creative potential and power to motion designers. In film and video, it involves the coordination and joining of multiple shots, each shot consisting of a series of frames that occupy screen space and time. In motion graphics, it is the process of linking two or more animation sequences or two or more views of the same sequence into a cohesive whole.

"To edit, means to organize pieces of film into a film, to 'write' a film with the shots, and not to select pieces for 'scenes.'"

—Dziga Vertov

Traditional "linear editing" involves a linear tape-to-tape process in which specialized equipment, such as videotape recorders (VTRs), switchers, and mixers, is used to sequence footage into a finished production. Today, the flexibility of "non-linear editing" allows you to digitally access and modify frames of footage without altering the original source. (In contrast, the "cut and glue" technique of film editing is destructive, since the actual film negative is cut.) Non-linear editing is performed on standard desktop computers or on specialized hardware systems (such as the Avid) that can process high-resolution data in real-time. Consumer-level video editing applications such as Final Cut Pro (Apple) and Adobe Premiere (Adobe), offer non-linear editing, compositing, and special effects tools, while motion graphics programs such as Adobe After Effects offer standard but less sophisticated editing capabilities. Some editing software can be downloaded for free, and others, like Microsoft's Windows Movie Maker or Apple's iMovie, are included with the "parent" operating system.

Editing involves two processes: selecting and sequencing. "Selecting" involves choosing actions or events that will be included in the final production. This choice depends upon contextual factors, such as the subject being communicated, the intent of the communication, the target audience, and the style that will be used to deliver the message. "Sequencing" involves linking actions or events together in a way that clarifies and intensifies the content to create a clear and memorable experience for viewers.

From classical Hollywood films to avant-garde filmmaking and experimental animation, different editing styles throughout history have defined narrative and non-narrative forms of filmmaking and have inspired trends in motion graphics.

Historical Perspective

During the 1920s, film theorists began to realize what editing could achieve, and it quickly became the most widely discussed technique in cinema. Sergei Eisenstein's early productions such as *Strike*, *Battleship Potemkin*, *October*, and *Old and New* influenced the attempt by young, experimental filmmakers to make editing their fundamental principle in the 1950s.

In the past, editing was a linear process that required careful planning. Today, simple cuts, inserts, and superimpositions can be performed digitally in any order, offering greater flexibility and precision in the timing and synchronization of events. Motion graphic designers can switch between multiple sources of footage more spontaneously and creatively.

A recent example of successful editing is director Carlos Lascano's film "Standing Up for Freedom" for Amnesty International (also discussed in Chapters 8, 10, 11, and 12). The piece commences with a close-up of a red flower growing in a meadow on a clear, sunny day. A prison wall builds across the frame and surrounds the flower. A new, dark environment without sunlight causes it to wilt and die among smoke and rubble. Flanked with barbed wire, the wall serves as the main canvas where the events of the story unfold. After picking a two-dimensional version of the flower, a young boy runs from several menacing figures that grow out of the ground. As he is overtaken by the figures, the scene transforms to show a wounded figure carrying the flower as he walks across the structure's walls, as he might carry the flame in a torch relay. The figure limps by a group of hooded Ku Klux Klansmen holding torches and moves into the space of a tattered poster, which is set afire by the Klansmen. Engulfed in flames, the figure, aware of his destiny, reaches his arm outside the poster and holds out the flower to release its petals. The petals are carried by a breeze into another space where the movie continues, featuring a group of prisoners being executed and a mother losing her baby. The hand of the boy at the beginning of the story reappears on the frame's right edge, holding up the flower as a beacon to halt an advancing line of army tanks. At this climactic moment, the music pauses and the wall crumbles. The word "freedom," composed of red carnation petals, accompanies the boy, who is now revealed as a three-dimensional character standing in the original pastoral setting holding the flower (**13.1**).

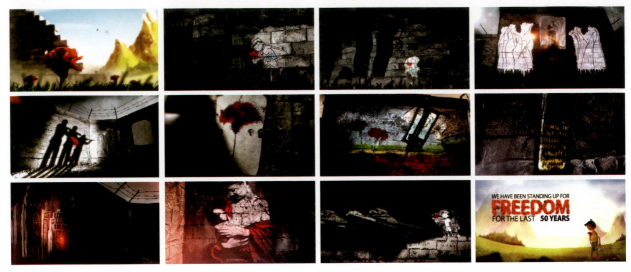

13.1
Frames from "Standing Up for Freedom," a film promoting Amnesty International. Courtesy of Eallin.

13.2
Frames from the opener for *Limca Book of Records*. Courtesy of Varun Chawla.

The opener for *Limca Book of Records*, a television series on India's Star News channel, shows how editing can set pace and establish mood (**13.2**). Based on a physical book (similar to the book *Guinness World Records*), the program celebrates the excellence of Indian culture and achievements across the globe. For the opener, filmmaker Varun Chawla conceived the idea of analog instruments that have been used to measure records. Cuts between shots were derived from the technical means behind how these tools work and were choreographed to the tempo of a percussive soundtrack that builds to a crescendo. Similar to Walter Ruttmann's *Berlin: Symphony of a Great City*, Varun created an orchestration of objects including a pendulum, a stopwatch, gear mechanisms, and typewriter keys, mixed with footage of a dilating pupil, a hand inserting film into a camera, and a finger pushing up the levels of a slider.

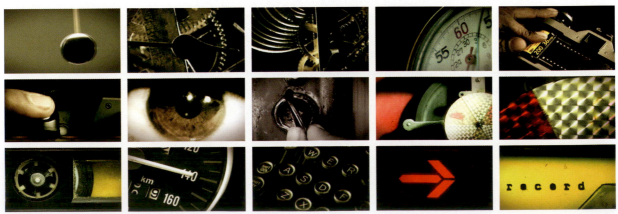

Cuts and Transitions

The "cut" has been the most widely used editing technique since the invention of film. It produces abrupt, instantaneous changes of space or time between images, actions, or events. Unlike transitions, cuts do not occupy time or space.

Cutting between images with different points of view or different types of framing can contribute to the emotional impact of a theme. If poorly used, cuts can create undesirable results that look like mistakes rather than intentional artistic decisions. Rhythmic cutting can help determine pace and regulate event density. For example, the frequency of cuts in an MTV spot or a short commercial might result in a sensory bombardment, whereas the limited number of cuts in a documentary nature film may preserve its modest, academic feel and sense of integrity.

In **figure 13.3**, simple cuts between segments of digitally projected images conform to subtle changes in the music to create a quiet sense of drama and suspense. In contrast, the rapid, rhythmic cuts in the typographic sequence in **figure 13.4** give a high intensity feel.

The soundtrack in music videos often aids motion graphic designers in determining where visual cutting should occur.

13.3
Frames from the opening titles for OFFF's BCN 06 festival. Courtesy of Renascent.

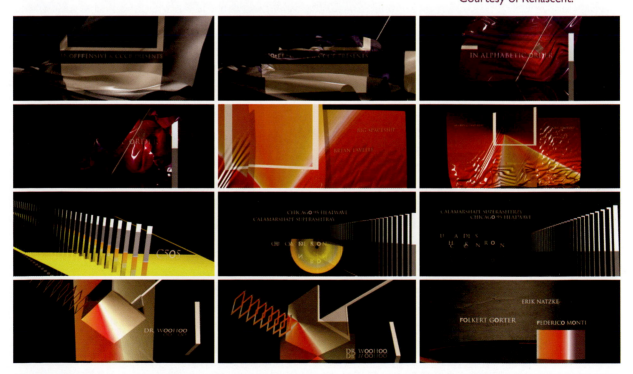

Edwin S. Porter's The Great Train Robbery (1903), a landmark of American silent film, is an early example of parallel editing. Many of the shots depend upon our ability to imagine that the crosscut scenes extend into off screen space where events continue to develop whether we are present to view them or not.

13.4
Frames from an ID for Insight, a company specializing in behind-the-scenes film production. Courtesy of Renascent.

"Crosscutting" involves cutting between different actions that occur at the same time to keep viewers informed of two or more events. In traditional chase scenes it can build tension by shifting back and forth between the pursuer and the pursued. As a result, both lines of action are tied together, indicating that they are concurrent. This technique can enrich narrative continuity and alter time by accelerating or slowing down the main action. It also gives viewers a range of knowledge that is greater than that of the subject. Although it creates some spatial discontinuity (discussed later in this chapter), it can link separate events together to produce a sense of cause and effect.

"Parallel editing" involves crosscutting between independent spaces or events to suggest that they are taking place simultaneously. It also creates a sense of omnipresence, giving viewers unrestricted access to onscreen and offscreen space by alternating between separate events. It can also create parallels by suggesting analogies, drawing the viewer

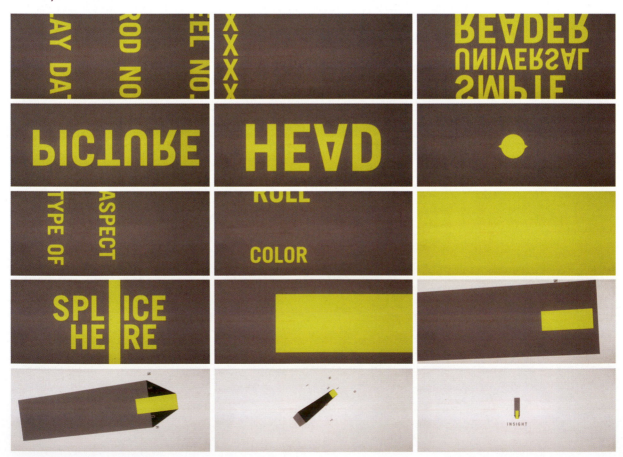

Cuts and Transitions

into the action. Parallel editing has been used to describe relationships between images and a corresponding soundtrack. The technique of "counterpoint" functions in the opposite way—to show relationships between images that are not parallel to the accompanying soundtrack. Both of these techniques have been used for creating suspense and altering the passage of time.

A "cutaway" shows an event or sequence of events that is unrelated to the main event. Its objective is to temporarily draw attention away from the action as it continues to unfold in offscreen space and time. For example, in *Heritage*, a personal film of mine about themes from the Old Testament, a sequence showing a close-up of a Torah reading precedes a shot of an Israeli dancer moving to the sound of his own voice. Cutaways are also used to establish symbolism. In "Heritage," they create a juxtaposition between intimate images that express Judaic spirituality, such as the Torah reading followed by the dancer, a flickering flame, and a rabbi reciting a prayer (**13.5**). The opening titles to the film *The Movie Hero* (2003) employ cutaway views between the main character, who believes that his life is a movie watched by an audience that only he can see, and images of movie theatre concessions (**13.6**).

Many believe that Russian film-maker Lev Kuleshov, who helped establish the basis for montage during the silent film era, pioneered the technique of parallel editing by linking together different shots of actors who seemed to be looking at each other, although they were filmed on different Moscow streets. Many filmmakers have employed the "Kuleshov effect" by juxtaposing shots of disparate events to create a cohesion between different spaces or time zones.

13.5
Frames from *Heritage*, a film by Jon Krasner. This sequence uses cutaways between shots of flames, a Torah reading, an Israeli dancer, and a rabbi reciting a prayer. © 2012 Jon Krasner.

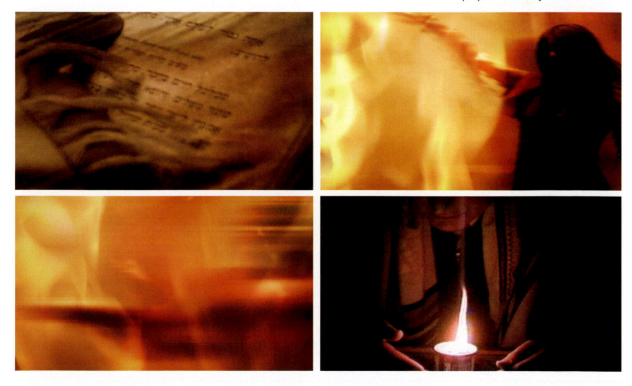

13.6
Frames from the opening titles to *The Movie Hero* (2003). Courtesy of Shadowplay Studio.

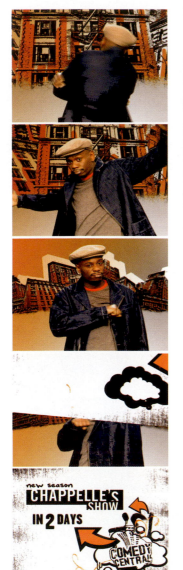

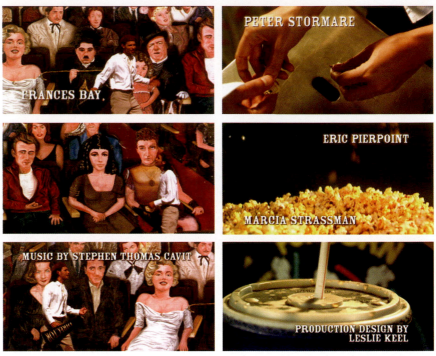

13.7
Frames from Comedy Central's *Chapelle's Show*. Courtesy of Freestyle Collective.

As an alternative to cutaways, "jump cuts" produce abrupt changes or noticeable jumps in the positions or movements of elements against a constant background. Alternatively, the ground can change abruptly while an element remains fixed in space. Because there is a visible change in the content, it becomes obvious that part of the composition has been cut out. The illusion of continuous time is broken.

Jump cuts became popular narrative devices during the 1960s and continue to be used to accentuate rhythm, abbreviate time, signal emotional stress, or cause viewers to be momentarily perplexed. In a series of promos for Comedy Central's hit series *Chappelle's Show*, a frequent use of jump cuts that alter the subject's movement and positioning, and camera views works in concert with bold graphic shapes to express the sharp, defiant humor of the series (**13.7**).

A "flash cut" is a rapid interchange between two shots to create a dramatic, psychological effect. Sometimes a single frame is enough to arouse fear or shock. Jump cuts and flash cuts are discussed later in this chapter with regard to creating temporal discontinuity.

Cuts and Transitions

In contrast to cuts, "transitions" can link a series of events by providing gradual changes between images or actions. They can be created by a camera during capture, produced optically in a lab, or generated digitally, and they play an influential role in the timing of events in a composition. It is essential that you exercise artistic discretion in using transitions appropriately and in moderation and avoid becoming overly dependent upon their effects.

The three most common types of transitions are "dissolves," "fades," and "wipes." Dissolves, frequently used to indicate the passage of time, involve smooth, gradual changes in opacity between two overlapping events. The ending frames of the first event incrementally blend with the opening frames of the next. This method of transition softens changes between the frames, producing the effect of one sequence melting into the other. (In sound editing, a dissolve is often referred to as a "crossfade.") Dissolves can aid continuity because they act as thematic or structural time bridges between events.

A dissolve's length can produce various effects and impact the tone of a presentation. For example, a slow dissolve can indicate a long time lapse, while a quick dissolve can convey the passage of a brief period of time. In a bumper for Showtime Networks, slow dissolves are used to enhance the concept of flowing silk (**13.8**).

If a dissolve is frozen midway, a "superimposition" results, producing ghosted images from two different sources. (In sound editing, stopping a crossfade would produce a mix of two different audio sources.)

In most motion graphics and digital editing applications, the parameters of built-in transitions can be altered in terms of their duration, size, or orientation, depending on the type of transition.

13.8
Frames from a bumper for Showtime Networks. Courtesy of Giant Octopus.

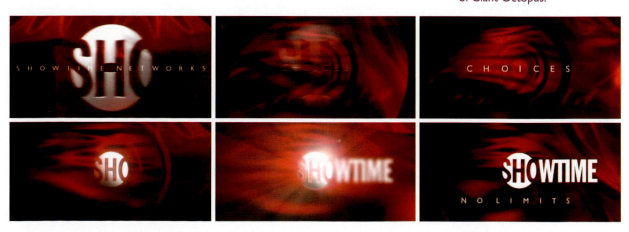

A "fade" is a dissolve from or to black (or any solid color), achieved by gradually increasing the exposure until the image reaches its full brightness capacity. A "fade-out" is obtained by decreasing the exposure until the last frame is completely black. Fades are generally used at the beginning or end of events to signify a major change in content, time, or space. Simply, they represent a distinct break in a story's continuity. The length of a fade is can affect timing and mood. In the opening title sequence to *Mansfield Park*, the use of fades between long sequences of events establishes the tone of the movie (**Chapter 7, figure 7.36, on p. 228**). The opening titles to *Moth* employ fades between strange transformations of rotating close-ups of light bulb filaments and the opening scene to indicate the passage of time (**13.9**).

13.9
Frames from the opening titles for *Moth*. Courtesy of Applied Works. © Amulet Films Limited 2004, www.amuletfilms.com.

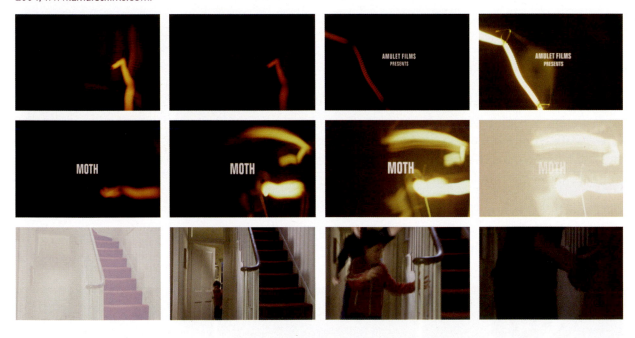

In a bumper for a weekly ice hockey series broadcast across NTL's cable network, short fades are emulated by players actually skating in and out of a theatre spotlight in a blacked-out ice hockey rink. Only small gaps are left between the actions, reflecting the passion and excitement of the game (**13.10**).

In a fictional product advertisement, Eric Eng at the Rochester Institute of Technology incorporated fades and dissolves between shots using various camera angles. This allowed him to focus on the subject's organic forms to express its sophistication and beauty (**13.11**).

13.10
Frames from the opening titles for *Inferno*. Courtesy of Applied Works. © 1997 Sportfact Ltd.

13.11
Frames from a fictional product ad by Eric Eng. Courtesy of Rochester Institute of Technology.

"Wipe transitions," common in the 1930s, involve an image pushing the previous image out of the frame through a horizontal, vertical, or diagonal movement. A "flip" (or "flip frame") is a type of wipe in which images appear like cards flipped one after another. Wipes can move in any direction, open any side, start in the center and move outward toward the frame's edges or vice versa. They can also begin as one shape and morph into another. (Split-screen effects are often created by wipes that are partially completed.)

In addition to standard dissolves, fades, and wipes, graphic transitions can flip, bounce, and crush their way into the frame. Clock wipes, checkerboards, and Venetian blinds are transitions that are usually included in consumer packages; more complicated transitions can be generated from black and white images in alpha channels. It is critical to exercise mature aesthetic judgment and use these transitions appropriately to maintain the integrity of your concept and design.

13.12

A linear wipe reveals new imagery in a specified direction. For example, at 90° the wipe travels from left to right.

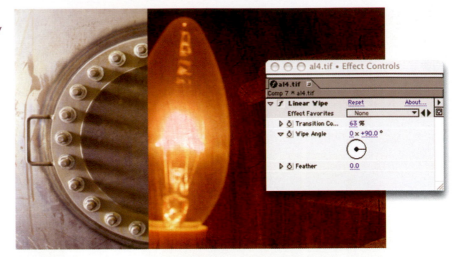

13.13

After Effects' gradient wipe references the luminance values of an overlying image.

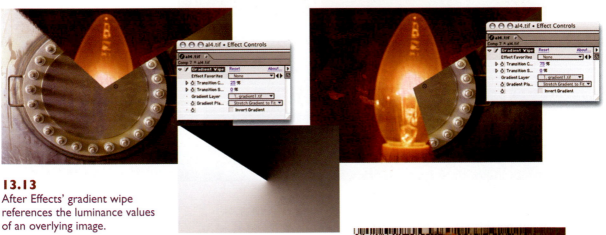

13.14

Adobe After Effects' block wipe creates the effect of an image disappearing in random blocks. This transition allows you to specify the pixel width and height of the blocks.

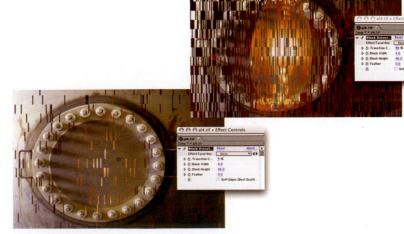

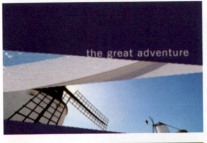
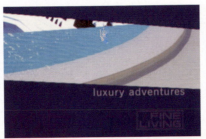
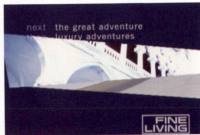
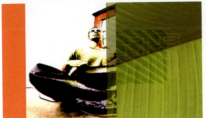
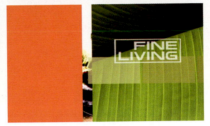
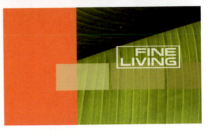

13.15
Susan Detrie's quiet, elegant, animated transitions for Fine Living Network consist of simple two-dimensional graphic planes that move fluidly across the screen at various angles. Courtesy of Fine Living Network and Susan Detrie.

Transitions can involve using images from one scene to introduce images or events in the next. The show opening for *Apna Khyal Rakhiyega* (**Chapter 12, figure 12.4, on p. 419**), for example, tells a seamless story through a continuous camera journey from an outdoor park scene, to a kitchen, to a young girl. Milk spilling out of a glass ends the first event and begins the second.

Another example is a design for an on-air package for the 2006 *Arion Music Awards* (**13.16**). The concept behind the project was to personify various categories of music through colorful animated illustrations. A ring of piano keys enters the frame to form a mask that encloses the underlying background imagery. The mask becomes smaller, transforming the imagery into the next scene that features female dancers wearing piano-like collars around their necks. A graphic close-up of a woman's profile enters the frame from the right and moves across the screen toward the left, its color shifting us into a new space. Another transition occurs when a medium shot of a male guitar player zooms into a space that becomes the last scene, featuring a television host that turns into the music video award, a golden trophy.

In a network rebrand for BET J, a spin-off cable channel of Black Entertainment Television, Freestyle Collective aimed to create a design that expressed the soul of jazz. A pair of musical symbols serve as a natural means of transition into a graphic cityscape (**13.17**).

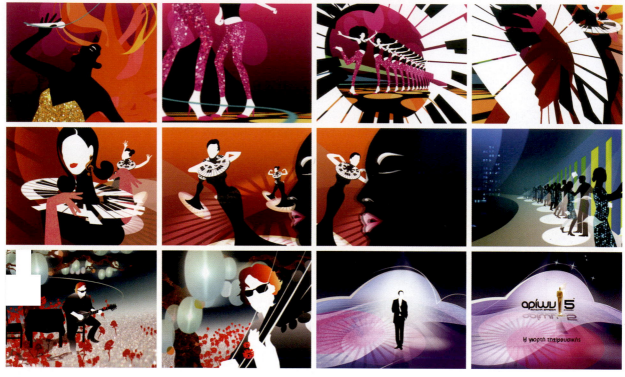

13.16
Frames from a trailer for the *Arion Music Awards*, the first corporate channel to launch on the Greek airwaves. Courtesy of Velvet.

13.17
Frames from a network rebrand for BET J. Courtesy of Freestyle Collective.

See also Chapter 3, figure 3.46, on p. 60.

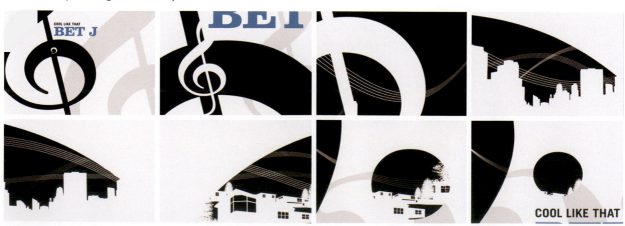

In a header for *50 anos bo es nada*, a documentary series that narrates the history of Spanish television, transitions are created by zooming into a portion of an image that becomes the ground for the next scene (**13.18**).

In Hillman Curtis' Flash advertisement for Craig Frasier/Squarepig.tv (**13.19**), graphic transitions are created by cutting or dissolving between an image at the end of a sequence and a similar image at the beginning of the next sequence.

13.18
Frames for *50 anos bo es nada*.
Courtesy of Ritxi Ostariz.

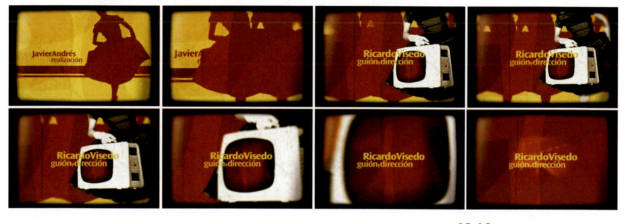

13.19
An online Flash advertisement for Craig Frasier/Squarepig.tv.
Courtesy of hillmancurtis, inc.

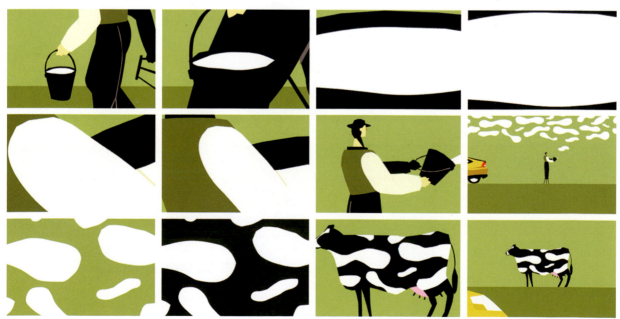

13.20
A VJ sequence for *Infinite Zoom– courtney pine*, by Kook Ewo.

The rectangular shapes of a slab serif typeface establish natural transitions between scenes.

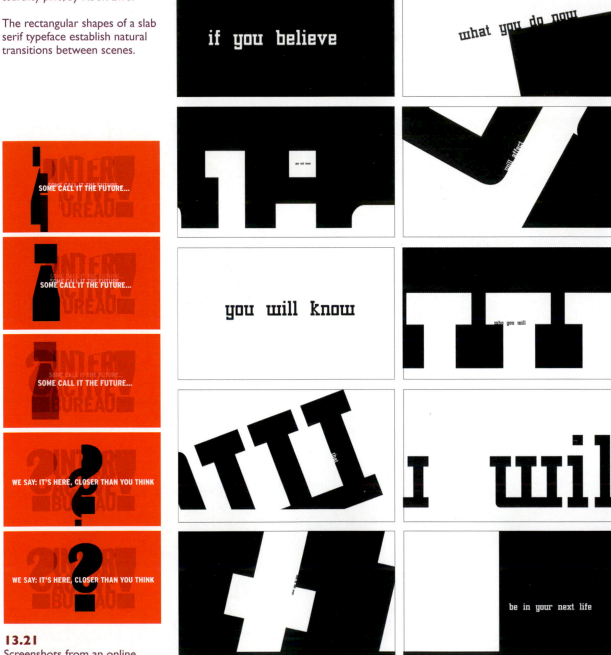

13.21
Screenshots from an online advertisement for Roger Black Interactive Bureau. Courtesy of hillmancurtis, inc.

Mobile Framing

"Secondary motion" (or "mobile framing") offers an alternative method of linking sequences of actions or events, rather than the standard cuts and transitions associated with editing. (Mobile framing is also discussed in **Chapter 6**.) **Figure 13.22**, for example, shows an unedited sequence of 3D animation that plays out continuously as the camera rotates our point of view to end with a frontal presentation of the subject.

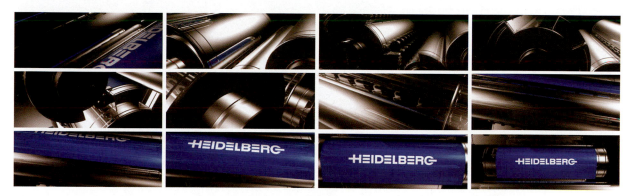

13.22
Frames from a logo animation for Heidelberg. Courtesy of Renascent.

Frame mobility can also impact our sense of a composition's pace and rhythm because it occupies time. The speed that the camera moves is an important consideration. A quick pan away from a subject can arouse curiosity or wonder, while an abrupt movement can induce surprise or shock. Music videos often organize the velocity of camera moves according to the underlying rhythm of a song.

The ending credits for *Silent Hill* (2006) demonstrate how camera motion helps drive the film's message and set the tone (**Chapter 2, figure 2.11, on p. 32**). Continuous zooming and panning creates a voyeuristic quality and unsettling feeling of being lost in the darkness. During the sequence's first phase, a range of unusual viewing angles and motions make the camera seem as if it were handheld. Later, a flashlight is introduced into the frame, moving through various three-dimensional spaces and illuminating portions of the environment.

For the original story behind the opening titles for the film *Splice* (2006), Kook Ewo conceptualized a passive, floating camera behaving like a simple weightless particle, moving in an amniotic fluid only in response to the random movements of its host. This powerful mise-en-scène approach would carry the audience from one location to another.

Because this concept was technically too complex, it was replaced by an "exploring robot" idea, in which the camera takes us on a visual journey inside a seemingly part-human, part-animal organism. A subtle depth-of-field effect was used to enhance the realism by giving the evolving particles a blurry aspect. **Figure 13.23** shows a wire-frame model that was used to set the camera movement.

13.23
Wireframe rendering from the making of the opening titles to *Splice* (2006). Courtesy of Kook Ewo.

See also Chapter 2, figure 2.10 on p. 31, Chapter 7, figure 7.32 on p. 225, and Chapter 10, figure 10.26 on p. 361.

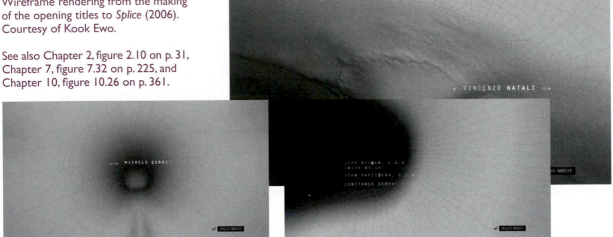

The camera movement in Honda's "Snow Trip" spot for the Crosstour leads us on a visual journey through a series of isolated vignettes of the great outdoors (**13.24**). The piece begins with a bird's eye view of the vehicle driving into a tunnel. The camera continues to move across the composition to show a closer view of the vehicle exiting the top of the frame. A snowflake flies into view, transitioning into the next scene in which we rush down a mountainside following a snowboard. A bottom view of the snowboard flows into a scene showing a male figure feeding a log from the back of his vehicle into a fireplace. The camera zooms into the flames and leads us up through the chimney and out into the final scene of a snowball fight.

Camera motion enhances the message that Ben Dansby of Kent State University wanted to convey about the imperial measurement system (**13.25**). Ben writes: "To emphasize the messy, large, diverse nature of the imperial system, I wanted the camera to be constantly moving, going from place to place. By the end of the piece, the camera has zoomed out so far to accommodate all the elements that the first objects we see, which initially appeared enormous, are now barely visible."

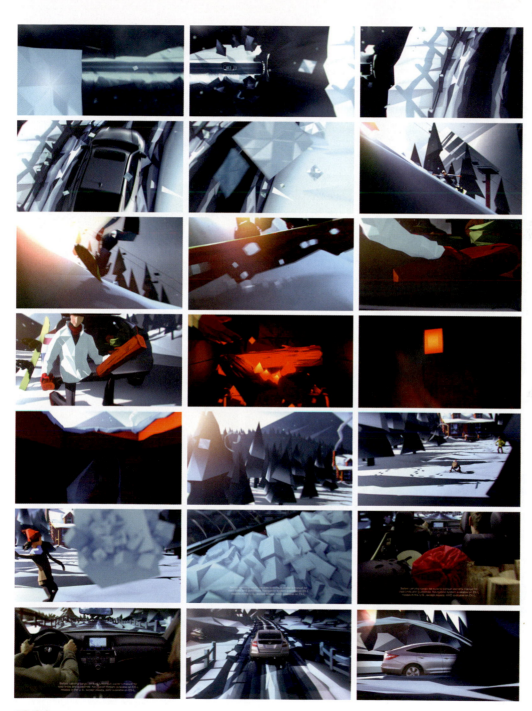

13.24
Frames from Honda's "Snow Trip" spot for the Crosstour. Courtesy of Elastic.

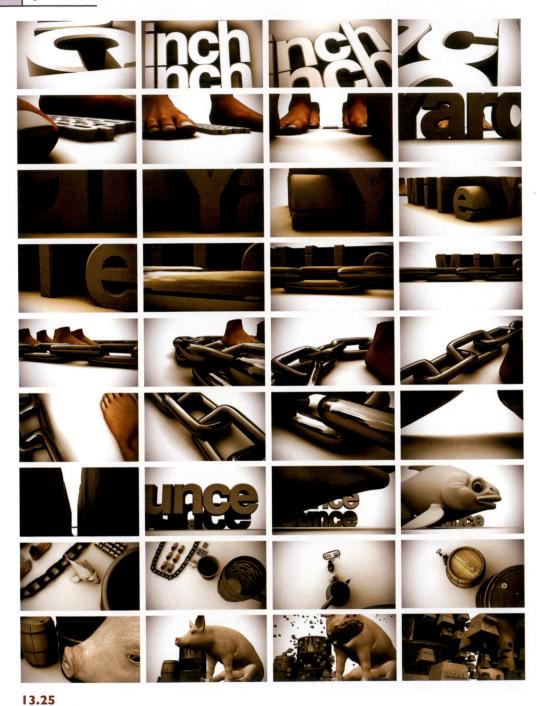

13.25
Frames from "Rethinking Measurements" by
Ben Dansby. © 2012 Kent State University.
Courtesy of Professor Gretchen Rinnert.

In a public service announcement assignment, Eric Celedonia explored the creative possibilities of camera movement with flat objects and typography (**13.26**). His animation summarizes how fair trade affects the lives of people across the globe. The use of camera movement throughout helps maintain the viewer's attention by making them feel as though they are exploring a very large space. Changing the angle and perspective also keeps the content exciting, fresh, and dynamic.

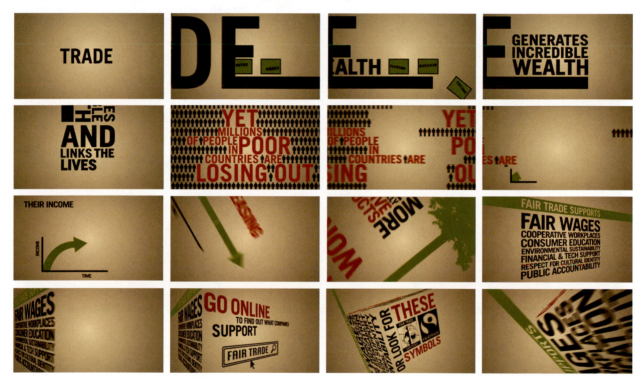

13.26
Frame from "Fair Trade" by Eric Celedonia. (C) 2012 Kent State University. Courtesy of Professor Gretchen Rinnert.

At Fitchburg State University, Justin Medas' motion identity uses frame mobility to convey the concept of a cubed object being inspected in someone's hand (**13.27**). The object enters the frame at the beginning of the animation. When it meets the implied ground, the camera takes over and spins the view around, allowing us to see every facet of the structure and decipher the text elements. In contrast, Nick Moreau's intermissions bumper for an annual student film screening uses uniform, linear camera movement and perspective. We move steadily through a retro, populated movie set featuring a range of individuals (including the director and a camera person) as neon silhouettes on a black background perform a variety of tasks. The camera remains focused on a slate as it passes through a succession of images (**13.28**).

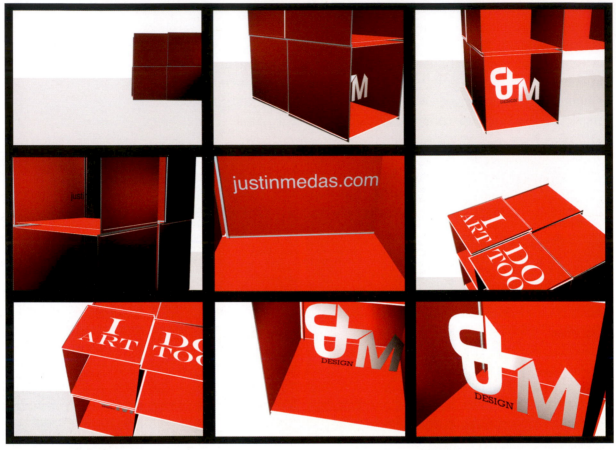

13.27
above: Animated ID by Justin
Medas. Courtesy of Professor Jon
Krasner, Fitchburg State University.

13.28
below: Bumper for *Visions*, by Nick
Moreau. Courtesy of Professor Jon
Krasner, Fitchburg State University.

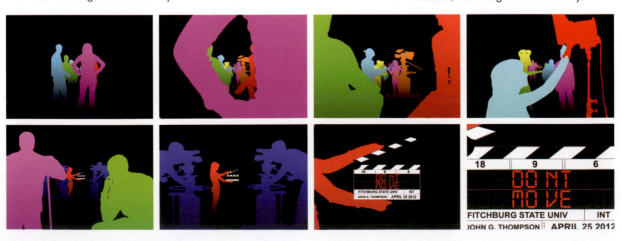

In a pitch for Nike Mercurial, a soccer boot designed to withstand all types of weather conditions, the concept of a single player on a soccer field who could mechanically shift positions in space was combined with the idea of massive slabs of concrete that could slide around like a Rubik's Cube to change the effect of gravity and confuse the viewer's orientation (**13.29**). Jon Saunders, the project's lead designer, states "we wanted it to feel like a highly dynamic sports sequence that Nike commercials are known for, but with a twist of this impossible shift in gravity and the field being another player that our hero has to deal with. We imagined starting with something that felt like a very straightforward sports commercial, then over the course of time we would break away from that adding in camera movements that played up our shifting gravity and finally revealing the giant mothership floating in space." In addition to the deliberate camerawork, oppositional weather conditions of rain and shine would be shown in a single frame. This Cubist-style approach of showing multiple moments. simultaneously reinforces the narrative by communicating the passage of time, and invites us to imagine the way the action might unfold.

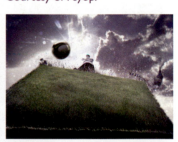
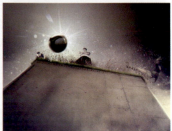
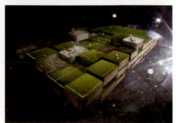

13.29
Frames from a storyboard pitch for the Nike Mercurial shoe. Courtesy of Psyop.

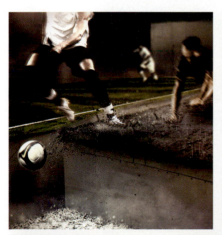
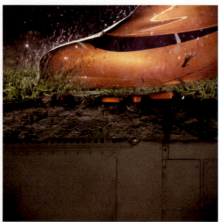
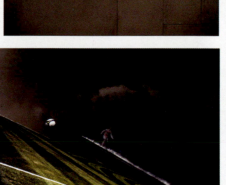

Establishing Pace

"Pace" is a vital yet elusive device that can add meaning to a message by controlling the duration of events onscreen. Fast paced films allow you to follow the basic story but entice you to watch again. Subtle events that are missed the first time can be enjoyed during a later viewing. Slower paced films such as documentaries ensure that information is delivered clearly the first time around without losing the audience's interest.

At Kent State University, the pacing of Catherine Zedell's promotional spot for *City of God* (2002) conveys the film's tense action and suspense (**13.30**). Catherine writes: "Most of the creative inspiration for this project came from the vibrant, fast-paced samba music of Brazil. The lively beat captures the feeling of suspense felt throughout the film. At the same time, there is a build up of excitement captured by the quickening of percussion instruments."

13.30
Frames from a promo for *City of God* by Catherine Zedell. © 2012 Kent State University. Courtesy of Professor Gretchen Rinnert.

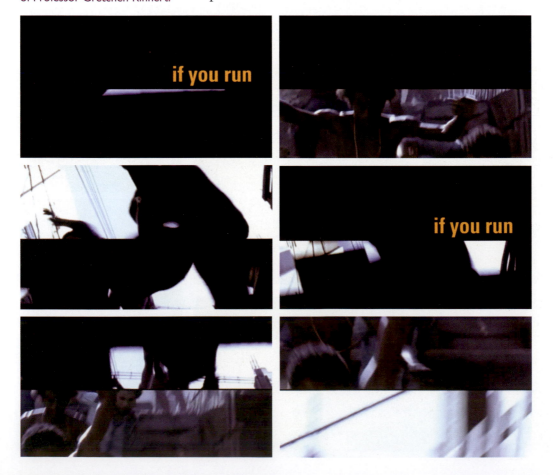

The pacing of the opening titles for the F5 festival 2009 (also discussed in Chapter 5, on page 55) was designed to adhere to the underlying rhythmic structure of the music. Transitions between shots establish ideal links between different "worlds." Additionally, smooth camera movements provide a counterpoint to the film's rhythmical editing (**13.31**).

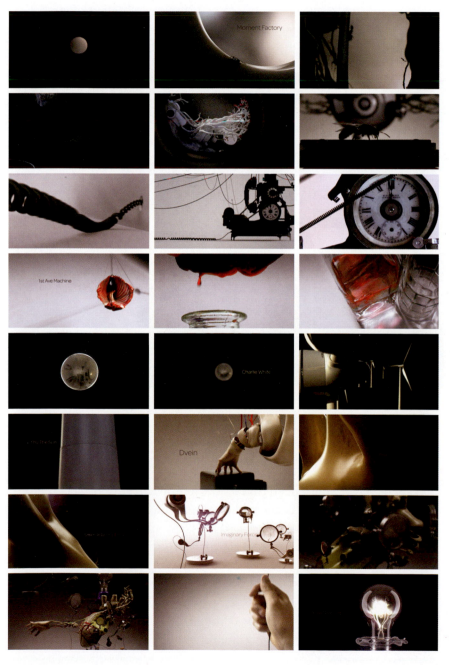

13.31
F5's 2009 opening titles.
Courtesy of Dvein.

13.32
Frames from the opening titles to *The Path to 9/11*, a miniseries that aired on ABC on September 10 and September 11, 2006. Courtesy of Digital Kitchen.

See also Chapter 3, figure 3.16, on p. 47.

A composition's pace can change over time to communicate different aspects of a story. In the opening titles to the television miniseries *The Path to 9/11* (2006), the pace picks up as the film progresses toward an extreme close-up of the World Trade Center. Each shot is heightened to inform us that an event is about to occur. Mundane scenes of a person's morning journey to work become transformed into images of large groups of people juxtaposed with close-ups of feet, hands, and bird's-eye views looking down into the city's streets (**13.32**).

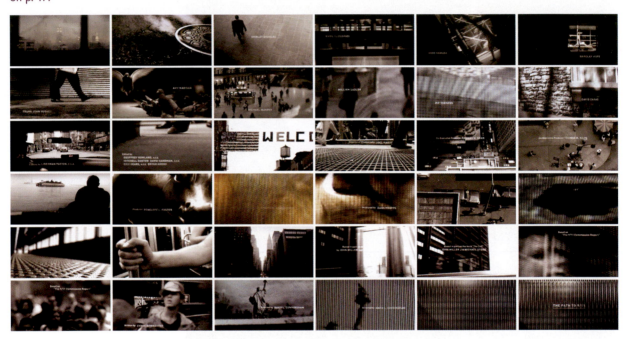

tempo and event density

In music, "tempo" refers to the speed that beats occur in each measure. In animation, tempo refers to the speed that events occur over time.

Most of us have experienced that a slow tempo can support a languid pace, while a fast tempo can establish a brisk one. Moderate tempos can reinforce a sense of positive, forward progress and can be applied to a wide range of styles, from the energy of a corporate presentation to the cheerful, good feelings of a travel spot. The tempo you choose can determine and regulate the number of cuts and transitions that will be applied to your composition, or the "event density." For example, the large number of cuts in many car commercials have a high-density, edge-of-the-seat impact, while a smaller number of cuts in a nature

If you are unsure of the subjective feel that you want for your composition's pace, try listening to different genres of music until you find one that has a prevailing tempo that expresses the mood of your concept.

documentary may generate a tranquil, serene atmosphere. David Carson's experimental film *End of Print* illustrates a high-density composition with short, rapid bursts of disassociated, disjointed images and typographic elements. Carson's precise, dynamic editing to the soundtrack creates an information overload (**13.33**). In contrast, the slow tempo of the titles to *The Path to 9/11* (**13.32**) is accompanied by minimal cuts between segments.

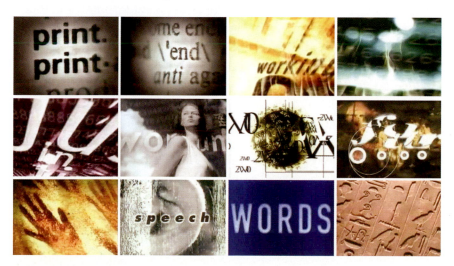

13.33
Frames from *End of Print*, based on the 1995 book of the same name by David Carson and Lewis Blackwell. © David Carson.

transition speed

The speed that transitions take place also helps establish and regulate pace. The duration of a transition that takes place *between* events may affect the composition's overall pace more than the style of transition you choose. Generally speaking, fast-paced compositions with rapid transitions across small ranges of frames can deliver snappy, energetic effects, while slow fades or dissolves that occur over long time intervals can produce a more deliberate and dignified feel.

Establishing Rhythm

Rhythm and pace are interrelated. In music, listening to repetitive beats and accents in a song can help you identify the song's rhythm. In motion graphics and film, a steady and consistent rhythm of changes between actions or scenes is predictable enough for viewers to feel subconsciously and tap their feet to. On the other hand, a rhythm with an inconsistent, variable pace can deliberately break up the predictable flow of events.

From traditional cinema to MTV, "rhythmic editing" (also referred to as "dynamic editing") has been applied to narrative and non-narrative forms of film and motion graphics. It has also been applied to both continuous and discontinuous approaches to editing. During the early twentieth century, avant-garde Cubist, Dadaist, and French Impressionist filmmakers subordinated narrative concerns to establish rhythmic patterns. (Even classical Hollywood cinema explored the rhythmic use of dissolves in montages.) Experimental filmmaker Martin Arnold took rhythmic editing to the extreme. Pièce Touchée (1989), an 18-second sequence taken from a 1950s American "B" movie, was reproduced frame by frame and manipulated according to its temporal and spatial progression. In Passage à l'acte (1993), a postwar family breakfast scene from the 1960s film, *To Kill a Mockingbird*, is transformed into a disturbing, compulsive, rhythmic sequence of repetitive movements and sounds. The sound of the opening and closing of the screen door mimics gunfire, and repeated shots of the family members who, like a broken record, yell out parts of words or twitch back and forth, seem to pulsate to an underlying, continuous, monotonous beat.

Historical Perspective

European avant-garde filmmakers often subordinated narrative to pure rhythmic editing. In French Impressionist films, rhythmic editing was often used to depict inner turmoil or violence. For example, the impact of the train crash in the film *La Roue* was conveyed through a series of accelerated shots that became shorter and shorter over time.

Rhythm was a key element in the work of Surrealist filmmakers, such as Hans Richter who combined improvisation and atypical camera usage with formal Constructivist design principles to produce continuous rhythmic themes throughout his films. Lev Kuleshov's *The Death Ray* (1926), Sergei Eisenstein's *October* (1927), and many of the films of Alfred Hitchcock also show how rhythm can dominate narrative.

When sound films became the standard, rhythmic editing was evident in musical comedies, dance sequences, and dramas. During the 1960s, fast cutting to a song's beat was used in television commercials for soft drinks and during the 1980s it was used in music videos. Rapid successions of stereotypical images were cut to match the soundtrack's rhythm.

continuous rhythm

In music and dance, most of us seem driven by discernable rhythms that are steady and constant. Many filmmakers and animators who have been inspired by avant-garde cinema and Eisenstein's experiments with montage have strived to create uniform rhythmic structures in their compositions.

A device that can establish steady, continuous rhythm is "timing." In music, timing differs from tempo in that it indicates the number of beats per measure. If you are a musician or have some knowledge of music theory, you may know that a 4/4 timing yields a different tap-of-your-foot rhythm than a 3/4 signature which, if played slowly, can feel like a waltz.

If you are editing to music, the timing of beats and accents can help determine a composition's underlying visual rhythm. Alternatively, if sound is not available you can recite a verse in your mind or listen to the beat of a metronome to create a sense of timing. In **figure 13.34**, the timing of the cuts between photographs of urban hipster scenes and dream-like live-action imagery is precisely edited to match the soundtrack. In a student project entitled *My Hero*, Eric Decker gave careful consideration to the cuts between segments and the timing with which various foods and condiments enter and leave the frame. Both are precisely edited to match the rhythm of the soundtrack (**13.35**).

In music, rhythm describes how sounds that vary in length and accentuation are grouped into patterns. The timing of notes is independent of the tempo that governs the composition's pace. If the beat changes so that you tap your foot faster or slower, the rhythm has not changed —only the tempo.

13.34
Frames from a network package for MTV K, the first premium channel in the MTV World family geared specifically toward young Korean-Americans. Courtesy of Freestyle Collective.

Combinations of live-action video, still photos, and vibrant animations are edited to match the soundtrack and evoke the young, cool lifestyle that has become synonymous with MTV culture.

See also Chapter 3, figure 3.45, on p. 5.

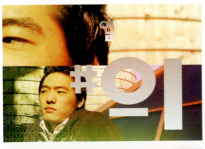
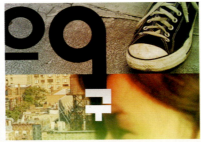
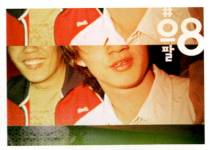
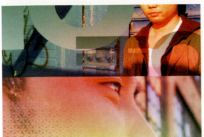
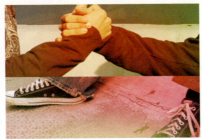
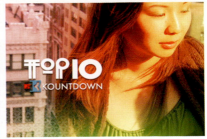

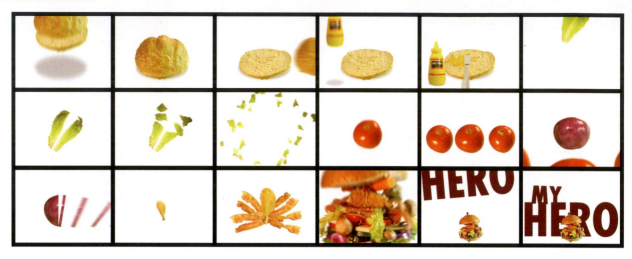

13.35
Frames from *My Hero* by Eric Decker. Produced in Dynamic Typography at the Rochester Institute of Technology. Courtesy of Professor Jason Arena.

Early cinema tended to rely on shots that were fairly lengthy. Shots eventually became shorter with the increased practice of continuity editing, and by the early 1920s, American films had average shot lengths of five seconds. The advent of sound film stretched this to about 10 seconds.

Another factor that should be considered when striving to establish continuous rhythm is "frame duration"—the length of time that images, actions, or events remain onscreen. This basic temporal consideration allows you to govern the amount of time that viewers see and interpret the content. An action or event can be as short as a single frame or as long as thousands of frames, running for many minutes. A simple way to construct a consistent rhythm is to make a composition's segments the same duration. Equal time intervals will produce a steady rhythm that unifies all elements (related or unrelated in meaning) into a cohesive whole. This means that the cuts and transitions used are also evenly distributed throughout. A silent viewing of Man Ray's avant-garde film "Emak-Bakia" (1926) illustrates this concept. The romantic, underlying musical rhythm that prevails throughout is largely due to the fact that the thematically related moving subjects on the screen are similar.

Cutting or transitioning between recurring matching or similar actions can also introduce uniform rhythm. This can help create structural continuity and maintain a sense of pace and cohesiveness in a composition. Experimental animations from the 1920s relied heavily on the concept of repetition to achieve rhythm. Fernand Léger's and Dudley Murphy's Cubist film, *Ballet mécanique* (1924), builds a rhythmic structure from juxtaposed mundane objects that are treated as motifs and repeated in different combinations in rapid succession. Repetitive, sequential movements of spinning bottles, faces, hats, and kitchen utensils are taken out of their original context, recurring in highly choreographed arrangements. This is accompanied by body gestures and facial expressions that seem mechanically orchestrated with the film's soundtrack. Graphic contrast, frame mobility, and rapid sequences of close-up shots illustrate a complete abandonment of the continuity system in favor of achieving a dance-like choreography of rhythm (**13.36**). In Viking Eggeling's *Symphonie diagonale* (1924), each movement is choreographed to a steady, mechanical tempo. Rhythm is articulated by the manner and speed by which geometric elements appear and disappear in the frame, along with the time for which they remain on the screen. In many instances, figures build over time, line by line, and varying shades of gray create the effect of images fading in and out to the underlying musical score (**13.37**). The arrangement of different themes within the piece can be compared, as the title suggests, to the orchestration of a symphony.

Uniformity of image and action was also a key element in Hans Richter's approach of combining spontaneous improvisation with formal organization. Throughout his Surrealist film, *Ghosts Before Breakfast* (1927), a strong underlying rhythm is maintained in the relative speeds that elements move from shot to shot. The numbers of characters or objects also remain constant throughout the film to preserve rhythm. For example, three men in one scene follow three hats in the previous scene. Additionally, shapes that fill the frame are spaced at equal intervals. In one particular scene containing five guns rotated to form a pinwheel image, the guns are equidistant from each another. The rhythm is also reinforced by the speed at which they turn. Recurring images of flying hats further establish a continuous rhythm throughout the composition.

In a bilingual on-air opener and program design for *DW Euromax* (**13.38**), objects such as violins, shoes, chandeliers, chairs, and fountain pens are strategically arranged into moving patterns or more complex abstract shapes. The elements move at constant speeds and are spaced at equal intervals. The repetition of these elements in consecutive segments ties the film together into a unified composition.

variable rhythm

Rhythm does not have to be uniform. It can change over time in order to vary the mood of a composition. Unlike dance music, where rhythm is steady and continuous, the variety of tempo during a piece of classical music characterizes its different phases.

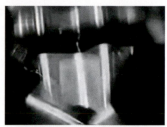
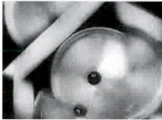
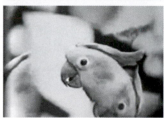
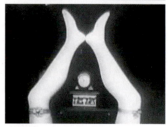

13.36
Fernand Léger and Dudley Murphy's *Ballet mécanique* (1924) shows a consistent rhythmic progression of abstract images and actions.

In musical arrangements, individual notes and durational sonic patterns of notes can repeat regularly to create unity. In classical music, a theme may be duplicated to give a piece a unique personality that differs from other arrangements. Without repetition, the composition can stray away aimlessly in too many directions, lacking a focus.

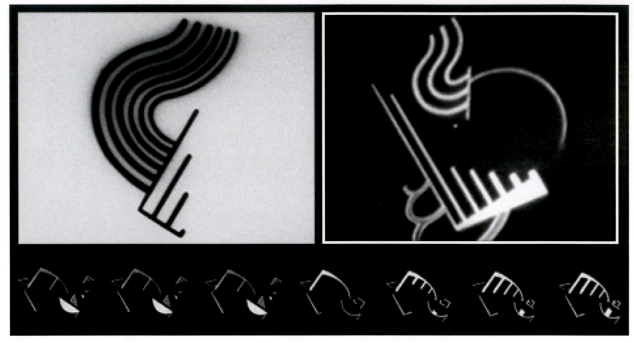

13.37
Filmstrip from Viking Eggeling's *Symphonie diagonale* (1924). Taking almost four years to complete, this animation showed a strong correlation between music and painting in the motions of figures created from paper cutouts and tin foil. Eggeling died in Berlin approximately two weeks after his film was released.

Variation in rhythm allows new material to be introduced. It can help break predictability and can be used to emphasize a particular point of interest. It can also allow you to simply stay in synch with the soundtrack, if your piece is a music video. Even if the "beat" of the soundtrack is steady, introducing changes in the way images and actions are presented, as well as in tempo, event density, and frame duration of content, can add variety. In Léger and Murphy's *Ballet mécanique*, the relative scale of objects in the frame changes through the use of close-up, medium close-up, and extreme close-up shots. Additionally, close framings are used to isolate and emphasize form and texture, while other framings, such as upside-down shots and masks, introduce rhythmic variation.

Emphasis can be used to mark an interruption in the fundamental flow of events in a composition. It can break predictability and define a point of focus. In music, emphasis is achieved by providing accents in order to make certain notes or combinations of notes stand out. In character animation, it is used to exaggerate movement. In motion design, it is used to contribute toward the visual hierarchy. For example, an element that flies or tumbles into the frame calls more attention to itself than one that moves slowly and uniformly.

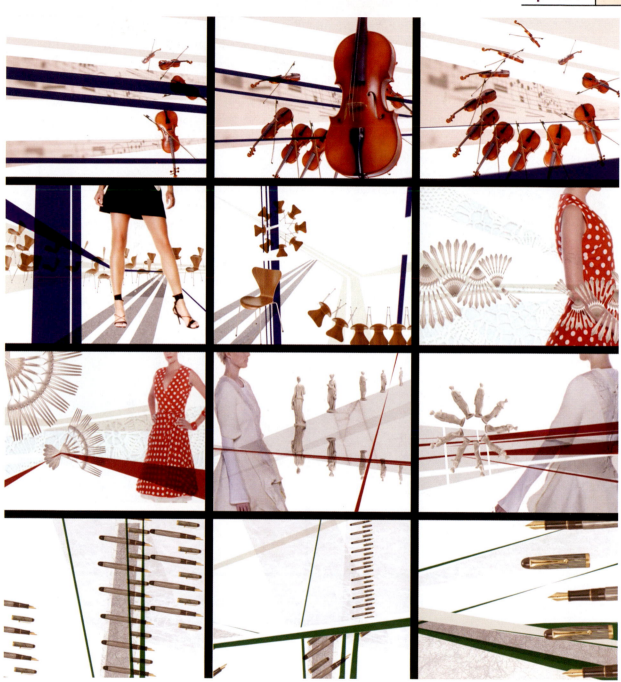

13.38
Frames from a program design for *DW Euromax*, a bilingual on-air program. Courtesy of Velvet.

Varying event frequency and tempo (or repeating the same event in a different way) can disrupt the viewer's normal expectations of the narrative, inviting them to focus on the actual process of assembling the story. One way to achieve this is by changing the tempo at which events are presented. This also offers a way to introduce rhythmic variation. Slow motion can interrupt a composition's flow by presenting a close-up of time (similar to holding your breath); fast motion can accelerate you forward in time.

In a television commercial for a Spanish supermarket, Dutch designer Joost Korngold explored how creating seamless transitions between groupings of pears and a glass of milk could illustrate the process of waking up in the morning, driving to work and starting the day. Based on a rough storyboard sketch, his challenge was to make the transitions exciting by combining the objects with camera motion. His use of fast, primary motion and accelerated camera moves creates an unpredictable rhythm against the underlying steady beat of the soundtrack (**13.39**).

13.39
Frames for "Eroski," a television commercial for a Spanish supermarket. Courtesy of Joost Korngold. © 2007 Renascent.

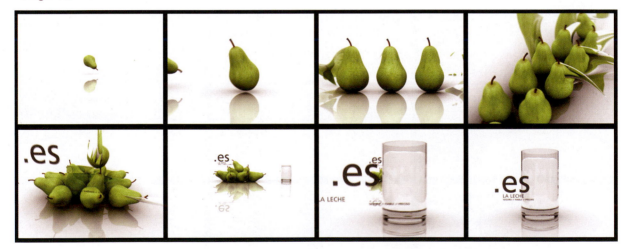

In a network package for MOJO (**Chapter 9, figure 9.34, on p. 328 and Chapter 7, figure 7.16, on p. 215**), discontinuous rhythm was deliberately used to create an edgy and almost disturbing feel, in order to arouse anticipation. (In fact, it was intended to evoke precisely the opposite reaction than the one you would get from watching the Hallmark Channel or a Martha Stewart special!) Rapid cuts between images occur at an unsteady pace, changing according to the soundtrack. Instead of using music, motion graphics company Flying Machine implemented pure sounds to create strong rhythmic contrasts. One particular segment shows a dramatic contrast in which a shot of a group of rapidly twisting and turning kitchen utensils is immediately followed by a slow pan of a sensuous female torso and a car. The repetition of events, such as alcohol being poured into a glass, film projections, and extreme close-ups of female body parts, occurs at an unpredictable rate to reinforce the element of surprise.

Varying frame duration for actions or events also allows you to introduce variety into a composition's rhythmic structure. Regardless of the time that elements "live" in the frame, if their onscreen durations are similar, the predictability of the pace can grow cumbersome if they are too long, or can become irritating if they are too short. (This is not always true. Similar durations of events can create a pleasing rhythm, as in Man Ray's "Emak-bakia.") Combining sequences with different frame lengths can create irregular rhythms. For example, shortening or lengthening each consecutive sequence can produce drama and tension, leading viewers to expect a change in narrative action. Mixing and matching short and long sequences can renew the audience's attention and refresh their interest. This means that the distribution of cuts and transitions that link a composition's segments is also variable.

Pauses can also vary rhythm and pace. A pause can be a series of black consecutive frames between two segments or a specified interval of time for which the action remains frozen on the screen. Pauses can also be used to give viewers time to rest between events, emphasize points of interest, create expectations or tension, and help regulate a viewer's perception of time.

Birth, Life, and Death

In Chapter 6, the terms "birth" and "death" are used to describe how elements are introduced into the frame and the manner in which they leave it. "Life" describes their duration or how long they live or reside in the frame. In sequencing, all of these factors need to be given considerable attention. The sequential or transitional continuity that is established in many of the storyboard designs in Chapter 10 is largely due to the method by which elements appear on the screen and how they leave it. This allows transitions between events to flow smoothly and be easily deciphered without even seeing their actual movement.

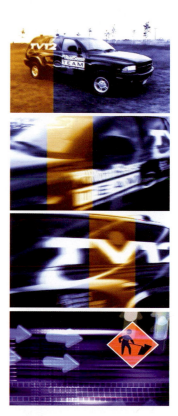

13.40
Frames from TV12's "ICBC Roadsense" PSA. Courtesy of Tiz Beretta and Erwin Chiong.

In this PSA promoting vehicle safety, a brisk tempo is established through rapid jump cuts that occur during a rotated and zoomed-in view of a Roadsense Team vehicle. The tempo then gives way to a steady, moderate pace that accompanies a layering of complex road signs that move uniformly across the screen.

Introduction and Conclusion

The importance of a story's beginning and conclusion cannot be overstated. Careful thought should be given to how you plan to capture your audience's attention and keep them engaged throughout the piece. Your opening and closing sequences should establish a strong start and a strong finish. They should be given at least twice as much attention as the middle of the composition. Beware of overloading these segments with too many effects and transitions; sometimes simplicity can be most effective (less is more).

Chapter Summary

The technique of editing involves coordinating and joining multiple images, actions, or events into a cohesive whole. "Cuts" produce instantaneous changes between scenes. "Parallel editing" involves joining separate events together to produce a sense of cause and effect. "Cutaways" are used to shift the viewer's attention away from the main action as it unfolds in offscreen space and time. "Jump cuts" produce abrupt changes in the positions or movements of elements, breaking the illusion of continuous time. "Transitions" allow for gradual changes between events. For example, "fades" are used to signify major changes in content, time, or space, representing distinct breaks in a story's continuity. "Mobile framing" through camera motion offers an alternative to cuts and transitions.

A composition's editing pace is based on the length of time events exist onscreen and the manner in which cuts and transitions are used to link them. Factors that help determine and govern pace are tempo, event density, and transition speed.

The technique of "rhythmic editing" can be used to create continuity or discontinuity. Presenting events in equally spaced time intervals produces a uniform rhythm. Varying a composition's tempo, changing the duration of onscreen events, or inserting pauses can strategically break predictability to maintain the interest of viewers.

Careful thought must be given to how elements are introduced into the frame, how long they exist in the frame, and how they leave the frame ("birth," "life," and "death"), and to your story's beginning and conclusion.

index

I

K